1994 BUYING GUIDE

Special year-end issue

The December 15, 1993, issue
of CONSUMER REPORTS
Volume 58, No. 13

The body of this book is made with recycled paper

▶Contents

7 — AUDIO & VIDEO GEAR
TV sets...11
VCRs...15
Laser-disc players 18
Camcorders......................................18
Remote controls...............................21
Receivers..22
Loudspeakers 25
Compact-disc players.....................27
Cassette decks................................29
Stereo headphones 32
Walkabout stereos 33
Audio tape 34
Ratings..36

59 — PHOTOGRAPHY
Cameras & lenses...........................60
Color print film..................................66
Film processing................................67
Video and photo tripods 68
Ratings..70

79 — MAJOR APPLIANCES
Microwave ovens.............................80
Ranges..83
Refrigerators....................................86
Dishwashers 89
Washing machines 91
Clothes dryers..................................93
Detergents & other laundry
 products 95
Ratings..98

111 — SMALL APPLIANCES
Food processors............................111
Blenders 113
Portable mixers..............................115
Coffee appliances 117
Toasters & toaster ovens..............119
Juicers & juice extractors 120
Slow-cookers..................................122
Pressure cookers 123
Indoor grills.....................................124
Ratings..126

139 — AUTOS
Recommended 1993 cars 140
Ratings of 1993 cars......................152
How to buy a new car 166
Should you lease? 169
How to buy a used car 170
Good & bad bets in used cars 173
Reliability records..........................178
Trouble indexes 218
Owner satisfaction 224

227 — PERSONAL PRODUCTS
Blood-pressure monitors..............228
Hearing aids 230
Eyeglasses.....................................232
Cribs & mattresses 234
Bathroom scales............................236
Dental products 237
Ratings..241

253 — RECREATION & EXERCISE
Exercise equipment 254
Running & walking shoes.............258
Bicycles...259
Ratings 262

267 YARD & GARDEN
Lawn mowers.................................268
String trimmers............................270
Garden hoses 272
Lawn sprinklers 273
Insect repellents..........................274
Ratings..276

291 HOME WORKPLACE
Telephones 292
Telephone answerers 297
Home fax machines 299
Computer software systems........301
Computer printers........................302
Ratings 304

311 HOME
Vacuum cleaners 312
Fans..315
Air-conditioners...........................317
Air cleaners..................................322
Water treatment...........................324
Lead in household water..............329
Paints, stains, & finishes..............330
Energy savers 335
Ratings..341

365 REPAIR HISTORIES

375 PRODUCT RECALLS

391 INDEX

Illustrations by Jeanne de la Houssaye

AUDIO/VIDEO

PHOTOGRAPHY

APPLIANCES

AUTOS

HEALTH

YARD

HOME WORKPLACE

HOME

REPAIR HISTORIES

RECALLS

ABOUT CONSUMERS UNION

Consumers Union, the publisher of CONSUMER REPORTS, is a nonprofit organization established in 1936 to provide consumers with information and advice on goods, services, health, and personal finance and to initiate and cooperate with individual group efforts to maintain and enhance the quality of life for consumers.

Consumers Union is a membership organization. Paid subscribers may become members in one of three ways: by written application; by sending in a nomination for the Board of Directors; or by voting in the annual election of CU's Directors (ballots are mailed to all paid subscribers). There is no financial or other obligation.

No advertising. We accept no advertising and buy all the products we test on the open market, so we are not beholden to any commercial interest. Our income is derived solely from the sale of CONSUMER REPORTS and our other publications and from nonrestrictive, noncommercial contributions, grants, and fees.

Our Ratings and reports are for the use of our readers. Neither the Ratings nor the reports may be used in advertising or for any commercial purpose. CU will take all steps to prevent commercial use of its material, its name, or the name of CONSUMER REPORTS.

Contributions. Contributions to Consumers Union are tax-deductible. Contributors of $1000 or more become Lifetime Members, receiving a lifetime subscription to CONSUMER REPORTS and other benefits. Bequests are another way to help ensure CU's programs. For information, write to Consumers Union, Box NR, 101 Truman Ave., Yonkers, N.Y. 10703-1057.

ABOUT CONSUMER REPORTS

CONSUMER REPORTS is published once a month. In addition, in December subscribers receive the Buying Guide as the thirteenth issue. Reproduction of CONSUMER REPORTS in whole or in part is forbidden without prior written permission (and is never permitted for commercial purposes).

About our Ratings. Ratings are based on laboratory tests, panel tests, reader surveys, and expert judgments of products bought in stores. Ratings are usually based on estimated overall quality without regard to price. If a product is judged high in quality and appreciably superior to other products tested, we give it a check rating (✓). If a product offers both high quality and relatively low price, we deem it A Best Buy.

A Rating applies only to the brand and model listed, not to other models sold under the same brand name, unless so noted. In a few cases, such as dishwashers and air-conditioners, we list "similar models," which are models judged comparable in performance to the tested model, based on the manufacturer's specifications.

We are unable to conduct special tests or provide information beyond what appears in CONSUMER REPORTS. We choose models to test after considering factors such as reader interest, the extent of a product's availability, current consumer expenditures, and new designs.

Subscriptions. U.S. rates: $22 for 1

year, $38 for 2 years, $54 for 3 years, $70 for 4 years, $86 for 5 years. Other countries: add $6 per year. (The Canadian rate is $35 if paying in Canadian dollars; Goods & Services Tax included GST #127047702.) For subscription service or to change a mailing address, write to Subscription Director, consumer reports, P.O. Box 53029, Boulder, Colo. 80322-3029. Please attach or copy your address from the back cover of a monthly issue.

Readers' letters. We welcome comments or questions about our reports. They should be sent to consumer reports, P. O. Box 2015, Yonkers, N.Y. 10703-9015. Note that constraints on staff time prevent us from responding individually.

Back issues. Back issues of CONSUMER REPORTS up to 11 months old are available as supplies permit from Back Issue Dept., CONSUMER REPORTS, P.O. Box 53016, Boulder, Colo. 80322-3016: Single copies of regular issues are $4; the Buying Guide is $10. Your local library may also have back issues on file.

Bulk reprints. Selected health and personal-finance reports are frequently available (10 copies minimum). For more information or for an order form, write to Consumers Union, Reprints Dept., 101 Truman Ave., Yonkers, N. Y. 10703-1057.

Other media. Copies of individual reports are available by fax or mail. See the index for ordering information and prices. CONSUMER REPORTS is available online through American Online, CompuServe, Dialog, Nexis, and Prodigy, and on CD-ROM. Reports are also available on microfilm from UMI, 300 N. Zeeb Rd., Ann Arbor, Mich. 48106. Address inquiries to Consumers Union, Electronic Publishing Dept., 101 Truman Ave., Yonkers, N.Y. 10703-1057.

ABOUT THE BUYING GUIDE

The Buying Guide collects, in one handy volume, buying advice and evaluations of hundreds of brand-name products. The new thumb index gives you fast access to its contents: information on automobiles, audio and video gear, household appliances, health and exercise items, yard and garden machines, home workplace equipment, home-care appliances, and photography equipment.

In addition to advice on specific products, the reports in the Buying Guide arm you with information about the choices you have to make, regardless of the brands and models you'll encounter in the stores.

The Buying Guide prepares you for buying a car, explaining how to negotiate with a dealer, recommending models, and giving reliability data on more than 300 cars. For those setting up a home-entertainment system, we explain how to set it up, choose a sound system, and hook up cable reception. For those setting up a home office, we provide basic information on telephones and answering machines plus the latest information on home fax machines and an overview of computer software systems.

Our reports offer up-to-date information on many other products as well— food processors, paints and stains, air-conditioners, fans, lawn mowers, vacuum cleaners, running and walking shoes, blood-pressure monitors, and a roundup of energy-saving measures for the cold season.

The Buying Guide also provides information on the reliability of brands, information available only from CONSUMER REPORTS. For reliability data on cars, see the Frequency-of-Repair charts beginning on page 178. For such products as refrigerators, washing machines, dishwashers, air-conditioners, lawn mowers, VCRs, and television sets, see page 365.

In addition, the Buying Guide includes a years' worth of a list of product recalls, defective products recalled by governmental agencies (published in the monthly issues of CONSUMER REPORTS from October 1992 through October 1993). See page 375.

You'll find a one-year index to CONSUMER REPORTS at the back of the book, following the index to the Guide. The date a report was published in CONSUMER REPORTS is also given at the top of each Ratings table. For copies of individual reports, check with your local library or see the ordering information in the index on page 393.

Availability. Because of the time required for testing and reporting, some of the models listed in the Ratings may no longer be available. Just before press time, however, we verify the availability of most of the products with the manufacturers. Products that have been discontinued are marked D in the Ratings. Such products may actually be still available in some stores. For some products, we've identified a "successor model" to the model that was tested. A successor, according to the manufacturer, is similar in performance to the item tested, but it may have different features. Such products are marked S in the Ratings.

Prices. Most prices are especially updated for the Buying Guide shortly before it goes to press. The prices we give, unless otherwise noted, are the manufacturers' approximate or suggested retail prices. Discounts may be substantial, particularly for electronics and photography equipment.

PRESIDENT: Rhoda H. Karpatkin.
BOARD OF DIRECTORS: James A. Guest, Chair; Jean Ann Fox, Vice Chair; Betty Furness, Secretary; Teresa M. Schwartz, Treasurer; Robert S. Adler, Carol M. Barger, Christine A. Bjorklund, Joan Claybrook, Clarence M. Ditlow, Michael Jacobson, Richard M. Kessel, Richard L. D. Morse, Sharon L. Nelson, Joel J. Nobel, Milton M. Pressley, Peter M. Sullivan, Julian A. Waller.

CONSUMER REPORTS (ISSN 0010-7174) is published 13 times a year by Consumers Union of the United States, Inc.,101 Truman Avenue, Yonkers, N.Y. 10703-1057. Second-class postage paid at Yonkers, N.Y., and at additional mailing offices. Canadian postage paid at Mississauga, Ontario, Canada. Canadian publications registration no. 9277. Title CONSUMER REPORTS registered in U.S. Patent Office. Contents of this issue copyright © 1993 by Consumers Union of the United States, Inc. All rights reserved under International and Pan-American copyright conventions. Reproduction in whole or in part is forbidden without prior written permission (and is never permitted for commercial purposes). CU is a member of the International Organization of Consumers Unions. Mailing lists: CU occasionally exchanges its subscriber lists with those of selected publications and nonprofit organizations. If you wish your name deleted from such exchanges, send your address label with a request for deletion to CONSUMER REPORTS, P.O. Box 53029, Boulder, Colo. 80322-3029. Postmaster: Send address changes to the same address.

▶ Audio & video gear

TV sets 11
VCRs 15
Laser-disc players 18
Camcorders 18
Remote controls 21
Receivers 22
Loudspeakers 25
Compact-disc players 27
Cassette decks 29
Stereo headphones 32
Walkabout stereos 33
Audio tape 34
Ratings 36

The idea of home theater—watching movies on a big-screen TV set with a good sound system—continues to change home-entertainment products:

■ Most big-screen TV sets are now stereo and can be connected to a sound system. More and more sets come with audio amplifiers capable of directly driving external loudspeakers. Many big-screen TV sets can switch among several video sources. Sets with a 27-inch screen are among the premier sellers, and large-screen sets are the fastest-growing part of the market.

■ Most stereo receivers these days are "audio/video" receivers, capable of serving as the switching center for a home-theater system. Many mid-priced models now come with special sound-effects abilities like Dolby Pro Logic. Pro Logic decodes and plays a special sound track through multiple speakers to add such ambience as the swoosh of airplanes or ricochets.

■ Speakers, once available only in pairs, are now available singly and in threes, the better to set up these ambience sound systems.

■ Hi-fi sound has become a common feature in VCRs, the machines that started home theater.

■ Laser-disc players, once considered something of a technological dodo, have taken on new life, primarily because they promise superb picture and sound quality.

■ Remote controls have shifted from being a handy accessory to being a product in their own right, often capable of day-to-day operation of the whole show.

At its fanciest, a home theater can cost more than a car. But setting up a home theater can be as simple as hooking up the TV set to a pair of powered speakers (price:

as little as $100) or adding a patch cord to connect the TV set to the stereo (about $5). Or you can update a component or two in your present setup. Even if you're building a system from scratch, you can do it for well under $2000 and still get good performance. Here's what to consider:

Decide which component is the heart of the system. Until recently, there was no choice. It had to be the stereo receiver, whether or not you watched TV and listened to music in the same room. But many big-screen TV sets can now directly drive external speakers plus switch among several video sources. For a TV-based system, plan on spending at least $500 for a 27-inch set with those audio and switching features.

If you already have a TV set with an audio output, you can set up a receiver-based system for much less. Because a receiver's amplifier is more powerful than what's currently built into TV sets, it can produce the best sound. And a receiver-based system is more versatile than a TV-based system. A separate receiver costs as little as $150. For an A/V model that decodes Dolby Surround sound, figure at least $250.

Choose the sound-effects package. You typically make this choice in buying a receiver, although some TV sets now come with sound-effects circuitry built in.

The most basic sound effect, of course, is a two-channel-stereo sound. All the configurations of surround-sound require at least one additional pair of speakers.

■ Dolby Surround, the at-home version of the Dolby Stereo used in movie theaters, deciphers the extra channels on the Dolby-encoded sound track of movie videos and a growing number of TV programs. It supplies a pair of rear speakers with a signal providing the sound effects and echoes that make the action seem to envelop you. The direction of the sound shifts to reflect the shifting action on screen.

■ Dolby Pro Logic represents a significant improvement over Dolby Surround. Pro Logic enhances the separation between the front and rear channels and separates some on-screen sounds for a center channel. That information goes to a fifth speaker, which is positioned above or below the TV set so that on-screen sound, usually dialogue, seems to be coming directly from the TV screen.

To drive the center channel, Pro Logic requires an additional amplifier. Most Pro Logic receivers have the amplifier built in; some low-end models have the Pro Logic circuitry, but not the amp.

■ Dolby 3 stereo, a relatively new feature found on many Pro Logic receivers, lets you experience some of the surround mode without using rear speakers. Sounds that would normally emanate from the rear speakers are rerouted to the front three speakers, but at a slightly lower volume than the sound for the front channels.

■ Ambience modes, which are found on most surround-sound receivers, are usually created with digital signal processing, which adds echo to the sound signal on the way to the rear speakers. By selecting "stadium," "concert hall," or "night club," you can simulate rooms with various acoustic characteristics.

Plan on spending at least $250 for a receiver that decodes Dolby Pro Logic, plus an additional $100 or so for the center-channel speaker.

Set up the speakers. Some TV sets have built-in "psychoacoustic effects," which enable speakers located only a couple of feet apart to simulate the spaciousness of full-blown stereo. Still, these effects can't compare with the sound produced by a set of good loudspeakers placed for maximum stereo effect. Expect to pay $350 to $400 for a main pair. The pair of "rear," adjunct speakers in a Dolby setup can be cheaper, since that channel carries only untaxing mid-range frequencies.

In a two-speaker setup, the speakers go on either side of the TV set. With the four speakers of a Dolby Surround system, the second pair should be pointed away from the listener, since you want the ambience sounds to seem as if they're coming from all around you. The fifth speaker in a Dolby Pro Logic setup goes near the TV screen.

Check the speaker and receiver specifications to be sure that components are compatible before you buy. Many high-quality speakers, particularly those of American origin, have an impedance rating of four ohms. (Impedance measures resistance to electric current.) But many receivers, particularly Japanese products, are designed to work with speakers rated at six ohms or more. Using the wrong speakers can overheat and damage receiver circuits, especially when playing steadily at high volumes. Multiple speakers complicate the picture. Two sets of speakers connected in parallel, as some receivers require for driving two sets, is a more difficult load than the same two sets connected in series, as other receivers require.

Choose the playback devices. At a minimum, a home theater needs a hi-fi VCR. Hi-fi models are fairly inexpensive, available at discount for less than $300. Laser-disc players are still generally more expensive—listing more than $500.

Consider the remote control. If all the components in a home theater are the same brand, there should be little problem in running the basic functions with just one remote, a "unified" remote, as it's called, that comes with TV sets and high-end VCRs. They can be bought separately, too, for $20 and up. But don't count on tossing out the remotes you've collected—you'll still need them to perform specialized functions. In a setup of mixed brands, you may want a universal remote, of either the "learning" or "code-entry" type.

Select the rest of the gear. To round out the home-entertainment possibilities, there are camcorders, tape decks, and CD players.

Several new technologies have appeared on the home entertainment scene during the past couple of years. Digital audio, represented by Philips's Digital Compact Cassette and Sony Corp.'s Mini-Disc, produces CD-quality sound with the ability to record as well as play. Interactive home multimedia devices, such as those marketed by Philips and Radio Shack, give the family TV set computerlike capabilities. Both types of technology are still expensive and their futures uncertain. Wait until the dust settles before investing in either.

Make connections. Connectors range from phono plugs to multipronged S-connectors; wires range from thin speaker wire to coaxial cable. Avoid thin speaker wire; ordinary lamp cord is better for hooking up speakers. Be sure to trim the ends of the wires carefully to keep the two wires from shorting together. Audio cables should be kept away from power cords to avoid excess hum.

Cable systems and home theater

Cable reception, theoretically perfect, can founder in three places: The signals transmitted by the cable company can be inferior; the distribution system—the cable and all the associated equipment—can degrade the signals; or the cable-converter box itself can introduce problems.

Cable boxes. Today's cable-ready sets are designed to present channels as if they were broadcast directly to the set's antenna. Cable boxes—set-top converters and de-scramblers—act as electronic go-betweens, one more link for signals to negotiate before they're fed to your TV set. Unfortunately, the boxes are sometimes a weak link. Many cable subscribers must use the boxes to get premium channels like HBO; in some systems, subscribers must use them to receive all channels.

Cable boxes often render a TV set's remote control useless for changing channels. You may need the cable company's remote—at perhaps a dollar or two in monthly charges—to change channels. One remedy: "code-entry" universal remotes, which work some brands of cable boxes.

Hooking up a VCR to a TV set with a cable box is apt to be cumbersome and to add a layer of complexity to programming the VCR. Further, the box can make it difficult or impossible to view two channels simultaneously on a set with the picture-in-picture (PIP) feature. In the worst cases, you may need *two* boxes in order to display PIP.

Cable sound. When cable systems were first being wired, no one envisioned that expectations of a TV set would change so. Less-than-superlative audio might have gone unnoticed before the days of hi-fi TV. Now, poor sound just gets reproduced more faithfully.

Even though you may watch programs that are broadcast in stereo and even though your TV set or VCR indicates it's receiving stereo signals, your cable company may not properly process the signal. If your "stereo" sound is practically mono, the problem is likely to be most noticeable with Dolby Surround and other ambience effects, which require clear stereo separation.

More annoying, noise can be introduced into the system—and the fancier the system, the worse it will sound. Buzz can come from the extra information that many cable systems use in scrambling the signal. If that's the problem, your only recourse is to complain to the cable company and hope that it will soon upgrade its equipment or switch to another scrambling method. Hum can result from electrical power leaking into the audio signal. That problem, which can be caused by voltage differences in electrical grounds, may be more easily solved by the cable company.

Some cable systems simulcast the audio track of their pay channels on a separate frequency in the FM band, with potentially far better sound quality; some systems also include the basic channels or at least the music channels, like MTV. Many A/V receivers are set up to receive such simulcasts. (The simulcasts are assigned broadcast frequencies where there are no local radio stations on the dial.) There may be an extra installation or monthly charge to hook up your stereo receiver to the cable.

Buying the gear

Our basic shopping advice is easily summed up: Shop around, and don't buy more than you think you need.

Home electronics equipment is often sharply discounted from the list price. The amount of discounting depends to some extent on where you buy. Audio/video salons tend to charge list or close to it; discount houses and mail-order sources usually provide better deals, but you have to know exactly what you want.

The benefits of spending more and moving up the brand line are often small but tangible improvements in performance, convenience, or versatility. Sometimes, however, you pay extra for a name and a look. Mass-market brands such as *RCA* and *Panasonic* in video and *Sony, Pioneer,*

Technics, and *JVC* in audio are widely available in stores and by mail, usually at a substantial discount. Prestige brands, such as *Proton* and *ProScan* video products, are sold primarily through specialty audio and video dealers, with little discounting. Some companies—Sony, RCA, and Panasonic among them—make separate lines of merchandise to reach both markets.

Our tests have shown no substantive performance advantage for the prestige brands. Indeed, prestige audio brands tend to give you fewer features for the money than mass-market brands. On the other hand, the control panels on many prestige products are models of simplicity.

Aficionados of hi-fi equipment have always put together a system one piece at a time, shopping carefully for just the right speakers or the cassette deck nonpareil. Our tests continue to support that strategy. A single company rarely excels at making every component.

Keep in mind, however, that the differences in performance we find between the best and the rest are often fairly small. Even "rack systems," the everything-provided audio systems that are snubbed by audiophiles, can, at their best, produce good sound.

The increasing interconnectedness of audio and video gear, however, may be a good reason to choose many or all components from the same manufacturer. Remote controls, for instance, may enjoy expanded capability if the components are of the same brand. And special taping conveniences built into modern cassette tape decks don't work without a same-brand compact-disc player.

TV sets

▶ **Ratings on page 36.**   ▶ **Repair records start on page 366.**

No sooner had the 27-inch set gained acceptance as the living-room standard than it began giving way to still larger sizes. Sets whose screens measure 31 to 52 inches diagonally represent the fastest-growing part of the television market. The greater involvement that comes with a larger screen size is not without its drawbacks, though: higher prices; larger space requirements; and for models with the largest conventional tubes, higher rates of repair. The larger models, especially those with a screen size of 27 inches or more, are typically designed to be part of an audio/video system. Such "monitor/receivers" generally have sufficient inputs and outputs for connection to the various other parts of the audio/video system.

Better pictures. Picture tubes have become better and brighter in recent years. More than 20 years ago, Sony introduced its breakthrough Trinitron system, with a grille-like metal screen inside the tube that allows greater brightness while keeping the image sharp.

Since then, various manufacturers introduced the Invar tube. The tube takes its name from Invar, the nickel-iron alloy used to make the tube's special shadow mask, a device that helps aim the electron beams at the phosphors of the tube. Ordinary shadow masks bend when they get hot, allowing the electron beams to go out of line and making the color blotchy and distorted. Invar, however, can stand up to the heat of all the electrons needed to create an exceptionally bright picture.

Companies often extol their sets' high

resolution. The current broadcast and cable-TV format allows at best for 330 lines of horizontal resolution, a measure of how sharply the tube can display closely spaced vertical lines.

To deliver a more detailed picture—one with more definition—the set needs more information than the existing broadcast signal provides.

The images on today's best TV screens are close to the best that's possible from broadcasts. Most of the sets we've tested can resolve 320 lines or so, good enough for most TV-watching. If a set lacks a comb filter, however, it may resolve only about 270 lines. S-VHS videotapes and laser-disc players can produce 400 to 425 lines, what any high-resolution TV set ought to reproduce if fed a high-quality signal directly.

The future of the medium lies a quantum leap away: HDTV (high-definition television). It will use an extra-wide screen with more scan lines to deliver images rivaling those seen at the movies, and it will provide CD-quality sound. HDTV sets aren't likely to turn up on store shelves until 1995 or later. Those sets are expected to be priced $1000 to $2000 more than conventional large-screen sets, at least until they become mass-market items. Under the latest government plan, broadcasters would send programming in two formats: conventional signals and high-definition. Thus, a set bought now won't become unwatchable with the coming of HDTV.

In the meantime, wide-screen conventional models ready for adaptation to HDTV are beginning to show up. These transitional models use IDTV (improved definition television), a technology that's been around for several years. IDTV paints the lines of the picture consecutively instead of alternately, effectively removing obtrusive scan lines from the image on the screen. Other signal-processing circuitry makes outlines and edges clearer. The result is a much improved picture.

The few IDTV sets on the market are expensive, priced hundreds of dollars more than conventional sets of similar size (screens of 32 or 35 inches).

Better sound. TV sound has also improved over the past decade. As stereo telecasts and hi-fi sound tracks on videotapes have become the norm, the ability to decode multichannel TV stereo (MTS) has also become commonplace.

Good sound starts with good fidelity—the ability to reproduce wide tonal range. Sound from the best TV sets now compares favorably with that of a decent compact component system.

But good tone quality alone cannot provide the sound effects that some movies beg for. Speakers are not far enough apart to produce stereo in all its glory.

The "side-firing" speakers on some TV sets offer a better illusion of stereo, as long as the set is not enclosed in cabinetry. More and more sets feature ambient sound, like Dolby Pro Logic and Dolby Surround, and have amplifiers built in to power the extra speakers Surround sound requires. Some sets offer electronically enhanced stereo, or "psychoacoustically" altered sound, as an alternative to hooking up external speakers. In those sets, electronics manipulate the audio cues reaching listeners' ears to promote the illusion of a wider sound stage, which can make dialogue sound unnatural. It's most effective in movies with exotic sound effects. The SRS (sound retrieval system) is a particularly effective two-speaker system.

The choices

In the world of television, screen size defines the subtype. There are other, oddball sizes and designs, but these are the main variations you'll find:

Mini. Color TV sets with screens of three inches or so are still in the fancy-gadget stage of evolution. The picture is provided by a liquid-crystal display (LCD) rather than by a regular TV set's cathode-ray tube. To look its best, the picture has to be viewed nearly straight on. Some LCD sets display fairly good pictures, but not as good as tube sets. Bright outdoor lighting makes the picture all but vanish, and even in shaded areas the picture is only marginally acceptable. Color mini sets are priced as high as a full-sized TV set: $150 to $800.

13-inch sets. Sets of this size aren't regarded as a household's main set, so manufacturers tend to make them plain (though the cabinets may be finished in "decorator colors"). As a rule, expect monophonic sound, sparse features, a remote control, and a price tag of $200 to $350.

20-inch sets. With corners squared off, most brands' 19-inch sets grew to 20 inches on the diagonal. Once the standard living-room set, TV sets of this size are increasingly regarded as a second set. Don't expect high-end picture refinements such as a comb filter and a high-performance picture tube. You can expect an acceptable to very good picture, stereo capability, and extra inputs to accept direct programming from a VCR and laser-disc player. This size set offers a wide array of features and typically sells for $250 to $500.

27-inch sets. The squared-off successor to the 25- and 26-inch set, this size ranges from no-frill versions to those heavy with features. It's usually the home's primary TV set. Such sets are priced from less than $400 to more than $1000. High-end models have fancy sound systems and complex but versatile remote controls.

31- to 40-inch sets. While their main selling point is their screen size, many also offer exotic features—such as the ability to recall customized picture and sound settings or picture-in-picture—not common on smaller sets. Prices range from less than $1000 to more than $3000. The largest

HOW MUCH SPACE FOR A BIG-SCREEN TV SET?

Before buying a big-screen set, you might ask, "Where can I put a 150-pound TV set?" Too wide and too heavy for the type of shelving that often holds electronic components, a 31- to 35-inch conventional set requires the kind of sturdy pedestal you see in ads or showrooms. At least a conventional set can fit in a corner. A four-foot-wide projection set works best when it's up against a wall. (If you change your mind about which wall, you won't have to call a mover: Casters are standard equipment.)

Any large-size set this size requires a viewing room with substantial depth. The appropriate range of viewing distance for a 31-inch screen is 6 to 14 feet; for a 35-inch screen, 7 to 14 feet; for a 50-inch set, 10 to 20 feet. Distances are measured from the screen; the set itself occupies another two or three feet of the room's length.

For each set, the closest distance is four times the screen height. We think that's the nearest a viewer can get before the picture's flaws begin to outweigh the benefits of the screen's size. (Some viewers do like to sit even closer, giving up picture quality for the pleasure of feeling a part of the on-screen action.) Sitting beyond the farthest distance, eight times each screen's height, some of the picture's details, and most of the impact of its size, are lost.

TV sets weigh hundreds of pounds.

Rear-projection sets. These offer still more picture area—40 to 70 diagonal inches—but less clarity than a conventional tube. You'll need a viewing distance of at least 10 feet for a 50-inch set, more for larger ones. You'll also have to be positioned more or less head-on, as brightness and color vary as you move left or right, up or down. The big-screen sets come with plenty of features, such as ambient sound and custom audio and video settings. Expect to pay anywhere from $1500 to over $3000.

Features and conveniences

Comb filter. This is circuitry that improves resolution and cleans up image outlines.

Remote control. Just about all TV sets come with an infrared remote control. The simplest such device may only switch the set on and off, change channels, and adjust volume. More versatile units can mute sound, shut the set off with a timer, block a channel from view, and control a VCR. For details, see the discussion of remote controls on page 21.

Electronic channel scan. Direct tuning, which lets you hop from one station to another, is standard. "Auto program" automatically inserts your active channels in the scan sequence. Most sets let you delete little-watched channels from the scan.

Cable ready. These sets have a coaxial cable jack on the back and can receive cable TV signals (except for scrambled premium movie channels) without using the cable company's decoder box. This feature is now commonplace. Higher-end models offer two cable (antenna) inputs, for basic and for scrambled channels.

MTS stereo. MTS (multichannel TV sound) means the set has a built-in stereo decoder and amplifier to reproduce stereo broadcasts. Some lower-priced 20-inch sets from RCA and GE create a pseudo-stereo sound instead of the standard MTS variety.

Inputs/outputs. Audio and video jacks are found mostly on sets 20 inches and larger. Many of the largest sets have more than a dozen. For hooking up a hi-fi VCR, laser-disc player, camcorder, or sound system, the TV set needs at least one video and one stereo audio input, and one stereo audio output.

The tests

Our standard panoply of TV tests includes lab measurements and viewer judgments. Experienced staffers evaluate key aspects of picture quality: clarity, color fidelity, and contrast. In addition, we test for a set's ability to handle less-than-perfect signals. Audio quality is measured similarly to the way we measure for sound-system components.

Reliability

The rule of thumb when it comes to repairs is, the larger the screen, the more likely the set will need a repair. According to our surveys, no single brand has been the most reliable across all set sizes. Among 19- to 20-inch and 25- to 27-inch sets, some of the more reliable brands have been *Panasonic, JVC,* and *GE.* See the Repair Histories, pages 366 and 367.

Buying advice

With good picture quality the norm these days, the choice of a TV set is likely to hinge on several other factors—features, reliability, price, or perhaps the design of the remote control. If it's possible, try out the remote functions in the store before buying the set, to see how convenient they are to use.

Don't put too much stock in comparisons of the picture you see on sets displayed in a store. You can't be sure that those TV sets are getting a uniform picture signal or that they have been uniformly adjusted.

VCRs

▶ Ratings on page 39. ▶ Repair records on page 366.

As VCRs become mature products, prices continue to fall and features trickle down from deluxe to basic models. Dramatic performance improvements await a future development, such as HDTV or digital video. For now, expect to wade through a flood of features, many of which are secondary to what most people need—good picture and sound quality.

These days, nearly all VCRs use the VHS format or its high-end variant, S-VHS. Three brands—*Emerson, Magnavox,* and *RCA*—account for nearly one-third of all VHS VCRs sold in the U.S. Other big brands include names such as *Panasonic, Sharp, JVC, Sony* and *Zenith.*

The Beta format has all but vanished; only Sony, its inventor, still sells Beta equipment, primarily to the TV industry, to Betaphiles, and to consumers outside the U.S. Newer formats such as 8mm and its cousin, Hi8, have come along to accommodate a new breed of small-sized camcorders, and a small number of VCRs that are sold in those formats. Like Beta-format machines, those formats do not accept VHS cassettes.

The choices

VCRs cost anywhere from less than $200 to more than $1000. Certain key features mark off rough price levels.

The basic VCR. While some very low-priced models exist that are just playback machines, VCP (videocassette players), the workhorse product among VCRs has been the low-priced ($200 to $300) two-head player with monophonic sound. Two play/record heads are all you need for everyday recording and playback.

Four-head models. An extra pair of heads offers some advantages: cleaner freeze-frames in the longer-play EP speed and sometimes a slightly better picture during regular playback. Four-head models outsell two-head models and may soon be regarded as the basic VCR. Four-head models start at about $250.

Hi-fi. Hi-fi stereo is resoundingly better than the older, "linear" stereo technology, which lays sound tracks along the edges of the tape. Hi-fi VCRs record the audio tracks as diagonal stripes across the tape's width under the video track. The result is near-CD sound quality, with virtually no flutter or noise and with excellent reproduction across a wide range of audio frequencies. Hi-fi VCRs use two extra heads on the drum and are sometimes referred to as "six-head" machines. Prices of $350 to $450 are typical.

Super VHS. You'll pay a premium of about $200 for this technical refinement. S-VHS gives a sharper picture than normal VHS. S-VHS also stands up better if you're making multiple tape-to-tape copies. To get the most from the S-VHS format, you need a source of S-VHS pictures, such as an S-VHS camcorder. The VCR must also be connected to a high-resolution TV set—preferably a model equipped with an S-video jack.

S-VHS is partially compatible with regular VHS—an S-VHS machine can tape and play in VHS mode, but an S-VHS tape can't be played in a regular VHS machine (although some conventional VHS machines offer "Quasi-S-VHS" playback capability to allow this). To record in S-VHS, you need special S-VHS tapes; the player automatically senses which type of tape and which mode to tape in.

S-VHS models generally are priced $600 to more than $1000.

Features and conveniences

Year by year, fancy features migrate down from higher-priced models to lower-priced ones.

Remote control. Even low-end models usually come with a remote. See the discussion on page 21.

HQ. HQ (high quality) refers to small technical refinements that reduce some of the video noise and other picture defects that a VCR can introduce into a recording. Virtually every VHS VCR has the HQ designation.

Easy programming. On-screen programming is almost universal. The VCR shows a menu on the TV screen that prompts you through the process of choosing times and dates for the programs you want to record, up to several days or weeks in advance.

Even though on-screen programming is a great improvement over previous methods, it's still too complicated for many people. So manufacturers keep devising new, easier ways to program. *VCR Plus*, widely sold as a separate product for $60, now comes incorporated in many VCRs. It enters the time and channel information automatically, using the special three- to seven-digit program code that appears in the TV listings of many newspapers and magazines.

Matsushita incorporates the Program Director, simplified programming controls, on the remote of most *Panasonic* models. On its *Quasar* models it's called "E-Z Dial Programming." You enter each piece of information—date, start time, stop time, and channel—by turning a dial. Then you send the information to the VCR with the Transmit button.

The newest wrinkle in programming is the voice-activated remote. It lets you call out the channel and time to record, but we found it unwieldy to use.

Camcorder jack. All VCRs let a camcorder of any format be plugged in. More and more models have the jack on the front of the VCR, where it's easy to reach.

Picture tricks. They include such features as multiple-speed slow-motion and fast-motion, frame advance, freeze-frame, and picture-in-picture capabilities. On the whole, we'd say that they're flashy gimmicks rather than truly useful additions.

Taping features. One-touch recording (OTR) simplifies taping. A tape-time-remaining indicator can save the frustration of running out of tape five minutes before the end of the movie. Index search lets you mark the tape and then move rapidly to the next mark. Real-time search or "go to" lets you enter the length of the taped program you want to skip and then speeds through the tape. A Skip button advances the tape in 30-second increments.

Tape-editing functions. Of interest mainly to those who make home videos, these include: flying erase heads, for glitch-free assemble edits; an Edit switch that boosts the signal when copying a tape to improve the quality of second-generation signals; a synchro-edit jack to coordinate a camcorder (of any format) or a second VCR used as a source; advanced editing features such as insert editing; a jog-shuttle control, which helps locate a tape segment by running the tape backward or forward at continuously variable speeds; audio and video dubbing abilities; and a character generator for adding written titles or captions.

The tests

CU's engineers check performance of each model at both SP (standard play) and EP (extended play) speeds. We make tapes on each machine, then play them back on laboratory monitors. A panel of staffers judges them for such factors as blurriness, graininess, streaking, and unnatural-looking edges to images.

In the laboratory, CU engineers measure the same tuner factors we check in TV sets—sensitivity to weak signals and selectivity for blocking out adjacent signals. Our audio tests measure the same factors we check on tape decks—flutter, signal-to-noise ratio, and frequency response. And of course, we evaluate how convenient each model is and its features.

Reliability

VCRs are finicky. According to our 1992 Annual Questionnaire, 14 percent of the machines bought from 1987 to 1992 have needed repair at least once. *Magnavox, Sylvania, Panasonic, GE,* and *Quasar* have been among the least troublesome brands. *Fisher* VCRs have needed repairs more often than any other brand. See the brand Repair Histories on page 366.

Buying advice

The current VCR market is replete with good performers. A two-head VCR or a basic four-head model is all you need if you're primarily interested in taping TV programs for viewing later. If you want to take advantage of movies with a stereo sound track or hook the VCR into your stereo system as part of a home theater, consider a hi-fi VHS model.

If you're interested in editing lots of tapes, check that the VCR and camcorder have compatible synchronization provisions. Unfortunately, there's no standardization of synchro-editing features.

VIDEO TAPE

It's not difficult—look for major brands and buy by price. Our tests show very little difference among major brands. We recommend stocking up on video tape whenever it is on sale. That may be fairly often, since manufacturers have shifted their focus from product innovation to packaging and promotion, including wider availability of the 130- and 160-minute cassettes for inveterate time-shifters.

One way the companies are trying to sell more video tape is by promoting special tape for special uses ("everyday," "special recording applications," and so forth). Our tests have shown little or no difference between the regular grade and the high-grade tapes. Nor is there any reason to pay extra for special "hi-fi" tape—a hi-fi VCR can record high-quality sound on any tape. (Our tests do show some small differences among brands when recording linear stereo tracks, but that's hardly ever used.)

Be wary of off-brand tapes. Even off-brand tapes that display legitimate VHS or 8mm logos, supposed assurance that manufacturing standards have been satisfied, can be substandard. It's ironic that at a time when the differences between major brands of videotape have all but disappeared, the assurances of the quality implied by the brand name itself have become more important.

Laser-disc players

Though they've never sold as well as VCRs, laser-disc players enjoy several potential advantages. As movie-playing machines, they can run rings around conventional VHS decks. The picture quality from laser discs can be higher, and sound quality is excellent. A player can rapidly skip to any desired portion of a program and, unlike tapes, discs don't wear with repeated use. Alas, disc players lack a VCR's versatility: You can't record on a disc (at least not yet), and the rental-movie market offers only limited disc selections. Mail-order clubs and retailers sell regular movies on disc for $20 to $30 apiece; special editions may cost $100 or more.

The choices

To ease consumers' qualms about the hodgepodge of disc formats that have arisen, manufacturers have made most of the players compatible with all formats (including CAV, CLV, and CD-V). Some models play only laser discs, others play audio compact discs, hence the term "combi player." Prices start at about $400 and range upward to more than $1000.

Features and conveniences

Double-sided play. This is a major convenience, but a pricey one. The feature plays both sides of a laser disc without having to flip the disc over by hand. It comes with machines selling for several hundred dollars more than a basic model.

CD changer. Available on some upscale models, this lets you play several CDs (but not laser discs) without pause.

Other features. There are many digital frills, including special video effects, esoteric means for preselecting tracks, and various methods for editing from disc to tape.

Buying advice

Picture quality is apt to be good with any model, so choose features first, then shop for the best price. Plan on building your own library of discs; there's not much of a rental market.

Camcorders

▶ **Ratings on page 45.** ▶ **Repair records on page 368.**

The choice is mainly between two lightweight formats—8mm and VHS-C—and their higher-resolution cousins—Hi8 and S-VHS-C—known as "high-band" formats.

Panasonic, the VHS-C market leader, plays up the format's compatibility with VHS VCRs, but the truth is, hooking up an 8mm camcorder to a TV set is very easy. The main advantage of 8mm is its longer playing time—two hours, versus 30 minutes for VHS-C at standard speed. Both formats have held their own in fierce competition; both are likely to stick around for the foreseeable future.

There are some 30 brands of camcorders on the market. A handful of manufacturers—Sony, Matsushita, Canon, Sharp, JVC, and RCA—account for most of the sales.

The choices

8mm. Small, light, easy to tote, 8mm is the hot format. Its "high-band" version is Hi8. Cassettes hold up to two hours.

(2.5-hour cassettes exist but are not readily available.) Sound quality is the equal of hi-fi models in the other formats. Cassettes cost about $5. For playback, you connect a cable from the camcorder to your TV or VCR. You can also connect the camcorder to your VCR to make copies or edit tapes in your VCR's tape format; 8mm VCRs are also available. Prices of 8mm camcorders range from about $700 to $2000 or more. Expect to pay $200 or so extra for Hi8.

VHS-C. JVC introduced this compact version of VHS. The high-band version is S-VHS-C. Cassettes are playable in a VHS VCR with an adapter (supplied with the camcorder) that will work with any VHS VCR. Cassettes hold just 30 minutes at fast speed, 90 minutes at slow speed, and are priced about $6 apiece; tapes with longer running times are reportedly on the way. Prices for VHS-C start at about $800, S-VHS-C at about $1200.

Full-sized VHS. This was the old standard, now fading. Models of this type are heavy and bulky, although some people prefer them for their stability. The high-band version is S-VHS. Standard VHS cassettes are widely available; T-120 (two-hour) tapes cost about $3 each. The camcorder can double as a VHS VCR to play rented movies. Full-sized VHS is the bargain format now, with prices of $700 or less on many models.

Features and conveniences

Standard features include: a motorized zoom lens that lets you make closeups of subjects within an inch of the lens; automatic exposure and sound-level controls; and a flying erase head that helps deliver clean scene changes even if you rerecord something.

Autofocus. Also standard. It keeps the image sharp as the subject or the camera moves. There are two types, infrared and contrast. In our tests, both worked well most of the time, but neither was infallible.

Automatic white balance. This circuitry keeps colors normal under different lighting conditions.

Color viewfinder. Found on a growing number of models, this lets you view scenes in color, but the picture is not as crisp or bright as the one provided by black-and-white viewfinders.

Electronic image stabilization. This feature tries to iron the jitters out of hand-held shots. EIS's effectiveness varies considerably from brand to brand. A video tripod is still the best tool for steady shots (see the report on tripods on page 68).

Digital gain-up. Helps create passable pictures in dim light. It works by slowing the shutter speed. The downside: Moving subjects or fast panning leaves a blur.

Sound. The 8mm format has audio capabilities inherently superior to all except hi-fi VHS and VHS-C models. The built-in mike in most camcorders is better suited for capturing speech than music.

Remote control. More and more commonplace, especially on 8mm models, a remote makes it easier to use the camcorder for playback and editing. It also works as an alternative to a self-timer.

Battery. Most camcorders get their power from a rechargeable nickel-cadmium (nicad) battery. That gives you about an hour of taping on a charge. Many models also offer batteries of smaller capacity (to save weight) or larger capacity (for longer shooting). Consider buying a spare (typically, about $60).

Nicad batteries temporarily lose some of their capacity if they're not periodically discharged fully before being recharged. To get around that, some models have a charger than can "dump" what's left of the battery's charge before the recharge.

Reset-to-auto switch. A single switch on some models restores all settings to their normal automatic mode so that you don't have to check each control.

Manual exposure control. Automatic exposure generally works well but doesn't offer the flexibility of a manual override.

Special picture effects. Simple effects, such as fade in and fade out and a range of shutter speeds, are standard. Effects found on models in the middle to top of brand lines include time lapse, freeze-frame, and other digital effects.

Title generator. Some models permit superimposing printed titles and captions created with a built-in character generator. Others let you photograph and superimpose titles from art work or signs. Most let you select a color for the title.

Connections. Camcorders usually come with all the cables and connectors needed to play back tapes through a TV set or copy them on a VCR. 8mm and VHS models can record from those sources as well; most VHS-C models cannot.

Date/time labeling. This lets you superimpose the date, the time, or both by pressing a button.

Wide-screen pictures. This feature lets you record images in a format similar to letterboxed movies. It's not especially useful, unless you have one of the pricey new TV sets with a 16:9 ratio picture tube.

The tests

We shoot a series of test subjects under a variety of lighting conditions and play the tapes for a panel of trained viewers to judge clarity, color accuracy, and low-light performance. Our audio tests for frequency response and flutter are done the way we test tape decks.

Reliability

Despite their low level of usage—an average of six hours per year for compact models our readers purchased since 1987, most of which had been owned for less than two years—one in 14 models needed repair. *Minolta* 8mm required the most repairs. Full-sized models purchased during the same period, most of which were more than two years old, were used about eight hours a year. They were less likely to need repair. See the brand Repair Histories on pages 368 and 369.

Buying advice

Picture quality overall is quite good. High-band models generally provide a slightly sharper picture than regular models. VHS and VHS-C are slightly more convenient for playback of tapes, but that's about their only advantage. Compared with VHS, 8mm and VHS-C cameras are much easier to lug around and the pictures are about as good.

With any type, you'll need a tripod for professional results. For fast panning, a tripod-mounted compact is more manageable than a tripod-mounted VHS model because the compact's viewfinder is at the rear. See page 68 for the report on tripods.

HOW OBJECTIVE IS CU?

Consumers Union is not beholden to any commercial interest. It accepts no advertising and buys all the products tested on the open market. CU's income is derived from the sale of CONSUMER REPORTS and other publications, and from nonrestrictive, noncommercial contributions, grants, and fees. Neither the Ratings nor the reports may be used in advertising or for any other commercial purpose. Consumers Union will take all steps open to it to prevent commercial use of its materials, its name, or the name of CONSUMER REPORTS.

Remote controls
▶ Ratings on page 57.

The remote control, a.k.a. the "zapper," has become a standard accessory on virtually every type of home-entertainment gear. Now it has become a product in its own right. As the remote's importance has grown—many functions of today's TV sets and VCRs can be performed only with the remote—designers have come up with better and better ways to make the device easier to use.

Some of the improved designs are obvious—buttons that are well spaced and differentiated by color and shape, large labels with good contrast, frequently used functions that are easy to find, and covers that hide little-used buttons. Other designs, like liquid-crystal displays or backlit labels, show a bit more enterprise. Don't expect to find the newest designs on the remote that comes with a cassette deck or CD-player, though; manufacturers reserve their best efforts for video remotes.

The choices

Remotes can be one of three types: dedicated, unified, or universal.

Dedicated remotes. These operate only the component they come packaged with, typically the cheapest TV sets, VCRs, and receivers. Remotes for cassette decks, CD players, and laser-disc players are generally product-specific, too.

Unified remotes. These also come packaged with a component, but offer more flexibility—they operate at least one other product of the same brand, although often in a limited way. Receiver remotes, for example, tend to have lots of buttons to control surround-sound, but only basic functions for a same-brand TV set.

Universal remotes. These are sometimes included with high-end TV sets, VCRs, and receivers, or are sold as a stand-alone product, with prices ranging from $20 to $250. They operate components from a variety of manufacturers.

Their appeal goes beyond that of cutting clutter. If you're looking to replace a lost remote, a universal remote control can cost less than a replacement from the manufacturer. Similarly, if a remote is broken, you can often buy a new universal model for less than it takes to repair the old device.

Universal remotes can be "code-entry" models, "learning" models, or both. Code-entry remotes, programmed with the codes for major-brand components, are easy to use: Just tell the remote which brand and model to emulate. But code-entry remotes often don't support the advanced commands needed for programming a VCR or for components that are more than a few years old.

Learning remotes mimic virtually any command found on other remotes, but are more complicated to set up. To program one, place it head-to-head with the remote whose commands you want it to acquire, then execute those commands. These remotes are typically more powerful, more complicated to learn, and more expensive than code-entry models.

Some models attempt to provide the best of both worlds: code entry to enable the remote to carry out simple commands, with learning keys for the advanced ones.

Features and conveniences

Buttons. The best designs differentiate buttons by size, shape, and color; the worst torture your eyes and fingers with row after row of identical minuscule buttons. Look for north/south buttons, for example, that control volume and channel. Often-used buttons, such as Mute on a TV set, or Pause on a VCR, should also be easy to spot at a glance.

Ergonomics. The best models are well balanced and can be used comfortably with one hand.

Commands. Well designed models let you operate components with a minimum of button-pressing or on-screen menu navigation. Avoid those that make you press the Enter key for something as simple as changing the channel.

Liquid-crystal display. The LCD typically indicates which component is being controlled and shows the command you've entered. It's a good idea, but most of the ones we've seen are hard to see in low light. Touch-sensitive LCDs confirm a command with a beep. Our home-use panel preferred the tactile feedback of regular push buttons.

Low-battery indicator. This warning is especially useful for a learning remote, which can be quite cumbersome to reprogram if the battery goes dead. When the time comes, most models give you a couple of minutes to make the switch.

The tests

We use the remotes with a variety of components from different manufacturers, evaluating convenience and design along with programming ease. To see how the products fare in real use, we also set up a home-use panel.

Buying advice

The simplicity of a code-entry universal remote limits it to only basic functions, which may be just fine for everyday use. Remotes of the learning variety are more difficult to use and tricky to program, but they handle more functions. Hybrid models combine the best of both types: easy setup with powerful functions.

Try to buy where you have return privileges in case the universal remote turns out not to control your components. In any event, don't throw away your old remote controls. You may need them to perform an arcane function or two—or to retrain a learning remote that loses its settings.

Receivers

▶ Ratings on page 41.

The receiver, heart of the audio system, has lately become the heart of the audio/video system as well. For a product that remained essentially unchanged for years, that's a big shift in capability.

In addition to acting as a switching center, a receiver amplifies audio signals from other components and its radio tuner. Receivers, particularly those without mechanical switches and knobs, use few moving parts and tend to last a long time. Our tests have shown that, regardless of price, the amplifier portion almost always performs very well. Where brands differ is in amplifier power output, in FM radio performance, and in the presence of such conveniences as input jacks for plugging in ancillary equipment.

A new technology that is starting to appear, known as RBDS (Radio Broadcast Data Service), allows FM tuners to display a station's call letters, music format, and other information on an LCD.

Receivers are sold under more than forty

brand names. Five brands—*Pioneer, Sony, Kenwood, Technics,* and *JVC*—account for nearly two-thirds of the market, however.

The choices

The premium charged for video capability depends on the brand. Some companies, such as Pioneer, Sony, and JVC, have switched virtually their entire lines over to audio/video receivers. Other companies retain audio-only receivers at the low end of their lines. Some prestige brands offer nothing but audio receivers, but even these are starting to recognize video functions as more than a frill.

Prices range from $150 to more than $1500. By spending more, you don't necessarily get better sound. You get:

Power. Low-end receivers may produce only 35 to 45 watts per channel of amplifier power, while higher-end models crank out 100 watts or more and come with a separate amplifier to drive the surround-sound speakers that are an essential part of a home theater.

How much you need depends on your speakers, the size of the room, and the type of music you play. The need for extra power is easily and often exaggerated. In most applications, 50 watts per channel is ample. Receivers in the 100-watt range are necessary only if you're driving multiple pairs of speakers at loud volumes in large spaces or are using speakers that are particularly inefficient. The box on page 24 can help you calculate your power requirements.

Sound. Two-channel stereo is the most basic sound effect, suited primarily to listening to music. For watching movies or videos, Dolby Surround or Dolby Pro Logic provides greater realism through special circuitry that deciphers the sound effects encoded on many movie videos. Dolby Surround adds a second pair of speakers that carry sound effects and echoes that make the action seem to surround you.

Dolby Pro Logic adds a fifth speaker to carry "center" sound from the direction of the TV screen. Look for a model that includes an amplifier for the fifth channel.

Dolby 3 Stereo, a feature on many Pro Logic receivers, lets you experience all five channels in the surround mode without the second set of speakers. Sounds that would normally emanate from the rear speakers are rerouted to the front three speakers and dispersed at slightly lower volume than the sounds for the other channels. The feature works, but rear speakers provide a more dramatic effect. Other sound effects include ambience modes, which simulate the acoustics of a stadium or concert hall and are now common on middle-of-the-line receivers.

Dolby Pro Logic models start at $250. See also the discussion about choosing a sound-effects package on page 8.

Audio/video switching. An A/V receiver is essentially a control center to select the component you want to hear—either a video source such as a TV set, VCR, or laser-disc player, or an audio source such as a CD, cassette tape, or radio. A remote control to handle most functions comes with all but the cheapest receivers these days.

Elaborate controls. A well-designed set of controls on a receiver should be sensibly arranged and clearly labeled. Mass-market receivers tend to accrete knobs, dials, levers, and lights as you move up the product line. More controls do more, but they make the product more complicated. Prestige brands, on the other hand, make a virtue of simplicity—no flashy display, perhaps no remote control, limited switching and dubbing capability, even on high-priced models.

Features and conveniences

Some receiver features—a pulsing bar graph of the sound "profile," say—may do more for a product's image and marketability than for its usefulness. Here's a rundown of the major features:

Graphic equalizer. This fancy tone control for contouring the sound starts showing up on low-priced models. Equalizers with less than seven adjustment levers, or "bands," as they are called, don't accomplish much more than regular bass and treble controls. Most high-end models now offer digital signal processing.

Digital electronic tuning. It's the standard method of radio tuning. It captures a station at its precise frequency, thus minimizing noise and distortion. Tuning is generally accomplished with an Up/Down Seek button that searches for the next listenable station along the dial. Handiest are tuners that step in increments of 200-kilohertz, the distance between FM channels in the U.S. Some models let you directly enter a station's frequency on a numeric keypad, the method we prefer. When you tune past either end of the band, wraparound tuning jumps automatically to the opposite end.

Remote control. These days, most receivers have ones, but those we've seen usually are riddled with rows and rows of undifferentiated buttons, the way video remote controls used to be.

Switched outlets. They let you plug other components into the receiver so that you can shut off the whole system when you turn off the receiver.

Tone-control bypass. It's useful for temporarily defeating tone settings so

HOW MUCH POWER DO YOU NEED?

Even inexpensive receivers have plenty of power. But if you want a idea of how much power a system actually needs, here's how to figure it:

Determine the "liveness" of your listening room. A space with hard floors, scatter rugs, and plain wood furniture will be acoustically live; one with thick wall-to-wall carpet, heavy curtains, and upholstered furniture, relatively dead. Locate the room size (in cubic feet) and type at right and note the multiplier. That figure, multiplied by a speaker's minimum power requirement, as noted in our speaker Ratings, gives the watts per channel needed.

Let's say you have a 4000-cubic-foot room with average acoustics and speakers that require 12 watts of power. Using the multiplier from the chart, 1.5, multiplied by the watts needed, 12, equals 18. At a minimum, you need an amplifier with 18 watts of power per channel to drive those speakers at moderately high volume. To be safe, double that figure. To do justice to CDs or demanding music, triple the figure, and look for a receiver that produces 50 watts or so.

POWER MULTIPLIERS

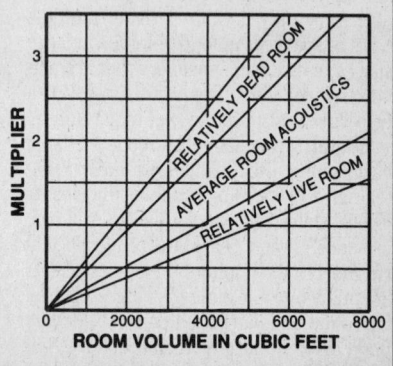

(Chart showing MULTIPLIER vs ROOM VOLUME IN CUBIC FEET, with lines for RELATIVELY DEAD ROOM, AVERAGE ROOM ACOUSTICS, and RELATIVELY LIVE ROOM; y-axis 1–3, x-axis 0–8000)

that you can listen to a recording in its pristine form.

Loudness switch. It boosts the bass when the volume is down to compensate for the human ear's insensitivity to bass at low volume. A variable control allows the most flexibility.

Mute switch. It reduces volume without changing the volume-control setting.

The tests

Our evaluation is based primarily on a standard battery of laboratory tests, chiefly of the FM tuner. A stellar tuner reproduces sound that's free of residual background noise and distortion. Sensitive enough to pull in weak signals, a receiver should also resist interference from electrical sources, aircraft, and other radio signals. We also consider convenience, especially of the control layout, and the usefulness of features.

Reliability

Receivers are stable components that typically last for years and years. Only 6 percent bought from 1987 to 1992 have needed repair, according to a recent reader survey.

Buying advice

If you want to power only a modest system purely for music listening, a low-end receiver, rated at 50 watts per channel, should be quite satisfactory. You should be able to find such receivers priced for $150 or less.

Although some low-priced models can handle a TV/VCR/stereo setup without a problem, you'll probably have to buy higher in the line if you want the receiver to be the heart of a home theater. Receivers in the $350-to-$450 range typically come with Dolby Pro Logic and enough jacks to accommodate a complicated system and enough power to run more than one set of loudspeakers.

Before buying any receiver, make sure it matches your other components and meets their power requirements. See "How much power do you need?" in the box at left.

Loudspeakers

▶ Ratings on page 52.

Good sound depends more on the loudspeakers than on any other component, so speakers are the last place to economize in setting up a system.

Speakers tend to differ most in their ability to handle the bass, which is most important if you listen to jazz, pop, or movie music. That doesn't mean speakers all sound the same—differences elsewhere in the audio spectrum give each model its own distinctive sound. That's where your own taste comes into play. Additionally, what you hear is affected by the size and furnishings of the room, by the speakers' placement, and even by the type of music.

There are more than 300 speaker brands, many of them from small, specialty companies and many of them American. The leading manufacturers are Radio Shack and Bose, which account for about one-quarter of all sales.

The choices

Classic loudspeaker configuration has not changed much in 30 years: a rigid box containing a large bass speaker, the woofer, and a much smaller treble speaker, the tweeter. There may also be a third speaker, the mid-range, that handles middle tones between the highs and lows. While most speakers direct all the sound out the front, others are designed to radiate some sound upward or to the rear, bouncing sound waves off a nearby wall.

To make a big, loud bass, a speaker needs a big woofer. Speaker manufacturers have long tried to design around that fact of physics, with some success. Some miniature speakers, for instance, can deliver more bass than their size would imply, though at the expense of volume. A newly popular type of speaker, the three-piece "subwoofer/satellite" system, separates the tweeter and mid-range speakers from the bass subwoofer. The tweeter and the mid-range speakers, which supply much of the stereo effect, are small and fit unobtrusively amongst furnishings, while the large bass section can be concealed behind a sofa or in a corner behind the TV set.

Prices for speakers run from $100 or so a pair to $1000 and up. What more money primarily buys, at every size level, is a deeper reach into the bass range. Here are the main choices:

Small speakers. Miniature speakers are smaller than a shoebox; they typically cost $100 and up per pair. Most of this type are seriously deficient in reproducing bass. A subclass of miniature speakers is called "powered" speakers; they have their own built-in amplifier.

Bookshelf speakers are the fastest growing type of loudspeaker. This size can fit on a bookshelf sideways, at the expense of about 1½ feet of books. Bookshelf speakers typically are priced $200 to $550 per pair. They're appropriate for undemanding listening in medium-sized rooms or as the second pair of speakers in a surround-sound system.

Ambience speakers are another type of small speaker and are typically priced less than $150 per pair. They are intended for use as the adjunct speakers in a Dolby Surround system. Many are sold singly, to serve as the center-channel speaker in a Dolby Pro Logic setup. These speakers don't need much bass capacity, as the bass in a Dolby system is carried by the main speakers.

Main speakers. Medium-sized models can fill a medium-sized room with loud sound, and a large room with fairly loud sound. When speakers reach this size, the woofer can be big enough to push the large volumes of air needed to reproduce a full, rich, loud bass sound. Figure on spending $300 or more for a decent pair.

Large speakers are necessary for filling a very large room, but they're overkill in a smaller setting. Speakers of this size can cost $700 to thousands of dollars. In this price range, you'll also find audiophile equipment, such as electrostatic speakers, in which tall, thin plastic diaphragms replace speaker cones.

Three-piece systems. Used as main speakers, these consist of two small satellite speakers connected to a separate bass module. The satellites have only mid-range and treble components and are positioned right and left. The bass module can be placed just about anywhere. On average, three-piece systems rendered sound less accurately than conventional speakers. Figure on spending $300 to $800.

The tests

Speaker performance is measured by laboratory instruments in an echo-free chamber and in a 14x23-foot carpeted, furnished room. For most speakers, we measure accuracy from a frequency of about 30 hertz in the bass to about 16,000 Hz in the treble and rate it on a 100-point scale. We don't rate ambience speakers at frequencies below 100 Hz.

Tweaking a receiver's tone controls can improve a speaker's accuracy and also help compensate for a room's acoustical drawbacks. Most listeners find it difficult to pick the more accurate of two models if the spread in our scores is eight points or less.

We also measure the minimum power the receiver must supply to a speaker to produce fairly loud sound in a medium-sized room.

Reliability

Loudspeakers are very stable components from which you can expect little trouble.

Buying advice

Buy the biggest high-accuracy speakers you can fit or afford. Money invested in speakers provides the biggest payoff.

Between types, speakers differ most in their ability to handle bass. Within a type, accuracy of the frequency response is most important. Differences in the audio spectrum give each model its own distinctive sound. So it's important to audition loudspeakers yourself. In an audio store's listening room, try to duplicate the speaker position you'll use at home. Compare only two pairs of speakers at a time; stay with the pair you prefer and judge it against the next. Take an LP or CD whose music you know well, one that gives both bass sounds and treble a workout.

It's also important to get return privileges in case the speakers don't sound satisfactory at home.

Once you have a model in mind, be sure your receiver will be able to supply enough power to the speakers and that speaker impedance is not too low for the amplifier to handle (see "Set up the speakers" on page 8 and "How much power do you need?" on page 24).

Compact-disc players

▶ Ratings on page 50.   ▶ Repair records on page 368.

Virtually every CD player we have tested is capable of reproducing superb hi-fi sound. All the traditional indicators of quality sound—wide dynamic range, accurate (flat) frequency response, and freedom from noise and distortion—can be taken for granted. The minor differences we've noted in sound-reproduction capabilities aren't apparent except to a laboratory instrument or an expert listener. Performance differences have been confined to how well the players overcome adverse conditions such as being bumped or playing a damaged disc. Recent models have gotten better at compensating for such problems.

Such perfection has helped the CD player conquer the world of sound. The technology of recording information for playback with lasers has also crept into the world of image. Laser-disc players typically also play CDs as well as the LP-sized laser discs. On the horizon are machines that play video compact discs. Kodak has recently introduced a system for putting still photos on CDs—"Photo CD." And CD players are increasingly sold packaged with computers as "CD-ROM" drives—to work as multimedia systems.

The world of home audio compact-disc players is very much dominated by Sony, which makes one of every four players sold in the U.S.. Other major brands include *Pioneer* (the leader in laser-disc players), *JVC*, and *Technics*.

The choices

Table-model components. These come as single-disc models and multiple-disc changers. Prices start around $100 for a low-end single-disc player, though most sell for between $150 and $300.

One changer design uses a "magazine," a slide-in box the size of a small, fat paperback book. Magazines typically hold six discs, but some models take more.

The alternative changer design is a carousel, holding five or six discs. That design has the advantage of being somewhat easier to load. Most carousels use a slide-out drawer, while a few others load from the top. Top-loading models cannot be sandwiched into a stack of other stereo components.

Portable players. Some are scarcely bigger than the disc itself; others are part of an overgrown boom box. Portable models sell from about $125 for a small, simple unit, to more than $300 for a fancy system. Basic models may have only rudimentary controls. More elaborate versions come with such features as a rechargeable battery pack, a built-in radio tuner, a cassette deck, or a panoply of controls similar to what you find on a table model. Many boom-box systems have detachable speakers with a bass-boost feature. Portables can easily be hooked into a sound system.

Features and conveniences

The CD world is rife with jargon referring to technical specifications, particularly those connected with the conversion of digital information to analog sound waves: "oversampling," "dual digital/analog converters," "bit stream" technology, triple laser beams, and so forth. None of that stuff is apt to make a difference you can consistently hear, our tests have shown.

The extras on a CD player don't always go hand-in-hand with price. Less expensive models may be just as generously endowed with features as more expensive ones.

Standard on all home compact models are features that let you play, pause, stop, select a track, and program selected tracks to play in the order you choose. (Changers let you skip from one disc to another.)

Also typical is a display that indicates which track is being played and the elapsed playing time. Common options, even on basic models:

Shuffle play. This mixes the playing order into a random sequence. Look for non-repeat shuffle.

Numeric keypad. It lets you program by punching in track numbers directly rather than fussing with Up/down buttons. It's common on remotes, less so on consoles.

Remote control. These are standard on all but the lowest-priced players. Look for one that's easy to use and whose buttons are logically organized.

Calendar display. It starts off by showing the number of each track on the disc; as the disc plays, the track numbers disappear one by one. Such a display is also handy for making tapes, since it reminds you which tracks you have already programmed.

On/off pause. It's handier than having to hit Play to resume playing.

Fade control. This makes the music fade out slowly, then stop.

Programming aids. Programming a CD player instructs the unit to play tracks in a particular order. Some players can even remember your programs. This feature, called Favorite-track selection or Custom file, involves the player's reading a code on each disc and filing your program for that disc under the code for later reference. Some models have a Delete-track function that will skip over unwanted tracks.

Taping aids. Taping is easiest with special features such as Auto-edit. When you punch in the recording time of one side of a tape, the CD player suggests a track order to fit the time. With a player that features synchronized recording, you don't even have to be present during the taping. You connect a cable from the player to a deck of the same brand that has Auto-reverse. When the deck is ready to record on the second side, it sends a signal to the CD player, and the taping resumes. Some models can search for the loudest passage on a disc, so you can set your recorder to the proper sound level. Running total adds up track time as you're programming the disc so that you can tell how many tracks will fit on the tape you're using.

Special effects. Digital signal processing, a technique that simulates the acoustics of a concert hall or stadium, is starting to appear on selected models.

The tests

In addition to making the usual sound checks, we see how well the players can cope with adversity: bumps and purposely defective discs. We also measure how fast the players can jump from track to track.

Reliability

The repair rate for most brands of compact-disc players bought from 1989 to 1992 has been about 5 percent, according to our readers' experiences. Of the two types of CD player, single-disc models have been slightly more trouble-free than changer models. Among the single-disc players, *Nakamichis* have experienced the most trouble. *Denon* had the worst record of the changers. For more information, see the brand Repair Histories on page 368.

Buying advice

Good audio performance from a compact-disc player is a given. Virtually every CD player we've tested can reproduce superb hi-fi sound. Product differences boil down to how they handle physical abuse (vibration, damaged discs) and to the presence of features.

Changer models are priced a little higher than single-play units but offer the convenience of hours of uninterrupted play. We prefer the carousel design of changer, since it's easier to load and unload than the magazine type.

If uninterrupted playing isn't crucial, consider a single-play model. You're likely to get more features for the money than you would with a changer.

Cassette decks

The cassette tape was originally developed for recording voices, not high-fidelity music, so it was born with a limited ability to capture the whole audible spectrum and burdened with a high level of background hiss. It has taken considerable technical cleverness to overcome those impediments. Now, the best of the modern cassette decks are able to reproduce music that's pleasing to any but the most critical listener.

Tape cassettes still outsell compact discs, an inherently superior medium, for obvious reasons. Cassettes—cheap, portable, and widely available—allow you to make your own recordings. But conventional tape has to compete against new digital technologies that play back and record:

■ Digital compact cassette decks (DCC), a new component that began appearing in stores last year, offer slightly better compatibility than other new media: DCC decks can play conventional cassettes as well as record and play digitally. For recording on digital tape, DCC relies on a data-compression process that leaves out the parts of a musical program that are masked by other sounds. In essence, it records only what you're apt to hear and ignores inaudible sonic information. DCC decks have copy-protection circuitry that creates perfect copies of CDs, but prevents copying those copies.

■ The Mini Disc, or MD, developed by Sony, is the first consumer-priced compact-disc-style medium that can record as well as play. Using data-compression technology similar to that used on digital compact cassettes, the Mini Disc is a 2½-inch disc that can play up to 74 minutes. The Mini Disc also incorporates copy protection circuitry.

■ Digital audio tape (DAT) cassettes have had a toehold in the U.S. for a couple of years. DAT delivers virtually the same fine high-fidelity sound as a compact disc. But, since the tiny DAT cassettes aren't compatible with conventional decks or CD players, a DAT or MD owner is faced with the prospect of building a new tape or CD library. Like DCC, DAT decks incorporate copy-protection circuits.

Promising as these new technologies seem, they won't send cassette tape the way of the LP record overnight. If you already have an extensive collection of tapes, it makes sense to stay with a conventional tape deck. If you choose the right deck, you won't sacrifice much in the way of performance. Some of the decks we've recently tested can deliver sound that approaches the quality of digital tape or CDs.

The choices

Component tape decks sell for $100 or so to well over $1000. To get a deck that performs well, expect to pay $200 to $500. Spend less, and you'll probably sacrifice performance. Spend more, and you'll get more features, which may not improve performance significantly.

You can also hook up most walkabout tape players to a stereo system. Their basic playing performance can be quite acceptable, although the small controls may not be very convenient.

Among component decks, there are two principal types:

Single-deck machines. They're generally regarded as serious machines, geared to the audio-buff market. We've found that the tape drive in a single-tape deck is often a cut above the drives in a comparably priced dual-deck machine.

Dual-deck machines. Also called "dubbing" decks, they lend themselves to making copies of tapes and to playing cassettes in sequence. For that convenience, you usually have to give up something in performance. In past tests, we've found that these decks tended to suffer more from flutter than single-deck models.

Features and conveniences

Here are features you're most likely to encounter:

Adjustable bias control. Modern tape coatings have the potential to deliver a wider dynamic range than the standard ferric oxide (Type I) tape. By increasing the "bias" (an ultrasonic signal the deck uses to reduce distortion), many decks can handle chromium dioxide (Type II) and metal (Type IV) tape. If a deck has Automatic tape-type switches, it is able to sense the type of tape loaded and switches bias accordingly. To fine-tune the bias setting, some decks have a manual control you set by ear. Some decks boast an Auto-bias control that fine-tunes the bias for you, which eliminates a lot of fiddling.

Noise-suppression circuits. Numerous techniques have been employed to mute tape hiss, including reformulating the tape itself. Most decks lean heavily on electrical signal-processing to reduce noise. To utilize the circuits, a tape must be recorded and played back with the circuitry.

Standard are Dolby B and Dolby C; virtually all prerecorded cassettes use Dolby B. Better still, though now available only on mid- to high-priced models, is HX Pro, which expands the treble range just about enough to capture the dynamic range of a CD, and the new Dolby S, which records at near-digital quality. Another system, dbx, has all but disappeared.

Auto-reverse. This feature reverses the tape automatically when it reaches the end, so you can hear both sides without having to flip the tape. Many dual-deck models can play both sides of two tapes in sequence, a feature called Relay play.

Music search. This feature locates a particular selection by looking for the silent gap between selections.

Tape scan. You can locate a desired selection on a tape by moving from song to song, playing the first few seconds of each.

Remote control. Remote controls for tape decks are probably less useful than for other components—you have to approach the machine anyway to insert or remove a cassette. The typical tape-deck remote is a small gadget with tiny buttons.

Recording-level meters. These days, meters are lighted bar graphs rather than swinging needles. If you do a lot of recording, look for a deck with 12 or so segments on its recording-level meter. Numerous segments make it easier to establish the peak level of the music you are recording and to set the appropriate level.

Three heads. A deck with three heads doesn't necessarily produce better recordings than one with two heads, but it is more convenient to use for recording. The third head makes it possible to monitor the recording as it is being made. On machines with bias adjustment, the third head also makes it easier to fine-tune the bias setting.

Record mute. This feature inserts a silence between selections when you record continuously, say from a CD or an LP. The silences act as signposts for the Music search and Scan features.

Quick reverse. This senses the leader tape at the end of a cassette, and immediately switches the tape's direction.

Dubbing. Dual decks dub, or copy, tapes at the press of a button. Many decks have an Edit dub feature that allows you to pause the recording deck while you change tapes or fiddle with the playback deck. A High-speed dubbing feature cuts recording time in half, but also degrades the music somewhat.

CD synchro. This feature helps coordinate recording from a CD. It requires using a CD player of the same brand as the tape deck. Pushing a Synchro button cues up the deck and starts recording the instant the music begins.

Buying advice

In our tests, low flutter and a wide dynamic range separate the best performers from the rest. We also found a wide range in convenience and ease of use as well as features.

If you plan to make a lot of tapes, look for a model with three heads, an adjustable bias control, and Dolby B, Dolby C, and HX Pro noise-suppression circuitry.

If you'll be taping CDs, you may want to pay a premium for Dolby S circuitry or at least Auto edit or Synchro edit features.

If you're interested in copying tapes, look for a dual-deck unit. For those who are primarily interested in playing tapes, make sure the deck is equipped with such features as Dolby B circuitry, plus Auto-reverse and Music search.

Stereo headphones

Headphones have come a long way in recent years. Some now rival the acoustic accuracy of high-quality loudspeakers, a feat made possible by careful acoustic design using a magnet-and-coil dynamic driver that functions like a miniature loudspeaker. Headphones suitable for use with home sound systems typically are priced at $50 to $150. The plastic and foam-rubber models designed for use with walkabout stereos are priced at $10 and up.

The choices

Headphones can sit on or around the ears. The best design for you may depend on the shape and size of your ears. Headphones also differ in how much of an acoustic cocoon they provide. Here are the types:

Closed-seal. These models keep out much of the surrounding sound, while letting out little of the sound that might disturb others.

Semi-open. Models of this design give you a reasonable chance of hearing the phone ring or the baby cry.

Open-seal. These models keep you in touch with your surroundings, but they leak a fair amount of sound.

Headphones also differ in their cord arrangements. The traditional Y-shaped cord, attached to both earpieces, makes the headphones a trifle hard to put on. Single-cord models are more convenient. Cords may be coiled or straight.

A few models do away with the cord, relying on infrared light to transmit the sound signal. Unfortunately, the infrared system may introduce background noise and interference. You also lose sound anytime something opaque comes between the headphones and the stereo.

Buying advice

Be sure the headphones are compatible with the impedances of your components. Receivers and CD players are usually no problem, but some cassette decks require high-impedance headphones. Equipment such as walkabout stereos may need high-sensitivity headphones to achieve satisfactory loudness.

With any headphones, it's easy to forget how loud the music has become. If sounds seem muffled and words are hard to distinguish after you've taken headphones off, you may have suffered temporary hearing loss. When those symptoms progress to a tickling sensation or ringing in your ears, there's a danger the hearing loss could become permanent.

WHAT THE RATINGS MEAN

- The Ratings typically rank products in order of estimated quality, without regard to price.
- A product's rating applies only to the model tested and should not be considered a rating of other models sold under the same brand name unless so noted.
- Models are check-rated (✓) when the product proved to be significantly superior to other models tested.
- Products high in quality and relatively low in price are deemed Best Buys.

Walkabout stereos

Walkabout stereos are now a familiar part of the American audio landscape. The typical walkabout has a cassette player and an AM/FM radio tuner, but you can buy walkabouts that have just one or the other. If you're willing to spend about $150, you can get a walkabout that plays CDs. There are also Sony Mini-Disc players for the audiophile who must have the latest in on-the-go digital sonic purity—and who doesn't mind spending $500 or so to get it.

The headphone cable on a walkabout acts as the FM antenna, so when you move, the signal strength reaching the antenna varies considerably. If you use the radio where stations are distant and signals weak, reception may be problematic, especially if you use the walkabout while jogging.

Sony invented the walkabout and remains the major brand. Other brands in the market: *Sanyo, Panasonic*, and *Aiwa*.

The choices

The name of the game in walkabouts is size; manufacturers have managed to cram decent sound and performance into machines little bigger than a couple of tape cassettes.

Radio/tape players. Unless you confine your listening to either tapes or radio, you'll want a walkabout that offers both functions. Those models average $50 or so, though feature-laden models go for $100 and up.

Tape players. The average cassette-only model costs about $25, and it's typically smaller and lighter than the units with radio tuners—a consideration if you plan to hook the player on your waistband while jogging. (The bounce of jogging causes noticeable flutter in these machines, though the act of running is likely to make critical listening impossible anyway.)

Radios. Most walkabouts with just a radio tuner are even cheaper (typically, less than $20) and lighter (no tape-drive mechanism).

Mini Discs. These play digitally recorded discs, therefore sharing many of the advantages of compact discs. Currently priced in the neighborhood of $500, they should eventually come down in price.

Features and conveniences

The typical radio/tape player has the basics you need to play a cassette (Play, Stop, Fast Forward, and Rewind) or tune in a station (AM/FM band, Tuning). Features beyond the basics include:

Autoreverse. If you're jogging and don't want to fumble with tape controls, it's handy to have the player automatically switch to the other side of the cassette.

Digital tuning. This allows precise tuning. The selected radio station is displayed on a small LCD screen.

Some models with digital tuning also have preset tuning that let you program for up to 16 of your favorite stations.

Bass booster. Sold under such names as "Megabass," this feature puts more oomph in the low range.

Water resistance. Sports models offer some protection from rain and sweat. Some models also claim moderate impact resistance.

Recording. Few models can record, but for people who want to tape lectures or interviews, a walkabout with a built-in microphone is a good choice.

Noise suppression. In our tests, units with Dolby B had significantly less tape hiss than those without it.

Other features. Models with Automatic stop turn themselves off after rewinding, to save the battery. On some models, unplugging the headphone stops the tape. A Hold button keeps you from accidentally turning the unit on or changing a station. Scan and Seek tuning make it easier to find radio stations. Dual headphone jacks let a friend listen in. Some models have a remote control.

Buying advice

Most walkabouts produce surprisingly good sound, roughly equivalent to what you would hear with a low-priced home audio system. When you pay more than $75, you get such conveniences as digital tuning with station-presetting capability, Dolby noise suppression, and a bass booster. Higher-priced walkabouts also tend to be more compact.

Don't buy more than you need. If radio reception where you live is weak, you may be better off with a unit that just plays tape. Or if you never listen to tapes, a radio-only model can save both money and considerable weight.

Sports models are typically bulkier than other walkabouts, but their cases provide some protection against water and occasional bumps and jolts.

Audio tape
▶ Ratings on page 55.

The beneficiary of countless improvements over the last 30 years, the best audio cassettes can handle the recording demands of a CD or other high-quality source.

In the years ahead, however, conventional cassette tape will have to compete with two new and inherently superior products—digital compact cassettes (DCC) and Mini Discs. DCC may represent the most immediate threat, because the new decks play conventional cassettes as well as the new type, so people with extensive tape libraries don't have to start all over. Both DCC and Mini-Disc recorders are still more expensive than a good analog cassette deck, and digital sound quality isn't essential for lots of situations, so the traditional cassette tape is likely to be around for years. Three brands dominate the U.S. market—*Maxell, TDK,* and *Memorex,* accounting for about two-thirds of sales.

The choices

The three main types of cassettes differ in the type of coating applied to the tape and the strength of the signal—known as the bias—needed for a tape deck to control distortion:

Type I ("normal"). This is the oldest type sold, as well as the lowest quality and, at $1 to $2.50 per tape, the lowest priced. Its ferric-oxide coating is easily overwhelmed by louder sounds and, when sounds are soft, it produces a background hiss. Type I tape is best for speech, nondemanding music such as background music, or recordings that will be played under less than ideal conditions, such as in a boom box.

Type II ("high bias"). This type, which uses a high-energy ferrite or chromium dioxide coating, minimizes tape hiss and handles higher frequencies better than Type I. Use this type to record FM broadcasts, to make tapes for the car from CDs, or to make tapes for a walkabout. Expect to pay $2 to $4 per cassette.

Type IV ("metal"). This is the highest grade of tape. Not all tape decks can produce a strong enough bias signal, when recording, to take advantage of its capabilities, but all should be able to play back tapes already recorded. Type IV tape is best for the most demanding applications, such as a live concert or music from a compact disc for listening at home. Prices range from about $3 to as much as $14 per tape.

Within the above types, manufacturers offer several grades of tape. Sony, for example, offers no less than five grades of Type II tape. Fancy, high-powered names, such as Turbo or Super, imply superior performances. Based on our tests, we wouldn't take the names too seriously.

Other considerations

Playing time. The time is indicated by the "C" number—C-60, C-90, and so forth. A C-90 tape plays 45 minutes per side. Tapes longer than C-90 haven't performed well in our tests, although they may be useful for recording two CDs or minimizing interruptions when taping a long speech.

Heat resistance. While the tape itself is reasonably tolerant of heat, the plastic carrying case may warp or come apart if it gets too hot. Temperatures inside a car can reach 130°F on a sunny day. We found that cassettes specifically designed to withstand such temperatures performed as advertised. Price: about $12 on average.

The tests

We use laboratory instruments to gauge each tape's ability to render sounds both loud and soft. We also measure how much distortion strong signals produce, check for dropouts (a measure of quality control) and verify the tape's ability to respond to the standard bias signal. Heat resistance tests are performed at temperatures ranging from 104° up to 221°.

Buying advice

There's no point wasting money on a fancy tape when you're just recording speech or making tapes for a boom box. Just about any Type I tape will do.

For reasonably high quality recordings—FM broadcasts, copying high-quality cassettes or LPs, or for playback in a walkabout player or a good car deck—higher-rated Type I and Type II tapes are fine. Save Type IV tapes for recording live music and copying CDs. And don't assume that the highest-priced brand is the best—in our tests, it wasn't.

HOW TO USE THE RATINGS

- Read the **article** for general guidance about types and buying advice.
- Read **Recommendations** for brand-name advice based on our tests.
- Read the **Ratings order** to see whether products are listed in order of quality, by price, or alphabetically. Most Ratings are based on estimated quality, without regard to price.
- Look to the **Ratings table** for specifics on the performance and features of individual models.
- A model marked Ⓓ has been discontinued, according to the manufacturer. A model marked Ⓢ indicates that, according to the manufacturer, it has been replaced by a successor model whose performance should be similar to the tested model but whose features may vary.

LARGE-SCREEN TV SETS

RATINGS: LARGE-SCREEN TV SETS

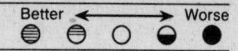

Better ◄——————► Worse
◉ ◒ ○ ◓ ●

▶ See report, page 11. From Consumer Reports, March 1993.

Recommendations: Among conventional sets, the 31-inch *Quasar SX3130FE*, $950, was a standout for high quality and attractive price. We judged it a Best Buy. Other top performers cost considerably more: the *Mitsubishi CS-35FX1* ($2500), *RCA F35100ST* ($1880), and *Toshiba CF3564B* ($1575). The clear choice among rear-projection sets is the *Hitachi 50UX10B*, $2600, which offers very good sound and the best picture. (Note: All have been discontinued but successor models are noted at right.)

Ratings order: Listed by types; within types, listed in order of overall score. Differences in score of seven points or less were not very significant. Models with identical scores are listed alphabetically. Price is the manufacturer's suggested retail; actual retail may be lower. [S] indicates tested model has been replaced by successor model; according to the manufacturer, the performance of new model should be similar to the tested model but features may vary. See right for new model number and suggested retail price, if available. [D] indicates model discontinued.

31, 32, AND 35-INCH CONVENTIONAL SETS

Brand & model	Price	Overall score	Clarity	Color fidelity	Black level	Brightness	Geometric distortion	Adj. channel rejection	Tone quality	Ease of set operation	Advantages	Disadvantages	Comments
Quasar SX3130FE, A Best Buy [D]	$950	90	◒	◒	◒	○	◒	●	◒	○	E,G,H,I,L,M,N,Q	i	C,L,M,N,DD
Toshiba CN3281B [S]	1499	88	◒	◒	◒	◒	◒	◒	○	◒	D,E,H,L,Q,R	—	A,L,M,P
Mitsubishi CS-35FX1 [D]	2500	86	◒	◒	◒	◓	○	◒	◒	◒	E,J,K,L,M,N,R	b,i	D,F,H,J,M,U,W
Panasonic CTP-3180SF [S]	1180	85	◒	◒	○	○	◒	●	◒	○	E,G,H,I,L,N	j	L,M,N,EE
Sony KV-32XBR35 [S]	1780	84	◒	◒	◒	○	○	○	○	◓	A,C,F,H,I,L,M,Q,R	b,d,e	E,L,M,P,CC,EE
RCA F35100ST [S]	1880	83	◒	○	◒	◒	◒	○	◒	◓	C,F,I,O,R	—	E,G,L,M,N,R,U
Toshiba CF3564B [S]	1575	83	◒	◒	◒	○	◓	○	◒	◓	E,L,Q	—	B,M,P,U,DD
RCA F31226ES [S]	1100	82	◒	◒	◒	◒	○	○	◓	◒	C,F,R	h	E,G,L,M,N,R
Zenith SJ3275BG [D]	1020	82	○	◒	○	○	◒	○	◒	○	L,R	a	G,I,K,R,W,Y,Z,AA
GE 31GT656 [D]	860	80	◒	◒	◒	○	◓	◒	○	◓	F,Q	—	G,L,N,R,DD

LARGE-SCREEN TV SETS 37

Brand & model	Price	Overall score	Clarity	Color fidelity	Black level	Brightness	Geometric distortion	Adj. channel rejection	Tone quality	Ease of set operation	Advantages	Disadvantages	Comments
Hitachi 31KX6B [D]	$890	79	○	◐	●	○	◐	◐	◐	○	E,G,M,Q	i	E,K,M,S,Y,Z,AA,BB,DD,EE
JVC AV31BM3 [S]	955	78	○	◐	●	●	◐	○	○	○	E,G,I,L,O,P	f,i	E,G,L,M,Y,AA,DD
Mitsubishi CS-31MX1 [S]	1300	78	◐	○	○	○	○	◐	○	◐	E,K,M,R	b,d,e,g	V,EE
Sears 43958 [S]	1500	76	○	◐	○	○	○	○	◐	○	F,I	—	G,L,N,R,U,DD
50- TO 52-INCH REAR-PROJECTION SETS													
Hitachi 50UX10B [D]	2600	72	○	○	◐	◐	○	◐	◐	○	H,B,R	a,b,c,d,e	A,L,M,Q,S,X
Pioneer SD-P5065 [D]	2680	68	◐	○	◐	◐	◐	◐	◐	◐	B,G,H,J,L,O,Q,R	a,j	A,I,L,M,O,X,DD,FF
RCA P52151WK [S]	2220	67	●	○	◐	◐	◐	◐	◐	◐	C,F,I,O,Q,R	a	G,L,M,N
Magnavox PN3052A [D]	2200	61	●	○	◐	○	○	◐	◐	○	E,L,N,O,R	a,c	F,M,DD
Mitsubishi VS-50VF2 [D]	3128	58	●	◐	◐	◐	◐	◐	◐	◐	E,H,J,K,L,M,R	a,i	F,M,T,W

Successor Models (in Ratings order)
Toshiba CN3281B is succeeded by CN32C90, $1999; Panasonic CTP-3180SF by CT-31SF10, $1499; Sony KV-32XBR35 by KV-32XBR36, $1999; RCA F35100ST by F35750ST, $2199; Toshiba CF-3564B by CF-35C40, $2199; RCA F31226ES by F31700GG, $1249; JVC AV-31BM3 by AV-31BM4, $1099; Mitsubishi CS-31MX1 by CS-31301, $1599; Sears 43958 by 43928, $1399; RCA P52151WK by P52750WK, $2799.

Performance Notes
All: • Have clearer pictures when fed high-quality video signals through S jack. • Have satisfactory freedom from audio noise and distortion. • Projection sets get dimmer at wider angles and as viewer moves up and down; are bright enough for viewing within about 45 degrees to left or right of center screen. • Conventional sets can be viewed within about 70 degrees to left or right of center.
Except as noted, all: • Have color correction judged fair or poor. • Have audio frequency response and separation judged very good or better. • Have remote operation judged very good or better.

Features in Common
All have: • On-screen menu to guide through features and adjustments. • At least 125 cable channels. • Automatic and manual channel bypass to eliminate unwanted channels. • Broadcast stereo and separate audio program (SAP). • Bass, treble, and balance tone controls. • In-home service warranty at least 90 days. • Comb filter for better resolution of fine detail. • Remote that controls same-brand VCR. • Sleep timer.
Except as noted, all have: • Screens measuring 31 to 32 in. (conventional sets) or 50 to 52 in. (rear-projection sets). • Remotes with ability to control more than 3 components. • Code-entry remote. • At least 2 audio inputs and 2 audio outputs. • At least 2 video inputs and 1 video output. • At least 2 S-input and no S-output. • At least 2 antenna inputs. • 2 powered speaker jacks. • Ability to make essential adjustments to picture or sound from remote and console. • Clock. • Fixed-volume and volume-controlled audio line outputs. • Some

Ratings continued ▶

LARGE-SCREEN TV SETS

degree of surround- or ambient sound. • Warranty 12/12/24 mo. on parts/labor/tube.

Key to Advantages

A–Cordless headphones with separate volume control; listen to audio from picture-in-picture or main screen. Helps hearing impaired.
B–Dolby Pro Logic Surround decoder.
C–SRS sound; produced particularly effective surround effect with only two speakers.
D–Headphone jack.
E–Channel-blockout feature with code access.
F–Each audio/video input retains its own settings; facilitates settings for different sources.
G–At least one audio/video setting can be programmed for a different viewer's preference.
H–One set of jacks on front of set; convenient for hooking up camcorder.
I–Can be programmed for timed on/off cycles.
J–Remote backlights its labels for dark rooms.
K–On-screen help menus easier to follow.
L–Switchable video noise reduction (VNR) to "smooth" noisy pictures.
M–Switch selects reddish or bluish background whites; others use mfrs.' preference.
N–Clock retains time for at least 10 min. during power interruption.
O–Can automatically scan active channels.
P–Switchable notch filter for cleaner outlines.
Q–Color correction judged good or very good.
R–Has picture-in-picture feature.

Key to Disadvantages

a–Noticeable color fringing at edges of objects.
b–Must use remote to reinstate deleted channel.
c–Cannot reset audio/video to factory settings.
d–Picture controls on remote only.
e–Tone controls on remote only.
f–No stereo or SAP indicators.
g–Picture distorts at low line voltage.
h–Audio separation judged worse than most.
i–Remote operation judged worse than most.
j–Remote operation judged only fair.

Key to Comments

A–Produces ambience sound effects like "stadium" and "concert hall."
B–Can't produce surround or ambience effects.
C–Requires extra speaker for surround effect.
D–Audio graphic equalizer.
E–Side-firing speakers improve stereo effect, but may limit set's placement.
F–Subwoofer line output.
G–Powered output can be used for main or surround speakers.
H–Detachable speakers.
I–Room-light sensor compensates for varying room brightness.
J–Console controls are inconveniently located at top rear of set.
K–Volume control sets only audio line output.
L–Demonstration mode for important features.
M–Can display stations' call letters.
N–Commercial skip timer lets viewer look at other channels during commercial.
O–No clock.
P–Menus in English, Spanish, or French.
Q–Second, simplified remote that controls only channel, volume, power, and input select.
R–Warranty 12/3/24 mo., parts/labor/tube.
S–Warranty 24/12/24 mo., parts/labor/tube.
T–Warranty 12/12/12 mo., parts/labor/tube.
U–Screen measures 35 in.
V–Has no learning or code entry.
W–Has learning remote.
X–Has remote that's both learning and code entry.
Y–Has 1 audio input.
Z–Has 1 audio output; 4 for **Sony**; 3 for **Pioneer**.
AA–Has 1 video input.
BB–Has no video output.
CC–Has 1 S-output.
DD–Has 1 antenna input.
EE–No external speaker jacks.
FF–5 speaker jacks for Dolby surround sound.

MID-PRICED VCRS

RATINGS MID-PRICED VCRs

Better ◄— ⊖ ⊖ ○ ⊖ —► Worse ●

▶ **See report, page 15.** From Consumer Reports, March 1993.

Recommendations: The best hi-fi VCRs: the *Sony SLV-595HF*, $470, and *Zenith VRS427HF*, $385. Both have VCR Plus. The *Sony* boasts more features and a friendlier remote; the *Zenith*, a better picture at SP speed. Top monophonic VCRs: *Panasonic PV-4214*, $320, and *RCA VR526*, $379. At SP both deliver good images; at EP speed, the *Panasonic* has the edge. That brand also has proven more reliable. (Note: Discontinued models that have successors are noted on page 40.)

Ratings order: Listed by types; within types, listed in order of overall score. Differences in score of six points or less were not very significant. Models with identical scores are listed alphabetically. Price is the manufacturer's suggested retail. **Notes to table:** Flutter score is for linear-track recording mode, at SP speed. ⓢ indicates tested model has been replaced by successor model; according to the manufacturer, the performance of new model should be similar to the tested model but features may vary. See page 40 for new model number and suggested retail price, if available. ⓓ indicates model discontinued.

Brand and model	Price	Overall score	Picture quality scores (SP/EP)	Programming ease	Features/convenience	Tuner: Adj. channel	Tuner: Fringe	Audio: Flutter	Programming, shows/days	Advantages	Disadvantages	Comments
MONOPHONIC VHS												
Panasonic PV-4214 ⓓ	$320	84	90/83	⊖	⊖	○	⊖	○	4/30	D,E,F,G,H,J,L,R	—	B,D,F,H,I,T
RCA VR526	379	82	88/74	⊖	⊖	⊖	⊖	○	8/365	A,D,K,Q,R	a	D,H,T
Sanyo VHR 5408 ⓓ	280	82	84/82	⊖	⊖	⊖	○	⊖	6/365	H,P,Q,R	j,k	D,H,T
Sharp VC-A66U ⓢ	340	82	85/91	○	⊖	⊖	○	⊖	8/365	N,O,R	a,d	B,D,E,H,J,P
Magnavox VR9142-AT ⓓ	285	79	87/83	○	⊖	⊖	⊖	◐	8/365	D,E,J,K,O	b,e,i	B,D,F,H,P
Quasar VH6420 ⓢ	330	79	89/76	○	⊖	●	⊖	●	4/31	E,J,L,M,P	a	D,F,H,I,T
JVC HR-VP46U	399	78	87/76	⊖	○	○	⊖	⊖	8/365	D,G,Q	a,b,g,h,i,k	B,D,G,H,K,P
Samsung VR5802 ⓓ	340	77	82/78	⊖	⊖	○	⊖	○	8/365	A,D,I,O,R	a,d,l	B,D,H,P,T
Emerson VCR4000	370	74	86/74	○	○	⊖	⊖	○	4/28	O,R	a,i,j	D,H,O,T
Goldstar GVRB445 ⓢ	247	73	84/72	○	⊖	⊖	⊖	⊖	8/365	I,R	a,d,i	D,E,F,H,P,S,T
HI-FI VHS (STEREO)												
Sony SLV-595HF ⓢ	470	87	87/85	⊖	⊖	⊖	⊖	○	8/31	A,E,K,M,O,P,Q,R	—	A,B,G,H,K,L,M,P
Zenith VRS427HF ⓢ	385	85	96/84	⊖	⊖	⊖	○	⊖	8/365	C,O,Q,R	d,e,f,m	A,B,D,H,R,T
Fisher FVH-4900 ⓓ	549	81	90/85	○	⊖	○	⊖	⊖	6/365	H,J,K,R	k	A,B,D,H,P,T

Ratings continued ▶

MID-PRICED VCRS

▶ *Ratings continued*

Brand and model	Price	Overall score	Picture quality scores (SP/EP)	Programming ease	Features/convenience	Tuner: Adj. channel	Tuner: Fringe	Audio: Flutter	Programming shows/days	Advantages	Disadvantages	Comments
RCA VR667HF	$549	81	87/70	◓	◓	◓	◓	○	8/365	A,B,D,H,J,K,N,Q	a,f	B,C,H,J,P,Q,T
General Electric VG4217 ⓢ	320	80	85/82	○	◓	◓	◓	◓	8/365	A,D,K,O,R	a,l	A,B,D,H,Q,T
Hitachi VT-F361 ⓢ	385	80	88/76	○	◓	◓	◓	◐	8/365	A,D,J,N,O,P,R	d	A,B,C,G,H,L
JVC HR-VP66U	550	80	86/83	◓	○	◓	○	◓	8/365	D,G,Q	a,b,g,h,i,k,l	A,B,D,G,H,K,P
Mitsubishi HS-U56 ⓢ	470	80	87/77	○	◓	◓	◓	◐	4/31	A,G,H,J,P,R	a,g	A,B,G,J,K
Toshiba M-648 ⓢ	350	80	89/83	○	◓	○	◓	◓	8/365	A,D,I,R	a,c,i,k,l	A,B,D,H,P,S
Panasonic PV-4260 ⒹⒹ	385	79	89/72	◓	◓	◓	◓	◓	4/30	E,F,G,J,K,L,M	e	A,D,F,H,I,T
J.C. Penney Cat. No. 855-2374 Ⓓ	300	78	89/78	○	◓	◓	○	◓	8/365	A,I,P,R	a,d,m	A,E,F,H,N,P,R,S,T
Magnavox VR9160 Ⓓ	330	78	87/80	○	○	◓	◓	○	8/365	E,J,O	b,e,i	A,D,E,F,H
Sears LXI Series 580.53485290 ⓢ	350	78	84/74	◓	◓	●	◓	◓	8/365	D,I,Q,R	a,i	A,C,E,F,H,P,S,T

Successor Models (in Ratings order)
Sharp VC-A66U is succeeded by VC-A68U, $400; Quasar VH6420 by VH6430C, $300; Goldstar GVRB445 by GVRD445, $330; Sony SLV-595HF by SLV-750HF, $549; Zenith VRS427HF by VRL427HF, $499; General Electric VG4217 by VG-4210, $399; Hitachi VT-F361 by VT-F372, $400; Mitsubishi HS-U56 by HS-U58, $470; Toshiba M-648 by M-649, $430; Sears 580.53485290 by 580.53484290, $299.

Features in Common
All have: • 4 or more heads. • Digital quartz tuner. • On-screen programming from remote. • Daily/weekly programming options. • Ability to play back at SP, LP, and EP. • Ability to record in SP and EP. • Tape counter with memory. • Automatic rewind at end of tape. • Automatic power on when a cassette is inserted. • Two-way speed search. • Monophonic audio capability on linear tracks. • Average to good signal-to-noise performance on SP and EP audio linear-track recordings. • Good freeze frames. • Tape counter that can count hours and minutes. • Ability to receive 125 cable channels.
Unless noted, all have: • Linear-track audio response judged better than average. • Remote control judged average or better than average. • Automatic channel set. • Remote control with numeric keypad.
All stereo VCRs have: • Ability to receive and record MTS stereo broadcasts with good separation and excellent frequency response.

Key to Advantages
A–Tape handling faster than average.
B–Built-in VCR Plus can control cable box.
C–Learning-type remote control.
D–Code-entry remote control.
E–Owner's manual better than average.
F–Has Program Director controls on console to simplify programming.
G–Can be programmed from console as well as from remote.
H–Can search for unrecorded segment.
I–Shows time remaining on tape.
J–"Go-to" feature searches tape by time.
K–Video-input device selection on console.
L–Can play, but not record, S-VHS tapes.
M–Console display easily seen from wider angles than average.
N–Has on-screen help.
O–Has skip search to skip commercials.
P–Has power backup.
Q–Has VCR Plus.
R–Has index search.

RECEIVERS

Key to Disadvantages
 a–Clock and counter combined on console.
 b–Tape-handling slower than most.
 c–No rear input video jacks.
 d–Owner's manual poorer than average.
 e–Tape counter only on screen.
 f–No seconds counter on console.
 g–No number keypad on remote.
 h–Remote clock separate from console's.
 i–No Pause on console.
 j–Lacks automatic channel set.
 k–Lacks toggle Pause control.
 l–Linear-track audio response judged only average.
 m–Remote judged worse than average.

Key to Comments
 A–Has SAP, for secondary audio program track.
 B–Unified-type remote.
 C–Has audio recording-level controls.
 D–No audio level meters.
 E–Display dim when power is off.
 F–Has on-screen calendar.
 G–Has multispeed shuttle.
 H–Tape speed can be programmed on unattended recordings.
 I–Childproof setting locks cassette door.
 J–Childproof setting disables controls.
 K–Jog-shuttle on remote.
 L–Jog-shuttle on console.
 M–Can use special cable with certain camcorders or VCRs to facilitate editing.
 N–Rudimentary character generator to add titles to videotapes.
 O–Console displays program settings.
 P–Front-mounted audio/video jacks for quick camcorder hookup.
 Q–Good assemble editing capability to put glitch-free segments end to end.
 R–Has headphone jack with vol. control.
 S–Automatic tape speed records in SP as long as possible, then switches to EP.
 T–Can record in LP speed.

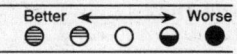

RATINGS RECEIVERS

Better ← ⊜ ⊜ ○ ⊝ ● → Worse

▶ **See report, page 22.** From Consumer Reports, March 1993.

Recommendations: Among Dolby Pro Logic models, look first at the three Best Buys; two have been discontinued and their successors noted on page 43. Any of the top three Dolby Surround models or the top nine non-surround receivers should make good choices.

Ratings order: Listed by types; within types, listed in order of overall score. Models with identical scores are listed alphabetically. Differences in score of five points or less are not significant. Price is the manufacturer's suggested retail; actual retail may be lower. Ⓢ indicates tested model has been replaced by successor model; according to the manufacturer, the performance of new model should be similar to the tested model but features may vary. See page 43 for new model number and suggested retail price, if available. Ⓓ indicates model discontinued.

Brand and model	Price	Overall score	FM tuner performance	AM tuner performance	Convenience	Measured power (8/6/4 ohm) [1]	Surround power [2]	Center power [3]	Advantages	Disadvantages	Comments
DOLBY PRO LOGIC MODELS											
Pioneer VSX-451, A Best Buy Ⓢ	$320	93	⊜	⊜	⊜	86/95/—	20	25	A,B,C,E	a,c	A,D,H,K, M,O,P,R
Sherwood RV-6010R, A Best Buy Ⓢ	380	93	⊜	⊜	⊜	113/86/106	18	30	E,H	a,c,e	A,D,E,H, K,M,R
Pioneer VSX-52 Elite	750	92	⊜	○	⊜	116/130/—	20	65	A,C,E,F	a,c	A,C,D,F, H,K,M,P, Q,R,S,T

Ratings continued ▶

42 RECEIVERS

▶ *Ratings continued*

Column headers: Brand and model | Price | Overall score | FM tuner performance | AM tuner performance | Convenience | Measured power (8/6/4 ohm) [1] | Surround power [2] | Center power [3] | Advantages | Disadvantages | Comments

Brand and model	Price	Overall score	FM	AM	Conv.	Measured power	Surr.	Center	Advantages	Disadvantages	Comments
Sony STR-GX69ES	$625	91	◐	◐	◐	118/93/114	25	25	E,G,H	—	A,D,G,H,K,M,P,S,V
Sony STR-D790, A Best Buy [S]	315	90	◐	◐	◐	86/100/—	20	20	A,B,C,E,H	c	A,D,H,K,L,P
JVC RX-807VTN [S]	450	89	◐	◐	◐	130/150/—	20	65	B,C,E,H	c,e	A,C,D,H,I,K,L,P,S
Yamaha RX-V660 [S]	699	89	◐	◐	◐	68/86/—	25	25	E,G	a	D,H,K,N,P,Y
Kenwood KR-V8540 [S]	505	88	◐	◐	◐	134/95/108	15	75	A,B,D,E,H	a	A,D,H,M,Q,S
Technics SA-GX530 [D]	355	88	◐	◐	◐	126/68/83	10	15	C	e	A,B,C,D,H,L,M,P,X,Y
Denon AVR-810 [D]	660	86	◐	◐	◐	81/95/—	30	30	E,H	a,e,h	D,E,H,J,N,P,S
Technics SA-GX730 [D]	560	81	◐	◐	◐	132/86/107	30	60	C,E	e	A,B,C,D,E,H,L,M,P

DOLBY SURROUND MODELS

Brand and model	Price	Overall	FM	AM	Conv.	Measured power	Surr.	Center	Advantages	Disadvantages	Comments
Sherwood RV5010R, A Best Buy [D]	240	93	◐	◐	◐	95/73/86	15	—	E,H	a,c,e	D,E,K,M,R
Onkyo TX-SV303PRO [S]	390	92	◐	◐	◐	91/109/—	12	0	A,E,G,H	—	D,F,G,H,K,N,R
Pioneer VSX401 [S]	285	90	◐	○	◐	109/122/—	20	—	A,E	a,c	C,D,K,O,P,R,X
Kenwood KR-V6040 [S]	285	87	◐	◐	◐	115/131/105	15	—	A,H	—	Q,U
Sony STR-D590 [S]	220	87	◐	◐	◐	65/75/—	10	—	A,E	c,f	D,P,X,Y
Philips FR920	269	78	○	○	○	61/68/—	10	—	A,B	b,c,f,i,k,l	D,K,M,P,U,X,Y

NON-SURROUND MODELS

Brand and model	Price	Overall	FM	AM	Conv.	Measured power	Surr.	Center	Advantages	Disadvantages	Comments
Onkyo TX-903 [S]	235	91	◐	◐	◐	65/78/92	—	—	A,G	—	G,K
Sherwood RX4010R, A Best Buy [S]	160	91	◐	◐	◐	66/61/61	—	—	G	a,c,d	K,M,R
Fisher RS-616, A Best Buy [D]	179	89	◐	◐	◐	67/74/—	—	—	A,G	c	K,Q,W
Kenwood KR-A5040	199	89	◐	◐	◐	96/67/84	—	—	A,H	a,c	M,Q
Pioneer SX251R	260	89	◐	◐	◐	55/61/—	—	—	A	a,c,j	K,O
JVC RX-307TN [S]	195	88	◐	◐	○	91/104/—	—	—	—	a,c,e,g,j	M,P,Q
Optimus STA-900 [S]	250	88	◐	◐	◐	84/94/—	—	—	G	c,d	K,M

RECEIVERS

Brand and model	Price	Overall score	FM tuner performance	AM tuner performance	Convenience	Measured power (8/6/4 ohm)[1]	Surround power[2]	Center power[3]	Advantages	Disadvantages	Comments
Technics SA-GX130	$230	87	◒	◒	○	73/80/—	—	—	—	a,c	M,O,P
Yamaha RX-360	249	87	◒	◒	◒	54/59/—	—	—	D,G	a,d	K
Denon DRA-345R	255	86	◒	◒	◒	52/58/—	—	—	D	a,d	P
Sony STR-D390 ⑤	170	86	◒	◒	◒	50/54/—	—	—	A,D,G	c	P,V
Philips FR910	219	78	○	◒	○	51/52/—	—	—	A,B	b,f,h,i,k	K,M,P

[1] Our measurements of watts-per-channel output at 3 typical impedances.
[2] The watts-per-channel output to the rear speakers, at 8 ohms, as stated by mfr.
[3] Mfr.'s 8-ohm rating for the Pro Logic channel.

Successor Models (in Ratings order)
Pioneer VSX-451 is succeeded by VSX-452, $389; Sherwood RV-6010R by RV-6030R, $475; Sony STR-D790 by STR-D711, $430; JVC RX-807VTN by RX-809VTN, $630; Yamaha RX-V660 by RX-V670, $749; Kenwood KR-V8540 by KR-V8050, $549; Onkyo TX-SV303PRO by TX-SV313PRO, $410; Pioneer VSX401 by VSX-402, $335; Kenwood KR-V6040 by KR-V6050, $359; Sony STR-D590 by STR-D511, $300; Onkyo TX-903 by TX-930, $290; Sherwood RX4010R by RX-4030R, $225; JVC RX-307TN by RX-309TN, $260; Optimus STA-900 by STA-2180, $250; Sony STR-D390 by STR-D311, $430.

Performance Notes
General: • Excellent frequency response, stereo separation, and AM rejection. • Channel balance and amplifier gain within expected range. *Amplifier:* • Excellent signal-to-noise ratio and freedom from distortion. *Phono preamplifier:* • Excellent signal-to-noise ratio and freedom from distortion. • Resistance to overload within expected range. • Input impedance of 100 to 300 picofarads, except as noted.

Features in Common
All have: • Digitally tuned FM and AM tuners. • 1 magnetic phono input. • Up/down seek tuning. • Tuner that automatically "wraps" from one end of the band to the other. • Headphone jack. • CD and tape inputs. • Connection for external AM and FM antennas. • Cabinet approx. 17 in. wide.
Except as noted, all have: • Bass and treble tone controls, not graphic equalizer. • Capability to accommodate 2 tape decks. • Tuning display readable from at least 30 degrees above horizontal. • Connection for 2 pairs of speakers. • Second pair of speakers connected in parallel when both pairs are switched on (a series connection may cause sound deterioration). • 2-yr. warranty.
Except as noted, all Pro Logic and surround models have: • At least 2 video inputs and 2 video outputs, and 6 audio inputs and 3 audio outputs.
Except as noted, all non-surround models have: • No video input or outputs.

Key to Advantages
A–Keypad allows direct entry of radio frequency.
B–Display can show station call letters.
C–Stores tone-control settings in memory.
D–Variable loudness control.
E–Provides variable delay to rear speakers.
F–Can show receiver status on TV screen.
G–FM/AM signal-strength indicator.
H–Direct flat-response tone-defeat switch.

Key to Disadvantages
a–Display not readable from above 30 degrees.
b–Power-on sequence judged inconvenient.
c–Speakers are connected in series if A+B on.
d–Only 1 recording output for tape deck.
e–Some jacks not coded red/white for left/right.
f–Lacks tape monitor.
g–Cannot turn off loudness compensation.
h–No terminals for 2nd pair (B) front speakers.
i–An external timer can't turn on receiver.
j–Speaker shorting test blew internal fuse.
k–Remote control inconvenient to use.

Ratings continued ▶

RECEIVERS

I–Has only one video input and one video output.

Key to Comments
A–Dolby 3 Stereo (in Pro Logic).
B–Tone control and parametric graphic equalizer.
C–7-channel graphic equalizer.
D–Has simulated/ambience surround modes.
E–Audio/video input jacks on front panel.
F–Can play 2 sources at once in different rooms.
G–Low phono-input capacitance may slightly degrade response with some cartridges.
H–Has pink-noise test for speaker volume.
I–Push-button volume control.
J–"S" video jacks.
K–Sleep timer.
L–Graphic analyzer display.
M–Can play 5 sec. (scan) of each station preset.
N–Pro Logic decoder without center amplifier.
O–1 yr. warranty.
P–Remote controls same brand of TV/VCR.
Q–Remote can select stations on either AM or FM band.
R–Has multi-room remote option.
S–Learning remote.
T–Code-entry remote.
U–Remote lacks rear speaker volume control.
V–Some labeled keys on remote don't apply to this model.
W–Has 2 video inputs and 1 video output.
X–Has at least 4 audio inputs.
Y–Has 2 audio outputs.

HOW TO USE THE RATINGS

- Read the **article** for general guidance about types and buying advice.

- Read **Recommendations** for brand-name advice based on our tests.

- Read the **Ratings order** to see whether products are listed in order of quality, by price, or alphabetically. Most Ratings are based on estimated quality, without regard to price.

- Look to the **Ratings table** for specifics on the performance and features of individual models.

- A model marked Ⓓ has been discontinued, according to the manufacturer. A model marked Ⓢ indicates that, according to the manufacturer, it has been replaced by a successor model whose performance should be similar to the tested model but whose features may vary.

CAMCORDERS

RATINGS CAMCORDERS

E ⊜ VG ⊖ G ○ F ◐ P ●

▶ **See report, page 18.** From Consumer Reports, March 1993.

Recommendations: The top-rated Hi8 *Minolta Pro 8-918*, $2300, and the Hi8 *Sony CCD-TR101*, $1800, provided fine picture quality except in very dim light. Repair history is a bonus for Sony models, but not for *Minolta*. Note that the *Minolta* is discontinued but may still be available. The top-rated S-VHS-C *Panasonic PV-S372*, $1599, is a bit heavy for a compact, but it's loaded with useful features. See below and page 46 for details.

Ratings order: Listed, in the table below and on pages 46 through 49, by format; within format, listed in order of overall score based mainly on picture quality and autofocus performance. Price is the manufacturer's suggested retail; actual retail may be lower. ⒹIndicates model discontinued.

Brand and model	Score	Price	Clarity Most favorable mode	Clarity Least favorable mode	Autofocus	Low light
8mm AND Hi8 MODELS						
Minolta Pro 8-918 (Hi8) Ⓓ	93	$2300	⊜	⊖	⊜	◐
Sony CCD-TR101 (Hi8)	93	1800	⊜	⊖	⊜	◐
Sony CCD-FX410 Ⓓ	83	860	⊜	—	⊜	○
RCA Pro870 Ⓓ	82	840	○	—	⊜	○
Hitachi VM-SP1A	79	1499	⊜	—	⊜	◐
Sharp VL-MX7U GY Ⓓ	78	1200	○	—	⊜	⊖
Canon E350	77	995	○	—	○	○
Fisher FVC-10	72	799	○	—	○	○
VHS-C AND S-VHS-C MODELS						
Panasonic PV-S372 (S-VHS-C)	96	1599	⊜	⊖	⊜	⊖
Panasonic PV-42 Ⓓ	92	1165	⊜	⊖	⊜	○
Magnavox CVN610AV	88	750	⊜	⊖	⊜	⊖
Quasar VM522 Ⓓ	87	739	⊜	⊖	⊜	○
JVC GR-AX50 Ⓓ	79	1000	○	◐	○	○
RCA CC177 Ⓓ	73	755	○	◐	○	○
Mitsubishi HS-CX7U (S-VHS-C) Ⓓ	72	1165	○	◐	◐	●

Features in Common
All have: • Automatic focus, exposure, and white balance. • Automatic audio-level control. • Flying erase head for seamless edits. • Time-used or time-remaining display. • Clock that can record time, date, or both in picture. • Automatic shutoff to save battery. • Low-battery warning. • Battery charger/AC power pack. • Cable or adapter for playback to TV set or VCR. • Viewfinder adjustment for near- or farsighted users. • Macrofocus for extreme close-ups. • Dew indicator and automatic camcorder shutoff when humidity high enough to damage heads. • Tripod socket.
All VHS-C and S-VHS-C models have: • Tracking control.
Except as noted, all: • Weigh between 1.8 and 2.5 lbs. with tape and battery.

Ratings continued ▶

46 CAMCORDERS

Except as noted, all have: • Power zoom but not manual zoom. • Non-motorized manual-focus option. • "Quick review" to let you see last few seconds of recorded tape. • Headphone jack. • External microphone jack. • Fade for picture (to black) and sound. • Input jacks for taping from VCR or TV. • Provision for operating from car cigarette-lighter socket. • Lens cap that attaches to camera strap. • Separate non-rechargeable clock battery. • Optical zoom ratio of 8:1 or 10:1. • Battery run-time of 50 to 70 minutes in our tests. • Battery recharge time of 50 to 65 minutes in our tests. • Very little flutter from varying tape speed. • Fastest shutter speed of 1/4000 sec. or faster. • Manual white-balance option.

RATINGS CAMCORDERS: THE DETAILS

▶ See report, page 18; Ratings table, page 44. From Consumer Reports, March 1993.

Minolta Pro 8-918 (Hi8)

Features: • Can be switched to manual exposure control. • Built-in character-generator titling. • 2-speed zoom (not mentioned in owner's manual). • Stereo sound. • Optional synchronizing cable for easier editing. • Momentary autofocus button. • Can be switched to manual zoom control. • Switch returns all functions to automatic mode. • Wind-noise-suppression setting. • Accessory shoe. • Self-timer starts recording after 10-second or selected delay; requires remote control. • Battery ran 90 minutes in our tests. • Wireless remote control. • Smaller-capacity battery available. • Time-lapse mode. • Short-burst animation mode. • Automatically zooms toward wide angle if can't find focus. • Noise-free picture in pause and 1/5-speed playback. • Can preset start and stop points to insert scene over previous recording. • LCD panel displays functions.

Disadvantages: • Relatively bulky—12½ inches long. • Heavier than most, 3.4 pounds. • Microphone response favors speech, poor for music. • Manual focus is motorized. • Under some conditions, doesn't shut off automatically to save battery. • No wired On-Off remote jack. • Battery took 100 minutes to recharge in our tests.

Sony CCD-TR101 (Hi8)

Features: • Can be switched to manual exposure control. • Picture-based titling; can scroll. • 2-speed zoom. • Stereo sound. • Image stabilizer reduces jiggles in picture. • Warns if heads clog during taping. • Switch returns all functions to automatic mode. • Viewfinder displays zoom and manual exposure setting. • LCD panel displays functions. • Wireless remote control. • Larger- and smaller-capacity batteries available. • Mosaic as well as conventional fade. • Can play in reverse at normal speed. • Can preset start and stop points to insert scene over previous recording. • Mike "zooms" with lens. • Records date and time in hidden form, displayed on demand in playback.

Disadvantages: • Autofocus doesn't work during wide-to-tele zooming. • Under some conditions, doesn't shut off automatically to save battery. • Low-contrast lettering on some controls is hard to read.

Comment: Nikon VN-750 ($1800 list) and Ricoh R-18H ($1799) are essentially similar.

Sony CCD-FX410

Features: • Backlight compensation. • 2-speed zoom. • Warns if heads clog during taping. • Momentary autofocus button. • Can beep at start and stop of taping. • Convenient single-cord setup for playback on TV set. • Viewfinder displays zoom settings. • Accessory shoe. • Wireless remote control. • Larger- and smaller-capacity batteries available. • Can play in reverse at normal speed; convenient for editing. • Can play at 1/5 normal speed. • Can preset start and stop points to insert scene over previous recording.

CAMCORDERS

Disadvantages: • Autofocus doesn't work during wide-to-tele zooming. • Under some conditions, doesn't shut off automatically to save battery. • Cover on clock battery not attached, easy to lose. • No manual white balance.

RCA Pro 870

Features: • Built-in character-generator titling. • Backlight compensation. • Optional synchronizing cable for easier editing. • Can be switched to manual zoom control. • Switch returns all functions to automatic mode. • Digital zoom ratio from 8:1 to 64:1 (but picture quality deteriorates above 8:1). • Zoom ratios above 8:1 displayed in viewfinder. • Wireless remote control. • Larger-capacity battery available. • Fades to white. • Can record "squeezed" images for 16:9-format TV.

Disadvantages: • No external microphone jack. • Autofocus doesn't work in extreme close-ups. • Under some conditions, doesn't shut off automatically to save battery. • Two dual-function buttons not dual-labeled. • No headphone jack. • No manual white balance.

Hitachi VM-SP1A

Features: • Backlight compensation. • Optional synchronizing cable for easier editing. • Digital zoom ratio from 8:1 to 64:1 (but picture quality deteriorates above 8:1, and autofocus doesn't work above 16:1). • Zoom ratios above 8:1 displayed in viewfinder. • Self-timer starts recording after 10-second delay and can record for 30 sec. or until stopped. • Wireless remote control. • Can superimpose any of 47 built-in graphics on picture. • Fades to white. • Can preset start and stop points to insert scene over previous recording. • Water-resistant shell; manufacturer says it floats and can be used in rain, though not under water. • Remote stores inside shell. • Can record "squeezed" images for 16:9 format TV.

Disadvantages: • Relatively bulky—9 inches long, 5 inches wide. • Heavier than most, 3.1 pounds. • Shell must be opened for operation with AC power

and for playback. • Manual focus is motorized. • No external microphone jack. • Viewfinder doesn't tip up or collapse for storage. • Under some conditions, doesn't shut off automatically to save battery. • No headphone jack. • No wired On-Off remote jack. • Cover on clock battery not attached, easy to lose. • Fastest shutter speed is 1/250-sec. • No manual white balance. • Case O-ring seals should be replaced yearly, according to mfr.

Sharp VL-MX7U GY

Features: • 2 lenses—zoom and fixed wide-angle; can switch, fade, or wipe from one to the other or record picture within a picture. • Backlight compensation. • 2-speed zoom. • Built-in lens cover. • Stereo sound. • Warns if heads clog during taping. • Charger can fully discharge battery before recharging. • Switch returns all functions to automatic mode. • Larger-capacity battery available. • Fades to white. • Color viewfinder. • Automatically zooms to wide angle if can't find focus. • Audio dynamic range slightly narrower than most.

Disadvantages: • Manual focus is motorized. • No external microphone jack. • Lacks button for automatic "quick review" of last few seconds of tape. • Under some conditions, doesn't shut off automatically to save battery. • No lock on power switch. • Low-contrast lettering on some controls is hard to read. • No headphone jack. • No wired On-Off remote jack. • Cover on clock battery not attached, easy to lose.

Canon E350

Features: • Picture-based titling. • Built-in character-generator titling. • During first minute, can automatically reset tape to reshoot scene. • 12:1 zoom. • Backlight compensation. • Stereo sound. • Manual zoom control. • Accessory shoe. • Wireless remote control. • Video light. • Larger-capacity battery available. • Fades to white. • Can search at 19 times normal speed.

Disadvantages: • Relatively bulky—12

Ratings continued ▶

inches long. • Autofocus doesn't work in extreme close-ups. • Viewfinder doesn't collapse for storage. • Under some conditions, doesn't shut off automatically to save battery. • No lock on power switch. • No wired On-Off remote jack. • Cover on clock battery and jacks not attached, easy to lose.

Fisher FVC-10

Features: • Accessory shoe. • Wireless remote control. • Switch returns all functions to automatic mode. • Charger can fully discharge battery before recharging. • Larger-capacity battery available. • Can play in reverse at normal speed.

Disadvantages: • No fade. • Autofocus doesn't work during wide-to-tele zooming. • No viewfinder warning of manual white-balance mode. • Manual focus is motorized. • No external microphone jack. • No AV input jacks for taping from VCR or TV. • Under some conditions, doesn't shut off automatically to save battery. • No wired On-Off remote jack. • Cover on clock battery not attached, easy to lose. • No manual white balance. • No optional adapter cord for operating from car battery.

Panasonic PV-S372 (S-VHS-C)

Features: • Can be switched to manual exposure control. • Picture-based titling. • 2-speed zoom. • Stereo sound. • Audio and video dubbing. • Optional synchronizing cable for easier editing. • Switch returns all functions to automatic mode. • Wind-noise-suppression setting. • Charger can fully discharge battery before recharging. • Battery ran 105 minutes in our tests. • Clock battery recharges from main battery. • Wireless remote control. • Accessory shoe. • Video light. • Time-lapse mode. • Can fade to white, black, or any of six colors. • Records VHS-index search mark automatically at power-up. • Can preset start and stop points to insert scene over previous recording. • LCD panel displays functions. • Audio dynamic range slightly wider than most.

Disadvantages: • Relatively bulky—12 inches long. • Heavier than most, 3.5 pounds. • Autofocus doesn't work during wide-to-tele zooming. • No AV input jacks for taping from VCR or TV. • Low-contrast lettering on some controls is hard to read. • Two dual-function buttons not dual-labeled. • No headphone jack. • Battery took 150 minutes to recharge in our tests.

Panasonic PV-42

Features: • Picture-based titling; titles can wipe or scroll. • Backlight compensation. • Audio and video dubbing. • Optional synchronizing cable for easier editing. • Switch returns all functions to automatic mode. • Battery ran 120 minutes in our tests. • Charger can fully discharge battery before recharging. • Clock battery recharges from main battery. • Accessory shoe. • Wireless remote control. • Video light. • Smaller-capacity battery available. • Can fade to white, black, or any of six colors. • Records VHS index search mark automatically at power-up. • Can preset start and stop points to insert scene over previous recording. • Digital zoom from 8:1 to 80:1 (but picture deteriorates above 8:1). • Special effects: freeze frame, strobe motion, mirror image. • Image stabilizer, but has little effect. • Audio dynamic range slightly narrower than most.

Disadvantages: • Heavier than most, 2.7 pounds. • No AV input jacks for taping from VCR or TV. • Two dual-function buttons not dual-labeled. • No headphone jack. • Battery took 120 minutes to recharge in our tests.

Magnavox CVN610AV

Features: • Backlight compensation. • Audio and video dubbing. • Optional synchronizing cable for easier editing. • Switch returns all functions to automatic mode. • Charger can fully discharge battery before recharging. • Larger-capacity battery available. • Clock battery recharges from main battery. • Records VHS-index search mark automatically at power-up. • Can preset start/stop points to insert scene over previous recording. • Audio dynamic range slightly narrower than most.

Disadvantages: No AV input jacks for taping from VCR to TV. • Two dual-function buttons not dual-labeled. • No headphone jack. • Moderate flutter.

Quasar VM522

Features: • Backlight compensation. • Audio and video dubbing. • Optional synchronizing cable for easier editing. • Switch returns all functions to automatic mode. • Accessory shoe. • Battery ran 120 minutes in our tests. • Charger can fully discharge battery before recharging. • Clock battery recharges from main battery. • Video light. • Smaller-capacity battery available. • Records VHS-index search mark automatically at power-up. • Can preset start/stop points to insert scene over previous recording. • Audio dynamic range slightly narrower than most.

Disadvantages: • No AV input jacks for taping from VCR or TV. • Two dual-function buttons not dual-labeled. • No headphone jack. • Battery took 115 minutes to recharge in our tests.

JVC GR-AX50

Features: • Color viewfinder. • Picture-based titling. • Audio and video dubbing. • Optional synchronizing cable to make editing easier. • Warns if heads clog during taping. • Can beep at start and stop of taping. • Switch returns all functions to automatic mode. • Can automatically record date/time on first scene after power-up. • Wind-noise suppression setting. • Accessory shoe. • Self-timer; requires optional remote control. • Carrying case. • Video light. • Larger-capacity battery available. • Time-lapse mode. • Short-burst animation mode. • Records VHS-index search mark at power-up. • Can record in 16:9 "letterbox" format. • Automatically zooms toward wide-angle if camcorder's circuitry can't find focus.

Disadvantages: • Manual focus is motorized. • No AV input jacks for taping from VCR or TV. • In some conditions, doesn't shut off automatically to save battery. • No lock on power switch. • Moderate flutter in our audio-quality tests. • No manual white-balance.

Comment: Price includes $100 for remote control.

RCA CC177

Features: • Switch returns all functions to automatic mode. • Can automatically record date/time on first scene after power-up. • Accessory shoe. • Charger can fully discharge battery before recharging. • Larger-capacity battery available. • Can record in 16:9 "letterbox" format. • Automatically zooms toward wide angle if can't find focus. • Manual white balance has 9 settings.

Disadvantages: • Relatively bulky—10½ inches long. • Fades picture only, not sound. • Autofocus doesn't work during wide-to-tele zooming. • Manual focus is motorized. • No external microphone jack. • No AV input jacks for taping from VCR or TV. • Under some conditions, doesn't shut off automatically to save battery. • No lock on Power switch. • Low-contrast lettering on some controls is hard to read. • No headphone jack. • No wired On-Off remote jack. • Moderate flutter.

Mitsubishi HS-CX7U (S-VHS-C)

Features: • Picture-based titling. • Backlight compensation. • Stereo sound. • Optional synchronizing cable to make editing easier. • Switch returns all functions to automatic mode. • Wind-noise suppression setting. • Records VHS-index search mark automatically at power-up. • Can record in 16:9 "letterbox" format. • Menu system for selecting certain settings. • Jack for optional wired remote. • Image stabilizer, but has little effect.

Disadvantages: • Microphone response favors speech, poor for music. • Manual focus is motorized. • No external microphone jack. • No AV input jacks for taping from VCR or TV. • Under some conditions, doesn't shut off automatically to save battery. • No headphone jack. • Cover on jacks not attached.

CD PLAYERS

RATINGS: CD PLAYERS

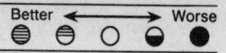

Better ◄──── ► Worse
⊜ ⊖ ○ ◐ ●

▶ **See report, page 27.** From Consumer Reports, March 1993.

Recommendations: The top-rated *Technics SL-PD927* (and its successor), $269 ($270), is a first-rate carousel changer that costs much less than some others. It's sparse with features, but is fine for just listening to CDs. If more features are desired, consider the *Sony CDP-C79ES* (or its successor), $480 ($570). Among magazine changers, we recommend the basic *Pioneer P-M701* (or its successor), $245 ($300), or two more feature-ladened models—the *Pioneer PD-M901* (or its successor), $315, and the *Sony CDP-C910*, $350.

Ratings order: Listed by types; within types, listed in order of overall score. All were excellent in sound quality. Differences in score of eight points or less were not significant. Models with identical scores are listed alphabetically. Price is the manufacturer's suggested retail; actual retail may be lower. Ⓢ indicates tested model has been replaced by successor model; according to the manufacturer, the performance of new model should be similar to the tested model but features may vary. See right for new model number and suggested retail price, if available. Ⓓ indicates model discontinued.

Brand and model	Price	Overall score	Changer capacity	Programming capacity	Disk-error correction	Track-finding speed	Bump immunity	Taping convenience	Key to features	Comments
CAROUSEL CHANGERS										
Technics SL-PD927, A Best Buy Ⓢ	$269	96	5	32	⊜	⊜	⊜	○	a,c,f,h,i	I,L,O,R
Philips CDC935	299	94	5	30	⊜	⊜	⊜	⊜	a,b,c,d,e,f,h,i	C,F,G,I,M,R,U,X,BB
Sony CDP-C79ES Ⓢ	480	94	5	32	⊜	⊜	⊜	⊜	a,b,d,e,f,g,h,j,k	B,E,F,G,J,S,T,Z,AA,CC
Carver SD/A-350 Ⓢ	345	92	5	32	⊜	⊜	⊜	◐	b,e,i,k	C,G,H,J,Q,U
JVC XL-F207TN	300	92	5	32	⊜	⊜	⊜	◐	e,f,k	F,I,J,R
Yamaha CDC-735	429	92	5	40	⊜	⊜	○	○	a,b,d,e,f,h,i,k	C,J,K,BB
Denon DCM-520	420	91	5	20	⊜	⊜	○	◐	a,b,d,e,f,i,j,k	C,J,T,V
Onkyo DX-C606	480	91	6	40	⊜	⊜	◐	○	a,b,c,e,f,i	E,F,N,P,R,S,V,Y
Sony CDP-C725 Ⓢ	365	91	5	32	⊜	⊜	○	⊜	a,b,d,e,f,g,h,j,k	B,E,G,J,S,T,Z,AA
Denon DCM-320 Ⓢ	275	90	5	20	⊜	⊜	○	◐	b,f,i	J,V
Onkyo DX-C206 Ⓢ	295	90	6	40	⊜	⊜	◐	○	b,c,e,f,i	F,L,N,P,R,V,Y
Sony CDP-C425	330	90	5	32	⊜	⊜	○	⊜	a,b,e,f,g,h,k	G,J,S,Z,AA

CD PLAYERS 51

Brand and model	Price	Overall score	Changer capacity	Programming capacity	Disk-error correction	Track-finding speed	Bump immunity	Taping convenience	Key to features	Comments
Yamaha CDC-625 [S]	$249	90	5	20	◐	◐	◐	◑	b,e,f,i,j	J,K,BB
Sherwood CDC-5010R [S]	250	88	5	32	◐	○	◐	◑	b,e,i,k	F,G,J,Q,R
Teac PD-D650 [D]	200	88	5	32	◐	○	○	◑	b,i,k	F,G,I,J,K,L,R
Marantz CC-52	349	85	5	32	○	○	◐	○	b,h,i,k	E,F,G,J,K,L,R,CC
Kenwood DP-R4440 [S]	210	84	5	20	◑	◐	◐	○	b,e,h,k	F,I,P,U
Fisher DAC243 [D]	190	82	5	32	○	○	○	○	b,h,i,k	F,G,J,K,L,R
MAGAZINE CHANGERS										
Pioneer PD-M901 [S]	315	92	6	40	◐	◐	○	○	b,d,e,f,h,j,k	B,F,G,I,J,O,Z
Sony CDP-C910	350	92	10	32	◐	◐	○	◐	a,b,d,e,f,g,h,j,k	E,G,J,S,T,Z,AA
Pioneer PD-M701, A Best Buy [S]	245	91	6	32	◐	◐	○	○	a,b,f,h,j,k	F,G,I,J,O,Z
Denon DCM-550	450	90	6	20	◐	◐	◑	◑	a,b,d,e,f,j,k	C,I,J,T
JVC XL-M407TN [S]	230	90	7	32	◐	○	○	◐	a,e,f,g,h,k	D,F,G,I,J,M,O,R
Pioneer PD-TM2 [S]	365	90	18	48	◐	◐	○	○	a,b,f,h,j,k	G,I,J,M,O,Z
JVC XL-M507TN [S]	275	88	7	32	◐	○	○	◐	a,e,f,g,h,k	D,F,G,I,J,M,O,R
Kenwood DP-M7740 [S]	270	86	7	20	○	◐	○	○	a,b,d,e,h,k	D,F,I,S,U,W
Kenwood DP-M5540 [S]	215	84	7	20	○	◑	○	○	a,b,e,h	A,D,F,I,L,U,W

Successor Models (in Ratings order)
Technics SL-PD927 is succeeded by SL-PD949, $270; Sony CDP-C79ES by CDP-C701, $570; Carver SD/A-350 by SD/A360, $400; Sony CDP-C725 by CDP-C735, $430; Denon DCM-320 by DCM-340, $300; Onkyo DX-C206 by DX-C210, $330; Yamaha CDC-625 by CDC-635, $299; Sherwood CDC-5010R by CDC-5030R, $275; Kenwood DP-R4440 by DP-R4450, $229; Pioneer PD-M901 by PD-M902, $450; Pioneer PD-M701 by PD-M702, $300; JVC XL-M407TN by XL-M09TN, $300; Pioneer PD-TM2 by PD-TM3, $520; JVC XL-M507TN by XL-M509TN, $380; Kenwood DP-M7740 by DP-M7750, $369; Kenwood DP-M5540 by DP-M5550, $229.

Features in Common
All: • Have Play, Pause, Stop, Track select, and Program functions. • Have audible scan (for shuttling rapidly through a track) free of pitch distortion. • Can repeat any or all discs. *Except as noted, all:* • Have remote control. • Have headphone jack. • Have 1-yr. warranty on parts and labor.

Key to Features
a–Keypad on console.
b–Time remaining on disc.
c–Fast scanning.
d–Favorite-track selection.
e–Calendar-type display.
f–Multiple-disc no-repeat shuffle.
g–Multiple-disc auto edit.
h–Single-disc auto edit.
i–Disc-changing while playing.
j–Volume control on remote.
k–Disc keypad on remote.

Ratings continued ▶

3-PIECE LOUDSPEAKERS

Key to Comments

A–No remote control.
B–Digital signal processor; ambience effect.
C–Coaxial connector for digital output.
D–Single-play drawer.
E–Fiber optical connector for digital output; useful with DAT.
F–Jack lets you operate player by using remote of same-brand receiver.
G–Music-sampling function.
H–Can repeat part of a track or disc.
I–Synchronizing jack for use with same-brand cassette deck.
J–Press switch to repeat whole track.
K–Index selection.
L–No headphone jack.
M–No scan feature on remote.
N–Running total of program time for tracks selected for taping.
O–Delete-track omits tracks you dislike.
P–Calendar display too far under viewing glass; readable only from head-on.
Q–No-repeat shuffle for 1 disc at a time.
R–Multiple-speed scan in play mode; slower speed at start of scan.
S–Music-peak finder for best recording level.
T–Both adjustable- and fixed-level analog outputs; permits use of receiver's or CD player's remote volume control.
U–Auto space; an aid in taping.
V–Carousel disc skip can turn either way, for easier disc selection.
W–No display of total time on disc.
X–Hitting Pause a second time resets track to beginning, instead of resuming play.
Y–Remote also controls **Onkyo** decks.
Z–Fade out/in; makes pauses less abrupt.
AA–Variable fade.
BB–2-yr. warranty on parts and labor.
CC–3-yr. warranty on parts and labor.

RATINGS   3-PIECE LOUDSPEAKERS

Better ◀——▶ Worse

▶ **See report, page 25.** From Consumer Reports, March 1993.

Recommendations: The best 3-piece systems can deliver extra-deep powerful bass or tolerate music played for long periods at window-rattling levels. Give first consideration to the top five systems. They are comparable but don't reproduce sound identically.

Ratings order: Listed in order of overall score. Differences in score of 8 points or less are not significant. Models with identical scores are bracketed and listed in order of tone-corrected accuracy. The first price or pair of prices are what we paid for the satellite/bass module or system. The second prices are the manufacturer's suggested retail. Satellite prices are per pair. ⓢ indicates tested model has been replaced by successor model; according to the manufacturer, the performance of new model should be similar to the tested model but features may vary. See page 54 for new model number and suggested retail price, if available. ⓓ indicates model discontinued.

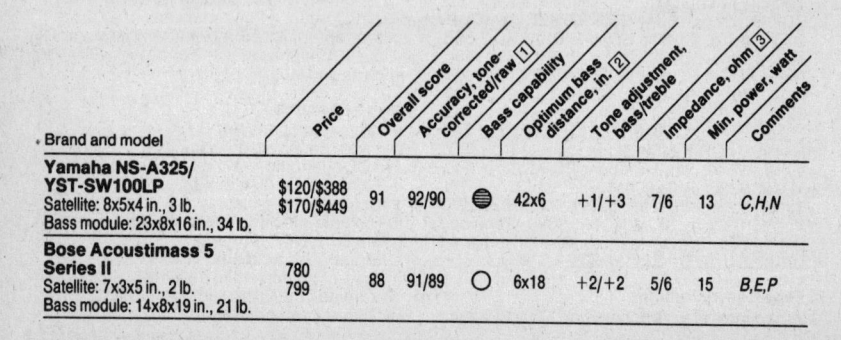

Brand and model	Price	Overall score	Accuracy, tone-corrected/raw [1]	Bass capability	Optimum bass distance, in. [2]	Tone adjustment, bass/treble	Impedance, ohm [3]	Min. power, watt	Comments
Yamaha NS-A325/ YST-SW100LP Satellite: 8x5x4 in., 3 lb. Bass module: 23x8x16 in., 34 lb.	$120/$388 $170/$449	91	92/90	◉	42x6	+1/+3	7/6	13	C,H,N
Bose Acoustimass 5 Series II Satellite: 7x3x5 in., 2 lb. Bass module: 14x8x19 in., 21 lb.	780 799	88	91/89	○	6x18	+2/+2	5/6	15	B,E,P

3-PIECE LOUDSPEAKERS

Brand and model	Price	Overall score	Accuracy, tone-corrected/raw [1]	Bass capability	Optimum bass distance, in. [2]	Tone adjustment, bass/treble	Impedance, ohm [3]	Min. power, watt	Comments
NHT Zero/SW-1V ⓢ Satellite: 9x6x6 in., 5 lb. Bass module: 20x8x13 in., 28 lb.	$200/$250 $200/$300	86	89/87	◒	54x36	−1/+2	6/8	30	C,K
Boston Acoustics SubSatSix ⓢ Satellite: 8x5x5 in., 4 lb. Bass module: 14x8x17 in., 18 lb.	450 500	85	90/83	◒	60x48	−1/+4	3/8	38	A,B,N,P
Design Acoustics PS55/PS-SW Satellite: 6x7x10 in., 7 lb. Bass module: 22x11x17 in., 38 lb.	220/340	84	87/82	◒	54x3	−3/+1	6/6	12	B,K
Allison MS-205 Ⓓ Satellite: 10x6x6 in., 7 lb. Bass module: 12x11x11 in., 17 lb.	449 499	83	91/81	○	42x24	0/+6	4/4	29	M
JBL Pro Performer Plus Ⓓ Satellite: 6x6x6 in., 3 lb. Bass module: 8x20x12 in., 21 lb.	260 439	83	91/82	○	18x6	+1/+6	3/8	19	C,J,L,O
Celestion 5/CS135 Satellite: 14x8x10 in., 11 lb. Bass module: 21x8x14 in., 21 lb.	395/259 399/259	83	90/78	◒	42x0	+2/+6	4/8	18	A,B,K
Bose Acoustimass 3 Series II Satellite: 4x5x5 in., 1 lb. Bass module: 8x8x15 in., 11 lb.	480 469	83	89/85	●	36x12	+2/+4	4/5	18	B,C,P
Advent Mini-Advent A1063 Satellite: 11x7x5 in., 5 lb. Bass module: 13x9x16 in., 21 lb.	330 289	83	86/86	○	60x12	0/+1	4/6	18	C,J,P
Cambridge Ensemble II Satellite: 8x6x5 in., 5 lb. Bass module: 14x8x17 in., 18 lb.	399 399	82	87/80	◒	48x12	−1/+6	4/—	36	B,C,N,P
Cambridge Ensemble 'Vinyl Clad' Satellite: 8x6x5 in., 5 lb. Bass module: 12x21x5 in., 16 lb.	499 499	80	84/82	○	42x24	+1/+3	4/—	36	A,D,N,P
JBL Pro III Plus Satellite: 10x6x6 in., 6 lb. Bass module: 16x14x14 in., 25 lb.	475 659	78	87/74	○	36x18	−1/+6	4/4	18	B,C,J
Celestion 1/CS135 Satellite: 11x6x9 in., 7 lb. Bass module: 8x21x14 in., 22 lb.	199/259 199/259	77	85/73	◒	24x12	+1/+6	4/8	29	A
Polk RM3000 Satellite: 7x4x5 in., 3 lb. Bass module: 13x20x13 in., 35 lb.	639 800	77	85/77	●	42x36	−1/+3	5/8	23	A,G,I
AR Athena System Satellite: 8x5x5 in., 3 lb. Bass module: 8x17x16 in., 27 lb.	510 599	77	84/76	○	42x24	−1/+4	4/6	23	C,G,P

Ratings continued ▶

3-PIECE LOUDSPEAKERS

▶ *Ratings continued*

Brand and model	Price	Overall score	Accuracy, tone-corrected/raw [1]	Bass handling	Optimum bass distance, in. [2]	Tone adjustment, bass/treble	Impedance, ohm [3]	Min. power, watt	Comments
Phase Tech PC 40/50 Mark II Satellite: 10x7x6 in., 8 lb. Bass module: 14x14x15 in., 31 lb.	$730	76	83/72	◒	18x12	+1/+6	4/6	29	A,G,O
Realistic Minimus 7W/ Subwoofer Satellite: 8x5x5 in., 4 lb. Bass module: 13x16x18 in., 27 lb.	120/140 120/150	75	83/71	◒	42x30	−6/+3	5/8	18	B,C,G,I,N
Infinity Micro II Satellite: 8x7x7 in., 4 lb. Bass module: 16x10x15 in., 24 lb.	619 799	75	82/73	○	54x36	−1/+5	4/7	29	C
Pioneer S-3D-K/SW-55 Satellite: 11x7x5 in., 4 lb. Bass module: 22x8x17 in., 28 lb.	379 550	74	82/73	◕	42x24	0/+6	6/8	19	A,B,O
Pinnacle PN5+/PN Sub+ [D] Satellite: 11x7x7 in., 7 lb. Bass module: 13x20x12 in., 28 lb.	169/229 329	74	80/68	◒	36x24	−6/+4	6/6	19	C,F,G,I,K
ADS SubSat 3 Satellite: 9x6x6 in., 7 lb. Bass module: 19x9x8 in., 18 lb.	650 769	71	81/70	◕	36x24	+1/+6	3/8	48	B,C,J,O
Altec Lansing System 3 Satellite: 9x4x4 in., 4 lb. Bass module: 10x20x12 in., 32 lb.	510 600	70	79/70	◕	30x18	−6/+2	6/4	15	B,N,P

[1] *Power response adjusted for a room's walls and floor: after tone-control adjustments/before tone-control adjustments.*

[2] *Our estimate of the distance bass module should be from side and back walls.*

[3] *Our measurement, then mfr.'s for speaker's resistance to electric current, which determines compatibility with a receiver.*

Successor Models (in Ratings order)
NHT Zero satellite is succeeded by SuperZero, $230; Boston Acoustics by SubSatSix Series II, $1000.

Features in Common
Except as noted, all: • Satellites available separately; judged average in accuracy when used without bass module. • Have spring-loaded connectors. • Connectors take stripped wire or single or double "banana" plugs.

Key to Comments
A–Satellites and bass module have binding posts instead of spring-loaded connectors. (**Boston Acoustics, Celestion,** and **Pioneer** use posts only on bass module.)
B–Satellite connectors don't take double-banana plugs.
C–Bass-module connectors don't take double-banana plugs.
D–Separate bass module for each channel.
E–Satellites have 2 drivers that can be directed separately.
F–Has switch to decrease output from satellites.
G–Bass module designed to be put flat on floor.
H–Bass module contains amplifier with bass-level and frequency-cutoff controls.
I–Bass module can be used as low stand.
J–Satellites also available separately.
K–Accuracy of satellites alone better than most.
L–Accuracy of satellites alone worse than most.
M–Comes with full warranty.
N–Screw slots for hanging on wall.
O–Comes with brackets for wall-mounting.
P–Comes with wires for connection to receiver.

AUDIO TAPES

RATINGS — AUDIO TAPES

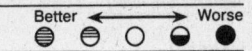

Better ◄———► Worse
⊜ ◒ ○ ◐ ●

▶ **See report, page 34.** From Consumer Reports, January 1993.

Recommendations: Just about any Type I tape will do for recordings for a cheap cassette deck in a noisy car, for a boom box, or for an answering machine. Choose higher-rated Type I and Type II tapes for recordings of a radio program, an LP record, or a CD to play in a quiet car, or to play in a walkabout. Higher-rated Type II and Type IV are for copying high-quality LPs, capturing live concerts, or copying CDs for critical listening. Under no circumstances, however, is the *TDK MA-XG* a good value; it cost us $14 apiece.

Ratings order: Listed by types; within types, listed in order of overall score. Differences in score of 10 points or less were judged insignificant. List price is the manufacturer's suggested retail price for a single tape. Paid is the manufacturer's suggested retail and the average price we paid. **Notes to table:** Key to **Bias shift:** + or ++ means higher-than-normal bias; a - or -- means lower than normal bias. Symbols to **Sensitivity shift** indicate how different the playback level will be than with "standard" tape at the same recording level. Increased sensitivity is indicated by +. Ⓓ indicates model discontinued.

Brand and model	Price, list/paid	Overall score	Midrange	Treble	Distortion	Uniformity/dropouts	Bias shift	Sensitivity shift	Comments
TYPE I ('NORMAL') TAPES									
Fuji DR-1	$1.99/$2.00	77	◒	◒	○	◒	++	0	F,G
Sony ES 1 Ⓓ	3.49/ 2.25	77	◒	◒	○	◒	++	0	C,F
Maxell UDI* Ⓓ	3.50/ 2.50	74	○	○	◒	◒	+	0	F
Maxell XLI-S* Ⓓ	4.00/ 3.00	74	○	○	○	◒	+	0	—
TDK DS-X	2.99/ 2.25	73	○	○	◒	○	0	0	F
TDK D	1.99/ 1.50	68	○	○	◒	○	+	0	—
BASF Ferro Extra I	0.99/ 1.00	67	○	○	○	◐	+	0	—
Maxell UR	1.79/ 1.75	67	◐	○	○	◒	0	0	—
Scotch CX	1.50/ 1.25	67	○	○	○	◒	0	0	—
Sony HF	1.69/ 1.75	67	○	○	○	◒	0	0	—
Realistic Supertape XR	1.99/ 2.00	66	○	○	○	○	+	0	D
Denon DX1	2.25/ 1.75	65	◐	○	○	◒	0	-	C
Memorex MRXI	2.29/ 2.50	64	◐	○	○	○	0	0	—
Scotch BX	1.25/ 1.50	64	◐	○	○	○	0	0	—
JVC GI	1.55/ 1.50	62	○	○	○	◐	0	0	—
Memorex dbs	1.59/ 1.50	61	◐	○	○	◐	-	0	—
Realistic Supertape LN	1.20/ 1.25	59	◐	○	○	●	-	0	D
K Mart KMC 90* Ⓓ	—/ 1.00	56	◐	○	◐	◐	-	0	E
Certon HD	1.79/ 1.25	44	●	◐	●	◐	0	+	E
Certon C/90 LN	0.80/ 0.50	41	●	◐	●	●	---	+++	E
TYPE II ('HIGH-BIAS') TAPES									
TDK SA-X	4.49/ 3.75	87	◒	◒	◒	◒	+	0	F

Ratings continued ▶

56 AUDIO TAPES
▶ *Ratings continued*

Brand and model	Price, list/paid	Overall score	Midrange	Treble	Distortion	Uniformity/dropouts	Bias shift	Sensitivity shift	Comments
Fuji DR-II	$2.99/$2.00	84	⊖	⊖	⊖	⊖	0	–	F,G
BASF Chrome Maxima II [D]	3.99/ 2.75	83	⊖	⊖	○	⊖	0	–	–
Maxell XLII-S	4.39/ 3.25	83	⊖	⊖	⊖	⊖	+	0	B,F
Sony ES II	3.99/ 2.25	83	⊖	⊖	⊖	⊖	0	0	F
Sony UX Turbo	3.99/ 2.50	82	⊖	⊖	⊖	⊖	0	0	A,F
Sony UX-Pro	4.29/ 4.00	81	⊖	⊖	⊖	⊖	0	0	–
BASF Chrome Super II	2.99/ 2.25	79	⊖	⊖	○	⊖	+	–	–
Maxell XLII	3.79/ 2.75	79	⊖	⊖	○	⊖	0	0	F
Fuji FR-IIx	3.99/ 2.00	78	⊖	⊖	⊖	⊖	0	0	F,G
Maxell UDII* [D]	4.00/ 2.75	78	⊖	⊖	⊖	⊖	0	0	F
TDK SD	2.99/ 2.50	78	⊖	⊖	⊖	⊖	0	0	F
Fuji FR-IIxPro	4.99/ 1.75	76	⊖	○	⊖	⊖	0	0	A
TDK SA	3.79/ 2.75	76	⊖	⊖	○	●	0	0	F
Denon HD6	3.25/ 2.25	75	⊖	⊖	○	⊖	0	0	F
Realistic Supertape M-II	4.79/ 4.75	75	○	⊖	⊖	⊖	0	–	D
Denon S-Port High (C-100)	2.50/ 2.25	74	○	○	○	⊖	0	0	F,G,H
Realistic Supertape HD	2.99/ 1.75	74	○	○	○	⊖	0	0	D
Sony ES II (C-100) [D]	4.49/ 3.25	74	⊖	○	⊖	○	+	0	–
TDK SA (C-100)	4.39/ 2.75	74	○	○	○	⊖	0	0	F
3M Black Watch 2020	3.99/ 3.50	73	○	⊖	○	⊖	0	–	–
Denon HD8	4.75/ 3.25	72	○	○	○	⊖	0	0	–
Sony CDit II (C-94)	2.99/ 2.00	72	○	⊖	○	⊖	0	0	F,G
Sony UX	3.19/ 2.75	71	○	⊖	●	⊖	0	0	–
Denon HD7	4.00/ 3.00	69	○	○	○	⊖	0	0	F
Memorex HBS II	2.59/ 2.25	68	○	⊖	●	●	0	0	–
TYPE IV ('METAL') TAPES									
Sony Metal-ES [D]	4.95/ 4.00	94	⊖	⊖	⊖	⊖	+++	–	–
Sony Metal Master	11.00/ 7.00	93	⊖	⊖	⊖	○	+++	–	B
TDK MA-XG	18.99/14.00	93	⊖	⊖	⊖	⊖	++	0	B
Fuji FR Metal	5.99/ 4.25	92	⊖	⊖	⊖	⊖	+	–	F,G
Maxell MX-S	5.29/ 4.00	89	⊖	⊖	⊖	⊖	++	0	B,F
Maxell Metal Vertex	14.99/13.25	89	⊖	⊖	⊖	⊖	++	0	B
TDK MA-X	5.29/ 4.50	88	⊖	⊖	⊖	⊖	++	0	–
Realistic Supertape M-IV	5.99/ 6.00	86	⊖	⊖	○	⊖	+++	0	D
Sony CDit IV [D]	3.49/ 2.75	86	⊖	⊖	○	⊖	+	0	F,G
Sony Metal-SR	3.49/ 3.00	86	⊖	⊖	⊖	⊖	+	0	–
TDK MA	3.99/ 3.50	86	⊖	⊖	⊖	○	+++	0	F
Denon S-Port Metal (C-100)	3.50/ 3.50	83	⊖	⊖	⊖	⊖	0	0	F,G,H
Maxell MX	3.99/ 3.00	83	⊖	⊖	⊖	○	++	0	–

UNIVERSAL REMOTE CONTROLS

Brand and model	Price, list/paid	Overall score	Midrange	Treble	Distortion	Uniformity/ dropouts	Bias shift	Sensitivity shift	Comments
3M Black Watch 4040	$4.59/$4.50	82	◐	◐	○	◐	+	0	—
Denon HD-M	5.50/ 3.25	82	◐	◐	○	◐	+	+	F
Memorex CDX IV	2.99/ 2.75	82	◐	◐	○	○	+	0	—
Denon MG-X (C-100)	9.95/ 9.00	81	◐	◐	○	◐	+	0	B

Performance Notes
Except as noted, all: • Cassettes and carrying cases were average in heat-resistance.

Key to Comments
A–Cassette and case much better than average in heat-resistance.
B–Cassette much better than average in heat-resistance.
C–Cassette better than average in heat-resistance.
D–Cassette worse than average in heat-resistance.
E–Cassette much worse than average in heat-resistance.
F–Cassette case has rounded edges.
G–"Slimline" case, somewhat thinner than most.
H–According to mfr., formulation has changed since we conducted our tests.

RATINGS | UNIVERSAL REMOTE CONTROLS

Better ← ● ◐ ○ ◐ ● → Worse

▶ **See report, page 21.** From Consumer Reports, December 1992.

Recommendations: To control video devices, consider *One For All 3 Big Easy* ($30) or *Sole Control SC-500* ($60); both remote controls were easy to program and the *Sole Control* even controlled complex functions. For controlling both video and audio products, look first at the top four: the *Memorex CP8 Turbo* ($90); the *Fox 600* ($60); the *One For All 12* ($99); the *RCA System Link RCU 100*, ($50). Models that are discontinued may still be available but hard to find.

Ratings order: Listed by types; within types, listed in order of overall score. Models with equal scores are listed alphabetically. Price is the manufacturer's suggested retail; actual retail may be lower. ⓢ indicates tested model has been replaced by successor model; according to the manufacturer, the performance of new model should be similar to the tested model but features may vary. See page 58 for new model number and suggested retail price, if available. ⓓ indicates model discontinued.

Brand and model	Overall score	Price	Components	Keypad Accessibility	Grouping	Differentiation	Visibility	Programming	Owner's manual	Code-entry Learning	Comments
VIDEO ONLY											
One For All 3 Big Easy	88	$30	4	◐	◐	◐	◐	◐	◐	✔	—	B,E,N
Sole Control SC-500 ⓓ	84	60	6	◐	○	◐	○	◐	◐	✔	—	A,B
Zenith MBR 3020 ⓓ	84	60	3	◐	◐	◐	◐	◐	◐	✔	—	I
Gemini Easy3	83	15	3	◐	◐	◐	◐	◐	◐	✔	—	I,N,W

Ratings continued ▶

UNIVERSAL REMOTE CONTROLS

Ratings continued

Brand and model	Overall score	Price	Components	Keypad Accessibility	Keypad Grouping	Keypad Differentiation	Visibility	Programming	Owner's manual	Code-entry	Learning	Comments
Memorex AV4 [D]	81	$40	4	●	●	◐	○	◐	◐	✓	—	B,E,L,N
VIDEO AND AUDIO												
Memorex CP8 Turbo [D]	90	90	8	◐	◐	◐	◐	◐	◐	—	✓	A,F,G,M,O
Fox 600	88	60	6	◐	◐	◐	◐	◐	◐	✓	✓	B,E
One For All 12	86	99	12	○	◐	◐	◐	◐	○	✓	—	A,B,D,E,G,H
RCA System Link RCU 100	86	50	5	◐	◐	◐	◐	◐	◐	✓	—	—
One For All 6	84	49	6	○	◐	◐	●	◐	○	✓	—	A,B,D,E
Philips The Smart One AK 9033	84	40	5	◐	◐	◐	◐	◐	○	✓	✓	A,B,E,N
Realistic Four in One 15-1904 [D]	83	40	4	○	○	○	○	◐	◐	✓	—	B,E
Gemini MAC 20 [S]	81	43	3	◐	◐	◐	◐	◐	◐	✓	✓	N,W
Realistic Eight in One 15-1903 [D]	80	100	8	○	●	○	●	◐	○	—	✓	A,F,G,M,O
Fox 800	79	100	8	◐	●	○	○	○	◐	✓	✓	A,C,E,F,M,N,P
Sole Control SC-2000	79	130	12	◐	●	◐	◐	◐	◐	✓	—	A,B
Mitsubishi M-X2541 [S]	77	150	8	◐	●	●	◐	◐	○	—	✓	F,J,K,O
Denon Unimote RC 770	76	150	17	●	●	●	○	○	○	—	✓	A,F,G,J,K,O,W
JVC Universal RM-S1	74	250	11	●	●	●	●	●	●	—	✓	A,B,C,F,J,K,P
Pioneer Smart Remote CU-AV200 [D]	70	185	13	○	●	◐	◐	◐	◐	✓	✓	G,J,N,O

Successor Models (in Ratings order)
Gemini MAC 20 is succeeded by MAC 15, $30; Mitsubishi M-X2541 by M-X2551, $150.

Features in Common
All: • Have range of at least 25 ft. • Remained functional after three 3-ft. falls onto linoleum-covered concrete floor. • Have estimated battery life of about 1 yr. in normal use.
Except as noted, all: • Have memory backup to hold settings for at least 2 min. when replacing batteries. • Have numeric keypad arranged like telephone number pad. • Have VCR menu.

Key to Comments
A–Low-battery indicator.
B–Light indicates remote is operational.
C–Beeper indicates remote is operational.
D–According to mfr., can be updated with new product codes at store.
E–Can systematically recall preprogrammed product codes.
F–Light for LCD display.
G–Can perform multiple commands from one button, as programmed by user.
H–Sleep timer.
I–No memory backup during replacement of batteries.
J–Numeric keypad not telephone style.
K–Preset codes handle only products from same manufacturer.
L–Controls several brands of CD and laser-disc players plus video equipment.
M–Has clock-timer.
N–Lacks ability to access VCR menu.
O–Has LCD display.
P–Has touch-sensitive LCD screen.

▶ Photography

Cameras & lenses	60
Color print film	66
Film processing	67
Video & photo tripods	68
Ratings	70

Camcorders will never entirely replace the still camera. Neither will electronic systems that rely on computer or compact discs and TV sets to store and display photographs electronically. There will always be a place for vacation snapshots, for wallet-sized pictures of loved ones, and for photos that mark life's rites of passage—birthdays, graduations, and weddings. And that means there will always be a market for cameras and the paraphernalia that goes with them—accessory lenses, tripods, and myriad attachments.

Blunder-proof, highly automated compact 35mm cameras have quickly become the amateur's best friend. Equipped with a moderate zoom lens, such cameras are almost as appealing and versatile as more "professional" single-lens reflex models. Disposable cameras—single-use models preloaded with print film—have also become so popular that roughly one disposable camera is sold for every regular camera. Some disposables even come equipped with flash for greater flexibility.

A sturdy tripod facilitates careful framing and the use of exposure settings that might cause blurring if the camera were handheld. For video work, a decent tripod is a must. A tripod specifically built for camcorder use can keep home videos from looking jumpy and jerky.

Of course, film is the most basic photographic tool. Although the *Kodak* brand is the most well known, other brands are available, sometimes for half the price. Processing film can be expensive and the quality can vary depending on the lab.

Shopping for photographic equipment is unusual in some ways. You'll find that few stores ask full list price for a camera or lens. Discounts depend on a store's competition and the amount of customer service and convenience it provides. For rock-bottom prices, check the mail-order ads in newspapers or camera magazines. Mail-order houses in New York and other big cities sell cameras and photography equipment sometimes for half the list price.

Watch for vendors who go beyond ordinary sales pressure into sharp, even illegal, sales practices. The classic trick is the familiar bait-and-switch: "We're all out of that one, but we have something better. . ." Protect yourself by refusing substitutes.

A variation on bait-and-switch is the tie-in. In this instance, you are told you cannot buy an item at a certain price unless you buy something else—a camera case, for instance. Try to find out beforehand which removable pieces—lens caps, straps, cases, and so forth—are standard on whatever it is you're buying. That way, you won't fall victim to "stripping," the practice of a store's stripping off standard equipment and then selling it back to you.

Some of the photo equipment available in this country, called "gray market" merchandise, is imported by someone other than the manufacturer's authorized U.S. subsidiary. That doesn't mean there's anything wrong with the goods—except that they may come with an "international" or camera-store warranty, which may complicate warranty service. A store may tell you your sales slip is your warranty. That means the store, not the manufacturer, assumes responsibility for the warranty period. Some stores may give you a choice of goods with or without a U.S. warranty. Unless the ad specifically says "U.S. warranty," assume the goods are gray market.

For gear with few moving parts and little likelihood of breakage, like tripods and lenses, forgoing the premium-priced U.S. warranty poses little risk. For cameras, whose repair can be expensive, we'd think carefully about the risk.

Cameras & lenses

▶ **Ratings of compact 35s on page 70.**

The 35mm format has become the standard for professional photographers, serious amateurs, and snapshooters alike. One reason for its appeal is the size of the negative—about 1x1½ inches, appreciably larger than negatives from disc and 110 cameras. Bigger negatives yield sharper enlargements. Another reason: the variety of film available. Lately, 35mm color films have become faster—better suited to low-light situations—and far less grainy, for better looking enlargements.

There are two basic types of 35mm cameras—the compact and the single-lens reflex, or SLR. In addition, 35mm "bridge" designs combine some characteristics of compacts and SLRs. They're aimed at photographers who want more than a compact but less than an interchangeable-lens SLR.

Compact 35s

Some are pocket-sized models; others, weighing over a pound and bristling with ergonomic bulges and bulky zoom lenses, would strain a coat pocket. Either way, compacts are nice for snapshooters with little or no photographic background. Automated film-loading features have made them almost as easy to use as disc and 110 snapshot cameras. List prices for most compacts range from about $40 to over $300.

CAMERAS & LENSES

Disposable cameras—single-use cameras preloaded with print film—appeared in the late 1980s and have become very popular. Some disposables can be used underwater; some take panoramic shots, for prints about twice as wide as ordinary snapshots. Some even have a flash or telephoto lens. They list for about $9 to $20, depending on type. You shoot the pictures, then return the entire camera for processing.

Lens. Early compact cameras were limited by their single fixed-focal-length lens. These days many compacts come with a zoom lens that goes from a wide-angle lens (say, 35 mm) to a modest telephoto (say, 105 mm) so that you can bring in more distant subjects and frame a scene even more tightly. Some models cover a more limited zoom range, say 35 mm to 70 mm; other dual-lens models just have a wide-angle setting, perhaps 28 mm, and a "normal" setting, 45 mm or 50 mm.

Exposure. Nearly all compacts have automatic exposure control to help assure proper exposure of the film: A built-in light meter sizes up the lighting and adjusts the aperture and shutter speed accordingly. The system strikes a balance between fast shutter speed (to prevent moving objects from blurring) and small aperture, or lens opening (to enhance overall sharpness). A few models have a backlight switch that lets you adjust the exposure when strong light comes from behind the subject. All but the most rudimentary compact cameras have a built-in flash; it's generally on the weak side, as flashes go. Most compacts fire their flash automatically when there's insufficient light. A few models let you turn off the flash for more natural-looking available-light photos.

Film handling. Most compact 35s have automatic film handling: You drop in the cartridge, pull out enough film to reach a certain mark in the camera, close the camera, and a motor automatically threads the film. The motor also advances the film after each shot and rewinds it when done.

All but the cheapest compact models read the film's sensitivity from the checkerboard DX-coding on the cartridge and appropriately set the exposure meter. Some can read only the most popular color-print film speeds, ISO 100 and 400, while some read the range of ISOs from 25 to 1600 or even 3200. If you plan to use a variety of film speeds, look for a camera that covers a wide range.

Focusing. Current compacts don't require you to focus. The simplest models, sometimes called focus-free, have fixed focus, like those in most 110 cameras and older box cameras. These cameras use very small lens apertures to keep all objects more than a few feet away in reasonably sharp focus. They can't take nonflash pictures in dim light like an autofocus camera.

Compact cameras that focus automatically typically list for more than $100. Autofocus systems set the lens for one of several distance zones. One zone might cover subjects 8 to 10 feet away; another, 10 to 14 feet away, and so on. Some models use only two distance zones (near and far) while some cameras cover a dozen or more. As a rule, the more zones, the better. Models with an infinity control—to get the focus at its farthest—are useful for shooting through glass or past an object in the foreground that otherwise might confuse the autofocus.

Viewfinder. Some compacts have a bright-frame viewfinder. Others have a sharp edge that frames the entire image. Both types are easy to use even with eyeglasses. Our tests have shown such viewfinders to be fairly accurate: What's visible in the frame is pretty much what is captured on film. Viewfinders with indistinct framing that shifts if you move your eye are the worst.

Flash. Built-in electronic flash is standard. Cameras have now been introduced that help reduce "red eye"—the demonic red glow that occurs when the flash bounces off a subject's retina. To avoid the red, some designs simply put the flash farther from the lens. Others turn on a light just before exposure, which makes the subject's pupils contract.

Limitations. Compact cameras can stymie an advanced photographer, who might want to use a variety of lenses or override the camera's automatic settings. Compact cameras usually don't allow such control. They don't even let you know which settings they've chosen for a picture. If you crave artistic control, compact cameras aren't for you. But many a snapshooter is happy to trade control for convenience and simplicity in a small package.

SLR cameras

Single-lens reflex cameras were once strictly for serious hobbyists and professionals—photographers who knew how to take advantage of the many ways possible to manipulate lenses, exposure controls, focus, and film types to create artistic effects. Recent innovations have automated so much of this that some SLRs can be as easy to work as a compact 35mm camera. But the main photographic value of an SLR remains not so much in the camera itself as in the additional lenses and paraphernalia you can add that transform the camera into a "system."

Lenses. The distinctive trapezoidal hump at the top of an SLR camera houses a prism mounted over a mirror, an arrangement that lets you see what the lens sees when you look through the eyepiece behind the hump. A built-in light meter also "sees" and evaluates what the lens sees.

The reflected image—the "reflex" in "single-lens reflex"—makes it practical to use a variety of lenses in addition to the "normal" 50mm or 55mm lens. Attach a

---

A GUIDE TO CAMERA AUTOMATION

Autofocus. Speeds up picture taking. May not work well in dim light or in scenes with little contrast or with repetitive graphic patterns.

Autofocus illuminator. A red beam shines on the subject to help the autofocus work in dim light.

Automatic zoom. On some compacts, the lens zooms in or out to maintain roughly the same composition as the camera-to-subject distance varies. On some models, the camera "guesses" the zoom setting you want from the distance away. The feature can be annoying on models where it's routinely on and must be manually turned off when you don't want to use it.

Autowinder. This feature typically threads, advances, and rewinds the film. A convenience that's popular.

'Creative expansion' cards. With this Minolta feature, plug-in chips provide special exposure modes. Cards are convenient for customizing camera settings, but they're also a nuisance to store and change.

Depth-of-field preview. This feature lets you see how much background and foreground will be sharp. May not work in all exposure modes and often too dim to see results.

Depth-of-field mode. An autofocus option that lets you select the nearest foreground and farthest background objects that you want to keep sharp. The camera then tries to adjust aperture and shutter accordingly. Takes the guesswork out of how the final photo will look.

super-wide-angle lens and you gain appreciable peripheral vision—excellent for panoramas or photographing groups in tight spaces. Switch to a telephoto lens and you're looking through a telescope—excellent for candid shots and bringing in distant objects without having to move in close. Or you can use a zoom lens for a whole range of views. What you see through the lens is what the film records when you press the shutter.

Thus, an SLR system gives you immense control over point of view and composition. But you're no longer talking about a $300 camera; an SLR system can easily cost several times the price of the camera alone.

For years, the lens typically sold with an SLR was a normal 50 mm lens. Now, that lens is likely to be a moderate-range zoom (35 mm to 105 mm or so). Our tests show that the quality of zoom lenses has improved markedly in recent years. Any lapses in sharpness are usually imperceptible except under high magnification.

Automatic exposure controls. Many SLRs are programmed to select both the aperture and shutter speed automatically. SLRs with aperture-priority exposure let you set the lens opening (f-stop) while they automatically select the shutter speed. Those with shutter-priority exposure do just the opposite. Most can be operated in a manual mode as well: Typically, an indicator in the viewfinder confirms when you've manually set a combination of aperture and shutter speed that works for a shot's lighting.

All the exposure systems rely on readings from a built-in light meter. Some systems (spot meters) check lighting only at the very center of the frame, where the subject is likely to be; others (center-weighted) consider the entire frame but give greater weight to the center; yet others (multipattern metering) average the frame's light reading in a more complex

---

Diopter adjustment. Adjusts viewfinder for moderate near- or farsightedness, so that eyeglass wearers with no astigmatism can focus and shoot without their glasses on. A nice feature for some.

DX film-speed reader. Reads the checkered code on 35mm cartridge to set film speed for proper exposure. Convenient—keeps you from ruining film if you forget to change meter settings. But some systems don't cover all common speeds.

Film-prewind feature. Shoots film "backwards" by first unwinding the entire roll from cartridge. As you shoot, film winds back into the light-tight film cartridge. If you accidentally open the camera in mid-roll, no more than one shot is ruined. A good idea.

Follow-focus mode. Sometimes called "servo" or "continuous focus," this feature keeps a moving subject in focus as long as you hold the shutter release partway down and keep the subject centered.

Programmed exposure. Automatically sets both aperture and shutter speed for proper exposure. Works well under all but trickiest lighting—a boon to novices and pros. Some programs favor background and foreground sharpness; others favor freezing fast action.

Trap-focus mode. After being focused manually, the camera automatically snaps any subject that moves into the center of the frame at the preset distance. This feature comes in handy for wildlife and candid photography.

manner. SLRs with more than one metering mode let a photographer select the mode used.

Automated film handling. This helps load, advance, and rewind the film. Most cameras with an autowinder also let you fire off a quick series of shots, as fashion and sports photographers are wont to do. Automatic DX-code readers set film speed.

Automatic focusing. Some people find focusing by hand and eye to be tedious and slow. Typically, the center of the viewfinder shows a split image whose halves you must align by turning the lens. Or you must try to sharpen a shimmering microprism ring surrounding the split-image circle in the center of the viewfinder.

Technology has solved the focusing problem as well. At the press of a button, computer chips and a miniature motor can now focus the lens in a split second, generally with pinpoint accuracy. You pay dearly for such convenience: Autofocus SLR camera bodies carry list prices of $300 to more than $2000. Manual-focus models start around $250 but go to more than $3000. An autofocus SLR with a zoom lens can easily list for well over $1500 (but discount prices are typically hundreds lower).

Flash. Most autofocus SLRs come with a small built-in flash, but manual-focus models require purchase of an external accessory flash. More powerful accessory flashes are also marketed for autofocus cameras.

Do you really need to spend the extra money for an autofocus SLR? No. Focusing an SLR is tricky only if you've never done it before. With just a little practice, the technique becomes second nature. The same is true of film loading and automatic-exposure control. If you're willing to spend the time to learn the photographic ropes, you can choose a basic SLR, which is the best SLR buy. Some camera makers no longer support their manual-focus cameras with a full line of lenses, however. If you want a zoom lens, say, for a manual SLR, you may have to settle for a different company's lens or for a secondhand lens.

'Bridge' cameras

These cameras bridge the gap between SLRs and compacts—they offer less user control than a typical SLR but more versatility than a typical compact camera. With list prices ranging from $500 to $900, these cameras are almost as expensive as a good SLR, but you don't get an SLR's flexibility.

Bridge cameras have a non-interchangeable zoom lens whose focal length generally spans 35 mm to 135 mm, a wider range than the zooms typical of compact cameras. Additional features include: a viewfinder that's sometimes the SLR type; programmed exposure; autofocus; built-in electronic flash (also found on most compacts and autofocus SLRs); and an autowinder with automatic film threading. Other features vary. With all their automation, bridge cameras are very easy to use. But so are most autofocus SLRs.

From what we've seen in our tests, the lenses on these cameras are about as good as that of a middling SLR zoom—very good, but not exceptional. The viewfinders, however, didn't let you frame scenes quite as accurately as you can with most SLRs. Framing errors of 15 or 20 percent picture area are typical.

People with the money and time to invest in learning photography will probably be happier with an SLR than with a bridge model. People with less photographic interest would probably be satisfied with a cheaper compact 35mm camera.

Flash units

Electronic flash units range from compact, low-powered models with limited features and list prices around $50, to high-powered, multifeatured models with list prices of more than $400.

A camera owner's choice is limited by problems of compatibility. Most camera manufacturers' flash units are dedicated: Each is designed for one or more models of the same camera brand and won't work satisfactorily with other brands, if at all. Consumers have to rely on salespeople or product literature to tell which flash does what with which cameras.

The expensive units usually offer more light output and special features. They calculate exposure automatically with your camera's metering system or let you override the setting manually. They can tilt toward the ceiling for "bounce" flash, a more pleasing effect than flatly lit head-on flash. Other features let you diffuse light or lighten shadows about faces.

In general, flash-units that go atop a camera are much less prone to red-eye.

The tests

Key camera tests are for sharpness, a function of the lens and focusing system, and for freedom from various lens shortcomings such as flare, distortion, and chromatic aberration.

Tests of exposure accuracy tell how capably a camera gauges lighting to adjust its shutter and aperture for a given scene and film. Accurate exposure is essential for shooting slides, but less so for print film, which is more forgiving of overexposure. Other tests gauge a camera's framing accuracy and the range and uniformity of its built-in flash.

Buying advice

Before you shop for a camera, decide how deeply you want to get involved in photography. If your commitment goes no further than recording everyday family events, a compact 35mm may be all the camera you need. For a dash of flexibility in framing your shots, consider a compact with a zoom lens.

If you are or expect to become knowledgeable about photography, consider an SLR without autofocus. Equipped with a 50mm lens, a manual-focus SLR lists for $350 to $800.

Whatever type of camera you decide on, select several models that have the features you want. In the store, hold each camera to your eye and check its view, controls, grip, and balance. That's the only way to tell whether you'll be comfortable taking pictures with it.

INFORMATION FROM CONSUMER REPORTS

Consumers Union provides information in a variety of ways. Its publications include CONSUMER REPORTS; Zillions, a CONSUMER REPORTS for Kids; two newsletters, On Health and The Travel Letter; and a book list of more than 100 titles. CU also offers used car prices by telephone, computer printouts of new car prices, fax copies of recent articles in CONSUMER REPORTS, and an electronic version of CONSUMER REPORTS on America Online, CompuServe, Dialog, Nexis, and Prodigy.

Color print film
▶ Ratings on page 78.

Kodak film dominates the photographic-film market in the U.S. Its yellow boxes enclose three of every four rolls of film sold. Despite *Kodak's* omnipresence, plenty of other brands exist—*Agfa, Fuji, Konica, Polaroid,* store brands such as *Focal,* and film from mail-order processing laboratories. Such brands sell for a lot less than *Kodak;* in some cases, half as much as *Kodak* film. A 24-exposure roll of *Kodak Gold Plus 200* is priced about $4.70. The same size of Polaroid's 200-speed film is priced about $2.30.

Neither *Kodak* nor *Fuji,* the next biggest brand, supply film to others to retail under other brand names. The only American company other than Kodak that makes film for the consumers is 3M Corporation, so any film except *Kodak* that's made in the U.S. is made by 3M. 3M film is sold as *Polaroid OneFilm,* K Mart's *Focal,* plus Kroger, Pathmark, Target, and other store brands.

Agfa is Germany's only consumer-film manufacturer, so private-label brands made in Germany are *Agfa* film.

The choices

Film speed ranges from ISO 25 to more than ISO 1600. Less sensitive ("slower") film demands more light but generally offers the most accurate colors and finest resolution. Film as slow as ISO 25 demands wide apertures or slower shutter speeds. Films have been improving, however, and today's top-speed rolls are both faster and better looking. Today, there's ISO 3200 film that allows you to shoot a candlelit dinner without using a flash unit.

As a general rule, the higher a film's speed, the higher its price. While faster films contain more silver, we think the cost differences have more to do with marketing considerations than the cost of materials.

The tests

Using ISO 100, 200, and 400 film, we shoot indoor and outdoor pictures with subjects and lighting similar to what most people use.

We send the film to each of five mail-order processing laboratories that were top rated in our last report on film processors (see the report opposite). When the 3½x5-inch prints come back, trained panelists judge them for color accuracy, graininess, contrast, and color saturation.

Buying advice

Among the ISO 100 films, six films produced the best pictures: *Polaroid High Definition, Fujicolor Super G, Kodak Gold Plus, Konica Super SR, Kodak Ektar,* and *ScotchColor.* In each ISO group, the film made by 3M—*ScotchColor* or a store-brand film, and *Polaroid OneFilm*—had more graininess than other films in their group.

Film is frequently a sale item, especially at peak shooting times like the holidays. We've seen advertised prices as low as $1.50 for a 24-exposure roll.

Buying film in multiple-roll packs is usually less expensive than single rolls. Store unopened film you won't use for a while in the refrigerator.

For the best quality pictures, use the slowest-speed film your shooting allows. Our tests of color print films showed better color rendition and finer grain, on average, with 100-speed films than with 200- or 400-speed films. The differences would be even more apparent if you were to make enlargements.

Film processing

All photofinishing companies—from local one-hour outlets to giant mail-order operations—use highly automated equipment. The machinery is geared to deliver good prints of average subjects captured under normal lighting. It can be easily foiled by out-of-the-ordinary conditions. And the folks running the machines don't always check the prints that come out. It's cheaper for the lab to redo botched jobs only when customers complain. But many never complain about printing errors.

Common lab mistakes include poor color balance, as evidenced by odd skin tones; overexposed prints, which look too dark; and underexposed prints, which look pale and washed out. On the other hand, muddy-looking prints due to underexposed negatives aren't the labs' fault.

Human errors at the lab include negatives marred by finger prints, dirt, or scratches; film inadvertently exposed to light during processing; and negatives chopped in half, for instance.

The choices

Mail-order labs. These businesses operate nationwide, with mailing envelopes that usually double as order forms. They're fairly low-priced—typically $3.50 to $7 for a set of 3½x5-inch prints from a 24-exposure roll.

Minilab chains. These outfits, often found in malls, can deliver prints within a few hours after you drop off film. Many promise one-hour service. You pay a premium price for quick turnaround, generally $10 to $15 for a 24-exposure roll.

Wholesale companies. These processors operate through supermarkets, discount centers, and drugstores. You may never even know the laboratory's name. Qualex is the dominant wholesaler. One of its branches is Kodalux, descended from Kodak's photofinishing operation. Its service is offered primarily through camera stores and prepaid mailers. Prices for wholesalers are comparable to those of the mail-order companies. Turnaround generally takes two days.

The tests

We take hundreds of photos—mainly landscapes and portrait shots—designed to challenge the photofinishers' equipment—using one kind of film (*Kodacolor Gold 100*). We shoot in various kinds of light—flash, incandescent, and fluorescent light indoors and sunny and cloudy skies outside. We deliberately over- and underexpose some shots. A tripod setup let us duplicate photos and exposures precisely on multiple rolls of film in multiple cameras.

Then we send the film to the processors, staggering sets of rolls over several months. We score print quality for all blunders, whether they're caused by a lab's machinery or its personnel.

Buying advice

Several mail-order labs—Mystic Color Lab, Skrudland Photo, Seattle FilmWorks, Kodalux, and Custom Quality Studio—served us best and have consistently done so over the past few years.

The better processors committed the fewest errors and returned prints generally within a week or two, all that for under $7. When we included wholesale labs and minilabs in a previous test, they were, on average, a notch or so poorer than the mail-order labs but still pretty good overall.

Unless you're in a terrible rush, stay away from the one-hour minilabs. They charged considerably more than mail-order and wholesale labs.

Video & photo tripods

▶ Ratings on page 76.

Today's fast films and quick shutter speeds create sharp pictures without "camera shake" even if hands aren't so steady. As a result, photo tripods have become primarily an artistic device, permitting sharp pictures at long exposure times and enabling you to compose a picture carefully and maintain that composition securely until conditions are absolutely right.

For camcorder owners, however, a good tripod is a necessity if you want your home videos to have a professional look. To achieve smooth panning (turning from side to side) or tilting (pointing the lens up or down), you need a video tripod.

A full-sized tripod is the most effective way to steady a camera, but there are other options: minipods, diminutive versions that fit into a camera bag or backpack; monopods, with one leg to rest on the ground or hoist above a crowd; car pods, which clamp onto rolled-down car windows; and shoulder pods, which brace a camera against the body the way you'd steady a rifle. Some pros carry a bean bag, which molds itself to various surfaces and on which a camera can rest steady.

The choices

Video tripods. Camcorders, as a rule, work better with tripods designed specifically for video use. Such tripods have a fluid pan head—viscous friction on the pan and tilt movements to ensure smooth motion. Further, you can adjust the amount of friction so that the camera sits still when you release the pan handle and yet moves smoothly when you push on it. (Mount a camcorder on a typical photo tripod and you'll see the difference. You must loosen and retighten tilt and pan locks frequently; it's also harder to follow the action without jerky motions.)

Mid-priced video models generally list for $100 to $150 and weigh around five pounds; some are a pound or so lighter. More expensive models tend to be taller and heavier; less expensive ones, shorter and lighter.

Photo tripods. Because these tripods are less complex mechanically, they're a bit cheaper than video tripods. Photo tripods list for about $75 to $120. They're also lighter, generally weighing three to four pounds.

Features and conveniences

A tripod has three principal parts: a pan head, which anchors the camera and controls its motion; a center column, which supports the pan head and periscopes up and down; and the legs.

Pan head. Video and still cameras need to pan from side to side and tilt up and down. A still camera should also be able to be tilted on its side to shoot in a vertical format. Some pan heads can perform all three operations, but some lack a side-tilting axis. You can use those tripods to take vertical shots, but to do so you must tip the pan head 90 degrees, loosen the camera-mounting screw, and rotate the camera.

Center column. A geared column lets you raise or lower the camera with a crank. The alternative, a simple tube that you adjust with one hand and lock with the other, works fine if the camera or camcorder isn't too heavy.

Legs. A tripod's telescoping legs can make it slower or faster to set up. We think legs in three sections work best. Units with more leg sections are more time consuming to set up; those with only two sections may be steadier but aren't as short when folded for carrying and storage.

Look for legs that lock with levers or knobs instead of collets, small threaded rings that tend to jam when dirty. Lever locks are fastest to operate.

Camera attachment. Most video tripods and some photo models have a quick-release insert—a small fitted plastic piece with a protruding screw—that's supposed to expedite the union of camera or camcorder and tripod. Instead of making the connection in the traditional way (by holding the camera over the tripod platform and tightening a screw from below), you screw the insert directly into the camera using a coin or screwdriver, then latch that combination onto a matching socket atop the pan head. In theory, the insert should speed setting up. Most such designs, we've found, make a camera less steady.

One feature that works well for camcorders is the use of a tiny pin found on the mounting platform of most video tripods and some photo models. The pin, which fits into a matching hole on the bottom of a camcorder, prevents the camera from twisting on the tripod during use. Few, if any, still cameras have a hole for the pin, however. Some pins retract, but some must be removed before you attach a still camera, a task that sometimes requires a screwdriver.

The tests

Key tests gauge freedom from vibration. For video models, we simulate up and down torque by releasing a weight suspended from a lever arm that we place between the camera and the pan head; we then play back the video tape frame by frame to measure the jumping and twitching of the recorded images.

For photo models, we use a system of mirrors and projected cross hairs to capture and analyze the jiggling as a 35mm camera shoots at a relatively slow shutter speed.

For both types of tripods, we also gauge speed and ease of use. Testers run through a drill using each model to compose a series of pictures in both vertical and horizontal formats.

Buying advice

Videos greatly improve when a tripod is used. Hand-held camcorder shots, particularly telephoto shots, are never really steady and rapidly become tiring to watch. (For more information on camcorders, see the report on page 18.)

A tripod is also a must for still photography in dim light or with long telephoto lenses, which magnify even the smallest vibration. With less demanding photography, a tripod lets you frame and compose your pictures precisely and permits sharp pictures at long exposure times.

In general, look for a tripod that is stable and sturdy and that allows for fluid pans and tilts. The surface on which the camera rests should be fairly large and made of a material like cork or textured rubber to keep the camcorder from twisting if there is no built-in video pin.

ABOUT PRICES IN THE BUYING GUIDE

Prices for most products have been updated for the Buying Guide. The prices we give, unless otherwise noted, are approximate or suggested retail as quoted by the manufacturer. Discounts may be substantial, especially for electronics and camera equipment.

COMPACT 35MM CAMERAS

RATINGS COMPACT 35MM CAMERAS

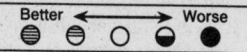

Better ⬤ ◐ ○ ◑ ⬤ Worse

▶ **See report, page 60.** From Consumer Reports, December 1992

Recommendations: We've organized the cameras below by focal-length range and type of exposure control. The lenses of the models in the first Ratings group offer the widest zoom range—typically, 35 mm to 105 mm. Those models sell for about $300. Models in the second Ratings group offer a zoom or a two-focal length lens with a more modest range—roughly 35 mm to 70 mm—cost about $200. The best models in the third group cost about the same but their lenses emphasize a slightly shorter, wider-angle range of focal lengths—typically, about 28 mm to 45 mm. Models in the fourth and fifth groups offer only one focal length, about 35 mm. The models in the fourth group offer automatic exposure while the simpler ones in the fifth group don't adjust shutter speed or lens aperture.

Brand and model	Score	Price	Weight, oz.	Film speeds, ISO	Focal lengths, mm	Smallest field, in.	Sharpness	Flare	Distortion	Chromatic aberration
MULTIPLE FOCAL LENGTH, AUTOMATIC EXPOSURE										
LONG FOCAL LENGTH										
Ricoh Mirai Zoom 3 [D]	81	$265	20	64-3200	35-105	6	⬤	○	◐	◐
Nikon Zoom-Touch 800	80	470	19	64-3200	37-105	7	⬤	◐	◐	◐
Olympus Infinity SuperZoom 3000	76	450	13	50-3200	38-110	4	⬤	○	◑	◐
Pentax IQ Zoom 105-R	76	437	19	25-3200	38-105	14	⬤	○	◐	◐
Konica AIBORG	75	510	21	25-3200	35-105	7	⬤	◑	◐	◐
Canon Sure Shot Megazoom 105 [D]	73	224	17	25-3200	35-105	5	○	◐	◐	◐
Yashica Zoomtec 105 Super	73	560	17	25-3200	35-105	5	○	◐	◐	◐
Samsung AF Zoom 1050	72	499	16	25-3200	38-105	10	⬤	○	◐	◐
MEDIUM FOCAL LENGTH										
Nikon Zoom-Touch 400 [S]	78	171	14	64-1600	35-70	10	⬤	◐	○	◐
Canon Sure Shot Megazoom 76 [D]	76	175	15	25-3200	38-76	8	⬤	○	◐	◐
Nikon Zoom-Touch 500S [D]	75	185	15	64-1600	35-80	9	⬤	◐	○	◐
Sigma Zoom Super 70	75	308	18	25-3200	35-70	13	⬤	◐	◐	◐

COMPACT 35MM CAMERAS

Better ⬅ ➡ Worse
● ◐ ○ ◐ ●

Ratings order: Listed by types based on focal-length range and type of exposure control; within types, listed in order of estimated quality. Models with equal overall scores are listed alphabetically. Bracketed models are essentially similar. The overall score is based mainly on judgments of picture quality and overall convenience. Differences of 10 points or less are not significant. Price is the manufacturer's suggested list. **Notes to table:** Film speeds are the range of speeds or the number. Focal lengths are the range or, for dual-focal-length models, one of two extremes (in parentheses). Framing accuracy shows the percentage of the final picture area included in the viewfinder frame. The lower the number, the less accurate the framing. ⓢ indicates tested model has been replaced by successor model; according to the manufacturer, the performance of new model should be similar to the tested model but features may vary. See page 74 for new model number and suggested retail price, if available. ⓓ indicates model discontinued.

Low-light capability	Film handling	Exposure uniformity	Range, ft.	Framing accuracy	Flash Compactness	Advantages	Disadvantages	Comments	Brand and model
									MULTIPLE FOCAL LENGTH, AUTOMATIC EXPOSURE
									LONG FOCAL LENGTH
●	◐	◐	18	85	◐	A,C,F,H,I,J,L	—	D,E,H,M,N,O,Q,X,Z,DD,FF,II,JJ	Ricoh Mirai Zoom 3 ⓓ
●	◐	◐	22	83	◐	A,C,D,E,F,G,H,I,J,L,M	z	E,K,L,N,Q,S,Z,BB,DD,II,JJ	Nikon Zoom-Touch 800
●	◐	◐	17	78	◐	A,C,E,F,G,H,I,J,L	d,z	B,E,N,S,Z,FF,II,JJ	Olympus Infinity SuperZoom 3000
●	◐	◐	16	92	◐	A,C,F,H,J	y,z	E,H,L,M,P,Q,S,T,U,Z,AA,DD,II,JJ	Pentax IQ Zoom 105-R
●	◐	◐	18	80	◐	C,E,F,G,H,I,J,L,M	s,y	F,G,H,K,L,M,N,O,P,Q,S,T,Z,DD,II	Konica AIBORG
●	◐	◐	15	76	◐	A,C,E,F,H,J,M	e,y,z	E,M,S,X,Z,DD,FF,II,JJ	Canon Sure Shot Megazoom 105 ⓓ
●	◐	◐	15	76	◐	A,C,E,F,H,J,M	e,y,z	E,M,S,X,Z,DD,FF,II,JJ	Yashica Zoomtec 105 Super
●	◐	◐	18	73	◐	A,C,F,H,J,L	z	E,L,M,N,P,Q,T,U,Z,AA,DD,II	Samsung AF Zoom 1050
									MEDIUM FOCAL LENGTH
●	◐	◐	15	74	○	A,C,D,E,F,H,J,L	z	E,Q,S,Z,II,JJ	Nikon Zoom-Touch 400 ⓢ
●	◐	◐	14	79	○	A,C,E,F,H,J,M	e,y,z	E,M,S,Z,DD,FF,II,JJ	Canon Sure Shot Megazoom 76 ⓓ
●	◐	◐	14	76	○	C,D,F,H,I,J	z	E,L,N,Q,Z,DD,II	Nikon Zoom-Touch 500S ⓓ
●	◐	○	19	71	◐	A,C,F,H,J,L,M	—	D,E,G,L,S,V,Z,DD,FF	Sigma Zoom Super 70

Ratings continued ▶

COMPACT 35MM CAMERAS

▶ *Ratings continued*

Brand and model	Score	Price	Weight, oz.	Film speeds, ISO	Focal lengths, mm	Smallest field, in.	Sharpness	Flare	Distortion	Chromatic aberration
Olympus Infinity Zoom 210 [D]	74	$186	14	50-3200	38-76	8	◓	◓	◯	◓
Yashica Zoomtec 70	74	330	13	50-1600	35-70	16	◓	◯	◯	◓
Canon Sure Shot Tele Max	72	190	9	25-3200	(38, 70)	10	◓	◓	◓	◓
Konica Big Mini BM-311Z	71	320	12	25-3200	35-70	16	◓	◯	◯	◓
Samsung AF Zoom 777i	71	369	15	25-3200	35-70	16	◓	◯	◯	◓
Ricoh Shotmaster Zoom Super [D]	70	219	14	64-3200	38-80	7	●	◓	◓	◓
Leica C2-Zoom [D]	69	430	13	25-3200	40-90	11	◓	◓	◐	◓
Minolta Freedom 70c	69	171	11	100, 400	35-70	11	◓	◓	◓	◓
Olympus Infinity Tele	68	200	11	50-1600	(35, 70)	13	●	◓	◓	◓
Rokinon 35AFZ	66	179	13	50-1600	35-70	16	◓	◯	◓	◓
SHORT FOCAL LENGTH										
Fuji Discovery Mini Dual QD Plus [D]	77	185	8	50-1600	(28, 45)	11	◓	◯	◓	◓
Olympus Infinity Zoom 220 Panorama [D]	73	217	14	50-3200	28-56	13	◓	◯	◯	◓
Vivitar 320Z Series 1	68	252	12	50-1600	38-60	20	◓	●	◓	◓
Yashica Twintec	67	235	11	100-400	(33, 53)	33	◓	◓	◯	◓
Minolta Freedom Dual C	61	171	11	100, 400	(28, 40)	19	◓	◓	◯	◓
SINGLE FOCAL LENGTH										
AUTOMATIC EXPOSURE										
Yashica T4	83	299	7	50-3200	35	11	◓	◓	◓	◓
Olympus Infinity Stylus	79	235	7	50-3200	35	11	◓	◯	◓	◓
Contax T2	78	1124	12	25-5000	38	22	◓	◓	◓	◓
Minolta Freedom Escort	77	188	7	50-3200	34	21	◓	◓	◓	◓
Konica Big Mini BM-201 [D]	76	171	8	25-3200	35	11	◓	◯	◯	◓
Leica Mini [D]	76	289	7	50-1000	35	22	◓	◓	◓	◓
Nikon One-Touch 200	73	142	9	100-1000	35	22	◓	◓	◓	◓
Canon Sure Shot Max	71	155	9	25-3200	38	20	◓	◓	◓	◓
Ricoh Shotmaster AF-P	71	119	9	100-1000	35	36	◓	◓	◓	◓
Canon Snappy LX	66	100	10	100, 400	35	55	◯	◓	◓	◓

COMPACT 35MM CAMERAS 73

Low-light capability	Film handling	Exposure uniformity	Range, ft.	Framing accuracy	Flash Compactness	Advantages	Disadvantages	Comments	Brand and model
◒	◒	◒	11	77	○	A,C,F,G,H,J	z	N,S,Z,DD,II,JJ	Olympus Infinity Zoom 210 [D]
◒	◒	◒	14	79	○	A,C,F,H,J,M	—	E,Z,AA,DD,FF,II,JJ	Yashica Zoomtec 70
◒	◒	◒	14	75	◒	A,C,E,F	e,g,u	E,JJ	Canon Sure Shot Tele Max
◒	◒	◒	16	76	◒	A,C,F,G,H,J,L,M	b,o	E,G,L,S,U,Z,DD,II,JJ	Konica Big Mini BM-311Z
◒	◒	○	20	72	○	A,C,F,H,J,L	—	E,M,N,P,Q,T,U,Z,AA,DD,II	Samsung AF Zoom 777i
◒	◒	◒	12	80	◒	A,C,E,F,H,J	—	E,H,M,O,U,Z,FF,II	Ricoh Shotmaster Zoom Super [D]
◒	◒	○	17	89	○	A,C,E,F,G,H,J	a	E,Z,GG,II,JJ	Leica C2-Zoom [D]
◒	◒	◒	14	68	◒	A,C,F	a	E,Z,II,JJ	Minolta Freedom 70c
◒	◒	◒	18	82	◒	C,F,H,J	—	E,Q,DD,II	Olympus Infinity Tele
○	◒	◒	13	85	●	C,F,G	p,z	E,II,JJ,LL	Rokinon 35AFZ
									SHORT FOCAL LENGTH
◒	◒	◒	11	82	◒	A,C,F,G,H,J,K,L	o	F,M,W,Y,Z,II,JJ	Fuji Discovery Mini Dual QD Plus [D]
◒	◒	◒	16	74	○	A,C,F,H,I,J	z	I,M,Q,S,Z,DD,II,JJ	Olympus Infinity Zoom 220 Panorama [D]
◒	◒	◒	10	81	○	C,G	p,r,z	C,U,II,JJ,LL	Vivitar 320Z Series 1
○	◒	◒	14	79	◒	C,J	h,p	E,U,HH,KK	Yashica Twintec
◒	◒	○	10	84	◒	—	m,u	E,W,II	Minolta Freedom Dual C
									SINGLE FOCAL LENGTH
									AUTOMATIC EXPOSURE
◒	◒	◒	10	74	◒	A,C,E,F,G,H,J,L	r	E,M,S,Z,II,JJ	Yashica T4
◒	◒	◒	12	78	◒	A,C,F,H,J	q,r	E,II,JJ	Olympus Infinity Stylus
◒	◒	◒	12	90	◒	A,C,F,G,H,J,L	e,y,z	E,G,L,Z,AA,BB,CC,II	Contax T2
◒	◒	◒	12	89	◒	A,C,F,H,J	o,r	C,E,S,Z,II,JJ	Minolta Freedom Escort
○	◒	◒	10	84	◒	C,F,H,J	o	E,L,S,Z,II,JJ	Konica Big Mini BM-201 [D]
◒	◒	○	11	88	◒	C,F,G,H,J,L	o,r	E,G,AA,II,JJ	Leica Mini [D]
◒	◒	◒	11	79	◒	A,F	—	Q,S,II,JJ,LL	Nikon One-Touch 200
◒	◒	◒	11	78	◒	A,C,E,F,G	e,g,u	E,JJ	Canon Sure Shot Max
○	◒	◒	11	92	◒	—	m,p	E,II,KK	Ricoh Shotmaster AF-P
○	◒	◒	9	80	◒	A	p	A,G,Q,JJ,LL	Canon Snappy LX

Ratings continued ▶

COMPACT 35MM CAMERAS

▶ *Ratings continued*

Brand and model	Score	Price	Weight, oz.	Film speeds, ISO	Focal lengths, mm	Smallest field, in.	Sharpness	Flare	Distortion	Chromatic aberration
Konica MT-100	66	$180	9	100, 400	34	45	◐	◐	◐	◐
Ansco Mini AF	64	170	8	100-1000	34	45	◐	◐	◐	◐
Kodak Star 835 AF	64	95	11	100, 400	34	46	◐	◐	◐	◐
Minolta Freedom AF35 [S]	60	92	10	100, 400	34	34	○	◐	○	◐
Fuji Discovery 80 [S]	59	83	10	100, 400	35	47	◐	◐	◐	◐
Kalimar Spirit AF [D]	58	70	10	100, 400	35	40	○	◐	○	◐
Kalimar Spirit 2 [D]	54	45	10	100, 400	35	55	○	○	○	◐
Samsung AF-200	52	79	11	100, 400	35	55	◑	◐	○	◐

NOT ACCEPTABLE

■ *All four tested samples of the following model had serious defects.*

| **Vivitar EZ200** [D] | — | 57 | 10 | 100, 400 | 35 | 40 | ● | ◐ | ◑ | ○ |

FIXED EXPOSURE

Yashica J Mini	63	115	9	100, 400	32	48	◐	◐	○	◐
Yashica Sensation [D]	61	67	10	100, 400	35	47	◐	◐	◐	◐
Konica TOP's	60	98	9	100, 400	34	57	◐	◐	◐	◐
Kodak Star 935	57	90	10	100, 400	35	43	◐	◐	◐	◐
Fuji DL-25 [S]	53	52	10	100, 400	35	55	◐	◐	◐	◐
Ricoh Shotmaster FF	53	89	10	100-1000	35	36	◐	◐	◐	○
Olympus Trip Junior [D]	49	52	9	100-400	33	38	◐	○	◐	◐
Minolta Freedom 50N	48	75	9	100, 400	35	55	○	○	○	○
Olympus AF Super [D]	40	76	10	100, 400	35	47	◑	◐	○	○

Successor Models (in Ratings order)
Nikon Zoom-Touch 400 is succeeded by 470, $232; Minolta Freedom AF35 by AF35R, $137; Fuji Discovery 80 by 80 Plus, $110; Fuji DL-25 by DL24 Plus, $80.

Features in Common
All have: • Automatic film loading, advancing, and rewinding. • Built-in electronic flash. • Low-light warning or automatic flash operation. • Shutter lock.
All autofocus models have: • Focus-hold.
Except as noted, all have: • Infrared autofocus system. • DX film-speed sensing. • Built-in lens cover. • Film-advancing indicator. • Self-timer that cancels after each use. • Tripod socket. • Single-frame film advance. • Shutter that locks if flash is not ready. • Window in camera back to show film type. • Neck strap. • Need for lithium battery.

Key to Advantages
A–Has "red eye" reduction feature.
B–Flash is far from lens to reduce "red eye."
C–Warns if subject is too close to focus.
D–Warns when subject is too far for flash.
E–Has multi-beam autofocus.
F–Has fill-flash capability.
G–Quieter than most.
H–Warns when batteries are weak.
I–Viewfinder has diopter adjustment for eyesight variation.
J–Has LCD display.
K–Prewinds film, reducing chances of ruined pictures.
L–Has infinity setting.
M–Rewinds faster than most.

Key to Disadvantages
a–Automatic zoom mode reactivates when

COMPACT 35MM CAMERAS

Low-light capability	Film handling	Exposure uniformity	Range, ft.	Framing accuracy	Flash Compactness	Advantages	Disadvantages	Comments	Brand and model
○	○	◐	9	81	◐	F,G	u,v	E,G,Z,II	Konica MT-100
◐	◐	◐	8	86	◐	F	m,n	C,Z,II,KK	Ansco Mini AF
○	○	◐	12	82	◐	—	h,m,p,v	Y,EE,LL	Kodak Star 835 AF
◐	◐	◐	8	81	◐	—	g,p,u	E,W,II,LL	Minolta Freedom AF35 [S]
○	●	◐	11	77	◐	—	h,p,w	E,J,Y,EE,JJ,LL	Fuji Discovery 80 [S]
○	○	◐	7	82	◐	—	h,l,p,v	E,J,Y,EE,II,JJ,KK	Kalimar Spirit AF [D]
○	○	◐	6	97	◐	—	c,h,p,v	A,E,J,Y,EE,KK	Kalimar Spirit 2 [D]
○	○	◐	6	74	◐	—	h,k,p,y	C,E,J,LL	Samsung AF-200
									NOT ACCEPTABLE
◐	○	○	7	56	◐	A,F	h,l,v	C,E,J,Y,EE,JJ,LL	Vivitar EZ200 [D]
									FIXED EXPOSURE
○	◐	○	10	91	◐	G,J	c,h,p	A,E,U,LL	Yashica J Mini
◐	●	◐	13	92	◐	—	e,f,h,m,v,x	C,E,J,Y,EE,JJ,LL	Yashica Sensation [D]
◐	◐	◐	8	76	◐	H	p	A,G	Konica TOP's
◐	○	◐	9	79	◐	B	c,h,p,v	A,C,J,Y,EE	Kodak Star 935
◐	●	◐	11	88	◐	—	c,h,p,w	A,C,J,Y,EE,LL	Fuji DL-25 [S]
◐	◐	◐	9	78	◐	L	c,h,j,p	A,E,R,LL	Ricoh Shotmaster FF
◐	●	◐	11	67	◐	—	c,e,f,h,j,v	A,J,Y,EE,LL	Olympus Trip Junior [D]
◐	◐	◐	10	83	◐	—	c,e,f,h	A,C,E,Y,EE,LL	Minolta Freedom 50N
◐	●	◐	10	64	◐	—	c,e,f,h,i,m,t,v,x	C,E,J,Y,EE,LL	Olympus AF Super [D]

you turn the camera on, a nuisance.
b–Zoom reverses only at ends of range.
c–Viewfinder hinders accurate framing.
d–May leak light if left in bright sunlight.
e–Flash must be turned on manually.
f–Flash must be turned off separately from camera.
g–Lacks flash-ready indicator.
h–Picture can be taken if flash isn't ready.
i–Lacks autofocus frame in viewfinder.
j–Lacks DX film-speed sensing.
k–Lacks indication that film is advancing.
l–Lens "vignettes," causing darkened corners.
m–Lacks focus-confirmation indicator.
n–Rewind noisier than most.
o–Lacks lens cover.
p–Automatic flash can't be turned off.
q–Flash close to lens, worsens "red eye."
r–Rewinds more slowly than most.
s–Viewfinder image poor at telephoto settings.
t–Inconvenient for left-eyed users.
u–Won't rewind film before end of roll.
v–Film must be advanced manually to first picture.
w–Rewind doesn't turn off automatically.
x–Rewind button must be held throughout rewind.
y–Self-timer doesn't cancel automatically.
z–Detachable battery-compartment cover could be mislaid.

Key to Comments
A–Fixed focus. (**Yashica J Mini** has two-position manual focus.)
B–Weatherproof.
C–Has wrist strap instead of neck strap.
D–Passive autofocus.
E–Available with date/time imprinter.

Ratings continued ▶

VIDEO & PHOTO TRIPODS

F–Available only with date/time imprinter.
G–Includes case.
H–Accepts optional electrical shutter-release cable.
I–Can be changed to panoramic format in mid-roll.
J–Has manually initiated rewind.
K–Displays approx. subject distance.
L–Has exposure-compensation control, useful with slide film.
M–Has backlight-compensation capability.
N–Has automatic zoom mode or modes.
O–TV mode sets shutter for pictures of TV screen.
P–Interval mode automatically takes shots at predetermined intervals.
Q–Self-timer can be set to take more than one picture.
R–Once set, self-timer cannot be cancelled before taking picture.
S–Can take time exposures with flash.
T–Can take multiple exposures on one frame.
U–Macro setting allows close-ups.
V–Optional "dedicated" flash attachment is more powerful than built-in flash.
W–Lacks window for checking film type.
X–Has separate lens cap.
Y–Lacks self-timer.
Z–Has shutter speeds of ¼-second or longer.
AA–Has Bulb setting for time exposures.
BB–Can be switched to manual focus.
CC–Has capability of aperture-priority exposure.
DD–Has switch for rapid-fire shooting.
EE–Lacks tripod socket.
FF–Wireless remote shutter release is optional.
GG–Has wireless remote shutter release.
HH–Also has waist-level viewfinder.
II–Automatic-exposure system allows use of slide film.
JJ–Easier than most for eyeglass wearers.
KK–Takes lithium or alkaline batteries.
LL–Takes alkaline batteries.

RATINGS VIDEO & PHOTO TRIPODS

Better ← → Worse

▶ See report, page 68. From Consumer Reports, August 1990.

Recommendations: For camcorder use, any of the top four video tripods would be a good choice. Our first choice is the *Bogen 3170*, $169. The best of the photo tripods is the *Bogen 3000*, $121.

Ratings order: Listed by types; within types, listed in order of overall score, based primarily on tests for steadiness and secondarily on convenience judgments. Differences in score of 7 points or less are not significant. Models with identical scores are listed alphabetically. Price is the manufacturer's suggested retail. Weights are to nearest ¼ lb. Heights are to nearest inch. ⓓ indicates model discontinued.

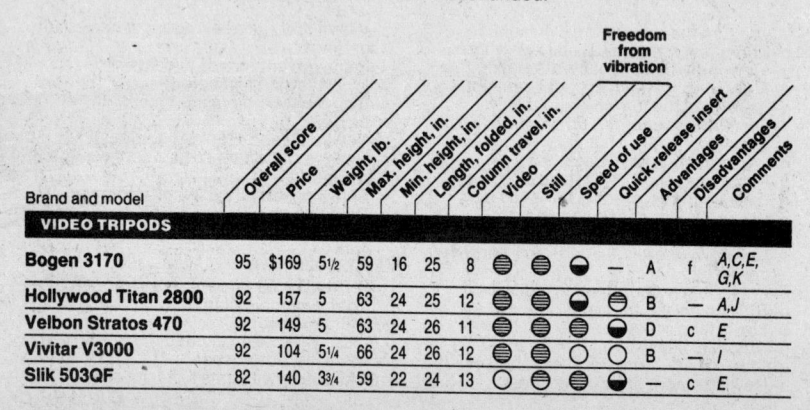

Brand and model	Overall score	Price	Weight, lb.	Max. height, in.	Min. height, in.	Length, folded, in.	Column travel, in.	Video	Still	Speed of use	Quick-release insert	Advantages	Disadvantages	Comments
VIDEO TRIPODS														
Bogen 3170	95	$169	5½	59	16	25	8	◐	◐	◖	—	A	f	A,C,E,G,K
Hollywood Titan 2800	92	157	5	63	24	25	12	◐	◐	◖	◐	B	—	A,J
Velbon Stratos 470	92	149	5	63	24	26	11	◐	◐	◐	◖	D	c	E
Vivitar V3000	92	104	5¼	66	24	26	12	◐	◐	○	○	B	—	I
Slik 503QF	82	140	3¾	59	22	24	13	○	◐	◐	◖	—	c	E

VIDEO & PHOTO TRIPODS

Brand and model	Overall score	Price	Weight, lb.	Max. height, in.	Min. height, in.	Length, folded, in.	Column travel, in.	Video	Still	Speed of use	Quick-release insert	Advantages	Disadvantages	Comments
Coast Coastar VTR-80 [D]	77	$130	4¼	62	24	25	15	○	◒	○	◒	—	d	D,E
Cullman T2502 [D]	75	145	4	63	24	24	16	○	◒	◒	◒	A	a	C,F
PHOTO TRIPODS														
Bogen 3000	95	121	4¾	58	16	24	8	◒	◒	○	—	A	f	B,C,E,G
Tiltall Junior LEO2 [D]	93	115	3¾	56	22	23	11	◒	◒	◒	—	A,C	e	C,G
Star-D D-29 Mini-Pro [D]	88	85	3½	56	22	23	11	◒	◒	◒	—	A	e	C,G
Velbon Victory 450	83	88	3¾	58	21	22	13	◒	◒	◒	—	A	b	H
Vivitar 980	83	88	4¾	66	24	25	13	◒	◒	●	—	B	—	I
Slik U100 Deluxe	77	89	3	57	22	23	13	◒	◒	○	—	—	—	E
Coast Coastar VTR-50RA [D]	74	80	2¾	60	21	22	13	◒	◒	◒	◒	B	—	H

Features in Common
All have: • Adjustable 3-section legs. • 1-piece adjustable column.
Except as noted, all have: • 3-way pan head with pan handle and side-tilt for vertical-format stills. • Geared column with adjustable friction control. • Leg braces and plastic yoke. • Convenient leg clamps that flip sideways to lock. • Rubber leg tips that retract to expose spikes. • Plastic control knobs.

Key to Advantages
A–Pan head can be positioned below center column; helpful for framing low-angle shots.
B–Has handy spring-loaded camcorder pin.
C–Has metal control knobs.
D–Has circular "bubble" level on pan head.

Key to Disadvantages
a–Center column can be moved even when locked; lacks stop to prevent accidental removal of column.
b–Legs tend to fold when tripod is lifted.
c–Camcorder pin must be reversed to use still camera.
d–No provision for storing camcorder pin when using still camera.
e–Has collet leg locks; requires much more time and finesse to operate than flip locks.
f–Knob-operated leg locks; slower than flip locks.

Key to Comments
A–Pan head lacks side-tilt for vertical-format stills.
B–Has versatile 3-way head with no pan handle.
C–Center column not geared; must be raised or lowered by hand.
D–Geared column has no friction-control adjustment.
E–Has rubber feet without spikes.
F–Feet flip to expose either rubber pads or teeth.
G–Has metal yoke; eliminates need for leg braces.
H–Leg clamps flip up to lock.
I–Leg clamps flip down to lock.
J–Has removable "bubble" level on tilt axis; judged fragile and of little use.
K–Has cork-covered mounting platform, a good alternative to camcorder pin.

COLOR PRINT FILM

RATINGS COLOR PRINT FILM

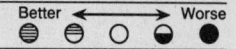

Better ◄———► Worse
⊜ ⊖ ○ ⊙ ●

▶ **See report, page 66.** From Consumer Reports, November 1993.

Recommendations: Among the 100 ISO films, the six top-ranking films produced the best pictures. In each group, the film made by 3M—*ScotchColor* or a store-brand film and Polaroid *OneFilm*—had more graininess than other films in their group.

Ratings order: Listed by types; within types, within estimated quality. Price is an average from a national survey for 24-exposure film sold in single-roll packs. Score is based on the color accuracy and graininess of 3½x5 inch prints processed by the five mail-order discussed in the film processing report (see page 67) and scored by a panel of trained CU staffers. Differences in score of less than 5 points are not significant.

Brand	Price	Score	Color	Graininess	Also sold as	Comments
ISO 100 FILMS						
Polaroid High Def.	$2.49	95	⊜	⊜	—	
Fujicolor Super G	2.91	94	⊜	⊜		110, 120, 126 formats.
Kodak Gold Plus	3.49	93	⊜	⊜		—
Konica Super SR	2.91	93	⊜	⊜		120 format.
Kodak Ektar	4.27	92	⊜	⊜		Some prints too high in contrast.
ScotchColor	2.69	92	⊜	⊜	K Mart Focal, Kroger, Pathmark, Target, York.	—
Fujicolor Reala	4.69	90	⊜	⊜		—
Agfacolor XRG	3.49	88	⊜	⊜	Clarkcolor, Walgreen's.	—
Signature Color	1.75	75	○	⊜		Respooled movie film.
ISO 200 FILMS						
Kodak Gold Plus	3.99	91	⊜	⊜		110 format.
Konica SR-G (ISO 160)	5.19	91	⊜	⊜		Some prints too low in contrast. 120, 220 format.
Polaroid OneFilm	2.28	90	⊜	⊜		110, 126, disc formats.
Fujicolor Super G	3.49	87	⊜	⊜		—
Konica Super SR	4.64	87	⊜	⊜		110, 126 formats. Some prints too low in contrast.
Agfacolor XRG	3.89	86	⊜	⊜	Clarkcolor, Mystic Color, Walgreen's, York.	110, 126 formats. Some prints too low in contrast.
ScotchColor	3.14	85	⊜	⊜	K Mart Focal, Kroger, Pathmark, Target.	Also in 110, disc formats.
ISO 400 FILMS						
Kodak Gold Plus	4.77	91	⊜	⊜	Kodak Gold Ultra (performed similarly).	110 format.
Fujicolor Super G	4.00	88	⊜	⊜	—	120 format.
Polaroid High Def.	3.04	83	○	⊜	—	—
ScotchColor	3.09	81	○	●	K Mart Focal, Kroger, Pathmark, Target, York.	—

▶Major appliances

Microwave ovens	80
Ranges	83
Refrigerators	86
Dishwashers	89
Washing machines	91
Clothes dryers	93
Detergents & other laundry products	95
Ratings	98

Consumers often acquire kitchen appliances the same way audio enthusiasts build sound systems: item by item from different manufacturers. Our tests over the years confirm the wisdom of that approach—no single company tops our major appliance ratings time after time.

Past satisfaction with a particular brand is no guarantee of future happiness either. Most of the top 25 appliance brands in the U.S. now come from the "Big Five": General Electric, Whirlpool, Maytag, Raytheon, and Frigidaire. General Electric brands include *GE, Hotpoint,* and *RCA.* Whirlpool owns *KitchenAid;* Maytag, the *Jenn-Aire, Magic Chef,* and *Admiral* brands. Raytheon sells *Amana* and *Speed Queen* machines; Frigidaire, *White-Westinghouse, Gibson, Kelvinator, Tappan,* and *Frigidaire* products.

To make the market even more confusing, companies may not manufacture all the brands they sell. Microwave ovens, for instance, are nearly all made by Japanese or Korean manufacturers.

Many stores now want to sell goods that take up less space and move faster than bulky ranges, refrigerators, and the like. So department stores have given up much of the major appliance business, except for microwave ovens. Although discount chains have taken up some of the slack, you'll generally find fewer places selling major appliances than in the past.

The price paid for a given appliance depends largely on where you live. In cities and suburban areas, where competition among mass merchandisers is keen, prices tend to be lower than elsewhere. Appliances are not discounted as sharply as audio and video equipment, but sales are common. Discontinued models, which are sometimes only slightly different from their newer replacements, may be a source of greater savings.

Kitchen and laundry appliances are not unlike most products—the more you pay, the more features you get. With major appliances, however, manufacturers can be hard-pressed to come up with genuine improvements. So you'll see distinctive design treatments given with trademarked names—"Spillguard," "Spacemaker," "Speed-Broil" and such—given prominent play in manufacturers' literature.

Some features actually make the products more useful or convenient. Electronic controls on major appliances add precision and versatility not possible with old-fashioned dials and switches. However, repair headaches sometimes come with that added electronic sophistication. Features like ice-makers and water dispensers in refrigerators and electronic controls on ranges, while useful, can make an appliance less reliable, as our brand Repair Histories show.

Manufacturers have long used style to sell products, but stylishness has new urgency as a selling tactic in these days of slumping housing starts and appliance sales. Currently trendy: white-on-white appliances and kitchen appliances that are designed to be installed flush with the surrounding cabinets. You pay a premium for the look, of course.

On the whole, new appliances are far stingier with energy than their predecessors. In fact, Federal standards for power-hungry refrigerators mandate that models built since 1993 be 25 percent more efficient than was permitted in 1990. New standards also require that dishwashers cut energy use. To check out energy costs, use the bright yellow energy-guide labels found on some major appliances. They provide an estimate of yearly energy costs based on national average utility rates and, in smaller print, other rates. They also compare the efficiency of a particular model with others like it.

A safety note: While manufacturers often warn against plugging major appliances into extension cords, many people do so anyway. The possibility of a short circuit or fire increases when an appliance is plugged into an extension cord incapable of handling the power load. If you must use an extension, buy one rated for the load.

Microwave ovens

▶ Ratings on page 101. ▶ Repair records on page 370.

The "zapper" provides a fast, convenient way to defrost frozen foods, warm leftovers, and bake potatoes. It doesn't heat up the kitchen, it's clean, and it saves energy. But it has its limitations. Microwave cooking doesn't do justice to roasts and other meats, and no self-respecting pastry chef would dream of baking in one. Our surveys show that few readers actually cook from scratch in a microwave oven.

The microwave-oven market is dominated by *Sharp*. Other big names include *Panasonic*, *Tappan*, *Sears Kenmore*, and *General Electric*.

The choices

Size and power. Microwave ovens come in small, medium, and large sizes—and in some lines, sizes in between. When appliance makers talk about "compact" or "large" ovens, they mean the size of the cooking cavity, which ranges from less than half a cubic foot to more than three times that. Inside dimensions, while roughly comparable to those outside, also reflect how efficiently the manufacturer has designed the cabinet. Some models are low and long; others have a more boxy shape. Big ovens typically sit on a countertop; smaller models may allow mounting under cabinets or over a range.

Size aside, the main difference between a big and small oven is the amount of power produced by the magnetron, the part that generates the high-energy microwaves that do the cooking. The power output of a full-sized oven is usually 650 to 900 watts, in mid-sized models, 600 to 800 watts. In small ovens, it's generally 500 to 700 watts.

More powerful ovens can heat food about one-third faster, a difference especially noticeable when cooking large quantities. In addition, many cookbooks and convenience-food package instructions are written solely for high-wattage ovens. (A less powerful model requires tinkering with the time or power levels specified in recipes and it may not do a very good job of cooking popcorn.)

Big ovens can accommodate lots of food—several containers of leftovers, two dinner plates, or a large casserole. But they take up lots of space—they're typically 22 to 24 inches wide and 15 to 19 inches deep. Figure on paying $180 to $300 for a large microwave.

The smallest ovens, just a bit larger and more expensive than a toaster oven, may be too small to hold some frozen dinners. But for basic chores, like popping corn or warming beverages or leftovers, you may not need more capacity. Small ovens sell for $150 or so.

Mid-sized ovens, a popular compromise, are quickly becoming the preferred size among consumers. Though they save just a few inches of counter space—they're typically 20 to 24 inches wide or less and 13 to 18 inches deep—they are considerably less bulky than a big oven. And there's little sacrifice in the way of capacity, power, or versatility. Mid-sized models are priced from about $170 to $225.

Microwave/convection ovens. Manufacturers have come up with various hybrid appliances designed to remedy the microwave oven's cooking deficiencies. The microwave/convection oven works fast, like an ordinary microwave. And like a traditional range oven, it browns food nicely. In convection cooking, air is heated by a concealed electric element and circulated inside the oven by a fan, crisping the outside as the heat works its way in. Most such ovens can be set for a full range of temperatures from 200° to 450°F. You can also use these models for conventional microwave cooking. Price is typically from about $350 to $650.

Features and conveniences

Bare-bones models have a mechanical rotary timer and no audible signal to tell you the food is ready. But as often happens, features once found solely on high-end products now grace smaller, cheaper models. Here's a rundown of what to look for when shopping:

Electronic controls. Most have electronic controls these days, an important feature since seconds count in using this appliance. (A mechanical timer could miss the mark by 20 or 30 seconds.) Touchpads vary in readability and ease of programming. On better models, numbers and letters are printed clearly, and the control pad is well labeled and laid out so that the buttons are near one another when an operation requires a sequence of commands. Good displays are large and well lit.

Programming the oven's automated features can be vexing. We like models with prompts that take you through each command step by step. Quick-cook keys minimize button-pushing. Look for one-button cooking: You press one key to start cooking. (Some models make you also hit a Cook or Time button. With a few models, you set the power level.)

Power levels. Most larger ovens have 10; some have 100. We find that five well-spaced settings are plenty. In a few inexpensive ovens, power remains constant. Models with a high-power default automatically cook at that power unless programmed otherwise.

Temperature probe. Like a meat thermometer, a temperature probe in a microwave oven monitors a food's internal temperature and either turns off the oven or switches to a lower "keep warm" setting when the preset temperature is reached. Few of CU's readers who own a probe said they actually use it, according to our surveys.

Moisture sensor. This keeps track of cooking progress by tracking the moisture level in the oven as the food releases steam. We think this type of sensor is much handier than a probe. It's especially useful when it works with Auto Reheat, shutting off the oven when the food is steaming. CONSUMER REPORTS readers say they don't often use these sensors either.

Multistage cooking programs. These programs tell the oven to cook at one power level for a while, then switch to another—helpful for going directly from Defrost to Cook or for recipes that call for 10 minutes at high power and 5 at a reduced setting. Basic models typically allow two programs; fancier models offer several.

Automatic defrosting. Any microwave can adequately thaw out food if you break apart defrosted pieces and turn the food occasionally. An automatic-defrost setting reduces the labor. With some ovens, the feature works by lowering the power level over the thawing period; with others, it works for a programmed time period, based on the item's weight. Some ovens signal when to turn the food or remove defrosted sections. They may also go into a "standing" mode periodically to let the temperature equalize. The models that thaw the best—without cooking parts of the food while leaving icy spots elsewhere—may not be the swiftest, since uniform thawing takes time. More than half our readers regularly use their oven's auto-defrost feature.

Programmed cooking. Electronic controls give a microwave oven various programming capabilities. Many models have shortcut buttons that adjust the cooking time and power level for specific tasks, such as Pizza, Popcorn, Beverage. Some models allow you to enter cooking instructions for your own recipes into computer memory or call up programmed instructions for a variety of foods at the touch of a button.

Turntable. Nowadays, most models have a turntable. A turntable improves heat distribution, but reduces an oven's usable space. A recessed or removable turntable doesn't cut down on space, but may create hard-to-clean nooks and crannies.

Conveniences. Inspect any oven, plain or fancy, for basic conveniences. Can you see through the window to check on the progress of a dish? A dim interior light, coarse screen, or light-colored door panel limits visibility. Does the oven have a shelf? It comes in handy for cooking more than one dish at a time. Other useful touches include a lip or tray to contain spills and a clearly written, logically organized instruction book.

The tests

Our evaluation includes a judgment of heating speed based on heating measured amounts of water for a fixed time interval, and a battery of cooking tests, most of them designed to gauge evenness of heating, a major concern in microwave cooking. We defrost ground beef, warm leftover mashed potatoes, and bake potatoes, popcorn, and brownies. With the bigger and fancier ovens, we prepare entrées like meat loaf and quiche. We also measure usable capacity and review conveniences.

Reliability

Mid-sized microwave ovens have been more reliable than full-sized models, our surveys show. Brands with the best repair records for microwave ovens bought between 1987 and 1992 include *Sanyo*, *Goldstar*, *Panasonic*, *Sharp* and *Quasar*. Worst by a healthy margin is *Whirlpool*. See the brand Repair Histories on page 370.

Buying advice

Consider how much space you have available and how you plan to use the oven. Given the smallest ovens' limited capacity and power, we suggest buying one only if your kitchen space is truly at a premium. In our opinion, mid-sized models give the best value for the money. Many are priced just a little more than small ovens but cook faster and come with more features. And they're still small enough to fit under a cabinet or sit on the kitchen counter without hogging it.

Look for clear, easy-to-use controls. If you're tempted by a model loaded with features, consider that most people end up never using a temperature probe or a moisture sensor.

Convection-oven cooking is free from many of the flaws of microwave cooking. But those flaws appear only when you use the microwave oven to cook food, not just heat. You'll have to learn new cooking methods to take advantage of a microwave/convection model. For broiling and baking, a regular oven is probably still the best choice.

Gas & electric ranges
▶ **Ratings on page 98.**   ▶ **Repair records on page 370.**

Today's "cooking center" may consist of a single basic range or a series of modular cooking appliances. Your choice depends largely on budget, personal preference, and cooking style. The kitchen layout, the fuel source, and the desired conveniences may also influence what you buy.

Whirlpool, *Sears*, and *GE* account for more than half of the electric ranges sold; other brands trail at a distance. *GE* is number one in gas ranges, with *Magic Chef*, *Sears*, and *Tappan* close behind.

Gas or electric?

This decision often depends on the utility hookup available. If you can choose gas or electric, but have no preference, here are a few points to keep in mind:

Gas burners respond quickly and let you see heat levels. Gas cooktops also remain usable in power outages. A gas cooktop isn't fussy about the flatness of the bottoms of pots. Sealed-burner units are fairly easy to clean. A gas range or cooktop is more expensive than a comparable electric model (there's more inside plumbing), but typically costs less to operate, especially now that automatic spark igniters have largely replaced pilot lights.

Electric cooktops, especially smoothtops, are easier to clean than conventional gas cooktops. Smoothtops require flat-bottomed pans. Ovens are typically bigger than in comparable gas models, and delivered more even broiling over a wider area in our tests. Electric ranges are also less likely to break down and need repair.

Configurations

The kitchen's cabinetry and floor plan will probably dictate the range's width, whether the range fits between counters, is built into the countertop and cabinets, or stands alone.

Freestanding models are the typical replacement ranges. These can be used either in the middle or at the end of a counter. You'll find more models available than with other types. Size varies from 20 inches wide to 40 inches wide, but most are 30 inches. Price: $200 to $1600.

Built-in models can be of two types: slide-ins that fit into a space between cabinets and drop-ins, which lack a storage drawer and fit into cabinets that are connected below the oven. Both types look "built in". Price: $500 to $2300.

Dual and combination ovens combine two methods of cooking in one oven or pair two ovens together. On dual-oven models, the second oven may be up top or alongside the first. Sometimes the second oven is a microwave. Microwaves can be built into the conventional oven, too, but that design is rarely seen nowadays. More often, a convection oven is built into the regular oven, with a fan to circulate hot air. That's supposed to cook faster and seal in the juices. Our tests showed that a convection oven was faster at roasting meat, but at the cost of reduced oven capacity.

A **cooktop/wall oven combination** can be placed anywhere there's counterspace, and it allows you to combine the instant on/off of a gas cooktop with the spaciousness of an electric oven. Cooktops come in all the types described in the next section. Some are modular, with pop-in grills, rotisseries, or other options. This combination typically costs more than an all-in-one range. Major brands: *GE, Jenn-Air, Sears, Magic Chef, Whirlpool*. Price: $150 to $1500 for cooktop, $250 to $2300 for wall oven.

Element and burner types

Gas cooktops can be made of glass or finished with enamel. The burners are topped with the familiar grates, but some models have sealed burners, with no space between them and the cooktop, which stops spills from seeping below.

Electric cooktops offer more choices:

Electric coil. Still the most common and least expensive type, and offers good low-heat cooking. It's fairly forgiving of warped and dented pots. The coils usually plug in, so it's easy to replace them when broken. Cleanup isn't the easiest, although spills usually burn off elements and no special care is required.

Solid element. Unlike electric coils, solid-disc elements remain gray even when very hot, so you may forget they're turned on. The discs are sealed to the cooktops, simplifying cleanup. Solid elements require perfectly flat pans and take a long time to heat up and cool down. Discs haven't performed as well or cleaned as easily as manufacturers hoped. They're on the way out.

Smooth cooktops are presently only available in electric, although a gas smoothtop is expected to be introduced shortly. Their flat design offers a clean, uncluttered look to the kitchen. Unlike the white smoothtops of the '70s, today's smoothtops are black or grayish white and made of a ceramic glass called Ceran, which is supposed to be more stain- and scratch-resistant. Patterned smoothtops, particularly the whitish gray ones, show smudges and fingerprints less than shiny black ones. Spills are easy to clean, but sugary foods, which could pit the glass, must be wiped up immediately. A special cleaner is recommended by manufacturers. Smoothtops come with radiant, halogen, or magnetic-induction elements.

Radiant element. This is essentially a coil below the glass. Indicator lights signal when the surface is hot, even if elements are off. A temperature limiter protects against overheating. For efficient heating, radiant burners require flat-bottomed pots about the same diameter as the heating element. The ones we've tested typically work a bit slower than coil burners, probably because they have a lower wattage.

Halogen elements. Usually found in combination with radiant elements, a halogen element consists of a quartz halogen lamp circled with resistance coils. This type reaches peak heat marginally faster than radiant burners, according to our tests. Pans should be flat-bottomed. The ones we've tested typically work a bit slower than coil burners, probably because they have a lower wattage.

Magnetic-induction elements. The most expensive type, limited in availability. A high-frequency electrical coil beneath the smoothtop surface heats the pot (not the cooktop surface) using magnetic induction. Removing the pot from the surface turns off the heat. Heat is instant on and off, much like gas cooking. Pots must be iron or steel (magnetic metal) but don't have to be flat-bottomed.

Features and conveniences

Self-cleaning oven. A high-heat cycle (usually two to four hours at temperatures as high as 1000°F) turns any accumulated goop into ash. When the cycle is complete, you wipe away the residue with a damp sponge. This worthwhile option adds $50 to $100 to an oven's price.

A "continuous-clean" oven uses a special textured surface to camouflage dirt and is claimed to dissipate grime. Plain porcelain enamel ovens must be cleaned with oven cleaner.

Cleanup. Features that facilitate cleaning: seamless corners and edges (especially where the cooktop joins the backguard; a glass backguard instead of a painted one (glass won't scratch as easily); a raised edge around the cooktop to contain spills; no chrome edges.

For a conventional range with coil elements or regular gas burners, look for deep wells and minimum clutter under the cooktop, which make cleanup easy. Make sure you can prop up or remove the cooktop for cleaning. Porcelain drip bowls are easier to clean than chrome ones.

Sealed elements or burners make cleaning easier. Smoothtops are easiest of all to clean but require special cleaners and care.

Oven capacity. Ovens in models with similar exterior dimensions often differ in capacity because of shelf supports and other protrusions. Some ovens won't let you cook casseroles on two racks at the same time. Ovens that double as convection ovens typically lose some space to the fan.

Oven controls. Dials are generally less expensive than electronic controls. They have the advantage of being simpler and more straightforward to operate than electronic controls. A nonelectronic control panel usually has an analog clock and, in many cases, it controls the timers that start and stop the oven for automatic cooking.

Touchpads or buttons, LED displays, and digital timers are the hallmark of electronic controls. The least complicated designs have prompts and a telephone-style keypad for direct entry of times. A design with a smooth surface is easiest to clean.

Cooktop controls. Dials are still the norm. Freestanding ranges have controls laid out on the background (electric) or in front of the cooktop (gas). On electric ranges, controls can be split left and right, with the oven controls between, an arrangement that gives some intuitive sense of which control works which element. Controls staggered right and left map better to front and back elements. Controls clustered in the center of the backguard typically allow a tall stock pot to set on a back element without blocking the controls. With gas ranges, only the oven controls are on the backguard, and usually don't interfere with the use of large pots.

Downdraft vents. These vents eliminate the need for a range hood. They're useful for island or peninsula installations but don't work well with sealed gas burners.

The tests

We judge speed of heating by the time it takes to bring measured quantities of water to a clear boil. To test simmering prowess, we melt baking chocolate in a heavy saucepan, keep it over low heat for 10 minutes, and check for scorching. We judge evenness of oven and broiler heating by baking cakes and broiling burgers. We evaluate self-cleaning ovens by baking on and then removing a special blend of gunk. We also assess cleanability and features.

Reliability

Electric ranges have been more reliable than gas models, according to our reader surveys over the years. Models with conventional control (dials) have been more reliable than ones with electronic controls.

Our most recent survey showed no meaningful difference among brands of electric ranges purchased from 1986 to 1992 for which we had enough reports—*Caloric, Frigidaire, GE, Hotpoint, Sears, Whirlpool,* and *White-Westinghouse.* Among gas ranges purchased between 1987 and 1992, we found a small but significant difference among six brands. For details, see the brand Repair Histories on page 370.

Buying advice

The least expensive type is a freestanding electric range. A typical 30-inch model with four coil elements and a self-cleaning oven sells for around $450 to $600; a comparable gas range sells for $500 to $700.

But gas has its advantages: It's cheaper to cook with gas than electricity; the heat is easily and directly controlled; and gas cooktops remain usable in a blackout.

For the more stylish specialized and modular units—built-ins, cooktop and wall ovens, cooktop and dual or combination ovens—you must pay a premium.

No matter what type of range you're considering, look for a model with logically placed, understandable controls and a simple, easy-to-clean cooktop.

Refrigerators

▶ **Repair records on page 371.**

Refrigerators, one of the biggest energy-consuming appliances in the home, have chalked up impressive gains in efficiency. Today's models work on about half or less of the energy of those from a decade ago. Responding to consumer demand and Government prodding, manufacturers continue to devise new ways to reduce energy use. In the future, refrigerators will be better insulated, boast an energy-thrifty compressor, and run on a refrigerant friendlier to the environment than chlorofluorocarbons, which are being phased out.

Efficiencies notwithstanding, a refrigerator's use of electricity still adds up over its expected 17-year life span. Your cumulative electricity bills can eventually amount to twice the appliance's purchase price, so shopping for high energy efficiency is just as important as shopping for a favorable price tag. Energy costs depend largely on the capacity and type of refrigerator you buy. But the design matters, too. Our tests regularly show a spread in the amount of electricity that similarly configured refrigerators consume.

Sears, GE, and *Whirlpool* account for more than half of the refrigerators sold; other brands are far behind.

The choices

These are the main types you'll find:

Top-freezer. The most common format, top-freezer models are generally least expensive to buy and cheapest to run; they also give you the widest choice of capacities, styles, and features. The eye-level freezer offers easy access to its contents. The fairly wide shelves in the refrigerator compartment make it easy to reach things at the back, but you have to bend or crouch to reach items stored on bottom shelves. Nominal capacity ranges from about 10 to almost 25 cubic feet; width ranges from 24 to 34 inches. A typical 20-cubic-foot unit sells for $650 to $850.

Side-by-side. These larger models (about 19 to 27 cubic feet, 30 to 36 inches wide) cost more to buy and run than other types. Advantages that may justify the expenditure: You can store food at eye level in both compartments. The tall, thin shape of the compartments makes it easy to find stray items (but hard to get at items in the back). Doors are narrower than those of a top-freezer model, requiring less clearance in front to swing open. The freezer is larger than in comparable top- or bottom-freezer models. Side-by-side models come in a fairly wide selection of capacities, styles, and features. Selling price: $900 to $2000, depending on size and features.

Bottom-freezer. These models, a tiny part of the market, give you fairly wide, eye-level shelves in the refrigerator and easy access to its contents, and a bigger freezer than that of top-freezer models with the same overall capacity. That advantage is offset by a pull-out basket, which reduces usable space in the freezer. Bottom-freezer models are more expensive ($900 to $1100) than top-freezer units and can be more expensive to run than other types. The lower position of the freezer means you have to crouch or bend to access it. And features such as an in-door water dispenser are unavailable. Nominal capacity: 20 to 22 cubic feet; width, about 32 inches.

Built-in refrigerators. Built-ins are expensive appliances (usually $2000 and more), sized from 10 to 33 cubic feet. Designed to be installed flush with the surrounding kitchen cabinets, they can be faced with custom door panels to match the cabinetry. To achieve that look, built-ins are only 24 inches deep, a half-foot shallower than conventional models; they're also taller and wider than typical refrigerators. Installation can be a major expense.

Compact models. At the other end of the scale are refrigerators with a nominal capacity of six cubic feet or less. The best-selling models of this type, popular in dormitories, offices, and playrooms, are cubes—scaled-down versions of regular-sized refrigerators. In this segment of the market, you'll find familiar appliance names, such as *General Electric* and *Whirlpool,* and also names known better for electronic products, such as *Sanyo* and *Goldstar*. Prices range from about $120 to $300.

Mechanically, compacts are old-fashioned. Freezers, typically within the refrigerator compartment, get no colder than 15° or 20°F and can keep ice cream for only a few hours before it goes soupy. If you

REFRIGERATORS

adjust the control to make the freezer colder, items in the refrigerator compartment freeze, too. These models don't automatically defrost. And if our experience is typical, the consumer has nearly a 25 percent chance of buying a model with a major problem, such as a bum thermostat.

Features and conveniences

When evaluating a regular refrigerator, we use a 70-item checklist to gauge how easy the unit would be to live with (the checklist for compacts has only 23 items). Minor items—poorly placed shelves, bins that don't glide smoothly—can mount up to major dissatisfactions in daily use.

Temperature controls. These are typically dials in the refrigerator area. With some designs, you may have to move food to make adjustments. Some models have additional controls—a louver or valve for crispers or meat-keepers. The effectiveness of these controls has varied greatly in our tests.

Electronic touchpad controls, available on high-end models, are usually easy to use. They indicate when a door is ajar, when the unit is excessively warm, and when to clean the coils. In addition, such controls can flag problems needing repairs.

Shelves and bins. The shelves in the refrigerator compartment can usually be rearranged; so can some freezer shelves and door shelves. Tempered-glass shelves, increasingly common, are preferable because they confine spills to one level. Sliding shelves help you find stray items. Removable bins are handy for ice cubes.

On top-of-the-line refrigerators, you may find such niceties as a utility shelf fitted with storage and serving containers that can pop right into the microwave oven; adjustable, extra-deep door shelves for holding gallon-sized food or beverage containers; movable retainers on door shelves for holding odd-shaped items; or a built-in beverage container with its own spigot.

No-frost operation. This is practically a given these days, except on compact models. Most self-defrosting models defrost about once a day, after their compressor has run for a fixed number of hours.

Ice and water. Ice-makers, ice dispensers, and water dispensers jack up a refrigerator's price by $100 to $250. The plumbing connections for ice-makers and dispensers also come in kit form for as little as $30 to $50. Such devices need to be used routinely to keep them in working order and to keep their contents tasting fresh.

An ice-maker can be a mixed blessing. It can take up a cubic foot of valuable freezer space and nearly double the chance that the unit will need repairs. Although the ice-maker is built-in, the refrigerator must still be connected to the home's cold-water line, a job do-it-yourselfers may be able to handle after checking local plumbing codes. Most ice-makers shut off when their bin is full or when you raise and lock a wire arm. Don't expect large quantities of ice: The models we've seen produce about four to six ice-trays' worth a day.

Through-the-door ice dispensers can drop just a few cubes into a glass or fill an ice bucket. We like the push-in cradle arrangement, modeled after certain soda fountains. Dispensers using overhead push buttons often send ice to the floor instead of into the glass. Don't expect to get lots of cold water from a dispenser—reservoirs typically hold about 1½ quarts.

Reliability

Refrigerators with an ice-maker are about twice as likely to need repairs as ones without, according to CONSUMER REPORTS readers. Among top-freezer models bought new between 1984 and 1992 even the most trouble-prone plain brand—*GE*—had a repair record that was comparable with the most reliable brands with an ice-maker—

Whirlpool, *Sears*, and *Frigidaire*. See the brand Repair Histories on page 371.

Buying advice

Decide on the type; then decide on capacity. Too large a model may be needlessly expensive, besides wasting space and energy. If your old model was big enough, then a similar-sized unit will probably suit your needs.

Kitchen space is another consideration. Check how much clearance the door or doors need in front and at the side. Some doors demand an extra foot on the side so that you can slide out bins and shelves.

To conserve energy, you should clean a refrigerator's condenser coil a few times a year with a special brush or a vacuum. When the coil collects dust, it becomes less effective at dissipating heat and may reduce efficiency. Some models locate the coil at the rear of the refrigerator; it gathers less dust there, but is hard to get at. Others models have the coil in front, located behind the grill at the bottom.

Small refrigerators such as compact models generally use energy less efficiently than larger models.

Dishwashers

▶ **Ratings on page 104.** ▶ **Repair records on page 369.**

An automatic dishwasher won't necessarily clean better than hand washing, but it could be a cheaper way to wash dishes. Modern dishwashers use relatively little hot water—less than you'd likely use if you're accustomed to washing dishes under a faucet spewing hot water.

Top-selling brands are *Sears*, *General Electric*, and *Whirlpool*; together they account for more than two-thirds of the dishwashers sold. Other major brands include *Maytag* and *KitchenAid*.

The choices

Basic dishwashers are priced about $300, but they're less popular than those that sell for $400 to $500. In that price range, you get electronic controls, specialized cycles, and better filtration systems. Spending more buys more sophisticated engineering and convenience features. State-of-the-art machines, priced at $750 and up, are European-made models. They're exceptionally energy efficient and quiet, and typically come with stainless-steel liners.

Nearly all models these days are built-in, under-counter models. Portable models have been declining steadily in sales. Mechanically, the two types are similar.

Built-in models. These units are permanently attached to a hot-water pipe, a drain, and electrical lines. They generally fit into a 24-inch-wide space under the countertop between two kitchen cabinets. A few compact models are designed to fit an 18-inch space.

Portable models. These have a finished exterior, wheels, a plug-in cord, and a hose assembly you attach to the sink faucet each time you use the machine. Most portables can be converted to an under-cabinet installation.

Features and conveniences

Controls. The choice is between manual or electronic. Neither type is superior, in our judgment. Simple models let you set everything with push buttons, or with buttons and a dial. Top-of-the-line models couple electronic touchpads with "systems monitor" displays. The circuitry displays the time for various dishwasher operations. Some displays flash warnings about clogged drains, blocked wash-arms, and so on. Some models have a hidden touchpad that locks the controls to keep kids from playing with them—a worthwhile feature.

Cycles. A cycle is a combination of washes and rinses. Normal or Regular generally comprises two washes and two or three rinses. A Heavy cycle can entail longer wash cycles, another wash, hotter water, or all of the above. A Light cycle usually includes one wash. Those three basic cycles are really all you need.

Extra cycles. With names such as Pot Scrubber, Soak and Scrub, and China and Crystal—these help justify a higher price tag. Regardless of what the names imply, a machine cannot scrub the way old-fashioned abrasive cleaners and muscle can. Nor can a dishwasher baby your heirloom crystal or good china. The machine jostles dishes, and the harsh detergents could etch them. Gold trim may be especially vulnerable.

Water-and energy-saving. European-made models are typically more frugal with water than conventional models. In our tests, the Euromodels used 5½ to 8½ gallons per wash compared with 7½ to 13 gallons used by conventional models.

Most of the energy a dishwasher uses is in the form of hot water from your water heater. Electricity to run the pump, motor, and heating element can be less than a dime's worth of electricity at average rates for efficient models. Helpful features include: a booster heater system that checks the water temperature, automatically heating it, if necessary (that allows you to keep your water heater at a lower, more economical setting); a Delay-Start setting that lets you program the dishwasher to do its work when off-peak energy rates are in effect. All dishwashers let you choose between a heated dry cycle and plain air drying. A few also use a blower to aid drying, though some machines do just fine without one.

Noise. Quiet operation is a major selling point. Dishwashers as a whole have become less raucous over the years. Insulating material and water pumps that run more quietly have helped. So has switching from porcelain to plastic tubs and redesigning the washer arms. In our most recent tests, the pricey Euromodels were the quietest; we could barely tell they were running. Only a few of the conventional models came close to be being as quiet.

Racks. Most racks hold the cups and glasses on top and the plates on the bottom. Some models have racks with folding shelves to let you add extra cups and glasses. Some models have provisions for adjusting the upper rack for tall glasses. Flatware baskets are typically in the main dish rack. *Whirlpool* machines place their baskets on the door.

The tests

We judge performance by how well a dishwasher cleans place settings soiled with some of the most challenging foods we can find: chili, spaghetti, mashed potatoes, fried egg yolk, peanut butter, raspberry jam, cheese spread, cornflakes and milk, oatmeal, stewed tomatoes, and coffee. We let soiled dishes stand in the machines overnight. We run many loads in each machine, half with 140° F water and half with 120° water. Most machines clean about the same with either water supply.

Reliability

Some of the more reliable brands, based on our readers' experience with dishwashers bought since 1987, have been *Magic Chef, Amana, Hotpoint, Whirlpool,* and

General Electric. See the brand Repair Histories on page 369.

Buying advice

We still find substantial performance differences among various brands of dishwashers—more than what we usually see with other major appliances. In our tests, price corresponded fairly closely with performance. So did quiet operation. Still, solid performers with dials and push buttons or electronic controls can be had for less than $500. Stay away from budget models.

When shopping, look at the racks with your dishes in mind. The unit's construction is important, too. A porcelain-coated steel interior resists abrasion better than plastic but is vulnerable to being chipped. Stainless steel can be dented but is the most durable finish.

Washing machines

▶ **Ratings on page 107.**   ▶ **Repair records on page 372.**

Over the years, washer design has improved to the point where, while there may be some differences, virtually any machine can be expected to wash clothes satisfactorily.

Nor are substantive changes expected when new Federal energy standards take effect in mid-1994. Models sold after that date will have to be more energy-efficient, but that's likely to be accomplished by simply eliminating warm-water rinses—a step worth taking on your own if your machine allows cold-water rinses.

New washers distinguish themselves cosmetically, with styling of the control panel, and with such conveniences as quiet operation, electronic touchpad controls, extra cycles, and larger capacity.

Manufacturers have also been forced to compete the old-fashioned way, price. Look for money-back guarantees, buy-back programs, and cash rebates.

Despite the multitude of brands in stores, just five companies dominate the U.S. laundry business. Maytag, known for its line of premium washers, is the parent company of *Magic Chef,* which makes machines sold under its own label as well as the *Admiral* and *Norge* nameplates. In addition to selling washers under its own marquee, Whirlpool makes the machines that sell as *Sears Kenmore, Roper,* and *KitchenAid.* General Electric washers bear the names *GE, Hotpoint,* and *RCA;* Frigidaire Company sells washers under the *Gibson, Kelvinator, White-Westinghouse,* and *Frigidaire* logos. *Amana* and *Speed Queen* washers are made by the Raytheon Corp. Four brands—*Sears, Whirlpool, Maytag,* and *GE*—account for most of the washers sold in the U.S.

The choices

Beyond brand names, washers vary by design and size, and range in price from about $200 to more than $800. Most models within a brand line are remarkably similar. They are often of the same design and boast the same basic components—washtub, agitator, transmission, pump, and so on. What can you expect for more money? Typically, more cycle and speed combinations, greater capacity, and a wider selection of water temperature and fill options.

Types. The basic choice is between top- and front-loaders. Top-loaders are the biggest sellers in this country. Front-loaders use water more efficiently than their cousins, but are more expensive and don't

WASHING MACHINES

hold as big a load. Their availability and selection is limited to *White-Westinghouse* and a few imported brands. And, they have a poor repair history.

Size. Most washers (and their companion dryers) are full-sized models, 27 inches wide. Tub capacities usually vary between "large" or "extra large." There are oddball models for special installations—models that piggyback with a dryer or have a built-in dryer on top, and "portable" rolling models that hook up to a sink.

Multiple speeds. Most washers have more than one wash/spin speed. A second, slower speed allows gentler handling for delicate items. Although some machines offer additional speeds, two speeds—a normal-speed agitation with normal spin and slow agitation/slow spin—are usually enough for most clothes.

Features and conveniences

High-priced models in a manufacturer's line come with more frills, not better performance. For example, controls that operate with buttons, levers, and dials may be slightly harder to manipulate than touchpads, which are often more complex and more expensive to service. Here are other options to consider:

Extra cycles. Regular, Permanent Press, and Delicate are all you usually need. The cycle you choose may also determine the speed and water temperature; though on many models, the choice is up to you. More expensive machines offer a Soak/prewash for badly soiled laundry or an extra rinse cycle at the end. You can get the same result manually by simply resetting the dial.

Temperature settings. You generally need only three wash temperatures: hot, warm, and cold, followed by a cold rinse. Though a warm wash-and-rinse is recommended for washable woolens, warm water doesn't rinse any better than cold water. And it wastes energy. Sears and Frigidaire equip a few of their washers with an electronic temperature sensor that measures incoming water temperature and blends hot and cold to reach preset targets. (Your adjusting the hot and cold spigots solves the problem as well.)

Water levels. The most economical way to wash is with a full load. When that's not practical, you can save water, detergent, and energy by lowering the fill level. On most large-tub models, the minimum fill requires roughly half as much water as the maximum fill, or 20 to 30 gallons per wash. A selection of three fill levels is enough.

Finish. More and more machines use plastic-based finishes for the washer's top and lid—not the traditional porcelain or baked enamel. The new coatings, with trademarked names like Dura-Finish or Enduraguard, are tougher than enamels, but softer than porcelain.

Tubs. More plastic is used inside the machines, too. Some washers have a plastic tub, which should wear as well as the porcelain-coated steel type. The polypropylene tub included with some models comes with a 25-year warranty.

Special features. Some machines have dispensers that release bleach and fabric softener at the appropriate time. Some include an alternate agitator that's supposedly kinder to delicates. Others boast a little basket that fits inside the main tub for very small loads. A "Suds-Saver" feature pumps the used wash water into an external tub for use with the next load.

The tests

To test washing ability, we wash uniformly soiled coths, comparing the color and shade before and after. We measure water and energy usage, tub capacity, noise, water extraction, and the ability to cope with unbalanced loads.

Washers vary a lot in the amount of noise they produce. They also vary in their consumption of water and electricity. Energy consumption hinges on the amount of hot water used, since heating water accounts for most of the energy cost of washing. At average utility rates, a typical top-loader (with an extra-large tub) doing six hot wash/cold rinse loads a week uses $112 worth of electrically heated water or $37 worth of gas-heated water a year. By contrast, a front-loader would consume only $42 in electricity, $14 in gas, for the same job. Washing in warm water would cut those costs by half.

Capacity depends on tub size and the design of the agitator. Our tests show washers deemed "extra large" can differ in capacity by as much as 50 percent.

Reliability

According to information from our reader survey, top-loaders from Hotpoint, Maytag, and General Electric purchased between 1984 and 1992 have been among the more reliable brands of washing machines. Front-loaders from White-Westinghouse have been the most trouble-prone. See the brand Repair Histories on page 372.

Buying advice

Look for a brand with a solid repair history. Top-of-the-line washers with fancy electronics and specialized settings don't provide the best value. You'll get best value by not buying more machine than you need. A three-cycle, two-speed model should be ample for most chores.

Most people choose a top-loading washer. They're easier to load and unload than front-loaders and hold more laundry. Installation and servicing are easier, too. If conserving energy and water is a priority, consider a front-loader.

Clothes dryers

▶ Ratings on page 109. ▶ Repair records on page 372.

Just about any modern dryer will dry clothes adequately, particularly if you're not terribly fussy about sorting your laundry. Performance differences show up mainly in extremes—drying a tiny load of delicates, say.

Like washing machines, clothes dryers tend to differ mainly in conveniences and capacity. Some machines do all the figuring for you; others make you learn the setting that works best for your laundry. The highly automated models may sell for hundreds more than the simpler ones.

The choices

As with washing machines, a handful of companies make a multitude of dryer brands. Whirlpool makes *Whirlpool* and *Sears* models; General Electric, *GE* and *Hotpoint*; Maytag, *Maytag*, *Magic Chef* and *Norge*. *White-Westinghouse*, *Frigidaire*, and *Gibson* are products of Frigidaire Company. Raytheon makes *Amana* and *Speed Queen* models. The biggest brands: *Sears, Whirlpool, GE,* and *Maytag*.

Dryer prices vary from under $200 to more than $600. Spend more, and you'll likely get electronic touchpad controls, greater drum capacity, more automatic settings, and a moisture sensor to control the drying time—not a thermostat, which is less precise. Here are the basic choices:

Gas or electric. If you have the choice, you're probably better off with a gas model. Gas models tend to cost around $50 more than comparable electric models, but you'll recoup that in lower operating costs. In our cost-comparison tests, based on average utility rates, we paid 14 cents to dry a 12-pound mixed load in a gas model, versus 44 cents in an electric one. The extra plumbing in a gas dryer, however, often makes it slightly more trouble-prone.

Size. Full-sized models are 27 to 29 inches wide with a drum of 5 to 7 cubic feet. Some brands offer only one size drum across the complete model line; others offer a larger drum in top-of-the-line machines. The bigger the drum, the more easily a dryer handles bulky items, such as a comforter. Manufacturers also make compact models, usually electric, with a capacity of about 3½ cubic feet. Compacts can often be stacked on a companion washer. They can be plugged into a regular outlet instead of a heavy-duty 240-volt line, but drying takes much longer than with a full-sized dryer. Compacts generally sell for less than $350.

Features and conveniences

Here's what to consider:

Cycles. Dryers typically offer two or three automatic drying cycles—Regular, Permanent Press, Knit/Delicate, for instance—as well as timed and unheated settings. A "More Dry to Less Dry" range on the automatic settings lets you fine-tune the setting based on the size and composition of each load. (That control helps retain dampness for easier ironing.) An automatic drying cycle reduces the chances of overdrying and saves energy; it can also reduce static cling. Low-end dryers may offer just a timed cycle.

Thermostat or moisture sensor. The oldest, simplest approach to automatic drying is to control the heat and the timer with a thermostat. The thermostat checks the load's dampness indirectly. As the clothes dry, air leaving the drum gets progressively hotter. When the temperature rises enough, the thermostat cycles off and the timer advances until the heat goes on again. The process is repeated until the heating part of the cycle has ended. Newer designs sense moisture more accurately, using sensors that touch the clothes to gauge dryness. Moisture sensors may be limited to more expensive models.

Controls. Top-of-the-line dryers come with electronic controls. Such controls make it simple to choose among many options, but they add a lot to the machine's price and are also expensive to repair. And they may not tell you as much as regular dial controls, which show roughly where you are in the cycle. Cheap models sometimes put too many choices on too few controls, which makes them hard to use.

Finish. Most dryers have a baked-enamel finish on the cabinet top and drum that's not as scratch-resistant as porcelain.

Added tumble time. Most dryers allow you to extend the period of cool tumbling after the end of the automatic drying cycle—anywhere from 15 minutes to a couple of hours. This useful feature, sometimes called "Wrinkle Guard" or "Press Guard," helps keep clothes from wrinkling if the cycle is completed and the dryer is not emptied right away.

Less useful is a "Wrinkle Remove" or similarly named feature that promises to save you some ironing. It takes clean, wrinkled clothes and puts them through a short spell of tumbling at low or no heat followed by a cool-down. The feature can be duplicated on any dryer with a temperature selector merely by setting the selector to low or no heat and the time to, say, 20 minutes.

Other features. Most models have a buzzer or other warning that sounds the end of the drying cycle; you may be able to disarm the signal or adjust loudness in some models. Some dryers also sound off when the lint filter needs emptying.

A drum light can be useful for hunting

down errant socks, even if the room has good lighting. Some dryers come with a special rack for drying items like sneakers without tumbling.

Most doors open to the right so that you can position the laundry basket under the opening. A door that opens down creates a handy shelf but forces you to stretch to reach into the drum.

The tests

We judge a dryer's prowess by seeing how it handles a number of assignments at the appropriate automatic settings. We dry large loads of towels, jeans, and shirts, and small heaps of underwear, shorts, shirts, and hand towels. We also fill the machines with permanent-press shirts, and do loads of delicates.

A good dryer should dry laundry thoroughly, without heating the fabrics too much. The machine should also turn off promptly when the clothes reach the degree of dryness selected.

Reliability

Our surveys show that the *Frigidaire* and *Magic Chef* models purchased between 1986 and 1992 have been significantly more trouble-prone than other brands of electric dryer. Among gas dryers, *White-Westinghouse* models have been most troublesome. See the brand Repair Histories on page 372.

Buying advice

If you have a choice between an electric or gas clothes dryer, opt for the gas. Although gas dryers are higher priced initially, they're much more efficient than electric models. The energy saved during the first year of ownership should offset the $50 or so price difference.

Look for a model that offers automatic drying cycles. Timed cycles are best just for small loads, which can confound the automatic setting on some machines. Models with a moisture sensor can further help reduce wasteful overdrying. But you'll have to spend an extra $30 to $40 to get that feature.

Whichever dryer you end up choosing, make sure to clean the lint filter regularly. Ideally, that's after every use. Lint that's allowed to build up in the exhaust duct could cause a fire.

Detergents & other laundry products

Industry giants Procter & Gamble, Colgate-Palmolive, and Lever Brothers spend millions of dollars a year promoting the idea that doing laundry is a complex task requiring many specialized products. But despite all the promises and claims for producing the fluffiest, cleanest laundry, all detergents clean clothes.

In fact, modern detergents clean fabric so thoroughly that they can leave clothes feeling scratchy. While line-dried clothes don't build up static, synthetics, especially, are prone to accumulate an electric charge in a dryer. Hence the need for fabric softeners, which also help with static.

The choices

Cleaning products come in a hodgepodge of forms. Liquids, powders, concentrates, sticks, sheets, pumps, and sprays. Each has its own characteristics.

Detergents. Modern laundry products work through the combined action of a number of key ingredients: surfactants, "builders," whiteners, enzymes, and all-fabric bleach.

Surfactants, or surface active agents, are dirt removers. They act much as soap does, emulsifying oil and grease and the dirt they bind, and allowing them all to be washed away. There are hundreds of such chemicals, which can be classed as three types. Anionic surfactants work best in hot, soft water and are very effective on oily stains and mud and clay. Nonionic surfactants, found in many liquids, are less sensitive to water hardness; they excel at ridding oily soils from synthetics at cool wash temperatures. Cationic surfactants are more common in fabric softeners and detergent/softener combinations.

Builders enhance the cleaning efficiency of the surfactants by softening the water. Phosphates, the quintessential builders, are found only in powdered detergents. Phosphates have taken the rap for spurring the growth of algae, which can eventually transform a lake into a bog in a process known as eutrophication. So they're banned in about a third of the country. Nonphosphorus powders may combine old-fashioned baking soda with extra ingredients to make up for the lack of phosphorus. Liquid detergents like *Wisk* and *Surf* contain water-softening chemicals such as sodium citrate.

Whitening agents, also known as optical brighteners, are colorless dyes that give laundry an added glow in sunlight and fluorescent light, making garments appear a bit brighter.

Enzymes help break down complex soils—especially proteins, such as in blood, egg, or grass stains—so that they can be more easily removed. Some people, however, may suffer skin irritation on contact with enzymes. You can generally tell if a detergent contains enzymes by checking the ingredient list for substances ending in the suffix "-ase."

All-fabric bleach, a popular addition to powders, is not as good at whitening as chlorine bleach, but it's gentler. All-fabric bleaches—sodium perborate tetrahydrate is the most common—are safe on most materials and dyes.

Not only do all detergents clean clothes, most also brighten, remove stains to some extent, and work in a variety of water temperatures. That's true whether or not a manufacturer decides to make any of those attributes a selling point.

There are some differences among detergents worth noting, however. Liquid detergents tend to be pricier than powders, but allow easier pretreatment of stains. Superconcentrated powders and liquids are the newest wrinkle in the detergent market. Packaged in easy-to-tote, compact containers a fraction the size of regular products, a concentrate can hold enough detergent for more than 40 loads.

Fabric softeners. By thinly coating a fabric's fibers with a waxy film, fabric softeners solve both the problem of static and the problem of clothes that are too clean. Humectant chemicals help the fabric retain moisture, neutralizing the static charge that otherwise causes cling. Lubricants in the softener let the fibers glide past each other, reducing wrinkling. They also separate a napped fabric's fibers and stand them on end, which makes a towel feel fluffy.

First marketed in the late 1950s, fabric softeners originally came as a creamy liquid, often pink, that you added during the washer's rinse cycle. Rinse liquids are still around, but these days they're competing against the convenience of products such as dryer sheets and detergent/softener combinations.

Dryer sheets are made of fiber or foam, impregnated with softener. You throw a sheet into the dryer along with the laundry. Heat releases the softener.

Combination products. "All-in-one"

DETERGENTS & OTHER LAUNDRY PRODUCTS

products—those with color-safe bleach, fabric softener, or stain-fighting enzymes—seem convenient, but the results leave something to be desired. Detergent/softener combinations, for instance, haven't done particularly well at cleaning or softening in our tests.

Detergent/softeners contain both products. The softener is present in the wash cycle, and the manufacturer relies on special chemicals to make sure it sticks around for the rinse cycle. Single-use packets of detergent-plus-softener contain detergent, which dissolves during the wash; the fibers of the bag are laced with softener and go into the dryer with the rest of the laundry.

Laundry boosters. Easiest to use for small stains are booster sticks, which come in a tube, like lipstick. You rub booster onto the stain, then launder in the usual way. Liquid boosters, like sticks, must be rubbed in—a chore if you have lots of stains. Aerosols and pump sprays are a bit easier to apply. You douse the stain, then wash the garment. Powders are the handiest for treating a large load. Instead of applying booster to the stained area, you simply pour it into the washer along with the detergent. Powders can also be used for presoaking.

Hand-laundry detergents. Specialty products like *Woolite* are promoted as a gentler alternative to regular detergents. Such products work, as our tests have shown, but so do dishwashing liquids, which are similar in composition to hand-laundry detergents except they lack whitening agents. The name-brand products charge a premium. Store-brand versions of these detergents cost less. But dishwashing liquids are the best buy.

Buying advice

On an ordinary load of laundry, the range of performance among detergents would be clean to cleanest—not dirty to clean. Some detergents work a bit better than others, especially on tough stains like tea, grass, and grape juice. On the other hand, we haven't found any detergent that works on used motor oil.

We've found little correlation in our tests between the price of a detergent and its cleaning ability. Look for special promotions, and buy what's on sale. You'll pay more for the convenience of liquids or premeasured packets. You'll also pay more for buying "green," although there's no evidence to suggest that so-called natural brands are any better for the environment than regular brands.

Almost all fabric softeners reduce static; dryer sheets are particularly good. On the whole, rinse liquids soften better than other types. Detergent/softener combinations are the least effective. Buy dryer sheets by price. Some store brands cost half as much as name brands but work about as well.

How Objective is CU?

Consumers Union is not beholden to any commercial interest. It accepts no advertising and buys all the products tested on the open market. CU's income is derived from the sale of CONSUMER REPORTS and other publications, and from nonrestrictive, noncommercial contributions, grants, and fees. Neither the Ratings nor the reports may be used in advertising or for any other commercial purpose. Consumers Union will take all steps open to it to prevent commercial use of its materials, its name, or the name of CONSUMER REPORTS.

ELECTRIC RANGES

RATINGS: ELECTRIC RANGES

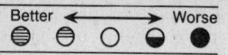

Better ◐ ◐ ○ ◐ ● Worse

▶ **See report, page 83.** From Consumer Reports, September 1993.

Recommendations: The *General Electric JBP45GR* was the only model that couldn't bake cakes well on two shelves. Differences among the other tested models were small. Use features, controls, and price to guide your choice.

Ratings order: Listed by types; within types, listed in order of overall quality based on how easy the cooktop was to clean, oven capacity, and performance. All are 30-inch free-standing, self-cleaning models. Price is the manufacturer's suggested retail. Color of the tested model is in bold. **Notes to table:** Key to colors: **A** = almond; **W** = white; **W/W** = white on white; **B** = black; **C/B** = chrome and black; **W/BD** = white with black drawer. Key to cooktop surface (smoothtops): **PBG** = patterned black glass; **PLBG** = plain black glass; **PB/PLG** = patterned black glass and plain glass; **BWPG** = black and white patterned glass. Cooktop drip bowls (conventional models): **C** = chrome; **P** = porcelain; **P/C** = porcelain/chrome. ⓢ indicates tested model has been replaced by successor model; according to the manufacturer, the performance of new model should be similar to the tested model but features may vary. See page 100 for new model number and suggested retail price, if available.

Brand and model	Price	Cooktop speed	Bake	Broil	Oven Size	Oven	Window	Available colors	Elements, watts	Cooktop surface	Comments
SMOOTHTOP MODELS											
DIAL CONTROLS											
Whirlpool RF366PXY	$729	◐	◐	◐	◐	◐	◐	A, **W**, W/W	1400; 1700; 2100; 2400	PBG	A,H,L,S,T,JJ
General Electric JB575GS ⓢ	640	◐	◐	◐	○	◐	○	**B**, W/W	1400; 1400; 1900; 1900	PBG	S,T,U,V,KK
Sears Kenmore 95629 ⓢ	680	◐	◐	◐	○	◐	—	**B**	1400; 1400; 1900; 1900	PLBG	E,Q,S,T,W,KK
ELECTRONIC CONTROLS											
Whirlpool RF396PXY	849	◐	◐	◐	◐	◐	◐	**A**, W, B, W/W	1400; 1700; 2100; 2400	PBG	A,C,H,S,X,Y,JJ
Frigidaire Elite REGC39BN ⓢ	675	◐	◐	◐	◐	◐	◐	**B**	1200; 1200; 2100; Dual 700/2100	PB/PLG	E,I,J,K,M,Z,AA,JJ,KK,LL
Tappan 31-5592-23	779	◐	◐	◐	◐	◐	●	**A**, W	1200; 1200; 2100; Dual 700/2100	PB/PLG	E,F,I,J,K,R,U,Z,BB,CC,JJ
General Electric JB578GS ⓢ	870	◐	◐	◐	○	◐	○	**B**, W/W	1400; 1400; 1900; Dual 1000/2400	PBG	J,U,KK

ELECTRIC RANGES

Brand and model	Price	Cooktop speed	Bake	Broil	Oven Size	Oven	Cleaning Window	Available colors	Elements, watts	Cooktop surface	Comments
Sears Kenmore 95929	$999	◐	⊖	⊖	○	⊖	○	B, W/W	1400; 1400; 1900; Dual 1000/2400	PBG	E,G,Q,S, DD,KK
RADIANT/HALOGEN ELEMENTS AND CONVECTION											
KitchenAid Supraba Selectra KERH507Y	1349	◐	⊖	○	◐	⊖	●	A, B, W/W	1400; 1800; 2200; 2400	BWPG	A,B,D,E,F, H,P,EE,AA, CC,MM
CONVENTIONAL MODELS											
DIAL CONTROLS											
Montgomery Ward KTM-4893	$499	⊖	⊖	⊖	⊖	⊖	◐	A, W	1500; 1500; 2600; 2600	C	I,J,K,U,Z, KK,NN
White-Westinghouse KF480N	410	⊖	⊖	⊖	○	⊖	○	A, W	1500; 1500; 2600; 2600	C	N,S,CC, FF,OO
Sears Kenmore 93421	569	⊖	⊖	⊖	○	⊖	○	A, W	1500; 1500; 2600; 2600	P	Q,S,T,DD
General Electric JBP26GR [S]	475	○	⊖	⊖	○	⊖	○	A, W, W/W	1325; 1325; 2350; 2350	P	S,T,U,V, GG,PP
Whirlpool RF365PXY	499	◐	⊖	⊖	⊖	⊖	⊖	A, W, W/W	1250; 1250; 2600; 2600	P	Q,S,T
ELECTRONIC CONTROLS											
Tappan 31-3962-23	509	⊖	⊖	⊖	⊖	⊖	◐	A, W, W/W	1500; 1500; 2600; 2600	C	I,J,K,U, Z,BB,CC
Caloric Prestige Series ESK3700	525	○	⊖	○	⊖	⊖	⊖	A, W, C/B, W/W	1500; 1500; 2600; 2600	P	G,J,K,O, Q,Z,AA, HH,LL
Sears Kenmore 93521	580	⊖	⊖	⊖	⊖	⊖	○	A, W/BD, W/W	1500; 1500; 2600; 2600	P	Q,S,DD
Frigidaire Elite REG38BN [S]	525	⊖	⊖	⊖	⊖	⊖	○	A, W/BD	1500; 1500; 2600; 2600	P/C	J,M,N,AA, CC,II,LL, OO
Whirlpool RF385PXY	599	◐	⊖	⊖	⊖	⊖	⊖	A, W, W/W	1250; 1250; 2600; 2600	P	S,X,Y
Hotpoint RB767GN	500	○	⊖	⊖	⊖	⊖	○	W/BD	1325; 1325; 2350; 2350	P	S
KitchenAid Selectra KERI500Y	699	○	⊖	○	○	⊖	◐	A, W/W	1500; 1500; 2600; 2600	P/C	P,AA,CC, EE,QQ
General Electric JBP45GR [S]	620	○	◐	⊖	○	⊖	○	A, W	1325; 1325; 2350; 2350	P	S,U,GG, PP

Ratings continued ▶

ELECTRIC RANGES

Successor Models (in Ratings order)
GE JB575GS is succeeded by JBP76GS, $650; Sears Kenmore 95629 by 55639, $699; Frigidaire Elite REGC39BN by FEF367CAB, $804; GE JB578GS by JBP79WS, $870; GE JBP26GR by JBP26GS, $475; Frigidaire Elite REG38BN by FEF364SA4, $615; GE JBP45GR by JBP45GS.

Key to Comments

A–Use and care video.
B–Comes with convection-use cookbook.
C–Comes with retractable-blade razor scraper for smoothtop cleaning.
D–Square outlines at each heat zone help to center pots and pans.
E–Cooktop relatively cool during use.
F–Cooktop relatively cool during self-cleaning.
G–Front of cooktop relatively cool during broil.
H–Bright light (one per heat zone) shows cooktop hot during and after use.
I–Metal panel above door and top of door get very hot during self-cleaning.
J–Porcelain-enamel broil-pan insert easy to clean.
K–Recessed bake elements judged very safe.
L–Large (11-qt.) pot cannot be centered on large rear heat zone.
M–Lines across oven window affect view.
N–Storage drawer wider than most; has curved, seamless corners for easy cleaning.
O–Storage drawer smaller than others.
P–Recessed handle makes storage drawer harder to open than others.
Q–Oven light must be turned on manually.
R–Cooktop light's housing not hinged; can fall off when changing bulb.
S–Cooktop controls split.
T–No self-clean lock indicator.
U–Cooktop controls hard to remove.
V–Has well-marked oven temperature control.
W–Bake/broil combined so can't broil at less than maximum temperature.
X–Prompts not helpful.
Y–Timer can't be set below 60 sec.
Z–Cooktop controls centered.
AA–Oven controls fast, convenient.
BB–Oven irksome to set.
CC–Self-cleaning locks door automatically.
DD–Knobs contoured and comfortable but hard to remove.
EE–Cooktop controls staggered with lights; easy to use.
FF–Oven can't be calibrated by cook.
GG–No protruding self-clean latch.
HH–Dull cooktop indicator.
II–Cooktop controls clustered left.
JJ–Cooktop contains spills.
KK–Has back seam.
LL–Glass backguard.
MM–Top doesn't show fingerprints.
NN–Chrome-trimmed sides.
OO–Shallow wells.
PP–Very deep wells.
QQ–Deep drip bowls.

How to Use the Ratings

■ Read the **article** for general guidance about types and buying advice.

■ Read **Recommendations** for brand-name advice based on our tests.

■ Read the **Ratings order** to see whether products are listed in order of quality, by price, or alphabetically. Most Ratings are based on estimated quality, without regard to price.

■ Look to the **Ratings table** for specifics on the performance and features of individual models.

■ A model marked Ⓓ has been discontinued, according to the manufacturer. A model marked Ⓢ indicates that, according to the manufacturer, it has been replaced by a successor model whose performance should be similar to the tested model but whose features may vary.

MICROWAVE OVENS

RATINGS — MICROWAVE OVENS

Legend: E ⊜ VG ⊖ G ○ F ◐ P ●

▶ **See report, page 80.** From Consumer Reports, December 1992.

Recommendations: The powerful *Panasonic NN-4471A*, $180, was the best small oven for small tasks—reheating food, heating beverages, and defrosting. The best mid-sized oven was the *Sharp R-3H83*, $223. It was the easiest oven to use and its keypad was sensibly laid out. (Even though the *Sharp* has been discontinued, it may still be available.)

Ratings order: Listed by sizes; within sizes, listed in order of estimated quality based on cooking, convenience, and features. Models that performed about equally are bracketed and listed alphabetically. Price is the manufacturer's suggested retail. Ⓢ indicates tested model has been replaced by successor model; according to the manufacturer, the performance of new model should be similar to the tested model but features may vary. See page 102 for new model number and suggested retail price, if available. Ⓓ indicates model discontinued.

Brand and model	Price	Turntable	Usable capacity, cu.ft.	Power output, watts	Heating speed	Automatic defrosting	Uniformity	Overall convenience	Advantages	Disadvantages	Comments
SMALL MODELS											
Panasonic NN-4471A [1]	$180	✔	0.4	720	⊜	—	⊜	◐	C,O	—	A,B,J,L
Amana C65T Ⓢ	156	✔	0.5	610	○	⊜	○	○	D,E,F,P	—	G,L
Samsung MW3500T Ⓢ	111	✔	0.5	610	○	⊜	○	○	D,E,F,P	—	G,L,V
Sharp R-2A82B Ⓓ	146	✔	0.4	530	◐	⊜	○	○	C,D,E,K,N,R	o	A,B,C,E,K
Sears Kenmore 89215	150	✔	0.4	570	◐	●	⊜	○	A,D,F,Q,S	e,h,n	B,E,H,K,R
GE JE690T Ⓢ	136	✔	0.5	580	○	—	○	◐	A,L,P	—	D,H,L,W,X
Sanyo EM604TW	190	✔	0.4	570	◐	●	⊜	◐	A,D,F,Q,S	e,h,n	B,E,H,I,K,R
Mont. Ward KSA-8066A Ⓓ	140	✔	0.4	570	○	●	○	○	C,D,E,N,R	o	A,B,C,E,K,L
GE JEM4KW Ⓢ	179	—	0.6	590	○	—	○	○	L,P	—	D,H,I,K,R,W,X
Frigidaire MCT690N	149	✔	0.5	540	◐	○	○	◐	F,M	c,k,l,o	A,F,G,T,X
Goldstar MA670M Ⓢ	$129	✔	0.5	560	◐	⊜	○	◐	A,F,M,S	l,o,q	E,F,H,I,V
Tappan 56-2180	150	✔	0.5	540	○	○	○	◐	F,M	c,k,l,o	A,F,G,Q,T
J.C. Penney 3208 Ⓓ	120	✔	0.3	560	◐	—	○	◐	M,P,Q	a,b,g,j,m,o,p	A,D,F,L,T

[1] We also tested the **Panasonic NN-4461A**, *$136*, identical except that it lacks a Memory feature. It scored the same as this model.

Ratings continued ▶

MICROWAVE OVENS

▶ *Ratings continued*

Brand and model	Price	Turntable	Usable capacity, cu.ft.	Power output, watts	Heating speed	Automatic defrosting	Uniformity	Overall convenience	Advantages	Disadvantages	Comments
Goldstar MA550M [D]	$152	✔	0.3	560	◐	—	○	●	M,P,Q	a,b,g,j,m,o,p	A,D,F,I,V
Emerson MT3060	100	✔	0.4	600	○	●	○	◐	B,F,K,N,P	a,b,e,f,g,i,j,l,o,p	B,E,I,T,U
Whirlpool MS1065XYQ [2]	139	—	0.5	530	●	●	○	◐	A,J	o	C,G,I,R
MID-SIZED MODELS											
Sharp R-3H83 [D]	223	✔	0.7	800	◐	◐	○	◐	C,D,E,F,G,I,K,M,N,S	—	E,K,M,O,P
Panasonic NN-5652A [D]	199	✔	0.6	800	◐	◐	◐	○	A,C,F,O,P,S	a	B,E,H,I,J,K,N
GE JEM27KWH [S]	171	—	0.8	770	◐	●	◐	◐	D,E,F,H,J,L,N,P,T	—	B,D,E,H,I,P,R,S,W,X
Sears Kenmore 89626	200	✔	0.6	720	◐	◐	○	○	A,D,F,H,K,S	d,h,l	B,F,H,K,L

[2] *This model was one of three, Whirlpool informed us, that might have a faulty computer chip. A faulty chip could cause the ovens to start and run by themselves but wouldn't affect performance. The other affected models are **MS1040XYQ** and **MS1065XYR**, with serial numbers between FGB01XXXXX and FGB26XXXXX. Whirlpool will replace the faulty chip. The company's customer service number is 800-253-1301.*

Successor Models (in Ratings order)
Amana C65T is succeeded by CW65T, $179; Samsung MW3500T by MW3500TM, $175; GE JE690T by JEG92T, $150; GE JEM4KW by JEMYKWA, $165; Goldstar MA670M by MA685, $220; GE JEM 27KWH by JEM27-LWH, $195.

Features in Common
All: • Are countertop models. • Operate on full power unless programmed otherwise. • Small ovens draw 950 to 1250 watts at full power. • Mid-sized ovens draw 1250 to 1400 watts at full power. • Pause when door is opened. • Show time of day when not in use. • Beep at end of cycle and when touchpads are pressed. • Have electronic controls with touchpad entry. • Have interior light that goes on when oven is in use. • Have door that opens to the left. • Have three-prong plug with cord at least 39 in. long. • Have removable glass tray. • Have painted-metal oven cavity. • Have push-panel latch release. • Have instruction manual with cooking guide. • Are 9 to 12 in. tall, 18 to 24 in. wide, 13 to 17 in. deep. • Have usable interiors of at least 6 in. high by at least 10½ in. in diameter.
Except as noted, all: • Can be programmed for, at most, 99 min., 99 sec. • Lack moisture sensor. • Lack temperature probe. • Use power level 0 for timer. • Have white cabinet. • Have black-screened window. • Have LED display. • Have 2 to 4 cooking stages (combinations of time and power level). • Have phone-style keypad. • Have light bulb that can't be changed by user. • Have 10 power levels. • Have warranty of 1 yr. on parts and labor, 5 yr. on magnetron.

Key to Advantages
A–Display especially bright.
B–Display characters extra large.
C–No need to press Cook or Time pad before regular timed cooking.
D–Shortcut setting for timed cooking.
E–Shortcut setting can extend time.
F–User need enter only weight for Auto Defrost.
G–Moisture sensor working in tandem with Auto Reheat worked well.
H–Temperature probe worked well.
I–Times of automatic programs adjustable.
J–Cooking guide printed on oven.
K–Comes with quick-reference guide.
L–Oven beeps and display shows "End" if

MICROWAVE OVENS

food is left in oven.
M–Display shows "End" if food is left in oven.
N–Has beverage-heating feature.
O–Memory button on **Panasonic NN-4471A** and **NN-5652A** can store frequently used power/time combinations.
P–Has separate kitchen timer feature.
Q–Turntable stops in same position it started.
R–Door latch can be operated with an elbow.
S–Child lock-out feature.
T–User can change light bulb.

Key to Disadvantages

a–Uses "count-up" method for setting time; less convenient than full keypad.
b–Power levels limited to two (**Emerson**) or three (**Goldstar**, **Penney**).
c–Keys harder to press than most.
d–Keys and program entry more confusing than most.
e–Auto Defrost doesn't vary power level.
f–Can't defrost manually.
g–Lowest power setting still too high: full power more than 40 percent of the time.
h–Lowest power setting still too high: full power more than 25 percent of the time.
i–Display is dim; red letters indistinct for colorblind people.
j–Only one cooking stage.
k–Power level not displayed and can't be recalled by pressing a button.
l–Door harder to open than most.
m–Door much harder to open than most.
n–Display recessed too deeply; hard to read without stooping.
o–Oven light stays off when door is opened.
p–Can't be set to cook longer than 30 minutes at a time.
q–Popcorn feature performed poorly.

Key to Comments

A–Black-on-gray LCD display; can't be seen in the dark.
B–Automatic cooking or reheating programs.
C–Quick or Special Defrost; user sets time; oven varies power level.
D–Has separate Defrost button with preset power level.
E–Popcorn feature.
F–Keep-warm feature.
G–Delay Start feature.
H–Delay Start uses timer or 0 power level; less convenient than setting actual start time.
I–White-screened window.
J–Six power levels.
K–No vents on top or sides; can be mounted flush with wall or kitchen cabinet.
L–Wood-grain cabinet.
M–Gray cabinet.
N–Calorie-calculator feature.
O–Beep signal can be turned off.
P–Numeric keys in two rows.
Q–Leaked microwaves when we intentionally caught a paper towel in the door, but still within FDA's safety limits.
R–Has optional kit for mounting under counter or cabinet.
S–Trim kit available for mounting oven within cabinetry.
T–2-yr. parts warranty.
U–7-yr. magnetron warranty.
V–8-yr. magnetron warranty.
W–10-yr. magnetron warranty.
X–In-home warranty service.

About Prices in the Buying Guide

Prices for most products have been updated for the Buying Guide. The prices we give, unless otherwise noted, are approximate or suggested retail as quoted by the manufacturer. Discounts may be substantial, especially for electronics and camera equipment.

DISHWASHERS

RATINGS DISHWASHERS

Better ← → Worse

▶ **See report, page 89.** From Consumer Reports, October 1993.

Recommendations: We judged the three Euromodels excellent, but we think you'll get much more for your money with one of the conventional models judged very good. Consider first the *Maytags* and the *KitchenAids* (as well as the *In-Sink-Erator*, a close relative). There is little of importance to choose among the five machines, save for price and noise level. You needn't limit yourself to the model listed. The Ratings also note models with similar wash systems, which are likely to wash much like the tested machines but whose features and noise levels may vary.

Ratings order: Within type, listed in order of overall performance. Price for the tested and similar models are from a national survey, except where marked with a * (price CU paid) or a ** (suggested list). **Notes to table:** Overall performance reflects all judged attributes, with washing the most important. The washing, energy consumption, and water use rating is based on performance using the Normal cycle. Ⓓ indicates model discontinued.

Brand and model	Price	Overall performance score	Washing	Noise	Energy	Water use, gal.	Cycle time, min.	Models with similar wash systems	Comments
CONVENTIONAL MODELS									
Maytag DWU9200AAX	$470	76	⊖	⊖	⊖	10.0	85	DWU7400AAX, $405; DWU7500AAX, $470; DWU9905AAX, $520; DWU9920AAX, $510	D,L,N,R,Z,AA, JJ,KK,LL,MM
Maytag DWU9920AAX Ⓓ	510	76	⊖	⊖	⊖	10.0	85	DWU7400AAX, $405; DWU7500AAX, $470; DWU9905AAX, $520; DWU9200AAX, $470	D,K,L,N,R,AA, BB,CC,DD,JJ, KK,LL,MM
KitchenAid KUDS230Y	635	75	⊖	⊖	⊖	7.5	85	KUDA230Y, $680; KUDD230Y, $400; KUDH230Y, $485; KUDP230Y, $540; KUDJ230Y, $475	N,R,W,DD,NN, OO,PP,QQ,LL RR
KitchenAid KUDJ230Y	475	71	⊖	○	⊖	7.5	85	KUDA230Y, $680; KUDD230Y, $400; KUDH230Y, $485; KUDP230Y, $540; KUDS230Y, $635	N,R,Z,NN,OO, PP,RR
In-Sink-Erator WS400	425	69	⊖	◖	⊖	7.5	85	WS-SUP, $540; WS-3000, $500	F,N,S,Z,NN,PP, RR
Sears Kenmore 15815	480	67	⊖	○	○	11.0	75	15715, $460**; 16711, $430; 16715, $450; 16755, $400; 16815, $520; 16911, $600; 16915, $570	D,F,L,U,V,AA, BB,CC,DD,FF, LL,MM,OO,PP, QQ,RR

DISHWASHERS

Brand and model	Price	Overall performance score	Washing	Noise	Energy	Water use, gal.	Cycle time, min.	Models with similar wash systems	Comments
Whirlpool DU9400XY [D]	$455	66	◒	○	◒	9.5	80	DU8700XY, $380; DU8750XY, $385; DU8900XY, $440; DU8950XY, $460; DU9450XY, $495; DU9700XY, $550**	D,F,K,N,Q,U,V, AA,BB,DD,GG, MM,OO,QQ,RR, UU
Sears Kenmore 16755	400	64	◒	○	○	11.0	75	15715, $460**; 15815, $480; 16711, $430; 6715, $450; 16815, $520; 16911, $600; 16915, $570	D,F,G,J,L,U,V, Y,Z,AA,LL,OO, QQ,RR,TT
Whirlpool DU8900XY [D]	440	63	◒	○	◒	9.5	80	DU8700XY, $380; DU8750XY, $385; DU8950XY, $460; DU9400XY, $455; DU9450XY, $495; DU9700XY, $550**	D,F,G,J,L,Q,U, V,Y,Z,AA,MM, OO,PP,QQ,RR, UU,
General Electric GSD2800S	470	61	◒	◒	◐	12.5	90	GSD1250R, $420*	D,J,K,N,Y,AA, BB,CC,DD,FF, JJ,LL,MM
Caloric DUS600WW	340	61	◒	○	○	12.5	90	DUS900, $570**	D,J,Q,U,Y,Z, JJ,LL,MM
General Electric GSD1250R [D]	420	59	◒	○	◐	12.5	115	GSD2800S, $470	D,J,L,U,Y,Z,JJ, LL,MM
Amana DU6000BR	420	59	◒	◐	◒	12.5	90	DU9010W/B, $500	J,L,Y,Z,DD,JJ, LL,MM
White-Westinghouse SU770NXR1 [D]	290	51	○	○	◒	10.5	95	—	D,J,L,Q,U,Z, LL,RR
Sears Kenmore 15745	420	51	○	○	◐	12.0	95	15515, $340**; 16715, $300	D,N,U,V,Z,QQ, RR,TT
Tappan (M. Ward) 61-1082-10 [D]	330	48	◐	◐	○	10.0	90	—	D,U,V,Z,LL,MM, QQ
Hotpoint HDA400S [D]	290	30	◐	◐	○	13.0	90	HD750S, $320	A,J,U,Z,JJ, MM,PP,VV
Roper WU5750Y2	285	30	●	◐	◒	9.0	85	—	B,D,G,J,T,U,Z, AA,EE,MM,SS
EUROMODELS									
General Electric Monogram ZBD4300SWH	930	85	◒	◒	◒	7.0	85	ZBD4100SBK, $1050**	C,E,J,L,N,R,Y, Z,AA,HH,KK,OO, QQ,RR
Asko Premier 1303	750	81	◒	◒	◒	5.5	65	Superior 1473, $880; Excellence 1503, $980	C,F,H,I,M,O,P, X,Z,AA,RR
Miele G572u	1000	80	◒	◒	◒	8.5	90	G572i, $1000; G590 u or i, $1250	C,T,X,Z,AA,II, RR

Ratings continued ▶

106 DISHWASHERS

Features in Common
All: • Have Heavy, Normal, and Light wash cycles (at least) plus a Rinse-and-Hold cycle. • Have Rinse-conditioner dispenser.
Except as noted, all have: • Have a self-cleaning filter or soil separator. • Have a flatware basket in lower rack. • Have push buttons and/or dials. • Have fold-down section(s) in upper rack for loading in two tiers. • Exposed elements (under lower rack) to heat water to 140F, when necessary. • Reversible front panels with up to four colors and capability to accept customer panels. • Plastic tub and door liner. • Parts/labor warranty of one year (10 years, tub/line).
Euromodels have: Stainless-steel tub and door liner.

Key to Comments
A–No filter or soil separator.
B–Filter required cleaning, every cycle.
C–Filter required occasional cleaning.
D–Cycle start can be delayed 2 to 12 hrs.
E–Requires custom door panels.
F–Cannot fit large plates, cutting boards, as easily as others.
G–First fill often shortened when advancing dial to start position (difficult to avoid on **Roper**).
H–Steamy after cycle ended.
I–Childproof door latch.
J–Detergent dumped when cycle reset.
K–Did not restart after electrical interruption.
L–Limited second year warranty.
M–2-yr. parts and labor warranty.
N–Limited 2- to 5-yr. warranty, some parts.
O–Limited 3- to 5-yr. warranty, some parts.
P–Limited 3- to 10-yr. warranty, tub and door liners.
Q–Limited 2- to 10-yr. warranty, tub and door liners.
R–20-yr. or more full warranty, tub and door liners.
S–Limited lifetime warranty, tub and door liners.
T–1-yr. full warranty only.
U–Plastic interior was stained in testing.
V–Utensil basket(s).
W–Hidden heating element; safer.
X–Cannot accept custom panel and lacks other color panels.
Y–Has china/crystal cycle.
Z–Push buttons and/or dial.
AA–Rinse-aid dispenser indicator.
BB–Electronic controls.
CC–Time displayed.
DD–Cycle reset slow.
EE–Fits large platters.
FF–Malfunctions displayed.
GG–No progress indication.
HH–Cycle reset slow, complex.
II–Some upper-rack supports fold.
JJ–Terraced upper rack so large platters fit underneath.
KK–Lower rack has fold-down shelf.
LL–Flatware-basket cover.
MM–Center tower.
NN–Porcelain tub.
OO–Upper rack adjusts.
PP–No upper-rack shelf.
QQ–Some upper or lower-rack tines fold and/or remove.
RR–Middle spray-arm.
SS–Two small flatware baskets; no handles.
TT–Flatware basket has awkward handle.
UU–Flatware rack on door; poor for cleaning.
VV–Flatware basket broke in tests.

ABOUT THE REPAIR HISTORIES

Thousands of readers tell us about their repair experiences with autos, appliances, and electronic items on the Annual Questionnaire. Using that unique information can improve your chances of getting a trouble-free car, washing machine, TV set, or other product. See the automobile Frequency-of-Repair charts starting on page 178 and the brand Repair Histories starting on page 365.

WASHING MACHINES

RATINGS WASHING MACHINES

Better ← → Worse
◉ ⊜ ○ ◐ ●

▶ **See report, page 91.** From Consumer Reports, November 1993.

Recommendations: The four top-loaders can do a lot of wash at a time, and do it well. And although they're wasteful of water and energy with small washes, they're reasonably efficient with full loads. The *Sears Kenmore 22841* delivered the cleanest washes but the trick is to use its Heavy Duty cycle. Consider the front-loading *White Westinghouse LT350R* only if water use is exceedingly critical or space limitations force stacking a dryer on the washer. The *Asko* is thoughtfully engineered and ecologically progressive compact washer but, at $1350, very expensive.

Ratings order: Listed by type; within type, listed in order of estimated quality. Price is the estimated average, based on prices paid nationally in late 1993. ⑤ indicates tested model has been replaced by successor model; according to the manufacturer, the performance of new model should be similar to the tested model but features may vary. See below for new model number and suggested retail price. ⑩ indicates model discontinued.

Brand and model	Price	Washing ability	Capacity	Water efficiency	Water extraction	Unbalanced loads	Noise	Ease of use	Servicing	Advantages	Disadvantages	Comments
TOP LOADERS												
KitchenAid KAWE860W	$555	⊜	◉	○	○	○	⊜	◉	⊜	B,C,K,L,P	f,i	E,I,J,L,Q,R,U,V,W
Whirlpool LSC9355A	500	⊜	◉	○	○	○	⊜	◉	⊜	C,J,K,L	f	H,J,L,P,Q,R,U,W
GE WWA8850R ⑩	395	○	◐	◉	○	○	⊜	⊜	●	B,C,I,K	—	H,J,M,O,Q,W,AA

■ *The following model was judged better than any other on its heavy-duty cycle, but worse than any other on its normal cycle. Scores are for Normal (on top) and Heavy Duty Cycle (on bottom).*

Sears Kenmore 22841	440	◐ / ⊜	⊜ / ⊜	◉ / ◐	⊜ / ⊜	○ / ○	○ / ○	⊜ / ⊜	⊜ / ⊜	A,B,C	g,k	H,K,L,P,Q,R,U,X
FRONT LOADERS												
ASKO 20003 ⑤	1,350	⊜	●	⊜	⊜	⊜	⊜	⊜	●	D,E,F,G,H,L,N,O	c,e,f,j	A,B,C,D,F,N,S,T,Y
White Westinghouse LT350R	650	○	◐	⊜	○	⊜	⊜	◐	●	J,M,O,P	a,b,d,f,h,j	B,G,M,R,Z

Successor Model
Asko 20003 is succeeded by 20004, $1350.

Features in Common
All: • Have variable water level controls. • Provide at least two agitation and spin speeds. • Are warranted for 1 year for parts and labor. *Except as noted, all:* • Operate on 120 volts. • Have bleach dispensers. • Have porcelain coated steel tub. • Have fabric softener dispensers. • Have instructions for use on bottom of lid. • Have automatic lint removal. • Have a lip on top to contain minor spills. • Have a max. drain height requirement of 72 in. • Cabinet tops and lids are painted. • Agitation and spin speeds are automatically chosen by selection of cycle or fabric.

WASHING MACHINES

Key to Advantages
A–Selectable electronic temperature control; can blend hot and cold water to a pre-set temperature.
B–Porcelain top and lid.
C–Has self adjusting legs at rear.
D–Has countdown timer to show remaining time for cycle.
E–Spin speed is adjustable from 600 to 1500 RPM.
F–Can set warm/hot wash water temperature in 5 degree increments between 30-95 degrees C (86-203 degrees F).
G–Has automatic detergent dispenser.
H–Softener dispenser much easier to use and clean than others.
I–Bleach dispenser judged better than others.
J–Has end-of-cycle signal.
K–Has automatic extra-rinse setting.
L–Has an automatic pre-wash cycle that goes into the regular cycle.
M–Has tub light.
N–Automatically adjusts water level.
O–Less lint than with others.
P–Removes sand better than others.

Key to Disadvantages
a–Coins accidentally left in with clothes can get caught in machine, requiring service.
b–Unit will spill water on floor if too much detergent is accidentally used.
c–Takes substantially more time than others for a cycle.
d–No bleach or fabric softener dispenser.
e–No bleach dispenser; chlorine bleach not recommended by manufacturer.
f–Lacks lip on top to help contain spills.
g–Lid does not open fully to lie flat; access from the left is hampered.
h–Cycle dial more difficult to use than others.
i–More cluttered and unclear markings on dial than others.
j–Lacks instructions on machine.
k–Does not remove sand as well as others.

Key to Comments
A–Electronic controls.
B–Door locks during operation.
C–Stainless steel inner and outer tub with extended warranty.
D–Electronic controls warranty extended to 5 years not incl. labor.
E–All parts warranted for two years.
F–All water or electrical distribution parts warranted for 3 yr. w/o labor.
G–All drive parts warranted for 5 yrs w/o labor.
H–Transmission parts warranted for 5 years w/o labor.
I–Transmission parts warranted for 10 years w/o labor.
J–Transmission warranty covers all parts.
K–Transmission warranty covers some parts.
L–Agitator has slots under vanes; readers have complained it snags laundry, did not happen during our tests.
M–Machine can be installed to a 96 in. drain height.
N–Machine can be installed to between 15 3/4 and 35 1/2 in. drain height.
O–User must clean lint filter.
P–Controls judged better than others for visually impaired users.
Q–Warm rinse available with hot wash.
R–Warm rinse available with warm wash.
S–Has delay start.
T–Requires 208/240 volts.
U–Washer tub warranted for 10 years not including labor.
V–Rust warranted for 5 years not including labor.
W–Lid opens back.
X–Lid opens left.
Y–Lid opens right.
Z–Lid opens down.
AA–Has separate wash/rinse speed selector.

ABOUT PRICES IN THE BUYING GUIDE

Prices for most products have been updated for the Buying Guide. The prices we give, unless otherwise noted, are approximate or suggested retail as quoted by the manufacturer. Discounts may be substantial, especially for electronics and camera equipment.

CLOTHES DRYERS

RATINGS **CLOTHES DRYERS**

E ⊜ VG ⊖ G ○ F ◐ P ●

▶ **See report, page 93.** From Consumer Reports, July 1993.

Recommendations: As in our 1992 report, the electric and gas *Maytags* (now with successor models, noted below) and the fancier *Sears* model, the *61951* this time proved the best dryers. But the top models from those brands tend to be expensive. All the tested models did a perfectly good job drying ordinary loads. Differences amount to noise level, cycle temperatures, and flexibility of controls. Choose among the rated dryers primarily on the basis of type (gas or electric) and price.

Ratings order: Listed by types; within types, listed in order of estimated quality. Price is the estimated average, based on prices paid in mid-1993. Ⓢ indicates tested model has been replaced by successor model; according to the manufacturer, the performance of new model should be similar to the tested model but features may vary. See below for new model number and suggested retail price, if available. Ⓓ indicates model discontinued.

Brand and model	Price	Drum volume	Mixed load (lg.)	Mixed load (sm.)	Permanent-press	Delicate fabrics	Noise	Convenience	Advantages	Disadvantages	Comments
ELECTRIC DRYERS											
Maytag LDE9900BC Ⓢ	$575	⊖	⊖	⊖	⊖	⊖	⊖	⊖	B,C,D,G	h,i	E,G,J,L,Q
Sears 61951	750	⊖	⊖	⊖	⊖	○	⊖	⊖	A,D,E,G	d	D,K,M,S
Sears 62931	600	⊖	⊖	⊖	⊖	○	⊖	⊖	E,G	a,d,e	A,B,S
Whirlpool LE9800XS	499	⊖	⊖	⊖	⊖	○	○	⊖	A,G	g,i	F,I,Q
KitchenAid KEYE860W	499	⊖	⊖	⊖	⊖	○	○	⊖	C,G	e,i,j	A,B,C,F,I, L,O,R
Amana LE4807 Ⓓ	440	⊖	⊖	⊖	⊖	○	○	⊖	B,D,E,F,G	f	C,E,H,N,S
General Electric DDE9500R Ⓢ	375	⊖	⊖	⊖	⊖	○	⊖	⊖	F	b,c,f,h	A,G,P,S
GAS DRYERS											
Maytag LDG9900BA Ⓢ	670	⊖	⊖	⊖	⊖	⊖	⊖	⊖	B,C,D,G	h,i	E,G,J,L,Q
Sears 72931	640	⊖	⊖	⊖	⊖	○	⊖	⊖	E,G	a,d,e	A,B,S
Whirlpool LG9801XS	499	⊖	⊖	⊖	⊖	○	○	⊖	A,G	g,i	F,I,Q
General Electric DDG9580R Ⓢ	385	⊖	○	⊖	⊖	⊖	○	⊖	F	b,c,f,h	A,G,J,P,S

Successor Models (in Ratings order)
Maytag LDE9900BC is succeeded by LDE9904, $640; General Electric DDE9500R by DDE9600R, $415; Maytag LDG9900BA by LDG9904, $670; General Electric DDG9580R by DDG9680R, $465.

Ratings continued ▶

110 CLOTHES DRYERS

Features in Common
All have: • Moisture sensor to gauge dryness during automatic drying cycles. • Automatic dryness-control cycles for Regular, Permanent Press, and Delicate fabrics. • No-heat setting. • Timed cycle with at least 60 min. drying time. • Drum light. • 4 leveling legs. • No power cord or plug included.
Except as noted, all have: Electronic controls with touchpads. • Automatic controls able to recognize already-dry loads and turn off dryer within 20 to 40 min. • Provision for choosing extended tumble period after automatic cycle. • Wrinkle Remove feature. • End-of-cycle signal, 2 to 5 sec. long, that can be adjusted or turned off. • Baked-enamel finish on cabinet top and drum. • Raised edge on top to contain spills. • Door that opens down. • Width of 28½ to 29 in. • Lint filter removable from inside the drum. • Drying rack, which can be placed in drum for drying without tumbling. • Ability to vent from rear, bottom, left, and right sides. • 1-yr. parts/labor warranty.

Key to Advantages
A–Automatic dryness control recognized already-dry loads and turned off dryer much sooner than most.
B–Automatic dryness control recognized already-dry loads and turned off dryer sooner than most.
C–Porcelain-coated top.
D–Programmable cycle memory.
E–Console light; makes controls easier to use.
F–Lint filter can be viewed and cleaned without removal.
G–Signals when lint filter is blocked.

Key to Disadvantages
a–Automatic dryness control failed to recognize already-dry loads and turn off dryer within 40 min.
b–Permanent-press "less dry" cycle begins in cooldown (no heat).
c–No drying rack.
d–Flap over lint-filter compartment may conceal absence of filter.
e–End-of-cycle signal judged too short (about 1 sec.).
f–End-of-cycle signal judged too long (more than 30 sec.).
g–End-of-cycle signal cannot be adjusted for loudness.
h–Drum light dimmer than most.
i–No raised edge on top of cabinet.
j–No-heat cycle limited to 20 mins.

Key to Comments
A–Rotary-timer dial instead of electronic control.
B–Dial provides continuous range of heat control in all cycles.
C–Extended-tumble period after automatic cycles cannot be turned off. **Amana** also has no "wrinkle remove" feature (but feature can be simulated).
D–Has additional cycles for towels and denim.
E–"Clean filter" message reminder lights up when machine is turned on.
F–Lint filter can be removed from top of cabinet.
G–Door opens to the right.
H–Door can be adjusted to open right or left.
I–Vents only from rear.
J–Can be vented to rear, left, or bottom.
K–Clothes hanger provided; mounts on cabinet.
L–2-yr. parts warranty.
M–3-yr. parts/labor warranty.
N–5-yr. parts/labor warranty.
O–5-yr. electrical element/cabinet assembly warranty.
P–5-yr. drum warranty.
Q–5-yr. electronic controls warranty.
R–10-yr. drum warranty.
S–27 in. wide.

ABOUT THE REPAIR HISTORIES

Thousands of readers tell us about their repair experiences with autos, appliances, and electronic items on the Annual Questionnaire. Using that unique information can improve your chances of getting a trouble-free car, washing machine, TV set, or other product. See the automobile Frequency-of-Repair charts starting on page 178 and the brand Repair Histories starting on page 365.

Small appliances

Food processors	111
Blenders	113
Portable mixers	115
Coffee appliances	117
Toasters & toaster ovens	119
Juicers & juice extractors	120
Slow-cookers	122
Pressure cookers	123
Indoor grills	124
Ratings	126

Beyond the novelty appliances and the trendsetters like food processors, small appliances didn't attract a lot of interest until the late '80s. That's when new designs gave new interest to coffee makers, blenders, mixers, and other previously boring small appliances.

The trend began in the early 1970s when Krups, the German appliance maker, redesigned the automatic drip coffeemaker pioneered by Mr. Coffee. Krups and another German company, Braun, have since redesigned small motorized kitchen items, creating new subtypes of appliances (such as handheld blenders) with a sleekly styled European look.

At the same time, a "retro" look has developed a following, notably with blenders and toasters styled in the chrome and colors of the 1950s.

Food processors

▶ **Ratings on page 128.**   ▶ **Guide to food fixers on page 116.**

Food processors, introduced by Cuisinarts Co. two decades ago, easily chop vegetables for a soup or stew. They also make quick work of salad fixings like onions, mushrooms, and cucumbers, and they're handy for such baking chores as crumbling graham crackers for a cheesecake crust and mixing pastry dough.

FOOD PROCESSORS

But for mashing potatoes or whipping cream, an electric mixer is preferable. And for liquefying foods, pureeing baby food, and concocting exotic drinks, nothing tops a standard countertop blender (see the chart on page 116).

The choices

Compact vs. full-sized. Food processors come in compact and full-sized versions, which vary widely in size. Since one manufacturer's "compact" may have a larger processing bowl than another's "full-size," we created our own definitions. Those we consider full-sized have a bowl that holds between 5¼ and 12¼ cups of food when filled to the brim. Price: around $35 to $300. Compacts, priced from around $30 to $95, hold from 2½ to 4¼ cups. Even by that measure of capacity, some compacts are taller than full-sized models.

Compact models demand a bit less kitchen space, and they're easy to lift and clean. If you need more quantity than a compact can handle, you can just make another batch. Full-sized processors are useful if you're an active chef with an ambitious menu or regularly make large meals.

Minis and shooters. Variations on the basic food-processor theme also exist. Miniature food choppers, which are priced from $20 to $35, chop, grind, and puree in small quantities—half a cup or so at a time. They cannot, however, slice or shred. Another option, the salad gun, is essentially a feed tube equipped with a motorized cone that holds a slicing or shredding blade. Though simple to clean and move around, these relatively inexpensive devices (starting at less than $30) tend to be less convenient and much less effective or versatile than a food processor.

Features and conveniences

Chute. With most machines, sliced or shredded food simply drops into a bowl, which must be emptied when full. Other machines use various means to keep food from filling the bowl: a separate chute you can attach to divert the flow of food, or a device that can "sling" food out of the bowl through an opening in the lid, into another container.

Bowl. All food processors have a transparent plastic work bowl, most with a convenient handle. Bowls can hold more dry food than liquids. Once filled to capacity with a thin liquid, a bowl will usually leak when the machine is processing.

Blades and disks. An S-shaped metal chopping blade and a slicing/shredding disk are standard. Some models have separate slicing and shredding disks. Additional attachments, either standard or optional, include thin and thick slicing/shredding disks, a cheese-grating disk, and a disk for cutting french fries. Attachments such as a plastic whipping accessory for cream, or a plastic dough-mixing blade are less worthwhile.

Feed tube and pusher. With most models, you slice or shred food by inserting it into a feed tube on the bowl's lid, with the help of a plastic pusher if need be. With some models, you have to trim food so it will fit in the tube. On a couple of models, the tube is big enough to swallow a medium-sized tomato and incorporates a slender tube for thin foods.

Controls and safety. For safety reasons, no food processor can be turned on unless lid and bowl are latched. Most compacts and all full-sized models have an On/off switch and a Pulse provision, which keeps the machine running as long as you depress a switch.

Some processors have touchpad controls instead of switches; others start whenever you move the lid in and out of a latch on the housing. On some models the switching mechanism may be part of the handle, an inconvenience that makes it easy to turn on the machine continuously instead of pulsing and vice versa.

One speed is all you should need for food processing. And that's what you'll find on all compacts and most full-sized models. Multiple speeds or variable speed controls are overkill.

Cleaning and storage. Machines with clean lines and no food-trapping gaps are easiest to clean. Tough to clean: large, convoluted feed tubes. Most components are dishwasher-washable. Be sure to place them on the top rack, away from the heating element. And don't let blades soak in water overnight—they may rust.

The tests

To judge the processors, we spend hundreds of hours chopping, slicing, shredding, and mixing more than 30 different foods. Our heavy-duty tasks include chopping, whipping, blending, and pureeing various foods. To judge grinding, we crush peanuts, graham crackers, and beef cubes. For the chopping and slicing tasks, we use carrots and prosciutto, among other foods. We follow manufacturers' suggestions but also experiment to get the best results.

Buying advice

Most people who own a food processor probably don't use it very often. If you're not an enthusiastic cook and don't make food for a crowd, a compact model should fill the bill nicely. But when you need to chop, puree, mix, or slice on a grand scale, you may be glad to have a full-sized processor around. A busy cook or baker of bread is best off with a full-sized model.

You needn't pay top dollar. Processors that come with a Cadillac price, such as the *Cuisinart* and *Waring Professional*, may be big and hefty, powerful, quiet, and well-appointed, but we found that less expensive models work quite well and may be more convenient.

Blenders

▶ **Ratings on page 126.** ▶ **Guide to food fixers on page 116.**

Blenders began gaining acceptance in the '30s, when Stephen J. Poplawski developed a gadget designed to make his favorite drink, the malted milk shake. Standard blenders today are much like their Depression-era prototypes, but innovative designs are reshaping the market.

The choices

Handheld models. In just a few years, sleek handheld models have emerged to challenge the traditional blender, capturing about a third of total sales. The original handheld models consisted of just the mixing apparatus, which you plunge into liquid in a glass or pitcher.

Handheld hybrids consist of a container that holds food or drink and a cylindrical hand grip with the motor housing inside and a blade shaft at the other end. A handheld model weighs only a couple of pounds, so it's fairly easy to maneuver. It's also convenient to use, since the blended food or drink may be eaten or sipped from the container. Handheld models are easy to clean by simply holding the blades under hot running water.

The handhelds are ideally suited to mixing drinks. Fitted with special attachments, a handheld model can also do such tasks as chop nuts and grind cheese. Prices range from about $20 to $80.

114 BLENDERS

Standard models. The standard blender—a mixing pitcher with a rotating blade driven by a motor in the pitcher's base—is more powerful than the handheld variety and hence more versatile. Besides mixing liquids, it can blend or chop some solid foods, grind peanuts into peanut butter, grate cheese, and make gazpacho. Standard models also boast more features than handheld models—generally a wide choice of speeds (the handheld ones usually offer only one or two), Pulse, and a continuously variable speed. Prices range from $20 to $150.

Features and conveniences

Controls. Fewer controls make cleaning the base easier and simplify operation. Handheld models are usually limited to one or two speeds—enough for mixing liquids. Especially handy is a continuously variable speed. On standard models, look for a wide range of speeds, not a lot of speed selections; a half-dozen speeds are enough for most chores. Pulse, which keeps the blades whirring only as long as you depress the control, is especially useful when it works with more than one speed. Most models have buttons, but more expensive ones boast touchpad controls, which should be a breeze to clean. A few models have a sliding-speed control with a lighted display.

Containers. Markings that aid measuring are an obvious convenience. Wide-mouth containers make cleaning and loading food easy. Handheld blenders come with plastic containers; standard models use plastic or glass. Plastic is lighter than glass but may not hold up as well in the dishwasher. Blend-and-store containers minimize cleanup.

Storage. Short or coiled cords are easy to store. Handheld units are small enough to fit into a drawer. A design that lets you stand the device on its head makes temporary storage easy; a rack makes long-term storage easy.

Accessories. Interchangeable blades extend the usefulness of handheld models beyond mixing liquids, making it possible to mince, whip, blend, beat, and chop.

The tests

We put all the blenders through a series of trials: whipping cream and blending diet drinks, milk shakes, and gazpacho soup. With the heftier standard blenders, we judge their prowess at grating Parmesan cheese and grinding peanuts into butter.

We also test for electrical leakage by spilling milk onto the base of each standard blender and then taking current readings at three points on the base.

Buying advice

A handheld model lets you mix and serve in the same container. If you make a lot of foamy drinks, it's your best choice. If your blending tasks go beyond merely mixing liquids, consider a standard blender. Differences among standard models tend to be slight, so let convenience, features, and price guide your choice.

ABOUT PRICES IN THE BUYING GUIDE

Prices for most products have been updated for the Buying Guide. The prices we give, unless otherwise noted, are approximate or suggested retail as quoted by the manufacturer. Discounts may be substantial, especially for electronics and camera equipment.

Portable mixers

▶ **Guide to food fixers on page 116.**

Portable mixers have earned a permanent place in the kitchen because of their convenience and versatility. Lightweight mixers excel at blending cake batter, mashing potatoes, and whipping cream. Heftier versions, introduced in recent years, can even handle bread dough.

Portable mixers come in plug-in or cordless (battery-powered) versions. Beyond that, models differ in three aspects: the power of the motor, the number of speeds, and the number of beaters.

The choices

Plug-in models. An unadorned, basic mixer selling for as little as $15 at discount, offers three to five speeds and interchangeable beaters. A new breed of muscular mixers is just a half-step down from powerful stand mixers, which are expensive and take up a lot of space. The advantage of a strong motor lies in its ability to keep the beaters turning through the stickiest dough, a challenge that could burn out a lesser machine. A special power-boost switch on some models often provides the extra muscle needed. The fancier models have price tags of up to $55.

Cordless models. Cordless mixers free you from the outlet box but when not in use, they must be kept on a charging base that's plugged into an outlet. Package claims suggest that cordless units pack lots of power. They don't. They're also expensive. Prices range from $35 to $70.

For choosing the right appliance for the task, see the chart on page 116.

Features and conveniences

Most portables weigh between 1¾ and 2¼ pounds. With time-consuming tasks, heavier models may begin to feel leaden. Too light a mixer, though, may lack muscle. In any event, a comfortable handle makes weight easier to bear.

Speeds. Though many models offer a generous number of speeds or even continuously variable speed, we've found that three well-spaced settings—slow, intermediate, and fast—are all you need. The slower the slow speed, in fact, the better to reduce the inevitable spattering.

Thumbwheel speed controls are more difficult to set than the typical On/off speed switch. It's better if the control is located toward the front of the handle; that way you can hold the mixer and adjust the speed singlehandedly. Look for a switch that's clearly labeled, located on top of the handle, and that can move sequentially from Off to Slow, Medium, and High.

Beaters. For most chores, beater shape doesn't much matter; for whipping cream, however, a wire whisk is best.

More important is the number of beaters: Some cordless models have only one beater and don't mix food as well as those models that have two.

Besides the basic beaters, some mixers come with such useful extras as a dough hook or a balloon whisk.

In general, stainless-steel whisks or wire beaters tend to be easier to clean and more corrosion-resistant than conventional chrome-coated ones.

Storage. A mixer with its beaters in place should be balanced enough to stand solidly on a countertop. Mixers with a narrow heel rest provide little stability.

A plug-in mixer doesn't take much space in a drawer or cupboard. Many mixers can be wall-mounted. Some models have clips on the housing to hold the beaters. A cordless model needs room near an outlet for the charging base.

Buying advice

If you bake, consider a powerful plug-in model, perhaps even a stand mixer. Although some portable mixers can manage dough, it takes quite a firm grip on the mixers to keep the dough hooks from recoiling. Many routine tasks leave cordless mixers wheezing.

Spending $50 on a mixer isn't necessary if you use it just to mash potatoes once in a while. For occasional use, a conventional plug-in portable will do nicely.

BUYING THE RIGHT FOOD FIXER

Not all food-fixers are equally adept at all chores. Here are the chores where the typical blender, handheld blender, portable mixer, stand mixer, and food processor stand out.

	Standard blender	Handheld blender	Portable mixer	Stand mixer	Food processor
Pureeing vegetables	✔				✔
Blending mayonnaise	✔				✔
Mixing frozen drinks	✔				
Making milk shakes	✔	✔			
Whipping cream			✔	✔	
Mashing potatoes			✔		
Mixing cake batter			✔	✔	
Mixing pie crust					✔
Mixing cookie dough				✔	✔
Kneading bread dough				✔	✔
Crumbling crackers					✔
Chopping, shredding, slicing vegetables					✔
Chopping parsley					✔
Grating Parmesan	✔				✔

Coffee appliances

Americans consume about one-third of all the coffee grown in the world—the equivalent of some 400 million cups a day. While some devotees boil their brew in a pot or swear by a percolator, the appliance of choice is a drip-style maker—usually an electric model.

Mr. Coffee pioneered the automatic drip machine in 1973. Now, two decades later, Krups, a European appliance manufacturer, and other European companies have transformed the coffee-maker into an appliance that is functional and yet has a sleekly styled European look.

Part of the coffee mystique holds that you can't make great coffee or espresso without grinding your own beans. Coffee grinders range from slim little choppers to coffee mills that are nearly as tall as a drip coffee-maker.

Drip coffee-makers

Among drip-style makers, there are two types: manual and electric. Both brew the same way.

The choices

Electric. Most automatic-drip machines have four parts: a water tank, a basket to hold filter and coffee, a carafe to catch the drippings, and a hot plate to keep the carafe's contents warm. Electric circuitry in the machine's base heats the water and hot plate. To brew a pot, you pour a measured amount of cold tap water into the tank and flip a switch.

Electric models come in various capacities, from junior-sized four-cuppers to full-sized machines that can brew 12 cups at once. List prices start at around $30.

Manual. The simplest manual-drip brewers basically consist of a cone, to hold the paper filter and coffee, and a glass carafe. To brew, you pour boiling water over the coffee. Price: $15 at most.

Features and conveniences

Carafe. The carafes that come with most drip coffee-makers are glass and are dishwasher-washable. That's important, because to make good-tasting coffee, the carafe must be kept squeaky clean.

Some carafes come with a glass-lined thermal carafe that doubles as a serving pitcher—no need to leave the carafe in place to keep the contents warm. An insulated carafe, however, is more delicate and therefore tougher to keep clean than a glass one. Some carafes have cup markings to help measure water.

Basket. With a basket that's attached to the coffee-maker, you needn't fiddle with hot grounds before you can serve the coffee—as you must with a basket that sits atop the carafe.

'Drip stop.' This keeps the last few drops from splashing on the hot plate when you remove the carafe.

Clock/timer. This automatically shuts off the hot plate. With some models, this feature automatically resumes brewing at the same time the next day, but we don't think it's a good idea since grounds in a coffee-maker will lose flavor overnight.

Features of questionable worth. Some heating systems say they lessen the need for descaling—purging the buildup of minerals in the coffee-maker's tank and tubes. A solution of water and vinegar does that job nicely. Nor do we see much point in brew-strength control to vary the potency of the coffee—it's quite enough to vary the amount of coffee used.

Buying advice

A coffee-maker should turn out consistently good-tasting brew. Most do that. Better models are also a pleasure to use.

Manual-drip coffee-makers can turn out a decent cup of coffee and list for $15 or less. Although less convenient, a manual coffee-maker is worth considering if you're short on counter space or simply want to minimize appliances.

Coffee grinders

There are two basic types of grinders: choppers and coffee mills.

The choices

Choppers. This type dominates. It's cylindrical in shape, and has a whirling blade that sits inside a small covered cup. Choppers are priced about $15 to $30.

Coffee mills. These grind the beans between a pair of wheels. They're somewhat bigger than choppers and are priced about $45 to $150.

Basic differences are in capacity, grinding speed, and operation.

Choppers can usually process enough beans in 15 seconds or less to make eight cups of drip-grind coffee. The mills are slower, typically taking 30 to 60 seconds; they're slower, since the beans must travel through the grinding wheels.

Anyone who has owned a coffee mill will vividly remember the racket it makes. A minute of a mill's noise is reason enough to consider a chopper.

Minor spills of grinds are inevitable. With a chopper, you use the lid to pour beans directly into the coffee-maker. Mills tend to be a bit messier than choppers, in part because you have to remove the ground-coffee holder.

Features and conveniences

Capacity. Brewing a full pot of coffee (10 5-ounce cups) requires approximately 2½ ounces of ground beans, just about a chopper's maximum. Mills hold enough for four to five pots.

Controls. Both devices are straightforward and simple to operate. For a chopper, a blade rotates as long as you maintain pressure on a switch or lid. Some people gauge grinding by counting off the seconds. Others let the motor turn until its noise changes from a crackle to a soft whine. With a mill, you pour the beans into a hopper, set a dial for the desired coarseness, and flip a switch.

Some mills have a timer and cup-portion control that doubles as an On/off switch; when enough beans have passed between the grinding wheels, the mill shuts off automatically. Once you find the right setting, the mill will deliver the same grind batch after batch.

Buying advice

Either type will do the job. In our experience, just about any chopper or grinder can mash beans fine enough to make good drip coffee. Grinding coffee doesn't demand great precision.

Choppers work just as well overall as fancy mills. And choppers cost a lot less, too. They don't hold as much as mills, but that's not important unless you regularly make more than 10 cups at a time.

It's important to wipe any grinder clean after each use. Oils left over from grinding can turn rancid, affecting the taste of the next batch.

# TOASTERS & TOASTER OVENS

Toasters & toaster ovens

A toaster's job is to make toast. Most models do that adequately. The toaster oven and toaster-oven broiler don't do the basic job better—many actually do it worse. Their particular strength lies in the ability to perform a variety of small cooking tasks: heating rolls and leftovers, making grilled sandwiches, baking potatoes. And they brown foods readily, unlike a microwave oven.

The choices

Toasters. The mechanics of the pop-up toaster haven't changed much since Toastmaster pioneered them in 1926. Until recently, the biggest difference among models was probably their capacity: either two or four slices. Now, however, there are models with a single elongated slot for toasting oversized slices, and models with wide slots for browning bagels, English muffins, and the like. We've found that the opening has to be at least 1⅛ inches wide for most thick items to fit. Some models advertised as "wide slot" have an opening no wider than the standard three-quarters of an inch. No four-slice toaster we've tested has done a good job with thick slices.

Other innovations include models designed for mounting under a kitchen cabinet (to free up counter space); an all-plastic housing, which remains cooler to the touch than traditional chrome; and electronic controls rather than a mechanical timer or electric thermostat. Prices range from around $15 to $60 for typical one- and two-slice machines and $30 to $60 for typical four-slice models.

For retro toast, Waring sells a four-slice luncheonette-style toaster that's straight out of the 1950s. The price is out of this world: $320.

Toaster ovens and toaster-oven broilers. Toaster ovens have elements that heat food from above and below. Toaster-oven broilers can also switch on their top element alone. Toaster ovens sell for about $40 to $65, toaster-oven broilers for about $45 to $130. More money usually buys sturdier components and such conveniences as "continuous clean" coating, fancy controls, and a slide-out crumb tray.

As toasters, the devices are lethargic, tending to leave bread underdone on the top and striped on the bottom. The most spacious models can accommodate six slices; the least roomy, just two. Bulky items like bagels and English muffins fit the oven easily enough, but often prove hard to toast.

As ovens, these devices aren't precise, even though they often have control knobs marked in degrees. Fluctuating temperatures are also common, a result of cycling by the heating element. But imprecision and variability don't matter much if you just want to warm up a snack or dinner.

As broilers, toaster-oven broilers often aren't hot enough. They lack heat high enough to turn out steaks and burgers that are well browned outside with a touch of pink inside. With some models, you end up with meat that's overcooked inside by the time the exterior is nicely browned. Broiling with any oven demands a watchful eye. Dripping grease can spatter, smoke, or cause a fire.

Features and conveniences

Controls. With most models, raising a lever interrupts toasting. Some toasters also have a control knob to raise the toast immediately; others have a "Keep-Warm" setting that lets the toast stay basking in the toaster's residual heat.

A well-designed four-slice toaster should have separate controls for each pair of slots.

That way you needn't heat all four elements just to toast a slice or two; you can vary doneness, too. Some toaster ovens and toaster-oven broilers have an On light. Some have elements that turn off when the door opens and stay off until the oven is turned on again. A timer that shuts off the machine and a mode-selector switch that keeps the oven and broiler from operating at the same time are also useful.

Cleanup. Something as elemental as a crumb tray can make toaster cleanup a snap. Next best: a slot on the bottom of the toaster through which crumbs can be shaken. With toaster ovens and toaster-oven broilers, a removable rack and a detachable door make for easy cleaning.

Removing baked-on stains is easiest with appliances that boast an unobstructed cooking cavity. Don't be overly impressed by models with a "continuous clean" interior. Such an interior supposedly absorbs and disperses food spatters. In reality, it mostly masks the buildup. On some cookers, the finish can impede travel of the toasting rack (a little vegetable oil on the edges keeps the rack moving freely).

A baking pan made of plated or porcelain-coated steel is sturdier and easier to scour than an aluminum one.

Buying advice

If you eat a lot of toast, buy a toaster. In general, we prefer the two-slice models. If your tastes run toward toasted bagels or thick hand-slices from crusty loaves, consider a machine that has wide slots. A four-slice model is good for cooking large quantities; look for a model with separate controls for each pair of slots.

If you eat a little toast but a lot of other foods that need browning, heating, or cooking, consider a toaster oven or a toaster-oven broiler. It won't make terrific toast, but it can make tuna melts, bake potatoes, warm rolls, broil a steak, and more. Look for features that make operation safe and cleaning easy. And be sure the model is roomy enough—some can't hold more than two slices of toast or two burgers.

Juicers & juice extractors
▶ Ratings on page 131.

Jack LaLanne and Jay "The Juiceman" Kordich are credited with the first food-fad of the 1990s—fresh-made juice. With the persistence of used-car salesmen and the fervor of televangelists, they convinced hundreds of thousands of people that juicing requires a gadget priced close to $300. Not so, according to our tests.

The choices

A top-quality extractor for vegetables and fruits should be priced less than $100; a citrus juicer, $25 or so. Here's how they differ and what you need to know:

Extractors. These machines get the juice out of tomatoes, grapes, celery, peaches, and other produce. To use them, you must peel citrus fruits, remove hard pits from peaches and plums, destem grapes, and cut everything into pieces small enough to fit a feed tube, like a food processor's, in the top of the extractor. Food travels from the tube to a whirling cutter disk (powered by a motor in the extrac-

JUICERS & JUICE EXTRACTORS

tor's base), and from there to a strainer, a pulp collector, and a spout, from which juice flows.

There are two types. Models with a separate cutter and strainer extract maximum juice. Models with a pulp ejector combine cutter and strainer and collect pulp in a separate bin. These models are easier to clean but tend to extract less juice.

Juice extractors range in price from $50 to almost $300.

Citrus juicers. They're designed for oranges, grapefruit, lemons, and limes. A typical electric juicer consists of a reamer set in the center of a strainer, a detachable pitcher, and a base to house the motor. Citrus juicers work in a straightforward way. You press cut halves of fruit onto a motorized reamer that extracts the juice. The juice flows to a pitcher, leaving the seeds and most of the pulp behind in the strainer. Most are priced at $30 or less, though we've seen one model with a price tag of $140.

Extractor features

Speeds. Most extractors have a single speed. Top-of-the-line models may boast two speeds: Low for soft fruits such as grapes and tomatoes and High, for hard foods such as apples and carrots.

Housing. Most models have containers made of plastic. More expensive models are stainless steel.

Feed tube. Look for a wide feed tube. The wider the tube, the less time you spend cutting the food into small chunks.

Controls. A simple On/off switch is best. Avoid designs where you rotate the housing to turn the unit.

Spout. Check the height to make sure it accommodates a glass or the size container you plan to use.

Citrus attachment. A few extractors include or sell separately an attachment to juice citrus fruit. Price: $30 to $40.

Pulp collection. Look for an extractor that permits you to see how much pulp has accumulated.

Cleanup. A pulp ejector, found on most models, helps by directing most of the pulp to an easily emptied receptacle. A pulp container that can be lined with a plastic bag eases the chore. One model we tested had a brushing system to sweep the embedded pulp out of the strainer.

In our tests, a dishwasher didn't always get parts clean. Models with a detachable, one-piece top were easiest to wash by hand.

Citrus-juicer features

Capacity. A citrus juicer's capacity is limited by the size of its juice container or its pulp-collection capacity. Capacities ranged from one to three cups in our tests.

Convenience. Some models come with a container to collect the juice; others have a spout under which you place a glass. Both methods worked well.

Several models have a reamer that reverses direction with changes in hand pressure. That feature made the juicers in our tests harder to use.

Cleanup. Citrus juicers are a breeze to clean. They have few parts and few corners and crevices to accumulate pulp.

The tests

To test extractors, we make a lot of juice from apples, carrots, and grapes and note how much juice and pulp are produced. (We also made juice from tomatoes, oranges, pineapples, celery, broccoli, and spinach to check if they could do it.)

We test citrus juicers by feeding them oranges, grapefruit, and lemons. We note how easy both types of appliances are to operate and clean.

Buying advice

You don't have to spend $300 if you favor a glass of carrot juice or an exotic fruit cocktail. Top extractors in our tests are priced lower than $100. Look for a model with the fewest components, nooks, and crannies—they're potential traps for pulp you have to clean whenever you use the extractor. An attachment to make citrus juice is a nice plus on an extractor.

If you want no more than a glass of fresh-squeezed O.J. with breakfast, buy a citrus juicer. Juicers are modestly priced, simple to use, and relatively easy to clean. Electric juicers are priced about $25. A manual juicer—the old-fashioned reamer or squeezer—is cheaper still, less than $10 in many cases. Lever-operated manual juicers are priced at about $40.

Slow-cookers

▶ Ratings on page 133.

If you have enough self-discipline to think about dinner at breakfast time, a slow-cooker can reward you with a stew or casserole that's ready when you come home. Their low cost, typically $20 at discount, helps make them a staple in many American kitchens.

The choices

Some of the slow-cookers you'll see in stores look pretty much like the metal-encased stoneware crockery cookers of the '70s. Others have a nonstick metal cooking vessel or a Corning Ware casserole-dish insert. A few are rectangular rather than the familiar round shape.

Some of the more expensive models—$40 or so—can hardly be called slow-cookers. With heating elements that go as high as 400°F, they're capable of tasks as diverse as popping corn, deep-frying potatoes, steaming asparagus, and simmering stew.

The typical slow-cooker holds four or six quarts. Other sizes are available: some that hold as little as one quart, designed for small portions, and some that hold as much as 12 quarts.

Features and conveniences

Heat settings. A model that only slow-cooks typically has just Low and High heat settings. Some have an Auto-shift option: It starts on High, then shifts automatically to Low. On Low, food cooks in about 10 to 12 hours, suitable for a dinner you start preparing on a weekday morning; on High, food cooks in about half the time, useful on a weekend when you can make the meal during the day. A model designed for more tasks than slow-cooking has a variable-temperature control. With either type, make sure the control's settings are easy to read.

Cooking vessel. Removable vessels make cleanup easier. The vessels are stoneware, CorningWare, or metal, and can be cleaned in the dishwasher. Depending on the material used, you may be able to use it to heat leftovers in a microwave or regular oven, or on a rangetop. With the vessel removed, some models cook at up to 400°, turning out fried foods. We also came across a couple whose nonstick-metal cooking base could be used as a mini-griddle.

Lids. Glass lids are usually easier to see through than plastic ones, which are apt to fog up during cooking. To see under a plastic lid, you must remove it, letting steam and heat escape.

Handles. The exterior of a slow-cooker can get hot, so large handles placed down on the cooker's sides are safest.

Owner's manual. Look for a manual that has slow-cooking recipes, or at least cooking times. Some models have a separate cookbook with recipes.

The tests

We test slow-cookers by cooking batches of beef stew in each one. The results were not quite a match for stews cooked in a regular oven or in a rangetop Dutch oven, but were still quite tasty. The meat emerged fork-tender; the vegetables retained their characteristic flavors and just enough crispness; and the dark reddish-brown sauce was thick and very flavorful.

We also measure the time it takes the slow-cookers to reach temperatures high enough to destroy bacteria. Food-safety experts say that a cooker should heat to 125° within three hours, and to 140° within four hours. Not all models meet those standards when heating thick beef stew, though more watery foods would heat up much faster. We don't think there's a significant risk of food poisoning from eating anything cooked in these appliances.

Buying advice

If slow-cooking is all you're after, choose a basic model with a removable vessel. On sale, they sometimes sell for less than $20. If you want a cooker/fryer or a slow cooker/mini-griddle, shop for the best combination of features, convenience, and price.

When using a slow-cooker, you can reduce any bacterial risk by following these practices: Keep raw ingredients refrigerated until you are ready to put them in the cooker. Thaw frozen meat or poultry before cooking. Don't overload the cooking vessel. And don't use a slow-cooker for warming leftovers.

Pressure cookers

▶ Ratings on page 135.

Long before the microwave oven, the pressure cooker promised to cut down on time spent cooking. But pot roast gave way to quiche and Big Macs, the microwave oven arrived, and the pressure cooker faded from the kitchen scene.

Now cookers are coming back, though on a modest scale. The new models offer improved safety and a healthy method of cooking, since they keep foods moist without the use of fats or cooking oils. Pressure cookers also allow speedy preparation of complete meals—outpacing even the microwave oven with some foods.

Two major makers of pressure cookers, National Presto and Mirro/Wearever, dominate sales of low-priced models, where prices range from $30 to $100. Imports account for the upscale market and include such names as Cuisinart, T-Fal, and Kuhn Rikon. Those prices range as high as $300.

The choices

The main differences are in size and materials. Size varies from 2 to 20 quarts. The larger sizes, 15- and 20-quart, are for large-scale cooking or canning. The most popular sizes are in the 5- to 6-quart range, big enough to fix meals for four or five.

Pressure cookers can be either aluminum or stainless steel. Stainless steel is more durable, easier to clean, and unlike aluminum, will not react with certain foods to change their taste and color. But it's heavier than aluminum. It's also vulnerable to discoloration and may scorch delicate foods such as fish or asparagus. By itself, it disperses heat unevenly, a problem manufacturers solve by sandwiching aluminum or copper between layers of stainless steel on the cooker's bottom.

Stainless steel models range in price from $80 for a 6-quart model to $260 for an 8-quart *Cuisinart*. Aluminum models are priced at $30 for a 3-quart model to $120 for an 8-quart model.

Features and conveniences

Safety. Pressure cookers are fitted with any of several devices to prevent pressure from rising dangerously. We found all types to be effective. Most cookers have a rubber plug on the lid that's ejected when pressure inside the pot is excessive. The best designs locate it under the handle so it can't shoot across a room. Blown plugs must be replaced. A few models have a metal plug that melts as pressure and temperature rise. When that happens, it, too, must be replaced. Another approach uses a small opening on the side of the lid to expose a section of the gasket, which high pressure releases. Some models have an additional pressure reliever, a valve on the cover or handle.

Multiple cooking pressures. Since cookers do their job fastest at highest pressures, multiple settings aren't usually useful. Some large-capacity models allow running at lower pressure, useful for certain canning and preserving chores.

Pressure release. If you mostly cook delicate foods, look for a model with a pressure-release valve. This allows rapid depressurizing and helps avoid overcooking. With models that lack such a valve, you simply run cold water from the sink over the cooker.

Rack/basket. Most cookers come with a rack for steaming vegetables or preparing meat and poultry dishes; others have a basket for that job, which makes loading and unloading small items much easier.

The tests

We operate each model repeatedly, as the manufacturer instructs, on gas and electric ranges, monitoring complete cycles of pressure buildup, control, and release. We measure heating speed, heat distribution, and overheating. To see how a model's safety features respond to excessive pressure, we simulate clogging of the main pressure regulator. We cook a variety of foods and evaluate the results.

Buying advice

A pressure cooker is best suited for hearty fare—it excels at cooking legumes, homemade soups, and stews.

Pressure cooking demands constant vigilance and frequent checks. Once mastered, it's a fast way to cook in an old-fashioned sort of way.

Indoor grills
▶ Ratings on page 137.

No one seriously maintains that indoor grilling is the same as backyard barbecuing. Barbecue grills are meant to generate smoke from fats and juices vaporizing on hot coals or rocks, adding that distinctive smoky flavor to the food. Indoor grills are designed to suppress smoke, if for no other reason than to keep the kitchen habitable. Even so, many Americans, either lacking the opportunity or the time, seem willing to forgo the flavors of outdoor grilling to grill indoors at the kitchen range or countertop.

The choices

The two main types—countertop and stove-top—produce very different results. The countertop models approximate cooking in an oven broiler, while the stove-top variety functions like a frypan.

Countertop grills. In much the same way as an oven broiler, these combine radiant heat from an electric element with hot air circulating around food held on a wire rack or grate; a reflector/drip pan directs heat to the food and catches the drippings. The effective cooking area ranges from about 75 to 150 square inches. Price: about $20 to $90.

Stove-top grills. These have a griddle, nestled in a drip pan, that fits over a range's burners or heating elements. The surface of the griddle slopes down from the center toward holes in the sides, to allow fats to drip away. The stove-top models come in two sizes, to fit over one or two elements. The effective cooking area is about 30 square inches and more than 100 square inches,respectively. Price: about $6 to $40.

Features and conveniences

Even heating. To increase your chances of getting a model that delivers heat evenly, make sure that the grate, reflector, and element are similarly sized. That way, food doesn't sit over a cool area.

Temperature control. It's easiest to control cooking with an electric grill if it has a temperature control. That control may have two heating positions, High and Low, or be continuously variable—the most useful arrangement.

Drip pan. On electric grills, look for a one-piece drip pan. There's less to clean on them than on ones that drain into the base or into a separate pan.

On stove-top models, drippings drain into a reservoir you fill with water, a rather awkward design. With single-burner models, the griddle sometimes tips into the water causing a spill. A porcelain drip tray lasts longer and makes clean-up easier.

Rotisserie. We came across only one model—a *Farberware*—with a motorized spit for slowly turning meat. It delivered excellent results.

Nonstick finishes. Stove-top grills usually come with a nonstick coating on the griddle, but its effectiveness varies. Some nonstick finishes were more helpful than others: the DuPont Teflon and Excaliber finishes on the *Burton* models.

Manufacturers' instructions say aluminum griddles are dishwasher safe, but we advise against washing them that way. Detergent may pit the metal.

The tests

We cooked hamburgers, chicken breasts, salmon steaks, and three-quarter-inch-thick steaks to test the grills' capabilities. Steaks and hamburgers need high temperatures to sear their surfaces, while chicken and fish need more moderate cooking temperatures so that they reach an even state of doneness. We also checked for convenience and for electrical safety.

Buying advice

Cooking on an electric indoor grill approximates barbecuing, without the special flavors of the real thing. If that appeals to you, look for a model that's likely to deliver even heating—one whose grate, reflector, and element are evenly sized. A continuously adjustable heat control makes it easy to control the temperature and a nonstick grate makes cleanup easier.

Cooking on a stove-top grill is more like sautéing than barbecuing. If that's what you're after, look for a model that doesn't tip (something you may not know till you get it home) and a double-burner model.

BLENDERS

RATINGS BLENDERS

Better ← → Worse

▶ **See report, page 113.** From Consumer Reports, June 1992.

Recommendations: Performance did not vary greatly among standard models. Let price, convenience, and features guide your choice. Among handheld models, the *Singer 795*, $25, is our favorite; we rated it A Best Buy. Even though it has been discontinued, it may still be available.

Ratings order: Listed by types; within types, listed in order of estimated quality. Price is the the manufacturer's suggested retail. Ⓢ indicates tested model has been replaced by successor model; according to the manufacturer, the performance of new model should be similar to the tested model but features may vary. See right for new model number and suggested retail price, if available. Ⓓ indicates model discontinued.

Brand and model	Price	Container[1]	Speeds	Diet drink	Milk shake	Whipped cream	Gazpacho	Parmesan cheese	Peanut butter	Convenience[2]	Advantages	Disadvantages	Comments
STANDARD													
Osterizer 852-20 Ⓢ	$40	G	12	◐	○	◐	◒	◒	◒	◒	C,M	—	H,W,Y
Osterizer 890-20 Ⓢ	42	G	7	◐	○	◐	◒	◒	◒	◒	D,M	—	H,X
Osterizer 887-20 Ⓢ	40	P	5	○	○	◐	◒	◒	◒	◒	D,M	—	H
Hamilton Beach 609W	25	G	6	○	○	●	◒	◒	◒	○	B,D,F,K,N	f	N,Y
Osterizer 5000-08 Ⓢ	69	G	1	○	○	◐	○	◒	◒	◒	E,F,I	h,j	H,V,Z
Waring NB5-1	54	P	2	◐	○	●	◒	◒	◒	◒	B,D,I,J,L	—	B,F,U,AA
Black & Decker HB15 Ⓓ	25	P	2	○	○	●	◒	◒	◐	◒	E,F,I,J,L,P	a,g	A,E,F,R
Hamilton Beach 722	20	P	6	○	○	●	◒	○	◒	◒	B,E,N	—	C,N
Hamilton Beach 5306B Ⓓ	52	G	2	○	○	○	◒	○	◒	◒	B,I,K	f,j	S
Sears 68175	37	G	14	○	○	●	◒	○	◒	◒	B,E,K,N	f	G,N,S,Y
Hamilton Beach 610W	25	P	14	○	○	◐	◒	○	◒	○	B,N	—	C,N,Y
NOT ACCEPTABLE													

■ *The following were judged Not Acceptable because of excessive leakage of electrical current in CU's tests.*

Singer 812 Ⓓ	22	P	12	○	○	●	◒	◒	◐	○	B,E,O	—	D,Y
Waring PKB10	146	G	2	○	○	◐	◒	◒	◒	◐	I	i,j	O,P
Waring VB70-1	21	P	4	○	○	●	◒	◒	◒	○	B,D,N,Q	i	E

BLENDERS

Ratings table — columns: Brand and model | Price | Container[1] | Speeds | Performance: Diet drink, Milk shake, Whipped cream, Gazpacho, Parmesan cheese, Peanut butter | Convenience[2] | Advantages | Disadvantages | Comments

HANDHELD

Brand and model	Price	Container[1]	Speeds	Diet drink	Milk shake	Whipped cream	Gazpacho	Parmesan cheese	Peanut butter	Convenience[2]	Advantages	Disadvantages	Comments
Singer 795, A Best Buy [D]	$25	P	2	◐	◐	○	○	—	—	○	G,R	b	L
Cuisinart CSB1 [D]	68	P	2	◐	◐	○	○	—	—	○	A,G,R	—	F,L,Q
Braun MR72 [D]	40	P	[3]	○	○	○	○	—	—	◐	G,M	—	I,K
Kitchenmate Daily	80	P	2	◐	◐	◐	○	—	—	◐	G,S	b,d,e	J,M,T
Hamilton Beach 250 [S]	23	P	1	◐	○	◑	○	—	—	○	G	—	F
Rival 951W [D]	25	P	2	○	○	◑	◐	—	—	◐	—	b,e	F
Waring HHB75-1	35	P	2	○	○	◑	◐	—	—	◐	—	b,e	F
Braun MR30 [D]	21	P	1	◑	○	○	○	—	—	◐	H	b,e	F
Moulinex 070 [D]	20	—	1	○	○	◑	○	—	—	○	—	c	—

[1] Key to container: G=glass; P=plastic.
[2] Rankings are relative with each category of blender.
[3] Continuously variable speed.

Successor Models (in Ratings order)
Osterizer 852-20 is succeeded by 4101/4102, $49; Osterizer 890-20 by 4112/4114, $39; Osterizer 887-20 by 4106/4111, $30; Osterizer 5000-08 by 4093, $69; Hamilton Beach 250 by 59700, $15.

Features in Common
All standard models: • Have removable blade assembly. • Have rubber feet to improve stability. • Are 12½ to 15½ in. tall.
Except as noted, all standard models: • Have 5-cup container, marked in 1-cup intervals, and handle. • Have removable insert in lid. • Have 3- to 3½-ft. cord. • Were relatively noisy. • Come with 1-yr. warranty.
Except as noted, all handheld models: • Come with clear plastic container that holds about 2 cups when full. • Have single 2-prong blade. • Can be rested temporarily on their flat top. • Come with 1-yr. warranty.

Key to Advantages
A–Container marked clearly in quarter-cups.
B–Container marked in half-cups.
C–Pulses on all 12 speeds.
D–Pulses on 2, 3, or 4 speeds.
E–Pulses on single speed.
F–Quieter than other standard blenders.
G–Storage rack for blender, blades, and container.
H–Has storage rack for blender.
I–Single On/off switch; base is easier to clean than most. See Disadvantage h.
J–Cord is coiled; easy to store.
K–Has wide-mouthed container; easy for loading food and cleaning.
L–Can chop ice without water, according to mfr.; our results were very good.
M–Very wide range of speeds.
N–Wide range of speeds.
O–Wide range of speeds at high rpm's.
P–Needs less counter space than others.
Q–Lid has built-in strainer.
R–Has blending, whipping, and chopping blades.
S–Has beating, whipping, mincing, and chopping blades.

Key to Disadvantages
a–Blades rusted after we "blended" water for several hours.
b–Container lacks markings.
c–Lacks container.
d–Container holds only a cup or so.
e–Container is opaque.
f–Hard to pour liquid without dribbling.
g–Processed carrots not smooth.
h–Protruding switch judged more likely than most to be damaged or turned on accidentally.
i–Blade unit hard to unscrew for cleaning.
j–Chrome-finished base highlights dirt.

Ratings continued ▶

FOOD PROCESSORS

Key to Comments
A–Marked 4-cup capacity.
B–Marked 4½-cup capacity.
C–Marked 5½-cup capacity.
D–Marked 6-cup capacity.
E–Container twist-locks on base.
F–Mfr. says plastic container dishwasher safe.
G–Has 2 blend-and-store containers.
H–Mfr. says container not dishwasher safe, but we washed it without damage.
I–Optional chopping attachment available.
J–Has grating and grinding attachments.
K–Comes with whisk attachment.
L–Safety guard around interchangeable blades makes it hard to remove them.
M–Available only from the distributor. For information call 800-344-4563.
N–Has 2-ft. cord.
O–Has 6-ft. cord; may be awkward to store.
P–Has 3-prong plug that can mitigate effects of leakage current when used with a grounded receptacle.
Q–18-mo. warranty.
R–2-yr. warranty.
S–3-yr. warranty.
T–90-day warranty against manufacturing defects. From 90 days to 12 years, mfr. will replace unit at 50 percent of cost.
U–5-yr. warranty on motor.
V–1-yr. warranty came with only 1 of 3 samples.
W–Essentially similar to **852-08**.
X–Essentially similar to **890-08**.
Y–Has speed-shift selector.
Z–Runs on a single speed, but will pulse on a lower speed.
AA–Hinged lid flips up.

RATINGS FOOD PROCESSORS   Better ← → Worse

▶ See report, page 111. From Consumer Reports, August 1992.

Recommendations: The top-rated model, the *Braun UK11*, $104, boasts generous capacity (11½ cups); except for noise, it got high marks in most tasks. The *Panasonic MK-5070*, $100, was nearly as good and much quieter.

Ratings order: Listed by types; within types, listed in order of estimated quality. Closely ranked models generally differed little in quality. Price is the manufacturer's suggested retail. **Notes to table:** Capacity is of dry food, with bowl filled to rim and S-shaped chopping blade in place. Ⓢ indicates tested model has been replaced by successor model; according to the manufacturer, the performance of new model should be similar to the tested model but features may vary. See right for new model number and suggested retail price, if available. Ⓓ indicates model discontinued.

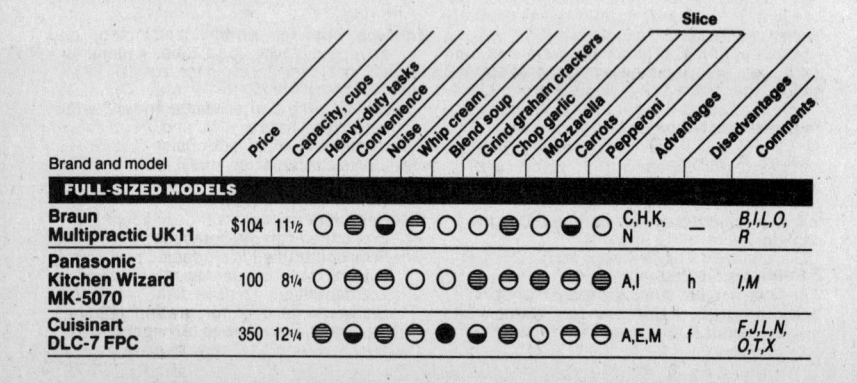

Brand and model	Price	Capacity, cups	Heavy-duty tasks	Convenience	Noise	Whip cream	Blend soup	Grind graham crackers	Chop garlic	Slice Mozzarella	Slice Carrots	Slice Pepperoni	Advantages	Disadvantages	Comments
FULL-SIZED MODELS															
Braun Multipractic UK11	$104	11½	○	◐	●	◐	○	○	◐	○	◑	○	C,H,K,N	–	B,I,L,O,R
Panasonic Kitchen Wizard MK-5070	100	8¼	○	◐	◐	○	◐	◐	◐	◐	◐	◐	A,I	h	I,M
Cuisinart DLC-7 FPC	350	12¼	◐	◑	◐	◐	●	◑	◐	◐	○	◐	A,E,M	f	F,J,L,N,O,T,X

FOOD PROCESSORS

Model	Price	Capacity, cups	Heavy-duty tasks	Convenience	Noise	Whip cream	Blend soup	Grind graham crackers	Chop garlic	Slice Mozzarella	Slice Carrots	Slice Pepperoni	Advantages	Disadvantages	Comments
Cuisinart Custom 11 DLC-8M	$250	10	⊖	●	⊖	○	⊖	○	⊖	○	⊖	○	A,E,M	f,i	F,I,J,N,O,T,X
Regal La Machine II K588GY	65	9½	○	⊖	●	○	●	○	○	⊖	⊖	⊖	B,K,M,N	—	A,W
Hamilton Beach 714W D	63	8	○	⊖	●	○	⊖	⊖	⊖	⊖	⊖	⊖	F,L,M	i	B,I,S
Waring Professional PFP15	350	7¾	⊖	●	⊖	○	○	○	⊖	⊖	○	⊖	—	e,i	F,H,J,R,X
Moulinex 305	80	6½	⊖	⊖	○	○	○	○	⊖	⊖	⊖	⊖	A,M,N	h	D,E,M,O,Q
Braun Multipractic MC100	65	6½	⊖	⊖	○	⊖	⊖	⊖	⊖	○	○	○	K,N	h,k	I
Braun Multipractic MC200	80	6½	●	○	⊖	○	⊖	○	⊖	○	⊖	○	K,N	h,k	D,I,M
Regal La Machine I K813GY	37	6½	⊖	○	⊖	○	●	⊖	○	○	○	●	K,M	h,i	A,O
Sunbeam Oskar 3000 14201 S	90	5½	⊖	⊖	●	○	⊖	⊖	⊖	○	⊖	○	D,N	d,i	C,G,M,U

COMPACT MODELS

Model	Price	Capacity, cups	Heavy-duty tasks	Convenience	Noise	Whip cream	Blend soup	Grind graham crackers	Chop garlic	Slice Mozzarella	Slice Carrots	Slice Pepperoni	Advantages	Disadvantages	Comments
Cuisinart Little Pro Plus	115	4¼	—	⊖	⊖	○	○	⊖	○	⊖	⊖	⊖	A,B,G,M	—	J,K,O,T
Black & Decker Shortcut CFP10	38	4¼	—	⊖	●	○	⊖	⊖	⊖	○	⊖	⊖	A,B,J,M	—	P,U
Black & Decker Handy Shortcut HMP30	30	2½	—	⊖	○	○	○	⊖	⊖	○	⊖	○	A,M	a,g	U
Sunbeam Oskar 14181 S	35	2¾	—	●	●	○	⊖	⊖	⊖	○	⊖	⊖	—	a,b,c,j	V

Successor Models (in Ratings order)
Sunbeam Oskar 3000 14201 is succeeded by 4818, $90; Sunbeam Oskar 14181 by 4817, $35.

Performance Notes

All were judged excellent to good at puréeing carrots, grinding peanuts, chopping carrots and prosciutto, slicing mushrooms. • Very good to good at grinding beef cubes. • Excellent to very good at shredding zucchini and cabbage.

Features in Common

All have: • See-through plastic chop/mix bowl and lid. • Effective safety-interlock switch. • Plastic food pusher. • Pads or feet under base.

Except as noted, all have: • Handle on chop/mix bowl. • Lid with feed tube. • Metal S-shaped chopping blade that rusted when soaked in salt water. • 1 metal reversible shredding/slicing disk with finger holes or other provision to aid removal and installation. • Separate On/off switch, Pulse provision, and 1 speed. • Cord between 3 and 4 ft. long. • 1-yr. repair/replacement warranty.

Key to Advantages

A—Controls well marked, easy to use.
B—Slicing/shredding disk easier and safer to mount and remove than most.
C—Has reversible thin/thick disks for slicing or shredding, disk for grating cheese, and disk for french fries. All worked well.
D—Coarse shredding disk worked well.

Ratings continued ▶

FOOD PROCESSORS

E–Feed tube handles slender and large-sized foods (but see Disadvantage f).
F–Can slice or shred food into bowl or expel it through lid's built-in chute.
G–Comes with both regular lid and chute for slicing or shredding.
H–Can process nearly 4 cups of liquid without leaks.
I–Can process 3 1/3 cups of liquid without leaks.
J–Can process 1 1/2 cups of liquid without leaks.
K–Blade stops instantly when switched off.
L–Chopping blade didn't rust.
M–All blades can be stored in bowl.
N–Has place to store cord.

Key to Disadvantages
a–Chop/mix bowl lacks handle.
b–Chop/mix bowl lacks feed tube; chute option cumbersome.
c–Lacks Pulse switch; for On/off and Pulse, lid must be rotated through latch on housing.
d–On/off/pulse switch on handle; inconvenient.
e–Touchpad On/off and Pulse switches require more effort than others.
f–Feed tube assembly hard to use and to clean.
g–Feed tube inconveniently narrow.
h–Blade inserts pose slightly greater danger of cut fingers than others.
i–Because these models leaked, we blended only a half-recipe of soup. The **Sunbeam, Hamilton Beach,** and **Waring** leaked most.
j–Leaked more than other compacts when processing liquids; held only 1/4 cup.
k–Hole on blade hub can admit foods, which can create a mess.

Key to Comments
A–Must lock On switch for continuous action.
B–2 speeds.
C–6 speeds.
D–Continuously variable speeds.
E–Feed tube has narrow side and wide side.
F–Feed tube at back of lid.
G–Bottom of bowl convex.
H–Has 3-prong plug.
I–Some or all parts not dishwasher safe.
J–Separate slice and shred disks.
K–Citrus juicer attachment.
L–Whisk attachment; the **Braun** has one, the **Cuisinart** a pair.
M–Plastic whip accessory.
N–Plastic dough-mixing blade.
O–Comes with hard plastic spatula.
P–Has insert to guide slim food down feed tube.
Q–Chopping blade comes with cover.
R–Cord 5 1/2 ft. long.
S–Cord 2 ft. long.
T–3-yr. repair/replacement warranty.
U–2-yr. repair/replacement warranty.
V–5-yr. warranty on motor.
W–Tallest model at 17 1/4 in.; may present storage problem.
X–Among heaviest models: **Waring,** 15 1/2 lb.; **Cuisinart DLC-7 FPC,** 14 3/4 lb.; **Cuisinart 11 DLC-8M,** 12 1/4 lb.

HOW TO USE THE RATINGS

■ Read the **article** for general guidance about types and buying advice.

■ Read **Recommendations** for brand-name advice based on our tests.

■ Read the **Ratings order** to see whether products are listed in order of quality, by price, or alphabetically. Most Ratings are based on estimated quality, without regard to price.

■ Look to the **Ratings table** for specifics on the performance and features of individual models.

■ A model marked Ⓓ has been discontinued, according to the manufacturer. A model marked Ⓢ indicates that, according to the manufacturer, it has been replaced by a successor model whose performance should be similar to the tested model but whose features may vary.

JUICE EXTRACTORS & JUICERS

RATINGS — JUICE EXTRACTORS & JUICERS

Rating symbols: E ◕ | VG ◖ | G ○ | F ◐ | P ●

▶ See report, page 120. From Consumer Reports, December 1992.

Recommendations: For fresh orange juice, consider the *Sanyo Just Juice Plus*, $20, the *Black & Decker Handy Juicer*, $20, or the *Krups Pressa Maxi*, $30. Those three made the largest batches of juice and are among the handiest to use. (Note: The *Sanyo* has been discontinued but may still be available.) Two juice extractors stood out for quality and price: the *Panasonic MJ-65PR*, $99, and the *Sanyo SJ3020*, about $75.

Ratings order: Listed by types; within types, listed in order of estimated quality. Ratings are not comparable between types. Except where separated by a bold rule, closely ranked models differed little in quality. Bracketed models, judged about equal in quality, are listed alphabetically. Price is the mfr.'s suggested retail. **Notes to table:** Key to types: **C** = centrifugal models; **CP** = centrifugal models with a pulp ejector. Ⓢ indicates tested model has been replaced by successor model; according to the mfr., the performance of new model should be similar to the tested model but features may vary. See page 132 for new model number and suggested retail price. Ⓓ indicates model discontinued.

Brand and model	Price	Type	Total extraction [1]	Juice extraction [2]	Capacity [3]	Convenience	Ease of cleaning	Ease of use	Advantages	Disadvantages	Comments
JUICE EXTRACTORS											
Panasonic MJ-65PR, A Best Buy	$99	CP	◖	◖	◖	◖	◖	—	E,K	c,h	—
Sanyo SJ3020, A Best Buy	75	CP	◖	◖	○	◖	○	—	G,K	a,h	B
Acme Supreme Juicerator 5001	206	C	◖	◖	◖	◐	◐	—	D	c,h,j	C,D,G,P
Kenwood JE-600	70	CP	○	◐	○	○	◖	—	A,B,F	b,i	A
Omega 1000	200	C	◖	◖	◖	◐	◐	—	D	b,c,h,j	C,D,F,P
Waring JE504-1	77	CP	○	◖	○	○	◖	—	—	c,d,h,i	K
Braun MP80	75	CP	○	◐	○	◐	○	—	A,C,H,I	—	—
Cuisinart JE-4	110	CP	○	◐	◖	○	◐	—	A,B,L	d,e,g	K
Hamilton Beach 395W	25	CP	○	◐	○	◐	◖	—	G	d,h,i	B
Juiceman II by Trillium	199	CP	◐	◐	◖	○	◐	—	I,J,M	f	H,J,K
Krups VitaMight 294	60	CP	○	○	○	◐	◐	—	A	d,l	—
Moulinex Deluxe 753	69	CP	○	◐	○	○	◐	—	A,B,I	c	—
Oster 323-08 Ⓢ	55	CP	●	●	◖	○	○	—	A,B,I,K	b,c,h	A,K
Tefal Juice Master 8310	60	CP	○	○	○	◐	◐	—	L	c,o	K
JUICERS											
Sanyo Just Juice Plus SJ60(W) Ⓓ	20	—	—	—	◖	○	—	◖	O,R	s	L
Black & Decker HJ28	20	—	—	—	◖	◖	—	○	B,O,R,S	—	I

[1] Amount of extracted juice by weight. [2] Volume of pulp-free juice.
[3] Amount of juice you can make before emptying machine.

Ratings continued ▶

JUICE EXTRACTORS & JUICERS

▶ *Ratings continued*

Brand and model	Price	Type	Total extraction [1]	Juice extraction [2]	Capacity [3]	Convenience	Ease of cleaning	Ease of use	Advantages	Disadvantages	Comments
Krups Pressa Maxi 293	$30	—	—	—	◒	◒	—	○	B,D,N,O,R,S	k,r	M
Oster 4100-08 [S]	19	—	—	—	●	○	—	◒	O,P,Q,R	t	L
Moulinex Citrus Fruit Press 918 [S]	21	—	—	—	○	○	—	◒	N	r,t	N,O
Bosch MCP1001 70	34	—	—	—	○	○	—	○	B	e,n,r	N
Kenwood JE-150	23	—	—	—	◒	○	—	●	B,D	k,m,s	E,N
Dazey Fruit Juicer FJ-24 [D]	32	—	—	—	◒	○	—	●	P,R	e,m,n	—
Hamilton Beach 379W [S]	17	—	—	—	●	○	—	○	O,Q	k,m,p,t	N,O
Salton Mini Squeeze JC-1 [S]	11	—	—	—	●	○	—	◒	B	e,k,m,q	L,N
Braun Citromatic MPZ4 [D]	17	—	—	—	●	●	—	◒	D	k,q,r	L,N
Waring Mighty Squeeze JC210-1	20	—	—	—	○	●	—	●	R	b,e,k,m,r,s,t	—

[1] Amount of extracted juice by weight.
[2] Volume of pulp-free juice.
[3] Amount of juice you can make before emptying machine.

Successor Models (in Ratings order)
Oster 323-08 is succeeded by 3161, $69; Oster 4100-08 by 3181, $23; Moulinex 918 by K76, $25; Hamilton Beach 379W by 66100, $15; Salton JC-1 by JC-1A, $15.

Features in Common
All extractors have: • Plastic motor housing, feed tube with pusher, lid that clamps or latches, and attached cord. • Metal grating disk. • Rubber feet. *Except as noted, all extractors have:* • Clear plastic lid. • Single speed. • Plastic juice container. • Fairly loud operation. • 1-yr. warranty. • Safety interlock to prevent operation when lid is removed. • Room for 4¾-in.-high glass.

All juicers: • Operate when fruit is pressed down on reamer. • Have plastic motor housing, plastic reamer, and plastic pulp strainer. *Except as noted, all juicers have:* • Plastic juice container with handle that shows juice level. • Plastic dust cover. • Reamer that reverses direction automatically. • Provision to store power cord. • 1-yr. warranty.

Key to Advantages
A–Can store cord.
B–Adjustable cord length.
C–Container can remove foam from juice.
D–Quieter than most.
E–User can clean strainer basket without disassembling entire unit.
F–On/off buttons light up.
G–Juice spout won't drip on counter.
H–Has food tray for easy tube feeding.
I–Separate pulp container.
J–Pulp container can hold scrap bag for easier cleaning.
K–Has small cleaning brush.
L–Has citrus-juicer attachment.
M–Includes instructional video/audio tapes.
N–Juice container has graduations.
O–Handles large fruit easily.
P–Juice can flow directly into glass.
Q–Very little spatter.
R–Includes brush for cleaning strainer.
S–Strainer has handle; easy to remove.

Key to Disadvantages
a–Upper housing and strainer basket were sometimes hard to remove.
b–Spatters more than others.
c–No juice container.
d–Feed tube smaller than most.
e–Noisier than most.
f–On/off switch gets easily stuck from juicing; is hard to clean.
g–Clips holding upper housing may break.
h–No safety interlock.
i–Has difficulty juicing unpeeled lemons.
j–Opaque lid hides accumulating pulp.
k–Opaque container hides juice level.
l–Hard to clean pulp under lid switch.
m–Reamer's reversal of direction can be disconcerting.
n–Narrow space around reamer.
o–Turns on by rotating housing.
p–Recessed strainer is hard to remove.

SLOW-COOKERS

q–Container dribbles when pouring.
r–No dust cover.
s–Has inconvenient handle or no handle.
t–No provision to store cord.

Key to Comments
A–2 speeds.
B–Spout too low for 4¾-in.-high glass.
C–Disposable filters available for strainer.
D–More parts to clean than others.
E–Graduations inside opaque container.
F–1-yr. warranty on blade; 10-yr. on other parts.
G–1-yr. warranty on blade; 5-yr. on other parts.
H–1-yr. warranty on blade and basket; 5-yr. on other parts.
I–2-yr. warranty.
J–Includes glass juice container.
K–Includes extensive recipe list.
L–Reamer turns in 1 direction only.
M–Juice container twist-locks onto base.
N–Reamer and strainer are single unit.
O–Long cord can't be shortened.
P–Has reset button for electrical overload protection.

RATINGS SLOW-COOKERS

Better ← → Worse

▶ See report, page 122. From Consumer Reports, January 1993.

Recommendations: In the top-rated group, the two *Rivals* are cheapest. Like most, the *3150* has a removable stoneware vessel; the *Rival 3753* has a Corning Ware dish. The pricier top models, *Dazey* and *Presto*, convert to cooker/fryers.

Ratings order: Listed in order of estimated quality, based on performance, convenience, and safety. Bracketed models, judged approximately equal in quality, are listed in order of increasing price. Price is the mfr.'s suggested retail. **Notes to table:** Key to cooking vessel: **RS**=removable stoneware; **NS**= nonremovable stoneware; **CD**=removable Corning Ware dish; **RM**=removable nonstick-metal; **NM**=nonremovable nonstick-metal. Key to settings: **L/H**=Low and High; **A**=automatic High to Low; **V**=variable. Ⓢ indicates tested model has been replaced by successor model; according to the mfr., the performance of new model should be similar to the tested model but features may vary. See page 134 for new model number and suggested retail price. Ⓓ indicates model discontinued.

Brand and model	Price	Cooking vessel	Settings	Capacity, qt. [1]	Weight, lb.	Advantages	Disadvantages	Comments
Rival Crock-Pot 3150	$30	RS	L/H	3½	8	G,I,J	b	A,E,F,I
Rival Crock-Pot 3753	35	CD	L/H	3	7	E,K	g,n	A
Dazey Chef's Pot Plus SFT3	40	RS	V	6/4	10	A,E,M	d,k	B,J
Presto Kitchen Kettle 06001	60	RS	V	6/4	10½	A,E,J	d,k	B,K
Rival Crock-Pot 3100	15	NS	L/H	3½	6¾	H	b,n,o	A,E,F,H,I
West Bend Slow Cooker 84624	23	RM	V	4	6	B,D,L	c,f,h,j	C,D,G,H
Hamilton Beach 415 Ⓢ	20	RS	L/H/A	4	9	E	b,e,m,n	G
Rival Crock-Pot 3154	33	RS	L/H	4	7½	I,J	b,i	A,E,F,H,I
West Bend Slow Cooker 84643 Ⓓ	37	NM	L/H	3½	2½	D	c,j,o,p	—
Hamilton Beach 417 Ⓢ	27	RS	L/H/A	6	11¾	E	a,e,m,n	G
Rival Crock-Pot 3656	40	RS	L/H	6	11¼	F,G,J	a,n	A,E,F,I
West Bend Slow Cooker 84646 Ⓓ	44	RM	V	6	6½	B,C,D,L	b,c,f,h,j,l	C,D,H

[1] *Capacity without liner/capacity with.*

Ratings continued ▶

SLOW-COOKERS

Successor Models (in Ratings order)
Hamilton Beach 415 is succeeded by 33400, $45; Hamilton Beach 417 by 33600, $55.

Features in Common
All: • Are roughly 7 to 11 in. high with lid. • Have 2- to 3-ft. cord. • Have plastic feet that did not get hot during cooking.
Except as noted, all: • Have drum-shaped metal housing with heating coils in its sides; two plastic handles; and permanently attached power cord. • Are rated 150 to 350 watts at highest setting. • Have plastic lid that made it difficult to watch food being cooked. • Became hot on the outside during cooking. • Heated fast enough to minimize risk of bacterial contamination. • Can be somewhat difficult to clean, although cooking vessel and lid go in the dishwasher. • Have 1-yr. repair/replace warranty.

Key to Advantages
A–With stoneware vessel removed, can be used as cooker/fryer. Outer pot of nonstick metal is fully immersible with temperature probe removed.
B–Heating base can be mini-griddle.
C–Has meat rack (but results were so-so).
D–Cooking vessel has nonstick coating.
E–Glass lid; lets you see food.
F–Low-slung handles make carrying easy.
G–Separate cookbook with many recipes.
H–Exterior stays relatively cool.
I–Relatively little stew stuck to vessel.
J–Vessel can go in microwave and regular oven.
K–Vessel can go in microwave and regular oven, under broiler, and on rangetop.
L–Vessel can go in regular oven and on rangetop; lid can be used as cooking dish in regular or microwave oven.
M–Vessel can go in microwave.

Key to Disadvantages
a–When filled, took longer than most to heat up, especially on Low.
b–When filled, took somewhat longer than others to heat up on Low.
c–Didn't do as well as others in cooking tests.
d–Has no slow-cook recipes.
e–Temp.-control marker hard to see.
f–Has no Off; you must pull plug.
g–Vessel a bit small; our beef stew spilled out when stirred.
h–Glass lid affords poor view. And water collected in lid during cooking can burn you when lid is removed (lid has handles but no knob).
i–Exterior gets hotter than most.
j–Metal handles get hot.
k–Metal probe receptacle gets hot.
l–Plastic temp.-control knob gets hot.
m–Small handles are close to housing; hands can get burned.
n–Cooking vessel harder to clean than most.
o–Cooking vessel not removable.
p–Plastic lid can't go in dishwasher.

Key to Comments
A–Choice of exterior and cooking-vessel colors and designs.
B–Rated at 1300 to 1400 watts; may need own branch circuit.
C–Base has plastic handles.
D–Removable cord.
E–Plastic lid can go in dishwasher.
F–Optional bread/cake pan, meat rack.
G–Optional meat rack.
H–Separate cookbook optional.
I–Braille edition of cookbook available.
J–Can be bought without stoneware cooking vessel as **DCP-6**.
K–2-yr. repair/replace warranty.

ABOUT PRICES IN THE BUYING GUIDE

Prices for most products have been updated for the Buying Guide. The prices we give, unless otherwise noted, are approximate or suggested retail as quoted by the manufacturer. Discounts may be substantial, especially for electronics and camera equipment.

PRESSURE COOKERS

RATINGS | PRESSURE COOKERS

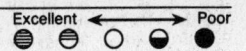

Excellent ⬅ ⬤ ◐ ○ ◑ ● ➡ Poor

▶ **See report, page 123.** From Consumer Reports, July 1993.

Recommendations: Worries over exploding pots need not be a consideration; every model handled overpressure safely. Models vary mainly by size and convenience. The top-rated *Innova 42001* is stainless steel but, at $100, expensive. The all-aluminum *Maitre's 80601*, $35, is a basic, competent cooker for much less. The smaller *Presto 01240*, $54, is also worth considering.

Ratings order: Listed in order of estimated quality, based mainly on convenience. Differences between closely ranked models were slight. Models judged equal in quality are bracketed and listed alphabetically. Price is the manufacturer's suggested retail. **Notes to table:** Pot material: **SS** = stainless steel; **A** = aluminum; **SS/A** = stainless steel and aluminum; **SS/C** = stainless steel and copper. Pressure regulator: **B** = built-in; **W** = weight. ⃟D indicates model discontinued.

Brand and model	Price	Pot material	Weight, lb.	Capacity, nominal/useful, qt.	Pressure regulator	Pressure release	Convenience	Advantages	Disadvantages	Comments
Innova 42001	$100	SS/A	7	6/3¾	W	◐	◐	B,C,E,F	—	—
Magefesa Rapid 2 Straight Side	127	SS/A	6	6/4	B	◐	◐	C,F	j	A,D,E
Maitre's 80601	35	A	4½	6/3¾	W	—	○	C,D,H	b,o	E
Presto 01240	54	A	3½	4/2½	W	—	◐	G	h,n	F
Presto 01260	62	A	4	6/3¾	W	—	◐	G	n	F
Presto 01360	99	SS	5	6/3¾	W	—	◐	G	e,h,n	F
T-Fal PCS6	99	SS/A	7	6.4/4¼	W	◑	○	A,F	j	D,E,I
Cuisinart C86-24	230	SS/C	7½	6/4¾	B	◐	◑	—	—	A,C
Presto 01340	90	SS	4½	4/2½	W	—	◐	G	e,n	F
Kuhn Rikon 3000	190	SS/A	6½	5.25/3½	B	◑	○	A,E	j,k	D,G
Mirro M-0534-50	26	A	3½	4/2¾	W	—	◐	—	b,h,j,n	B
Aeternum 750	105	SS	4½	5.5/3½	W	◑	○	—	f,j,m,n,o	A,H
Mirro M-0536	40	A	5	6/4	W	—	○	—	c,g,j,n	—
Farberware C8806	150	SS/A	7	6/4¼	B	—	◑	F	j	A,C
Hawkins Futura	110	A	5½	5.25/3	W	○	◑	—	a,f,j,n	A
Wearever 059803	45	A	6	8/6	W	—	○	—	d,j,n	C
Hawkins	39	A	4	6.9/4¼	W	◑	◑	—	a,b,f,j,n	A
Wearever 053603	30	A	5	6/4	W	—	◑	—	b,g,j,n	C

■ *The following model was downrated due to possible ejection of hot food when using pressure release.*

| Chantal SLPC6-22N ⃟D | 210 | SS/A | 6½ | 6.3/4 | B | ● | ○ | A,F | j,l | A,C |

Ratings continued ▶

PRESSURE COOKERS

Features in Common
Except as noted, all have: • Automatic, pressure-sensitive locking mechanism. • At least 1 overpressure device. • Long plastic handle and short helper handle, usually plastic, on the opposite side. • Cooking pressure of between 12 and 15 pounds per square inch (psi) above standard atmospheric pressure. • Maximum fill-level mark. • Cooking rack. • 5-yr. warranty.

Key to Advantages
A–Heat distribution better than most.
B–Pressure release easiest to use.
C–Overpressure devices better than most.
D–Easiest to open and close.
E–Easier to carry than most.
F–Has steaming basket instead of cooking rack.
G–Has cooking guide affixed to pot.
H–Scalding during fast depressurization less likely than with other models that lack pressure release.

Key to Disadvantages
a–Steam may scald fingers when you position pressure-regulating weight on the cover.
b–Took longer than most to heat up on smoothtop range.
c–Took much longer than most to heat up on smoothtop range.
d–Could not bring to pressure on smoothtop range.
e–Uneven heat distribution may burn food in spots.
f–Unusual cover design; harder to open and close than most.
g–Small helper handle makes it difficult to carry loaded pot. **Wearever** helper handle gets hot.
h–Lacks helper handle.
i–Large metal screw under handle very hot to the touch.
j–Lacks fill-level mark.
k–Lacks alignment mark on cover to help position lid.
l–Can be opened when still under slight pressure; ejection of hot food possible.
m–Pressure release awkward to use. Possibility of scalding.
n–Overpressure device needs replacing if activated.
o–Lacks cooking rack or steaming basket.

Key to Comments
A–Has manual locking mechanism.
B–Recommended fill level of 3/4 full.
C–Has 3 pressure settings: 5 to 8, 10 or 12, and 15 or 17 psi.
D–Has 2 pressure settings: 8, and 15 or 16 psi.
E–1-yr. warranty.
F–2-yr. warranty.
G–10-yr. warranty.
H–Tested samples lack warranty.
I–Has removable countdown timer of up to 59 minutes.

What the Ratings Mean

■ The Ratings typically rank products in order of estimated quality, without regard to price.

■ A product's rating applies only to the model tested and should not be considered a rating of other models sold under the same brand name unless so noted.

■ Models are check-rated (✓) when the product proved to be significantly superior to other models tested.

■ Products high in quality and relatively low in price are deemed Best Buys.

INDOOR GRILLS

RATINGS — INDOOR GRILLS

Key: E VG G F P

▶ **See report, page 124.** From Consumer Reports, February 1993.

Recommendations: Electric grills best approximate barbecuing. The *Sunbeam's* cooking performance and attractive price ($45) earned it Best Buy status. Stove-top grills approximate sauteeing. For that, consider the *Burton Double Stove Top Grill*, $40.

Ratings order: Listed in order of estimated quality. Bracketed models were judged about equal in quality. Except where separated by a bold rule, closely ranked models differed little in quality. Price is the manufacturer's suggested retail. Ⓢ indicates tested model has been replaced by successor model; according to the manufacturer, the performance of new model should be similar to the tested model but features may vary. See page 138 for new model number and suggested retail price, if available. Ⓓ indicates model discontinued.

Brand and model	Price	Size (HxWxD, in.)	Cooking area, effective sq. in.	Steak, rare/well-done	Burgers, rare/well-done	Heating evenness	Cleaning ease	Advantages	Disadvantages	Comments
ELECTRIC GRILLS										
Dazey DSG-132	$68	4¼x16¼x12¼	109	◐/○	○/◐	○	◐	G,K	i	B
Farberware R4550	100	7x18x11 [1]	151	○/◐	◐/◐	◐	○	I	I	C,J
Sunbeam Griffo 4758, A Best Buy	45	4¾x12½x12¾	112	◐/◐	◐/◐	●	○	C,D,F	h,m	G
Maverick M-90	65	4x13x14½	138	○/◐	○/◐	○	○	D,F	—	G
Rival 5760 Ⓓ	35	5½x14¼x14¼	125	◐/◐	○/◐	○	◐	—	I	K
Rival 5750	38	5½x12¾x12¾	77	◐/◐	◐/◐	●	◐	—	—	—
Tefal 39090 Ⓓ	89	7x22¼x12	102	○/◐	○/◐	●	◐	D,H,I	—	D,E
Contempra ECB-25	30	5x11¾x11¾	77	○/◐	○/○	◐	◐	—	g,h	—
Contempra ECB-41	35	5¼x13¾x13¾	127	◐/◐	◐/◐	◐	◐	G	f,g,h	—
Contempra ECB-72	40	4¼x15¼x12¼	126	○/◐	◐/◐	○	◐	—	h,n	—
Regal K6708	53	6¼x13¾x11¼	89	○/◐	◐/◐	◐	●	D,I,J	q	C
NOT ACCEPTABLE: *The following model was judged Not Acceptable due to excessive electrical leakage.*										
Maverick M-80 Ⓢ	50	3½x12¾x12¼	113	○/◐	◐/◐	○	○	F	—	G

[1] 14½x24x11 in. with rotisserie in place.

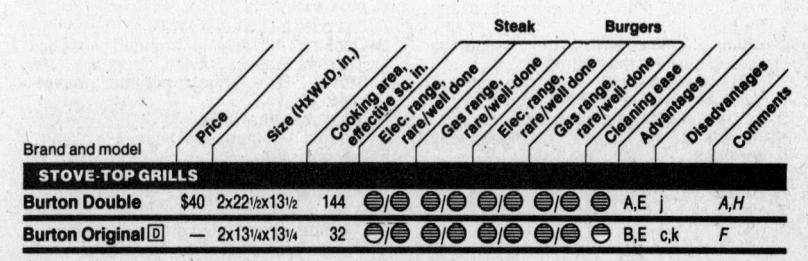

Brand and model	Price	Size (HxWxD, in.)	Cooking area, effective sq. in.	Steak Elec. range rare/well done	Steak Gas range rare/well done	Burgers Elec. range rare/well done	Burgers Gas range rare/well done	Cleaning ease	Advantages	Disadvantages	Comments
STOVE-TOP GRILLS											
Burton Double	$40	2x22½x13½	144	◐/◐	◐/◐	◐/◐	◐/◐	◐	A,E	j	A,H
Burton Original Ⓓ	—	2x13¼x13¼	32	○/◐	◐/◐	◐/◐	◐/◐	◐	B,E	c,k	F

Ratings continued ▶

INDOOR GRILLS

▶ *Ratings continued*

Brand and model	Price	Size (H×W×D, in.)	Cooking area, effective sq. in.	Elec. range, rare/well done	Gas range, rare/well done	Elec. range, rare/well done	Gas range, rare/well done	Cleaning ease	Advantages	Disadvantages	Comments
Maverick S-10	$20	1¾×12¾×12¾	31	◒/◒	◒/◒	◒/◒	◒/◒	●	E	c	B,G
Mr. Stove MG 06013	10	1¾×13×13	34	◒/◒	◒/◒	◒/◒	◒/◒	○	—	b,e	B,F

■ *Cooking tests of the following models were conducted at low heat per manufacturers' instructions (see story).*

Mr. Stove DG-06000	15	2×21¼×12¼	102	●/○	◒/◒	●/○	◒/◒	◒	—	b,e	A,B,F,I
Metro 1035 ⃞D	6	1¾×12¾×12¾	29	●/○	◒/◒	●/◐	◒/◒	◒	—	b,c,p	B,F,I
Metro 1076 ⃞D	10	1¾×21½×12½	113	●/●	◒/◒	●/○	○/◒	◒	—	a,b,d,e,o,p	A,B,F

Successor Model
Maverick M-80 is succeeded by D-2800, $50.

Features in Common
Except as noted, all: • Were judged very good to excellent at grilling salmon steaks.
Except as noted, all electric models: • Were judged very good to excellent at minimizing smoke. • Have fixed, chromed-steel wire grates, ceramic base. • Have 2-prong plug. • Lack temp. control. • Have 1-yr. warranty.
All stove-top models: • Claim to be suitable for gas and electric stoves. • Were judged fair to good at minimizing smoke when cooking at high heat (but improved significantly when used at low). • May be washed in dishwasher, according to mfr.
Except as noted, all stove-top models: • Have aluminum griddle, painted-steel drip pan. • Cooked evenly.

Key to Advantages
A–"Excalibur" cooking surface, judged much more durable than others.
B–Teflon II coating, judged more durable than most others.
C–Porcelain-coated steel grate with small holes; better than other electrics' grates for fish.
D–Heating element/reflector assembly judged sturdier than others.
E–Porcelain-coated steel drip pan.
F–Infinitely variable temperature control.
G–2-position temperature control.
H–Grate's height can be changed while cooking.
I–Height of grate can be adjusted.
J–Drip pan; can double as small frying pan.
K–Nonstick coating on grate eased cleanup.

Key to Disadvantages
a–Electric range burned paint on drip tray.
b–Drip pan rusted during tests.
c–Griddle tips easily into drip tray.
d–Steel griddle; developed more hot spots than aluminum ones.
e–Does not fit well on electric ranges.
f–Reflector and heating element can easily fall into base while cooking.
g–Small drip pan; if tipped, can easily spill grease through open bottom of unit.
h–Harder to assemble than most.
i–Heating-element support fell off repeatedly during assembly.
j–Too much water recommended in tray.
k–Too little water recommended in tray.
l–Power cord judged hard to plug in and remove from unit.
m–Produced more smoke than other electrics.
n–Heating element doesn't attach firmly.
o–Overly high heat may damage griddle.
p–Should not be preheated; limitation degraded cooking performance with fish from fair to poor.
q–Sharp edges; could cut user's hand.

Key to Comments
A–Fits over 2 stove burners.
B–Cooking surface: unbranded nonstick (**Dazey, Metro**); "Xylan" nonstick (**Mr. Stove**); "Blue Ribbon" nonstick (**Maverick S-10**).
C–Stainless-steel base.
D–Porcelain-coated steel base.
E–3-prong plug.
F–No warranty.
G–2-yr. warranty
H–20-yr. warranty.
I–Cleanup judged fair if grill used on High.
J–Comes with rotisserie.

▶ Autos

Recommended 1993 cars	140
Ratings of 1993 cars	152
How to buy a new car	166
Should you lease?	169
How to buy a used car	170
Good & bad bets in used cars	173
Reliability records	178
Trouble indexes	218
Owner satisfaction	224

Given the average selling price of a new car—$17,000—car shoppers must be better prepared than ever when considering this most expensive of regular purchases. To that end, we provide information on three key issues: performance, price, and reliability.

Performance. We present performance information, drawn from our most recent road tests, in two forms: a list of Recommended cars, with descriptions, and hierarchical Ratings. For those who want more information on recently tested models, the Ratings tell you the issue date of the last full report in consumer reports and the order number for reports available by fax (see page 393).

Price. Because a car's sticker price frequently represents an asking price, not a selling price, one shopper may pay $1000 or more than another for the same car. A car typically costs the dealer about 85 percent of the sticker price, and if you know how to negotiate, the dealer may let you have it for close to cost. The report on page 166 takes you through the process.

The selling price for a used car depends on the car's condition and accessories, the region of the country, and whether the sale is private or through a dealer. Although any used car is a risk, it also can offer the best value. Compared with a new car, a used car costs less, depreciates more slowly, and is cheaper to insure. The report on page 170 tells you what you need to know.

Reliability. You can better your odds of getting sound transportation by choosing a car that our readers report as having a good reliability history. The trouble indexes, which start on page 218, sum up the detailed Frequency-of-Repair records, which begin on page 178.

The recommended 1993 cars

The summary descriptions of the models we recommend in the following pages are listed alphabetically. In general, recommended models are those that performed competently in recent tests and have proved at least reasonably reliable. (In a few cases, we recommend models not recently reported on—because they've been reliable and because we've had favorable experience with them either in the past or presently.)

We divide the following car models into seven categories. Small cars provide basic, general transportation. Sporty cars include performance-oriented coupes, sports cars, and convertibles. Compact cars provide practical transportation for small families. Mid-sized cars are the classic "family car." We've divided them into two groups—those that cost less than $25,000 and those that cost more. Large cars are big and bulky, with comfortable seating for up to six. Small passenger vans are the successors to the station wagon. Sport-utility vehicles are increasingly popular as runabouts and all-purpose family wagons.

Small cars

Excellent ◄──────► Poor

Acura Integra

The sportiest sedan designed by Honda. Superb handling and braking. The 1.8-liter Four transmission provides brisk acceleration. Overdrive automatic transmission usually shifted smoothly. Front-seat comfort ◔; rear-seat ◑. Controls and displays ◔. Climate-control system ◔. Excellent predicted reliability. Due for redesign in 1994.

Mercury Tracer
Ford Escort

Both the Tracer and the Escort are average all-around performers, much better in the GT, LX-E, and LTS versions. The standard 1.9-liter Four provides leisurely acceleration. The 1.8-liter Four in the more expensive LX-E, GT, and LTS versions is peppier. The basic Escort handles competently, though steering response is a little sloppy. Poor brakes. The LX-E's taut suspension makes the car feel nimble, but the car's tail wags in emergency maneuvers. The LX-E's ride is stiff and uncomfortable. Front-seat comfort ◔; rear-seat ○. Controls ◔; displays ●. Climate-control system ◔. Average predicted reliability. The rear seatback sections fold to enlarge trunk.

Geo Prizm

Formerly a virtual twin of the Toyota Corolla, the redesigned Prizm has a slightly firmer ride, and it tends to come with less standard equipment and costs less than the Toyota. For best performance, choose the 1.8-liter Four over the base-level 1.6-liter Four, and choose the five-speed manual transmission over the automatic. The Prizm's body rolls a bit less than the Corolla's during cornering, and the steering responds more crisply, but lifting off the accelerator during hard cornering can make the tail wag. The antilock brakes stop the car short, though not always entirely straight, on wet and dry roads. The ride is never punishing, but large bumps make their presence known a bit more forcefully than in the Corolla. Front-seat comfort ◔; rear-seat ◑. Controls and displays ●. Climate-control system ●. Excellent predicted reliability.

Honda Civic

Perennially one of our favorite small cars, the Civic was redesigned in 1992. Expect peppy acceleration from the basic 1.5-liter Four, and even peppier performance from the 1.6-liter "VTEC" Four. The ride is firm on smooth pavement, active on back roads. The noise level is relatively high. Routine handling was good; emergency handling, smooth. The brakes stop short and straight. Front-seat comfort is ◒; rear-seat ◓. Controls and displays ●. Climate-control system ●. Excellent predicted reliability.

Mazda 323
Mazda Protegé

Getting left behind by new competitors. The 323 is the two-door version; the Protegé, the four-door. The 1.8-liter Four in the Protegé gives peppy acceleration. Overdrive automatic transmission shifts smoothly except during brisk acceleration. Crisp, responsive handling in normal driving, but controlling tail wag sometimes took skillful steering when the car was nearing its limits. Braking is excellent. For added performance, consider the LX version, with a more powerful engine and other sports-oriented equipment. Front-seat comfort ◒; rear-seat ○. Controls and displays ●. Climate-control system ●. Excellent predicted reliability.

Nissan Sentra

The Sentra's sporty looks could make you forget it's an economy car. Its smooth, quiet ride would have made this model a very desirable small car if not for the tight, uncomfortable rear seat. Acceleration is adequate with the standard 1.6-liter Four, and fuel mileage is impressive. (With the SE-R version's 2.0-liter Four, performance is brisk.) The four-speed automatic shifts quite smoothly. Handling is stable and controllable in abrupt emergency maneuvers, but somewhat sloppy during hard cornering under power. Stopping distances are rather long. The interior is as quiet as in many large cars. Front-seat comfort ◒; rear-seat ●. Controls and displays ◒. Climate-control system ●. Excellent predicted reliability. The trunk is large for a small car.

Saturn

Exceptional reliability, unusual in a domestic car. The 1.9-liter Four in the base versions (SL and SL1) provides impressive fuel economy, but it's noisy and the acceleration is pokey. Much nicer are the higher-line versions, with their peppier engine, more closely spaced gears and sportier suspension. The optional automatic transmission shifts smoothly. Handling is nimble and precise, but the ride is stiff. Along with its driver's-side air bag, the Saturn retains its motorized shoulder belts, which tend to entangle anyone getting in or out carrying packages. Front-seat comfort ○; rear-seat ◓. Controls and displays ◒. Climate-control system ◒. Excellent predicted reliability data. Plastic body panels are dent-resistant and easy to replace when damaged.

Subaru Impreza

New in 1993, it replaces the crude and tinny Subaru Loyale sedan (the Loyale station wagon lives on into 1994). We'd opt for the LS version of the Impreza, with automatic transmission and antilock brakes. Without antilock brakes, stopping distances are very long on wet pavement and control is poor. The steering is nicely weighted and responsive. The LS model's larger tires and more suspension provides crisp and nimble handling. The ride is smooth and gentle on the highway, somewhat jittery on bad roads. Front-seat comfort ◒; rear-seat ◓. Controls and displays ◒. Climate-control system ◒. New model; no reliability data.

RECOMMENDED CARS

Toyota Corolla

This has long been one of our recommended cars. It's an able performer, thoughtfully appointed, with an excellent reliability record. Formerly twins, the Corolla and the Geo Prizm still share the same powertrains, platform, and many body parts. The redesigned Corolla has a firmer ride than its predecessor, tends to come with more standard equipment, and is priced higher. For best performance, choose the 1.8-liter Four over the base-level 1.6-liter Four, and choose the five-speed manual transmission over the automatic. Safe and predictable handling. The suspension damps out the biggest road irregularities, but the highway ride feels a little jiggly. Front-seat comfort ◐; rear-seat ◐. Controls and displays ◐. Climate-control system ◐. Excellent predicted reliability.

Compact cars

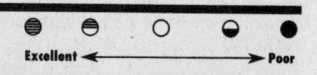

Excellent ← → Poor

BMW 325i

The 325i version does everything a sports sedan should do: Its 2.5-liter Six accelerates powerfully, and the optional four-speed automatic shifts smoothly. A manual setting lets you hold any gear, useful when starting out on slippery roads. Rear-wheel drive. Precise, nimble handling. Crisp and responsive emergency handling. Firm but well-controlled ride. Brakes superbly. Front-seat comfort ◐; rear-seat ○. Controls ◐; ◐ displays. Climate-control system ◐. Average predicted reliability.

Honda Accord

One of the best-selling models in the U.S. Acceleration with the 2.2-liter Four is as strong as that of many compacts' V6. Electronically controlled automatic transmission shifts a bit abruptly and whines. Smooth, nimble handling. Short, straight stops, but the antilock brakes pulse obtrusively. Firm, nervous ride; somewhat better with a full load. Rather noisy inside. Low but comfortable front seats, with excellent driver visibility. Front-seat comfort ◐; rear-seat ○. Controls ◐; displays ◐. Climate-control system ◐. Excellent predicted reliability. Redesigned in late 1993.

Infiniti G20

The 2.0-liter Four is powerful and relatively economical. The optional four-speed automatic transmission shifts smoothly in normal driving, more aggressively during hard acceleration. The G20's relatively light weight makes the car feel especially nimble, but handling can be tricky at the limit. Stiff but not punishing ride. Front-seat comfort ◐; rear-seat ○. Controls and displays ◐. Climate-control system ◐. Excellent predicted reliability. The trunk is roomy, but it's awkward to access. The 1993½ version boasts dual airbags.

Mazda 626

A good compact sedan that scores well in all our important tests. The top-of-the-line ES comes with a smooth and powerful V6. The four-speed automatic transmission, however, sometimes shifts abruptly; we prefer the five-speed manual transmission. The antilock brakes stop the car short and straight on dry roads, but wet-pavement distances are rather long. The lower-priced LX sedan is a better bet for the value-minded; it comes with a four-cylinder engine and all-weather tires. Responsive handling. Smooth ride even on poor roads. Front-seat comfort ◐; rear-seat ◐. Controls and displays ◐. Climate-control system ◐. New model; no reliability data. The split rear seatback folds to expand the trunk.

Mitsubishi Galant

A desirable model that combines crisp, sporty handling with comfortable seating, both front and rear. The 2.0-liter Four accelerates responsively. Electronically controlled automatic transmission shifts smoothly except during light acceleration at low speeds. Electronic steering in the GS version lets you adjust steering effort. Excellent brakes. Firm, nervous ride. Provided mediocre driver protection in Government crash tests. Front- and rear-seat comfort ◐. Controls and displays ◓. Climate-control system ◓. Excellent predicted reliability. Redesign available in late 1993.

Nissan Altima

Introduced as a 1993 model, the Altima should have been state of the art. While it tested out decently overall, it falls down in handling and ride. Its driving behavior is safe but ungainly. The Altima leans noticeably when cornering, plowing ahead through hard, tight turns. Overall, its handling remains predictable. The antilock brakes stop short and straight on wet and dry pavement. The ride is always jittery and busy. The 2.4-liter Four accelerates quite quickly, but it buzzes and hums while gathering speed. Front-seat comfort ◐; rear-seat ○. Controls and displays ○. Climate-control system ◓. New model; no reliability data.

Subaru Legacy

This competent but unexciting model has changed little since its 1989 introduction. The Legacy is the only mid-priced compact to offer all-wheel drive; though pricey, that option significantly improves traction on slippery roads. The four-cylinder engine delivers adequate acceleration; a turbo version is available. The four-speed automatic transmission shifts quite smoothly. The antilock brakes stop straight and fairly short. Handling is steady during routine driving, but handling can be tricky at during abrupt emergency maneuvers. Smooth, quiet ride. The trunk is large, and folding down the rear seats makes it even larger. Front-seat comfort ◐; rear-seat ○. Controls and displays ◐. Climate-control system ◓. Better than average predicted reliability.

Sporty cars

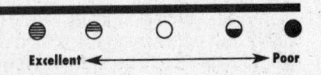

◓ ◐ ○ ◒ ●
Excellent ← → Poor

Chevrolet Camaro

The Camaro and its cousin, the Pontiac Firebird, were redesigned in 1993 but remain big rear-wheel-drive muscle cars. The drivetrain determines the personality of both of these cousins. The basic version comes with a 3.4-liter V6 and five-speed transmission, which is by no means pokey. But the more expensive V8 is powerful and effortless. Both versions ride decently for a sporty car, but the V8 feels noticeably firmer. Very good braking. Wide roof pillars block much of the driver's view to the right rear, and both the front and rear ends are invisible to the driver. Front-seat comfort ◐; rear-seat ●. Controls and displays ○. Climate-control system ◓. New model; no reliability data.

Dodge Stealth
Mitsubishi 3000GT

Mitsubishi's answer to the Chevrolet Corvette. These exotic siblings deliver superlative performance, especially with the 3.0-liter twin-turbo V6 and all-wheel drive in the highest-trimline version. The R/T Turbo offers quick steering response and traction, competent cornering, extraordinarily short stops, and blazing acceleration. Front-seat comfort ◐; rear-seat ●. Controls ○; displays ◓. Climate-control system ◓. Average predicted reliability.

Ford Probe GT
Mazda MX-6

Both models were redesigned for 1993. Though their bodies are different, they share many mechanical parts. The higher price line of each make is a step up in performance from the base four-cylinder version. Their smooth V6 engine accelerates with authority. Choose the five-speed transmission; the automatic transmission in our 1993 model shifted abruptly. Handling is very smooth and predictable. The Probe feels a bit crisper; the MX-6 rides a bit more comfortably. Front-seat comfort ◓ in the Mazda, ○ in the Ford; rear-seat ● in both (but good for a coupe). Controls and displays ◓. Climate-control system ◓ in the Ford, ○ in the Mazda. New models; no reliability data. Generous luggage room under the Probe's hatchback, and folding the rear seatbacks extends the luggage area. The MX-6 is a coupe with a conventional trunk.

Honda Prelude

Honda redesigned the Prelude in 1992 and added a high-performance VTEC engine as an option in 1993. The five-speed manual transmission shifts slickly and precisely, but depressing the clutch pedal requires a stretch. The steering feels nicely weighted and responsive. The car handles well. Braking is respectable, though not outstanding. The ride is jiggly, though well controlled even on rough pavement. The cabin is quiet for a sporty car. Front-seat comfort ◓; rear-seat ●. Controls and displays ○. Climate-control system ○. Excellent predicted reliability. Space for storage and luggage is limited.

Mazda MX-3

This small, agile coupe was introduced in 1992. A 1.6-liter Four is standard in the base version. Even with the smooth, free-revving 1.8-liter V6 that's optional in the GS version, it lacks the acceleration of such competitors as the Nissan NX 2000 and Saturn SC. The gears makes the engine rev faster than necessary. Steering is accurate and precise, and the tires grip well. But the ride is very stiff and noisy. The optional antilock brakes are especially needed in this model; the standard brakes work well on dry roads; but wet-pavement stopping distances are rather long. Front-seat comfort ○; rear-seat, ●. Controls ◓; displays ◓. Climate-control system ◓. Better than average predicted reliability.

Mazda MX-5 Miata

A two-seat convertible that feels much like the Austin-Healeys, Triumphs, and MGs of the 1950s and 1960s—including their harsh and noisy ride. The Miata, however, is weathertight and reliable. (A removable plastic hardtop is optional.) The 1.6-liter Four provides peppy performance and impressive fuel economy. A crisp-shifting five-speed manual transmission has a stubby shifter and short shift pattern. Nimble handling, precise and direct steering, and powerful brakes. The driver's foot room around the pedals is limited. Front-seat comfort ◓; no rear-seat. Controls and displays ◓. Climate-control system ◓. Excellent predicted reliability.

Mazda RX-7

The RX-7 is a two-seater styled after classic sports cars of the past. Acceleration, braking, and handling from the rear-wheel drive chassis are superb. The stiff suspension produces an exceptionally hard, uncomfortable ride. Relentlessly noisy. Access is awkward even for a sports car. Front-seat comfort ◓; no rear seat. Controls ○; displays ◓. Climate-control system ◓. New model; no reliability data. Luggage space is minimal, too. An R1 version is available for those who want maximum performance; it comes with a stiffer suspension and minus leather upholstery and power accessories.

RECOMMENDED CARS

Nissan NX 1600
Nissan NX 2000

The Nissan Sentra sedan provides many of the parts for this model. The NX 2000 is one of the best of the moderately priced sporty cars. Its 2.0-liter Four accelerates with authority, and the five-speed manual transmission shifts smoothly and crisply. The Nissan NX 1600 is similar; its 1.6-liter Four lacks the larger engine's punch, but it should provide better fuel mileage. The NX 2000 handles nimbly and precisely and takes tight corners smoothly and predictably. Stops are short and straight. The ride is stiff and choppy. Getting in and out is awkward. Front-seat comfort ◓; rear-seat ●. Controls ◓; displays ◒. Climate-control system ◓. Excellent predicted reliability. The NX models have been dropped for 1994.

Nissan 300ZX

This two-seater is everything a sports car should be. It's remakably smooth and easy to drive. The 3.0-liter V6, with twin turbochargers, runs flawlessly and delivers blazing acceleration without noticeable turbo lag. The five-speed manual transmission shifts crisply and precisely. Routine handling of this rear-wheel drive model is near perfect; during emergency maneuvers, it's crisp and quick. The antilock brakes stop short and straight. Front-seat comfort ◓; rear-seat ●. Controls and displays ○. Climate-control system ◒. Average predicted reliability. The cargo bay is relatively roomy for a sports car.

Pontiac Firebird

The last major change for the Firebird/Camaro cousins occurred 11 years ago—an eternity in the auto industry. But the 1993 redesign was worth the wait. The basic V6 delivers respectable acceleration; the V8, effortless acceleration. The Firebird's steering felt a bit smoother, quicker, and more precise than the Camaro's. Very good braking. Wide roof pillars block much of the driver's view to the right rear, and both the front and rear ends are invisible to the driver. Front-seat comfort ◓; rear-seat ●. Controls and displays ◒. Climate-control system ◒. New model; no reliability data.

Saturn SC

The SC2 is the sporty coupe version of the Saturn SL2 with its own unique front-end styling. The twin-camshaft 1.9-liter Four combines quick acceleration with fast, nimble, and precise handling. At steady speeds, the Saturn is notably quiet inside. The taut suspension makes for a stiff, sometimes jarring ride. Front-seat comfort ○; rear-seat ●. Controls ◒; displays ◒. Climate-control system ◒. Excellent predicted reliability. Plastic body panels are dent-resistant and easy to replace when damaged.

Subaru SVX

The SVX is more a touring coupe than a sports car. It offers the stability and slippery-road traction of all-wheel drive and the comfort and quietness of a luxury sedan, along with a high level of technical sophistication. A 3.3-liter Six and smooth-shifting four-speed automatic transmission deliver ample acceleration. Normal handling feels very stable and predictable, but emergency handling isn't precise. The divided side windows make it hard to reach through the window and the Auto Up feature on the driver's side window could squeeze an unwary finger or a child's neck. Front-seat comfort ◓; rear-seat ●. Controls ◓; displays ◒. Climate-control system ◒. Average predicted reliability.

RECOMMENDED CARS

Mid-sized cars under $25,000

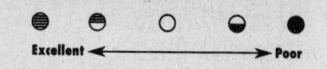

Excellent ◄──────► Poor

Ford Taurus
Mercury Sable

The Taurus and its sibling, the Mercury Sable remain in the front rank of domestic sedans. They deliver fine all-around performance, comfortable seating, and reasonable fuel economy. The standard-equipment four-speed automatic shifts smoothly. These models handle very well in normal driving, though sluggishly in hard turns at the track. At anything below highway speed, the steering feels much too light. The interior is quiet except for wind noise. The heavy-duty suspension caused frequent jiggles and some side-to-side rocking on bumpy roads. Front-seat comfort ●; rear-seat ◐. Controls ◐; displays ●. Climate-control system ●. Average predicted reliability.

Nissan Maxima

The Maxima remains a competent and well-rounded sedan. It provides precise handling, sporty acceleration, a large measure of comfort, and a full complement of safety equipment. Nissan has moved the Maxima upscale to separate it further from the compact Nissan Altima. The SE model gets a more powerful 3.0-liter V6. Front-seat comfort ●; rear-seat ○. Controls ●; displays ◐. Climate-control system ●. Excellent predicted reliability.

Toyota Camry

The best mid-sized car selling for under $25,000. It drives effortlessly, like a luxury car. In fact, the V6 version scored virtually identically, overall, with Toyota's luxury Lexus ES300 model, with which it shares its engine, driveline, and chassis. The Camry doesn't have the panache of the Lexus name—but it offers far better value. The 3.0-liter V6 is smooth, quiet, and strong, but the 2.2-liter Four is no slouch. Stops are short and straight. Front-seat comfort in the Four ◐, in the V6 ●; rear-seat comfort in both ○. Controls and displays ●. Climate-control system ●. Excellent predicted reliability.

Mid-sized cars over $25,000

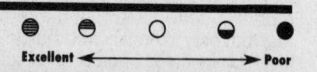

Excellent ◄──────► Poor

Acura Legend

The Legend, with its strong 3.2-liter V6, accelerates impressively and smoothly, especially for a car of its size and weight. But expect only about 20 mpg overall—on premium fuel. The four-speed automatic transmission sometimes shifts with a thump. The car handles predictably but not nimbly in normal driving. Considerable body lean and mediocre tire grip limited the speed through our avoidance maneuver. Stops are straight, though relatively long. The ride is fairly taut but well controlled and quiet. Front-seat comfort ●; rear-seat ○. Controls ●; displays ●. Climate-control system ◐. Excellent predicted reliability.

BMW 535i

A sporty package. Responsive acceleration from the 3.5-liter inline Six and superb handling make this rear-wheel-drive sedan a pleasure to drive. The 1994 versions—the 530i and 540i—share the same body as the 535i but sport an all-aluminum V8. Exceptionally smooth-shifting overdrive automatic transmission. One of the shortest dry stopping distances we've recorded. Road-hugging ability on winding back roads comes at the expense of a rather stiff ride. Skittery on slick roads. Front-seating comfort ●; rear seating ○. Controls ○; displays ●. Climate-control system ●. Excellent predicted reliability.

RECOMMENDED CARS

Cadillac Seville

The Seville was designed to compete with the more sophisticated sedans from Mercedes, BMW, Lexus, and Infiniti. The heart of that redesign is the "Northstar system"—a combination of a 4.6-liter aluminum V8, an electronically controlled four-speed auto transmission, a traction-control system and, in the STS version, an "active" suspension that reacts to road conditions. Faster acceleration than many performance cars. Our STS handled securely if not quickly. Smooth ride on good roads deteriorates on poor ones. Front-seat comfort ◐; rear-seat ○. Controls and displays ◐. Climate-control system ◐. Average predicted reliability.

Infiniti J30

The J30 is essentially a four-door luxury coupe that sacrifices sporty handling for a gentle ride and near-absolute isolation from the road. A 3.0-liter V6 drives the rear wheels, delivering smooth and responsive acceleration, and the four-speed auto transmission shifts smoothly. The car leans noticeably in tight turns, and the rear tires break loose fairly easily on slippery surfaces. Tail wag is tricky to control in abrupt maneuvers. The antilock brakes stop the car short and straight. Smooth and quiet ride. Front-seat comfort ◐; rear-seat ◑. Controls and displays ◐. Climate-control system ◐. The trunk is small, and its high sill makes loading difficult. Excellent predicted reliability.

Infiniti Q45

This is the top-of-the-line Infiniti. The first generation Q45 scored points for its performance-car acceleration and superb handling. The new Q45 sacrifices performance for a quieter, refined ride. The 4.5-liter V8 provides excellent acceleration. Antilock brakes stop short and straight. A quiet ride. Handling is very good. Traction control tames the skittishness of the rear-wheel drive. Front-seat comfort ◐; rear-seat ◑. Controls ◐; displays ◐. Climate-control system ◐. Excellent predicted reliability.

Lexus ES300

This sophisticated upscale model feels much like the bigger and costlier Lexus LS400, but nimbler and sportier. The ES300 shares its engine, driveline, and chassis with the V6 version of the Toyota Camry, which sells for about $7000 less. Not surprisingly, those two models scored virtually the same, overall, in our tests. The 3.0-liter V6 accelerates powerfully and the four-speed automatic transmission shifts imperceptibly. Rides smoothly and very quietly. The steering feels too light during normal driving, but predictable handling during abrupt accident-avoidance maneuvers inspires confidence. The brakes stop the car short and straight on wet and dry pavement. Front-seat comfort ◐; rear-seat ○. Controls and displays ◐. Climate-control system ◐. Large trunk. Excellent predicted reliability.

Lexus LS400

This luxury sedan combines a sophisticated, modern powertrain with a lush, quiet, leather-wrapped interior. Virtually everything under the hood is electronically controlled. Not a "driver's car," it isolates the driver from the road. Fine acceleration and exceptionally smooth shifting. Very light, almost numb, steering and soft suspension. Emergency handling is sure-footed but not quick. A smooth, quiet ride. Front-seat comfort ◐; rear-seat ◐. Controls and displays ◐. Climate-control system ◐. Excellent predicted reliability.

Lexus SC400

This is the two-door luxury-coupe version of the flagship Lexus LS400 luxury sedan. The refined and powerful aluminum V8, with rear-wheel drive, delivers plenty of acceleration, and the suspension handles winding roads as nimbly as that of a fine sports car. A sophisticated and effective traction-control system minimizes wheel spin. The ride is firm, but the suspension soaks up most road bumps without fuss. The Lexus SC300 looks virtually the same as the SC400. Its spirited Six isn't as smooth as the V8, but the car costs thousands less. Front-seat comfort ◐; rear-seat ◑. Controls and displays ◐. Climate-control system ◐. Excellent predicted reliability.

Lincoln Continental

Since 1988, this model has been a front-wheel-drive mid-sized car built on the Ford Taurus/Mercury Sable platform. The 1995 model year will bring about a complete redesign. Like other Lincoln models, this one comes with most accessories as standard equipment. Acceleration is leisurely. Handling and steering was a little sluggish when we tested it a few years ago but this year's suspension modifications may improve matters. Front-seat comfort ●; rear-seat ◐. Controls ◐; displays ●. Climate-control system ◐. Huge trunk that's conveniently shaped and nicely finished. Average predicted reliability.

Lincoln Mark VIII

This rear-wheel-drive luxury coupe replaced the nine-year-old Mark VII in 1993. A powerful aluminum V8, an electronically controlled transmission, and a fully independent suspension delivers as smooth a ride as you'll find. The traction assist works only at low speeds, and a heavy foot on the throttle easily overwhelms it. The steering feels overly light at low speeds, but it's surprisingly agile for such a large car. Front-seat comfort ◐; rear-seat ◑. Controls and displays ●. Climate-control system ◐. New model; no reliability data.

Mazda 929

The 929 retains its traditional rear-wheel drive, but all else is state of the art. The 3.0-liter V6 takes off aggressively from standstill, a trait that can produce disconcerting wheel spin on slippery roads. The four-speed automatic transmission shifts very smoothly. Handling is smooth and steady in normal driving, but loose and queasy during hard cornering. The brakes perform admirably on dry and wet roads. Very quiet and comfortable ride. The front seats could use more side support during hard cornering. Front- and rear-seat comfort ◐. Controls and displays ●. Climate-control system ●. Skimpy trunk. Better than average predicted reliability.

Volvo 850GLT

This sporty yet highly practical and competent sedan has a responsive 2.4-liter, five-cylinder engine, mounted sideways. The four-speed automatic transmission usually shifts smoothly. Traction control is a worthwhile option. A stiff, choppy ride. Steering response isn't particularly quick, but steering effort is just right. Safe and predictable handling. On dry pavement, the 850GLT stopped shortest of any car we've ever tested; wet-pavement stops were also short. Front-seat comfort ●; rear-seat ◐. Controls and displays ●. Climate-control system ●. Safety features: dual air bags, five three-point safety belts with pretensioners, antilock brakes, side-impact reinforcement, a built-in rear child safety booster seat. New model; no reliability data.

Volvo 940/960

Both models share the same boxy body, which excels as a people-carrier. It provides easy access, exceptional comfort for four or even five, a wealth of safety features, and a cavernous trunk that makes it ideal for family vacations. In short, it's a nice design overall—but the Volvo 850 is even nicer, and cheaper. The 960 series comes with a 2.9-liter in-line Six; the 940 series has a 2.3-liter Four, with or without a turbocharger. The six-cylinder version provides enthusiastic performance. An automatic-locking differential limits wheel spin on slippery surfaces. Previous Volvo sedans have never handled nimbly, and this model is no exception. Handling is safe and predictable. Stops are short and straight. The ride is taut and smooth. Front-seat comfort ●; rear-seat ◐. Controls ◐; displays ●. Climate-control system ●. Better than average predicted reliability.

RECOMMENDED CARS

Large cars

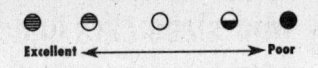

Excellent ◄——————► Poor

Eagle Vision
Chrysler Concorde
Dodge Intrepid

These triplets, code-named "LH," are high-rated among large cars. They seem to be well made, with a solid body structure. The 3.3-liter V6 accelerates responsively; the optional 3.5-liter V6 packs even more punch, but it's noisier. The automatic transmission shifts quite smoothly. With any of the three available suspensions, the Concorde and its brethren handle nimbly. The stiffest suspension provides the sportiest handling, along with the firmest ride. The mid-level "touring" suspension is probably the best choice for most drivers. Front- and rear-seating comfort ◐. Controls and displays in the Chrysler and Eagle ◐; in the Dodge ○. Climate-control system in the Chrysler and Eagle ○; in the Dodge ◐. New model; no reliability data.

Ford Crown Victoria/
Mercury Grand Marquis

These twins are big freeway cruisers with a V8, the traditional full frame, and rear-wheel drive. They ride very well, especially when fully loaded. Huge trunk and substantial trailer-towing capability. 4.6-liter engine accelerates quite well. Steering response is fairly good but provides little feel of the road. For improved handling, consider the optional Handling and Performance Package and traction assist. Optional antilock brakes work well on dry payment, somewhat less well on wet pavement. Front- and rear-seating comfort ◐. Controls and displays ◐. Climate-control system ◐. Average predicted reliability.

Oldsmobile 88 Royale
Buick Le Sabre

Overall personality depends on equipment. With the standard suspension, both are typical of a big car, in the worst sense of the term. Quiet, floating ride on most roads; sloppy on rough roads. The optional touring suspension makes for much more responsive handling, much like that of the Pontiac Bonneville, cousin to the 88 Royale and Le Sabre. The 3.8-liter V6 accelerates responsively and returns relatively good fuel mileage. The four-speed automatic transmission shifts extremely smoothly. The brakes stop well on dry pavement, not so well on wet pavement. Front- and rear-seating comfort is ◐. Controls on the Olds ○ (the Buick is somewhat better); displays ◐. Climate-control system ●. Better than average predicted reliability.

Pontiac Bonneville

It's our top-rated large car by a small margin, but that recommendation depends in part on trim line and options. The SE version with the optional firm suspension and large touring tires handles especially well. The ride feels tight, almost European. The Bonneville responds precisely and quickly to its steering, delivers enthusiastic acceleration, and the four-speed automatic transmission shifts responsively and smoothly. The optional antilock brakes work well on dry pavement, but worse than average on wet pavement. Front- and rear-seating comfort ◐. Controls and displays ●. Climate-control system ◐. Better than average predicted reliability.

Mid-sized cars under $25,000

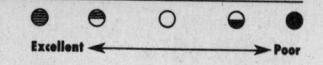

Excellent ◄———► Poor

Chevrolet Lumina APV
Oldsmobile Silhouette
Pontiac Trans Sport

The Lumina APV performs competently, overall, as do its siblings, the Oldsmobile Silhouette and Pontiac Trans Sport. The optional seating layout for seven passengers is especially versatile: the five modular seats fold, shift, or can be easily removed. The 3.1-liter V6 and three-speed automatic gives adequate acceleration; the optional 3.8-liter V6 and four-speed automatic provide much better performance. Handling is nimble in normal driving, reasonably controllable in emergency maneuvers. Excellent bumper protection. Front-seat comfort ◉; middle-seat ○; rearmost-seat ◉. Controls ◉; displays ◉. Climate-control system ●. Average predicted reliability.

Dodge Caravan
Plymouth Voyager

For years these twins were our benchmark minivans. The competition is stiffer nowadays, but Chrysler Corporation's models remain competitive. The 3.3-liter V6 delivers plenty of acceleration. The automatic sometimes shifts too often; a five-speed manual is available in some versions. Like most vans, handling is sluggish. Optional, stiffer suspensions improve handling somewhat. Traction, already quite good, improves markedly with optional all-wheel drive. Front- and middle-seat comfort ◉; rearmost-seat ◉. Controls and displays ○. Climate-control system ◉. Average predicted reliability.

Ford Aerostar

The Aerostar is a sound choice for heavy-duty work, whether that means carrying six or seven passengers or towing a trailer. Credit its powerful 4.0-liter V6, optional in some versions, and its roomy cargo compartment, especially in the stretched version. (The 3.0-liter V6 provides adequate acceleration in the standard-length versions of the Aerostar.) The four-speed automatic sometimes can shift abruptly. The all-wheel-drive version handles more sure-footedly than the ponderous rear-wheel-drive version, especially on slippery roads. Front- and middle-seat comfort ◉; rearmost-seat ○. Controls ◉; displays ●. Climate-control system ◉. Average predicted reliability. The Aerostar will be replaced by the Windstar, a front-wheel-drive minivan, in late 1994.

Mercury Villager
Nissan Quest

The Villager and its sibling, the Nissan Quest, are our top-rated minivans and they're the most carlike of the ones we've tested. They have significantly less cargo room than, say, the Dodge Caravan/Plymouth Voyager twins. The 3.0-liter V6 delivers plenty of power, and the four-speed automatic generally shifts smoothly. We strongly recommend the optional trailer-towing package for its extra engine cooling and conventional spare tire, as well as its increased towing capacity. The ride is quite smooth and quiet, and handling is nimble and precise. The Villager's ride is a bit softer than the Quest's, but its handling isn't quite as crisp; the optional heavy-duty suspension provides a slight edge in handling. The standard (except in the Quest) antilock brakes stop well. Annoying motorized belts. Front-and middle-seat comfort ◉; rearmost-seat ○. Controls and displays ◉. Climate-control system ●. New models; no reliability data.

Toyota Previa

If you use a van mostly to carry people, this is a good choice. It has nice balance, responsive steering, and a quiet ride. The 2.4-liter Four strains when the van is fully loaded. The four-speed automatic transmission shifts back and forth annoyingly between third and fourth gears on uphill slopes. The All-Trac four-wheel-drive option is worthwhile for its extra traction in poor driving conditions. The Previa feels secure in routine driving and reasonably steady in hard turns at the track. But wide roof pillars and third-row head restraints reduce the driver's view, and the downward-curving body panels hamper the driver's ability to gauge tight clearances. Front- and middle-seat comfort ◒; rear-seat ◐. Controls ◒; displays ●. Climate-control system ◒. Excellent predicted reliability.

Sport-utility vehicles

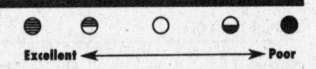

● ◒ ○ ◐ ●
Excellent ◄─────────► Poor

Ford Explorer
Mazda Navajo

The Explorer has been the best-selling sport-utility vehicle in the U.S. Big and roomy, the four-door version easily seats five. The Mazda Navajo, which only comes as a two-door, is essentially similar to the Explorer. The 4.0-liter V6 delivers peppy performance, and the four-speed automatic transmission shifts smoothly. A convenient button on the dash engages four-wheel drive; the system lacks a center differential, so it's unsuited for dry pavement. Handling is ponderous but predictable. We strongly recommend the optional limited-slip rear axle, which helps control rear-wheel spin in turns, and the optional trailer-towing package, with its additional engine cooling. Front-seat comfort ◒; rear-seat ○. Controls ◒; displays ●. Climate-control system ◒. Average predicted reliability.

Isuzu Trooper

Introduced in 1992 as a replacement for the Trooper II, the new Trooper is more civilized than its boxy predecessor. A high-output 3.2-liter V6 is standard in the LS version; it runs well, but it can't push the heavy Trooper along very quickly. The part-time four-wheel drive lacks a center differential, so it isn't suitable for use on dry pavement. Handling is sloppy even in routine driving, and the car leans a lot in turns. Stops are straight but longer than usual with four-wheel antilock brakes, and nosedive is severe. Front- and rear-seat comfort ◒. Controls and displays ◒. Climate-control system ◒. Insufficient reliability data.

Jeep Grand Cherokee

The Grand Cherokee scored highest overall in its class, but we won't know for a while whether this relatively new, upscale model will be reliable. Other Jeeps have been troublesome in the past. The Grand Cherokee comes in various two- and four-wheel-drive permutations; we recommend the Quadra-Trac option, a sophisticated full-time all-wheel-drive system. The 4.0-liter Six provides good acceleration, and the 5.2-liter V8 is even more powerful. The four-speed automatic transmission shifts smoothly. Handling is precise and stable, though a bit clumsy. Stops are reasonably short. The Jeep rocks annoyingly from side to side on bumpy roads, but the cabin is as quiet as in most sedans. Front- and rear-seat comfort ◒. Controls ◒; displays ●. Climate-control system ●. New model; no reliability data.

RATINGS OF 1993 CARS

RATINGS | 1993 SMALL CARS

Ratings order: Models are listed in order of estimated quality, based on road and track tests and on judgments of comfort and convenience. The mpg data refer to the car equipped as tested; see the last full report for details. **Notes to table:** Predicted reliability:

Make & model	Trim lines	Overall score	Version tested	Predicted reliability	Overall mpg
Saturn	SL, SL1, SL2, SW1, SW2	◯ ◒	SL2 1.9/4 Auto/4 SW2 1.9/4 Auto/4	⊜ ⊜	27 27
Geo Prizm	Base, LSi	◯	LSi 1.8/4 Man/5	⊜	33
Honda Civic	CX, DX, LX, EX, VX, Si	◯	EX 1.6/4 Auto/4	⊜	29
Toyota Corolla	Standard, Dlx, LE DX Wagon	◯ ◯	LE 1.8/4 Auto/4 DX 1.8/4 Auto/4	⊜ ⊜	30 28
Subaru Impreza	Base, L, LS	◯	L 1.8/4 Man/5	New	29
Mitsubishi Expo LRV	LRV Base, AWD, Sport, 4-Dr Base, AWD, SP	◯	LRV Sport 2.4/4 Auto/4	New	24
Nissan Sentra	E, XE, GXE, SE, SE-R	◯	GXE 1.6/4 Auto/4	⊜	28
Ford Escort	Base, LX, LX-E, GT LX Wagon	◯ ●	LX-E 1.8/4 Auto/4 LX 1.9/4 Auto/4	◯ ◯	27 27
Mercury Tracer	Base, LTS		Base 1.9/4 Auto/4	◯	29
Toyota Tercel	Standard, Dlx, LE	◒	Std. 1.5/4 Man/4	⊜	35
Plymouth Sundance **Dodge Shadow**	Base, Duster Base, ES	◒	Base 2.2/4 Man/5	◯ ◯	28 —
Dodge Colt **Eagle Summit** **Plymouth Colt**	Base, GL DL, ES, LX, 4WD Base, GL, SE, 4WD	◒	ES 1.8/4	⊜ ⊜ ⊜	— 34 —
Hyundai Elantra	Base, GLS	◒	GLS 1.6/4 Auto/4	●	25

[1] *Optional in one or more models.* [2] *Standard in one or more models.*

RATINGS OF 1993 CARS 153

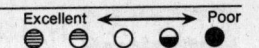

Excellent ◄——————► Poor

ID=insufficient data. Major options: **S**=standard; **NA**=not available; **O**=option; **Dlr**=Dealer; **Pkg**=part of package. Body styles: **C**=coupe; **CN**=convertible; **H**=hatch; **S**=sedan; **W**=wagon; **R**=regular; **E**=extended; **2W**=2-door wagon; **4W**=4-door wagon.

Air bag, driver/passenger	Antilock brakes	Automatic transmission	Air-conditioning	Body styles	Comments	Last full report
S/NA	O	O	O	S	A good performer with impressive reliability. SL2 is best choice. See Sporty Cars for coupe.	May '92
S/NA	O	O	O	W		Sep. '93
S/NA	O	O	O	S	A competent performer. Newly designed for 1993.	Aug. '93
S [1]	NA [2]	O	Dlr	C,H,S	Good performer. Good resale. Tested EX model has the more powerful engine and antilock brakes.	May '92
S/NA	O	O	[2]	S	Refined and capable small car. Typical Toyota virtues of high quality and high resale.	Sep. '93
S/NA	O	O	O	W		
S/NA	[1][2]	O [2]	[2]	S,W	LS most desirable version.	Aug. '93
NA/NA	[1]	O	O	W	Smooth riding and comfortable. Roomy, tall wagon. LRV is smaller than Expo.	Sep. '93
[2]/NA	[1]	O	[2]	C,S	A strong performer in this class, with the best ride. Cramped rear seat.	May '92
NA/NA	NA	O	O	H,S	The LX-E model has a more powerful engine and sports suspension. Nippy handling, but stiff ride. Might be hard to find.	May '92
NA/NA	NA	O	O	W		
NA/NA	NA	O	O	S,W	Tracer tested in its basic version. LTS is Tracer equivalent of Escort LX-E.	May '91
S/NA	O	O	O	C,S	Inexpensive and reliable transportation, nothing more.	Mar. '91
S/NA	O	O	O	H,S	Aging models based on K-car platform. To be replaced next year. Shadow also has a convertible model.	Mar. '91
S/NA	O	O	O	H,S		
NA/NA	[1]	O	O	C,S	Newly redesigned for 1993. Cars are basic transportation. Wagons are desirable. ABS is vital in all versions.	Aug. '93
NA/NA	[1]	O	O	C,S,W		
NA/NA	[1]	O	O	C,S,W		
NA/NA	NA	O	Pkg	S	A bit better than the Excel, but still not competitive.	May '92

RATINGS OF 1993 CARS

RATINGS: 1993 COMPACT CARS

Ratings order: Models are listed in order of estimated quality, based on road and track tests and on judgments of comfort and convenience. The mpg data refer to the car equipped as tested; see the last full report for details. **Notes to table:** Predicted reliability:

Make & model	Trim lines	Overall score	Version tested	Predicted reliability	Overall mpg
BMW 3-Series	318i, 318is, 325i, 325is	◒	325i 2.5/6, Auto/4	○	21
Infiniti G20	—	◒	2.0/4, Auto/4	◒	24
Mazda 626	DX, LX, ES	◒	ES 2.5/V6 Auto/4	New	24
Honda Accord	DX, LX, EX, SE	◒	EX 2.2/4, Auto/4	◒	24
Mitsubishi Galant	S, ES, LS	◒	ES 2.0/4, Auto/4	◒	24
Subaru Legacy	L, LS, LSI, SPORT	○	LS 2.2 flat 4 Auto/4	◒	22
Nissan Altima	XE, GXE, SE, GLE	○	GLE 2.4/4 Auto/4	New	23
Audi 90	S, CS, CS Quatt	○	CS Quattro Sport 2.8/V6 Man/5	New	22
Chrysler Le Baron	LE, Landau	○	LE 3.0/V6, Auto/4	○	23
Plymouth Acclaim	—	○	2.5/4, Auto/3	○	24
Dodge Spirit	Highline, ES	○		○	
Ford Tempo	GL, LX	○	LX 2.3/4, Auto/3	◉	24
Mercury Topaz	GS			◉	
Buick Skylark	Custom, Limited, Gran Sport	◉	GS 3.3/V6, Auto/3	ID	21
Oldsmobile Achieva	S, SL	◉	S 2.3/4, Auto/3	ID	24
Pontiac Grand Am	SE, GT	◉	GT 2.3/4 HO, Man/	ID	25
Volkswagen Passat	GL, GLX	◉	GL 2.0/4, Auto/4	●	24
Chevrolet Corsica	LT	◉	LT 2.2/4, Auto/3	◉	25
Chevrolet Beretta	Base, GT, GTZ			◉	
Pontiac Sunbird	LE, SE, GT	●	LE 2.0/4, Auto/3	●	24
Chevrolet Cavalier	VL, RS, Z24			●	

1 *Standard in one or more models.* 2 *Dealer installed in some models.*

RATINGS OF 1993 CARS

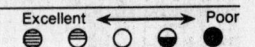

Excellent ◄────► Poor
◉ ⊖ ○ ⊝ ●

ID = insufficient data. Major options: **S** = standard; **NA** = not available; **O** = option; **Dlr** = Dealer; **Pkg** = part of package. Body styles: **C** = coupe; **CN** = convertible; **H** = hatch; **S** = sedan; **W** = wagon; **R** = regular; **E** = extended; **2W** = 2-door wagon; **4W** = 4-door wagon.

Air bag, driver/passenger	Antilock brakes	Automatic transmission	Air-conditioning	Body styles	Comments	Last full report
S/NA	S	O	S	C,S,CN	Pure driving fun—everything a sports sedan should be. Expensive as used car.	Feb. '92
S/S [3]	S	O	S	S	Accent on handling and performance. Sort of a Japanese BMW. Significant mid-year changes.	Aug. '91
S/NA	O	O	O [1]	S	New for 1993, similar to the sporty MX-6. V6 desirable.	June '93
S/NA	NA [1]	O	S [2]	C,S,W	A top performer. But only the pricey EX and SE come with antilock brakes. New for 1994.	Mar. '92
NA/NA	NA	O [1]	O	S	A desirable model that was replaced last summer.	July '91
S/NA	S	S	S	S,W	A steady performer. Most versions AWD only.	June '93
S/NA	O	O	O [1]	S	Average performer.	June '93
S/NA	S	O	S	S	New in 1993, with a larger and more useful trunk. Extensive warranty.	May '93
S/NA	O	S	O [1]	S	In performance, personality, and reliability, it's no match for the better compacts.	Mar. '92
S/NA S/NA	O O	O O [1]	O O	S S	Competent though unexceptional cars. Twins to LeBaron.	June '91
O/NA O/NA	NA NA	O O	O O	S S	These twins are still no more than journeymen performers.	May '91
NA/NA	S	S	O	C,S	Disappointing, especially for cars newly designed for 1992.	June '92
NA/NA NA/NA	S S	O [1] O	O O	C,S C,S	Crash-test results especially bad. Best overall performance in V6 versions.	June '92 June '93
NA/NA	NA [1]	O	S	S,W	A disappointing car; some high spots, but riddled with annoyances. V6 more desirable.	July '91
S/NA S/NA	S S	O O	O O	S C	Unimpressive performer. A classic rental car.	June '92
NA/NA NA/NA	S S	O O [1]	O O	C,S,CN C,S,W,CN	Despite improvements, this decade-old design can no longer compete, except in price.	May '91

[3] 1993½ models only.

RATINGS OF 1993 CARS

RATINGS 1993 SPORTY/SPORTS CARS

Ratings order: Models are listed in order of estimated quality, based on road and track tests and on judgments of comfort and convenience. The mpg data refer to the car equipped as tested; see the last full report for details. **Notes to table:** Predicted reliability:

Make & model	Trim lines	Overall score	Version tested	Predicted reliability	Overall mpg
Nissan 300ZX	Base, 2+2, Turbo	◒	Turbo 3.0/V6 Man/5	○	21
Chevrolet Corvette	LT1, ZR1	◒	LT1 5.7/V8, Man/6	●	17
Dodge Stealth	Base, ES, R/T, R/T Turbo	◒	R/T Turbo 3.0/V6	○	20
Mitsubishi 3000GT	Base, SL, VR-4		Man/5 AWD	○	
Mazda RX-7	Base, Touring, R-1	◒	1.3/R Turbo, Man/5	New	19
Ford Probe	Base, GT	◒	GT 2.5/V6, Man/5	New	24
Mazda MX-6	Base, LS		LS 2.5/V6, Auto/4	New	24
Chevrolet Camaro	Base, Z28	○	Base 3.4/V6, Auto/4	New	19
Pontiac Firebird	Base, Formula, TransAm	◒	Trans Am 5.7/V8, Auto/4	New	17
Subaru SVX	LS, LS-L, XR	◒	XR 3.3/6 Auto/4 AWD	○	19
Saturn	SC1, SC2	◒	SC2 1.9/4, Man/5	◒	29
Mazda MX-5 Miata	Base, Ltd. Ed.	◒	1.6/4, Man/5	◒	29
Nissan NX	1600, 2000	◒	2000, 2.0/4, Man/5	◒	28
Honda Prelude	S, Si, Si 4WS, VTEC	○	Si 2.3/4, Man/5	◒	26
Mazda MX-3	Base, GS	○	GS 1.8/V6, Man/5	◒	28
Eagle Talon	DL, ES, TSi Turbo, TSi Turbo AWD	○	TSi 2.0/4 Turbo Man/5 AWD	○	21
Mitsubishi Eclipse	Base, GS, GS Turbo, GSx			○	
Plymouth Laser	Base, RS, RS AWD			○	
Geo Storm	Base, GSi	○	GSi 1.6/4, Man/5	○	28
Toyota Paseo	—	●	1.5/4, Man/5	◒	34
Hyundai Scoupe	Base, LS, Turbo	◐	LS 1.5/4, Man/5	●	32
Honda Civic del Sol	S, Si	◐	Si 1.6/4 Man/5	◒	32
Mercury Capri	Base, XR2	●	Base 1.6/4, Man/5	●	28

[1] *Standard in top-line model only.* [2] *Available in top-line model only.*

RATINGS OF 1993 CARS

Excellent ⬅ ➡ Poor

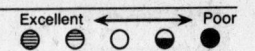

ID=insufficient data. Major options: **S**=standard; **NA**=not available; **O**=option; **Dlr**=Dealer; **Pkg**=part of package. Body styles: **C**=coupe; **CN**=convertible; **H**=hatch; **S**=sedan; **W**=wagon; **R**=regular; **E**=extended; **2W**=2-door wagon; **4W**=4-door wagon.

Air bag, driver/passenger	Antilock brakes	Automatic transmission	Air-conditioning	Body styles	Comments	Last full report
S/NA	S	O	S	H,C	Slick, sleek and highly competent. Best overall sports car.	Sep. '92
S/NA	S	NC	S	C,CN	Brutally powerful, technically sophisticated. High resale.	Sep. '92
S/NA	[1]	O	Pkg	H	The R/T Turbo performs well despite its weight. Front-wheel drive more reliable than AWD.	Apr. '92
S/NA	[1]	O	S	H		
S/NA	S	O	S	H	Exceptional handling and braking. Tight cockpit. R1 too stiff.	Sep. '92
S/NA	O	O	O	H	Both have excellent handling with smooth responsive V6. Avoid rough-shifting auto. transmission.	Jan. '93
S/NA	O	O	O	C		Jan. '93
S/S	S	O	O	H	New for 1993 and much improved.	Oct. '93
S/S	S	O	O	H		Oct. '93
S/NA	S	S	S	C	A grand touring car, not sports car.	Sep. '92
S/NA	O	O	O	C	A spunky coupe with decent handling. Very reliable.	July '92
S/NA	[1]	O	[1]	CN	British sports-car fun, Japanese reliability. Expensive used.	Oct. '93
S/NA	[2]	O	O	H	One of the best small sporty cars. Discontinued for 1994.	July '92
S/S [1]	[1]	O	Dlr [1]	C	Punchy 4-cylinder. Very capable chassis.	Jan. '93
NA/NA	[2]	O	O	H	Excellent handling and smooth V6. Cramped quarters.	July '92
NA/NA	[3]	O	Pkg	H	Has all the right pieces, but getting old. AWD helps handling as well as traction, though it's less reliable than 2WD.	Jan. '93
NA/NA	[4]	O	O	H		
NA/NA	[2]	O	Pkg	H		
S/NA	NA	Pkg	O	H	Sporty looking economy car.	Oct. '91
S/NA	O	O	O	C	Econobox heart.	July '92
NA/NA	NA	O	Pkg	C	Rather crude. Good tires, weak chassis. Poor resale.	Oct. '91
S/NA	NA	O	Dlr	C	A removable roof panel makes it an open coupe.	Oct. '93
S/NA	NA	O	O	CN	Sporty looking, not much fun. Poor quality, poor resale.	Apr. '91

[3] Not available in base model. [4] GS Turbo only, standard in GSX, not available otherwise.

RATINGS: 1993 MID-SIZED CARS OVER $25,000

Ratings order: Models are listed in order of estimated quality, based on road and track tests and on judgments of comfort and convenience. The mpg data refer to the car equipped as tested; see the last full report for details. **Notes to table:** Predicted reliability:

Make & model	Trim lines	Overall score	Version tested	Predicted reliability	Overall mpg
Lexus LS400	—	◒	4.0/V8, Auto/4	◒	19
Lexus ES300	Sport Sedan	◓	3.0/V6, Auto/4	◓	20
Volvo 850 GLT	Base, Touring	◓	Touring 2.4/5 Auto/4	New	22
Volvo 940 / Volvo 960	Base, S, Turbo / —	◓	960, 2.9/6, Auto/4	◓	20
Infiniti Q45	Q45, Q45a, Q45t	◓	Q45a 4.5/V8, Auto/4	◓	17
BMW 5-Series	525i, 525i Touring, 535i	◓	535i, 3.4/6, Auto/4	◓	17
Lincoln Continental	Executive, Signature	◓	Signature 3.8/V6 Auto/4	○	18
Mazda 929	—	◓	3.0/V6, Auto/4	◓	20
Infiniti J30	—	◓	3.0/V6 Auto/4	◓	20
Lexus SC	300, 400	◓	400 4.0/V8 Auto/4	◓	19
Acura Legend	Base, L, LS	◓	L 3.2/V6, Auto/4	◓	20
Mitsubishi Diamante	ES, LS	◓	LS 3.0/V6, Auto/4	◐	20
Lincoln Mark VIII	—	◓	4.6/V8 Auto/4	New	19
Cadillac Seville	Base, Touring Sedan	◓	Touring Sedan 4.6/V8 Auto/4	○	17
Cadillac Eldorado	Base, Sport Coupe, TC	●	4.9/V8 Auto/4	○	15
Acura Vigor	LS, GS	○	GS 2.5/5, Auto/4	◓	23
Jaguar XJ6	Base, Vanden Plas	○	Base 4.0/6 Auto/4	ID	18
Audi 100	Base, S, CS, CS Quattro, CS Quattro Wagon	◐	S 2.8/V6, Auto/4	ID	21

[1] *Base model only.* [2] *Standard in top-line model.*

RATINGS OF 1993 CARS 159

Excellent ◀──────▶ Poor

ID=insufficient data. Major options: **S**=standard; **NA**=not available; **O**=option; **Dlr**=Dealer; **Pkg**=part of package. Body styles: **C**=coupe; **CN**=convertible; **H**=hatch; **S**=sedan; **W**=wagon; **R**=regular; **E**=extended; **2W**=2-door wagon; **4W**=4-door wagon.

Air bag, driver/passenger	Antilock brakes	Automatic transmission	Air-conditioning	Body styles	Comments	Last full report
S/S	S	S	S	S	Competes successfully with the world's top luxury cars.	Nov. '93
S/NA	S	O	S	S	Scored only slightly better overall than Toyota Camry V6.	Feb. '92
S/S	S	O	S	S	New. Front-wheel drive with numerous safety features.	May '93
S/S	S	S	S	S,W	Very comfortable. Lots of safety features. A fine family sedan.	Aug. '92
S/S	S	S	S	S	Slick and powerful. Handling not as crisp as previous models.	Nov. '93
S/NA	S	S	S	S,W	It can't be surpassed for driving fun with its responsive handling and supple suspension.	June '90
S/S	S	S	S	S	Big and roomy, with all the amenities Detroit can muster.	June '90
S/S	S	S	S	S	A Japanese Jaguar. Competent handling. Small trunk.	Aug. '92
S/S	S	S	S	S	A slick, new model. Rear-wheel drive. Desirable.	May '93
S/S	S	O [1]	S	C	Coupe version of Lexus LS400. 300 model has Six cylind. engine.	July '93
S/S	S	O	S	C,S	Smooth and refined. A roomy and comfortable sedan.	Aug. '92
S/NA	O [2]	S	S	S,W	Technological tour de force but reliability problems.	Feb. '92
S/S	S	S	S	C	New for 1993 with 32-valve V8. Rear-wheel drive.	July '93
S/S	S	S	S	S	STS version with Northstar V8 aimed at world's best.	Nov. '93
S/S	S	S	S	C	Top models now have Northstar V8. Luxurious and fast.	July '93
S/NA [2]	S	O	S	S	Accelerates vigorously, but comfort takes a back seat.	Feb. '92
S/NA	S	S	S	S	British elegance.	Nov. '93
S/S	S	O	S	S,W	Needs considerable improvement. Fussy and idiosyncratic. Excellent warranty.	Aug. '92

RATINGS OF 1993 CARS

RATINGS | 1993 MID-SIZED CARS UNDER $25,000

Ratings order: Models are listed in order of estimated quality, based on road and track tests and on judgments of comfort and convenience. The mpg data refer to the car equipped as tested; see the last full report for details. **Notes to table:** Predicted reliability:

Make & model	Trim lines	Overall score	Version tested	Predicted reliability	Overall mpg
Toyota Camry V6	Dlx, LE, XLE, SE	◐	LE 3.0/V6, Auto/4	◐	21
Toyota Camry 4	Dlx, LE, XLE	◐	Dlx 2.2/4, Auto/4	◐	24
Ford Taurus	GL, LX, SHO	◐	LX 3.8/V6, Auto/4	○	20
Mercury Sable	GS, LS		LS 3.8/V6, Auto/4	○	20
Nissan Maxima	GXE, SE	◐	SE 3.0/V6, Auto/4	◐	21
Chrysler New Yorker	Salon	○	Salon 3.3V6,	○	21
Dodge Dynasty	Base, LE		Auto/4	◐	
Buick Regal	Custom, Limited, Grand Sport	◐	Custom 3.8/V6, Auto/4	○	20
Olds Cutlass Supreme	S, Intn'l Series, Special Edition			◐	—
Pontiac Grand Prix	LE, SE, GT, STE			○	—
Chevrolet Lumina	Base, Euro, Z34	●	Base 3.1/V6, Auto/4	◐	22

[1] *Base model only.* [2] *Standard in top-line model.*

READING A TIRE

You can tell a lot about a tire by the coding molded into the sidewall. The U.S. Department of Transportation requires tire makers to state the following on passenger-car tires:

Size. A typical size designation is P185/70R14 87S. The "P" is for passenger-car tire.

The "185" is the nominal width of the tire's cross section in millimeters. And the "70" indicates the height of the sidewall—or, more precisely, the ratio of sidewall height to cross-section width. Thus on a 185/70R14 tire, the height of the sidewall is about 70 percent of 185 mm, or 130 mm.

The "R" stands for radial-ply construction. The "14" is the diameter, in inches, of the metal wheel that the tires are designed to fit.

The "87S" is a service designation consisting of a load index and speed symbol. The speed symbols are as follows: S stands for 112 mph; T for 118; U for 124; H for 130; V for 149; Z for 149+.

Load and pressure. Say the designation is "Max load 590 kg (1301 lbs) @ 240 kPa (35 psi) max press." If the tire is inflated to 35 pounds per square inch, the maximum recommended pressure, it can safely support 1301 pounds.

Tread wear. An index based on how quick-

RATINGS OF 1993 CARS

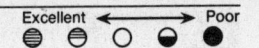

Excellent ◄——————► Poor

ID=insufficient data. Major options: **S**=standard; **NA**=not available; **O**=option; **Dlr**=Dealer; **Pkg**=part of package. Body styles: **C**=coupe; **CN**=convertible; **H**=hatch; **S**=sedan; **W**=wagon; **R**=regular; **E**=extended; **2W**=2-door wagon; **4W**=4-door wagon.

Air bag, driver/passenger	Antilock brakes	Automatic transmission	Air-conditioning	Body styles	Comments	Last full report
S/NA	O	S	O [1]	S,W	One of the better values. While the V6 model is better, the Four is quite competent and much more economical. Desirable used car.	Mar. '93
S/NA	O	O [1]	O [1]	S,W		Mar. '92
S/O	O	S	O [2]	S,W	Still among the best of domestic models. Decent performers that have remained reliable.	Mar. '92
S/S	O	S	S	S,W		Mar. '93
S/NA	O	O	S	S	Performance, practicality, and reliability in one package.	Aug. '91
S/NA	O	S	S	S	Some of the last Chrysler K-cars. The new LH models outperform them in essentially every way.	Jan. '91
S/NA	O	S	O	S		
NA/NA	O [2]	S	S	C,S	These GM models have been improving in reliability. Their overall performance, however, has not been up to the best in this class. Oldsmobile has a convertible model.	July '91
NA/NA	O	S	S	C,S		
NA/NA	O [2]	S	S	C,S		
NA/NA	O [2]	S	O [2]	C,S	Your basic rental car. Not an inspired performer.	June '91

ly the tread wears under conditions specified by the Government, relative to a "standard" tire. The index won't tell you how long the tire will last on your car; driving conditions vary too much. But a tire with a tread-wear index of 200 should wear about twice as long as one with an index of 100 under like conditions.

Traction. A measure of the tire's ability to stop on wet pavement. Grades range from A (highest) to C (lowest).

Temperature. A measure of the tire's resistance to heat buildup under simulated high-speed driving. Again, grades range from A (highest) to C (lowest).

Note that the tire maker, not the DOT, performs the tests for tread wear, traction, and temperature. Snow-tire markings are not required to include those indices.

Date of manufacture. Every passenger tire carries a DOT identification number—for example, DOT B9PA B55X 103. The last three digits identify the week and year of manufacture. For example, "103" means the tenth week of 1993. That date is important for two reasons: Tire compounds harden with age, so you should look for a tire made no more than a year ago. Also, when tires are recalled, the date of manufacture can help determine whether the tire is affected by the recall. For recalls of tires, see page 390.

RATINGS OF 1993 CARS

RATINGS | 1993 LARGE CARS

Ratings order: Models are listed in order of estimated quality, based on road and track tests and on judgments of comfort and convenience. The mpg data refer to the car equipped as tested; see the last full report for details. **Notes to table:** Predicted reliability:

Make & model	Trim lines	Overall score	Version tested	Predicted reliability	Overall mpg
Pontiac Bonneville	SE, SSE, SSEi	◓	SE 3.8/V6 Auto/4	◓	20
Eagle Vision	ESi, TSi	◓	TSi 3.5/V6, Auto/4	New	21
Chrysler Concorde	—	◓	3.5/V6, Auto/4	New	21
Dodge Intrepid	Base, ES	○	Base 3.3/V6, Auto/4	New	21
Ford Crown Victoria	Standard, LX	○	LX 4.6/V8, Auto/4	○	20
Mercury Grand Marquis	GS, LS			○	
Oldsmobile 88 Royale	Base, LS	○	LS 3.8/V6, Auto/4	◓	19
Buick LeSabre	Custom, Ltd.			◓	
Chevrolet Caprice Classic	Base, LS	◐	Base 5.0/V8, Auto/4	●	18
Buick Roadmaster	Base, Ltd.	◐	Base 5.7/V8, Auto/4	●	17

[1] Standard in top-line model.   [2] Includes traction control

RATINGS | 1993 SPORT/UTILITY VEHICLES

Make & model	Trim lines	Overall score	Version tested	Predicted reliability	Overall mpg
Jeep Grand Cherokee	Base, Laredo, Ltd., Grand Wagoneer	◓	Laredo 4.0/6 Auto/4	New	16
Ford Explorer	XL, Sport, XLT, Bauer	◓	Bauer 4.0/V6 Auto/4	○	15
Mazda Navajo	DX, LX			○	
Isuzu Trooper	S, LS, RS	◓	LS 3.2/V6 Auto/4	New	15
Jeep Cherokee	Base, Sport, Country	○	Country 4.0/6 Auto/4	◐	17
Mitsubishi Montero	Base, RS, LS, SR	○	LS 3.0 V6 Auto/4	New	15
Isuzu Rodeo	S, LS	◐	LS 3.1/V6 Auto/4	●	15
Oldsmobile Bravada	—	◐	4.3/V6 Auto/4	◐	18

[1] Standard on Limited and Grand Wagoneer.   [2] Optional on top-line models.

RATINGS OF 1993 CARS

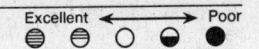

Excellent ←——→ Poor

ID=insufficient data. Major options: **S**=standard; **NA**=not available; **O**=option; **Dlr**=Dealer; **Pkg**=part of package. Body styles: **C**=coupe; **CN**=convertible; **H**=hatch; **S**=sedan; **W**=wagon; **R**=regular; **E**=extended; **2W**=2-door wagon; **4W**=4-door wagon.

Air bag, driver/passenger	Antilock brakes	Automatic transmission	Air-conditioning	Body styles	Comments	Last full report
S/NA [1]	S	S	S	S	Best of GM's H-bodies. Optional suspension recommended.	Jan. '92
S/S	O [1]	S	S	S	Chrysler's newest, and potentially best models. Ride and handling competent even in base-suspension versions, although touring suspension is even better.	Mar. '93
S/S	S	S	S	S		Mar. '93
S/S	O	S	O	S		Mar. '93
S/O	O [2]	S	S	S	RWD. Not as nimble as the FWD models. Has superior trailer-towing ability. Quiet.	Jan. '92
S/S	O [2]	S	S	S		
S/NA	S	S	S	S	With optional suspensions, would perform nearly as well as the Pontiac Bonneville.	Jan. '92
S/NA	S	S	S	S		
S/NA	S	S	S	S/W	RWD. Clumsy and soft. Optional suspension or LTZ package recommended.	Jan. '91
S/NA	S	S	S	S/W	RWD. Interior package not as efficient as in Buick LeSabre.	Jan. '92
S/NA	S	O [1]	O [1]	4W	Latest safety features and good performance. V8 available.	Nov. '92
NA/NA	S	O	O	2W, 4W	The most popular SUV. Roomy, but lacks modern AWD.	Nov. '92
NA/NA	S	O	O	2W		
NA/NA	O [2]	O	O [3]	2W, 4W	Civilized and refined. Lacks modern AWD. Clumsy handling.	Nov. '92
NA/NA	O	O [4]	O	2W, 4W	Price competitive, but rather crude and dated.	Sep. '91
NA/NA	O [3]	O [3]	O	4W	Lacks power, has tricky emergency handling.	Nov. '92
NA/NA	S [5]	O	O	4W	Made in USA. New engine may solve reliability problems.	Sep. '91
NA/NA	S	S	S	4W	An expensive S-10 Blazer, but still crude.	Sep. '91

[3] *Standard on top-line model(s) only.*   [4] *Requires 4.0 liter engine.*   [5] *Rear-wheel antilock only.*

RATINGS | 1993 SMALL PASSENGER VANS

Ratings order: Models are listed in order of estimated quality, based on road and track tests and on judgments of comfort and convenience. The mpg data refer to the car equipped as tested; see the last full report for details. **Notes to table:** Predicted reliability:

Make & model	Trim lines	Overall score	Version tested	Predicted reliability	Overall mpg
Mercury Villager	GS, LS	◒	GS 3.0/V6 Auto/4	New	20
Nissan Quest	XE, GXE	◒	GXE 3.0/V6 Auto/4	New	19
Dodge Caravan	2WD:Base, SE, LE, ES	◒	SE FWD 3.0/V6 Auto/3	○	20
	4WD:SE, LE, ES		ES FWD 3.3/V6 Auto/4		19
Plymouth Voyager	2WD:Base, SE, LE, LX			○	
	4WD:SE, LE, LX				
Dodge Grand Caravan	2WD:Base, SE, LE, ES	◒	LE AWD 3.3/V6 Auto/4	◐	17
	4WD: SE, LE, ES				
Plymouth Grand Voyager	2WD: Base, SE, LE			◐	—
	4WD:SE, LE				
Chrysler Town & Country	FWD, AWD			◐	—
Ford Aerostar	2WD:XL, XL+, XLT, Eddie Bauer	◒	Std. XLT 2WD 3.0/V6 Auto/4	○	18
	4WD:XL, XL+, XLT, Eddie Bauer		Ext. EB E-4WD 4.0/V6 Auto/4		16
Toyota Previa	2WD:Deluxe, LE	◒	LE 2.4/4 Auto/4	◒	21
	4WD:Dlx All-Trac, LE All-Trac		LE All-Trac 2.4/4 Auto/4		18
Pontiac Trans Sport	SE	○	SE 3, 1/V6 Auto/3	○	17
Chevrolet Lumina APV	Base, LS			○	—
Oldsmobile Silhouette	—			○	—
Volkswagen EuroVan	CL, GL, MV	◐	GL 2.5/5 Auto/4	New	17
Mazda MPV	2WD/4, 2WD/V6, 4WD/V6	◐	4WD 3.0/V6 Auto/4	○	16
Chevrolet Astro	2WD, AWD	●	Ext. LT AWD 4.3/V6 Auto/4	◐	15
GMC Safari	2WD, 2WD XT, AWD, AWD XT			◐	

[1] *Standard in top-line model(s).* [2] *Rear antilock brakes only.*

RATINGS OF 1993 CARS

Excellent ← → Poor

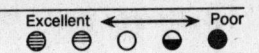

ID=insufficient data. Major options: **S**=standard; **NA**=not available; **O**=option; **Dlr**=Dealer; **Pkg**=part of package. Body styles: **C**=coupe; **CN**=convertible; **H**=hatch; **S**=sedan; **W**=wagon; **R**=regular; **E**=extended; **2W**=2-door wagon; **4W**=4-door wagon.

Air bag, driver/passenger	Antilock brakes	Automatic transmission	Air-conditioning	Body styles	Comments	Last full report
NA/NA	S	S	O [1]	R	New for 1993. Drives most like a passenger car. Flexible seating, but rather modest cargo area. Smooth handling.	Feb. '93
NA/NA	O	S	S	R		Feb. '93
S/NA	O	O [1]	O [1]	R	Versatile, usable cargo area, up-to-date safety features. Best handling with Sport suspension. Facing many new tough competitors, but still holding its own.	Feb. '91
S/NA	O	S	O [1]	R		Feb. '93
S/NA	O	O [1]	O [1]	R		
S/NA	O	S	O [1]	R		
S/NA	O	S	O [1]	E	A flexible people and cargo carrier, but reliability is poorer than for the short versions. AWD adds security in bad weather.	Oct. '92
S/NA	O	S	O [1]	E		
S/NA	S	S	S	E		
S/NA	S [2]	O [1]	O [1]	R,E	Gets more refined every year. Comfortable seating, large cargo area. E-4WD recommended.	Feb. '91
	S [2]	S		R,E		Oct. '92
S/NA	S	O [1]	O [1]	R	Although somewhat underpowered, the Previa rides and handles well. Easy convertability.	Oct. '92
				R		
NA/NA	S	S	O	R	Clever seating package with easy-to-remove seats. Smart choice is 3.8 V6 with 4-speed automatic. Long snout takes getting used to.	
NA/NA	S	S	O	R		Feb. '91
NA/NA	S	S	S	R		
NA/NA	O	O	O [1]	R	Excellent passenger seating and huge cargo area, but not much else to recommend it. Clumsy delivery truck.	Feb. '93
S/NA	S [2]	S	O	R	Small cargo capacity. Tricky emergency handling. 4WD recommended.	Oct. '92
NA/NA	S	S	O	R,E	Poor ride and clumsy handling. Bad crash test results. Large cargo area and towing capacity. Awkward driving position.	Oct. '92
				R,E		

How to buy a new car

Traditionally, a new car's selling price is arrived at through bargaining between the buyer and the dealer. But enough people find the rug-bazaar atmosphere of that transaction so unpleasant that a new type of sales strategy has emerged—the one-price policy. Dealers with such a policy set a nonnegotiable, take-it-or-leave-it price, which is generally well below the normal sticker price but well above their own cost. One manufacturer, General Motors, has organized a one-price system for its Saturn division that applies to all Saturn cars, nationwide. Saturn's success has inspired more than 1000 new-car dealers to adopt one-price selling on their own, and several automakers are trying the no-dicker sticker on selected models.

The no-haggle price, we've found, isn't the lowest price. While the preset price is usually discounted from the manufacturer's sticker price, it's discounted less than it might have been for a buyer who knows how to drive a hard bargain. Bargaining can save an extra $200 to $300, judging by our shopping experience. People who don't know how to bargain hard or who hate the process, however, may consider that extra cost worthwhile. And a no-haggle price offers the comfort of knowing the price is the same for everyone.

Decide on the model

Falling in love with a car is a poor bargaining strategy. Unless the salesperson believes you are willing to walk out and shop elsewhere, he or she has little incentive to offer you the lowest possible price.

Whether you plan to bargain or not, first decide on the type and style of car that best suits your needs. Then narrow the field to comparable makes and models in your price range. (The Ratings of the 1993 cars and the Frequency-of-Repair information can help you select the best models.)

Next, decide on the equipment you want in your new car. Most models are sold in two or more trim lines (basic, deluxe, etc.). Each trim line has a different base price and selection of standard equipment.

In some cases, a higher trim line may cost less than dressing up a basic model with all the options you want. Sometimes, too, the options you want aren't available with the base model. But you may pay for extras you don't want with the higher line.

Often, option packages bundle together some useful and some frivolous equipment. If you want all or most of the extras, though, it's usually cheaper to buy a package than to buy options à la carte.

Automakers' brochures, available at dealerships, provide plenty of information about trim lines and options, but they don't say a word about prices. For that, you're left to the fanciful figures on the window sticker or to better sources outside the showroom.

Learn the dealer's costs

If you're prepared to bargain over price, try to negotiate up from what the car cost the dealer rather than down from the sticker price. With the sticker price and the cost factor listed in the Ratings charts in the April issue of CONSUMER REPORTS, you can get a pretty good idea of what the dealer paid the factory for the vehicle.

More precise information is available from the Consumer Reports New Car Price Service, which provides printouts for any make, model, and trim line. (For ordering information, see the box on page 168.) Each printout notes the standard equipment, list price, and dealer cost of the basic car. It itemizes, by invoice number, all available factory-installed options and options

BUYING A NEW CAR

packages, giving list prices and dealer cost.

The service lists current cash rebate offers, including unadvertised rebates to dealers. Since the dealer has the option of pocketing that rebate or passing all or part of it on to the consumer, knowledge of such offers is useful leverage when you bargain.

Using the printout, you can prepare a worksheet that describes the car you want, its dealer cost, and its list price. Include the complete name of the car—make, model, and trim line—and next to it, the dealer cost and list price from the printout. Under that, in columns, list the invoice number and name of each option you want, its dealer cost, and its list price. At the bottom of each column, write in the destination charge from the printout. Finally, total both columns. The difference between the two totals is the room for negotiation.

If there's a factory-to-dealer rebate on the car, subtract its value from the dealer cost tally. (In effect, such a rebate reduces the dealer cost.) If there's a factory-to-customer rebate, the check will be mailed directly from the manufacturer to you. Or if you prefer, you can sign it over to the dealer as part of the down payment.

How much over dealer cost should you expect to pay? It depends on the car. Vehicles in great demand command a higher markup. Some luxury cars and sporty models may command a premium. But on a mid-priced sedan in good supply, you may have to pay as little as $150 to $300 over cost. Five hundred dollars over invoice is still a reasonable deal. (Dealers sometimes even sell cars below cost because they receive an additional payment, called a holdback, from the manufacturer at year's end. That typically amounts to 2½ to 3 percent of the base sticker price.)

Resist add-ons

The price you're quoted during initial negotiations, however, may not be the bottom line. Dealers have come up with an amazing array of add-ons designed to improve their profits.

The most common are "packs"—extras added by the dealer or regional distributor to pad the price of the car. One of the most common is a "protection package" that includes a fabric finish, a paint sealant, rustproofing, and undercoating. These are of little or no value to the car buyer, but very profitable for dealers.

Some packs on popular cars are nothing but a dealer's demand for profit over and above that built into the manufacturer's price structure. If a sticker lists ADP, ADM, or AMV, be aware that those are abbreviations for "additional dealer profit," "additional dealer markup," and "additional market value." Don't pay them.

Another costly extra is an extended warranty, also commonly referred to as a service contract or mechanical breakdown insurance. Given the three-to-seven-year warranty common with today's new cars, an extended warranty is not worthwhile unless the model has had an unreliable history.

Some dealers charge a "conveyance" or "document" fee, a charge for the paperwork involved in selling and registering the car. Some charge $10 to $20 for filling the gas tank. You can refuse to pay.

Many dealers add an advertising surcharge—of as much as $400 per car—to cover regional advertising by the area's dealer association. (National advertising is included in the car's price.) If the dealer insists on charging such a fee to cover costs, ask to see proof on the invoice. The fee won't appear on the window sticker.

Occasionally, a salesperson may point out that your figures don't include dealer preparation. In most cases, they shouldn't. Dealer preparation is almost always included in the base price of the car.

All too often, dealers will mention packs and fees at the end of the bargaining, when it's time to sign the sales contract. Then, when the dealers cut the price of a pack or waive a fee, buyers feel they're getting a break. They're not.

Keep the deal simple

Don't discuss trade-ins or financing until you have a firm price quote.

Trade-in. Salespeople usually ask whether you have a trade-in early in the negotiations. Your answer should be "no." You'll have plenty of time to reconsider later. If you talk trade-in too soon, the dealer can sour a good deal on the new car with a bad deal on the old one—or vice versa. The numbers become so garbled you don't know how much you paid for the new car or got for the old one.

Selling your old car privately can be troublesome, but you'll probably get more for it. Whether you decide to trade your old car or sell it privately, you should have a good idea of its market value. You can learn what your car is worth by calling Consumer Reports Used-Car Price Service, which provides up-to-date price information for your area (see page 172).

Financing. When sales are sluggish, dealers often try to boost business by offering below-market-rate loans from the car manufacturer. Compared with typical bank rates, promotional rates can save hundreds of dollars over the life of a loan. In many cases, however, low-rate financing applies only to particular models or to short-term loans.

If low-interest financing isn't available on the car you want, don't accept the dealer's financing until you've shopped around. Credit unions, banks, or even some auto-insurance companies may offer more favorable terms.

Read the contract

Take time to read the sales contract—including the fine print—before signing. If you see something you don't like—or if you don't see something that should be included—ask to have changes made.

If you'll be turning in your old car on delivery of the new one several weeks later, the sales contract might allow the dealer to reappraise your car at that time. That's reasonable. Many things can happen to your car that might affect its value in the intervening weeks .

Make sure the sales contract states that you have the option to void the agreement and get your down payment back if something goes wrong (failure to deliver by the specified date, for example). And make sure an officer of the dealership signs the agreement. The salesperson's signature alone may not be binding.

NEW CAR PRICE SERVICE

Consumer Reports New Car Price Service gives you the facts you need to get a better deal on a new car. Here's what you get:

■ A computer printout showing the current list price and dealer's invoice for the car and all factory-installed options.

■ Current information on factory-to-dealer and factory-to-customer rebates.

■ A list of options recommended by the CONSUMER REPORTS auto engineers.

To order by mail, write Consumer Reports New Car Price Service, Box 8005, Novi, MI 48376. To order by phone, call (303) 745-1700. Visa and Mastercard accepted. Please know the make, model, and exact style of the vehicle(s). Price: $11 for one car; $20 for two; $27 for three; $5 for each additional.

Should you lease?

Since 1988, the number of leased cars in the U.S. has risen 50 percent. One in every five new cars is now leased. Leases may seem attractive, because they offer what looks like low monthly payments. But leasing deals are not necessarily as attractive as they first appear. Leasing contracts vary widely in their wording and provisions, and many people end up shelling out far more money than they anticipated.

The low payments act as bait, but the contract itself often includes such charges as a high down payment, fees for "excess wear and tear," and per-mile charges for anything over a low specified allowance. Getting out of a lease early can sometimes cost several thousand dollars in addition to the price of the car.

When a lease makes sense

If you want to drive a new car and lack the cash for a substantial down payment, or if regular monthly payments required to purchase a new car are out of reach, leasing may be worth considering.

Even then, however, leasing may turn out to be a financially sensible arrangement only if you drive close to but not more than the number of miles allowed during the lease. Typically, that's about 15,000 miles a year. Additional miles may cost as much as 25 cents each.

Shopping for a lease

A lease price should be negotiated just as doggedly as the purchase price of a new car. You'll be able to negotiate more effectively if you follow the procedure outlined in the preceding report "How to Buy a New Car" to determine a fair price for the car and calculate a monthly lease payment based on that rather than the car's sticker price. It pays to shop around. Most lease companies will give quotes over the phone.

Note that leases from a manufacturer are generally cheaper than those offered by independent leasing companies. Leasing cars is one way a carmaker gets rid of excess stock, and low payments are used as an incentive. A carmaker may also be less tempted to hit you with unexpected charges because of concern about ill will

Virtually all leases these days are closed-ended, meaning you have no obligation to buy the car at the end of the lease term. If you come across an open-end lease, avoid it. If you have the option to buy at lease end, check the market value of the car before deciding. And if you want to buy the car, try to negotiate a price that is as close as possible to the car's wholesale value.

There is no standard leasing contract but some widely used provisions are portents of trouble:

Steer clear of leases that run more than four years or that require substantial security deposits and up-front money. Avoid leases with short mileage terms (12,000 miles a year or less), or that require mandatory insurance or costly low deductibles ($500 or less) on your own insurance. Also avoid end-of-lease "disposition" or "termination" fees. Refuse disability insurance, which would cover the payments if you can't because of illness (it's generally overpriced and hard to collect on). A leasing company may also try to sell you "gap" insurance, which covers the differnce between the value of the car and what you owe on the lease in case the car is stolen or destroyed. That insurance is worth having, but not at the $450 or more some companies charge for the term of the contract. A few hundred dollars is a fairer price, and some companies throw it in for nothing. Try negotiating this charge.

How to buy a used car

The average new car costs more than $17,000 and depreciates by nearly 30 percent in the first year. A used car costs an average of $8000 and depreciates more slowly.

The used-car marketplace, however, can be an unsavory bazaar. Prices are highly elastic and subject to haggling. Paint and polish can be liberally applied to mask evidence of wear and tear, and odometers are frequently rolled back to hide the car's true mileage. Warranties are skimpy, if available at all. Finding out how much a car has suffered usually entails a good bit more than the proverbial kick in the tires.

Although you can't eliminate the risk when buying a used car, you can better your odds of getting sound transportation by learning how to shop.

What to consider

First, figure out what kind of car suits your life-style and budget. Four-door sedans and station wagons usually provide the best used-car value. Chances are they've been driven and maintained more prudently than high-performance models. Convertibles, sporty coupes, and luxury models remain pricey even when used.

Next, consider cars that have held up well in the past. Our Frequency-of-Repair records, based on readers' experiences with more than 583,000 cars, trucks, and vans, describe the reliability history of 1987 through 1992 models. The better the car scored in the past, the less likely it is to have problems in the future. From those data, we have derived a list of reliable used cars (see page 173). We used the same data to identify models to avoid (see page 176). However, the older the car, the less important our records and the more important is your inspection.

To find out how much a model sells for in your area, you can use the Consumer Reports Used-Car Price Service described in the box on page 172. Price information also appears in various printed guides, which are available in public libraries.

Where to buy

Franchised new car dealers are among the most trustworthy sources for late-model used cars. They often retain only the best trade-ins for resale, and they frequently provide a warranty and have the service facilities to back it up. Of course, a car dealership's substantial overhead means that you'll often pay more there than you would elsewhere.

Independent used-car dealers offer lower prices, but the inventory at such establishments is apt to be less desirable. Rejects from new-car dealers or weary specimens from police or taxi fleets are not uncommon. If you shop an independent dealer, choose one that's been in business locally for some time, and check it out with the Better Business Bureau. Avoid the come-and-go "gypsy" operators found in some poor neighborhoods.

Cars repossessed by lenders are periodically auctioned off. Check newspapers for advertisements. Such cars may not have had the best care, though. Auto-rental agencies such as Hertz, Avis, and National offer some cars to the public. While these cars may have been driven long and hard, most have had the advantage of regular servicing. And some companies provide a limited warranty. You can call the agencies' toll-free numbers to learn the location of their nearest used-car lot.

The Federal Trade Commission requires every used car sold by a dealer to display a "Buyer's Guide" label containing warranty information. Besides that, only Connecticut,

BUYING A USED CAR

Massachusetts, Minnesota, New York, and Rhode Island have effective lemon laws to protect buyers from dealers who sell faulty merchandise. Protection extends to all but the oldest and cheapest used cars.

You can often get the best deal if you buy a car from an individual, because there is no dealer overhead and markup figured into the price. But in a private sale you normally get no guarantee, so it's best to buy from someone you know and trust. If you shop for a car through a newspaper ad, ask about the car's condition and mileage, if it's been in a wreck, and why it's being sold. Also ask if the seller is a dealer. If so, and the advertisement omitted that fact, watch out—you could be dealing with an unethical operator.

Looking for trouble

Never buy on looks alone. After you've found a car that catches your fancy, give it a thorough inspection—on the lot, on the road, and at the service station. Bring along a friend to help troubleshoot.

Here's what to look for:

Fluids. When the engine is cold, open the radiator cap and inspect the coolant; it shouldn't be rusty. Greenish stains on the radiator denote pinholes. To check the transmission, warm up the engine and remove the dipstick. The fluid should be pinkish; it shouldn't smell burned or contain metal particles.

Leaks. Puddles or stains beneath the car are a bad sign. So is excessive residue of lubricants on the engine, transmission, hoses, or other underhood components.

Body. Rust is ruinous. Check the wheel wells and rocker panels, the door edges, and the floor of the trunk. Rust can also hide beneath blistered paint. Fresh welds in the car's underbody point to an accident. So does ripply body work, a part whose color or fit doesn't seem to match, and new paint on a late-model car. Fresh undercoating on older cars also is a giveaway.

Tires and suspension. A car with fewer than 25,000 miles should have its original tires. Uneven tread wear may merely indicate poor alignment, but it might signal serious suspension damage. Grab the top of each tire and shake it. If there's play or a clunking sound, suspect loose or worn wheel bearings or suspension joints. Bounce the car a few times by pushing down each corner. When you let go, the car should rise and then settle. If it keeps bouncing, the struts or shock absorbers need replacing.

Interior. A saggy driver's seat means heavy use. Excessively worn or brand new pedals might signal high mileage. Musty odors suggest a water leak, a costly fix that may be hard to find.

The road test

Plan to spend at least half an hour driving the car at various speeds on a variety of roads. But before you turn on the ignition, unlock the steering and turn the wheel. It shouldn't have much free play. Check the safety belts and all the controls and accessories. Have your helper verify that all exterior lights, including brake and reverse lights, are working properly.

Engine. The car should start easily and pick up smoothly. Pings or knocks may be corrected with higher-octane fuel or a tune-up. Or they could signal costly problems. Ask a mechanic.

Transmission. A manual transmission shouldn't grab suddenly and make the car buck. An automatic shouldn't slam into gear or slip as you drive.

Brakes. Speed up to 45 mph on a flat stretch of empty road. Apply the brakes firmly. The car should stop quickly, evenly, and in a straight line. Repeat the exercise. To check for leaks in the brake system, press firmly on the pedal for 30 seconds. It shouldn't sink to the floor.

Alignment. Have someone stand behind the car while you drive straight ahead. The front and rear wheels should line up. Forget about the car if it scuttles sideways; it probably has a bent frame. Veering to one side may be less serious; the wheels may simply need alignment.

Exhaust. Blue exhaust smoke from the tailpipe means the car is burning oil—a potentially costly fix. Billowy white smoke is serious as well. That means water is entering the combustion chamber. White vapor emerging briefly from the tailpipe on a cold morning is nothing to worry about. Black smoke generally means that the fuel system needs adjustment.

Comfort, noise. Suspension work might be in order if the car bounces or rattles over rough road at moderate speeds. Sputtering sounds from beneath the chassis indicate exhaust-system leaks.

A car that's passed muster to this point is ready to be examined by a reliable mechanic. If you don't have one, consult the Yellow Pages for an auto diagnostic center. The National Highway Traffic Safety Administration (800-424-9393) can tell you if the model has ever been recalled. Also, check the Product Recalls chapter on page 375 for recalls of cars published in CONSUMER REPORTS from October 1992 through October 1993. If the car has been recalled, ask the seller for proof that the problem was corrected.

To get a general idea of what you should pay for a used car, you can look at any of the used-car guides available at public libraries. However, you can get more specific information about what used cars sell for in your area from the Consumer Reports Used-Car Price Service (see the box below).

USED-CAR PRICE SERVICE

Consumer Reports Used-Car Price Service quotes purchase and trade-in prices over the telephone for 1985 to 1993 cars, vans, and light trucks. (Prices for '93 models will be available beginning in January 1994.) The service provides up-to-date price information that takes into account the caller's region of the country, the vehicle's mileage, major options, and general condition. For many models, it offers the vehicle's Trouble Index, based on CU's Frequency-of-Repair data (also on pages 178 through 223).

The telephone number for the price service is 1-900-446-1120. The call costs $1.75 a minute and must be made from a touch-tone phone. Expect the call to take five minutes or more. You'll be charged on your phone bill. Have the following facts about the car on hand when you call: model name or number, model year, mileage, number of cylinders, the car's general condition, and major options, such as air-conditioning, cassette radio, or power sun roof.

This service is not available in Alaska, Hawaii, or Canada and in certain areas of the continental U.S.

Good & bad bets in used cars

The list of reliable used cars includes 1987 to 1991 models whose overall reliability records were better than average for their model year, according to our Frequency-of-Repair records (see page 178).

The list of used cars to avoid includes '87 to '91 models whose overall reliability records are considerably worse than the average for their model year.

Problems with the engine, engine cooling, transmission, driveline, clutch, and body rust—troubles likely to be serious and costly to repair—weighed more heavily than other problems in forming these lists.

The reliable cars are grouped by price as reported in the April 1993 CONSUMER REPORTS. Most are likely to have dropped to a lower price by 1994. Prices are Mid-western averages for cars with average mileage, and with air-conditioning, AM/FM cassette stereo, and automatic transmission. (Prices for sporty cars, pickups, and sports-utility vehicles are for manual transmission.) Luxury cars were priced with leather seats, sunroof, and CD player.

RWD = rear-wheel drive; FWD = front-wheel drive; 2WD = two-wheel drive; 4WD = four-wheel drive.

Reliable used cars

$2500-$3500
88 Chevrolet Nova (FWD)
87 Chevrolet Nova (FWD) [2]
88, 89 Ford Festiva
87 Honda Civic (2WD)
88 Nissan Sentra (2WD)
87 Plymouth Caravelle

$3500-$4000
87 Chrysler Le Baron GTS
88 Mazda 323 (2WD)
87 Mazda Pickup (2WD)
89 Mercury Tracer
87 Nissan Pickup 4 (2WD)
88 Pontiac Fiero 4 [2]
87 Toyota Corolla FX-16 [2]
87 Toyota Tercel (2WD)

$4000-$4500
88 Chevrolet S10 Pickup V6 (2WD) [2]
89 Dodge Colt/Plymouth Colt (2WD)
87 Dodge Ram 50 Pickup 4 (2WD)
90 Ford Festiva
87 Honda CRX [2]
89 Isuzu Pickup 4 (2WD)
88 Mazda Pickup (2WD)

87 Nissan 200SX 4
87 Nissan Stanza Wagon (2WD)
87 Toyota Corolla (2WD)
88 Toyota Pickup 4 (2WD)
88 Toyota Tercel (2WD)

$4500-$5000
88 Chrysler Le Baron GTS
89 Eagle Summit
88 Honda Civic (2WD)
89 Mazda 323 (2WD)
87 Mazda 626 [1]
88 Nissan Pickup 4 (2WD)
87 Nissan Stanza [2]
87 Toyota Corolla SR5 (RWD)
87 Toyota Tercel Wagon (4WD)

$5000-$6000
87 Acura Integra
89 Dodge/Plymouth Colt Vista Wagon (2WD)
90 Dodge Colt/Plymouth Colt (2WD)
88 Dodge Ram 50 Pickup 4 (2WD)
87 Dodge Ram 50 Pickup 4 (4WD)

90 Eagle Summit
91 Ford Festiva
87 Ford LTD Crown Victoria
89 Ford Probe 4 [1]
87 Ford Thunderbird V6, V8
87 Honda Accord
88 Honda Civic Wagon (4WD)
90 Mazda 323 (2WD)
88 Mazda 626 [1]
89 Mazda Pickup (2WD)
87, 88 Mazda Pickup (4WD)
87 Mercury Grand Marquis
89 Nissan Pickup 4 (2WD)
87, 88 Nissan Pickup V6 (2WD)
89 Nissan Sentra (2WD)
88 Nissan Stanza Wagon (2WD)
87 Toyota Celica (2WD)
88 Toyota Corolla (2WD)
88 Toyota Corolla FX-16
87 Toyota MR2
89 Toyota Pickup 4 (2WD)
89 Toyota Pickup V6 (2WD)
89 Toyota Tercel (2WD)

Listings continued ▶

GOOD & BAD BETS IN USED CARS

$6000-$7000
91 Dodge Colt/Plymouth Colt (2WD)
89 Dodge Ram 50 Pickup 4 (2WD)
88 Dodge Ram 50 Pickup 4 (4WD)
89 Dodge Spirit 4 Turbo
91 Geo Metro
90 Geo Prizm
88 Honda CRX
89 Honda Civic (2WD)
91 Isuzu Pickup 4 (2WD)
88 Mazda MX-6 [1]
88 Mazda MX-6 Turbo [1]
90 Mazda Pickup (2WD)
87 Mazda RX-7 [2]
90 Mitsubishi Mirage
87 Nissan Maxima [2]
90 Nissan Pickup 4 (2WD)
89 Nissan Pickup V6 (2WD)
88 Nissan Pulsar NX
90 Nissan Sentra (2WD)
88 Nissan Stanza
89 Plymouth Acclaim 4 Turbo
88 Pontiac Fiero V6 [2]
87 Toyota Camry 4 (2WD)
88 Toyota Celica (2WD)
89 Toyota Corolla (2WD)
90 Toyota Pickup 4 (2WD)
88 Toyota Pickup 4 (4WD)
88 Toyota Pickup V6 (4WD)
90 Toyota Tercel (2WD)

$7000-$8000
88 Acura Integra
88 Buick Electra
89 Dodge Ram 50 Pickup 4 (4WD)
91 Eagle Summit
88 Ford LTD Crown Victoria
91 Geo Prizm
88 Honda Accord
89 Honda CRX
87 Honda Prelude
87 Lincoln Continental (RWD)
87 Lincoln Mark VII
91 Mazda 323 (2WD)
89 Mazda 626 [1]
89 Mazda MX-6 [1]
91 Mazda Pickup (2WD)
89, 90 Mazda Pickup (4WD)
90 Mazda Protegé (2WD)
88 Mercury Grand Marquis
91 Mitsubishi Mirage
88 Nissan Maxima [2]
91 Nissan Pickup 4 (2WD)
89 Nissan Pickup 4 (4WD)
89 Nissan Stanza
88 Toyota Camry 4 (2WD)
90 Toyota Corolla (2WD)
89 Toyota Corolla All-Trac (4WD)
88 Toyota MR2
91 Toyota Pickup 4 (2WD)
90 Toyota Pickup V6 (2WD)
91 Toyota Tercel (2WD)
87 Volkswagen Cabriolet

$8000-$9000
89 Acura Integra
87 BMW 528e
89 Buick Le Sabre
91 Geo Storm
90 Geo Tracker (4WD) [2]
90 Honda Civic (2WD)
90 Honda Civic Wagon (4WD)
87 Lincoln Town Car
88 Mazda 929
89 Mazda MX-6 Turbo [1]
91 Mazda Pickup (4WD)
89 Mercury Grand Marquis
89 Mitsubishi Galant 4 (2WD)
89 Nissan 240SX
90 Nissan Pickup 4 (4WD)
90 Nissan Pickup V6 (2WD)
91 Nissan Sentra (2WD)
88 Oldsmobile Toronado
90 Plymouth Laser (2WD) [2]
90 Subaru Legacy (2WD) [1]
89 Toyota Camry 4 (2WD)
88 Toyota Camry All-Trac 4 (4WD)
88, 89 Toyota Camry V6
89 Toyota Celica (2WD)
91 Toyota Corolla (2WD)
90 Toyota Corolla All-Trac (4WD)
88 Toyota MR2 Supercharged
89 Toyota Pickup 4 (4WD)
91 Toyota Pickup V6 (2WD)
87 Volvo 740 Sedan, Wagon
87 Volvo 740 Sedan, Wagon Turbo [2]

$9000-$10,000
87 Acura Legend [2]
88 BMW 528e [2]
89 Buick Riviera
90 Eagle Talon (2WD) [2]
89 Ford LTD Crown Victoria
89 Honda Accord
90 Honda CRX
91 Honda Civic (2WD)
90 Mazda 626
90 Mazda MX-6
91 Mazda Protegé (2WD)
88 Mazda RX-7 [2]
90 Mitsubishi Eclipse (2WD) [2]
88 Nissan 300ZX
91 Nissan NX 1600
87 Nissan Pathfinder V6 (4WD)
91 Nissan Pickup V6 (2WD)
89 Nissan Pickup V6 (4WD)
89 Pontiac Bonneville
90 Subaru Legacy (4WD) [1]
91 Subaru Loyale (4WD)
88 Toyota 4Runner 4 (4WD)
91 Toyota Corolla All-Trac (4WD)
88 Toyota Cressida
90 Toyota Pickup 4 (4WD)
89 Toyota Pickup V6 (4WD)
88 Toyota Supra
89 Toyota Van (2WD)
88 Volvo 240 Sedan, Wagon
88 Volvo 740 Sedan

GOOD & BAD BETS IN USED CARS

$10,000-$12,000
90, 91 Acura Integra
88 Acura Legend [2]
87 BMW 535i
91 Buick Century
90 Buick Le Sabre
88 Cadillac Eldorado
88 Cadillac Seville
91 Eagle Talon (2WD)
90 Honda Accord [1]
91 Honda CRX
91 Honda Civic Wagon (4WD)
89, 90 Honda Prelude
88 Lincoln Town Car
91 Mazda 626
89 Mazda 929
90 Mazda MX-5 Miata
91 Mazda MX-6
91 Mitsubishi Eclipse (2WD)
90, 91 Mitsubishi Galant 4 (2WD)
89 Mitsubishi Montero V6
90 Nissan 240SX
88 Nissan 300ZX Turbo
89 Nissan Maxima
91 Nissan NX 2000
88 Nissan Pathfinder V6 (4WD)
90 Nissan Pickup V6 (4WD)
91 Nissan Stanza
90 Nissan Stanza [2]
90 Nissan Van
90 Oldsmobile Eighty-Eight
91 Plymouth Laser (2WD)
91 Saturn SC Coupe
91 Saturn Sedans
91 Subaru Legacy (2WD)
88, 89 Toyota 4Runner V6 (4WD)
90 Toyota Camry 4 (2WD)
89 Toyota Camry All-Trac 4 (4WD)
90 Toyota Camry V6
90 Toyota Celica (2WD)
88 Toyota Land Cruiser Wagon
91 Toyota Pickup 4 (4WD)
91 Toyota Pickup V6 (4WD)
90 Toyota Pickup V6 (4WD) [1]

89 Toyota Van (4WD)
89 Volvo 240 Sedan
88 Volvo 740 Wagon

$12,000-$15,000
89 Audi 100
89 BMW 325i
88 BMW 535i [2]
91 Buick Le Sabre
89 Cadillac De Ville/Fleetwood (FWD)
89 Cadillac Seville
91 Honda Accord
91 Honda Prelude
89 Lincoln Town Car
91 Mazda MPV 4
91 Mazda MX-5 Miata
89 Mazda RX-7 [1]
89 Mazda RX-7 Turbo
90 Mitsubishi Montero V6 [2]
91 Nissan 240SX
90 Nissan Maxima [2]
89 Nissan Pathfinder V6 (4WD)
90, 91 Saab 900
91 Subaru Legacy (4WD)
91 Toyota Camry 4 (2WD)
90, 91 Toyota Camry All-Trac 4 (4WD)
91 Toyota Camry V6
91 Toyota Celica (2WD)
89 Toyota Cressida
89 Toyota Land Cruiser Wagon
91 Toyota MR2
89 Toyota Supra
89 Volvo 240 Wagon

$15,000-$20,000
89, 90 Acura Legend [2]
90 Audi 100
90 Cadillac De Ville/Fleetwood (FWD)
91 Infiniti G20
90, 91 Infiniti M30
90, 91 Lexus ES 250
89 Mercedes-Benz 190E 2.6
91 Nissan Maxima
90, 91 Nissan Pathfinder V6 (4WD)
90, 91 Saab 900 Turbo

90, 91 Toyota 4Runner V6 (4WD)
90, 91 Toyota Cressida
91 Toyota MR2 Turbo
91 Toyota Previa (2WD)
91 Toyota Previa All-Trac Van (4WD) [2]
91 Volvo 740 Sedan, Wagon
90 Volvo 740 Sedan, Wagon Turbo
91 Volvo 940 Wagon

$20,000-$25,000
89, 90 BMW 525i, 535i
89 BMW 535i
91 Mercedes-Benz 190E 2.3
91 Toyota Land Cruiser Wagon
91 Volvo 740 Sedan, Wagon Turbo
91 Volvo 940 Sedan
91 Volvo 940 Sedan, Wagon Turbo

$25,000-$30,000
91 Acura Legend [2]
91 BMW 525i
90 BMW 535i
90 Infiniti Q45
90 Lexus LS 400
91 Mercedes-Benz 190E 2.6
89 Mercedes-Benz 300E (2WD)
87 Mercedes-Benz 420 SEL

$30,000 AND UP
91 BMW 535i
91 Infiniti Q45
91 Lexus LS 400
89-91 Mercedes-Benz 300CE, 300TE (2WD)
90, 91 Mercedes-Benz 300E (2WD)

[1] *Manual transmission only.*
[2] *Automatic transmission only.*

Listings continued ▶

Used cars to avoid

ACURA
91 Legend [1]

BUICK
87 Century
87 Regal V6 (RWD)
91 Riviera
91 Roadmaster Estate Wagon
87, 89 Skyhawk
87, 88 Somerset, Skylark

CADILLAC
91 Eldorado

CHEVROLET
89-91 Astro Van V6 (2WD)
90 Astro Van V6 (4WD)
87-91 Blazer
88-91 S10 Blazer V6 (2WD)
87-91 S10 Blazer V6 (4WD)
87-91 Camaro
90, 91 Caprice V8
87, 88, 91 Cavalier 4
87, 91 Cavalier V6
87 Celebrity 4
88 Celebrity V6
88-91 Corsica, Beretta 4
88-91 Corsica, Beretta V6
87-91 Corvette
90 Lumina 4
91 Lumina V6
89-91 C/K10-20 Pickup V6
87-91 C/K10-20 Pickup V8 (2WD)
87-91 C/K10-20 Pickup V8 (4WD)
88-91 S10 Pickup 4 (2WD)
90, 91 S10 Pickup V6 (2WD)
88-91 S10 Pickup V6 (4WD)
87, 88 Spectrum
87-91 Sportvan V8
87-91 Suburban (2WD)
87-91 Suburban (4WD)

CHRYSLER
90 Imperial
91 Le Baron Sedan V6
88 Le Baron Coupe, Convertible 4
87, 88 Le Baron Coupe, Convertible 4 Turbo
90 Le Baron Coupe, Convertible V6
89, 90 New Yorker (FWD) V6

DODGE
89 Grand Caravan 4
90, 91 Caravan V6 (2WD)
91 Caravan V6 (4WD)
88-91 Grand Caravan V6 (2WD)
91 Grand Caravan V6 (4WD)
91 Dakota Pickup V8
87-89 Daytona 4
90, 91 Monaco
87, 89 Omni, America, Charger
87-89 Ramcharger V8
87, 91 Ram B150-250 Van, Wagon V8
89, 90 Ram D/W 100-250 Pickup V8
87 Shadow Turbo
91 Stealth Turbo (4WD)

EAGLE
88-91 Premier V6
91 Talon Turbo (4WD)

FORD
87-91 Aerostar Van (2WD)
90, 91 Aerostar Van (4WD)
87-91 Bronco V8
87-90 Bronco II (4WD)
87-91 Club Wagon Van V8
87-89 Escort
91 Explorer (2WD)
91 Explorer (4WD)
87, 88 F150-250 Pickup 6 (2WD)
87-91 F150-250 Pickup 6 (4WD)
87-91 F150-250 Pickup V8 (2WD)
87-91 F150-250 Pickup V8 (4WD)
87-90 Mustang 4
90, 91 Mustang V8

91 Probe 4 [2]
90 Probe V6 [2]
90 Ranger Pickup V6 (2WD)
90, 91 Ranger Pickup V6 (4WD)
87-89 Taurus 4
89, 90 Taurus SHO V6
87-90 Tempo 4 (2WD)
90 Thunderbird Supercharged V6
91 Thunderbird V8

GMC
87, 88 S15 Jimmy 4
88-91 S15 Jimmy V6

HYUNDAI
87-91 Excel
89-91 Sonata

ISUZU
87, 88 I-Mark
91 Rodeo V6
87 Trooper II 4
89, 90 Trooper, Trooper II V6
91 Trooper V6 [2]

JAGUAR
87-90 XJ6

JEEP
88, 90 Cherokee 4 (4WD)
90, 91 Cherokee, Wagoneer 6 (4WD)
87-91 Wrangler 6

LINCOLN
88-90 Continental (FWD)
91 Town Car

MAZDA
89, 90 MPV V6 (2WD)
90 MPV V6 (4WD)
91 Navajo (4WD) [2]

MERCURY
91 Capri
90 Cougar V6
87 Sable V6
87-90 Topaz 4 (2WD)

GOOD & BAD BETS IN USED CARS

MITSUBISHI
91 3000GT Turbo (4WD)
91 Eclipse Turbo (4WD)

NISSAN
87 Van

OLDSMOBILE
87 Eighty-Eight
87 Ninety-Eight
91 Custom Cruiser Wagon
87, 88 Cutlass Calais 4
87 Cutlass Calais V6
90 Cutlass Supreme 4 (FWD)
89 Cutlass Supreme V6 (FWD)

PLYMOUTH
87 Horizon, Turismo, America
87 Sundance Turbo
89 Grand Voyager 4
90, 91 Voyager V6 (2WD)
91 Voyager V6 (4WD)
88-91 Grand Voyager V6 (2WD)
91 Grand Voyager V6 (4WD)

PONTIAC
87 6000 4
87 6000 V6 (2WD)
87 Bonneville
87-91 Firebird
88, 89 Grand Am 4
87 Grand Am V6
89, 90 Grand Prix V6 (FWD)
88, 89 LeMans
87, 89, 91 Sunbird 4

SAAB
88, 89 9000 Series

SUBARU
87, 88 Coupe, Sedan, Wagon (2WD)
87, 88 Sedan, Wagon Turbo

VOLKSWAGEN
88-91 Golf, GTI
88, 91 Jetta
90, 91 Passat
87 Vanagon (2WD)

[1] *Manual transmission only.*
[2] *Automatic transmission only.*

BATTERY BASICS

There are three principal types of batteries on the market today: **Low-maintenance** batteries have caps or covers over their cells to permit periodic checking and refilling. **Maintenance-free** batteries are designed to reduce water loss further; indeed, some have no refill caps. On the downside, maintenance-free batteries may not fare as well as low-maintenance batteries after deep discharges. The **dual** type is a new design. It typically combines a low-maintenance battery with separate backup cells that can be activated to supply emergency power.

Size. Manufacturers further categorize batteries by group size—24, 26, 34, and so forth—which denotes the size of the case (but has no direct bearing on the power output). You probably won't find the group-size number in your car's owner's manual, so you may have to check the label on the old battery or refer to the battery dealer's handbook.

Cold-cranking amps. In addition, manufacturers rate the cold-cranking amperage (CCA) of their models. The CCA is the amount of current a battery should be able to deliver at 0°F without dropping below a certain cutoff voltage for 30 seconds. That translates into the battery's ability to supply power long enough to start your car in below-freezing weather. Two popular power ranges: batteries with a CCA of 455 to 550 and 600 to 650.

Frequency-of-repair records, 1987-1992

The following charts provide the most comprehensive picture available of auto reliability. The data come from subscribers to CONSUMER REPORTS, who tell us each year about their auto problems. The 1992 Annual Questionnaire on which these records are based brought in reports about 583,000 vehicles, reflecting subscribers' experiences between April 1991 and March 1992.

How to read the charts. The symbols reflect the percentage of cars with problems reported for each trouble spot, explained below, in each model year. Our calculations include a standardization to minimize differences due to mileage. For twins (essentially identical models sold under different nameplates) data are pooled.

The 1992 models were generally less than six months old, with an average of only 3000 miles. In our judgment, those cars should score ⊖ in all trouble spots; a score of ○ or worse is a sure sign of trouble in a car that new. In older models, scores of ○ are not necessarily cause for alarm, but scores of ◐ or ● reflect too many problems for most trouble spots.

KEY TO PROBLEM RATES	
⊖	2.0% or less
⊖	2.0% - 5.0%
○	5.0% - 9.3%
◐	9.3% - 14.8%
●	More than 14.8%
✻	Insufficient data
☐	Not applicable

Trouble spot	Includes
Engine	Rings, cylinders, pistons, bearings, valves, camshaft, turbocharger, drive belts or chain; oil leaks; engine overhaul.
Engine cooling	Radiator, heater core, water pump; overheating.
Fuel system	Stalling or hesitation; carburetor, choke, fuel pump, fuel injection, computer, fuel leaks, emission controls.
Ignition system	Spark or glow plugs, coil, distributor, timing, electronic ignition; too-frequent tuneups; engine knock or ping.
Automatic transmission	Transaxle, gear shifter, linkage; leaks, malfunction, or failure.
Manual transmission	Gearbox, gear shifter, linkage; leaks, malfunction, or failure.
Clutch	Lining, pressure plate, release bearing, linkage.
Driveline	Drive joints, drive axle, differential, wheel bearings, drive shaft, four-wheel-drive components.
Electrical system	Starter, alternator, battery, switches, controls, instruments, lights, radio, horn, accessory motors, electronics, wiring.
Steering/suspension	Linkage, power-steering unit, pump, wheel alignment, springs or torsion bars, ball joints, bushings, shocks, strut assembly.
Brakes	Power-boost and hydraulic systems; linings, discs, drums; antilock system; malfunction.
Exhaust system	Exhaust manifold, muffler, catalytic converter, pipes, leaks.
Body rust	Corrosion, pitting, perforation.
Paint	Fading, discoloring, chalking, peeling.
Body integrity	Air and water leaks, wind noise, rattles and squeaks.
Body hardware	Window, door, seat mechanisms; locks, seat belts, head restraints, sunroof.
Air-conditioning	Compressor, expansion valves, leakage, fans, electronics.

RELIABILITY RECORDS

TROUBLE SPOTS	Acura Integra '87–'92	Acura Legend '87–'92	Acura Vigor '87–'92	Audi 5000, 100 '87–'92
Engine				
Engine cooling				
Fuel system				
Ignition system				
Auto. transmission				
Man. transmission				
Clutch				
Driveline				
Electrical system				
Steering/suspension				
Brakes				
Exhaust system				
Body rust				
Paint				
Body integrity				
Body hardware				
Air-conditioning				

TROUBLE SPOTS	BMW 318i '87–'92	BMW 325 Series (2WD) '87–'92	BMW 5 Series '87–'92	BMW 7 Series '87–'92
Engine				
Engine cooling				
Fuel system				
Ignition system				
Auto. transmission				
Man. transmission				
Clutch				
Driveline				
Electrical system				
Steering/suspension				
Brakes				
Exhaust system				
Body rust				
Paint				
Body integrity				
Body hardware				
Air-conditioning				

Few ←— **Problems** —→ Many   * Insufficient data

180 RELIABILITY RECORDS

Buick Century / Buick Electra, Park Ave., Ultra / Buick Le Sabre / Buick Regal V6 (RWD)

Trouble Spots	Century '87-'92	Electra/Park Ave./Ultra '87-'92	Le Sabre '87-'92	Regal V6 RWD '87-'92
Engine				
Engine cooling				
Fuel system				
Ignition system				
Auto. transmission				
Man. transmission				
Clutch				
Driveline				
Electrical system				
Steering/suspension				
Brakes				
Exhaust system				
Body rust				
Paint				
Body integrity				
Body hardware				
Air-conditioning				

Buick Regal V6 (FWD) / Buick Riviera / Buick Roadmaster / Buick Roadmaster Estate Wagon

Trouble Spots	Regal V6 FWD '87-'92	Riviera '87-'92	Roadmaster '87-'92	Roadmaster Estate Wagon '87-'92
Engine				
Engine cooling				
Fuel system				
Ignition system				
Auto. transmission				
Man. transmission				
Clutch				
Driveline				
Electrical system				
Steering/suspension				
Brakes				
Exhaust system				
Body rust				
Paint				
Body integrity				
Body hardware				
Air-conditioning				

RELIABILITY RECORDS

Trouble Spots Reliability Chart

Trouble Spots	Buick Skyhawk '87–'92	Buick Somerset, Skylark '87–'92	Cadillac Brougham (RWD) '87–'92	Cadillac De Ville, Fleetwood (FWD) '87–'92
Engine				
Engine cooling				
Fuel system				
Ignition system				
Auto. transmission				
Man. transmission				
Clutch				
Driveline				
Electrical system				
Steering/suspension				
Brakes				
Exhaust system				
Body rust				
Paint				
Body integrity				
Body hardware				
Air-conditioning				

Trouble Spots	Cadillac Eldorado '87–'92	Cadillac Seville '87–'92	Chevrolet Astro Van V6 (2WD) '87–'92	Chevrolet Astro Van V6 (4WD) '87–'92
Engine				
Engine cooling				
Fuel system				
Ignition system				
Auto. transmission				
Man. transmission				
Clutch				
Driveline				
Electrical system				
Steering/suspension				
Brakes				
Exhaust system				
Body rust				
Paint				
Body integrity				
Body hardware				
Air-conditioning				

Few ←—Problems—→ Many   * Insufficient data

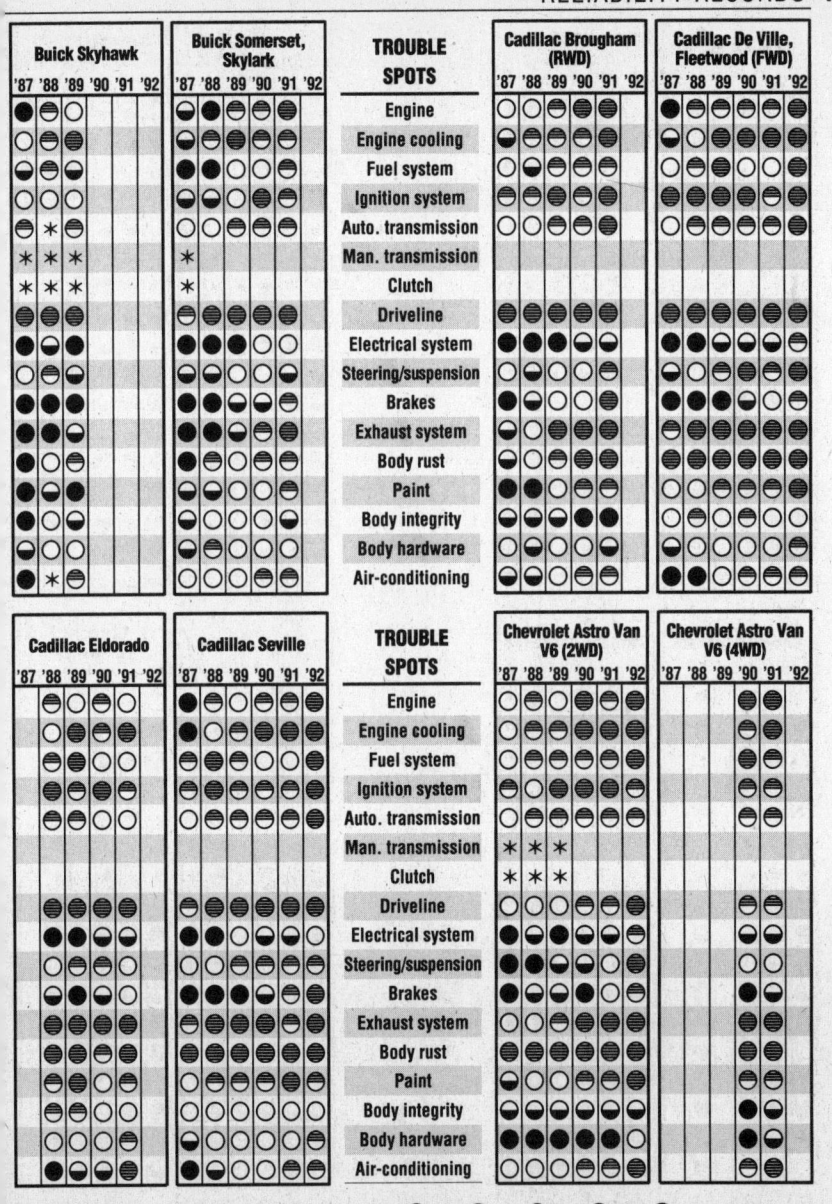

RELIABILITY RECORDS

Chevrolet Blazer / Chevrolet C/K10-20 Pickup V6 / Chevrolet C10-20 Pickup V8 (2WD) / Chevrolet K10-20 Pickup V8 (4WD)

Trouble Spots	Blazer '87–'92	C/K10-20 V6 '87–'92	C10-20 V8 2WD '87–'92	K10-20 V8 4WD '87–'92
Engine				
Engine cooling				
Fuel system				
Ignition system				
Auto. transmission				
Man. transmission				
Clutch				
Driveline				
Electrical system				
Steering/suspension				
Brakes				
Exhaust system				
Body rust				
Paint				
Body integrity				
Body hardware				
Air-conditioning				

Chevrolet Camaro / Chevrolet Caprice V8 / Chevrolet Cavalier 4 / Chevrolet Cavalier V6

Trouble Spots	Camaro '87–'92	Caprice V8 '87–'92	Cavalier 4 '87–'92	Cavalier V6 '87–'92
Engine				
Engine cooling				
Fuel system				
Ignition system				
Auto. transmission				
Man. transmission				
Clutch				
Driveline				
Electrical system				
Steering/suspension				
Brakes				
Exhaust system				
Body rust				
Paint				
Body integrity				
Body hardware				
Air-conditioning				

RELIABILITY RECORDS

Chevrolet Celebrity 4, Chevrolet Celebrity V6, Chevrolet Corsica/Beretta 4, Chevrolet Corsica/Beretta V6

TROUBLE SPOTS	Celebrity 4 '87–'92	Celebrity V6 '87–'92	Corsica/Beretta 4 '87–'92	Corsica/Beretta V6 '87–'92
Engine				
Engine cooling				
Fuel system				
Ignition system				
Auto. transmission				
Man. transmission				
Clutch				
Driveline				
Electrical system				
Steering/suspension				
Brakes				
Exhaust system				
Body rust				
Paint				
Body integrity				
Body hardware				
Air-conditioning				

Chevrolet Corvette, Chevrolet Lumina 4, Chevrolet Lumina V6, Chevrolet Lumina APV Van

TROUBLE SPOTS	Corvette '87–'92	Lumina 4 '87–'92	Lumina V6 '87–'92	Lumina APV Van '87–'92
Engine				
Engine cooling				
Fuel system				
Ignition system				
Auto. transmission				
Man. transmission				
Clutch				
Driveline				
Electrical system				
Steering/suspension				
Brakes				
Exhaust system				
Body rust				
Paint				
Body integrity				
Body hardware				
Air-conditioning				

Few ← Problems → Many   * Insufficient data

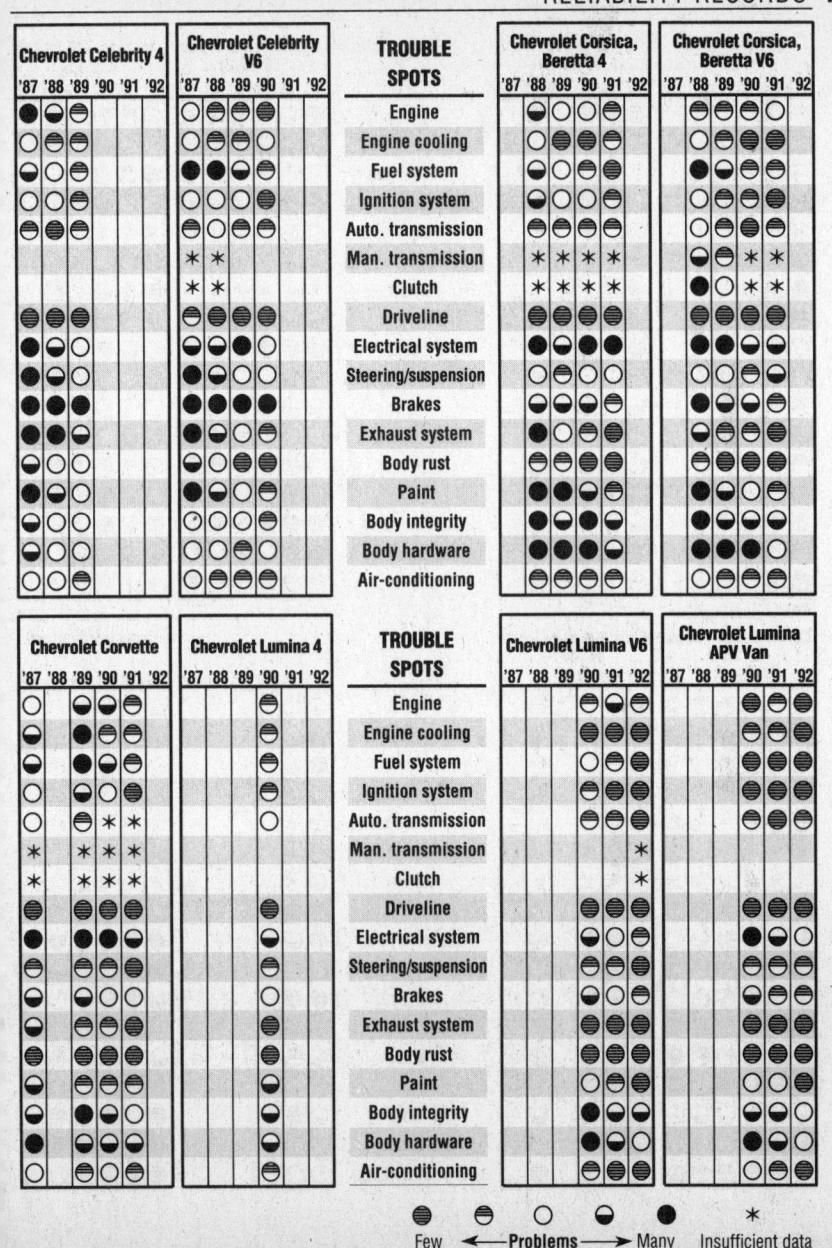

RELIABILITY RECORDS

Chevrolet Nova (FWD) / Chevrolet S10 Blazer V6 (2WD) / Chevrolet S10 Blazer V6 (4WD) / Chevrolet S10 Pickup 4 (2WD)

TROUBLE SPOTS	Nova (FWD) '87–'92	S10 Blazer V6 (2WD) '87–'92	S10 Blazer V6 (4WD) '87–'92	S10 Pickup 4 (2WD) '87–'92
Engine				
Engine cooling				
Fuel system				
Ignition system				
Auto. transmission				
Man. transmission				
Clutch				
Driveline				
Electrical system				
Steering/suspension				
Brakes				
Exhaust system				
Body rust				
Paint				
Body integrity				
Body hardware				
Air-conditioning				

Chevrolet S10 Pickup V6 (2WD) / Chevrolet S10 Pickup V6 (4WD) / Chevrolet Spectrum / Chevrolet Sportvan V8

TROUBLE SPOTS	S10 Pickup V6 (2WD) '87–'92	S10 Pickup V6 (4WD) '87–'92	Spectrum '87–'92	Sportvan V8 '87–'92
Engine				
Engine cooling				
Fuel system				
Ignition system				
Auto. transmission				
Man. transmission				
Clutch				
Driveline				
Electrical system				
Steering/suspension				
Brakes				
Exhaust system				
Body rust				
Paint				
Body integrity				
Body hardware				
Air-conditioning				

RELIABILITY RECORDS 185

Symbols legend: ◒ Few ← Problems → ● Many ✻ Insufficient data

Chevrolet Sprint

Trouble Spot	'87	'88	'89	'90	'91	'92
Engine	○	○				
Engine cooling	○	◒				
Fuel system	○	○				
Ignition system	◒	◒				
Auto. transmission	✻	✻				
Man. transmission	◒					
Clutch	◒	○				
Driveline	◒					
Electrical system	○	◒				
Steering/suspension	◒					
Brakes	●	●				
Exhaust system	○	○				
Body rust	●	●				
Paint	◒	◒				
Body integrity	●	●				
Body hardware	○	○				
Air-conditioning	◒	✻				

Chevrolet Suburban (2WD)

Trouble Spot	'87	'88	'89	'90	'91	'92
Engine	◒	○	◒	◒	◒	
Engine cooling	●	●	◒	◒	◒	
Fuel system	●	○	◒	◒	◒	
Ignition system	◒	◒	◒	◒	◒	
Auto. transmission	○	○	○	◒	◒	
Man. transmission	✻	✻	✻	✻		
Clutch	✻	✻	✻	✻		
Driveline	○	○	○	◒	◒	
Electrical system	●	●	●	◒	◒	
Steering/suspension	◒	○	◒	◒	◒	
Brakes	●	◒	◒	◒	○	
Exhaust system	○	◒	◒	◒	◒	
Body rust	●	●	●	●	◒	
Paint	●	●	●	●	●	
Body integrity	●	●	●	●	●	
Body hardware	●	●	●	●	●	
Air-conditioning	●	◒	◒	○	◒	

Chevrolet Suburban (4WD)

Trouble Spot	'87	'88	'89	'90	'91	'92
Engine	◒	○	◒	◒	◒	
Engine cooling	◒	○	○	◒	○	
Fuel system	●	○	◒	◒	○	
Ignition system	◒	◒	◒	◒	◒	
Auto. transmission	◒	○	○	◒	◒	
Man. transmission	✻	✻	✻	✻		
Clutch	✻	✻	✻	✻		
Driveline	◒	◒	○	○	◒	
Electrical system	●	●	◒	◒	◒	
Steering/suspension	●	●	●	●	○	
Brakes	●	●	●	●	○	
Exhaust system	◒	◒	◒	◒	◒	
Body rust	●	●	●	●	◒	
Paint	●	●	●	●	●	
Body integrity	●	●	●	●	●	
Body hardware	●	●	●	●	●	
Air-conditioning	◒	○	○	◒	◒	

Chrysler Fifth Avenue (RWD)

Trouble Spot	'87	'88	'89	'90	'91	'92
Engine	◒	◒				
Engine cooling	○	◒				
Fuel system	●	●				
Ignition system	◒	◒				
Auto. transmission	○	○				
Man. transmission						
Clutch						
Driveline	◒	◒				
Electrical system	●	●				
Steering/suspension	●	●				
Brakes	●	●				
Exhaust system	●	●				
Body rust	●	●				
Paint	●	●				
Body integrity	●	●				
Body hardware	●	●				
Air-conditioning	●	○				

Chrysler Imperial

Trouble Spot	'87	'88	'89	'90	'91	'92
Engine				○		
Engine cooling				◒		
Fuel system				○		
Ignition system				◒		
Auto. transmission				◒		
Man. transmission						
Clutch						
Driveline				◒		
Electrical system				●		
Steering/suspension				●		
Brakes				●		
Exhaust system				◒		
Body rust				●		
Paint				◒		
Body integrity				○		
Body hardware				○		
Air-conditioning				○		

Chrysler Le Baron Sedan 4

Trouble Spot	'87	'88	'89	'90	'91	'92
Engine	◒	◒				
Engine cooling	◒	○				
Fuel system	●	○				
Ignition system	○	○				
Auto. transmission	○	○				
Man. transmission						
Clutch						
Driveline	◒	◒				
Electrical system	●	●				
Steering/suspension	●	○				
Brakes	●	●				
Exhaust system	●	●				
Body rust	●	●				
Paint	●	●				
Body integrity	●	●				
Body hardware	●	○				
Air-conditioning	●	○				

Chrysler Le Baron Sedan V6

Trouble Spot	'87	'88	'89	'90	'91	'92
Engine				◒	◒	
Engine cooling				◒	◒	
Fuel system				◒	◒	
Ignition system				◒	◒	
Auto. transmission				○	◒	
Man. transmission						
Clutch						
Driveline				◒	◒	
Electrical system				○	○	
Steering/suspension				◒	◒	
Brakes				◒	◒	
Exhaust system				○	◒	
Body rust				◒	◒	
Paint				◒	◒	
Body integrity				○	○	
Body hardware				◒	◒	
Air-conditioning				◒	◒	

Chrysler Le Baron Coupe & Conv. 4

Trouble Spot	'87	'88	'89	'90	'91	'92
Engine	◒	◒	○			
Engine cooling	○	○	◒			
Fuel system	◒	◒	◒			
Ignition system	◒	◒	◒			
Auto. transmission	○	◒	◒			
Man. transmission	✻	✻	✻			
Clutch	✻	✻	✻			
Driveline	◒	◒	◒			
Electrical system	●	●	○			
Steering/suspension	●	●	◒			
Brakes	●	●	●			
Exhaust system	○	●	◒			
Body rust	●	●	●			
Paint	●	○	◒			
Body integrity	●	●	◒			
Body hardware	●	●	◒			
Air-conditioning	●	●	◒			

RELIABILITY RECORDS

Trouble Spots

Trouble Spots	Chrysler Le Baron Coupe & Conv. 4 Turbo '87–'92	Chrysler Le Baron Coupe & Conv. V6 '87–'92	Chrysler Le Baron GTS Hatchback '87–'92	Chrysler Le Baron GTS Hatchback Turbo '87–'92
Engine				
Engine cooling				
Fuel system				
Ignition system				
Auto. transmission				
Man. transmission				
Clutch				
Driveline				
Electrical system				
Steering/suspension				
Brakes				
Exhaust system				
Body rust				
Paint				
Body integrity				
Body hardware				
Air-conditioning				

Trouble Spots	Chrysler New Yorker, E-Class 4 (FWD) '87–'92	Chrysler New Yorker, E-Class 4 T'bo (FWD) '87–'92	Chrysler New Yorker V6 (FWD) '87–'92	Chrysler Town & Country Van (2WD) '87–'92
Engine				
Engine cooling				
Fuel system				
Ignition system				
Auto. transmission				
Man. transmission				
Clutch				
Driveline				
Electrical system				
Steering/suspension				
Brakes				
Exhaust system				
Body rust				
Paint				
Body integrity				
Body hardware				
Air-conditioning				

RELIABILITY RECORDS

Trouble Spots by Model and Year

Trouble Spots	Dodge 600 '87–'92	Dodge Aries '87–'92	Dodge Caravan 4 '87–'92	Dodge Caravan 4 Turbo '87–'92
Engine				
Engine cooling				
Fuel system				
Ignition system				
Auto. transmission				
Man. transmission				
Clutch				
Driveline				
Electrical system				
Steering/suspension				
Brakes				
Exhaust system				
Body rust				
Paint				
Body integrity				
Body hardware				
Air-conditioning				

Trouble Spots	Dodge Grand Caravan 4 '87–'92	Dodge Caravan V6 (2WD) '87–'92	Dodge Caravan V6 (4WD) '87–'92	Dodge Grand Caravan V6 (2WD) '87–'92
Engine				
Engine cooling				
Fuel system				
Ignition system				
Auto. transmission				
Man. transmission				
Clutch				
Driveline				
Electrical system				
Steering/suspension				
Brakes				
Exhaust system				
Body rust				
Paint				
Body integrity				
Body hardware				
Air-conditioning				

Legend: Few ←— Problems —→ Many   ✱ Insufficient data

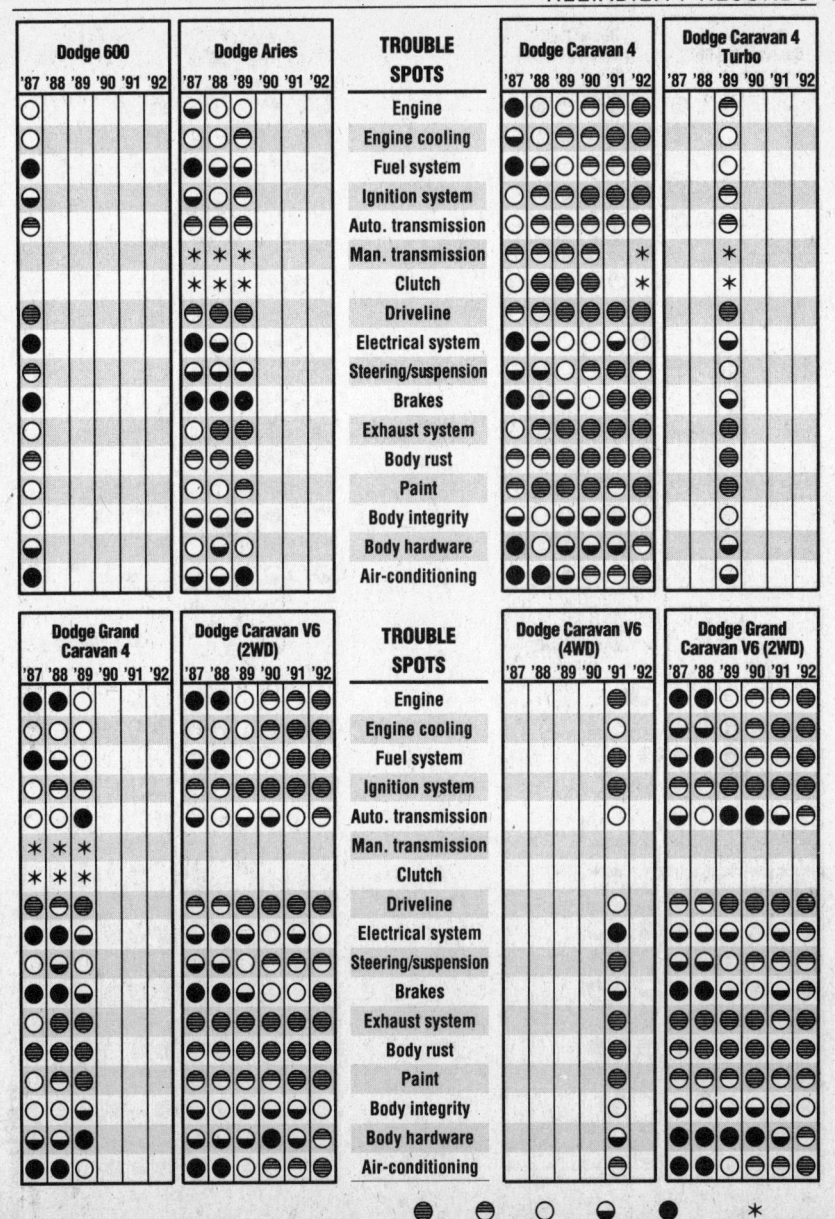

RELIABILITY RECORDS

Trouble Spots	Dodge Grand Caravan V6 (4WD) '87–'92	Dodge Colt, Colt Wagon (2WD) '87–'92	Dodge Colt Vista Wagon (2WD) '87–'92	Dodge Colt Vista Wagon (4WD) '87–'92
Engine				
Engine cooling				
Fuel system				
Ignition system				
Auto. transmission				
Man. transmission				
Clutch				
Driveline				
Electrical system				
Steering/suspension				
Brakes				
Exhaust system				
Body rust				
Paint				
Body integrity				
Body hardware				
Air-conditioning				

Trouble Spots	Dodge Dakota Pickup V6 (2WD) '87–'92	Dodge Dakota Pickup V6 (4WD) '87–'92	Dodge Dakota Pickup V8 '87–'92	Dodge Daytona 4 '87–'92
Engine				
Engine cooling				
Fuel system				
Ignition system				
Auto. transmission				
Man. transmission				
Clutch				
Driveline				
Electrical system				
Steering/suspension				
Brakes				
Exhaust system				
Body rust				
Paint				
Body integrity				
Body hardware				
Air-conditioning				

RELIABILITY RECORDS 189

Dodge Dynasty V6 '87–'92	Dodge Lancer '87–'92	TROUBLE SPOTS	Dodge Monaco '87–'92	Dodge Omni, America, Charger '87–'92
		Engine		
		Engine cooling		
		Fuel system		
		Ignition system		
		Auto. transmission		
		Man. transmission		
		Clutch		
		Driveline		
		Electrical system		
		Steering/suspension		
		Brakes		
		Exhaust system		
		Body rust		
		Paint		
		Body integrity		
		Body hardware		
		Air-conditioning		

Dodge Ram 50 Pickup 4 '87–'92	Dodge Ram B150-250 Van, Wagon V8 '87–'92	TROUBLE SPOTS	Dodge Ram D/W 100-250 Pickup V8 '87–'92	Dodge Ramcharger '87–'92
		Engine		
		Engine cooling		
		Fuel system		
		Ignition system		
		Auto. transmission		
		Man. transmission		
		Clutch		
		Driveline		
		Electrical system		
		Steering/suspension		
		Brakes		
		Exhaust system		
		Body rust		
		Paint		
		Body integrity		
		Body hardware		
		Air-conditioning		

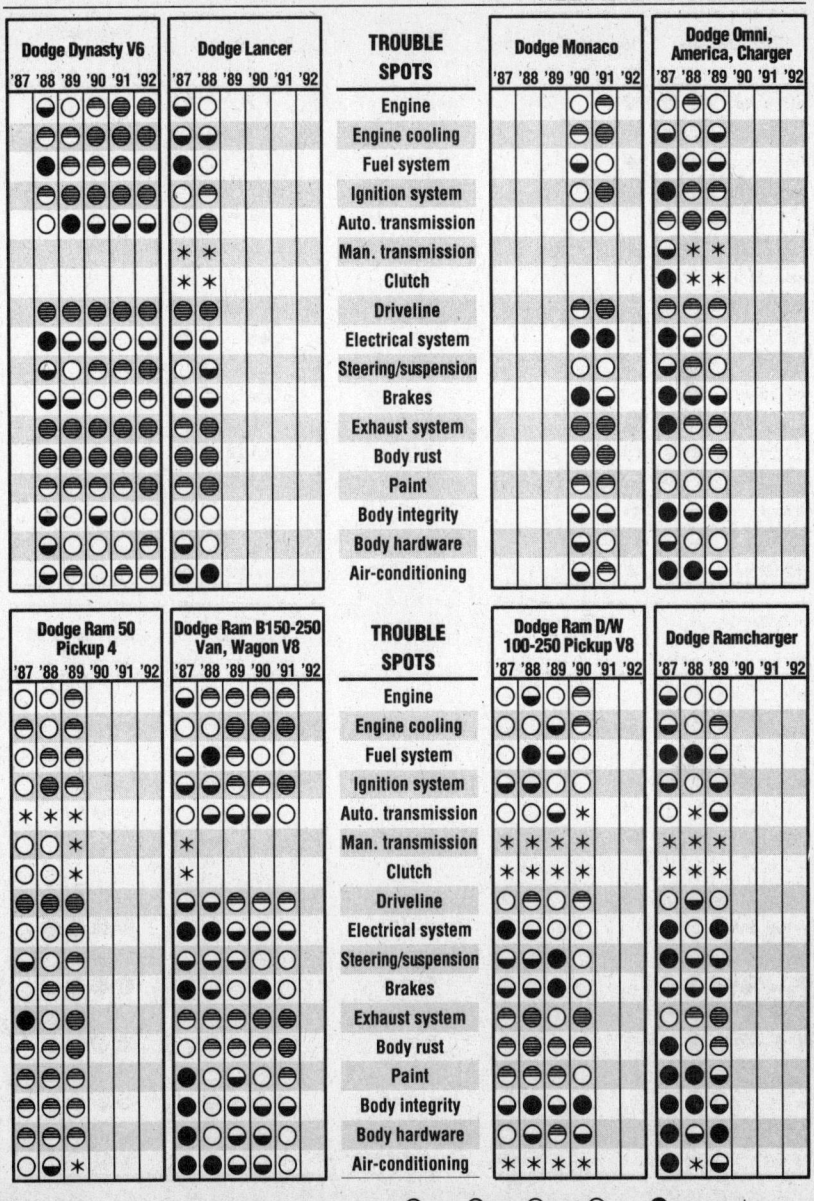

Few ← Problems → Many   * Insufficient data

190 RELIABILITY RECORDS

	Dodge Shadow '87–'92	Dodge Shadow Turbo '87–'92	TROUBLE SPOTS	Dodge Spirit 4 '87–'92	Dodge Spirit 4 Turbo '87–'92
			Engine		
			Engine cooling		
			Fuel system		
			Ignition system		
			Auto. transmission		
			Man. transmission		
			Clutch		
			Driveline		
			Electrical system		
			Steering/suspension		
			Brakes		
			Exhaust system		
			Body rust		
			Paint		
			Body integrity		
			Body hardware		
			Air-conditioning		

	Dodge Spirit V6 '87–'92	Dodge Stealth (2WD) '87–'92	TROUBLE SPOTS	Dodge Stealth Turbo (4WD) '87–'92	Eagle Premier V6 '87–'92
			Engine		
			Engine cooling		
			Fuel system		
			Ignition system		
			Auto. transmission		
			Man. transmission		
			Clutch		
			Driveline		
			Electrical system		
			Steering/suspension		
			Brakes		
			Exhaust system		
			Body rust		
			Paint		
			Body integrity		
			Body hardware		
			Air-conditioning		

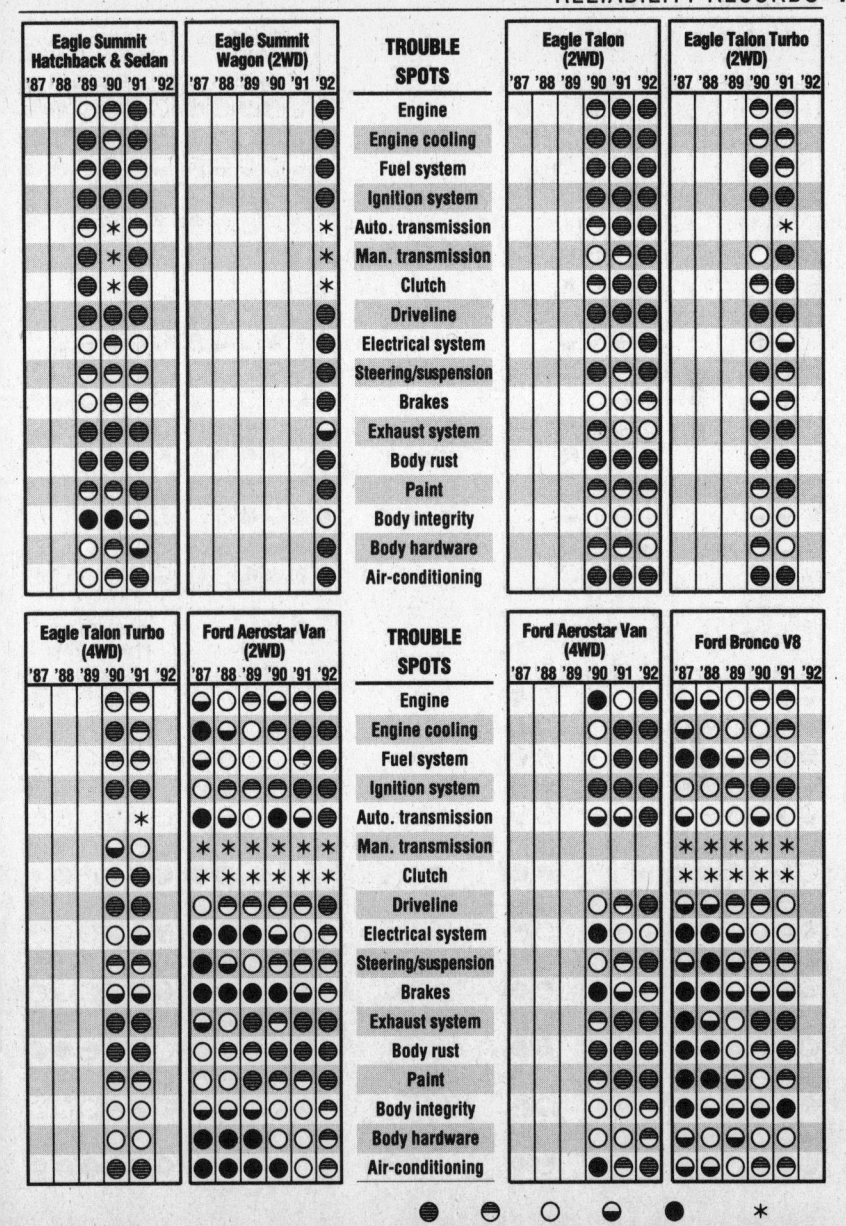

RELIABILITY RECORDS 191

TROUBLE SPOTS	Eagle Summit Hatchback & Sedan '87-'92	Eagle Summit Wagon (2WD) '87-'92	Eagle Talon (2WD) '87-'92	Eagle Talon Turbo (2WD) '87-'92
Engine				
Engine cooling				
Fuel system				
Ignition system				
Auto. transmission				
Man. transmission				
Clutch				
Driveline				
Electrical system				
Steering/suspension				
Brakes				
Exhaust system				
Body rust				
Paint				
Body integrity				
Body hardware				
Air-conditioning				

TROUBLE SPOTS	Eagle Talon Turbo (4WD) '87-'92	Ford Aerostar Van (2WD) '87-'92	Ford Aerostar Van (4WD) '87-'92	Ford Bronco V8 '87-'92
Engine				
Engine cooling				
Fuel system				
Ignition system				
Auto. transmission				
Man. transmission				
Clutch				
Driveline				
Electrical system				
Steering/suspension				
Brakes				
Exhaust system				
Body rust				
Paint				
Body integrity				
Body hardware				
Air-conditioning				

Few ← Problems → Many   * Insufficient data

RELIABILITY RECORDS

Ford Bronco II (2WD) — '87 '88 '89 '90 '91 '92
Ford Bronco II (4WD) — '87 '88 '89 '90 '91 '92
Ford Club Wagon Van V8 — '87 '88 '89 '90 '91 '92
Ford Crown Victoria, LTD Crown Victoria — '87 '88 '89 '90 '91 '92

TROUBLE SPOTS

- Engine
- Engine cooling
- Fuel system
- Ignition system
- Auto. transmission
- Man. transmission
- Clutch
- Driveline
- Electrical system
- Steering/suspension
- Brakes
- Exhaust system
- Body rust
- Paint
- Body integrity
- Body hardware
- Air-conditioning

Ford Escort — '87 '88 '89 '90 '91 '92
Ford Explorer (2WD) — '87 '88 '89 '90 '91 '92
Ford Explorer (4WD) — '87 '88 '89 '90 '91 '92
Ford F150-250 Pickup 6 (2WD) — '87 '88 '89 '90 '91 '92

TROUBLE SPOTS

- Engine
- Engine cooling
- Fuel system
- Ignition system
- Auto. transmission
- Man. transmission
- Clutch
- Driveline
- Electrical system
- Steering/suspension
- Brakes
- Exhaust system
- Body rust
- Paint
- Body integrity
- Body hardware
- Air-conditioning

RELIABILITY RECORDS 193

Ford F150-250 Pickup 6 (4WD) — '87–'92
Ford F150-250 Pickup V8 (2WD) — '87–'92
Ford F150-250 Pickup V8 (4WD) — '87–'92
Ford Festiva — '87–'92

TROUBLE SPOTS: Engine, Engine cooling, Fuel system, Ignition system, Auto. transmission, Man. transmission, Clutch, Driveline, Electrical system, Steering/suspension, Brakes, Exhaust system, Body rust, Paint, Body integrity, Body hardware, Air-conditioning

Ford Mustang 4 — '87–'92
Ford Mustang V8 — '87–'92
Ford Probe 4 — '87–'92
Ford Probe 4 Turbo — '87–'92

Legend: Few ← Problems → Many, * Insufficient data

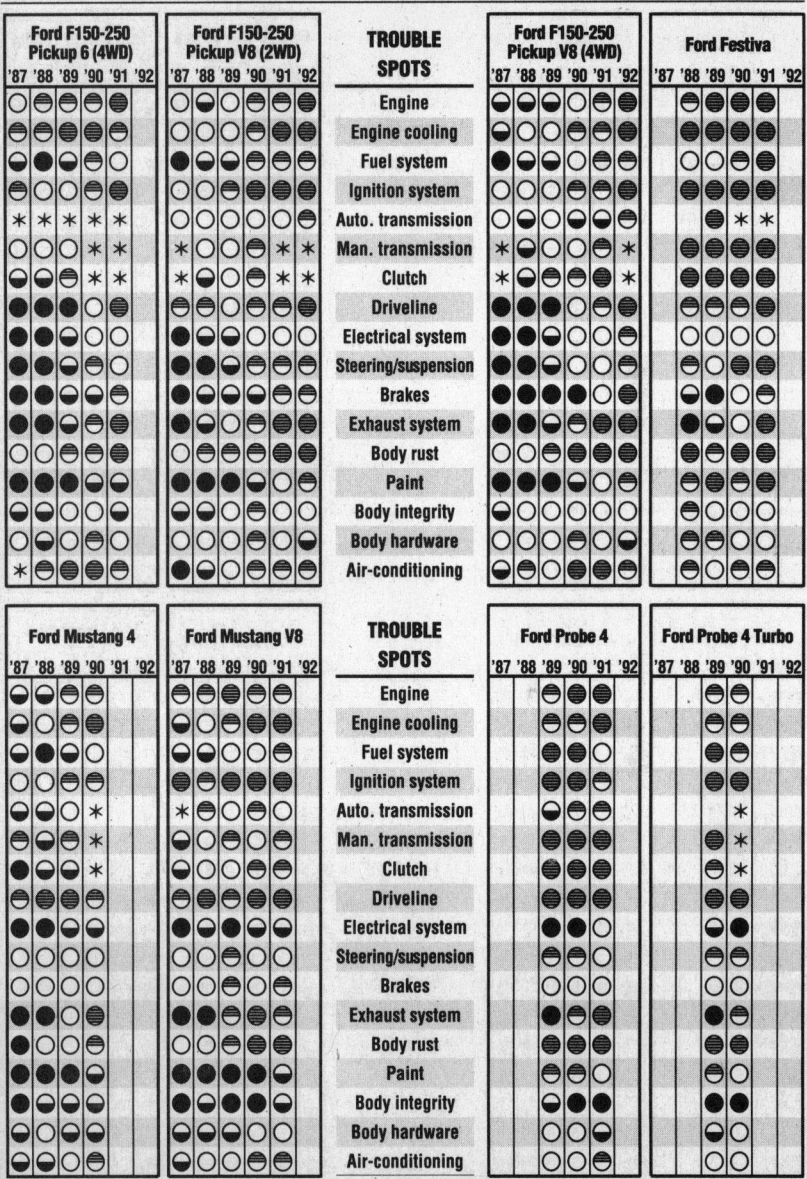

RELIABILITY RECORDS

TROUBLE SPOTS	Ford Probe V6 '87–'92	Ford Ranger Pickup 4 (2WD) '87–'92	Ford Ranger Pickup V6 (2WD) '87–'92	Ford Ranger Pickup V6 (4WD) '87–'92
Engine				
Engine cooling				
Fuel system				
Ignition system				
Auto. transmission				
Man. transmission				
Clutch				
Driveline				
Electrical system				
Steering/suspension				
Brakes				
Exhaust system				
Body rust				
Paint				
Body integrity				
Body hardware				
Air-conditioning				

TROUBLE SPOTS	Ford Taurus 4 '87–'92	Ford Taurus V6 '87–'92	Ford Tempo 4 (2WD) '87–'92	Ford Thunderbird 4 Turbo '87–'92
Engine				
Engine cooling				
Fuel system				
Ignition system				
Auto. transmission				
Man. transmission				
Clutch				
Driveline				
Electrical system				
Steering/suspension				
Brakes				
Exhaust system				
Body rust				
Paint				
Body integrity				
Body hardware				
Air-conditioning				

RELIABILITY RECORDS

Ford Thunderbird V6 — '87 '88 '89 '90 '91 '92
Ford Thunderbird Supercharged V6 — '87 '88 '89 '90 '91 '92
Ford Thunderbird V8 — '87 '88 '89 '90 '91 '92
Geo Metro — '87 '88 '89 '90 '91 '92

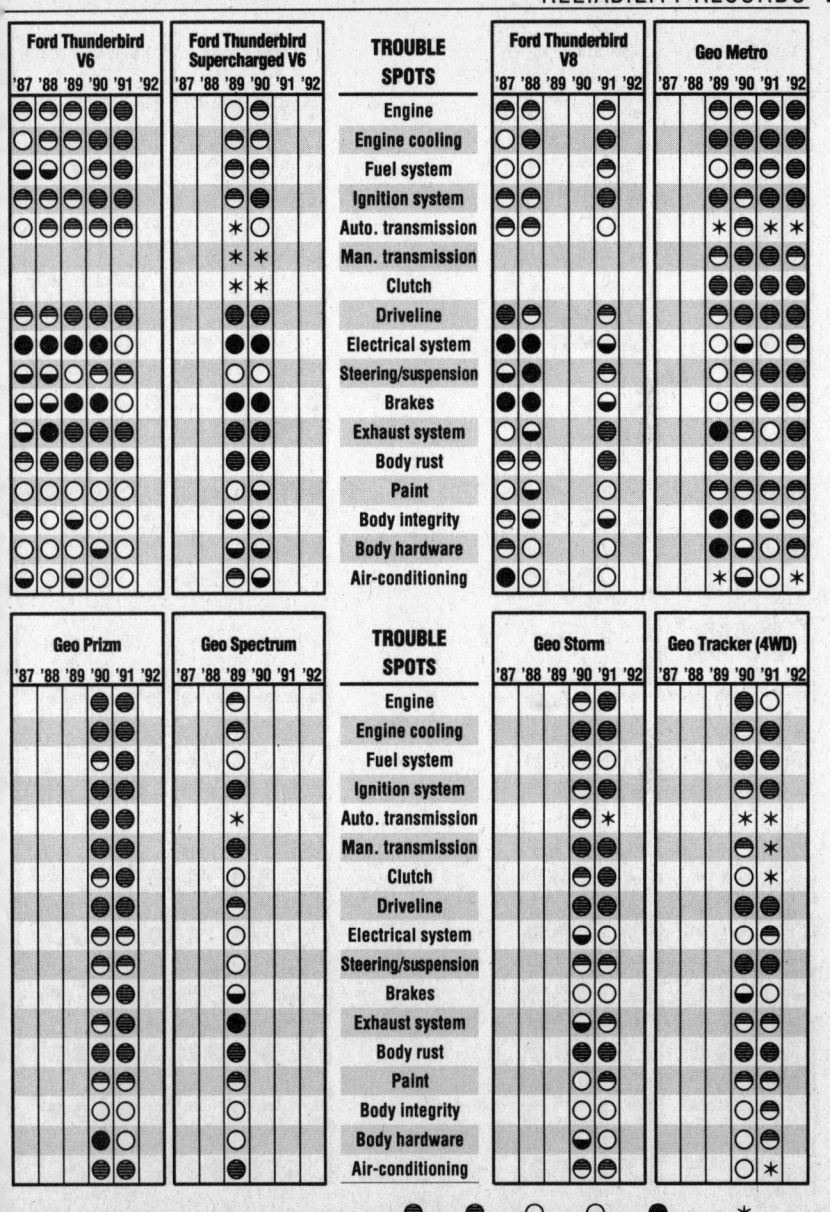

Trouble Spots	T-Bird V6	T-Bird SC V6	T-Bird V8	Geo Metro
Engine	◐ ◐ ◐ ◐ ◐ ◐	— — ○ ◐ ◐ —	◐ ◐ — ◐ ◐ ◐	— — ● ◐ ◐ ●
Engine cooling	○ ◐ ◐ ◐ ◐ ◐	— — ◐ ◐ ◐ —	○ ○ — ◐ ◐ —	— — ◐ ◐ ◐ ◐
Fuel system	◐ ● ○ ◐ ◐ —	— — ◐ ◐ ◐ —	○ ○ — ◐ ◐ —	— — ○ ◐ ◐ ●
Ignition system	— ◐ ◐ ◐ ◐ —	— — ◐ ◐ ◐ —	— — — ◐ ◐ —	— — ◐ ◐ ◐ ●
Auto. transmission	○ ◐ ◐ ◐ ◐ ◐	— — ✱ ○ — —	◐ ◐ — ○ — —	— — ✱ ◐ ✱ ✱
Man. transmission	— — — — — —	— — ✱ ✱ — —	— — — — — —	— — ◐ ◐ ◐ ◐
Clutch	— — — — — —	— — ✱ ✱ — —	— — — — — —	— — ◐ ◐ ◐ ◐
Driveline	◐ ◐ ◐ ◐ ◐ —	— — ◐ ◐ — —	◐ ◐ — ◐ ◐ —	— — ◐ ◐ ◐ ◐
Electrical system	● ● ● ● ○ —	— — ● ● — —	◐ ● — ◐ ◐ —	— — ○ ◐ ◐ ◐
Steering/suspension	— ◐ ◐ ◐ ◐ —	— — ○ ○ — —	— — — ◐ — —	— — ○ ◐ ◐ ◐
Brakes	◐ ● ◐ ● ○ —	— — ● ● — —	◐ ● — ◐ — —	— — ○ ◐ ◐ ◐
Exhaust system	◐ ● ● ◐ ◐ —	— — ◐ ◐ — —	◐ ○ — ◐ ◐ —	— — ● ◐ ◐ ◐
Body rust	◐ ◐ ◐ ◐ ◐ —	— — ◐ ◐ — —	◐ ◐ — ◐ — —	— — ◐ ◐ ◐ ◐
Paint	○ ○ ○ ○ ○ —	— — ○ ◐ — —	○ ○ — ◐ — —	— — ◐ ◐ ◐ ◐
Body integrity	◐ ○ ◐ ○ ◐ —	— — ◐ ◐ — —	◐ ◐ — ○ — —	— — ● ◐ ◐ ◐
Body hardware	○ ○ ◐ ○ ◐ —	— — ◐ ○ — —	◐ ○ — ○ — —	— — ● ◐ ○ ◐
Air-conditioning	◐ ○ ◐ ○ ◐ —	— — ● ◐ — —	◐ ◐ — ○ — —	— — ✱ ◐ ○ ✱

Geo Prizm — '87 '88 '89 '90 '91 '92
Geo Spectrum — '87 '88 '89 '90 '91 '92
Geo Storm — '87 '88 '89 '90 '91 '92
Geo Tracker (4WD) — '87 '88 '89 '90 '91 '92

Trouble Spots	Geo Prizm	Geo Spectrum	Geo Storm	Geo Tracker (4WD)
Engine	— — — ◐ ◐ —	— — ◐ — — —	— — — ◐ ◐ —	— — — ◐ ○ —
Engine cooling	— — — ◐ ◐ —	— — ◐ — — —	— — — ◐ ◐ —	— — — ◐ ◐ —
Fuel system	— — — ◐ ◐ —	— — ○ — — —	— — — ◐ ○ —	— — — ◐ ◐ —
Ignition system	— — — ◐ ◐ —	— — ◐ — — —	— — — ◐ ◐ —	— — — ◐ ◐ —
Auto. transmission	— — — ◐ ◐ —	— — ✱ — — —	— — — ◐ ✱ —	— — — ✱ ✱ —
Man. transmission	— — — ◐ ◐ —	— — ◐ — — —	— — — ◐ ◐ —	— — — ◐ ✱ —
Clutch	— — — ◐ ◐ —	— — ○ — — —	— — — ◐ ◐ —	— — — ○ ✱ —
Driveline	— — — ◐ ◐ —	— — ◐ — — —	— — — ◐ ◐ —	— — — ◐ ◐ —
Electrical system	— — — ◐ ◐ —	— — ○ — — —	— — — ◐ ○ —	— — — ○ ◐ —
Steering/suspension	— — — ◐ ◐ —	— — ○ — — —	— — — ○ ○ —	— — — ◐ ◐ —
Brakes	— — — ◐ ◐ —	— — ◐ — — —	— — — ○ ○ —	— — — ◐ ○ —
Exhaust system	— — — ◐ ◐ —	— — ● — — —	— — — ◐ ◐ —	— — — ◐ ◐ —
Body rust	— — — ◐ ◐ —	— — ◐ — — —	— — — ◐ ◐ —	— — — ◐ ◐ —
Paint	— — — ◐ ◐ —	— — ◐ — — —	— — — ○ ◐ —	— — — ◐ ◐ —
Body integrity	— — — ○ ○ —	— — ○ — — —	— — — ○ ○ —	— — — ◐ ◐ —
Body hardware	— — — ● ○ —	— — ○ — — —	— — — ◐ ◐ —	— — — ◐ ◐ —
Air-conditioning	— — — ◐ ◐ —	— — — — — —	— — — ◐ ◐ —	— — — ○ ✱ —

● ◐ ○ ◐ ●   ✱
Few ←—Problems—→ Many   Insufficient data

196 RELIABILITY RECORDS

Trouble Spots	GMC S15 Jimmy 4 '87-'92	GMC S15 Jimmy V6 '87-'92	Honda Accord '87-'92	Honda Civic (2WD) '87-'92
Engine				
Engine cooling				
Fuel system				
Ignition system				
Auto. transmission				
Man. transmission				
Clutch				
Driveline				
Electrical system				
Steering/suspension				
Brakes				
Exhaust system				
Body rust				
Paint				
Body integrity				
Body hardware				
Air-conditioning				

Trouble Spots	Honda Civic Wagon (4WD) '87-'92	Honda CRX '87-'92	Honda Prelude '87-'92	Hyundai Excel '87-'92
Engine				
Engine cooling				
Fuel system				
Ignition system				
Auto. transmission				
Man. transmission				
Clutch				
Driveline				
Electrical system				
Steering/suspension				
Brakes				
Exhaust system				
Body rust				
Paint				
Body integrity				
Body hardware				
Air-conditioning				

RELIABILITY RECORDS 197

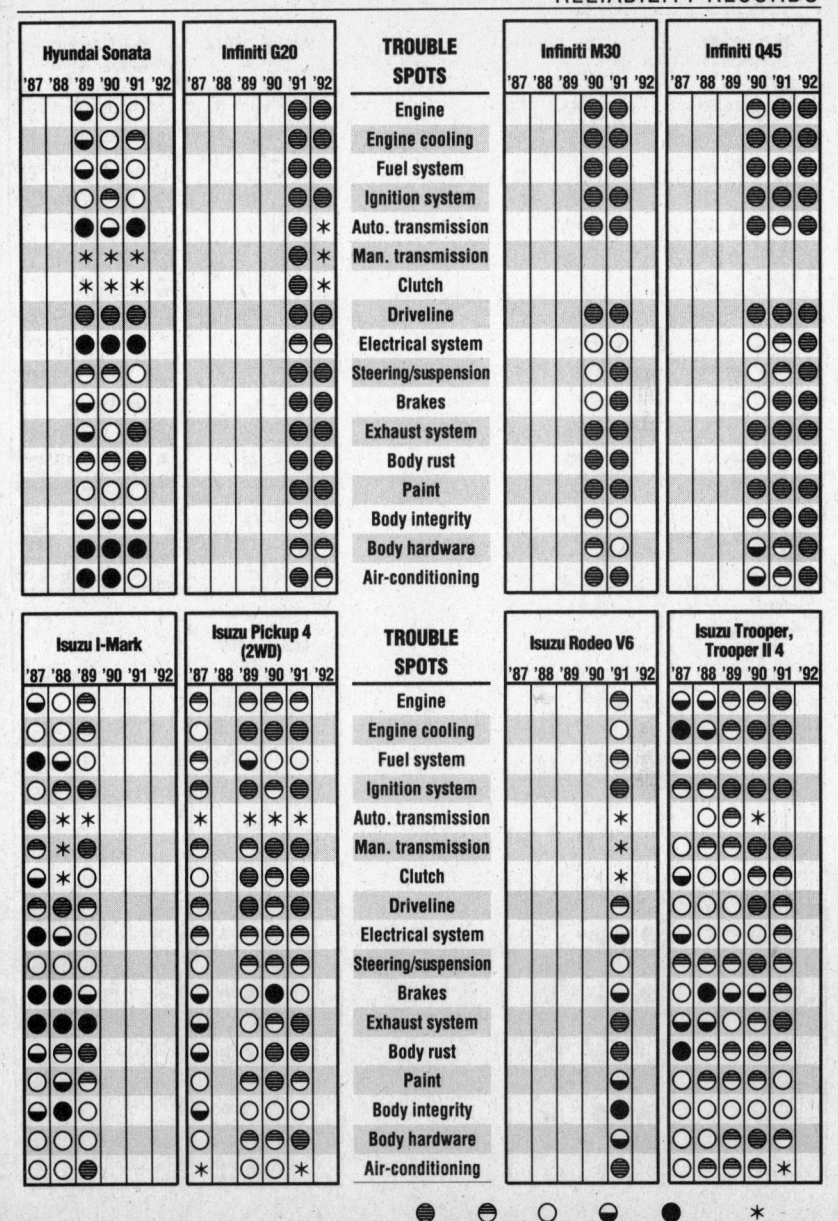

TROUBLE SPOTS

Trouble Spot	Hyundai Sonata '87-'92	Infiniti G20 '87-'92	Infiniti M30 '87-'92	Infiniti Q45 '87-'92
Engine				
Engine cooling				
Fuel system				
Ignition system				
Auto. transmission				
Man. transmission				
Clutch				
Driveline				
Electrical system				
Steering/suspension				
Brakes				
Exhaust system				
Body rust				
Paint				
Body integrity				
Body hardware				
Air-conditioning				

Trouble Spot	Isuzu I-Mark '87-'92	Isuzu Pickup 4 (2WD) '87-'92	Isuzu Rodeo V6 '87-'92	Isuzu Trooper, Trooper II 4 '87-'92
Engine				
Engine cooling				
Fuel system				
Ignition system				
Auto. transmission				
Man. transmission				
Clutch				
Driveline				
Electrical system				
Steering/suspension				
Brakes				
Exhaust system				
Body rust				
Paint				
Body integrity				
Body hardware				
Air-conditioning				

Few ← Problems → Many   Insufficient data

RELIABILITY RECORDS

Trouble Spots	Isuzu Trooper, Trooper II V6 '87–'92	Jaguar XJ6 '87–'92	Jeep Cherokee 4 (4WD) '87–'92	Jeep Cherokee, Wagoneer 6 (4WD) '87–'92
Engine				
Engine cooling				
Fuel system				
Ignition system				
Auto. transmission				
Man. transmission				
Clutch				
Driveline				
Electrical system				
Steering/suspension				
Brakes				
Exhaust system				
Body rust				
Paint				
Body integrity				
Body hardware				
Air-conditioning				

Trouble Spots	Jeep Comanche Pickup 6 '87–'92	Jeep Wrangler 6 '87–'92	Lexus ES 250 '87–'92	Lexus ES 300 '87–'92
Engine				
Engine cooling				
Fuel system				
Ignition system				
Auto. transmission				
Man. transmission				
Clutch				
Driveline				
Electrical system				
Steering/suspension				
Brakes				
Exhaust system				
Body rust				
Paint				
Body integrity				
Body hardware				
Air-conditioning				

RELIABILITY RECORDS

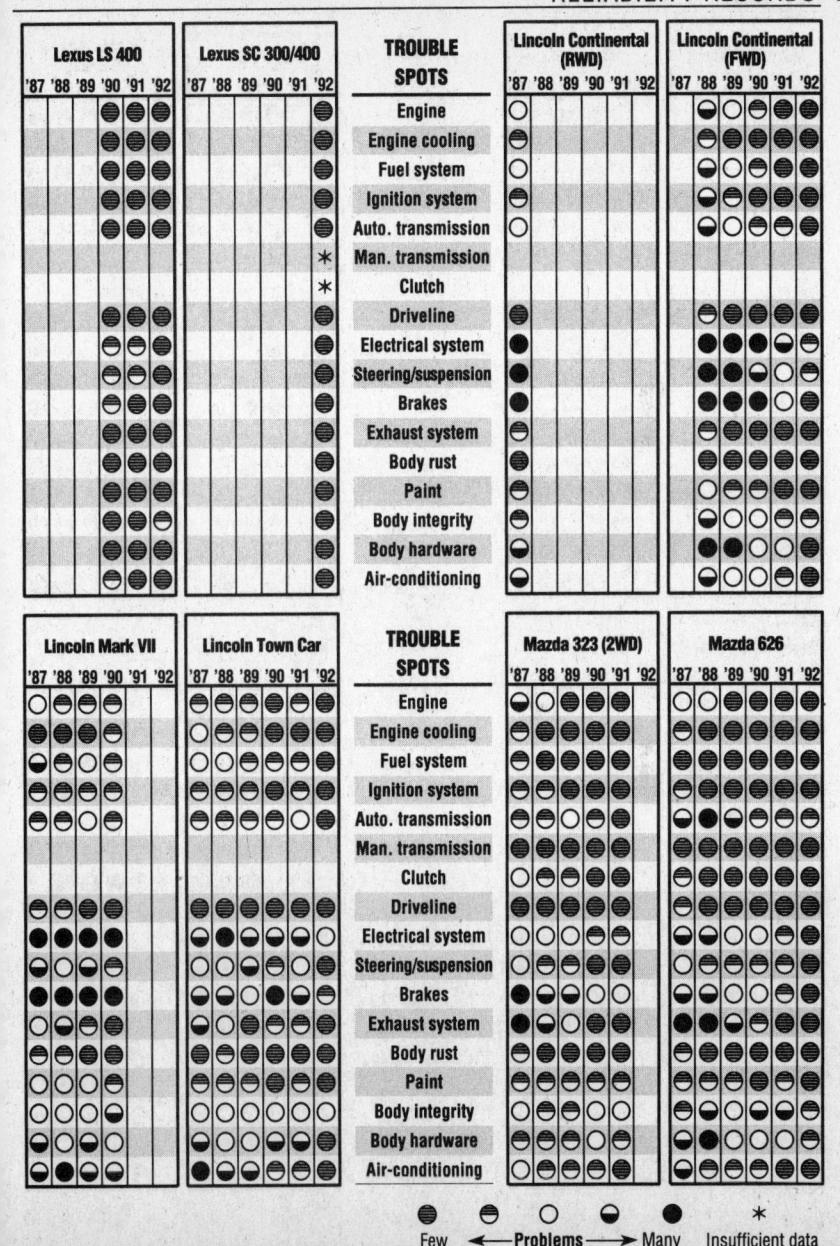

Trouble Spots

Trouble Spots	Lexus LS 400 '87–'92	Lexus SC 300/400 '87–'92	Lincoln Continental (RWD) '87–'92	Lincoln Continental (FWD) '87–'92
Engine	'90–'92 data	'92 only	'87 few	'87–'92
Engine cooling				
Fuel system				
Ignition system				
Auto. transmission				
Man. transmission		*		
Clutch		*		
Driveline				
Electrical system				
Steering/suspension				
Brakes				
Exhaust system				
Body rust				
Paint				
Body integrity				
Body hardware				
Air-conditioning				

Trouble Spots	Lincoln Mark VII '87–'92	Lincoln Town Car '87–'92	Mazda 323 (2WD) '87–'92	Mazda 626 '87–'92
Engine				
Engine cooling				
Fuel system				
Ignition system				
Auto. transmission				
Man. transmission				
Clutch				
Driveline				
Electrical system				
Steering/suspension				
Brakes				
Exhaust system				
Body rust				
Paint				
Body integrity				
Body hardware				
Air-conditioning				

Few ← **Problems** → Many   * Insufficient data

RELIABILITY RECORDS

Mazda 626 Turbo / Mazda 929 / Mazda MPV 4 / Mazda MPV V6 (2WD)

Trouble Spots	626 Turbo '87–'92	929 '87–'92	MPV 4 '87–'92	MPV V6 (2WD) '87–'92
Engine				
Engine cooling				
Fuel system				
Ignition system				
Auto. transmission				
Man. transmission				
Clutch				
Driveline				
Electrical system				
Steering/suspension				
Brakes				
Exhaust system				
Body rust				
Paint				
Body integrity				
Body hardware				
Air-conditioning				

Mazda MPV V6 (4WD) / Mazda MX-3 / Mazda MX-5 Miata / Mazda MX-6

Trouble Spots	MPV V6 (4WD) '87–'92	MX-3 '87–'92	MX-5 Miata '87–'92	MX-6 '87–'92
Engine				
Engine cooling				
Fuel system				
Ignition system				
Auto. transmission				
Man. transmission				
Clutch				
Driveline				
Electrical system				
Steering/suspension				
Brakes				
Exhaust system				
Body rust				
Paint				
Body integrity				
Body hardware				
Air-conditioning				

RELIABILITY RECORDS 201

TROUBLE SPOTS	Mazda MX-6 Turbo '87–'92	Mazda Navajo (4WD) '87–'92	Mazda Pickup '87–'92	Mazda Protege (2WD) '87–'92

TROUBLE SPOTS	Mazda RX-7 '87–'92	Mercedes-Benz 190 '87–'92	Mercedes-Benz 300 6 (2WD) '87–'92	Mercedes-Benz 300 6 TurboDiesel (2WD) '87–'92

Trouble spots (both tables): Engine, Engine cooling, Fuel system, Ignition system, Auto. transmission, Man. transmission, Clutch, Driveline, Electrical system, Steering/suspension, Brakes, Exhaust system, Body rust, Paint, Body integrity, Body hardware, Air-conditioning

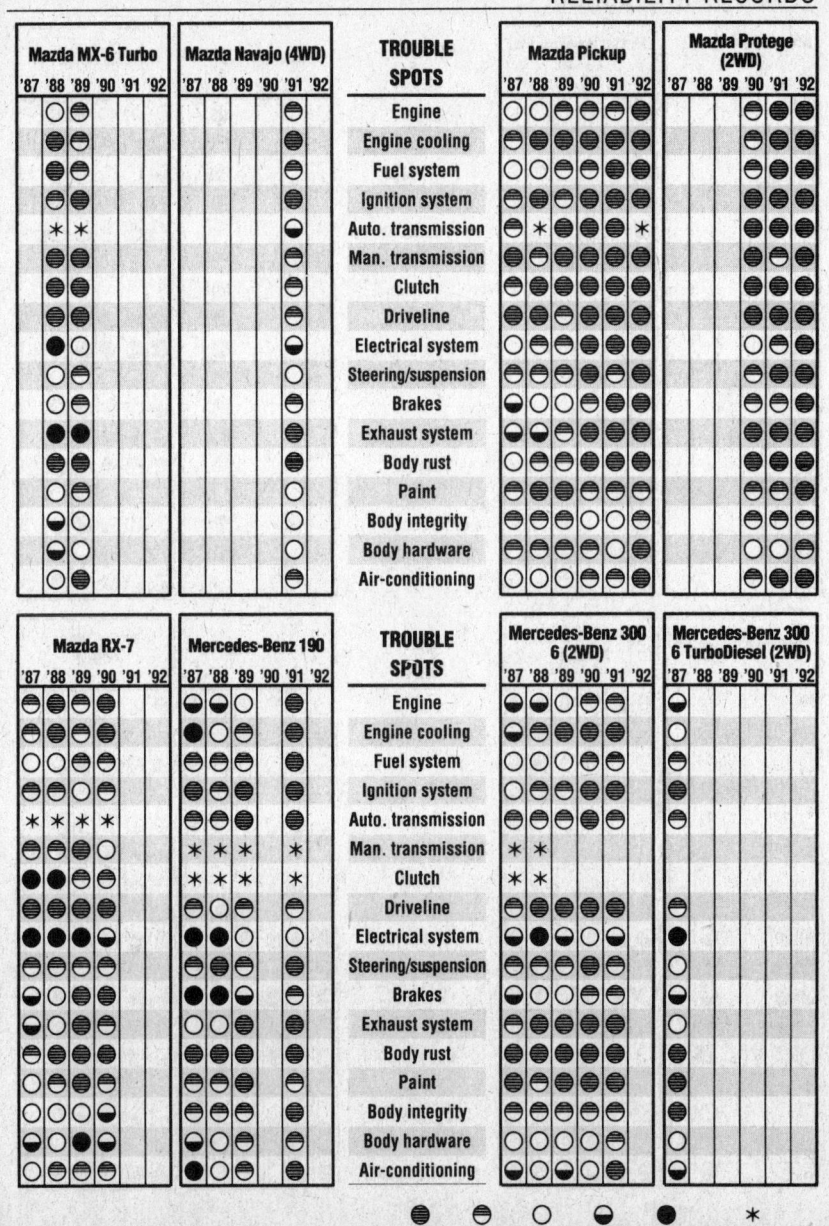

Legend: Few ←—Problems—→ Many   ∗ Insufficient data

RELIABILITY RECORDS

Trouble Spots	Mercedes-Benz 420 S Class '87-'92	Mercedes-Benz 560 S Class '87-'92	Mercury Capri '87-'92	Mercury Cougar V6 '87-'92
(Reliability chart with symbols — not transcribed in detail)

Trouble Spots	Mercury Cougar V8 '87-'92	Mercury Grand Marquis '87-'92	Mercury Sable V6 '87-'92	Mercury Topaz 4 (2WD) '87-'92
(Reliability chart with symbols — not transcribed in detail)

Trouble spot categories (both tables):
- Engine
- Engine cooling
- Fuel system
- Ignition system
- Auto. transmission
- Man. transmission
- Clutch
- Driveline
- Electrical system
- Steering/suspension
- Brakes
- Exhaust system
- Body rust
- Paint
- Body integrity
- Body hardware
- Air-conditioning

RELIABILITY RECORDS

Trouble Spots by Model and Year

Trouble Spots	Mercury Tracer '87-'92	Mitsubishi 3000GT (2WD) '87-'92	Mitsubishi 3000GT Turbo (4WD) '87-'92	Mitsubishi Diamante '87-'92
Engine		●●	●	●
Engine cooling		●●	●	●
Fuel system		●●	●	●
Ignition system		●●	●	●
Auto. transmission		○ *		●
Man. transmission		● *	◐	
Clutch		● *		
Driveline		●●		●
Electrical system		○ ●	◐	●
Steering/suspension		●●	○	●
Brakes		●●	●	●
Exhaust system		●●	●	○
Body rust		●●	●	●
Paint		●●	●	●
Body integrity		◐ ○	●	●
Body hardware		○ ●	●	●
Air-conditioning		●●	●	●

Trouble Spots	Mitsubishi Eclipse (2WD) '87-'92	Mitsubishi Eclipse Turbo (2WD) '87-'92	Mitsubishi Eclipse Turbo (4WD) '87-'92	Mitsubishi Expo LRV (2WD) '87-'92
Engine			●●	●
Engine cooling			●●	●
Fuel system			●●	●
Ignition system			●●	●
Auto. transmission		*	*	*
Man. transmission		○ ●	◐ ○	*
Clutch		○ ●	●	*
Driveline				
Electrical system		○ ◐	○ ●	●
Steering/suspension		●●	●●	●
Brakes		○ ●	●●	●
Exhaust system			●●	◐
Body rust		●●	●●	●
Paint		●●	●●	●
Body integrity		○ ○	●●	○
Body hardware		●○	●●	●
Air-conditioning		●●	●●	●

Legend: ● Few ← Problems → ● Many ● Insufficient data (*)

RELIABILITY RECORDS

TROUBLE SPOTS

Trouble Spot	Mitsubishi Galant 4 (2WD) '87–'92	Mitsubishi Galant Sigma V6 '87–'92	Mitsubishi Mirage '87–'92	Mitsubishi Montero V6 '87–'92
Engine				
Engine cooling				
Fuel system				
Ignition system				
Auto. transmission				
Man. transmission				
Clutch				
Driveline				
Electrical system				
Steering/suspension				
Brakes				
Exhaust system				
Body rust				
Paint				
Body integrity				
Body hardware				
Air-conditioning				

Trouble Spot	Mitsubishi Pickup 4 (2WD) '87–'92	Nissan 200SX 4 '87–'92	Nissan 240SX '87–'92	Nissan 300ZX '87–'92
Engine				
Engine cooling				
Fuel system				
Ignition system				
Auto. transmission				
Man. transmission				
Clutch				
Driveline				
Electrical system				
Steering/suspension				
Brakes				
Exhaust system				
Body rust				
Paint				
Body integrity				
Body hardware				
Air-conditioning				

RELIABILITY RECORDS 205

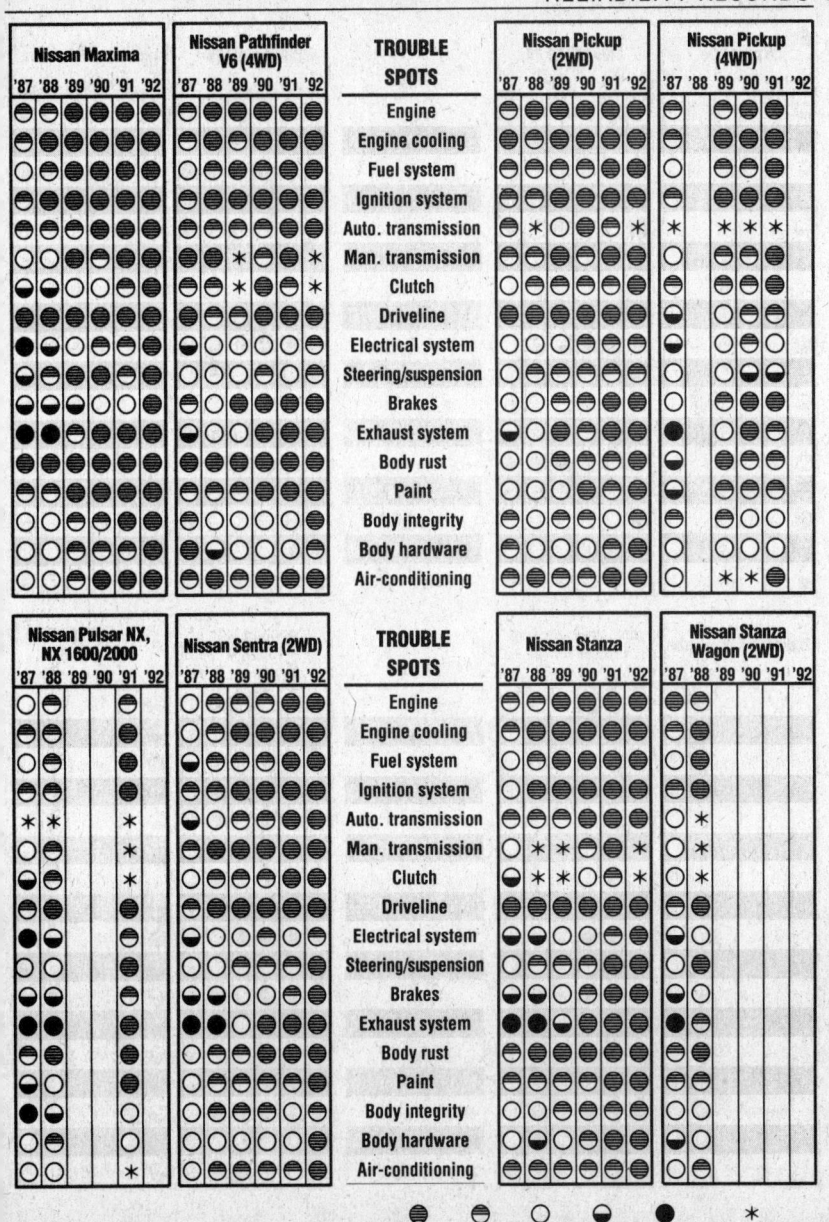

TROUBLE SPOTS	Nissan Maxima '87-'92	Nissan Pathfinder V6 (4WD) '87-'92	Nissan Pickup (2WD) '87-'92	Nissan Pickup (4WD) '87-'92
Engine				
Engine cooling				
Fuel system				
Ignition system				
Auto. transmission				
Man. transmission				
Clutch				
Driveline				
Electrical system				
Steering/suspension				
Brakes				
Exhaust system				
Body rust				
Paint				
Body integrity				
Body hardware				
Air-conditioning				

TROUBLE SPOTS	Nissan Pulsar NX, NX 1600/2000 '87-'92	Nissan Sentra (2WD) '87-'92	Nissan Stanza '87-'92	Nissan Stanza Wagon (2WD) '87-'92
Engine				
Engine cooling				
Fuel system				
Ignition system				
Auto. transmission				
Man. transmission				
Clutch				
Driveline				
Electrical system				
Steering/suspension				
Brakes				
Exhaust system				
Body rust				
Paint				
Body integrity				
Body hardware				
Air-conditioning				

Few ← Problems → Many   * Insufficient data

RELIABILITY RECORDS

TROUBLE SPOTS	Nissan Van	Oldsmobile 88	Oldsmobile 98	Oldsmobile Achieva

(Reliability ratings chart for model years '87–'92 across trouble spots: Engine, Engine cooling, Fuel system, Ignition system, Auto. transmission, Man. transmission, Clutch, Driveline, Electrical system, Steering/suspension, Brakes, Exhaust system, Body rust, Paint, Body integrity, Body hardware, Air-conditioning.)

TROUBLE SPOTS	Oldsmobile Bravada	Oldsmobile Custom Cruiser Wagon	Oldsmobile Cutlass Calais 4	Oldsmobile Cutlass Calais V6

RELIABILITY RECORDS 207

TROUBLE SPOTS	Oldsmobile Cutlass Ciera 4 '87–'92	Oldsmobile Cutlass Ciera V6 '87–'92	Oldsmobile Cutlass Supreme 4 (FWD) '87–'92	Oldsmobile Cutlass Supreme V6 (FWD) '87–'92
Engine				
Engine cooling				
Fuel system				
Ignition system				
Auto. transmission				
Man. transmission				
Clutch				
Driveline				
Electrical system				
Steering/suspension				
Brakes				
Exhaust system				
Body rust				
Paint				
Body integrity				
Body hardware				
Air-conditioning				

TROUBLE SPOTS	Oldsmobile Silhouette Van '87–'92	Oldsmobile Toronado '87–'92	Plymouth Acclaim 4 '87–'92	Plymouth Acclaim 4 Turbo '87–'92
Engine				
Engine cooling				
Fuel system				
Ignition system				
Auto. transmission				
Man. transmission				
Clutch				
Driveline				
Electrical system				
Steering/suspension				
Brakes				
Exhaust system				
Body rust				
Paint				
Body integrity				
Body hardware				
Air-conditioning				

Few ← Problems → Many   * Insufficient data

RELIABILITY RECORDS

TROUBLE SPOTS	Plymouth Acclaim V6 '87-'92	Plymouth Caravelle '87-'92	Plymouth Colt, Colt Wagon (2WD) '87-'92	Plymouth Colt, Vista Wagon (2WD) '87-'92
Engine				
Engine cooling				
Fuel system				
Ignition system				
Auto. transmission				
Man. transmission				
Clutch				
Driveline				
Electrical system				
Steering/suspension				
Brakes				
Exhaust system				
Body rust				
Paint				
Body integrity				
Body hardware				
Air-conditioning				

TROUBLE SPOTS	Plymouth Colt, Vista Wagon (4WD) '87-'92	Plymouth Horizon, Turismo, America '87-'92	Plymouth Laser (2WD) '87-'92	Plymouth Laser Turbo (2WD) '87-'92
Engine				
Engine cooling				
Fuel system				
Ignition system				
Auto. transmission				
Man. transmission				
Clutch				
Driveline				
Electrical system				
Steering/suspension				
Brakes				
Exhaust system				
Body rust				
Paint				
Body integrity				
Body hardware				
Air-conditioning				

RELIABILITY RECORDS 209

Plymouth Reliant						Trouble Spots	Plymouth Sundance					
'87	'88	'89	'90	'91	'92		'87	'88	'89	'90	'91	'92

(Reliability chart comparing Plymouth Reliant, Plymouth Sundance, Plymouth Sundance Turbo, Plymouth Voyager 4, Plymouth Voyager 4 Turbo, Plymouth Grand Voyager 4, Plymouth Voyager V6 (2WD), and Plymouth Voyager V6 (4WD) across model years '87–'92 for the following trouble spots:)

- Engine
- Engine cooling
- Fuel system
- Ignition system
- Auto. transmission
- Man. transmission
- Clutch
- Driveline
- Electrical system
- Steering/suspension
- Brakes
- Exhaust system
- Body rust
- Paint
- Body integrity
- Body hardware
- Air-conditioning

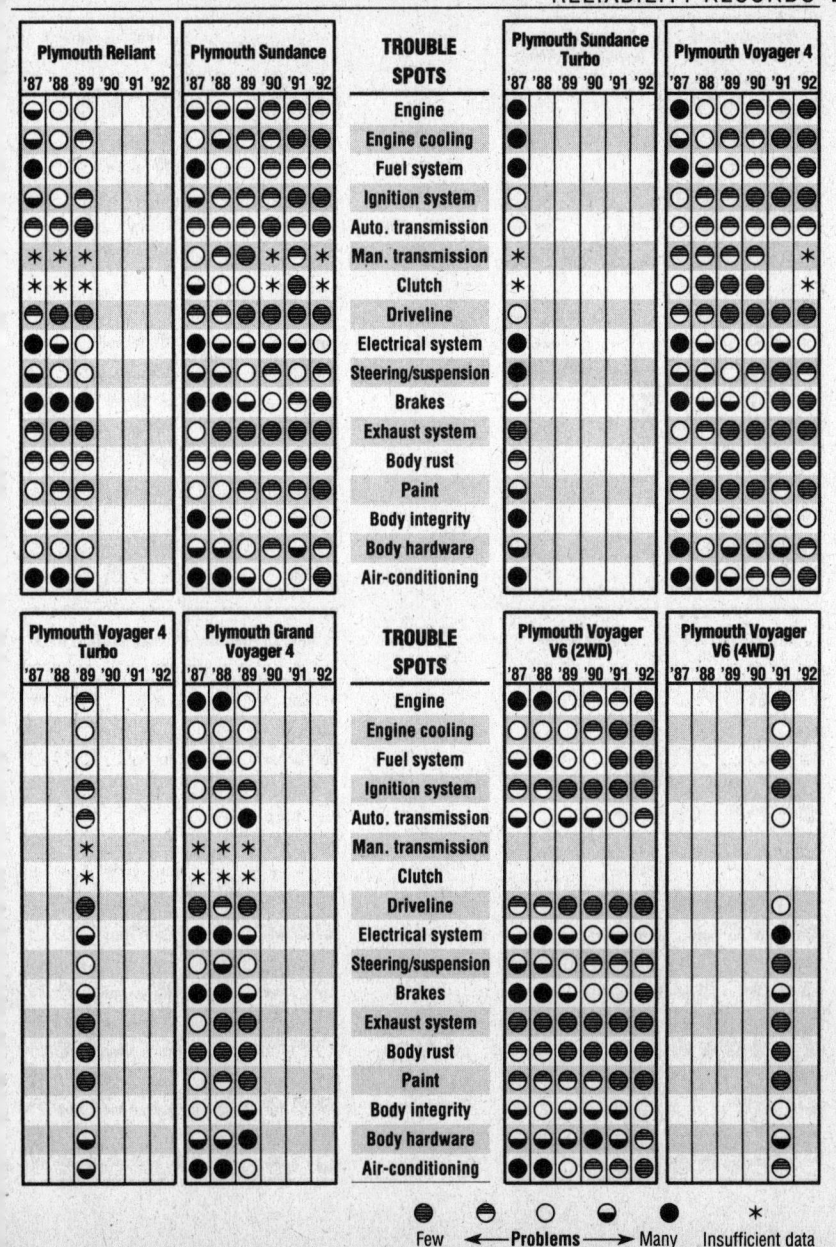

Legend: ⬣ Few ← Problems → Many ● ✱ Insufficient data

210 RELIABILITY RECORDS

Plymouth Grand Voyager V6 (2WD)

Trouble Spot	'87	'88	'89	'90	'91	'92
Engine	●	●	○	◐	◐	◐
Engine cooling	●	◐	○	◐	◐	◐
Fuel system	●	●	○	◐	◐	◐
Ignition system	●	◐	○	◐	◐	◐
Auto. transmission	◐	○	●	◐	◐	◐
Driveline	◐	◐	◐	◐	◐	◐
Electrical system	◐	◐	◐	○	◐	◐
Steering/suspension	●	●	○	◐	◐	◐
Brakes	●	●	●	◐	◐	◐
Exhaust system	●	●	●	◐	◐	◐
Body rust	◐	◐	◐	◐	◐	◐
Paint	●	●	●	◐	◐	◐
Body integrity	●	●	●	◐	◐	○
Body hardware	●	●	●	◐	◐	◐
Air-conditioning	●	●	○	◐	◐	◐

Plymouth Grand Voyager V6 (4WD)

Trouble Spot	'87	'88	'89	'90	'91	'92
Engine					◐	◐
Engine cooling					◐	◐
Fuel system					○	◐
Ignition system					◐	◐
Auto. transmission					◐	◐
Driveline					◐	◐
Electrical system					◐	○
Steering/suspension					○	◐
Brakes					●	◐
Exhaust system					◐	◐
Body rust						
Paint						
Body integrity						
Body hardware						
Air-conditioning					◐	◐

Pontiac 6000 4

Trouble Spot	'87	'88	'89	'90	'91	'92
Engine	●	○				
Engine cooling	◐	◐				
Fuel system	◐	○				
Ignition system	◐	○				
Auto. transmission	◐	◐				
Man. transmission	*	*				
Clutch	*	*				
Driveline	◐	◐				
Electrical system	◐	◐				
Steering/suspension	●	●				
Brakes	●	●				
Exhaust system	●	●				
Body rust	◐	◐				
Paint	●	◐				
Body integrity	○	○				
Body hardware	○	○				
Air-conditioning	○	◐				

Pontiac 6000 V6 (2WD)

Trouble Spot	'87	'88	'89	'90	'91	'92
Engine	○	○	◐	◐	◐	◐
Engine cooling	◐	◐	◐	◐	◐	
Fuel system	●	◐	◐	◐	◐	
Ignition system	○	○	◐	◐	◐	
Auto. transmission	○	◐	◐	◐	◐	
Man. transmission	*	*				
Clutch	*	*				
Driveline	◐	◐	◐	◐	◐	
Electrical system	●	●	◐	◐	◐	
Steering/suspension	●	●	◐	◐	◐	
Brakes	●	●	●	◐	◐	
Exhaust system	●	●	●	◐	◐	
Body rust	◐	◐	◐	◐	◐	
Paint	●	◐	◐	◐	◐	
Body integrity	○	○	◐	◐	○	
Body hardware	○	○	○	○	◐	
Air-conditioning	○	◐	◐	◐	◐	

Pontiac Bonneville

Trouble Spot	'87	'88	'89	'90	'91	'92
Engine	○	◐	◐	◐	◐	◐
Engine cooling	◐	○	◐	◐	◐	◐
Fuel system	●	○	○	◐	◐	◐
Ignition system	○	◐	◐	◐	◐	◐
Auto. transmission	●	○	◐	◐	◐	◐
Driveline	◐	◐	◐	◐	◐	◐
Electrical system	●	●	●	◐	○	○
Steering/suspension	●	●	●	◐	◐	◐
Brakes	●	●	◐	◐	◐	◐
Exhaust system	●	○	◐	◐	◐	◐
Body rust	◐	◐	◐	◐	◐	◐
Paint	●	●	◐	◐	◐	◐
Body integrity	●	◐	◐	○	◐	◐
Body hardware	●	●	○	◐	◐	◐
Air-conditioning	◐	◐	◐	◐	◐	◐

Pontiac Fiero

Trouble Spot	'87	'88	'89	'90	'91	'92
Engine	◐	○				
Engine cooling	◐	◐				
Fuel system	◐	◐				
Ignition system	◐	◐				
Auto. transmission	*	*				
Man. transmission	*	*				
Clutch	*	*				
Driveline	◐	◐				
Electrical system	●	◐				
Steering/suspension	◐	◐				
Brakes	◐	○				
Exhaust system	○	○				
Body rust	○	◐				
Paint	○	◐				
Body integrity	○	◐				
Body hardware	◐	◐				
Air-conditioning	◐	◐				

Pontiac Firebird

Trouble Spot	'87	'88	'89	'90	'91	'92
Engine	○	◐	○		◐	
Engine cooling	●	◐	◐		◐	
Fuel system	●	●	●		◐	
Ignition system	○	◐	○		◐	
Auto. transmission	◐	*	◐		◐	
Man. transmission	*	*	*		*	
Clutch	*	*	*		*	
Driveline	◐	◐	◐			
Electrical system	●	●	●		○	
Steering/suspension	◐	◐	○			
Brakes	◐	◐	◐			
Exhaust system	●	●	●			
Body rust	◐	◐	◐			
Paint	●	●	●		◐	
Body integrity	●	●	●		◐	
Body hardware	●	●	●		◐	
Air-conditioning	◐	○	◐		◐	

Pontiac Grand Am 4

Trouble Spot	'87	'88	'89	'90	'91	'92
Engine	◐	●	○	◐	◐	◐
Engine cooling	◐	◐	◐	◐	◐	◐
Fuel system	●	◐	◐	◐	◐	◐
Ignition system	◐	◐	◐	◐	◐	◐
Auto. transmission	◐	◐	◐	◐	◐	◐
Man. transmission	*	*	◐	*	*	*
Clutch	*	*	◐	*	*	*
Driveline	◐	◐	◐	◐	◐	◐
Electrical system	●	◐	◐	○	○	◐
Steering/suspension	●	●	◐	◐	◐	◐
Brakes	●	●	●	◐	◐	◐
Exhaust system	●	●	●	◐	◐	◐
Body rust	◐	◐	◐	◐	◐	◐
Paint	●	◐	◐	◐	◐	◐
Body integrity	●	●	○	◐	◐	◐
Body hardware	●	●	○	○	◐	◐
Air-conditioning	◐	◐	◐	◐	◐	◐

RELIABILITY RECORDS

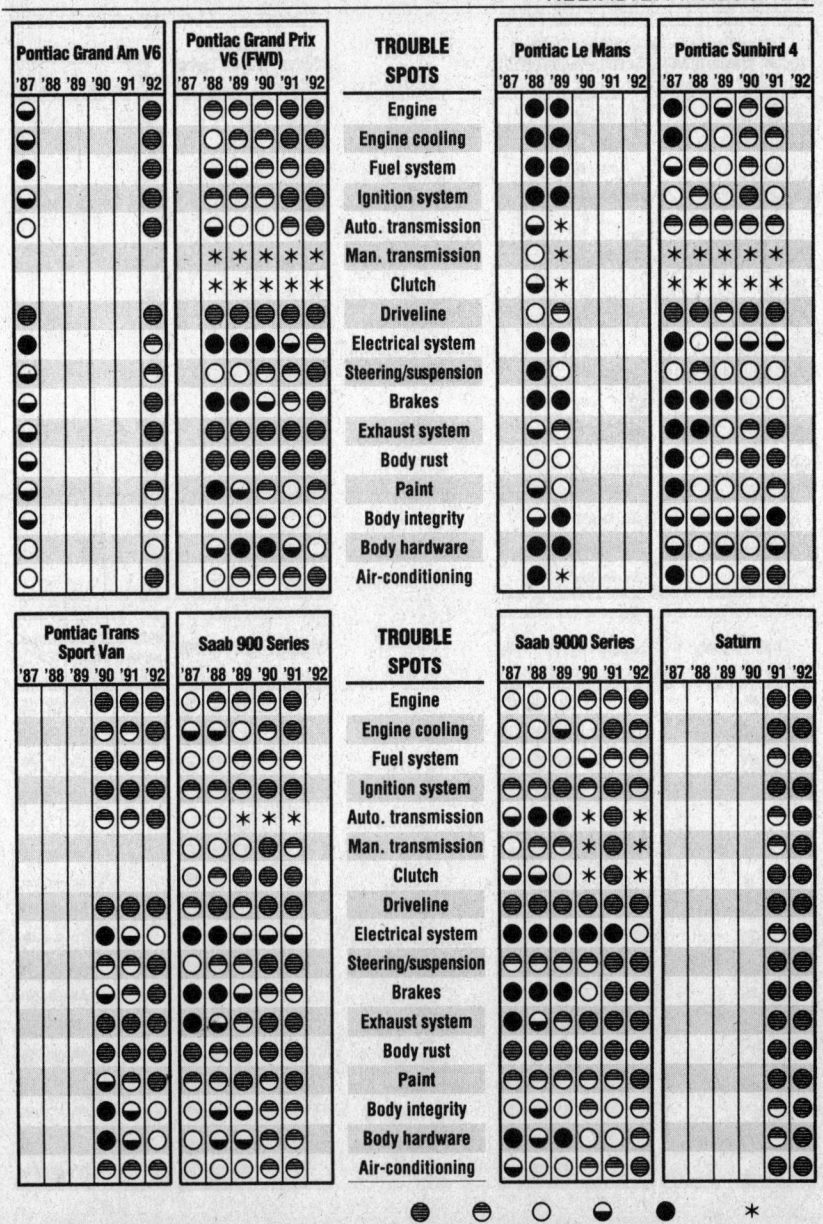

Pontiac Grand Am V6 | Pontiac Grand Prix V6 (FWD) | Pontiac Le Mans | Pontiac Sunbird 4

Trouble Spots	Grand Am '87-'92	Grand Prix '87-'92	Le Mans '87-'92	Sunbird '87-'92
Engine				
Engine cooling				
Fuel system				
Ignition system				
Auto. transmission				
Man. transmission				
Clutch				
Driveline				
Electrical system				
Steering/suspension				
Brakes				
Exhaust system				
Body rust				
Paint				
Body integrity				
Body hardware				
Air-conditioning				

Pontiac Trans Sport Van | Saab 900 Series | Saab 9000 Series | Saturn

Trouble Spots	Trans Sport '87-'92	Saab 900 '87-'92	Saab 9000 '87-'92	Saturn '87-'92
Engine				
Engine cooling				
Fuel system				
Ignition system				
Auto. transmission				
Man. transmission				
Clutch				
Driveline				
Electrical system				
Steering/suspension				
Brakes				
Exhaust system				
Body rust				
Paint				
Body integrity				
Body hardware				
Air-conditioning				

Few ← Problems → Many ✳ Insufficient data

RELIABILITY RECORDS

Subaru Coupe, Sedan, Wagon (2WD) — '87–'92

Trouble Spot	'87	'88	'89
Engine	●	●	◓
Engine cooling	◓	◓	◓
Fuel system	○	◓	○
Ignition system	◓	◓	○
Auto. transmission	○	○	◓
Man. transmission	◓	◓	*
Clutch	●	●	*
Driveline	◓	◓	◓
Electrical system	◓	○	○
Steering/suspension	◓	◓	◓
Brakes	◓	◓	◓
Exhaust system	◓	◓	●
Body rust	◓	◓	◓
Paint	◓	◓	◓
Body integrity	○	○	◓
Body hardware	○	○	◓
Air-conditioning	○	○	◓

Subaru Coupe, Sedan, Wagon (4WD) — '87–'92

Trouble Spot	'87	'88	'89
Engine	●	●	◓
Engine cooling	◓	◓	◓
Fuel system	◓	◓	◓
Ignition system	◓	◓	◓
Auto. transmission	◓	○	*
Man. transmission	◓	◓	◓
Clutch	○	○	●
Driveline	◓	◓	◓
Electrical system	○	○	◓
Steering/suspension	◓	◓	◓
Brakes	◓	◓	◓
Exhaust system	●	◓	●
Body rust	◓	◓	◓
Paint	◓	◓	◓
Body integrity	◓	◓	◓
Body hardware	◓	◓	◓
Air-conditioning	◓	◓	◓

Subaru Coupe, Sedan, Wagon Turbo — '87–'92

Trouble Spot	'87	'88
Engine	●	●
Engine cooling	●	◓
Fuel system	○	◓
Ignition system	○	◓
Auto. transmission	*	*
Man. transmission	○	*
Clutch	●	*
Driveline	◓	◓
Electrical system	◓	○
Steering/suspension	○	◓
Brakes	◓	○
Exhaust system	◓	◓
Body rust	◓	○
Paint	◓	◓
Body integrity	○	○
Body hardware	○	○
Air-conditioning	○	◓

Subaru Hatchback — '87–'92

Trouble Spot	'87
Engine	●
Engine cooling	◓
Fuel system	◓
Ignition system	◓
Auto. transmission	*
Man. transmission	
Clutch	◓
Driveline	◓
Electrical system	○
Steering/suspension	◓
Brakes	◓
Exhaust system	●
Body rust	◓
Paint	◓
Body integrity	
Body hardware	
Air-conditioning	◓

Subaru Justy — '87–'92

Trouble Spot	'88	'89
Engine	◓	◓
Engine cooling	○	●
Fuel system	◓	●
Ignition system	○	●
Auto. transmission		*
Man. transmission	○	*
Clutch	◓	*
Driveline	◓	◓
Electrical system	◓	○
Steering/suspension	◓	◓
Brakes	◓	◓
Exhaust system	●	●
Body rust	○	○
Paint	○	◓
Body integrity	◓	○
Body hardware	◓	◓
Air-conditioning	*	*

Subaru Legacy (2WD) — '87–'92

Trouble Spot	'90	'91	'92
Engine	●	●	◓
Engine cooling	●	●	◓
Fuel system	●	●	◓
Ignition system	●	●	◓
Auto. transmission	◓	○	◓
Man. transmission	◓	●	*
Clutch	◓	●	*
Driveline	●	●	◓
Electrical system	○	◓	◓
Steering/suspension	◓	◓	◓
Brakes	●	◓	◓
Exhaust system	●	●	◓
Body rust	●	●	◓
Paint	●	●	◓
Body integrity	○	◓	◓
Body hardware	◓	●	◓
Air-conditioning	●	◓	◓

Subaru Legacy (4WD) — '87–'92

Trouble Spot	'90	'91	'92
Engine	◓	●	◓
Engine cooling	◓	●	◓
Fuel system	◓	●	◓
Ignition system	◓	●	◓
Auto. transmission	◓	●	◓
Man. transmission	◓	●	◓
Clutch	◓	●	◓
Driveline	◓	●	◓
Electrical system	○	◓	◓
Steering/suspension	◓	●	◓
Brakes	◓	●	◓
Exhaust system	◓	●	●
Body rust	◓	●	◓
Paint	◓	●	◓
Body integrity	◓	●	◓
Body hardware	○	●	◓
Air-conditioning	◓	●	●

Subaru Loyale Coupe, Sedan, Wagon (2WD) — '87–'92

Trouble Spot	'90	'91	'92
Engine	◓	●	◓
Engine cooling	◓	●	◓
Fuel system	◓	○	◓
Ignition system	◓	●	◓
Auto. transmission	*	○	*
Man. transmission	*	*	*
Clutch	*	*	*
Driveline	◓	●	◓
Electrical system	○	◓	◓
Steering/suspension	◓	●	◓
Brakes	◓	●	◓
Exhaust system	●	●	●
Body rust	◓	●	◓
Paint	◓	●	◓
Body integrity	◓	●	◓
Body hardware	○	●	◓
Air-conditioning	○	●	◓

RELIABILITY RECORDS 213

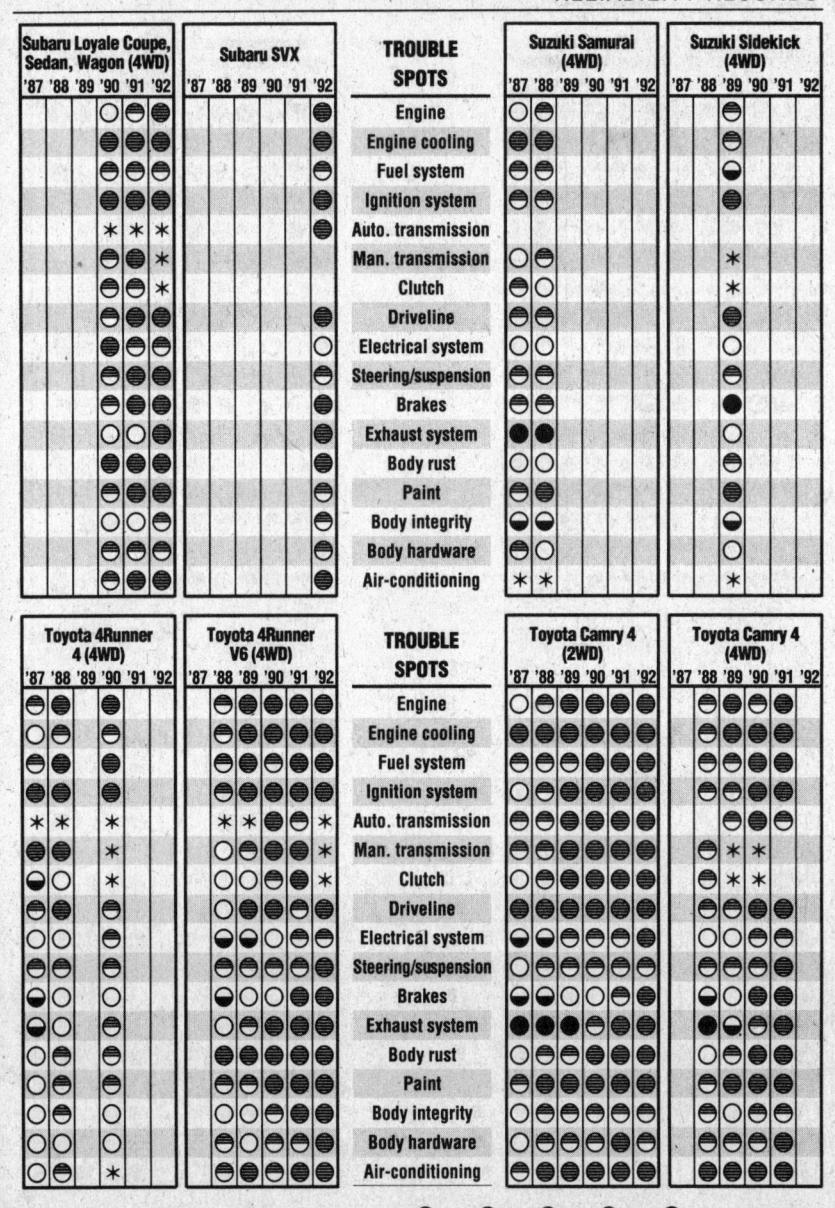

Subaru Loyale Coupe, Sedan, Wagon (4WD) '87–'92	Subaru SVX '87–'92	TROUBLE SPOTS	Suzuki Samurai (4WD) '87–'92	Suzuki Sidekick (4WD) '87–'92
		Engine		
		Engine cooling		
		Fuel system		
		Ignition system		
		Auto. transmission		
		Man. transmission		
		Clutch		
		Driveline		
		Electrical system		
		Steering/suspension		
		Brakes		
		Exhaust system		
		Body rust		
		Paint		
		Body integrity		
		Body hardware		
		Air-conditioning		

Toyota 4Runner 4 (4WD) '87–'92	Toyota 4Runner V6 (4WD) '87–'92	TROUBLE SPOTS	Toyota Camry 4 (2WD) '87–'92	Toyota Camry 4 (4WD) '87–'92
		Engine		
		Engine cooling		
		Fuel system		
		Ignition system		
		Auto. transmission		
		Man. transmission		
		Clutch		
		Driveline		
		Electrical system		
		Steering/suspension		
		Brakes		
		Exhaust system		
		Body rust		
		Paint		
		Body integrity		
		Body hardware		
		Air-conditioning		

Few ← Problems → Many   * Insufficient data

RELIABILITY RECORDS

Toyota Camry V6 / Toyota Celica (2WD) / Toyota Corolla (2WD) / Toyota Corolla (4WD)

TROUBLE SPOTS	Camry V6 '87	'88	'89	'90	'91	'92	Celica 2WD '87	'88	'89	'90	'91	'92	Corolla 2WD '87	'88	'89	'90	'91	'92	Corolla 4WD '87	'88	'89	'90	'91	'92
Engine	○	●	●	●	●	●	○	○	●	●	●	●	●	●	●	●	●	●			●	●	●	●
Engine cooling	●	●	●	●	●	●	●	●	●	●	●	●	●	●	●	●	●	●			●	●	●	●
Fuel system	●	●	●	●	●	●	○	●	●	●	●	●	○	●	●	●	●	●			●	●	●	●
Ignition system	●	●	●	●	●	●	○	●	●	●	●	●	●	●	●	●	●	●			●	●	●	●
Auto. transmission	○	●	●	●	●	●	●	●	●	●	●	●	●	●	●	●	●	●			✳	✳	✳	✳
Man. transmission	✳	●	✳	✳	✳	✳	●	●	●	●	●	●	●	●	●	●	●	●			●	✳	✳	✳
Clutch	✳	○	✳	✳	✳	✳	○	●	●	●	●	●	○	●	●	●	●	●			●	✳	✳	✳
Driveline	●	●	●	●	●	●	●	●	●	●	●	●	●	●	●	●	●	●			●	●	●	●
Electrical system	●	○	○	○	●	●	●	●	○	○	○	●	○	○	○	○	●	●			●	●	●	●
Steering/suspension	○	●	●	●	●	●	○	●	●	●	●	●	○	●	●	●	●	●			●	●	●	●
Brakes	●	●	●	●	●	●	●	●	●	●	●	●	●	●	●	●	●	●			○	●	●	●
Exhaust system	●	●	●	●	●	●	●	●	●	●	●	●	●	●	●	●	●	●			●	●	●	●
Body rust	●	●	●	●	●	●	●	●	●	●	●	●	●	●	●	●	●	●			●	●	●	●
Paint	●	●	●	●	●	●	●	●	●	●	●	●	●	●	●	●	●	●			●	●	●	●
Body integrity	○	●	●	●	●	●	○	○	●	●	●	●	○	●	●	●	●	●			●	○	●	○
Body hardware	○	●	●	●	●	●	○	●	●	●	●	●	○	●	●	●	●	●			●	○	●	●
Air-conditioning	●	●	●	●	●	●	●	●	●	●	●	●	●	●	●	●	●	●			●	✳	●	●

Toyota Corolla FX, FX-16 / Toyota Corolla SR5 (RWD) / Toyota Cressida / Toyota Land Cruiser Wagon

TROUBLE SPOTS	FX/FX-16 '87	'88	'89	'90	'91	'92	SR5 RWD '87	'88	'89	'90	'91	'92	Cressida '87	'88	'89	'90	'91	'92	Land Cruiser '87	'88	'89	'90	'91	'92
Engine	●	●					○						●	●	●	●	●				○	●		●
Engine cooling	●	●					○						●	●	●	●	●				○	●		●
Fuel system	●	○					○						○	○	●	●	●				●	○		●
Ignition system	●	●					○						●	●	●	●	●				●	●		●
Auto. transmission	●	●					✳						●	●	●	●	●				●	●		●
Man. transmission	●	●					✳						✳											
Clutch	●	●					✳						✳											
Driveline	●	●					●						●	●	●	●	●				○	●		●
Electrical system	○	○					●						●	●	○	○	○				●	●		●
Steering/suspension	○	●					○						○	●	●	●	●				●	●		●
Brakes	●	●					●						●	○	●	●	●				○	○		●
Exhaust system	●	●					●						○	●	●	●	●				○	●		●
Body rust	●	●					●						●	●	●	●	●				●	○		●
Paint	○	●					○						●	●	●	●	●				●	●		●
Body integrity	○	○					○						●	●	●	●	●				●	○		○
Body hardware	●	●					●						●	●	●	●	●				○	●		●
Air-conditioning	●	●					○						●	○	○	●	●				●	●		●

RELIABILITY RECORDS

Toyota MR2 / Toyota Paseo / Toyota Pickup 4 (2WD) / Toyota Pickup 4 (4WD)

Trouble Spots	MR2 '87	'88	'89	'90	'91	'92	Paseo '87	'88	'89	'90	'91	'92	Pickup 4 2WD '87	'88	'89	'90	'91	'92	Pickup 4 4WD '87	'88	'89	'90	'91	'92
Engine	◐	◐			●							●	●	●	●	●	●	●	●	●	●	●	●	●
Engine cooling	○	○	●		●							●	○	●	●	●	●	●	○	●	●	●	●	●
Fuel system	●	●	●		●							●	●	●	●	●	●	●	●	●	●	●	●	●
Ignition system	●	●	●		●							●	●	●	●	●	●	●	●	●	●	●	●	●
Auto. transmission	∗	∗			∗							●	○	●	●	●	●	∗	∗	∗	∗	∗	∗	∗
Man. transmission	●	∗	●		●							●	●	●	●	●	●	●	●	●	●	●	●	∗
Clutch	●	∗	●		●							●	◐	○	●	●	●	●	◐	○	●	●	●	∗
Driveline	●	●	●		●							●	●	●	●	●	●	●	●	●	●	●	●	●
Electrical system	○	○	●		○							●	●	●	●	●	●	●	●	●	●	●	●	●
Steering/suspension	○	○	●		●							●	●	●	●	●	●	●	●	●	●	●	●	●
Brakes	○	○	●		●							●	○	○	○	○	●	●	○	○	●	●	●	●
Exhaust system	●	◐	●		●							●	●	●	●	●	●	●	●	●	●	●	●	●
Body rust	●	●	●		●							●	●	●	●	●	●	●	●	⬤	●	●	●	●
Paint	○	●	●		●							●	○	●	●	●	●	●	○	●	●	●	●	●
Body integrity	◐	●	●		○							●	●	●	●	●	●	●	●	●	●	●	●	●
Body hardware	○	●	●		●							●	●	●	●	●	●	●	●	●	●	●	●	●
Air-conditioning	○	●	●		●							●	●	●	●	●	●	●	●	●	●	●	●	∗

Toyota Pickup V6 (2WD) / Toyota Pickup V6 (4WD) / Toyota Previa Van (2WD) / Toyota Previa Van (4WD)

Trouble Spots	V6 2WD '87	'88	'89	'90	'91	'92	V6 4WD '87	'88	'89	'90	'91	'92	Previa 2WD '87	'88	'89	'90	'91	'92	Previa 4WD '87	'88	'89	'90	'91	'92
Engine			●	●	●	●		●	●	●	●	●					●	●					●	●
Engine cooling			●	●	●	●		●	●	●	●	●					●	●					●	●
Fuel system			●	●	●	●		●	●	●	●	●					●	●					●	●
Ignition system			●	●	●	●		●	●	●	●	●					●	●					●	●
Auto. transmission			●	●	●	●		∗	∗	∗	●	∗					●	●					●	●
Man. transmission			●	●	●	●		●	●	●	●	∗					∗	∗					∗	∗
Clutch			○	●	●	●		●	○	●	●	∗					∗	∗					∗	∗
Driveline			●	●	●	●		●	●	●	●	●					●	●					●	●
Electrical system			●	●	○	●		●	●	○	●	●					●	●					●	●
Steering/suspension			○	○	○	●		●	●	○	●	●					●	●					●	●
Brakes			◐	○	●	●		●	●	●	●	●					●	●					●	●
Exhaust system			●	●	●	●		○	●	●	●	●					●	●					●	●
Body rust			●	●	●	●		●	●	●	●	●					●	●					●	●
Paint			●	●	●	●		●	●	●	●	●					●	●					●	●
Body integrity			●	●	●	●		●	●	●	●	●					●	●					○	●
Body hardware			●	●	●	●		●	●	●	●	●					●	●					○	●
Air-conditioning			●	●	●	●		∗	●	●	●	∗					●	●					●	●

● Few ← **Problems** → Many ⬤   ∗ Insufficient data

216 RELIABILITY RECORDS

Trouble Spots	Toyota Supra '87-'92	Toyota Supra Turbo '87-'92	Toyota Tercel (2WD) '87-'92	Toyota Tercel Wagon (4WD) '87-'92
Engine	○ ○ ◐	● ● ◐	○ ○ ◐ ◐ ● ●	◐
Engine cooling	◐ ● ◐	● ● ●	◐ ○ ◐ ◐ ● ●	○
Fuel system	◐ ◐ ◐	◐ ◐ ◐	◐ ◐ ◐ ○ ◐ ●	◐
Ignition system	◐ ◐ ◐	◐ ◐ ◐	◐ ◐ ◐ ◐ ◐ ◐	◐
Auto. transmission	◐ * *	◐ * *	◐ ◐ ◐ ◐ ◐ *	*
Man. transmission	◐ * *	◐ * *	◐ ◐ ◐ ◐ ◐ ◐	◐
Clutch	○ * *	◐ * *	◐ ◐ ◐ ◐ ◐ ◐	◐
Driveline	◐ ◐ ◐	◐ ◐ ◐	◐ ◐ ◐ ◐ ◐ ◐	◐
Electrical system	● ◐ ○	◐ ○ ○	◐ ◐ ◐ ◐ ◐ ◐	◐
Steering/suspension	○ ◐ ◐	○ ○ ○	◐ ◐ ◐ ◐ ◐ ◐	○
Brakes	◐ ○ ○	○ ◐ ◐	● ● ◐ ◐ ● ●	●
Exhaust system	○ ◐ ◐	○ ○ ○	● ● ◐ ◐ ● ●	◐
Body rust	○ ◐ ◐	◐ ◐ ◐	◐ ◐ ◐ ◐ ◐ ◐	○
Paint	○ ◐ ◐	○ ◐ ◐	◐ ◐ ◐ ◐ ◐ ◐	◐
Body integrity	○ ○ ◐	◐ ◐ ◐	○ ◐ ◐ ◐ ◐ ◐	◐
Body hardware	○ ○ ◐	◐ ◐ ◐	○ ◐ ◐ ◐ ◐ ◐	○
Air-conditioning	● ◐ ○	● ○ ◐	◐ ◐ ◐ ◐ ◐ ◐	◐

Trouble Spots	Toyota Van '87-'92	Volkswagen Cabriolet '87-'92	Volkswagen Fox '87-'92	Volkswagen Golf, GTI '87-'92
Engine	◐ ◐	○	◐ ◐ ◐ ◐	○ ○ ◐ ◐
Engine cooling	◐ ◐	○	● ● ◐ ○	● ◐ ◐ ◐
Fuel system	◐ ◐	◐	○ ◐ ◐ ◐	◐ ● ● ◐
Ignition system	◐ ◐	◐	◐ ◐ ◐ ◐	◐ ○ ○ ◐
Auto. transmission	◐ ◐	*	◐ ◐	○ * * * *
Man. transmission	◐ *	*	◐ ◐ ◐ ◐	◐ ◐ ◐ * *
Clutch	◐ *	*	○ ○ ◐ ◐	◐ ◐ ◐ * *
Driveline	◐ ◐	◐	◐ ◐ ◐ ◐	◐ ◐ ◐ ◐
Electrical system	● ◐	◐	● ● ◐ ◐	● ● ● ●
Steering/suspension	○ ◐	○	◐ ◐ ● ●	● ● ● ●
Brakes	◐ ◐	◐	● ● ● ●	● ● ● ●
Exhaust system	◐ ◐	◐	◐ ◐ ◐ ◐	◐ ◐ ◐ ◐
Body rust	◐ ◐	○	○ ◐ ◐ ◐	◐ ◐ ◐ ◐
Paint	◐ ◐	◐	● ◐ ○ ○	◐ ◐ ◐ ◐
Body integrity	◐ ○	◐	◐ ◐ ◐ ◐	◐ ◐ ● ●
Body hardware	◐ ○	○	○ ○ ◐ ●	◐ ◐ ◐ ◐
Air-conditioning	● ◐	*	* ○ ◐ *	◐ ◐ ◐ ◐

RELIABILITY RECORDS

Trouble Spots by Model and Year

Trouble Spots	Volkswagen Jetta '87-'92	Volkswagen Passat '87-'92	Volkswagen Vanagon (2WD) '87-'92	Volvo 240 Series '87-'92
Engine				
Engine cooling				
Fuel system				
Ignition system				
Auto. transmission				
Man. transmission				
Clutch				
Driveline				
Electrical system				
Steering/suspension				
Brakes				
Exhaust system				
Body rust				
Paint				
Body integrity				
Body hardware				
Air-conditioning				

Trouble Spots	Volvo 740 Series '87-'92	Volvo 740 Series Turbo '87-'92	Volvo 760 Series Turbo '87-'92	Volvo 940 Series '87-'92
Engine				
Engine cooling				
Fuel system				
Ignition system				
Auto. transmission				
Man. transmission				
Clutch				
Driveline				
Electrical system				
Steering/suspension				
Brakes				
Exhaust system				
Body rust				
Paint				
Body integrity				
Body hardware				
Air-conditioning				

Few ← Problems → Many   * Insufficient data

Trouble indexes, 1987-1992

The Trouble Index summarizes each model's reliability, as reported by respondents to the Consumers Union 1992 Annual Questionnaire.

The data for the trouble indexes come from readers' responses that cover experiences with more than 583,000 cars, trucks, and vans. Vehicles from the 1987 through 1992 model years were included, with reports on how they held up for the one-year period between April 1991 and March 1992. Respondents told us about serious problems in any of 17 potential trouble spots. The details for each trouble spot are shown in the Frequency-of-Repair records (see page 178). The scores for the index show how each model compares with the average model of the same model year in the number and severity of reported problems.

We combine the problems reported for all trouble spots to calculate an overall problem rate for each model in each model year. The scores in the table show how each overall rate compares with the average rate for all models of the same model year. In order to score ◐ or ◒, a model had to differ from the model-year average by at least 15 percent; to score ● or ◉, the difference had to be at least 35 percent.

Because problems with the engine, engine cooling, driveline, transmission, clutch, and body rust tend to be more difficult and costly to repair, we weighted those problems more heavily than others. We included a standardization in our calculations to minimize differences due to mileage. For some of the models identified as twins—that is, essentially identical models sold under different nameplates—data are pooled.

In the listing below, a ✳ means we didn't have sufficient data to evaluate that year's car. A dash means that the model wasn't made in that year. RWD = rear-wheel drive; FWD = front-wheel drive; 2WD = two-wheel drive; 4WD = four-wheel drive; 4 or 6 = four- or six-cylinder engine; V6 or V8 = six- or eight cylinder engine.

Model	'87	'88	'89	'90	'91	'92
Acura Integra	◉	◉	◉	◉	◉	◉
Acura Legend	◉	◉	◉	◉	◉	◉
Acura Vigor	—	—	—	—	—	◉
Audi 5000, 100	○	✳	◉	◉	◉	✳
BMW 318i	—	—	—	—	○	✳
BMW 325 Series (2WD)	◉	○	◉	○	✳	○
BMW 5 Series	◉	○	◉	◉	◉	✳
BMW 7 Series	✳	◐	✳	✳	✳	✳
Buick Century	○	◉	◉	◉	◉	○
Buick Electra, Park Ave., Ultra	○	◉	◉	○	○	◐
Buick Le Sabre	○	◉	◉	◉	◉	○
Buick Regal V6 (RWD)	◐	—	—	—	—	—
Buick Regal V6 (FWD)	—	○	○	○	○	○

Model	'87	'88	'89	'90	'91	'92
Buick Riviera	✳	✳	◉	◉	◐	✳
Buick Roadmaster	—	—	—	—	✳	●
Buick Roadmaster Estate Wagon	—	—	—	—	●	✳
Buick Skyhawk	●	○	○	—	—	—
Buick Somerset, Skylark	◐	◉	○	○	◐	✳
Cadillac Brougham (RWD)	○	○	◉	○	○	✳
Cadillac De Ville, Fleetwood (FWD)	○	◉	◉	◉	○	○
Cadillac Eldorado	✳	◉	◉	○	◐	✳
Cadillac Seville	○	◉	◉	○	○	○
Chevrolet Astro Van V6 (2WD)	○	○	◐	○	◐	●

Legend: ● Much better than average | ◖ Better than average | ○ Average | ◗ Worse than average | ⬤ Much worse than average

Model	'87	'88	'89	'90	'91	'92
Chevrolet Astro Van V6 (4WD)	—	—	—	◗	◗	*
Chevrolet Blazer	⬤	⬤	⬤	⬤	◗	*
Chevrolet C/K10-20 Pickup V6	*	○	⬤	⬤	⬤	○
Chevrolet C10-20 Pickup V8 (2WD)	◗	◗	⬤	⬤	⬤	⬤
Chevrolet K10-20 Pickup V8 (4WD)	⬤	⬤	⬤	⬤	⬤	⬤
Chevrolet Camaro	◗	◗	◗	*	⬤	*
Chevrolet Caprice V8	○	○	○	◗	⬤	⬤
Chevrolet Cavalier 4	⬤	○	○	○	⬤	⬤
Chevrolet Cavalier V6	⬤	○	○	○	⬤	*
Chevrolet Celebrity 4	○	○	○	*	—	—
Chevrolet Celebrity V6	○	○	○	◗	—	—
Chevrolet Corsica, Beretta 4	*	◗	◗	⬤	○	*
Chevrolet Corsica, Beretta V6	*	◗	◗	◗	◗	*
Chevrolet Corvette	○	*	⬤	⬤	◗	*
Chevrolet Lumina 4	—	—	—	○	*	*
Chevrolet Lumina V6	—	—	—	○	⬤	◗
Chevrolet Lumina APV Van	—	—	—	○	○	◗
Chevrolet Nova (FWD)	◖	◖	—	—	—	—
Chevrolet S10 Blazer V6 (2WD)	○	○	◗	*	⬤	*
Chevrolet S10 Blazer V6 (4WD)	○	⬤	⬤	⬤	⬤	◗
Chevrolet S10 Pickup 4 (2WD)	○	◗	⬤	*	⬤	*
Chevrolet S10 Pickup V6 (2WD)	◖	◖	○	◗	⬤	⬤
Chevrolet S10 Pickup V6 (4WD)	○	◗	⬤	*	⬤	*
Chevrolet Spectrum	◖	○	—	—	—	—
Chevrolet Sportvan V8	◖	⬤	⬤	⬤	⬤	*
Chevrolet Sprint	○	◖	—	—	—	—
Chevrolet Suburban (2WD)	⬤	⬤	⬤	⬤	⬤	*
Chevrolet Suburban (4WD)	⬤	⬤	⬤	⬤	⬤	*
Chrysler Fifth Avenue (RWD)	○	◖	*	—	—	—
Chrysler Imperial	—	—	—	⬤	*	*
Chrysler LeBaron Sedan 4	○	○	—	—	*	*
Chrysler LeBaron Sedan V6	—	—	—	◗	⬤	*
Chrysler LeBaron Coupe, Conv. 4	○	○	○	*	*	*
Chrysler LeBaron Coupe, Conv. 4 Turbo	◖	⬤	○	*	*	*
Chrysler LeBaron Coupe, Conv. V6	—	—	—	◗	○	*
Chrysler LeBaron GTS Hatchback	◖	◖	*	—	—	—
Chrysler LeBaron GTS Hatchback Turbo	○	*	*	—	—	—
Chrysler New Yorker, E-Class 4 (FWD)	○	—	—	—	—	—
Chrysler New Yorker, E-Class 4 T'bo (FWD)	◖	○	—	—	—	—
Chrysler New Yorker V6 (FWD)	—	○	◗	◗	○	◖
Chrysler Town & Country Van (2WD)	—	—	—	*	*	◖
Dodge 600	◖	*	—	—	—	—
Dodge Aries	○	○	○	—	—	—
Dodge Caravan 4	○	○	○	◖	◗	◖
Dodge Caravan 4 Turbo	—	—	○	*	—	—
Dodge Grand Caravan 4	○	◖	⬤	—	—	—
Dodge Caravan V6 (2WD)	○	○	○	○	◗	◖
Dodge Caravan V6 (4WD)	—	—	—	—	⬤	*
Dodge Grand Caravan V6 (2WD)	○	⬤	⬤	⬤	⬤	○
Dodge Grand Caravan V6 (4WD)	—	—	—	—	⬤	⬤
Dodge Colt, Colt Wagon (2WD)	⬤	⬤	⬤	⬤	*	

219

TROUBLE INDEXES

Model	'87	'88	'89	'90	'91	'92
Dodge Colt Vista Wagon (2WD)	○	○	◒	✳	✳	—
Dodge Colt Vista Wagon (4WD)	○	○	✳	✳	✳	—
Dodge Dakota Pickup V6 (2WD)	◒	◒	○	○	◒	○
Dodge Dakota Pickup V6 (4WD)	◒	◒	○	○	✳	✳
Dodge Dakota Pickup V8	—	—	✳	—	●	●
Dodge Daytona 4	◒	◒	●	✳	✳	✳
Dodge Dynasty V6	—	○	○	○	○	●
Dodge Lancer	○	◒	✳	—	—	—
Dodge Monaco	—	—	—	●	●	●
Dodge Omni, America, Charger	●	○	◒	✳	—	—
Dodge Ram 50 Pickup 4	◒	◒	◒	✳	✳	✳
Dodge Ram D/W 100-250 Pickup V8	○	○	◒	●	✳	✳
Dodge Ramcharger	●	●	●	✳	✳	✳
Dodge Ram B150-250 Van, Wagon V8	◒	◒	◒	●	●	✳
Dodge Shadow	○	○	○	○	○	◒
Dodge Shadow Turbo	●	✳	✳	✳	✳	✳
Dodge Spirit 4	—	—	○	◒	○	○
Dodge Spirit 4 Turbo	—	—	◒	✳	✳	✳
Dodge Spirit V6	—	—	○	◒	○	○
Dodge Stealth (2WD)	—	—	—	—	◒	◒
Dodge Stealth Turbo (4WD)	—	—	—	—	●	✳
Eagle Premier V6	—	●	●	●	●	✳
Eagle Summit Hatchback & Sedan	—	—	◒	◒	◒	✳
Eagle Summit Wagon (2WD)	—	—	—	—	—	○
Eagle Talon (2WD)	—	—	—	◒	◒	○
Eagle Talon Turbo (2WD)	—	—	—	◒	◒	✳
Eagle Talon Turbo (4WD)	—	—	—	○	◒	✳
Ford Aerostar Van (2WD)	●	●	◒	●	●	○
Ford Aerostar Van (4WD)	—	—	—	●	●	○
Ford Bronco V8	●	●	●	◒	●	✳
Ford Bronco II (2WD)	✳	○	○	✳	—	—
Ford Bronco II (4WD)	◒	◒	◒	●	—	—
Ford Club Wagon Van V8	●	●	●	●	●	●
Ford Crown Victoria, LTD Crown Victoria	◒	◒	◒	◒	○	○
Ford Escort	◒	◒	◒	◒	○	○
Ford Explorer (2WD)	—	—	—	—	◒	◒
Ford Explorer (4WD)	—	—	—	—	◒	○
Ford F150-250 Pickup 6 (2WD)	◒	◒	◒	○	◒	●
Ford F150-250 Pickup 6 (4WD)	◒	●	●	○	●	✳
Ford F150-250 Pickup V8 (2WD)	○	◒	◒	○	◒	◒
Ford F150-250 Pickup V8 (4WD)	●	●	●	●	●	●
Ford Festiva	—	◒	◒	◒	◒	✳
Ford Mustang 4	●	●	●	◒	✳	✳
Ford Mustang V8	○	○	○	◒	◒	✳
Ford Probe 4	—	—	○	○	◒	✳
Ford Probe 4 Turbo	—	—	○	○	✳	✳
Ford Probe V6	—	—	—	◒	○	✳
Ford Ranger Pickup 4 (2WD)	○	○	○	◒	○	●
Ford Ranger Pickup V6 (2WD)	○	○	○	○	◒	●
Ford Ranger Pickup V6 (4WD)	○	○	◒	●	●	●
Ford Taurus 4	●	●	●	○	○	○
Ford Taurus V6	◒	○	○	○	◒	○
Ford Tempo 4 (2WD)	●	●	●	◒	○	✳
Ford Thunderbird 4 Turbo	◒	○	—	—	—	—
Ford Thunderbird V6	◒	◒	○	○	○	✳
Ford Thunderbird Supercharged V6	—	—	○	●	✳	✳
Ford Thunderbird V8	◒	◒	—	—	●	✳
Geo Metro	—	—	○	○	◒	○

● Much better than average ◐ Better than average ○ Average ◑ Worse than average ⬤ Much worse than average

Model	'87	'88	'89	'90	'91	'92
Geo Prizm	—	—	—	●	◐	*
Geo Spectrum	—	—	○	—	—	—
Geo Storm	—	—	—	○	◐	*
Geo Tracker (4WD)	—	—	—	*	◐	○	*
GMC S15 Jimmy 4	◐	◐	—	—	—	—
GMC S15 Jimmy V6	○	◐	●	●	●	*
Honda Accord	◐	◐	◐	◐	◐	◐
Honda Civic (2WD)	◐	◐	◐	◐	◐	◐
Honda Civic Wagon (4WD)	◐	◐	*	◐	◐	—
Honda CRX	◐	◐	◐	◐	◐	*
Honda Prelude	◐	◐	◐	◐	◐	◐
Hyundai Excel	●	●	●	●	●	*
Hyundai Sonata	—	—	●	●	●	*
Infiniti G20	—	—	—	—	◐	◐
Infiniti M30	—	—	—	◐	◐	*
Infiniti Q45	—	—	—	—	◐	◐
Isuzu I-Mark	◑	○	○	—	—	—
Isuzu Pickup 4 (2WD)	◐	*	◐	○	◐	*
Isuzu Rodeo V6	—	—	—	—	●	*
Isuzu Trooper, Trooper II 4	●	○	○	◐	○	—
Isuzu Trooper, Trooper II V6	—	—	●	◐	○	*
Jaguar XJ6	*	●	●	○	*	*
Jeep Cherokee 4 (4WD)	*	◐	○	◐	*	*
Jeep Cherokee, Wagoneer 6 (4WD)	○	○	◐	●	●	○
Jeep Comanche Pickup 6	*	○	○	*	*	*
Jeep Wrangler 6	●	◑	●	◐	*	◐	*
Lexus ES 250	—	—	—	◐	◐	—
Lexus ES 300	—	—	—	—	—	◐
Lexus LS 400	—	—	—	◐	◐	◐
Lexus SC 300/400	—	—	—	—	—	◐
Lincoln Continental (RWD)	◐	—	—	—	—	—
Lincoln Continental (FWD)	—	●	●	◑	◐	◐
Lincoln Mark VII	◐	◐	○	○	*	*
Lincoln Town Car	●	◐	◐	◐	◑	◐
Mazda 323 (2WD)	◐	◐	◐	◐	◐	*
Mazda 626	◐	◐	◐	◐	◐	◐
Mazda 626 Turbo	◐	○	*	*	*	—
Mazda 929	—	◐	◐	◐	◐	◐
Mazda MPV 4	—	—	○	○	◐	◐
Mazda MPV V6 (2WD)	—	—	○	○	◐	◐
Mazda MPV V6 (4WD)	—	—	*	●	◐	*
Mazda MX-3	—	—	—	—	—	◐
Mazda MX-5 Miata	—	—	—	◐	◐	◐
Mazda MX-6	—	◐	◐	◐	◐	◐
Mazda MX-6 Turbo	—	◐	◐	*	*	*
Mazda Navajo (4WD)	—	—	—	—	●	*
Mazda Pickup	◐	◐	◐	◐	◐	◐
Mazda Protege (2WD)	—	—	—	◐	◐	◐
Mazda RX-7	◐	◐	◐	○	*	—
Mercedes-Benz 190	○	○	◐	*	◐	*
Mercedes-Benz 300 6 (2WD)	◐	◐	◐	◐	◐	◐
Mercedes-Benz 300 6 TurboDiesel (2WD)	◐	—	—	*	*	*
Mercedes-Benz 420 S Class	●	*	*	*	*	—
Mercedes-Benz 560 S Class	◐	*	*	*	*	—
Mercury Capri	—	—	—	—	●	*
Mercury Cougar V6	◐	◐	○	●	◐	◐
Mercury Cougar V8	◐	○	—	—	◐	*
Mercury Grand Marquis	◐	◐	◐	○	○	○
Mercury Sable V6	◑	○	○	○	◐	○
Mercury Topaz 4 (2WD)	●	●	●	●	○	*
Mercury Tracer	—	◐	◐	—	○	○
Mitsubishi 3000GT (2WD)	—	—	—	—	◐	◐
Mitsubishi 3000GT Turbo (4WD)	—	—	—	—	●	*
Mitsubishi Diamante	—	—	—	—	—	◐
Mitsubishi Eclipse (2WD)	—	—	—	◐	◐	○

TROUBLE INDEXES

Model	'87 '88 '89 '90 '91 '92
Mitsubishi Eclipse Turbo (2WD)	— — — ◐ ◐ ✻
Mitsubishi Eclipse Turbo (4WD)	— — — ○ ◐ ✻
Mitsubishi Expo LRV (2WD)	— — — — — ○
Mitsubishi Galant 4 (2WD)	○ — ● ● ● ●
Mitsubishi Galant Sigma V6	— ◐ ✻ ✻ — —
Mitsubishi Mirage	✻ ✻ ○ ◐ ◐ ✻
Mitsubishi Montero V6	— — ● ● ✻ ✻
Mitsubishi Pickup 4 (2WD)	● ● ✻ ✻ ○ ✻
Nissan 200SX 4	◐ ✻ — — — —
Nissan 240SX	— — ● ● ● ✻
Nissan 300ZX	◐ ● ✻ ○ ○ ✻
Nissan Maxima	● ● ● ● ● ●
Nissan Pathfinder V6 (4WD)	● ● ● ● ● ●
Nissan Pickup (2WD)	● ● ● ● ● ●
Nissan Pickup (4WD)	◐ ✻ ◐ ◐ ○ ✻
Nissan Pulsar NX, NX 1600/2000	○ ◐ ✻ ✻ ◐ ✻
Nissan Sentra (2WD)	● ● ● ● ● ●
Nissan Stanza	● ● ● ● ●
Nissan Stanza Wagon (2WD)	● ● — — — —
Nissan Van	● ✻ ✻ ◐ — —
Oldsmobile 88	◐ ○ ● ◐ ○ ○
Oldsmobile 98	○ ● ● ◐ ○ ◐
Oldsmobile Achieva	— — — — — ●
Oldsmobile Bravada	— — — — ○ ✻
Oldsmobile Custom Cruiser Wagon	○ ◐ ○ ✻ ● ✻
Oldsmobile Cutlass Calais 4	○ ◐ ○ ○ ◐ —
Oldsmobile Cutlass Calais V6	◐ ✻ ✻ ✻ ✻ —
Oldsmobile Cutlass Ciera 4	○ ○ ○ ○ ✻ ✻
Oldsmobile Cutlass Ciera V6	○ ○ ○ ◐ ○ ◐
Oldsmobile Cutlass Supreme 4 (FWD)	— — — ● ✻ —
Oldsmobile Cutlass Supreme V6 (FWD)	— ○ ◐ ● ○ ●
Oldsmobile Silhouette Van	— — — ○ ◐ ✻
Oldsmobile Toronado	✻ ◐ ✻ ○ ✻ ✻
Plymouth Acclaim 4	— — ○ ◐ ○ ○
Plymouth Acclaim 4 Turbo	— — ● ✻ — —
Plymouth Acclaim V6	— — ○ ◐ ○ ◐
Plymouth Caravelle	◐ ✻ — — — —
Plymouth Colt, Colt Wagon (2WD)	○ ● ● ● ● ✻
Plymouth Colt Vista Wagon (2WD)	○ ○ ◐ ✻ ✻ ○
Plymouth Colt Vista Wagon (4WD)	○ ○ ✻ ✻ ✻ ✻
Plymouth Horizon, Turismo, America	◐ ○ ○ ✻ — —
Plymouth Laser (2WD)	— — — ◐ ◐ ○
Plymouth Laser Turbo (2WD)	— — — ◐ ◐ ✻
Plymouth Reliant	○ ○ ○ — — —
Plymouth Sundance	○ ○ ○ ○ ○ ◐
Plymouth Sundance Turbo	● ✻ ✻ ✻ ✻ ✻
Plymouth Voyager 4	○ ○ ○ ◐ ◐ ◐
Plymouth Voyager 4 Turbo	— — ○ ✻ — —
Plymouth Grand Voyager 4	○ ◐ ● — — —
Plymouth Voyager V6 (2WD)	○ ○ ○ ○ ◐ ○
Plymouth Voyager V6 (4WD)	— — — — ● ✻
Plymouth Grand Voyager V6 (2WD)	○ ◐ ● ● ● ○
Plymouth Grand Voyager V6 (4WD)	— — — — ● ●

Legend	
◒ Much better than average	◓ Better than average
○ Average	◑ Worse than average
● Much worse than average	

Model	87	88	89	90	91	92
Pontiac 6000 4	◓	○	*	*	*	—
Pontiac 6000 V6 (2WD)	○	○	○	◓	*	—
Pontiac Bonneville	●	○	◓	◓	◓	○
Pontiac Fiero	○	◓	—	—	—	—
Pontiac Firebird	◓	●	●	*	●	*
Pontiac Grand Am 4	○	○	◓	○	○	◓
Pontiac Grand Am V6	◓	—	—	—	—	○
Pontiac Grand Prix V6 (FWD)	—	○	◓	○	○	◓
Pontiac Le Mans	—	●	●	*	*	*
Pontiac Sunbird 4	●	○	○	○	●	*
Pontiac Trans Sport Van	—	—	—	○	○	○
Saab 900 Series	○	○	○	◓	◓	*
Saab 9000 Series	○	◓	●	—	○	○
Saturn	—	—	—	—	●	◓
Subaru Coupe, Sedan, Wagon (2WD)	◓	◓	◓	—	—	—
Subaru Coupe, Sedan, Wagon (4WD)	◓	◓	○	—	—	—
Subaru Coupe, Sedan, Wagon Turbo	●	●	*	—	—	—
Subaru Hatchback	○	*	*	—	—	—
Subaru Justy	*	○	○	*	*	*
Subaru Legacy (2WD)	—	—	—	○	◓	◓
Subaru Legacy (4WD)	—	—	—	◓	◓	◓
Subaru Loyale Coupe, Sedan, Wagon (2WD)	—	—	—	○	◓	○
Subaru Loyale Coupe, Sedan, Wagon (4WD)	—	—	—	◓	◓	○
Subaru SVX	—	—	—	—	—	◓
Suzuki Samurai (4WD)	◓	◓	*	*	*	*
Suzuki Sidekick (4WD)	—	—	○	*	*	*
Toyota 4Runner 4 (4WD)	◓	◓	*	◓	*	*
Toyota 4Runner V6 (4WD)	—	◓	◓	◓	◓	◓
Toyota Camry 4 (2WD)	◓	◓	◓	◓	◓	◓
Toyota Camry 4 (4WD)	—	◓	◓	◓	◓	—
Toyota Camry V6	—	◓	◓	◓	◓	◓
Toyota Celica (2WD)	◓	◓	◓	◓	◓	◓
Toyota Corolla (2WD)	◓	◓	◓	◓	◓	◓
Toyota Corolla (4WD)	—	*	◓	◓	◓	*
Toyota Corolla FX, FX-16	◓	◓	—	—	—	—
Toyota Corolla SR5 (RWD)	◓	—	—	—	—	—
Toyota Cressida	◓	◓	◓	◓	◓	*
Toyota Land Cruiser Wagon	*	◓	◓	*	◓	*
Toyota MR2	◓	◓	*	—	◓	◓
Toyota Paseo	—	—	—	—	—	◓
Toyota Pickup 4 (2WD)	◓	◓	◓	◓	◓	◓
Toyota Pickup 4 (4WD)	◓	◓	◓	◓	◓	◓
Toyota Pickup V6 (2WD)	—	—	◓	◓	◓	*
Toyota Pickup V6 (4WD)	—	◓	◓	◓	◓	◓
Toyota Previa Van (2WD)	—	—	—	—	◓	◓
Toyota Previa Van (4WD)	—	—	—	—	◓	◓
Toyota Supra	◓	◓	◓	*	*	*
Toyota Supra Turbo	○	○	○	*	*	*
Toyota Tercel (2WD)	◓	◓	◓	◓	◓	◓
Toyota Tercel Wagon (4WD)	◓	*	—	—	—	—
Toyota Van	◓	*	◓	—	—	—
Volkswagen Cabriolet	◓	*	*	*	*	*
Volkswagen Fox	○	○	○	○	*	*
Volkswagen Golf, GTI	◓	◓	◓	◓	◓	*
Volkswagen Jetta	○	◓	◓	◓	◓	◓
Volkswagen Passat	—	—	—	●	●	*
Volkswagen Vanagon (2WD)	●	*	*	*	*	*
Volvo 240 Series	◓	◓	◓	○	○	◓
Volvo 740 Series	◓	◓	◓	◓	◓	*
Volvo 740 Series Turbo	◓	○	○	◓	◓	*
Volvo 760 Series Turbo	◓	*	○	*	—	—
Volvo 940 Series	—	—	—	—	◓	◓

Owner satisfaction

"Would you buy that car again?" is a question we ask hundreds of thousands of CONSUMER REPORTS subscribers on each year's Annual Questionnaire. As might be expected, owner satisfaction starts to slip as a car ages. On average, the newest cars in our survey—the 1992 models—won a 94 percent vote of confidence from owners. That average drops to 90 and 88 percent for 1991 and 1990 models, respectively. Satisfaction scores for the worst cars plunge even more dramatically after only a year or two of ownership.

With satisfaction so uniformly high for 1992 cars, we turned our attention to the 1991 models. The table below presents the percentage of our readers who say they would, considering such factors as price, performance, reliability, comfort, enjoyment, etc., buy their car again. Generally, differences of six percentage points or more are meaningful. We haven't included cars no longer available in 1993 and cars with too few votes to be judged reliably.

Small cars

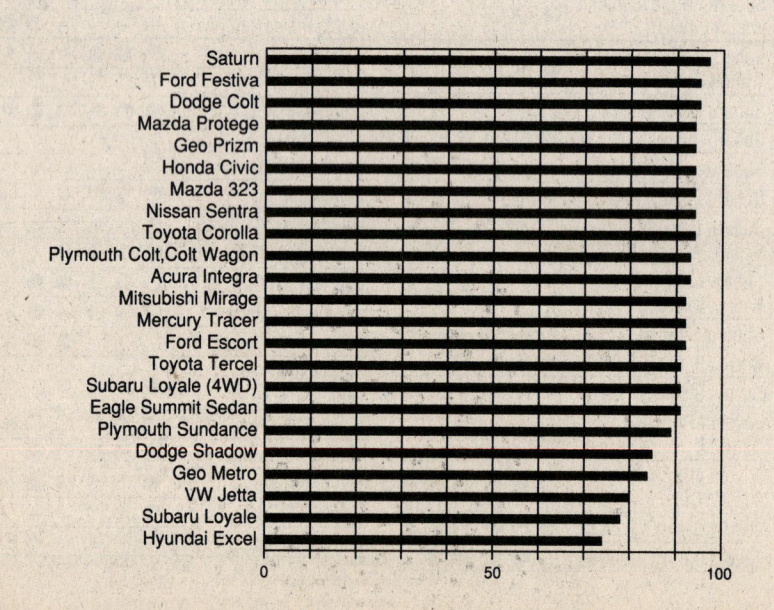

Model	
Saturn	
Ford Festiva	
Dodge Colt	
Mazda Protege	
Geo Prizm	
Honda Civic	
Mazda 323	
Nissan Sentra	
Toyota Corolla	
Plymouth Colt, Colt Wagon	
Acura Integra	
Mitsubishi Mirage	
Mercury Tracer	
Ford Escort	
Toyota Tercel	
Subaru Loyale (4WD)	
Eagle Summit Sedan	
Plymouth Sundance	
Dodge Shadow	
Geo Metro	
VW Jetta	
Subaru Loyale	
Hyundai Excel	

OWNER SATISFACTION **225**

Sporty cars

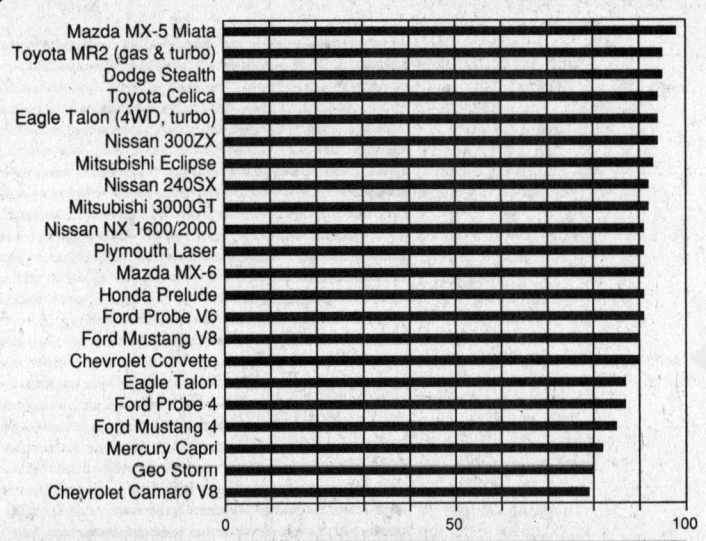

Model	
Mazda MX-5 Miata	
Toyota MR2 (gas & turbo)	
Dodge Stealth	
Toyota Celica	
Eagle Talon (4WD, turbo)	
Nissan 300ZX	
Mitsubishi Eclipse	
Nissan 240SX	
Mitsubishi 3000GT	
Nissan NX 1600/2000	
Plymouth Laser	
Mazda MX-6	
Honda Prelude	
Ford Probe V6	
Ford Mustang V8	
Chevrolet Corvette	
Eagle Talon	
Ford Probe 4	
Ford Mustang 4	
Mercury Capri	
Geo Storm	
Chevrolet Camaro V8	

Compact cars

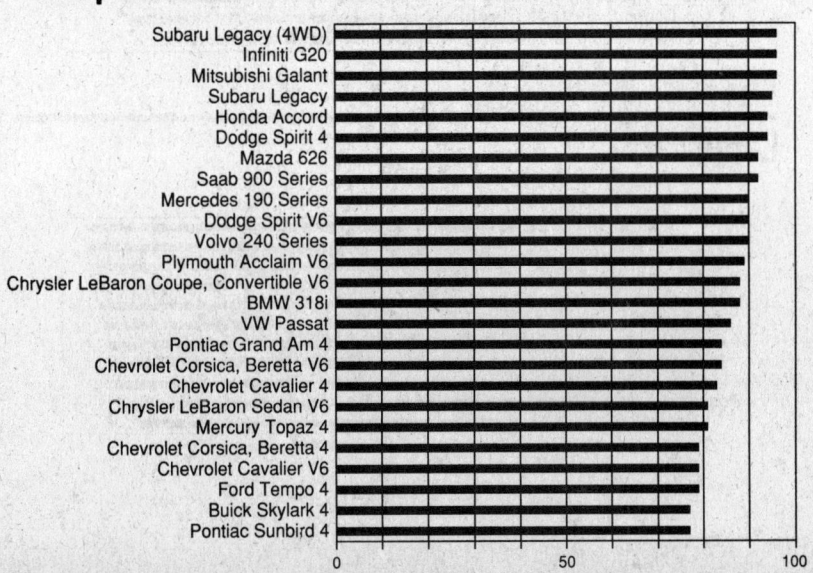

Model	
Subaru Legacy (4WD)	
Infiniti G20	
Mitsubishi Galant	
Subaru Legacy	
Honda Accord	
Dodge Spirit 4	
Mazda 626	
Saab 900 Series	
Mercedes 190 Series	
Dodge Spirit V6	
Volvo 240 Series	
Plymouth Acclaim V6	
Chrysler LeBaron Coupe, Convertible V6	
BMW 318i	
VW Passat	
Pontiac Grand Am 4	
Chevrolet Corsica, Beretta V6	
Chevrolet Cavalier 4	
Chrysler LeBaron Sedan V6	
Mercury Topaz 4	
Chevrolet Corsica, Beretta 4	
Chevrolet Cavalier V6	
Ford Tempo 4	
Buick Skylark 4	
Pontiac Sunbird 4	

Mid-sized cars

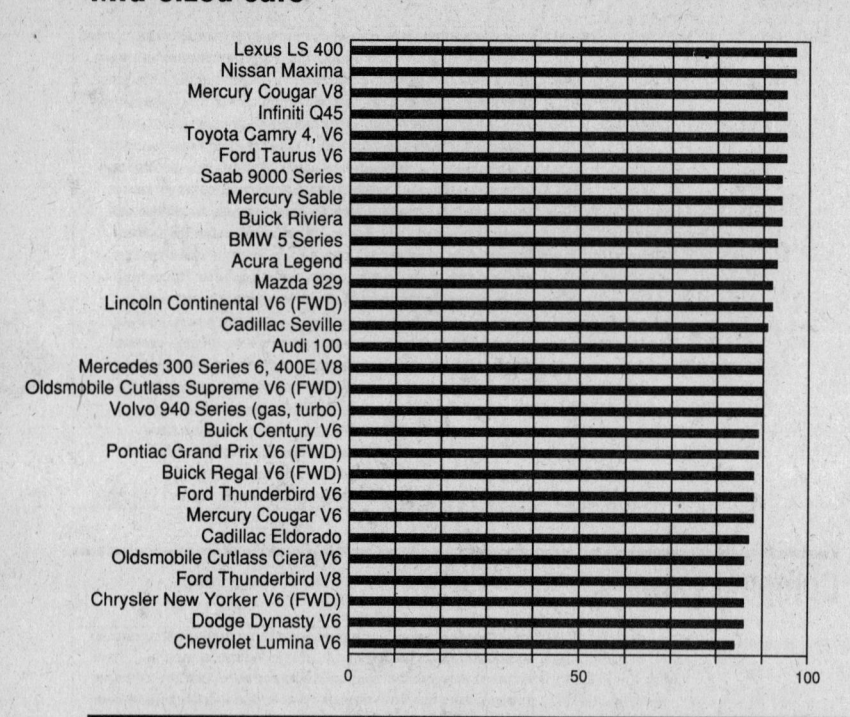

Model	
Lexus LS 400	
Nissan Maxima	
Mercury Cougar V8	
Infiniti Q45	
Toyota Camry 4, V6	
Ford Taurus V6	
Saab 9000 Series	
Mercury Sable	
Buick Riviera	
BMW 5 Series	
Acura Legend	
Mazda 929	
Lincoln Continental V6 (FWD)	
Cadillac Seville	
Audi 100	
Mercedes 300 Series 6, 400E V8	
Oldsmobile Cutlass Supreme V6 (FWD)	
Volvo 940 Series (gas, turbo)	
Buick Century V6	
Pontiac Grand Prix V6 (FWD)	
Buick Regal V6 (FWD)	
Ford Thunderbird V6	
Mercury Cougar V6	
Cadillac Eldorado	
Oldsmobile Cutlass Ciera V6	
Ford Thunderbird V8	
Chrysler New Yorker V6 (FWD)	
Dodge Dynasty V6	
Chevrolet Lumina V6	

0   50   100

Large cars

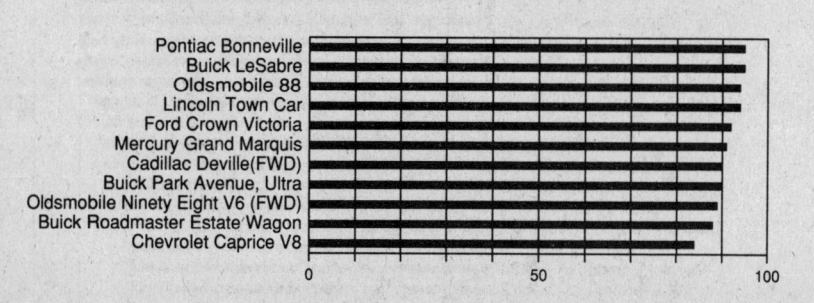

Model	
Pontiac Bonneville	
Buick LeSabre	
Oldsmobile 88	
Lincoln Town Car	
Ford Crown Victoria	
Mercury Grand Marquis	
Cadillac Deville (FWD)	
Buick Park Avenue, Ultra	
Oldsmobile Ninety Eight V6 (FWD)	
Buick Roadmaster Estate Wagon	
Chevrolet Caprice V8	

0   50   100

▶Personal products

Blood pressure monitors	228
Hearing aids	230
Eyeglasses	232
Cribs & mattresses	234
Bathroom scales	236
Dental products	
Toothpaste	237
Mouthwash	238
Electric toothbrushes	239
Oral irrigators	239
Ratings	241

An ounce of prevention is worth a pound of cure. Public-health experts reckon that a dollar spent avoiding illness pays off many times over compared with the cost of being sick. While not all illnesses can be prevented, many can; others can be mitigated or kept in check.

Eyesight and hearing are two key senses that often demand increased attention as people age. Periodic eye exams are particularly crucial for older people and others prone to the potentially blinding eye problems of diabetes, high-blood pressure, and glaucoma. Many less severe sensory problems can be corrected with eyeglasses and hearing aids. Buying either device, however, has never been straightforward—you can spend a lot of money and get little value.

A blood-pressure monitor is a wise investment for people with hypertension. Taking regular readings at home can help you learn how well your efforts—drugs, diet, exercise—are working. Another good investment is a bathroom scale, considering the health benefits overweight people will reap by dropping a few pounds and watching their weight conscientiously.

Prevention is also the key to good oral health. Routine and conscientious brushing and flossing remain the best weapons against tooth decay and gum disease. And an electric toothbrush is more effective than an old-fashioned brush because, in the same amount of time, it does a more complete cleaning. Dental irrigators are worthwhile for people with braces or extensive bridgework who find it difficult to brush and floss.

The littlest consumers, infants, shouldn't be overlooked, either. For them, many injuries occur in cribs, accidents that modern cribs aim to avoid.

Blood-pressure monitors
▶ Ratings on page 241.

For people diagnosed with hypertension, a home blood-pressure monitor can show whether drugs or alternatives to drug therapy—diet and exercise—are working, and how well. For those who do need drug treatment, home monitoring can help the doctor determine the lowest effective dose that minimizes any side effects.

A home monitor also allows patients to chart their progress in controlling pressure, a powerful motivator for staying with a treatment regimen. Home monitoring can be especially useful for people whose blood pressure is driven up by the stress of having a doctor measure it. More typical readings are likely to be obtained at home.

For all those reasons, the National High Blood Pressure Education Program, a Government-sponsored effort, endorses home blood-pressure monitoring for people with documented hypertension, provided monitoring is done in collaboration with a physician and is not used as a means of self-diagnosis.

Blood pressure, the force exerted by the blood against the walls of the arteries, has traditionally been described as height: the number of millimeters that arterial pressure can push a column of mercury up a vertical tube, abbreviated as "mmHg."

Traditionally, a nurse or doctor wraps an inflatable cuff around the upper arm and inflates it by pumping a rubber bulb. The cuff becomes a tourniquet, cutting off blood flow below the elbow. While gradually deflating the cuff, the nurse listens with a stethoscope to the arm's main artery. As blood returns to the lower arm, the onset and cessation of sounds from the artery mark "systolic" pressure, the arterial force as the heart pumps, and "diastolic pressure," the pressure between heartbeats, which is lower. Blood pressure is given as the systolic figure over the diastolic, as in 120/80 mmHg, more or less "normal."

The choices

To take your own pressure at home, some monitors make you do all the things the doctor or nurse does. Others use electronic circuitry, which simplifies the matter considerably.

Mechanical aneroid models. These are simple mechanical monitors that use a round dial-type pressure gauge. (Home devices no longer use a mercury column— "aneroid" means "without liquid.") They're relatively cheap at $20 to $30 and can be quite accurate if used properly. Proper use is the big drawback—you must don the cuff, pump it, and listen carefully to the artery as you turn a valve to slowly deflate the cuff, all the while keeping an eye on the gauge's needle. The procedure takes practice but isn't impossible. It demands good eyesight and hearing and the dexterity to do things with one hand.

Electronic models. These sense pressure changes in the cuff—no stethoscope is needed—and pass data to a microchip in their console, which calculates the systolic and diastolic pressures automatically and flashes your blood pressure and pulse rate on a digital display. No human judgment is required. The circuitry can sometimes err—if you move your arm, say—but an error code is displayed or the reading is so outlandish that it's obviously a mistake.

The cheapest electronic monitors, priced about $40 to $60, require you pump the cuff with a rubber bulb; deflation is handled automatically. More expensive models—

ranging from $60 to as high as $200—inflate cuffs automatically. You put on the cuff and select a starting pressure, somewhat higher than your expected systolic reading. You then push a button, and the monitor does the rest.

Recently, electronic monitors have appeared that take readings from the index finger, so you needn't even roll up your sleeve. You slip the finger into a loop, and the machine does its thing. Electronic finger monitors range in price from $140 to $160.

Features and conveniences

All arm models have a D-ring to make it easier to don the cuff with just one hand—you form a loop and pull the cuff snugly around your arm, then fasten it with the plastic-loop closure. The ends of some cuffs, however, can easily slip out of the metal bar if they don't have a retaining device sewn in. Some cuffs were made of limp material, were difficult, or were otherwise cumbersome to handle in our tests.

Features that make mechanical gauges easier to use include the stethoscope's sensor already sewn in place on the cuff (so you needn't hold it down). Also, a sturdy metal deflation valve that works smoothly is easier to control than the plastic valves on some mechanical models.

Some electronic models feature highly readable displays—big, clear numbers three-quarters of an inch high.

The tests

An inaccurate monitor can give a false sense of security, alarm unnecessarily, or adversely affect your treatment. So we first checked each unit's gauge, disconnected from the cuff, to see how accurately it registered known pressures. Most were highly accurate.

For mechanical models, the gauge's accuracy determines the best that a unit can work—the rest is up to the user's skill.

For electronic models, the circuitry also affects readings, no matter how accurate the gauge. As a result, we involved a cross-section of staffers in an extensive use test with those models. We modified the tubing so that a nurse could take a simultaneous reading with a mercury gauge and stethoscope. By taking multiple readings at each sitting and comparing the nurse's figures with each monitor's, we were able to assess each model's variability from one reading to another.

Buying advice

Mechanical models offer the best value if you're comfortable with them. They cost as little as $20 and generally proved more accurate than electronic arm models, provided they're used correctly. With practice, most people should have little trouble perfecting the technique.

The best electronic arm models can be as accurate as better mechanical units, or nearly so. Those that inflate automatically are easiest to use but most expensive. If you don't trust your ability to master a mechanical model, but don't want to pay top dollar, a good compromise is an electronic arm model whose cuff you inflate manually. Such models sell for about half the price of an automatic model.

With any arm model, you need the right size cuff to get accurate readings. People with large upper arms—more than 13 inches around—may have trouble with the cuffs supplied. Larger cuffs are available from medical supply houses or from the manufacturer at extra cost.

Stay away from electronic finger models. Because the finger is smaller than the arm and farther from the heart, more factors can interfere to give false readings. Our tests found the finger monitors' readings grossly variable. As a result, we judged them Not Acceptable.

Hearing aids

People with poor eyesight rarely hesitate to wear glasses or contacts, yet many with poor hearing are slow to be examined and loath to wear a hearing aid. Vanity may well stand between them and keener hearing. Or hearing loss may have developed so gradually—and they've adapted so deftly—they hardly realize they have a problem.

Recent developments in hearing-aid design have produced increasingly smaller units, some barely visible. Circuitry can be tailored to unique patterns of hearing losses encompassing a variety of listening situations.

You should first consult a physician, to rule out any medically correctable cause. The precise testing needed to fit a hearing aid may be done by an audiologist, a nonphysician specialist with graduate training in the measurement and treatment of hearing impairment; or by a hearing-aid dealer, who will generally have less formal education and less diagnostic equipment, but who may have more practical experience in fitting aids.

The hearing-aid dispenser uses an audiometer to determine your ability to detect pure tones of various frequencies and your ability to understand speech. The device helps track the faintest sounds audible (your threshold) and the loudest you can tolerate without pain. The difference between the two is called the dynamic range.

People suffering from age-related hearing loss typically have trouble with consonant sounds like s, t, f, and th, which demand good high-frequency hearing to discriminate. Other types of hearing loss, especially that from noise damage, involve a narrowed dynamic range—if you turn up the TV just slightly to hear better, it seems the characters are now shouting. A hearing exam should pinpoint whether the disorder is sensorineural (so-called nerve deafness) or a conductive loss (more a physical blockage), which bears on the correction.

The choices

All hearing aids consist of a tiny microphone, amplifier, and speaker, and a battery to power them. Depending on the type you buy, the aid may be able to block or filter background noise, control electronic feedback, cut amplification in noisy settings, and provide an extra power boost when needed. Nearly all aids fall into one of three types:

Behind the ear. A curved case that fits behind the ear houses microphone, speaker, and amplifier; a short tube conducts sound to an earpiece that fits inside the ear. The cases of some newer models are about an inch long and not noticeable if hair covers the tops of your ears. Because this type of aid is larger than others, it can hold bigger, longer-lasting batteries, pack more circuitry for better sound quality, and offer controls that are easier to adjust. The design, outside the ear, protects components from wax and so may make the aid more reliable overall than other types. Expect to pay $500 to $700 for a basic unit. Some optional circuitry can bring the price to $1000 or even $2000.

In-the-ear. A custom-molded housing contains all components and fits directly in the ear. The controls and battery are far smaller than in a behind-the-ear aid and thus require more dexterity. Batteries may have to be changed weekly rather than monthly, as in behind-the-ear models. (Hearing-aid batteries cost about $1 apiece, bought in bulk.) Expect to pay $700 to $1000 or more, depending on options.

Canal aids. These are even smaller and fit entirely within the ear canal. Since they're barely visible from the outside, they have great cosmetic appeal. But they have all the problems of the in-the-ear design—you'll need lots of dexterity to change batteries, for example, and you'll have to clean the hearing aid often. It may need more frequent repairs because of wax buildup on tiny components. The design also renders these aids too weak to correct for severe hearing loss. Expect to pay $700 to $1000 or more.

Features and conveniences

Sophisticated circuitry takes a hearing aid beyond being a simple amplifier that boosts all sounds indiscriminately. Here are some of the available options:

Digital programming. Microchips can amplify different frequencies to different degrees, to fit the user's pattern of hearing loss. Some models let you choose several profiles depending on the environment—a quiet car versus a noisy restaurant, say. Some models divide the sound spectrum into more bands, for more precise correction, much as a graphic equalizer does. This option, which can bring an aid's price to $1000 or $2000, is best geared to those with moderate to severe loss who need to hear well in a variety of backgrounds and who have tried a conventional aid unsuccessfully. It can also help people particularly sensitive to loud or low-pitched sound. Such circuitry is especially power hungry, requiring as much as one battery a week.

K-amp. This patented circuitry is a cheaper and less complex system that aims to do what digital programming does: selectively amplify sounds depending on their frequency, thus providing clear sound with less distortion. Price: $100 to $200 extra.

Telecoil. Some behind-the-ear models have a telecoil, or T-switch, for phone conversations. Flipping the switch turns off the aid's microphone and uses the aid's circuitry to directly pick up signals from the telephone earpiece and amplify them. The system eliminates the feedback many people experience when using conventional hearing aids with a telephone. All public telephones and newer models of home phones are compatible with telecoil circuitry. The feature adds about $50 to the overall price.

Automatic gain control. This option can control distortion caused by background noise and keeps loud noises from becoming uncomfortably loud. It also allows wearers to move between noisy and quiet situations without having to adjust the aid's volume. Price: $100 to $150 extra.

Automatic signal processing. This circuitry helps reduce distortion caused by background noise by amplifying low-frequency sounds less than the higher-frequency sounds of conversation. Price: $50 to $80 extra.

Buying advice

Big commissions may cause a hearing-aid dealer to steer you to one type or brand, so it's wise to avoid dealers who sell only one brand. It's also wise for you to get a copy of your hearing-test results—you may have to pay extra, so ask first. That way you can comparison shop.

Make sure the dispenser you choose can work with you over several visits to find the right hearing aid, teach you to use and maintain it, and then be available to service it in the months and years to come.

Choose an aid of a size and type appropriate for your physical capabilities. A tiny device may look cosmetically attractive, but the small controls are a poor choice for people with limited manual dexterity.

It's a good idea to buy from a dealer who offers a trial period of at least 30 days (this is the law in several states). And be clear about what is included in the price. Some dispensers charge separately for the hearing aid and fitting, or for follow-up visits.

The Veterans Administration evaluates hearing aids every year to decide which manufacturers to buy from. Its list is far from complete—many new, high-tech devices are missing—but it's a reliable guide. Any aid the VA has found acceptable is satisfactory, but don't assume that an aid *not* on the VA list is defective. To get a copy, request "Hearing Aids," publication IB-11/78A from Veterans Affairs, Forms and Publications Department, 6307 Gravel Ave., Alexandria, Va. 22310.

Eyeglasses

▶ **Ratings of eyeglass stores on page 243.**

There are many more places selling glasses and many more frames to choose from than ever before. There are also more lens choices beyond plastic—special-purpose materials, lens coatings, and optical designs.

The industry's retailing extremes are the "superstore" and the warehouse store. Superstores, often run by large optical chains like LensCrafters and Pearle Vision, are eyeglass emporiums where consumers can have their eyes tested, choose from thousands of frames and, for many prescriptions, have glasses made within about an hour. LensCrafters and Pearle Vision together run more than 1500 stores and cover most states. Warehouse operations, like The Price Club, take a no-frills, mass-merchandising approach—a more limited frame selection sold in smaller facilities, perhaps with no optometrist on duty and no in-store lab. Of course, private practitioners—optometrists and ophthalmologists—still examine eyes and sell glasses.

Where to buy

First decide where to buy your glasses —from a private ophthalmologist or optometrist, an independent optician, or a larger optical chain. In a 1992 survey of 71,000 CONSUMER REPORTS subscribers who had bought spectacles in the previous two years, readers whose glasses came from a private practitioner were the most satisfied. Some chains, however, got marks nearly as high in overall satisfaction.

Two further reasons favored the private practitioners: Readers had slightly fewer problems with glasses purchased from doctors than with those from the average chain. And more readers felt they got a more thorough eye exam from private eye doctors than from doctors with the chains. While private optometrists and ophthalmologists excel in service, the optical chains excel in frame selection and speed.

The choices

Besides selecting a frame, you'll need to make decisions about the lens material, coatings, and optical design.

Lens materials. *Regular plastic,* actually a hard resin called CR-39, is the most widely used material; it is half the weight of glass and more impact resistant. *High-index plastic* is at least 30 percent thinner than CR-39, a boon for the very nearsighted, whose lenses can be thick at the edges; it can cost twice the price of regular plastic or more. *Polycarbonate lenses* are about as thin as high-index but extremely impact resistant, a plus for children and people who play sports; polycarbonate's price is about one-third higher than regular plastic

Lens treatments. *Scratch protection,* about $20, is a must for anyone who handles glasses roughly (polycarbonate lenses are soft and always need this coating). *UV protection* comes from a gray dye that shields wearers from the sun's harmful ultraviolet rays, rays associated with the formation of cataracts. The protection, about $20, is most important for those who spend lots of time in strong sunlight. *Antireflection coating,* about $40, cuts glare and is good for night driving and computer work.

Lens designs. People who need *bifocals* can choose from two traditional styles: *flat-top,* with a small closeup field at the bottom, or *Franklin style,* where the entire bottom is ground to the near prescription, giving good wide-field vision up close. A better choice for some: New *progressive lenses* ("no-line bifocals") gradually change lens power to give a continuous range of clear vision as eyes move from the lens's top (distance vision) to bottom (close); importantly, the middle of the lens covers an arm's-length range, good for computer workers. Progressive lenses cost about twice as much as regular bifocals. *Aspheric* lenses are typically for farsighted people, who must wear bulging convex lenses; their optical design creates a flatter lens that can make eyes look more natural.

Buying advice

There are advantages to having your eyes checked by an optometrist or ophthalmologist not connected with any store. Private doctors have no particular incentive to prescribe new glasses and are more likely to be objective about problems you may have with glasses bought elsewhere.

Eyeglass prices vary considerably from chain to chain. The readers surveyed were generally happiest at the places that charged the least. Some chains offer straightforward pricing for complete eyeglasses; others charge a la carte for frames, lenses, and various lens options, tacking on surcharges for oversize lenses, coatings, and higher-power prescriptions.

FITTING A FRAME

Good eyeglass fit is crucial, though there's no guarantee that the person behind the counter is a trained optician (only about half the states have licensing requirements). Here are some tips:

■ Lenses must be positioned properly in frames—with optical centers directly over the pupils—to prevent eyestrain and headaches; it's especially important with progressive lenses and strong prescriptions.

■ Avoid oversized frames, which require oversized lenses that can add weight, distort vision, catch glare, and cost more than regular-sized lenses. Oversized lenses in many prescriptions are apt to be thick at the edges, too.

■ Temple pieces should not pinch or touch the head until they reach the tops of ears. The sides should be long enough to wrap behind the ears and positioned at a level above or below eye pupils, to avoid blocking peripheral vision. Hinges should be sturdy. Springs can prevent the sides from bowing outward over time.

■ The bridge should not be too tight or too wobbly for the nose. Soft silicon pads are comfortable and less likely than hard plastic to let glasses slide down when you sweat, but makeup can make silicon dirty. Hard pads on springs are another option.

■ If you or your children play sports, get special sports frames, which resemble goggles. They're stronger than "dress" frames and have no hinges or bridge that can snap to injure eyes.

■ Polycarbonate lenses, the most impact-resistant lens material, is a good all-around choice. It's thinner than regular plastic and inherently offers protection from harmful UV light.

Cribs & mattresses
▶ **Ratings of cribs on page 251.**

Because babies spend so much time sleeping, cribs should be not only comfortable, but safe and secure. The previous generation of crib design contributed to tens of thousands of accidents and upwards of 150 deaths each year, often when an infant's limbs, head, or neck got caught between slats that were set too wide apart or when active babies tumbled from cribs with sides not tall enough to safely contain them.

Government-mandated safety standards, in place since 1973, have fixed those problems by specifying acceptable measurements for slat separation, crib height, and mattress fit, among other factors. Additional voluntary safeguards, followed by most leading crib makers, supplement the Government effort.

Cribs

The largest manufacturer of cribs is Child Craft. Other common brands are *Simmons, Bassett, Welsh, Cosco,* and *Evenflo.*

Prices for cribs range from less than $100 up to $600. You can find cribs in varied furniture styles, but that's cosmetic. The key choice involves the number of dropsides. Cribs with two give you easy access to baby from either side. Models built with only one dropside are often $100 or less and work just as well if the crib will be set up against a wall.

Features and conveniences

Safety. You generally needn't worry about the safety of new cribs, though occasionally a new model may slip past Federal standards. In our tests, we found one such model, an import, and judged it Not Acceptable. Since that time, that model has been redesigned to meet Federal standards. For an extra measure of assurance, look for cribs that bear the seal of the Juvenile Products Manufacturers Association. They comply with mandatory Federal and voluntary safety standards. A crib without the seal, however, is not necessarily less safe.

Assembly. Some cribs are easier than others to assemble. The simplest take only 10 minutes to assemble and don't require tools; most take a half hour and demand basic tools.

Casters. Look for spherical or hooded casters, to help roll the crib smoothly. Avoid narrow disk-shaped casters.

Dropsides. We like the dropsides that operate with only one hand; that allows you to hold onto baby with your free arm as you work the dropside. Many models use a foot treadle or rod or a combination of both to lower and raise the sides.

Mattress height adjustments. You should also be able to adjust the mattress's height easily. As infants grow into toddlers, it's important that a crib's sides remain high enough to protect them, which you do by lowering the mattress support.

The tests

Our convenience tests gauge how easy it is to set up a crib, operate the dropsides, adjust mattress height, and roll the crib along flooring. We assess each model's durability by raising and lowering each dropside up to 2000 times, which simulates

CRIBS & MATTRESSES

about 2½ years' use, and by checking for loose or broken hardware.

Buying advice

Models with a single dropside are usually cheaper than those with two dropsides. If you plan to locate the crib against a wall, you may want to save money by buying a single dropside. Choose a double dropside if you want access from either side. A double dropside also gives you a backup, should one dropside mechanism break.

Crib mattresses

Buying a mattress for a baby is much like buying one for an adult—you typically want to get the firmest one you can find. In addition, a baby's mattress must keep out wetness and resist punctures and tearing.

The choices

The basic choice is between foam and innerspring models. Prices range from about $30 to more than $100. Foam is usually less expensive and easier to lift, a consideration when changing sheets. Innerspring models usually keep their shape better, though high-density foam can be just as good.

Features and conveniences

Look for high-density foam or stiff innerspring construction. A high coil count doesn't necessarily mean a firm mattress.

Better mattresses offer quilted vinyl ticking or multiple layers of vinyl laminated together and reinforced with nylon, an especially sturdy and waterproof construction. Fabric binding to join the top, bottom, and sides allows air to escape and helps relieve pressure that might otherwise weaken or split seams, as a child moves about. Vent holes also serve to relieve pressure and help keep a mattress fresh by allowing odors to escape.

Buying advice

Select the firmest mattress you can find, foam or innerspring. Check by squeezing the center and edges. Look for double- or triple-laminated ticking, fabric binding along the seams, and plenty of vent holes.

SIZING UP CRIB SAFETY

Some 50 children a year die and 13,000 others are injured because of unsafe cribs. Often the blame lies in older, hand-me-down cribs. It may be wiser to buy a new crib than to wonder and worry about a used one, especially if the crib is more than 20 years old. Parents using older cribs or uncertain about a new model they're considering should be wary of:

- Protruding corner posts, which can snag a string or necklace around the neck or catch a garment.
- Ornamentation that can break into small parts that can choke.
- Decorative cutouts on a crib's end panel, which can trap.
- Slats more than 2⅜-inches apart, which can strangle.
- Mattresses that don't fit snugly and can thus trap and suffocate; if two adult fingers can fit between the mattress and the frame, the mattress is too small or the crib too big.

Bathroom scales

▶ Ratings on page 248.

Many bathroom scales tell you the bad news with an electronic digital display. Some talk and have a memory, reminding you what you weighed last time. However, most still measure mechanically.

The choices

Bathroom scales differ primarily in how they measure weight and by price. You can pay as little as $12 or as much as $230. We came across four ways to measure weight: a spring mechanism, a strain-gauge, a hydraulic device, and the balance-beam.

Most use a calibrated spring to measure weight. Levers under the platform transmit the force of your weight to the spring, which stretches in proportion to the weight imposed. The spring moves the scale's dial or pointer or governs the digital display.

The only truly electronic bathroom scale is the strain-gauge type. When you step on the scale, your weight bends a small steel beam. As the beam deflects, it stretches a wire, causing a change in the wire's electrical resistance proportional to your weight. A microchip monitors the resistance, translating it into a signal for the digital display.

A less common type uses fluid. Stepping on the platform of a hydraulic scale forces fluid from one compartment to another. The changing fluid pressure provides the weight reading.

The balance-beam method, which is used in some expensive models, resembles the scale many doctors use. This upright scale has movable weights you slide across two bars until its beam is balanced horizontally.

Features and conveniences

Legible display. Most digital displays are easier to read than the analog dials. Their displays usually have colored LEDs (light-emitting diodes), with lighted numbers against a dark background.

Zeroing. You have to check analog scales periodically to make sure the dial or pointer is resting on zero. Dials can drift when not in use. Resetting is a matter of turning a thumbwheel or knob. Some models are hard to adjust, we found. Most digital models zero automatically.

User-friendly edges and surfaces. Look for models with finished, smooth edges and corners. The platform mat should be comfortable to the feet and easy to clean. Step on the scale to make sure your feet don't block the display.

The tests

To test the accuracy and consistency of bathroom scales, we pile 25-pound weights on each scale's platform to reach several adult-level weights between 100 and 225.

To verify accuracy, we compare the tested scales' readings with a known weight. And to check consistency, we repeat the test five times with each scale at each weight level.

Buying advice

Don't let "professional" designations sway you into spending more money than you have to. Our tests show that some so-called professional models were less accurate than inexpensive ones. In fact, spending more doesn't buy greater accuracy or consistency. We found accurate and dependable scales for less than $20.

Cold, heat, and high humidity can compromise the accuracy and consistency of any bathroom scale. Consider keeping your scale in a room other than a bathroom.

Dental products
▶ **Ratings start on page 244.**

Routine brushing and flossing still remain the best weapons to fight plaque. But some of the new products may help. Electric toothbrushes have been transformed into fast-whirring, high-tech "plaque removers" that can clean teeth quite efficiently. Toothpaste formulas have also undergone changes—to offer better cleaning or control tartar or help those with sensitive teeth. Other claims, such as pledges of whiter teeth, are less substantial.

Mouthwashes have proliferated, and no longer is "fresh breath" their raison d'être. Some rinses now play up their medicinal benefits, promising to help teeth and gums over and above ordinary brushing and flossing.

An appliance that makes similar claims, the oral irrigator, delivers a pressurized, pulsating stream through a thin nozzle that you direct against teeth and gums. Irrigators, however, are specialized tools that are not for everyone. *Water Pik* is the major brand.

Toothpaste

Several newer dentifrices rely on old-fashioned baking soda, a mild abrasive and cleaner. Plans for futuristic formulas include antibacterial agents to control plaque germs. The two toothpaste giants, Colgate-Palmolive (maker of *Colgate*) and Procter & Gamble *(Crest)* are now awaiting approval from the U.S. Food and Drug Administration of just such a formula. The controversial germ-fighter, triclosan, is currently used in deodorants in the U.S. and in toothpastes abroad. Another brand, *Viadent*, already includes a plaque-fighting agent extracted from the bloodroot plant.

The choices

We counted 10 toothpaste types on store shelves. Here's how they differ:

Regular paste. Effective fluoride formulas to prevent tooth decay.

Extra-strength paste. One brand, *Extra Strength Aim,* packs about 50 percent more fluoride than most other toothpastes, which could help cavity-prone individuals.

Antiplaque paste. All toothpastes fight plaque with brushing action. *Viadent* does contain a plaque-fighting chemical. The antiplaque agents in some mouthwashes are stronger, however, and can reduce plaque and mild gum disease better than toothpaste.

Antitartar paste. These products contain chemicals to slow the buildup of tartar, the rock-hard deposit formed when plaque unites with minerals in saliva. But unlike plaque, tartar is generally harmless. And these pastes cannot remove tartar that's already on teeth—that demands professional cleaning.

Desensitizing paste. Receding gums expose softer dental tissue that can make teeth sensitive to heat, cold, or pressure. Special ingredients can block the pain.

Smokers' paste. These products are sometimes more abrasive than regular toothpaste, in order to fight tobacco, coffee, tea, and other stubborn stains.

Children's paste. In flashy colors and unusual flavors, like tutti-frutti, these products are sweet from sorbitol and saccharin, non-nutritive sweeteners. But using sweeteners to encourage kids to brush isn't a good idea. Children should be taught not to swallow any toothpaste, to avoid ingesting fluoride.

'Natural' paste. *Tom's of Maine* and other natural brands boast only natural ingredients and flavors.

Soda paste. Baking soda, riding its reputation for treating gum disease, has been added as a mild abrasive and cleaner.

Whitening paste. Special ingredients are supposed to make teeth "whiter." They cannot—the best any toothpaste can do is leave teeth the shade they look after a dental cleaning. Natural tooth color ranges from white to yellow. (Cosmetic bleaching by a dentist can whiten tooth enamel, but its safety has been questioned by the FDA.)

Buying advice

If possible, brush at least twice daily with a fluoride toothpaste and use floss. If your teeth and gums are in good shape, you can use just about any fluoride dentifrice. People with receding gums should choose a toothpaste of moderate or low abrasiveness to avoid abrading the exposed roots.

Abrasiveness sometimes goes hand-in-glove with cleaning, but not always. Steer clear of pricey whitening toothpastes with offbeat ingredients—they might irritate some mouths in the long run, say CU's dental consultants.

Mouthwash

To combat odors, mouthwashes mask offensive odors with pleasant-smelling ingredients such as mint and cinnamon. Unfortunately, the fix is only temporary. Bad breath, particularly when from a systemic source like garlic or onion that you've eaten or from mouth or respiratory infections, typically returns within an hour of using mouthwash.

The choices

Breath-freshening isn't the only reason to use mouthwash. Some brands deliver additional benefits:

Plaque fighters. Proven plaque-fighting chemicals can help finish the job you start with toothbrush and floss by curbing the oral bacteria that produce plaque. Such rinses can help reverse gingivitis, too.

The American Dental Association has so far certified two basic plaque-fighting formulas: *Peridex*, a prescription rinse with chlorhexidine, a powerful antibacterial; and a nonprescription rinse based on other ingredients used in *Listerine Antiseptic* and a number of private-label look-alikes, like *K Mart Antiseptic*.

Other plaque-fighting chemicals may also work. *Viadent* toothpaste and rinse both contain a plant extract that curbs plaque significantly when used twice daily.

Anticavity rinses. Fluoride rinses found in brands such as *Act, Fluorigard,* and *Listermint* can benefit those who are especially prone to cavities.

Antitartar rinses. With the same chemicals as in antitartar toothpaste, these slow the buildup of new tartar above the gumline. They can help the people who accumulate tartar most rapidly between dental cleanings and who don't normally use tartar-control dentifrice.

Buying advice

Don't count on mouthwash to freshen breath very long. Most mouthwashes deliver only in the short term. Choose a product by flavor and price. If you need extra help curbing plaque, gingivitis, tartar, or cavities, choose a special-purpose rinse.

Electric toothbrushes

The American Dental Association—and many dentists—used to hold that any toothbrush could potentially clean teeth well—it depended solely on an individual's diligence. Now, the ADA has been convinced that, for most people, an electric brush takes off more plaque than a regular brush.

CU's dental consultants believe most people can be trained to use a manual brush with excellent results, but most don't brush well enough or long enough. Electric brushes help by covering more area faster.

The choices

The typical electric toothbrush moves in small circles or ellipses, which simulate good hand-brushing techniques. You can also buy fancier "plaque removers" whose whirring, geared business ends bear only slight resemblance to a conventional toothbrush. The simplest electric brushes can be had for around $30. Complex designs generally sell for $80 to $100.

Features and conveniences

Ease of use. A brush should be easy to set up and maintain—or you won't use it. Some models have finicky internal gearing that must be rinsed and kept clean, lest it clog with toothpaste residue.

Handle. Look for one whose weight and design are comfortable to grip for two minutes, the time brushing should take.

Controls. Make sure they're easy to work. A soft-touch button or slider switch is easier to manage than a small button. Some brushes offer two or three speed settings, to adjust brushing vigor.

Charging time. The longer the time between charging, the more practical a model is for traveling. We found a wide range of "run down" times, from nearly an hour to about six minutes. If counterspace is at a premium, be sure to consider the size of the charging stand.

Extra heads. Some models include extra heads, often color-coded, for multiple users.

The tests

Electric toothbrushes are judged by dental professionals and by a panel of ordinary people who use each model. In the lab, we check for electrical hazards; we found two models that failed.

Buying advice

Choose a model that's easy to maneuver in the mouth, easy to set up, and easy to maintain. A little bleeding from gums should be expected at first. People especially prone to infection—those given antibiotics routinely before dental work—should check with their dentist before using an electric toothbrush.

Brush heads wear out—some in as little as two or three months. The price of replacements can be considerable—$10 or more for some designs.

Oral irrigators

People with extensive dental work—fixed bridges, braces, implants, crowns—often find it difficult to clean their mouths with just brush and floss. An irrigator can flush debris away. For those with advanced gum disease, the dentist may order irrigation twice a day as an adjunct to treatment.

One study found that once-a-day irrigation with plain water was as effective in controlling gingivitis as was twice-a-day rinsing with a powerful antibacterial mouthwash. That's impressive evidence that irrigation works to improve gums. Irrigation with an antimicrobial solution or mouthwash works even better than irrigation with plain water.

The choices

Most models sold are *Water Piks,* which are more alike than different. Other brands tend to be similar, too. Irrigators cost about $40 to $70, depending on features.

Features and conveniences

Flow control. The best arrangement for adjusting the stream's force is a button-dial on the handset that lets you do everything with just one hand. Less convenient arrangements have the dial on the base or a valve that must be twisted on the handpiece.

Reservoirs. Capacity varies from 12 to 35 ounces. The larger the reservoir, the better. Some models include a spare smaller reservoir to hold medicated solutions.

Tips. Deluxe irrigators offer two kinds of snap-on tips: blunt tips for regular irrigation above the gumline and pointy tips to irrigate pockets below the gumline. However, some pointy tips can scratch gums if not used properly.

Wall mounting. Because of the motor's vibration, an irrigator can "walk" across a bathroom counter. Mounting the unit on a wall eliminates that hazard and makes sure things stay put. Some models include mounting hardware.

The tests

We test irrigators much as we do electric toothbrushes, using a panel of staffers and three professionals. We also check for electrical leakage: Two models failed.

Buying advice

Most people don't need an irrigator. People with extensive bridgework and braces and people with gum disease might find it useful as a supplement to brushing and flossing. Some people simply like the gum massage irrigation provides. Anyone considering an irrigator should first consult with a dentist, since there is some potential to harm gums, cheeks, or tongue, or to drive debris deeper into a periodontal pocket, which might cause an abscess.

Irrigators are more alike than different. Choose by features and price.

HOW TO USE THE RATINGS

- Read the **article** for general guidance about types and buying advice.
- Read **Recommendations** for brand-name advice based on our tests.
- Read the **Ratings order** to see whether products are listed in order of quality, by price, or alphabetically. Most Ratings are based on estimated quality, without regard to price.
- Look to the **Ratings table** for specifics on the performance and features of individual models.
- A model marked Ⓓ has been discontinued, according to the manufacturer. A model marked Ⓢ indicates that, according to the manufacturer, it has been replaced by a successor model whose performance should be similar to the tested model but whose features may vary.

BLOOD-PRESSURE MONITORS 241

RATINGS BLOOD-PRESSURE MONITORS

Better ◀——▶ Worse
● ◔ ○ ◕ ●

▶ See report, page 228. From Consumer Reports, May 1992.

Recommendations: Look first to the mechanical monitors for the best value. They are the least expensive type and, if used correctly, are generally more accurate than electronic models. Anyone with poor eyesight, hearing, or dexterity, however, should consider the easier-to-use electronic models.

Ratings order: Listed by types; within types, listed in order of estimated quality, based mainly on consistency in use. (Models judged Not Acceptable are listed alphabetically.) Except where separated by a bold rule, closely ranked models differed little in quality. Price is the manufacturer's suggested retail.

Brand and model	Price	Self-inflating	Consistency; systolic/diastolic	Ease of use	Instructions	Advantages	Disadvantages
MECHANICAL MODELS							
Marshall 104	$30	—	◔/◔	◔	◔	B	k,q,r,s,u
Omron HEM-18	30	—	◔/◔	◔	○	B	c,k,q,r,s,u
Walgreens 2001	20	—	◔/◔	◔	◔	J	c,k,r,s
Lumiscope 100-021	30	—	◔/◔	●	◔	—	h,j,k,l,s,u
Sunmark 100	22	—	◔/◔	◔	○	—	h,j,k,q,r,s,u
Sunbeam 7627-10	31	—	○/◔	●	○	J	h,i,j,k,l
ELECTRONIC ARM MODELS							
Omron HEM-704C	130	✔	◔/◔	◔	◔	A,C,E,F,I,J	—
Sunbeam 7621	62	—	◔/◔	○	◔	D	g,t
Sunbeam 7650	115	✔	◔/◔	◔	◔	C,D,E	b,d,e,t
Lumiscope 1081	100	✔	◔/◔	◔	◔	C,D,E,H	b,e,o,t
Marshall 91	118	✔	◔/◔	◔	◔	H	m,p
AND UA-701	45	—	◔/◔	○	◔	D,H	b,c,e,g,t
Omron HEM-713C	90	✔	◔/○	◔	◔	J	m,p
Sunmark 144	48	—	◔/◔	○	◔	—	m,p,r
Omron HEM-413C	52	—	◔/○	○	◔	—	m,p,r
Walgreens 80WA	40	—	◔/○	○	◔	J	m,p,r
Marshall 80	60	—	◔/○	○	◔	H,J	m,p,r
Lumiscope 1065	60	—	◔/○	○	●	D,G,H	d,k,o,p,t
AND UA-731	79	✔	◑/◔	◔	◔	C,D,E,H	e,o,t
Radio Shack Micronta 63-663	50	—	◑/◑	○	◔	—	m
Lumiscope 1060	60	—	◑/◑	○	●	D,G,H	k,o,p,t

Ratings continued ▶

BLOOD-PRESSURE MONITORS

▶ *Ratings continued*

Brand and model / Price / Self-inflating / Consistency; systolic/diastolic / Ease of use / Instructions / Advantages / Disadvantages

ELECTRONIC FINGER MODELS
NOT ACCEPTABLE

■ *The following models were judged Not Acceptable because of the great variability in the readings they gave. Listed alphabetically.*

Brand and model	Price	Self-inflating	Consistency	Ease of use	Instructions	Advantages	Disadvantages
Lumiscope 1083	$130	✔	●|◐	⊖	⊖	—	f,n,p
Marshall F-89	138	✔	●|◐	⊖	⊖	—	a,p
Omron HEM-815F	130	✔	●|◐	⊖	◯	—	a,p
Sunbeam 7655-10	156	✔	●|◐	⊖	⊖	—	f,n,p

Features in Common

Except as noted, all: • Come with storage case or pouch. • Have cuff fitted with metal D-ring to facilitate donning 1-handed. • Measured pressure accurately to within 2 mmHg or less in lab tests. • Allow for rapid cuff deflation in emergency.
All mechanical models: • Have dial-type gauge about 2 inches in diameter. • Include stethoscope, usually with sensor attached to cuff to aid in correct placement.
Except as noted, all mechanical models: • Have loop on cuff from which to hang gauge (used in 2-person operation).
All electronic models: • Have liquid-crystal digital readout. • Measure pulse rate (accurate to within 2 beats per minute in tests, except where noted). • Have low-battery indicator.
All self-inflating models: • Automatically deflate cuff when measurement is completed.
Except as noted, all electronic models: • Have push-button On/Off switches. • Do not include batteries.

Key to Advantages

A–Cuff somewhat easier to don than most.
B–Stethoscope sounds somewhat easier to hear than most.
C–User can preset any of 4 inflation pressures.
D–Deflation rate can be adjusted; unusual in electronic models.
E–Very large, clear digital readout.
F–Self-contained in hard case, with storage area for cuff, tubing; also protects On/Off switch from accidentally turning on.
G–On/Off slider switch; less likely to be turned on inadvertently when packing unit for storage.
H–Oversized cuff available.
I–Instruction summary in cover of case.
J–Cuff has prominent mark to aid in correct placement on arm.

Key to Disadvantages

a–Average error substantially greater than most in use tests.
b–Average error slightly greater than most in use tests.
c–Gauge slightly less accurate than most when checked in lab against known pressures.
d–Pulse-rate measurement slightly less accurate than most.
e–End of cuff sometimes slipped out of D-ring.
f–Adjusting finger cuff somewhat difficult.
g–Some testers found cuff harder than others to inflate.
h–Plastic deflation valve flimsy and hard to adjust, which can affect readings.
i–Stethoscope not attached to cuff; makes 1-person operation relatively inconvenient.
j–Plastic stethoscope yoke: May be uncomfortable for some users.
k–Deflation valve must be closed manually each time cuff is inflated.
l–No assembly instructions.
m–Digital readout a bit harder to read than most; user must lean forward.
n–Systolic and diastolic readings not separated; numbers can run together.
o–Instructions lack advice that unit should be used in consultation with a physician.
p–No carrying case or pouch.
q–Pouch too small to hold monitor and stethoscope easily.
r–Instructions in relatively small print.
s–Cuff more cumbersome to apply than most because of attached tubing; **Lumiscope's** cuff is made of floppy material and was hard to keep spread out on the arm.
t–Cuff lacks mark or other indication to aid in correct placement on arm.
u–Cuff lacks loop on outside from which to hang gauge in 2-person operation.

EYEGLASS STORES

RATINGS — EYEGLASS STORES

Better ← → Worse

▶ See report, page 232. From Consumer Reports, August 1993.

Recommendations: Big chains offer one-stop shopping with an eye test, but there are advantages to having your eyes checked by an optometrist or ophthalmologist not connected with any store. For convenience and large selection, three chains—*For Eyes, Frame-n-Lens,* and *Price Club Optical*—offer good prices and were especially liked by our readers. The quickest were *EyeMasters, Lenscrafters,* and *Opti-World*.

Ratings order: Listed in order of overall satisfaction with buying eyeglasses, based on responses to CU's 1992 Annual Questionnaire. Of 71,000 readers who had bought glasses in the previous two years, nearly 15,000 had bought from one of the chains rated below. Each chain was evaluated by at least 200 respondents. Results reflect the experience of our readers, not necessarily that of all eyeglass buyers. **Notes to table:** Differences of about 3 points in overall score are meaningful. Eyeglass price: the median price readers reported having paid for a complete pair of eyeglasses. The margin of error is $3 for the largest chains to $10 or $15 for the smaller chains. Key to extra charges: ✔=extra charge; —=no extra cost; **V**=charge varies.

Company	Overall score	Eyeglass price	Frame selection	Time to make lenses	Employee service	Oversized	High-power	Antiscratch	Location
Private offices [1]	79	$158	○	○	◐	V	V	V	All states
Price Club Optical [2]	77	112	○	◐	○	—	—	—	Ariz., Calif., Colo., Conn., Md., N.J., N.M., N.Y., Pa., Tex., Va.
For Eyes	76	98	○	◐	○	—	—	✔	Calif., Fla., Ga., Ill., Mass., Md., N.J., Pa., Va., Wash., D.C.
Frame-n-Lens	75	88	○	○	◐	—	—	✔	Calif.
Visionworks	74	171	◐	◐	◐	—	—	—	Fla., Md., N.C., S.C., Va.
Opti-World	73	161	◐	◐	◐	—	—	V	Ala., Fla., Ga., Minn., N.C., S.C.
Vision World	72	96	○	○	○	—	—	✔	Conn., Fla., N.Y., N.J., Va.
Eye World	71	158	◐	◐	○	—	✔	—	Mass., N.H., N.Y., R.I.
LensCrafters	71	182	◐	◐	○	—	✔	—	Most states
Sterling Optical	70	137	○	○	○	V	V	V	Calif., Colo., Conn., Del., Fla., Ill., Ind., Iowa, Me., Md., Mass., Mo., N.H., N.J., N.Y., Pa., Va., W.Va., Wash., D.C., Wis.
NuVision	69	154	○	○	○	—	✔	✔	Ind., Mich., N.J.
EyeMasters	69	192	◐	◐	○	✔	✔	✔	Ala., Ariz., Fla., Idaho, Iowa, Kan., La., Mo., Neb., N.M., Okla., Tenn., Tex., Wash.
Empire Vision Center	68	113	○	○	◐	V	V	✔	N.Y.

[1] *Average responses from 23,000 readers who bought from private practitioners.*
[2] *$25 annual membership fee required for warehouse store.*

Ratings continued ▶

ORAL IRIGATORS

▶ *Ratings continued*

Company	Overall score	Eyeglass price	Frame selection	Time to make lenses	Satisfaction with Employee service	Oversized	High-power	Antiscratch	Location
Pearle Vision Center	68	$173	○	○	○	✓	✓	✓	Most states
Cohen's Fashion Opt.	67	187	○	○	○	✓	✓	V	Conn., Fla., Mass., N.J., N.Y.
Texas State Optical	66	175	○	○	○	—	—	✓	Ark., La., Okla., Tex.
Sears Optical	66	166	○	◐	○	—	—	✓	All states
D.O.C. Center	66	188	○	○	○	—	—	✓	Fla., Md., Mich., Mo., Ohio, Wis.
Royal Optical	63	146	◐	●	◐	V	✓	✓	Ala., Ariz., Ark., Colo., Fla., Ga., Idaho, Ill., Ind., Iowa, Kan., Ky., La., Md., Mich., Miss., Mo., N.M., Ohio, Okla., Ore., Pa., Tenn., Tex., Utah, Va., W.Va., Wyo.

[1] *Average responses from 23,000 readers who bought from private practitioners.*
[2] *$25 annual membership fee required for warehouse store.*

RATINGS ORAL IRRIGATORS

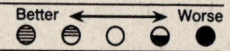

Better ◀———▶ Worse

▶ **See report, page 239.** From Consumer Reports, September 1992.

Recommendations: If you're willing to mount your irrigator on the wall, our condition of Acceptability, you might try the *Colgate Via-Jet Periodontal Irrigator 7500*; our panelists judged it best overall. It has been discontinued but may still be available. Otherwise, we recommend one of the three *Water Pik* irrigators.

Ratings order: Listed in order of overall performance, based on judgments of CU's user panel. Price is the manufacturer's suggested retail. ⓢ indicates tested model has been replaced by successor model; according to the manufacturer, the performance of new model should be similar to the tested model but features may vary. See right for new model number and suggested retail price, if available. ⒹⒹ indicates model discontinued.

Brand and model	Price	Reservoir, fl. oz.	Dimensions (WxDxH), in. [1]	Overall performance	Cleaning	Instructions	Ease of use	Advantages	Disadvantages	Comments
Water Pik Professional Dental System WP-32W	$60	35	7x4x7½	◐	◐	◐	◐	A,B,F	—	A,B,F,I
Water Pik Family Dental System WP-30W	50	35	7x4x7½	◐	◐	◐	◐	F	—	F,I
Water Pik Personal Dental System WP-20W	40	25	5½x4x7½	◐	◐	◐	◐	F	a,b	C,F,I

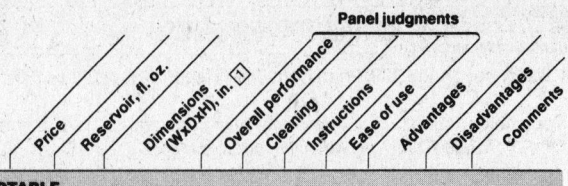

ORAL IRRIGATORS

Panel judgments: Price / Reservoir, fl. oz. / Dimensions (WxDxH), in. [1] / Overall performance / Cleaning / Instructions / Ease of use / Advantages / Disadvantages / Comments

Brand and model

CONDITIONALLY ACCEPTABLE

■ *The following models were judged Conditionally Acceptable due to excessive electrical leakage in our tests. They should only be used with their wall mount.*

Brand and model	Price	Reservoir	Dimensions	Overall	Cleaning	Instructions	Ease of use	Advantages	Disadvantages	Comments
Colgate Via-Jet Periodontal Irrigator 7500 [D]	$60	25	8½x4½x7	◐	◐	◐	◐	C,D	c	A,B,D,G,I
Sunbeam Dental Water Jet 6282-100 [S]	61	12½	8½x4¼x5½	○	○	◐	◐	E	d,e	E,G,H,I

[1] *The width and depth, plus the height in use, to the nearest quarter-inch. The tank on the Water Pik WP-32W and WP-30W detach and serve, inverted, as a dust cover. That reduces overall height 3 in.*

Successor Model

Sunbeam Dental WaterJet 6282-100 is succeeded by 6282-200, $50.

Features in Common

Except as noted, all: • Have 1-yr. warranty on all parts except irrigator tips. • Supply 4 regular tips, which can be stored in or on base. • Have American Dental Association's seal as acceptable when used as an adjunct to brushing, flossing, and regular professional care. • Run on 120-volt AC. • Have continuous pressure-adjustment control. • Have control on handpiece to stop water flow temporarily without changing pressure setting. • Do not include wall mount. • Have adequately long power cord and water hose.

Key to Advantages

A–Includes secondary 10-oz. reservoir for periodontal rinses.
B–Sulcus (pointy) tips supplied have soft points, judged safer to use.
C–Large, clearly marked pressure-control knob.
D–Judged somewhat less noisy than most.
E–Tips are a bit easier to change than those on other models.
F–Reservoir has permanent volume markings in ounces and milliliters.

Key to Disadvantages

a–Provision for storing only 2 tips on base unit; 1 stores in handpiece, thus increasing overall height.
b–Hose connecting handpiece to base judged short, making unit less convenient to use than most.
c–Sulcus (pointy) tips supplied have hard points, judged more likely to scratch gums.
d–Stopping water flow temporarily at handpiece—to switch hands, say—requires user to change pressure setting.
e–Lacks markings on pressure-control knob to help reset pressure to accustomed level.

Key to Comments

A–3-yr. warranty.
B–Includes 2 regular (blunt) and 2 sulcus (pointy) tips, the latter for irrigation below the gumline or into periodontal pockets.
C–Includes 2 regular (blunt) tips only.
D–Includes wall-mounting hardware.
E–Wall mount must be ordered from the distributor for $3.25.
F–Wall mount must be ordered from mfr. for $2.75.
G–Lacks the American Dental Association seal.
H–Judged easier to use for people with limited use of fingers and wrist or difficulty grasping.
I–Replacement-tip prices. **Water Piks:** Pik Pocket Tip PP-3, 2 for $10; Jet Tip JT-4, 4 for $4. **Colgate Via-Jet:** 4 for $5. **Sunbeam:** 2 for $5.

ELECTRIC TOOTHBRUSHES

RATINGS — ELECTRIC TOOTHBRUSHES

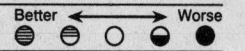

Better ◐ ◑ ○ ◐ ● Worse

▶ See report, page 239. From Consumer Reports, September 1992.

Recommendations: Our test panel and consultants gave highest marks to the *Braun Oral-B Plaque Remover*, which we check-rated.

Ratings order: Listed in order of overall performance, based on judgments of CU's user panel. Price is the manufacturer's suggested retail for the basic unit and for extra brushes (number of extra brushes shown in parentheses). [D] indicates model discontinued.

Brand and model	Price	Price, extra brushes	Handset weight, oz.	Speeds	Brushes, supplied/stored on base	Overall performance	Ease of use	Changing brushes	Cleaning brushes	Charge capacity [1]	Advantages	Disadvantages	Comments
✓Braun Oral-B Plaque Remover D5545	$99	$10(1)	6	1	4/4	◐	◐	◐	◐	◐	A	—	A,B,D,G,H
Water Pik Automatic Toothbrush AT-10W [D]	45	5(4)	6	1	4/4	○	◐	◐	◐	◑	—	—	—
Teledyne Water Pik Plaque Control PC-2000W [D]	50	5(4)	6	1	4/4	○	◐	◐	◐	◑	—	a	—
Interplak Voyager TK-2 [D]	99	13(1)	5	3	1/2	○	○	○	○	[2]	B	b	C,D,E,F,L
EpiDent C2500 [D]	79	17(2)	7	2	2/2	◑	◐	◐	○	◐	D	c,d	F,M
DentiBrush BT-691-10	35	7(4)	3	1	2/—	◑	◐	◐	◐	◐[3]	D	a,e	B,I,N,Q
Interplak Plus PB-6	90	13(1)	7	3	4/4	◑	○	◐	●		C	—	D,J,K

CONDITIONALLY ACCEPTABLE

■ The following model was judged Conditionally Acceptable due to excessive electrical leakage in immersion test; it should be used only with its wall mount.

| Sunbeam Automatic Angle Toothbrush 4205 | 50 | 5(2) | 5 | 2 | 4/4 | ○ | ◐ | ○ | ◐ | ◐ | B | — | A,O,P,Q |

NOT ACCEPTABLE

■ The following model was judged Not Acceptable due to excessive electrical leakage in immersion test; a wall mount is not available.

| Plak Trac PT-100 | 30 | [4] | 3 | 1 | 2/4 | ○ | ◐ | ○ | ◐ | ○ | — | — | — |

[1] An estimate of how long each brush will run after its batteries have been fully charged.
[2] Plug-in model, powered on house current—no batteries.
[3] Based on tests with a typical rechargeable nickel-cadmium "C" cell; a regular alkaline cell would perform even better.
[4] Brush head holds 2 multitufted disks, which may be replaced independently of the head.

ELECTRIC TOOTHBRUSHES

Performance Notes
All: • Clarity of instructions was judged excellent or very good. • Ease of set-up was judged excellent or very good.

Features in Common
Except as noted, all: • Carry American Dental Association seal as effective cleansing devices. • Have 1-yr. warranty on all parts except brushes and brush heads. • Run on built-in rechargeable batteries, not replaceable by user, and include charging stand (base unit), which is connected to house current. • Use 120-volt AC only. • Have adequately long power cord. • Do not include wall mount.

Key to Advantages
A–Timer light flashes after about 2 min. to signal adequate brushing time.
B–Built-in voltage converter for foreign travel.
C–Automatically shuts off if excess pressure is exerted on teeth or gums.
D–Battery can be replaced by user.

Key to Disadvantages
a–Panelists noted excessive vibration when brushing.
b–Coiled power cord only 4 feet.
c–Brush head is bulky, judged hard to maneuver inside mouth.
d–Push-button switch must be held down to operate—judged inconvenient.
e–Some samples had defective battery contacts and didn't work.

Key to Comments
A–Wall mount included.
B–Judged easier to use for people with limited dexterity or ability to grip.
C–Oversized control button available at no cost from manufacturer; makes it easier to change speeds.
D–The American Dental Association has allowed brush to claim significant dental plaque and gingivitis reduction.
E–Foreign plug adapters not available from mfr.; must be obtained elsewhere.
F–Judged harder to use for people with limited dexterity or ability to grip.
G–30-day return/refund privilege.
H–Warranty terms not stated on or inside package.
I–90-day warranty limited to defective material or workmanship; $5 charge.
J–Wall mount not supplied but available from mfr. at no charge.
K–Storage clips for additional brush heads available from mfr. at no charge.
L–Travel case can store 2 brush heads.
M–Battery charger is separate unit, not a charging stand; the design eliminates the possibility that the charger will be accidentally immersed when plugged in.
N–No charger; uses 1 "C" flashlight battery.
O–Wall mount holds 4 brush heads as well as charger.
P–Travel kit with foreign plug adapters available from mfr.
Q–Lacks American Dental Association seal.

INFORMATION FROM CONSUMER REPORTS

Consumers Union provides information in a variety of ways. Its publications include CONSUMER REPORTS; Zillions, a CONSUMER REPORTS for Kids; two newsletters, On Health and The Travel Letter; and a book list of more than 100 titles. CU also offers used car prices by telephone, computer printouts of new car prices, fax copies of recent articles in CONSUMER REPORTS, and an electronic version of CONSUMER REPORTS on America Online, CompuServe, Dialog, Nexis, and Prodigy.

BATHROOM SCALES

RATINGS: BATHROOM SCALES

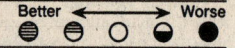

Better ⬤ ◐ ○ ◑ ⬤ Worse

▶ **See report, page 236.** From Consumer Reports, January 1993.

Recommendations: The *Health O Meter 840*, $50, earned top-rating for its sample-to-sample consistency and high overall performance. Choose from the next seven high-rated models for accuracy and repeatability—the ability to give the same reading for a given weight time after time. Two models stood out for low price and high quality: the *Counselor Digital 850*, $22, and the *Borg Digital 9855*, $23.

Ratings order: Listed in order of estimated quality. Except where separated by a bold rule, closely ranked models differed little in quality. Price is the manufacturer's suggested retail. **Notes to table:** Key to type: **ST** = strain-gauge; **S** = spring; **H** = hydraulic. Key to display: **D** = digital; **C** = conventional rotating dial and fixed needle; **S** = speedometer-type with fixed dial and spinning needle. [D] indicates model discontinued.

Brand and model	Price	Type	Display	Repeatability [1]	Accuracy [2]	Display clarity	Ease of setting zero	Advantages	Disadvantages	Comments
Health O Meter 840	$50	ST	D	⬤	○	⬤	⬤	A,C,F,G,H,K	p	C,D,E,F,J,N,U
Thinner MS-7	50	ST	D	⬤	○	○	⬤	B,C,D,G,H	h	E,F,K,M,U
Metro The Thin Scale 9800	50	ST	D	⬤	◐	◐	⬤	A,C,F,G,K	h,l,n	C,F,J,R
Borg Hot Dots 9144	28	S	D	⬤	○	⬤	⬤	B,C	p	S
Sunbeam Digital 12657	49	ST	D	⬤	◐	⬤	⬤	C,D	h,l	—
Counselor Digiscale 2121	40	ST	D	⬤	○	⬤	⬤	B,C,D	e,h,i,n	S,U
Salter Electronic 971	50	ST	D	⬤	⬤	○	⬤	B,C,F,G,I	a,l,m	C,D,E,F,J,P
Counselor Digital 850, A Best Buy	22	S	D	⬤	○	○	⬤	B,C	a,m	A,R
Counselor Accucycle 1100	32	S	D	⬤	◑	⬤	⬤	C,K	e,n	E,S
Health O Meter 811	30	ST	D	⬤	○	⬤	●	C,D,F,G,H,I,K	b,p	D,E,F,J
Health O Meter 190	79	ST	D	⬤	◐	⬤	⬤	C,H,K	a,e,f	D,F,H,L,U
Metro Big Dial 1000	50	S	S	⬤	⬤	○	⬤	A,F,G,K	g,k	H,J
Borg Digital 9855, A Best Buy	23	S	D	⬤	⬤	○	⬤	C,F	e,m	R
Health O Meter 1706	20	S	D	⬤	◑	⬤	⬤	C,D	a	F,L
Sunbeam Thin Maxi 12573	29	S	D	⬤	◑	⬤	⬤	C,D	a,e,f	O
Sunbeam Eclipse II 12756	22	S	D	⬤	○	⬤	⬤	—	a	Q
Metro Digital 1600	25	S	D	⬤	○	○	⬤	C	e,m,n	Q
Seca Doctor's Scale 760	120	S	S	⬤	○	◑	○	G,J,K	g	H
Polder Swing Marble 6130	18	S	C	⬤	○	●	○	F	p	S,Q

BATHROOM SCALES

Brand and model	Price	Type	Display	Repeatability [1]	Accuracy [2]	Display clarity	Ease of setting zero	Advantages	Disadvantages	Comments
Health O Meter 1715	$35	S	D	⊖	○	⊖	⊖	G,K	a,b,e	—
Medixact Hydraulic 6400 ☐	65	H	S	○	⊖	◐	○	C,G,H	g	G,H
Metro Fashion 9500	20	S	C	⊖	⊖	◐	○	E,F	k,l,m,n,o,p	—
Counselor Monterey Wicker 410	14	S	C	⊖	○	◐	●	F,G	g,j	R
Sunbeam Thin Speedometer 12280	25	S	S	⊖	○	◐	●	—	g,k,o,q	G
Polder Tic Tac Toe 6200	24	S	C	○	⊖	◐	○	—	a,l,m,n	Q
Medixact Proshape 6500	35	S	S	⊖	◐	○	●	G,K	b,f,g,k,n	H,K,T
Sunbeam Granite Square 12509	15	S	C	○	◐	◐	○	—	b	C,O,Q
Counselor Leatherette 97	10	S	C	○	○	◐	●	—	b,d	—
Salter Hampshire White 424	17	S	C	○	◐	●	○	—	a,g,l,m	C,O
Health O Meter Professional 150	50	S	S	○	○	○	○	G,K	b,g	G,H
Sunbeam The Classic 12200	25	S	C	○	◐	◐	●	K	e,g	C,O
Counselor 550	22	S	C	○	⊖	○	●	F	a,d,g,n	S
Krups Family Data 881 ☐	60	S	S	○	◐	◐	○	G,J	b,d,e,g,n	G,I,O
Krups Fitness Sport 830 ☐	30	S	C	◐	○	◐	○	G	c,d,e,g,k	R,Q
Borg 3300	12	S	C	◐	◐	○	○	F	a,d,g	O
Terraillon Eyedrop T1180	28	S	C	○	◐	◐	○	—	a,b,g,l,m	O,P
Health O Meter 50	10	S	C	○	●	◐	○	—	a,b,e,g,k,l	—
Metro Fashion 2000	12	S	C	○	●	◐	○	—	a,l,m,n	O
Health O Meter 180	20	S	S	◐	◐	◐	●	—	a,b,c,e,f,g,k,l,m,o	B,G,O

[1] *The ability to give consistent readings for the same weight.*
[2] *The ability to accurately display the weight of object being weighed.*

Features in Common

All will suffer in accuracy and repeatability when subjected to abnormally hot or cold temperatures, when exposed constantly to high humidity, when used on a rug, and when your weight is not centered on the scale platform.

Except as noted, all have: • Readout interval of 1 lb. • Steel base and square or rectangular platform. • Claimed maximum capacity of 300 lb. or more (up to 330 lb.). • Sample-to-sample variability of 1 to 3 percent in accuracy and ½ to 1½ lb. in repeatability. • Tendency to rust or creak after exposure to high humidity. • Sharp edges in battery compartment or on bottom of unit. • 5-yr. warranty.

Except as noted, all digital-display models: • Have red LED digits. • Are activated by tapping toe on button, small lever, or scale platform. • Delay readings after user steps on platform, but only by 6 sec. or less. • Give minimum readings of 6 to 13 lb. • Have tare-measurement capability (for weighing held objects). • Use 9-volt battery (not included). • Have low-battery indicator.

Key to Advantages

A–Showed less than 1 percent sample-to-sample variability in accuracy overall.
B–Showed less than ½-lb. sample-to-sample variability in repeatability overall.
C–Consistently repeated same readings for weights under 100 lb.

Ratings continued ▶

BATHROOM SCALES

D—Consistently repeated same readings for weights over 225 lb.
E—Accurate to within ½ percent with weights under 100 lb.
F—Accurate to within ½ percent with weights over 225 lb.
G—No sharp edges.
H—Did not rust during humidity tests or creak afterward.
I—Judged easier to clean than most.
J—Padded mat; very comfortable to bare feet.
K—Platform easily accommodates large feet.

Key to Disadvantages
a—Showed more than 3 percent sample-to-sample variability in accuracy in parts of its weight range.
b—Showed more than 1½-lb. sample-to-sample variability in repeatability in parts of its weight range.
c—Off in repeatability by more than 1 lb., on average, for weights under 100 lb.
d—Off in repeatability by more than 1 lb., on average, for weights over 225 lb.
e—Off in accuracy by more than 2 percent, on average, for weights under 100 lb.
f—Off in accuracy by more than 2 percent, on average, for weights over 225 lb.
g—Zero settings often shifted after weighings.
h—Allows little time for weighing; turns off only 10 sec. after being turned on.
i—Takes more than 6 sec. to display weight after user steps on platform.
j—Textured mat judged very hard to clean.
k—Dirt couldn't be removed from display area.
l—Tended to slide on dry floor fairly easily.
m—Tended to slide on wet flooring fairly easily.
n—Less stable than most.
o—Large feet will partially block display.
p—Bumps or ridges around edge of scale are uncomfortable to bare feet.
q—Mat was peeling off base on 2 of 3 new samples.

Key to Comments
A—According to mfr., this is the same model as **Borg Digital 9855**, but it performed somewhat differently.
B—Also sold as **Health O Meter 181** and **182**, identical to tested model except for color.
C—Displays weight in kilograms or pounds.
D—Standing on platform causes unit to turn on, adjust zero setting, and display weight.
E—Unlike most digital-readout models, can measure weights of 5 lb. or less.
F—Unlike most digital-readout models, has no tare-measurement capability.
G—Has 5 color-coded markers to record weights.
H—Horseshoe-shaped platform.
I—Oval platform.
J—Plastic base.
K—Add-on plastic feet claimed to promote accurate weighings on carpet, but did not do so in our tests.
L—Battery included.
M—Has LCD display. Uses "lifetime" lithium battery (but if new battery is required, replacement must be performed at "authorized service center").
N—Uses 4 AA batteries.
O—Maximum claimed capacity less than 300 lb. (between 260 and 288 lb.).
P—1-yr. warranty.
Q—3-yr. warranty.
R—7-yr. warranty.
S—10-yr. warranty.
T—"Lifetime" warranty.
U—Readout interval ½ lb.

ABOUT PRICES IN THE BUYING GUIDE

Prices for most products have been updated for the Buying Guide. The prices we give, unless otherwise noted, are approximate or suggested retail as quoted by the manufacturer. Discounts may be substantial, especially for electronics and camera equipment.

RATINGS FULL-SIZED CRIBS

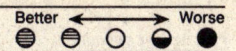

Better ◐ ◉ ○ ◒ ● Worse

▶ **See report, page 234.** From Consumer Reports, May 1993.

Recommendations: The best of the double-dropside models was the *Child Craft 16101*, $295. It was very easy to operate and very durable. The second-rated *Simmons Victoria*, $559, has a dropside release that gave some parent testers trouble; be sure to try it out in the store. Of the single-dropside models, the *Sears 37017/Okla Homer Smith* (or its successor), $159, is a better value than the *Tracers Bobby*, $325.

Ratings order: Listed by types; within types, listed in order of estimated quality, based mainly on convenience and durability. Closely ranked models differed little in quality. Models judged equal in quality are bracketed and listed alphabetically. Price is the manufacturer's suggested retail. **Notes to table:** Finish: **W** = white; **C** = cherry; **M** = maple. Dropside type: **HF** = requires one hand and one foot to release; **HL** = one hand and one leg; **1H** = one hand; **2H** = two hands. ⓢ indicates tested model has been replaced by successor model; according to the mfr., the performance of new model should be substantially similar to the tested model but features may vary. See page 252 for new model number and suggested retail price. ⒹＤ indicates model discontinued.

Brand and model	Price	Finish	Dropside type	Convenience	Durability	Comments
DOUBLE-DROPSIDE MODELS						
Child Craft 16101	$295	W	HF	◉	◉	B,N
Simmons Victoria 4727	559	C	1H	◐	◉	B,C,K,S
Bassett 5004-1507	199	M	HF	◐	◉	C,J,Y
Bassett 5068-1512	329	M	HF	◐	◉	G,H,J,M,U,Y
Simmons Avella 1290	389	W	HF	◐	◉	B
Simmons Turin 1403	399	W	HF	◐	◉	B
J.C. Penney 393-1920/ Stork Craft Monarch III Ⓓ	229	W	2H	○	◉	B,C,I,W,Z,AA
Delta 4-530-1	199	W	2H	◐	○	B,E,T,U,W,X,AA
Sears 50226/Evenflo 017322	200	C	HF	◐	○	B,P
SINGLE-DROPSIDE MODELS						
Tracers Bobby 9201	325	W	HL	◐	◉	A,B,C,T,U,V,X
Sears 37017/Okla Homer Smith ⓢ	159	W	HF	◐	◉	B,O,V,X
Child Craft 13641-18	200	W	HF	◐	◉	J,V
Nelson 11-210	99	M	HF	◐	◉	J,R,Y
Nelson 18-110	119	W	HF	◐	◉	C,J,Y
Cosco T14-WHO Euro Crib	149	W	HL	◐	○	B,C,Q,U,W,X,CC
Sears/Evenflo 012614 ⓢ	99	M	HF	◐	○	B,C,P
Welsh 7452	99	M	HF	◒	○	J
Okla Homer 80023 Nod A Way ⓢ	169	M	2H	◒	○	J,L,R,X

Ratings continued ▶

252 FULL-SIZED CRIBS

▶ *Ratings continued*

Brand and model / Price / Finish / Dropside type / Convenience / Durability / Comments

CONDITIONALLY ACCEPTABLE

■ *The following model was judged Conditionally Acceptable provided that drawer stops are installed.*

| Child Craft 15591 Crib 'n' Bed | $599 | W | 2H | ● | ◉ | D,F,L,BB |

Successor Models (in Ratings order)
Sears 37017 is succeeded by Lynwood 30562, $160; Sears/Evenflo 012614 by Jenny Lind 30038/37, $120/$130; Okla Homer 80023 by 80029, $90.

Features in Common
All: • Require assembly. • Claim to meet Federal safety standard.
Except as noted, all: • Are wood. • Measure 53-56 in. long, 30-33 in. wide, and 44-54 in. high. • Have interior dimensions of about 52 in. by 28 in. at mattress-support height levels. • Require tools to assemble. • Have casters. • Have metal mattress support with spring suspension.

Key to Comments
A–Lockable casters; help prevent rolling.
B–Hooded or spherical casters; rolled smoother than disk-shaped casters.
C–Assembly instructions easier than most.
D–Base-mounted drawers help prevent child from crawling under crib.
E–Lacks instructions for adjusting mattress support (though it's easy to figure out).
F–Lacks casters.
G–Dropside-mechanism screws hard to install.
H–Metal caster supports bent under weight of crib in motion and prevented casters from turning. Replacement casters worked fine.
I–Casters tended to fall out of legs.
J–Disk-shaped casters; rolled less smoothly than other types.
K–Dropside mechanism easy to use, but requires practice. Also, some panelists could not release mechanism.
L–Dropside mechanism is difficult to release.
M–Dropside slightly heavy.
N–Thin, rod-type dropside-release treadle hurt bare foot in use, some panelists said.
O–Protruding dropside rod could snag clothing or hurt child playing near or under crib.
P–Our samples had sharp edges on mattress-support hangers.
Q–Can't adjust mattress-support height by following instructions.
R–Knobby spindles hurt fingers reaching in to remove standard-sized mattress.
S–Mattress support had burrs, which made height adjustment difficult.
T–Adult's foot could bang into bottom edge of end boards when moving crib.
U–Crib interior length is approx. 51 in. (**Bassett 5068-1512**) or approx. 53 in. (**Cosco, Bellini, Tracers Bobby, Delta**).
V–Crib interior width is approx. 29 in.
W–Does not require tools for assembly.
X–Requires simple tools to adjust mattress support.
Y–Has hexhead tool to adjust mattress support.
Z–Sample with 1991 manufacturing date had difficult-to-operate dropside release. Sample made more recently had improved release.
AA–Has pressboard (**J.C. Penney/Stork Craft**) or wooden (**Delta**) mattress support.
BB–68 in. long by 30 in. wide by 40 in. high.
CC–Metal crib.

Recreation & exercise

Exercise equipment:
- Home gyms 254
- Treadmills 255
- Exercise bikes 256
- Stair climbers 256

Running & walking shoes 258
Bicycles 259
Ratings 262

Exercise can strengthen the heart, improve circulation, help control weight, reduce cholesterol, ease hypertension, reduce stress, increase muscle tone, and improve sleep. It can also be fun, but that's hard for some people to believe. Their early exposure to exercise was gym-class calisthenics and team sports enjoyed by a few and dreaded by others.

Schools can help by providing physical activities that everyone can enjoy. If children learn that exercise is fun, there's a better chance they'll do it all their lives.

Almost any form of exercise will give you some health benefits. Bowling, golf, fishing, and gardening may not get your pulse pounding, but they're a lot better than watching TV. If you want to build muscle tone, no one has improved on resistance training such as weightlifting.

For cardiovascular benefit, you have many aerobic exercises from which to choose. Among the best: running, brisk walking, biking, rowing, swimming, stair climbing, cross-country skiing, aerobic dance.

The standard words of caution apply. If you're out of shape, have a medical problem that could affect your ability to exercise, or are over 40, it's best to consult a doctor before starting out. Don't try to do too much the first few times. Start with a short workout at moderate effort level and gradually add to duration and intensity. If you feel pain at any point, stop and walk until the pain goes away; if it doesn't, call it a day. Stretch—without bouncing or jerking—before and after each workout.

Finally, don't feel that all your recreation has to have a significant physical effect. There's nothing wrong with doing something simply because it's relaxing. It's called recharging your batteries.

Exercise equipment

▶ **Ratings of home gyms on page 265; stair climbers on page 262.**

You can achieve fitness without buying an expensive machine. All you really need is a good pair of sneakers (these days called athletic shoes) and the will to use them regularly. The scenery and fresh air of an outdoor workout can do a lot to keep you from getting bored while exercising. But Americans love gadgets, leading many to the conviction that if only they had the right equipment, the key to health and long life would be theirs. Hence, an industry supplying treadmills, exercise bikes, stair climbers, and other home-gym equipment.

Workouts on an exercise machine have advantages. You can use it when bad weather might otherwise encourage sloth. You can exercise in the privacy of your own home, even in the dead of night. There's no risk of injury from potholes, dogs, muggers, or cars. Terrain doesn't determine the effort you must expend. You can stop anytime without being miles from home. And you may be able to get a better workout, since a good machine makes it easy to maintain your aerobic target heart rate (60 to 85 percent of 220, minus your age).

Exercise machines vary in the kind of workout they give. Some machines work just the lower body. Others can improve the tone of the whole body. But if your reason for exercising is to achieve cardiovascular fitness, the kind of exercise matters less than the amount of effort you put into it, as long as you are using the larger muscle groups. Your choice should be governed by personal preference and what you can afford. When weighing price versus benefits, keep in mind that a machine you don't enjoy is likely to turn into an expensive coat rack.

Before settling on any machine, it's a good idea to ask your doctor if you're making the right choice. Some people with back problems, for example, might be advised to avoid rowing machines. Those with knee problems might be warned away from stair climbers. The obese should probably avoid running on a treadmill, although walking is okay.

Home gyms

Some multi-station home gyms are essentially scaled-down versions of the expensive machines used in health clubs. They typically consist of padded seats or benches, some form of mechanical resistance, and various levers that you move in order to work against the resistance. Each machine has its own set of "stations" where you can do a specific exercise, some for the upper body, others for the lower.

The gyms provide the resistance in one of several ways: with a stack of weights on a bar so they can't fall; with hydraulic or pneumatic "shock absorbers;" with rubber bands of varying thickness; with flexible rods; or with a centrifugal brake. All, CU found, are capable of providing an effective workout. But then so are free weights—at much lower cost. But home-gyms allow you to do some exercises that you can't do with free weights and you don't need an assistant to catch the weight should you lose the strength to support it.

Home gyms are sold primarily in department stores and through mail-order catalogs. *DP* (Diversified Products) is by far the biggest brand; it and two others—*Soloflex* and *Weider*—account for more than half of all U.S. sales.

Price. Home gyms that let you perform a complete range of upper- and lower-body exercises are priced typically between $300 and $1000. Spending more buys better construction—heavier-gauge metal, more durable moving parts. You can also expect smaller-increment resistance changes and a wider range of resistance settings. More expensive gyms are likely to offer more comfortable stations and more stations, so that more than one person can use the machine simultaneously.

Exercise value. You can combine the muscle-enhancing benefits of a home-gym workout with the heart-strengthening benefits of aerobic exercise by "circuit training"—performing different strengthening exercises in rapid succession continuously for 20 minutes or more. But on some home gyms, you have to take a long pause between exercises to reconfigure the equipment; the more and longer you pause, the less the aerobic value. Of course, you can always do your aerobic exercising on another machine (or by jogging outdoors, say) and use the gym for just your muscle-building workout.

If you had to choose just one of the two types of workout, choose the aerobic one first. But there's value in all-around muscle-building, too—to help protect the body from injury, to make everyday tasks like carrying groceries easier, and to help improve performance in sports.

Features and conveniences. A gym should be versatile enough to work all muscle groups and simple enough to use without extensive reference to the owner's manual. It should also be challenging enough to provide a real workout yet comfortable enough to keep workouts free of pain.

Look for a design that lets you get in and out of the stations easily. Changing resistance is easiest on gyms with weight stacks and elastic bands. For circuit-training workouts, choose a model that lets you zip from one exercise to another with little fussing. Watch out for models with potential pinch points. Finally, take note of a machine's size. Make sure it's a machine that fits into the space you have—some of them are quite bulky.

If possible, try out a gym before you buy. You may not fit in each station well or it might put you body in a position that risks injury. Some machines may not offer enough range of motion; others not enough resistance or too large an increment between increasing resistance levels.

Treadmills

In essence, a treadmill is a belt stretched between two rollers and driven by a motor. Most treadmills let you adjust the incline to simulate hills and increase the strenuousness of the workout. A monitor tells you how fast you're going, how far, and for how long, and sometimes such useful things as heart rate and an estimate of the calories burned.

Machines vary in the type and size of motor. The type of motor—AC or DC—affects the way the machine works. An AC motor runs at full speed all the time, relying on a transmissionlike pulley system to vary the speed of the walking belt. Most such models can start up at full speed—a rude surprise if you're standing on the belt at the time. The speed of a DC motor can be regulated, so machines with a DC motor avoid this problem.

In any case, straddling the belt is the recommended way to start up. Once you're on the belt, all models, whether AC or DC, let you gradually turn up the speed as you start to walk.

Motor sizes vary from half a horsepower to one horsepower or more. The more power, the better the ability to handle heavy loads or high speeds. Walking or jogging can be done on any unit, but running requires a treadmill that goes at least 5 mph.

Inexpensive brands include *Proform*, *Vitamaster*, *Sears*, *Tunturi*, *Voit*, and *DP*.

Precor, Trotter, and Quinton make expensive versions.

Price. The machines most consumers buy range from about $400 to $1000. The more you spend, the bigger the motor, the wider and longer the belt, and the higher the top speed. Higher-priced machines have automatic incline adjustments and easy-to-use controls. The kind of treadmill used in health clubs, which can cost thousands of dollars, is built even better. The typical machine priced under $500 is designed for walking, not running; the top speed is likely to be less than 5 mph. The least expensive machines, we found in our tests, often suffer such ills as worn drive mechanisms, faulty controls, and balky motors over time.

Exercise value. Walking at a brisk pace, jogging, and running are excellent aerobic conditioners. Increasing the incline can boost the exertion level of even a 3-mph walk to an aerobic level for a regular runner. Walking and running improve lower-body muscle tone, but do nothing for the upper body.

Features and conveniences. A slow minimum speed makes starting safer. Automatic incline adjustments are helpful; treadmills that use pins to change the slope are a bother. A long, wide belt and full-length handrails make for comfortable, safe use.

Exercise bikes

There are two main types of exercise bikes: single- and dual-action models. As you pedal "single-action" models, you drive a resistance device, such as a flywheel affixed with a brake. The main advantage of a flywheel bike is that you can change resistance with the twist of a knob.

"Dual-action" models can give you an upper- and lower-body workout. As you pedal, you also pump handlebars back and forth with your arms. Models vary according to how they apply resistance. Some have their handlebars coupled with the pedals; as you move the handlebars the pedals rotate. Others use hydraulic shock absorbers for arm resistance. Most use a fan for resistance, but some use a flywheel instead. To increase resistance on a fan model, you move arms and legs faster. While you're pedaling, the fan can cool you—in theory. But some models, we've found, produce barely a zephyr.

There are a couple of variations as well. Recumbent models let you sit in a chairlike seat rather than perch on a bike seat. That arrangement works the hamstring muscles more than an upright bike and is helpful for people who have back problems or trouble with balance—or who just find a bicycle seat too uncomfortable.

If you already own a bike, you can convert it and save yourself money. Training stands are typically priced less than $200.

Exercise bikes are made by bicycle companies such as Schwinn and Ross, as well as companies that first made their name in the exercise-equipment field, like Tunturi and Vitamaster. Lifecycle and Precor make home and health-club models that include programmable "courses" of hills and flats.

Price. Most models range from about $100 to $700. Health-club type bikes can cost upward of $1000 or more. Bikes that cost less than $150 tend to be flimsy and jerky, we've found.

Exercise value. Cycling is an excellent aerobic conditioner. And it can actually be easier to maintain a steady activity level on an exercise bike than a bicycle, on which you may alternately pedal hard and coast.

Features and conveniences. The flywheel should rotate smoothly and the resistance control should be easy to work. The seat should be well padded and comfortably shaped. A monitor keeps track of your speed, how far you've "traveled," and the time. Pedal straps let your legs work on the upstroke as well as the downstroke.

On dual-action models, "coaster" pedals let your feet momentarily stop while your arms do the work.

Stair climbers

Most stair climbers are essentially levers attached to a resistance device. Your legs pump the levers as if you were climbing stairs. A monitor displays steps-per-minute, time, and calories burned.

There are two types of stair climbers: steppers, the more common kind, and ladders. On a stepper, you mimic the action of climbing stairs; on a ladder, you look as though you're ascending a ladder.

Dual-action models work arms as well as legs. Additionally, models vary according to how they apply resistance—with a hydraulic piston, flywheel, drive train, or fan. On many models, the "steps" are linked—as one goes down, the other goes up. Other models have independently moving step, which gives a better workout.

Stairmaster and *Lifestep* are leading brands of health-club models; *DP, Tunturi, Precor,* and *Sears* are popular brands among the home models.

Price. Stair climbers range in price from less than $100 to more than $3000, but many models meant for home use sell for less than $500.

Exercise value. Aerobic plus muscle toning. Since your feet stay on the levers, stress on the knees is less than it would be for going up and down a real flight of stairs.

Features and conveniences. Look for pedals and handles positioned so you can maintain a comfortable posture; smooth pedal motion; a stable machine; monitors that are clear and versatile but not overly complicated; easy-to-adjust resistance; pedals that provide a comfortable and secure stance; and comfortable handles.

The tests

In addition to thoroughly examining the way a device works and how it's put together, testers use each piece of equipment, sometimes extensively. When appropriate, we devise machines to supplement the human workouts. We also check convenience factors such as how easy any monitors are to use; comfort factors such as how much a treadmill vibrates; and safety factors such as the security of seat-adjustment pins.

Buying advice

To get an idea of the type of machine that's best for you, try some out. Health clubs typically have several.

Once you've settled on a type, try several models if you can. Be alert for things like loose parts, grating noises, and anything that causes discomfort, particularly in regard to how you fit on the machine. Inquire about return privileges in case you don't like it once it's home. If the machine can't be easily transported, make sure in-home service is available.

The more expensive machines, we've found, generally run more smoothly, have a greater range of speeds or motions, and can be expected to stand up to harder use than the cheaper ones. Very inexpensive machines typically suffer from shoddy workmanship, cheap materials, and poor design. But you can find poor design in machines at the high end as well, particularly in the form of overly complicated monitors.

Running & walking shoes

They're not called sneakers anymore. These days, if you're an athlete or just physically active, you buy special shoes suited (or so they say) to your activity. Good shoes can reduce the risk of injury from running or walking, a risk that is likely to increase the more you weigh and the more miles you cover.

The major athletic-shoe manufacturers like Nike and Reebok spend many millions on advertising. Those two companies account for about half of the athletic shoes sold in this country. Other brands you will encounter in the stores and on the road include names like *New Balance*, *Avia* and *Saucony*. Walking shoes are also made by "sensible shoe" companies such as *SAS*, *Rockport*, and *Dexter*.

Athletic shoes are sold by mail as well as in athletic footwear, sporting goods, and department stores; unless you're sure of your size and brand preference, buy at a store with knowledgeable salespeople and where you can try the shoes on.

The choices

Although walking is the main activity for which consumers say they buy athletic shoes, walking shoes rank third in sales, after basketball and cross-training shoes. Running shoes rank fifth.

Athletic shoes are priced from under $20 to $150 or so. The typical athletic shoe consists of a breathable upper; a toe box (the front of the upper) that's big enough so you can wiggle your toes; a heel counter and heel stabilizer to cup the heel and control lateral motion; a thin foam insole (a.k.a. sockliner) for some cushioning; a midsole that provides most of the cushioning and support; and an outsole, the bottom of the shoe, made of durable material with lugs, grooves, or a waffle pattern for traction.

Walking shoes are priced from under $20 to over $100. Many have a "rocker" profile, turned up slightly at the front and beveled at the heel. Running shoes sharply turn up at the front. Both types stress shock absorption in their design, while shoes for basketball, aerobics, and court sports also stress lateral support.

Features and conveniences

Comfort. A comfortable shoe has good arch support and adequate, but not overly spacious, toe room. It doesn't pinch or cause pain during or after exercise and is free of protrusions that can chafe the opposite leg. Its heel pad cushions, but doesn't restrict, the Achilles tendon.

Cushioning. The cumulative toll from thousands of footstrikes during a run can cause painful and disabling bone and joint injuries. Cushioning in a running shoe, especially the midsole, absorbs some of the shock. Walking causes less impact, but a walking shoe still needs cushioning. Manufacturers use a variety of midsole materials, including compressed gas, plastic foam, silicone gel, and rubber balls.

Flexibility. Proper walking or running form calls for the foot to land on the heel and roll forward, bending at the base of the toes as it pushes off. A shoe should be flexible enough to allow that bending to take place easily.

Stability. Many people's feet roll to the inside when they walk or run (called pronation); some roll to the outside (supination). Some shoes are designed to help control either tendency without clamping your foot like a boot.

Ventilation. Porous materials in the shoe's upper let sweat evaporate and reduce the chance of foot or shoe odor.

Other features. Reflective tabs make

you more visible to motorists at night. Some shoes have lacing systems that let you adjust shoe tightness more precisely. The weight of running or walking shoes can vary by several ounces; over a long run, the differences add up.

Buying advice

If you're buying athletic shoes just to wear to the supermarket, almost any brand will do. But serious athletes should be a little choosy. Find a store that has knowledgeable salespeople and sells a number of brands. (Friends who are runners or fitness walkers may be able to recommend a store.)

Use the following tips to help narrow the selection:

■ Find out if you're a pronator or supinator by looking for wear on your present shoes—when looked at from the back, a pronator's shoes will tilt to the the inside, a supinator's shoes will tilt to the outside. If the shoe doesn't tilt at all, you have a neutral running or walking style, and don't need shoes with special motion control. Ask the salesperson for a shoe that's right for your style.

■ Shop at the end of the day (when feet are their largest), and wear the socks you'll wear for workouts.

■ If your feet are different sizes, buy for the larger foot. Use an insert to fill any gaps in the other shoe.

■ Look for defects in workmanship such as a shoe that tilts to one side. Check to see if seams and layers of shoe material are poorly attached.

■ Run or walk a few steps and stop short to see if your feet slide inside the shoes, a sign that the shoes are too big. Check for adequate toe room by pushing down at your longest toe—there should be a thumbnail-sized space. Make sure the heel counter is snug around the back of your foot. Test the flexibility of the shoes by going up and down on your toes; the shoes should bend easily.

Bicycles

Walk into a bicycle store and you'll see a profusion of models across a broad range of types. All these types and variants of types reflect the specialization that has occurred in the past decade or so. More and more, manufacturers cater to several distinct classes of bike rider: recreational, fitness, commuter, racer, around-town, or off-road. Which bike is best for you depends on where and how you ride.

The choices

Bike prices range from about $100 for a discount-store clunker up to thousands for an elite model. Expect to pay $200 to $600 for a competent model. The world of bicycles can be divided into three main types:

Mountain bike. This is the most popular type sold in the U.S. With the help of fat, knobby tires, 26-inch-diameter wheels, flat handlebars, a sturdy frame, and, in some cases, a shock-absorbing suspension, the mountain bike moves competently over rough terrain but can feel a bit ungainly on pavement.

Road bike. This lightweight, thin-tired bike designed for racing or touring comes with "drop" handlebars. Fast and efficient, but not as comfortable as some people like, it doesn't ride as well on rough surfaces as other types. Although road bikes are the best choice if you ride fast or ride far, primarily on smooth pavement, they've declined in popularity.

Hybrid bike. Introduced in the late '80s and making great strides in popularity, this type uses a lightweight frame, flat handlebars, and moderately knobby tires to marry a mountain bike's strength and comfort with a road bike's efficiency. A hybrid is a good choice for commuters or those who travel a dirt road now and then.

Features and conveniences

Frame. The diamond-shaped chassis—the foundation of a bicycle—determines whether the bike will fit you. The frame is a major factor in the bike's weight and handling ability.

Frames are made from a variety of materials: heavy steel on the cheapest bikes; lightweight aluminum or carbon fiber, or exotic metals like titanium on the most expensive bikes. Frames for the typical $300-to-$600 model are chromium-molybdenum steel or lightweight aluminum. Chromoly mountain and hybrid bikes weigh about 30 pounds; a carbon-fiber road bike can weigh as little as 18 pounds. A frame's stiffness and geometry also affect a bike's performance.

Handlebars. Their size and shape influence riding efficiency and comfort. The bent-over posture required by road bikes, and to a lesser extent, by performance-oriented mountain bikes and hybrids, reduces wind resistance and shocks from bumps. That posture also lets muscles work more efficiently. But such benefits are unimportant for casual rides on pavement, where an upright position is likely to be preferred.

DON'T FORGET THE HELMET

Whether you ride your bike 30 miles a day or 30 miles a year, a helmet, adjusted for a snug fit, should be worn on every ride. For our last report (May 1991), we tested helmets in a cross-section of styles and sizes. Most of our high-rated helmets were no-shell models. They generally performed best in all our tests except those for penetration resistance.

For maximum protection, a snug fit is critical. Here's how to check:

Buy the smallest size that fits comfortably. Use the sizing pads (included with most helmets) to refine the fit. Put the helmet on, and try to push it to the sides, front, and back. If it moves enough to create a gap between your head and the pads, use thicker pads. If the helmet is still loose, get a smaller one that touches your head at the crown, sides, front, and back.

Adjust the straps. With the helmet level across your forehead just above your eyebrows, the front strap should be close to vertical. The back strap should lie straight, just below the ear, without any slack. Straps should meet just below the hinge of the jaw, in front of the ear.

Test the fit. With the chin strap buckled, the helmet shouldn't move when you shake your head or push from the sides, front, or back. If it does, use thicker pads or select a smaller helmet. The helmet shouldn't roll back or forward on your head when you push up on the front or back. If it does, tighten the straps. The chin strap should feel tight when you open your mouth.

Gears. These let you pedal comfortably despite changes in road slope. With three sprocket wheels in front and six to eight in the rear, most mountain bikes and hybrids have 18 to 24 speeds. Off-road, we consider 18 the minimum needed. On pavement, 12 or 14 speeds are usually enough.

Just as important as the number of gears are a bike's highest and lowest gear numbers. These numbers sum up the interaction between the front and rear gears, and the wheel size. For challenging off-road rides, the lowest should be 28 or less. A road bike for general use should have a low of 40 or less. High gears around 100 help speed you downhill on roads.

Shifters. These cause the derailleurs to move the drive chain from one sprocket wheel to another. Long a deterrent to would-be riders, old-fashioned "friction" shifters can be difficult to master until you develop a feel for them. "Indexed" shifters make changing gears far easier.

The most convenient indexed shifters are the "push-button" or "wishbone" type found on many mountain bikes and hybrids. One caveat for off-road riding: If these shifters are thrown out of alignment by a fall, they cannot revert to friction shifting. Above-the-bar levers offer indexing with a friction mode as backup. For rough riding, that type may be the wiser choice.

Brakes. Road bikes typically use caliper brakes, poised over the tire. Most mountain and hybrid bikes have cantilever brakes mounted directly on the front wheel fork and the seat or chain stay. According to our tests, both types are able to stop a bike quickly and controllably. If you ride in wet weather, avoid steel-rimmed wheels. In our wet-brake tests, they required a greater distance to stop than did wheels with aluminum rims.

Tires. A major factor in handling ability, they are easily changed to suit the terrain. For rough trails, they should be at least 1.9 inches wide, with very aggressive treads. Such tires produce a "buzzy" ride on pavement, though; smoother tires are better on paved roads.

Saddle. This won't affect performance much, but may limit how often or how long you ride. Look for one that's comfortable. Saddles are easy to change—don't let a poor saddle stop you from buying an otherwise good bike. Some manufacturers claim that seats filled with siliconelike "gel" reduce shock and vibration. But our testers—of both sexes—have found them no more comfortable than other types of bike seats.

Buying advice

Bicycle models and components change every year, but the basic characteristics of a good bike remain the same. Last year's model may prove a good buy with no compromise in performance or features.

Narrow the field by selecting among bikes with frames that fit the rider. To find the right size, the rider should straddle the crossbar with both feet flat on the floor. Allow 3 inches clearance between crossbar and crotch for mountain bikes, 2 inches for hybrids, and 1 inch for road bikes. We recommend that both men and women buy a bike with a crossbar if they intend to ride more than just casually.

Most of a bike's components can be easily changed by the dealer. Before buying, ride the bike over varying terrain to make sure you like how it handles; that your posture, the saddle, and the pedals feel comfortable; and that the brakes respond evenly, without grabbing, as you increase hand pressure on the brake levers.

STAIR CLIMBERS

RATINGS — STAIR CLIMBERS

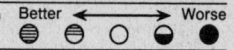

Legend: Better ← ⬤ ◕ ○ ◐ ● → Worse

▶ **See report, page 256.** From Consumer Reports, May 1992.

Recommendations: If a "stepper" climber is your preference, give first consideration to the *CSA E541*. Nearly as good was its brandmate the *CSA E512*, which we judged A Best Buy. To add an upper-body workout, we recommend the *Precor 730e* (or its successor). If you prefer a "ladder" climber, consider the *BMI/Helix SC8000*.

Ratings order: Listed by types; within types, listed in order of estimated quality based on ergonomics, performance, reliability, and safety. Closely ranked models are similar in quality. Price is the manufacturers' suggested retail. Ⓢ indicates tested model has been replaced by successor model; according to the manufacturer, the performance of new model should be similar to the tested model but features may vary. See right for new model number and suggested retail price, if available. Ⓓ indicates model discontinued.

STEPPERS

Brand and model	Price	Action [1]	Ergonomics	Rigidity, stability	Smoothness	Resistance adj.	Monitor's ease of use	Reliability	Safety	Advantages	Disadvantages	Comments
CSA E541	$400	S	⬤	⬤	⬤	⬤	⬤	⬤	○	C,D,E,F,J,L,N,O,R	z	N,Q,T,AA,JJ,MM,OO
Precor 730e Ⓢ	650	D	⬤	⬤	●	⬤	⬤	⬤	○	F,H	j	B,D,V,X,FF,GG,KK,LL
Precor 725e Ⓢ	625	S	⬤	⬤	○	◐	○	⬤	○	H,N	—	G,R,FF,GG,JJ,KK,PP
CSA E512, A Best Buy	160	S	○	○	⬤	●	⬤	⬤	⬤	A,F	k,p,r	H,X
Spirit 766UBC	395	S/D	○	⬤	⬤	◐	⬤	⬤	○	F,H,N	d,l,q,r,bb	A,B,E,G,T,Z,JJ,MM
Precor 718e Ⓢ	399	S	⬤	⬤	⬤	◐	⬤	○	○	A,G,H	s,w	G,V,X,FF,GG,KK,LL
Spirit 660	459	S	○	⬤	⬤	◐	⬤	⬤	○	A,H,N,O	g,q,r,v,bb	G,T,Z,JJ,MM,PP
Wynmor Wynstep 17-W690 Ⓓ	360	S	⬤	⬤	⬤	⬤	⬤	⬤	○	A,G,M,N,Q	b,cc	F,G,M,Q,JJ,KK,MM,OO
Tunturi C401 Ⓓ	219	S	○	⬤	⬤	⬤	○	○	○	D,H	a,q,x,dd	G,M,X,DD,JJ,KK,MM,NN
Quinton Cross Country Climber	549	D	○	○	○	○	○	⬤	○	D	f,r,z,cc	C,D,M,O,T,CC,EE,JJ,PP
Impex QS900SR Ⓓ	149	S	○	○	⬤	◐	○	○	○	H	r,w	H,X,FF
Impex SNT600 Ⓓ	199	D	○	⬤	◐	○	○	⬤	○	A,G,H	r,w	B,E,T,Z,BB,JJ,MM
Lifestyler (Sears Cat. No. 28552) Ⓓ	180	S	○	○	○	◐	⬤	○	○	E	b,q,t,w,z	H,M,R,S,U,Y,JJ,KK,MM,NN
BMI 4500 Ⓓ	129	S	◐	○	○	○	○	○	○	H	a,v,w	H,T,Z

STAIR CLIMBERS

Brand and model	Price	Action [1]	Ergonomics	Rigidity, stability	Smoothness	Resistance adj.	Monitor's ease of use	Reliability	Safety	Advantages	Disadvantages	Comments
Stamina Stepper 975 [D]	$94	S	○	○	◐	◐	○	●	○	H	b,o,w,y,bb	H,T,Z,GG,KK,MM
ProForm Airobic Trainer [D]	299	S	○	○	◐	◐	◐	●	○	A,D,I	b,g,cc	H,J,K,P,W,FF,II,NN,QQ
BMI 8660 [D]	199	D	○	○	◐	◐	◐	○	○	A,H,N	a,e,r,w,z,cc	B,D,T,Z,JJ,MM
DP Quantum 17-0629 [D]	222	S	◐	●	◐	◐	◐	○	○	E,G,M,Q	b,p,w,y,z,bb,cc	G,Q,FF,JJ,KK,MM,OO
Lifestyler 3000p (Sears Cat. No. 28502) [D]	230	S/D	○	○	◐	◐	○	○	○	J	j,n,q,t,w,y,z,cc	B,E,H,R,S,U,Y,JJ,KK,MM,NN
LADDERS												
BMI/Helix SC8000	229	S/D	○	◐	○	◐	◐	◐	○	A,B,G,J,N,O	a,c,g,i,n,r,u,v,aa,cc	B,E,H,I,X,HH,JJ,MM
Tunturi C614 [D]	699	S/D	◐	◐	○	◐	◐	◐	○	A,H,J,K,P	c,h,i,k,m,n,q,s,u,v,aa,cc	B,E,G,L,X,JJ,KK,MM,NN
Impex MC1000 [D]	225	D	◐	●	◐	○	○	○	◐	—	a,b,c,h,r,u,x,z,aa,cc	B,E,M,X,BB,HH,JJ,MM

[1] S = single-action; D = dual-action; S/D = single or dual action.

Successor Models (in Ratings order)
Precor 730e is succeeded by 731e, $500; Precor 725e by 721e, $475; Precor 718e by 715e, $325.

Features in Common
All: • Require assembly. • Can be tipped over backward during careless use. • Ladder-type climbers have movable arm pegs with two positions for users of different heights.
Except as noted, all: • Have dependent pedal motion (stepping down on one raises the other). • Have up/down timer. • Have counter that tracks steps taken. • Have lever-type pedals that pivot reasonably high on the support column. • Have variable resistance levels. • Use shock absorbers for resistance, adjustable by moving each absorber's mount backward or forward along its pedal lever. • Include electronic monitor. • Can be tipped to side during careless use. • Provide toll-free number for parts and service.
Except as noted, all monitors: • Use AA batteries. • Shut off automatically when not in use. • Scan through functions. • Beep at set tempo.

Key to Advantages
A–Less apt to tip to side than most.
B–Three hand-peg positions.
C–Handrail has forearm rests and adjusts for height and fore-and-aft positions.
D–Easier than most to assemble.
E–Wheels make model easier to move than most.
F–Quieter than most.
G–No room-light reflections on monitor.
H–Manual and/or markings on unit warn of danger to fingers from moving parts.
I–Resistance can be adjusted by preset program or manually without stopping exercise.
J–Resistance adjusted with single knob that controls both pedals; no need to stop exercise.
K–Pedal straps allow pulling as well as pushing.
L–Simulates exercise bicycle with optional seat.
M–Calorie counter more accurate than most.
N–Wide pedals; relatively comfortable.
O–Pedals stay horizontal through entire stroke.
P–Pedals can pivot to stay horizontal.
Q–Displays actual pulse; sounds alarm if pulse rises or sinks below preselected target range.
R–Displays actual pulse; sounds alarm if pulse exceeds preselected target level.

Ratings continued ▶

Key to Disadvantages

- a–No warnings in manual or on machine to keep children away.
- b–Low-pivoting pedals may slant foot uncomfortably and may pinch careless bystander.
- c–Open trolley track poses a pinching hazard.
- d–Moving handles can pinch user's fingers against stationary handlebar.
- e–Moving handles can injure bystander at pivot and shock-absorber mount.
- f–Beginners can lose balance when mounting.
- g–Irregular pedal action can cause discomfort to knees.
- h–Knees can bang into frame.
- i–Single-action handlebar too low.
- j–Arm levers can brush chest during deep step.
- k–Pedals smaller or narrower than most.
- l–Large diameter of single-action handlebar can make it uncomfortable to grasp.
- m–Room-light reflections can obscure the display.
- n–Resistance settings not indexed.
- o–Resistance settings tend to slip.
- p–Must unscrew knob under pedal and reposition shock absorber to change resistance.
- q–Cramped display or small markings make monitor hard to read.
- r–Beeps at each step; may be annoying.
- s–Actual step-per-minute rate can exceed capacity of display.
- t–No auto-off; monitor drains batteries if left on.
- u–Monitor is positioned too high or low for easy viewing.
- v–No toll-free telephone number for parts and service.
- w–Pedal cable or rope broke in reliability test.
- x–Shock absorbers leaked oil in reliability test.
- y–Replacing broken cable is difficult.
- z–Monitor may not count small steps.
- aa–Harder to move around than most.
- bb–Harder to assemble than most.
- cc–Noisier than most.

Key to Comments

- A–Available as single-action machine without electronic display (Model **766**).
- B–Arms can be used either actively or passively.
- C–Arms must be used actively.
- D–Step down with your right foot and the right arm lever moves away from you.
- E–Step down with your right foot and the right arm lever moves toward you.
- F–Can use with back against support, facing away from machine, but poor body position or low resistance makes workout ineffective.
- G–Has front rail or handlebar.
- H–Has side rails.
- I–Flywheel resistance.
- J–Fan resistance.
- K–Fan cools face, but may dry eyes.
- L–Drum-brake resistance.
- M–Resistance adjusted by dial on each shock absorber; stop workout to make adjustment.
- N–Hydraulic oil-transfer resistance.
- O–Monitor is optional.
- P–Electronic display and resistance adjustments need 120-volt AC; adaptor included.
- Q–Monitor measures pulse with ear clip.
- R–Monitor gives visible, not audible, cadence.
- S–Monitor displays all functions at same time.
- T–Pushing pedal turns monitor on.
- U–Monitor has graphic display of workout.
- V–Monitor cannot be turned off.
- W–Monitor shows total distance in miles and step rate in mph.
- X–No auto-shutoff on monitor, but LCD display uses little power.
- Y–Monitor uses 9-volt battery.
- Z–Monitor uses flat-cell batteries.
- AA–Folds, but folding mechanism tends to jam.
- BB–6-mo. warranty on shock absorbers.
- CC–5-yr. warranty on frame.
- DD–Sold as **C405** at Herman's sports stores.
- EE–Available with electronic monitor for $587.
- FF–Timer on monitor only counts up.
- GG–Monitor has step odometer.
- HH–Monitor counts total distance plus total steps.
- II–Monitor tracks total distance only.
- JJ–Beeps or flashes at a cadence you try to match.
- KK–Displays number of steps per minute.
- LL–Displays both average and maximum cadence for workout.
- MM–Calorie counter indicates calories burned so far.
- NN–Calorie counter estimates the number per minute you are burning.
- OO–Calorie counter also counts down to zero from a preset total.
- PP–Pedals move independently.
- QQ–Displays speed in mph.

HOME GYMS 265

RATINGS HOME GYMS

▶ **See report, page 245.** From Consumer Reports, November 1993.

Recommendations: The best overall, the *BMI 9700* and the *Marcy Apex Plus* ($499 and $699, respectively) were only good. The *Soloflex*, the most expensive gym, was merely fair.

Ratings order: Listed in order of overall score, based primarily on a gym's ergonomics (its ability to accommodate different body types) performing the eight exercises in our tests: leg extension, leg curl, chest (bench) press, butterfly, pulldown, shoulder press, triceps extension, biceps curl. Dimensions are height by weight by depth. Prices are manufacturer's retail for the basic gym. Resistance range is as specified by the manufacturer; the full range may not be available for all exercises. All gyms come unassembled. ⓓ indicates model discontinued.

BMI 9700, $499
Overall score: 56
Size: 85x58x90 in.
Resistance: Weight stack, 10-330 lb.
Changing set-up: Minimal change required—excellent for circuit training.
Summary: Very good for triceps extension and biceps curl; fair for leg curls; poor for shoulder press; good for all other exercises.
Comments: Very easy to change resistance, but resistance increments may be too large for some users on some exercises. Has vertical knee-raise station for abdominal workout and dips, and hand grip and leg strap for one-arm and one-leg exercises. During our severe durability tests, some pulleys broke. Assembling and moving were very difficult.

Marcy Apex Plus, $699
Overall score: 55
Size: 82x38x95 in.
Resistance: Weight stack, 10-200 lb.
Changing set-up: Minimal change required—excellent for circuit training.
Summary: Same ergonomic scores as the *BMI* except only fair for biceps curl.
Comments: Almost as user-friendly as the *BMI*, and like that gym, has hand grip and leg strap let you do one-arm and one-leg exercises. Very easy to change resistance, but resistance increments may be too large for some users on some exercises. Lacks the *BMI*'s option of vertical knee raises and dips. Emerged in very good condition from our durability test. Assembling and moving were very difficult.

ProForm Edge 3001, $399 ⓓ
Overall score: 49
Size: 82x58x66 in.
Resistance: Shock absorber, 30-250 lb.
Changing set-up: Some exercises require minor change; very good for circuit training.
Summary: Good ergonomics for chest press, butterfly, pull-down; very good for triceps extension; fair for leg extension; poor for leg curls, shoulder press, and biceps curl.
Comments: The *Edge* has an electronic monitor and control for changing resistance; this is the only tested gym that you plug in. You can change resistance easily without getting up. Minimum resistance may be too high for beginners. You can do abdominal crunches and back extensions on the *Edge*. Has an independent-action stair climber. Was in very good condition after durability test.

Weider Cross Trainer Master Gym, $374 ⓓ
Overall score: 48
Size: 80x43x87 in.
Resistance: Weight stack, 10-200 lb.
Changing set-up: Some exercises require minor changes; very good for circuit training.
Summary: Very good for triceps extension and biceps curl; good for pull-downs; poor for shoulder press; fair for other exercises.
Comments: Changing resistance is easy, but resistance increments may be too large for some users on some exercises. Hand grip and leg strap allow one-arm and one-leg exercises. The pull-down bar's cable is too short for all but short users to do shoulder press standing up. Has independent-action stair climber. Two bolts on the butterfly arms can dig into users' forearms. Durability test broke some pulleys. Difficult to move. Took

almost five hours to assemble—you may want to spend extra on in-home assembly.

Schwinn Bowflex Pro, $900
Overall score: 48
Size: 74x70x63 in.
Resistance: Flexible rods, 5-210 lb.
Changing set-up: Easy, but a bit slow; good for circuit training.
Summary: Good for upper body ergonomics except for pull-down, which was poor. Fair for all others.
Comments: Varying resistance is easy—you change the number or thickness of rods hooked to the machine's cables. But hold on while you're changing them—the rods can deliver a painful smack if you let go. Resistance increments were small enough for even weak beginners. Grips allow one-arm and one-leg exercises. A sliding seat (included) turns the *Schwinn* into a rowing machine. The *Schwinn*'s bench was the only one tested that was low enough for a proper, feet-on-the-floor chest press. Its cables let you move your arms or legs in whatever motion you want, but that freeform method can make for an unstable feeling in some exercises, especially the lat pull-down. Getting into and out of position for some exercises is difficult. Was in very good condition after our durability test.

Nordic Flex Gold, $999
Overall score: 46
Size: 75x49x75 in.
Resistance: Centrifugal brake, 0-450 lb.
Changing set-up: Awkward and slow. Poor for circuit training.
Summary: Very good ergonomics for pull-downs; good for butterfly and shoulder press; poor for chest press; fair for everything else.
Comments: Lacks scale to tell you how many pounds of resistance you're moving, though an accessory electronic power meter ($150, not tested) provides some indication of workout intensity. You can do dips, pull-ups, and Roman sit-ups on the *Flex Gold*. To change lever speed and resistance ranges, you re-route cables through different pulleys—if you can remember the right pattern. Changes in resistance levels within each range is continuous. The press arms move in a somewhat unnatural straight-up-and-down motion. The bench was wobbly, and the heavy butterfly arms could pinch fingers while being attached or removed. The durability test didn't change the performance.

Soloflex, $995 plus $200 for leg curl/extension attachment and $200 butterfly attachment
Overall score: 43
Size: 72x42x65 in.
Resistance: Rubber bands, 10-350 lb.
Changing set-up: Awkward and slow. Poor for circuit training.
Summary: Good for pull-down, butterfly, shoulder press; poor for chest press; the rest were fair.
Comments: It takes a limber body just to wiggle into position for the chest press, so tight is the space below the bar. The press bar moves in an arc motion that can push you off balance. The bench is wobbly without the optional leg exercise arm in place, an unexpected flaw in a machine so expensive. The heavy butterfly arms can swing around while you're attaching or removing them, trapping fingers. And the gym can tip forward if you attach only the leg exercise arm and sit at the end of the bench. (Attaching other accessories restores balance.) You can do dips, pull-ups, and Roman sit-ups. Resistance was easy to change, with small increments between resistance levels. Bands lost some elasticity during our durability test. Very quiet to use.

Trimax, $650 plus $325 for leg extension/curl setup and $250 for butterfly attachments
Overall score: 42
Size: 64x51x89 in.
Resistance: Hydraulic cylinders, 0-500 lb.
Changing set-up: Not difficult, but somewhat slow. Good for circuit training.
Summary: Good for leg extensions, chest press, pull-downs; the rest were fair.
Comments: When you move the cylinders' attachment point (not always easy), you change the resistance range and the speed at which you can operate the exercise levers. The resistance increments are continuous within each range. But the *Trimax* doesn't tell you how many pounds you're lifting. Pulse monitor (not tested) can indicate workout intensity. You do leg curls while sitting; it's more effective to do them lying down. Press arms move in an arc motion that can push you off balance. Applies resistance to muscle group in one direction. Cuts exercise time but may feel strange. Cams that connect the shocks to the butterfly arms can pinch an inattentive bystander. If you need to change height on the butterfly arms, you'll need a wrench. Our durability test wore out the cylinders.

▶ Yard & garden

Lawn mowers	268
String trimmers	270
Garden hoses	272
Lawn sprinklers	273
Insect repellents	274
Ratings	276

Homeowners who take on the chores of lawn and garden maintenance need a lot of equipment. The list starts with a lawn mower and includes hoses, sprinklers, and perhaps a timer to fit a watering schedule into a busy life. It includes an assortment of hand tools and perhaps various power tools, including a weed trimmer.

The lawn mower and maybe a string trimmer might be considered essential pieces of power equipment for anyone with a lawn. Other power tools probably won't see action more than once or twice a year for homeowners with less than a half acre of yard. Renting makes more sense for those items. It eliminates the need to store a bulky tiller or cultivator and a cuts down on maintenance chores such as changing spark plugs and oil and sharpening blades.

Whether you rent or buy, follow the tool's safety rules. They're typically printed at the front of the owner's manual. Electric tools shouldn't be used when conditions are wet. Disconnect the power before handling the blade. Gasoline-powered tools deserve special caution—they're capable of killing or severely injuring their operator or people in the vicinity. Fill the fuel tank carefully, after the engine has cooled. Don't handle the blade of a machine unless the engine is stopped and the ignition disabled. In general, don't operate any power tool with children or pets close by. Wear sturdy shoes, long pants and, when it's appropriate, ear and eye protection.

In many parts of the U.S., an effective insect repellent heads the list of products essential to working—or playing—in the yard. We tested herbal and deet repellents against mosquitos, stable flies and deer tick nymphs, the carriers of Lyme disease.

Lawn mowers

▶ **Ratings start on page 276.**   ▶ **Repair records on page 373.**

Some people with postage-stamp lawns use powerful lawn tractors to cut the grass. And a few hardy souls with vast expanses of green still doggedly perform the weekly mowing chore with a manual reel mower. But it makes more sense to buy a machine that matches the lawn.

The terrain and the landscape also affect the decision. A very hilly half-acre may need a different machine from one that's flat. A lawn dotted with trees and flower beds calls for a walk-behind mower of some type. Even the simplest, flattest lawn will need trimming with a walk-behind mower or string trimmer.

Lawn-mowing machines range from $100 you-push-it-yourself reel mowers to versatile 20-horsepower lawn tractors priced upward of $5000. Sears and Murray sell about half the lower-priced mowers. Other big names in the mower business—Toro, Lawn-Boy, Snapper, Ariens, Honda, John Deere—concentrate on the high end of the market.

More and more people are choosing a new lawn-mowing option—the mulching mower or mulching attachment. A mulcher chops clippings into small pieces and blows them down into the turf, hastening the return of nutrients to the soil and reducing the likelihood that the clippings will smother the grass. With no bags of clippings to empty, the mowing job becomes easier, but you may have to mow more frequently to avoid clipping too much grass. Some models that mulch can convert to bag-using or chute-using mowers or tractors.

Where rainfall is scarce, there is reason to decide against a lawn. You can use half as much water by choosing among less thirsty grasses and plants. For more information, contact your local Cooperative Extension or a local nursery or garden center.

Safety

The Consumer Product Safety Commission requires manufacturers to equip walk-behind mowers with a deadman control that stops the blade when you let go of a handle. Such requirements seem to have helped make mowing safer. Walk-behind mower-related injuries have dropped to about half what they were just ten years ago. Still, thousands of people receive treatment in hospital emergency rooms every year because of an injury caused by a lawn mower or lawn tractor. When you mow, follow these rules:

■ Mow only when and where it's safe. Don't mow when the grass is wet; your foot can slip under the mower. Push a mower across a slope, not up and down; if you have a riding mower or tractor, travel up and down, not across. If the slope is more than about 15 degrees, don't mow at all; the mower can get away from you or the ride-on could tip over. Consider planting a different groundcover.

■ Dress for the job. Wear sturdy shoes and close-fitting clothes.

■ Prepare the area. Pick up toys, hoses, rocks, and twigs. Banish anyone nearby, including pets—flying objects can be hurled from the mower.

■ Use gasoline carefully. Fill the mower's fuel tank before you start, while the engine is cold. Before you refill, wait for the engine to cool (unless you're using a riding model whose tank is located away from the engine).

■ Keep hands and feet away from moving parts.

LAWN MOWERS

- Don't defeat safety devices.
- Don't let young children use a mower or tractor.
- Don't let children ride a tractor.

The choices

Choose a type of mower according to the size and nature of your yard.

Manual reel mower. The original lawn mower has been brought up-to-date with lightweight alloys and plastic parts. A series of blades linked to the wheels slice the grass. For small lawns, up to about 5000 square feet, this is a quiet, no-pollution solution. But it's impractical for all but a small, level lawn. Price: $100 or less.

Electric mower. The electric versions of the power mower use an electric motor to spin the blade while you push. For lawns up to about one-quarter acre, a quiet, fairly low-cost solution. Look for models with a rear grass-catcher—they work better than models whose bags are side mounted.

The power cord does get in the way, and it limits the range. A device to guide the cord across the handle when you change mowing direction keeps the cord from tangling. A new variation does away with the cord—the battery-powered electric. A full charge can cut about ¼-acre.

The relatively low engine power makes electrics slower and less effective in tall grass than gasoline-powered mowers. Price: $120 to $300 for corded models; $350 to $500 for battery models.

Push-type power mower. The typical basic gasoline-powered mower is best suited for mowing flat lawns up to about one-half acre and trimming larger lawns. It has a one-cylinder, four-stroke, 3½-hp engine that spins a 20- to 22-inch blade. A few models use a two-stroke engine, which requires a gasoline/oil fuel mixture—and emits more pollutants.

Look for a deadman control that stops the blade but not the engine when you release the handle (called a blade-brake/clutch), rather than a control that stops both. A blade-brake/clutch is generally found on higher-priced models, but it's worth the cost. Some models come with oversized rear wheels for smoother rolling on rough terrain. Many mulching models are available. On convertible or regular models, a rear grass-catcher bag is easier to maneuver around trees than a side bag. A mower with a deck that extends outboard of its wheels has a better chance of trimming close to a wall or fence than one whose wheels stick out. Metal wheels should hold up better than plastic ones. A folding handle allows compact storage. Electric start eliminates tugging on a rope starter. Price: $100 to $600.

Self-propelled mower. These mowers use the same general design as push-type mowers, but the engine also powers the front or rear wheels. This type is much easier to use, especially on hilly lawns, than push-type power mowers. It's good for lawns about one-half acre.

Look for the same features mentioned for push-type mowers, plus variable drive speeds and a clutch that lets you "feather" the mower into gear rather than abruptly starting it. Price: $200 to $800.

Riding mower. These junior tractors suit lawns about one-half to one acre. They typically use an 8- to 10-horsepower engine to power the wheels and a 30-inch blade. They can hold a large grass-catcher, and most have an electric starter. Most offer a mulching conversion kit.

Look for one deadman control to stop the engine and/or blade if you dismount, another to stop the engine if you dismount with the mower in gear. Price: $1000 to more than $2000.

Tractor. For lawns one acre or larger, this is the homeowner's version of the farmer's workhorse. Small versions—called lawn tractors—typically use a 12- to 14-hp engine, mounted in the front, to power the wheels and a 38- to 45-inch cutting deck with two or three blades. Large versions—garden tractors—use a 16- to 20-hp engine. Mulching kits are often available, as are many other attachments, including such accessories as snow plow and thrower, cultivator, leaf vacuum, and cart.

Look for positive gear-shift detents or for a hydrostatic transmission, which permit continuously variable speed. Make sure there are deadman controls similar to those we recommend for riding mowers. Price: $900 to $4000 for lawn tractors, $2000 to $5000 for garden tractors.

The tests

CU tests mowers early each year, as soon as the new models become available. When grass at our New York headquarters is brown and dormant in winter, we test mowers at a college campus in Florida. We assess each model's adeptness at several tasks: cutting evenly, dispersing clippings without clumping, cutting tall grass, and getting the clippings into the grass-catcher bag. For mowers that mulch the clippings, we see how well they chop and disperse the grass.

We also look for designs that ease or hinder the chore and for anything that increases the risk of injury.

Reliability

The repair rate for most brands of mowers varied by type of mower, according to our readers. The more complex the mower, the higher the probability that it will need repair. Our readers report that about 11 percent of electric and push-type mowers purchased since 1988 needed repairs. On the other hand, self-propelled mowers and lawn tractors were repaired at nearly twice that rate during the same time period. See the chart on page 373.

Buying advice

Don't buy more mower than you need. Lawn mowers are heavily promoted in the spring, but the best prices are found after the Fourth of July. No matter when you buy, expect to pay more at a hardware store or specialty mower shop than at a home center, discount store, or catalog retail outlet. But smaller stores typically offer better service, more knowledgeable assistance, and a higher-quality line of mowers.

String trimmers

▶ Ratings on page 282.

The whine of power string trimmers is now part of the suburban weekend serenade. String trimmers, either electric- or gasoline-powered, trim what's beyond the mower's reach, effortlessly cleaning up tough weeds and tall grass. A trimmer works by spinning a plastic line fast enough to slice through leaf and stem but with too little inertia to hurt seriously a wayward foot. Still, a lashing from the whirling line can draw blood from bare skin, and the line can fling dirt and debris with considerable force. And gasoline trimmers typically generate around 100 decibels of noise, enough to warrant use of hearing protection. Wear long pants, sturdy shoes, and goggles.

The choices

Gasoline-powered. The heaviest, most powerful type cuts a swath 15 to 18 inches wide. These models weigh 9 to 15 pounds, enough to require two-handed operation.

STRING TRIMMERS

Price: $80 to more than $300.

Two-handled electric. Some trimmers cut as well as gasoline-powered models, although the need for an extension cord limits the range. They cut a swath 10 to 17 inches wide and weigh less than 10 pounds. Price: $35 to $80.

One-handled electric. For light trimming, these models cut a swath 8 to 10 inches wide and weigh about three pounds. Price: $35 or less.

Wheeled string trimmer. These gasoline-powered machines tackle areas of wood or plantings that are too large or rough for a power mower or that would require prolonged use of an ordinary trimmer. They cut a swath 17 to 18 inches. Price: $400 and up.

Battery-powered. These trimmers offer freedom from both an extension cord and gasoline. They run for about 20 minutes on a charge, typically with less power than plug-in electric trimmers. They cut a swath 6 to 9 inches and weigh 3 to 5 pounds. Price: $35 to more than $100.

Features and conveniences

Bump-feed string advancement. You tap or bump the trimmer head on the ground, and the line advances. A metal cutter on the head shears off any excess line. Not as common but even more convenient, is automatic line-advance.

Brush-cutter blade. A metal blade that can be substituted for the string to cut woody vines up to an inch thick.

Good engine/motor location. With larger trimmers—those weighing nine pounds or more—good balance is critical to ease of use. One of the best indicators of good balance is an engine or motor mounted high on the shaft, above the handle.

Shoulder strap. For heavier models, this is another way to improve balance. It also takes some load off arms.

Pivoting trimmer head. For edging with most models, you have to orient the unit so the line spins vertically. A pivoting head makes edging easier by letting you grip both handles in their regular position.

Translucent fuel tank. On gasoline-powered models, this makes the fuel level easy to check.

The tests

We allow tough grass, goldenrod, ragweed, timothy, and clover to take over our test lawn and then attack it with each trimmer. Larger models are also tried on mature weeds with stiff, seed-encrusted stalks and on wild-grape and morning-glory vines.

To simulate trimming by a wall, we line up rows of 4x4s and let the grass grow tall. For trimmers that seem capable of the chore, we use them for edging the grass along a sidewalk.

Throughout the testing, our engineers assess the trimmers' balance, handling, vibration, noise, and ease of feeding out plastic line and changing line spools. For gasoline-powered models, they also assess ease of starting and servicing.

Buying advice

If your property is large, or if you must tackle heavy growth, consider a gasoline-powered model. But if the tether of an extension cord isn't a problem, a two-handled electric model may make more sense. For trimming a small, well-tended plot, a one-handled electric or a battery-powered trimmer is fine.

Garden hoses
▶ Ratings on page 288.

Whatever you use a hose for—washing the car, filling the swimming pool, or watering the garden—you want one that is flexible, deploys without kinking, and that does not unduly restrict the flow of water. Manufacturers' labeling doesn't help much in this search. Their labels include "good," "better," and "best" designations that have no universally accepted meaning. They tout impressive bursting strengths, although just about any hose can handle normal water pressure without bursting. Some promise lifetime guarantees. Are they superior to models whose makers warrant their product for only a year or two, or not at all? How many people actually make use of a hose warranty, anyway?

The choices

Garden hoses range in price from $3 to $160. They come in varying lengths and diameters. Fifty feet is by far the most common length, and ⅝-inch is the most common diameter. That diameter is a good all-round choice. Half-inch hoses, either in 50- or 100-foot lengths, are suitable for most sprinklers and nozzles. But they may constrict water flow if hooked up in more than two 50-foot lengths. Three-quarter-inch hoses let you reach beyond 150 feet or supply lots of water fast.

Features and conveniences

Materials. Hoses are made of four basic materials, none inherently better than the others. Vinyl is the most common; often low-priced, it can be harder to coil in cool weather than hoses made of other materials. Rubber hoses have a reputation for quality, but we found little reason in our tests to justify their generally higher price. Rubber/vinyl, also common, is designed to look and feel like rubber. They are likely to handle better than all-vinyl hoses and

---

HOSE ACCESSORIES

Water timers
Timers screw onto the faucet. They can be mechanical or electronic. Either type will turn the water off after a set length of time. Most electronic timers can also select the day and the hour to start the watering. In general, the more scheduling options a timer offers, the harder it is to program and the higher the price. We think most people would be adequately served by a $15 mechanical model; electronic timers are priced between $30 and $90.

Quick-connect couplings
A quick-connect hose coupling makes it easier to connect a hose to a faucet or a sprinkler to a hose. That saves trips back to the faucet and simplifies changing nozzles and hook up to a sprinkler. It attaches to the threaded fittings at both ends of the hose and to the faucet and the hose accessories. In our tests, metal couplings ($4 to $7 a pair) attached and detached more easily, withstood more abuse, and restricted water flow less than plastic ones ($2 to $4).

cost less than all-rubber ones. Nylon hoses are rare these days.

Reinforcement. Except for the cheapest models, all hoses are reinforced. One or more layers of nylon or rayon fabric is sandwiched between the vinyl or rubber layers. The fabric may be knit, wrapped in a spiral or dual-spiral pattern, or a combination of knit and spiral. We found no benefit to the type of fabric—any kind of reinforcement helps strengthen the hose and makes it easier to use.

Faucet fittings. An octagonal hose-end fitting, or a fitting with a plastic collar, either winged or round, is easier to attach to and remove from the faucet than a plain round knurled fitting.

The tests

To test for bursting strength, we warm the hoses to simulate a day of lying in the sun, clamp off one end, and then run the pressure up. We test resistance to pulling by clamping a 150-pound weight at one end of a short length of hose and attaching the other end to a faucet fitting. All those that don't tear are then subjected to a second burst-strength test to see if the pulling has weakened them. We also coil the hoses under varying temperatures and check their tendency to kink in use.

Buying advice

The ⅝-inch size offers the widest selection of lengths. The best values are reinforced models made of vinyl. The easiest to use are reinforced vinyl/rubber models. Buy a half-inch hose only for short faucet-to-sprinkler reaches, and a ¾-inch hose only if you need more than 150 feet.

As with much yard and garden equipment, you'll find the best prices off season.

Lawn sprinklers
▶ Ratings on page 285.

Sprinklers come in various forms suitable for different shaped lawns and gardens. Prices typically range from $4 to $40.

The choices

There are five basic types: stationary, impulse, rotary, traveling, and oscillating sprinklers. Each has its uses.

Stationary. These are probably the most well known and least expensive type. They come in a variety of shapes: spots, rings, salt shakers, and turrets. Price: $2 to $5.

Impulse. This is the most versatile type. They cover a very wide area, or, with an adjustment, a small area. A spring-loaded flapper deflects the stream of water and turns the sprinkler's nozzle a few degrees each time it flaps. A set of stops lets you water a whole circle or an arc as narrow as 30 degrees. Other controls let you reduce the upward angle of the stream or break the stream into a spray; both reduce the diameter of the coverage. Price: $4 to $35.

Rotary. These sprinklers whirl like a pinwheel, with two or three nozzles spreading a circular spray over a smaller area than impulse models. Some rotary sprinklers let you adjust the angle of the nozzle arms or the type of spray to reduce the area covered; others have a fanlike deflector that makes the water cover a square pattern. Price: $5 to $25.

Traveling. A mobile version of the rotary sprinkler. This type lets you tailor the coverage to your lawn's shape to some extent. Most have a spray arm linked by gears to tractor-type wheels; as the nozzles whirl around, the tractor base slowly drives along, using the hose as its guide. Price: $65 to $125.

Oscillating. On this type, a curved tube with holes or tiny nozzles slowly moves back and forth, watering a rectangular pattern about the same size as that covered by rotary models. All models let you make the rectangle shorter; some also let you make it narrower. Price: $10 to $40.

Features and conveniences

Easy adjustments. To avoid watering the house or driveway, look for a sprinkler that makes it easy to adjust the pattern size and shape. Avoid impulse models whose deflectors have to be adjusted directly by hand (you get splashed). Also inconvenient are rotary models whose pair of nozzles lack labels to assist in setting them at the same angle.

Quick-connect couplings. Some models come with quick-connect hose couplings that snap rather than screw the sprinkler onto the hose (see the box on page 272).

Bases. Some sprinklers are mounted on a sled base, while others are mounted on a spike. A spike may be more convenient than a sled base on uneven ground or in the garden. But keep in mind that a spike may be difficult to push into hard, dry soil.

Other accessories. Some sprinklers include a timer or a rain gauge to help you know when you've watered enough.

The tests

To measure size and evenness of coverage, we set up 299 laboratory cylinders over a 36-by-66-foot grid and pump water at standard household pressure through a 50-foot, $5/8$-inch hose. We run each sprinkler for a set time, and then measure the water in each cylinder. We also note how easy each sprinkler is to adjust.

Buying advice

Choose a model that's right for your lawn. An impulse model covers the largest area—typically, a 70-foot-diameter circle—but slowly. It might take 10 to 14 hours to put down an inch of water over that space. For a smaller lawn, a rotary or oscillating model will do the job in two to five hours. If your lawn has an irregular shape, look for a model with pattern adjustments.

Insect repellents

An effective insect repellent can discourage mosquitos and flies from landing on treated skin or clothing. To do that, most bug repellents use N, N-diethyl-meta-toluamide, a chemical nicknamed "deet." First synthesized in the 1950s, deet has emerged as the most effective active ingredient to repel a wide variety of crawling and flying insect pests. And some makers of repellents claim that deet also protects against ticks. But deet has its drawbacks, as explained at right.

The big brands in the repellent market are *Off!*, *Deep Woods Off!* and *Cutter*, all deet-based products. Their sales account for 85 percent of insect repellents sold.

Competing with deet are several herbal products. The most widely used active ingredient in herbal products is citronella. Others include pennyroyal, clove, bay, balsam, and peppermint oil.

Other considerations

Amount of deet. Deet concentration for most repellents ranges from below 10 to 40 percent, but some products have higher deet levels—as much as 95 or 100 percent. Lately, concern over deet's safety has prompted the introduction of, or renewed interest in, low- and non-deet products, some marketed for children. Combination sunscreen-repellents may contain deet or other active ingredients. A few products claim to use a "controlled release" technology that slows deet's evaporation. Avon's *Skin-So-Soft* bath oil does not claim to be an insect repellent, but many people swear it keeps mosquitoes away.

Form. Repellents come in aerosol and pump sprays, lotions, creams, and waxy sticks. Aerosols are easy to apply but wasteful. Lotions and creams are easier to control, but can be messy.

The tests

Repellents are tested on real arms, with real pests—two species of mosquitos and stable flies. And due to the concern over Lyme disease, we also test the repellents on deer-tick nymphs.

Buying advice

For the most part, our tests showed that products with the highest deet concentrations lasted the longest against mosquitos and stable flies. But because excessive use of deet can pose some risk, such products should be used sparingly. Products with only 20 to 25 percent deet performed adequately in our tests; they might be a better choice, especially for children.

"Natural" products and products without deet, including *Skin-So-Soft*, provided little or no protection against mosquitoes. All of the tested products provided adequate protection from the flies.

No deet repellent was fully protective against deer tick nymphs. Tests by the U.S. Army and the U.S. Department of Agriculture showed permethrin, which you apply to clothing, to be safe and effective.

THE DOWNSIDE OF DEET

Deet is a powerful chemical that's readily absorbed into the bloodstream. Most people use it without incident, but there have been a few cases when its use resulted in seizures or even death. Employees of Everglades National Park have reported episodes of confusion, irritability, and insomnia after repeated and prolonged use of deet. A more common side effect is a rash in people with sensitive skin.

Here's how to minimize exposure:

■ Use a low-deet product and apply it sparingly. Apply more as necessary.

■ Don't apply repellent near eyes, on lips, or on broken skin. (To apply a spray to your face, spray your palm, then spread the repellent carefully.)

■ Avoid breathing a repellent spray. Don't use it near food.

■ Once it's not needed, wash repellent off with soap and water.

■ On children, use a product containing less than 20 percent deet, and keep it out of their reach. Don't apply it to a young child's hands, which often wind up in the mouth.

■ Treat your clothes instead of your skin. Note that deet can damage spandex, rayon, and acetate, as well as the plastic in sunglasses and vinyl car seats.

You can also use other, nonchemical precautions: Tuck pants cuffs into boots or socks; stay to the center of hiking paths, away from high grass; and inspect yourself after leaving an infested area.

276 LAWN TRACTORS & RIDING MOWERS

RATINGS — LAWN TRACTORS & RIDING MOWERS

E ⊖ VG ⊖ G ○ F ◐ P ●

▶ **See report, page 268.** From Consumer Reports, June 1993.

Recommendations: The *Honda H4013SA*, the top-rated tractor, has almost everything going for it except its price—$3150. Two tractors priced at about $1700—the *Lawn-Boy 81180* and the *Toro/Wheel Horse 71180*—faltered when cutting tall grass but otherwise did everything just about as well as the *Honda*. (The *Honda* and the *Toro/Wheel Horse* have been discontinued but may still be available.) Also worth considering are two hydrostatic-drive tractors, the *White* ($1399) and the *MTD* ($879). Among riding mowers, we recommend the *John Deere* and the *Honda*, both priced about $1800.

Ratings order: Listed by types; within types, listed in order of estimated quality. Except where separated by bold rules, closely ranked models differed little in quality. Bracketed models are essentially equal in quality and are listed alphabetically. Price is the manufacturer's suggested retail price for the mower, the grass-catcher kit, and the mulching conversion kit. Incl. means accessory is included in the price of the basic machine. ⑤ indicates tested model has been replaced by successor model; according to the manufacturer, the performance of new model should be similar to the tested model but features may vary. See right for new model number and suggested retail price, if available. ⑩ indicates model discontinued.

TRACTORS WITH GEAR DRIVE

Brand and model	Mower	Catcher kit	Mulching kit	Safety	Clippings dispersal	Tall grass	Vacuuming	Capacity of catcher	Mulching dispersal	Handling	Advantages	Disadvantages	Comments
Honda H4013SA ⑩	$3150	$350	$62 ①	⊖	◐	⊖	⊖	⊖	—	⊖	A,E,H,I,L,P	u,v,y	B,J
Simplicity Broadmoor 12.5G ⑩	2950	360	110	⊖	⊖	⊖	⊖	⊖	○	⊖	B,G,J,O,Q	h,p,s,t	B,J
John Deere STX38 ⑤	2349	309	69	⊖	⊖	⊖	⊖	○	○	⊖	A,H,J,O,R,S	e,n,u,y	B,J
Lawn-Boy 81180	1699	269	Incl	⊖	⊖	◐	⊖	⊖	⊖	⊖	C,F,H,I,K,M,N,O,Q,S	d,e,g,h,p,r	F,J
Toro/Wheel Horse 71180 ⑩	1699	269	Incl	⊖	⊖	◐	⊖	⊖	⊖	⊖	C,F,H,I,K,L,M,N,O,Q,S	d,e,g,h,p,r	F,J
MTD I660F	879	199	89	⊖	◐	⊖	⊖	○	○	○	A,C,I,N	b,d,e,l,m	E
White LT12 ⑩	1399	239	89	⊖	○	⊖	⊖	○	○	⊖	A,C,H,I	b,d,e,m	E
Cub Cadet 1225 ⑩	2299	299	119	◐	◐	⊖	⊖	⊖	⊖	○	C,J,K,N,O,R,S	a,d,l	E
Murray 40707	899	159	30	⊖	○	⊖	○	○	○	◐	A,H,I,M,R	c,d,i,r,v,x	D,F
Troy-Bilt 13025	2099	302	300	◐	○	◐	○	⊖	○	○	C,J,O,R,S	a,d,e,g,i,q,s,t	B,G,I

LAWN TRACTORS & RIDING MOWERS

Brand and model	Mower (Price)	Catcher kit	Mulching kit	Safety	Clippings dispersal (Free discharge)	Tall grass	Vacuuming	Capacity of catcher	Mulching dispersal	Handling	Advantages	Disadvantages	Comments
Lawn Chief 440	$1099	$199	$79	◉	○	○	◉	◓	◉	○	M,N	a,c,d,e,g,k,m,v	F

NOT ACCEPTABLE
■ *The following tractors with gear drive can easily be kicked into gear and drive away when operator dismounts.*

Brand and model													
Dynamark D3912070 [D]	838	199	40	●	○	○	◉	◉	○	○	M	c,d,g,k,o,q,v	F
Murray 38702	868	159	30	●	○	◉	◉	◉	○	◓	A,H,M,Q,R	c,d,i,j,o,r,v,x	D,F
Sears Craftsman 25511	1000	230	60 [1]	●	◉	◉	◉	◉	○	—	A,H,N,O,R	c,d,i,j,o,r,v,x	B,D,F,H,K

TRACTORS WITH HYDROSTATIC DRIVE

Cub Cadet 1330 [D]	2999	299	119	◉	◓	◉	◉	◉	◉	○	C,J,K,N,O,R,S	l,w	B,E,J
Simplicity Broadmoor 12.5H	3450	360	110	◉	◉	◉	◉	◉	○	○	B,G,J,O,Q	h,j,p,s,t	A,B,J
White LT125 [D]	1799	239	89	◉	◉	◉	◉	◉	◉	○	C,H	—	E
MTD I600F	1099	199	89	◉	◓	◉	◉	◉	◉	◉	C,N	e	E
Bolens 13024 [D]	2799	302	300	◉	◉	○	◉	○	◉	◉	C,J,O,S	e,g,i,j,q,s,t,v,w	B,G,I

REAR-ENGINE RIDING MOWERS

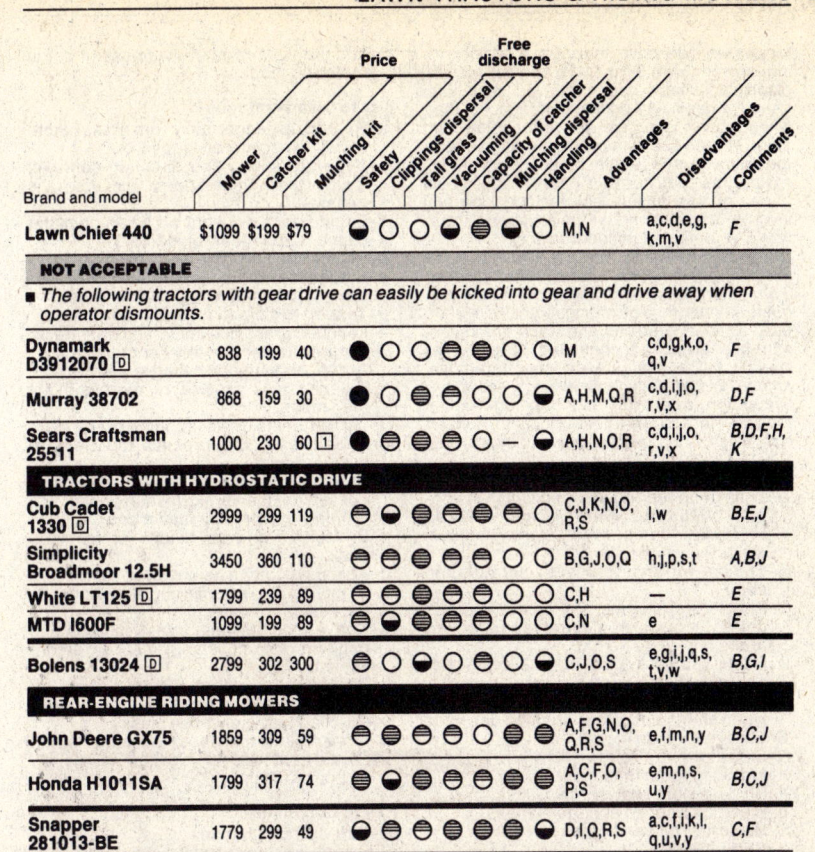

John Deere GX75	1859	309	59	◉	◉	◉	◉	◉	○	◉	A,F,G,N,O,Q,R,S	e,f,m,n,y	B,C,J
Honda H1011SA	1799	317	74	◉	◓	◉	◉	◉	◉	◉	A,C,F,O,P,S	e,m,n,s,u,y	B,C,J
Snapper 281013-BE	1779	299	49	◓	◉	◉	◉	◉	○	◉	D,I,Q,R,S	a,c,f,i,k,l,q,u,v,y	C,F
Murray 30550	727	159	30	◉	○	○	○	◉	◉	◉	A,M,R,S	c,d,e,g,i,m,o,r,u,v	C,D,F,J

[1] *Mulching kit not available in time to be tested.*

Successor Model
John Deere STX38 is succeeded by STX38, $1999.

Performance
Except as noted, all: • Were judged good in evenness of cut in free-discharge mode, with catcher, and in mulching mode. • Were judged excellent or very good at vacuuming with catcher in place.

Features in Common
All have: • Cutting swath of 36-40 in. (tractors) or 28-30 in. (riding mowers). • Side-discharge mower deck with deflector for grass chute. • Electric starter. • Interlock to prevent engine from starting when blades are engaged. • Interlock that stops blades if operator dismounts. • 5 to 7 speeds, with lowest speed between 1 and 1½ mph and highest speed between 4½ and 6 mph (hydrostatic-drive models have continuously variable speed controls). • Adjustable seat. • Dimensions of about: 4x7½ ft. (tractors), 3½x7 ft. (riding mowers); 2 ft. less in length without catcher. *Except as noted, all have:* • 12- to 13-hp,

Ratings continued ▶

1-cylinder, side-valve, four-stroke engine (riding mowers have 9- to 11-hp engine). • Twin-blade, adjustable-height mower deck with gauge wheels. • Additional interlocks that, when mower is in gear, prevent engine from being started and shut off engine when operator dismounts. • Single brake/clutch pedal. • Opt. grass catcher with 2 cloth bags. • Fuel gauge or translucent tank for checking fuel level. • Headlights. • 2-yr. parts-labor warranty. • 5-yr. or more ignition warranty.
Except as noted, all: • Were relatively noisy (94 to 97 decibels). • Blades stopped less than 3 sec. after operator dismounted. • Had adequately smooth clutch engagement. • Were easy to steer on turns and track on course. • Brakes produced controlled stops at all speeds. • Grass bags were easy to remove, empty, and replace. • Converted easily between free-discharge and bagging without tools. • Were somewhat difficult to convert from free-discharge or bagging to mulching.

Key to Advantages
A–Little or no rearing up when clutch is popped (**Murray, Sears,** and **Honda H1011SA** come with front counterweight).
B–Engine won't start unless operator is in seat.
C–Engine stops when operator dismounts unless mower in neutral and parking brake on.
D–Blade stopped less than 2 sec. after operator dismounted.
E–Alarm warns that parking brake is on when shifting into gear (ignition on).
F–Less noisy than most.
G–Small turning circle (under 4 ft.).
H–More leg room than most.
I–Shifting more precise than most.
J–Electric switch to engage blades.
K–Blade-height easier than most.
L–Comfortable seat.
M–Conversion to mulching less difficult than most. Not even blade change required for **Toro/Wheel Horse** and **Lawn-Boy** tractors.
N–Easy fueling.
O–Oil draining convenient.
P–Very smooth clutch engagement.
Q–Judged very good in evenness of cut in free-discharge mode.
R–Judged very good in evenness of cut with catcher in place.
S–Judged very good in evenness of cut in mulching mode.

Key to Disadvantages
a–Reared up dangerously with grass catcher full, especially on slopes.
b–Separate speed and direction controls; inadvertent high-speed reverse is possible.
c–Engine does not shut off when operator dismounts (in gear, blades off).
d–Engine can be started while in gear.
e–Blades took more than 3 sec. to stop.
f–Less stable than most in uphill turns.
g–Tended to clog during tall-grass test.
h–Mulched grass accumulated under deck.
i–Abrupt clutching or drive engagement.
j–Abrupt braking at mowing speed.
k–Steering less precise or more difficult than most.
l–Large turning circle (about 6 to 7 ft.).
m–Too little leg room, clutch too close to seat, or both.
n–Separate brake and clutch pedals, less convenient than brake/clutch pedal.
o–Shifting less precise than most.
p–Difficult to engage blades or to move deck.
q–Adjusting cutting height inconvenient.
r–Emptying or installing grass bags or buckets inconvenient.
s–Conversion between free-discharge and bagging or to mulching relatively inconvenient.
t–Fueling inconvenient with catcher on.
u–Lacks fuel-level indication.
v–Oil-changing likely to be messy.
w–More difficult than most to push by hand.
x–Clutch hard to reach for short people.
y–Lacks headlights.

Key to Comments
A–Two-cylinder engine.
B–Engine has overhead valves.
C–Single-blade deck.
D–Plastic grass-catcher buckets.
E–Won't cut in reverse, safer but less convenient.
F–No gauge wheels on deck.
G–3-yr. warranty.
1–1-yr. warranty.
I–3-yr. ignition warranty.
J–2-yr. ignition warranty.
K–1-yr. ignition warranty.

SELF-PROPELLED MOWERS 279

RATINGS SELF-PROPELLED MOWERS

E VG G F P

▶ **See report, page 268.** From Consumer Reports, June 1992.

Recommendations: If your lawn is big enough or hilly enough to warrant buying a self-propelled mower, we recommend a model with a blade-brake/clutch safety system. You can't go wrong with any of the 11 such models tested. Our first choice is a rear-bagger, the *Lawn-Boy M21BMR*, or its successor the *10591*.

Ratings order: Listed by types; within types, listed in order of estimated quality. Bracketed models, judged about equal, are listed alphabetically. Unless separated by a bold rule, closely ranked models differed little in quality. The price is the manufacturer's suggested retail price for the mower equipped with the attachments to bag, disperse, or mulch clippings. ⓢ indicates tested model has been replaced by successor model; according to the manufacturer, the performance of new model should be similar to the tested model, but features may vary. See page 281 for new model number and suggested retail price, if available. ⓓ indicates model discontinued.

REAR-BAGGING MODELS WITH BLADE-BRAKE/CLUTCH

Brand and model	Price	Evenness	Vacuuming	Bag capacity	Evenness (chute)	Dispersal	Mulch dispersal	Handling	Convenience	Speeds	Advantages	Disadvantages	Comments
Lawn-Boy M21BMR ⓢ	$800	E	E	E	E	E	E	E	E	3	B,D,E,F,I,K,N,O,Q,U,V	n,q	A,F,G
Honda HR215HXA	815	E	E	E	E	G	G	E	E	9	A,D,I,K,L,N,O,U,V	ee	C,F,G,K,O
John Deere 14SB	709	E	E	E	E	G	G	VG	E	5	A,E,F,I,L,N,O,R,S,T,U,V	e,s	F,G,K,O
Ariens LM21SB 911047 ⓓ	719	E	E	E	E	VG	G	G	E	Inf	D,I,K,L,N,U,V	a,f,dd,ii	D,E,H
Honda HR215SXA	758	E	E	E	E	G	G	G	E	3	A,I,K,L,N,O,U,V	e,q,ee	F,G,K,O
Kubota W5021SC	749	E	E	E	G	E	E	E	E	2	A,F,I,J,L,M,N,O,T,V	e,t,dd,gg	F,G,K,O
Lawn-Boy S21BST ⓓ	699	E	E	G	E	E	E	E	G	1	D,E,F,I,T	h,m	A,F,H,I,M
Toro GTS Recycler 20107	599	E	G	G	E	F	E	G	E	3	E,I,L,M,O,T,U	d,t,dd,ii	E,F,G,I
Snapper P21508B ⓢ	595	G	E	E	G	G	F	E	G	6	A,B,D,F,J,K,L,O,U,V	r,dd	E,H,O
Yard-Man 122898 ⓢ	538	G	G	E	E	G	—	E	G	6	D,F,I,L,N	m,v,x,aa,bb,dd,ii	H
Homelite HSB21P5C/ UT-30149 ⓓ	532	E	E	E	E	F	—	G	G	2	F,I,O	q,s,t,bb,dd,gg	E,F,G

Ratings continued ▶

SELF-PROPELLED MOWERS

▶ *Ratings continued*

Brand and model	Price	Evenness	Vacuuming	Bag capacity (With catcher) Evenness	Dispersal	Mulch dispersal	Handling (With chute)	Convenience	Speeds	Advantages	Disadvantages	Comments
REAR-BAGGING MODELS WITH ENGINE-KILL											
Husqvarna R53S2 [S]	$690	◕	◕	◕	—	—	—	○	○	Inf	D,E,J,K,N,P,T,U,V	j,m,n,u	A,F,G
Toro 20216	$499	◕	◕	○	◕	◔	—	○	○	3	E,L,M,O,U,V	d,t	E,F,G
Cub Cadet 848E	599	◕	○	◕	◕	◕	◔	◕	○	6	C,D,F,N,P,V	j,m,r,aa,bb,ii	E,H,M,O
Snapper P21509B [S]	574	○	○	◕	◕	○	○	◕	○	6	A,B,D,F,J,K,L,O,U,V	r,y	E,H,O
White 848R Lawncycler [D]	459	○	◕	◕	◕	◕	◕	◕	○	6	D,F,N,P	j,m,aa,bb,ii	E,H,O,M
Dynamark C2105-500 [D]	375	◕	◕	◔	—	—	◕	○	○	5	E,M,N,O,P	a,k,l,u,v,aa,gg	E,G,L,O
Homelite HSD20P/UT-30152 [D]	467	◕	◕	○	◕	○	○	◕	◔	1	A,E,F,H,V	o,p,y,ff	E,F,H,M,N,O
Noma Signature Series C2105-520	439	◕	◕	◔	—	—	◕	○	○	5	E,M,N,O,P,T	a,k,l,u,v,aa,gg	E,G,K,L,O
Murray 21711 [S]	288	◕	○	◕	◕	◔	—	○	◔	1	E,N,O,P,V	i,m,n,bb	D,E,G,L
Wheeler WRRBQSP-21 [D]	386	○	◕	◕	◕	◕	◕	◕	◔	1	A,D,O	l,u,w,aa,hh	G,L,M
Rally BP410 [D]	309	◕	◕	○	—	—	—	●	◔	1	N,O,P	f,g,h,k,l,p,u,bb	D,E,G,N
Garden Pride 101-9221 [S]	299	◕	●	◔	—	—	—	●	◔	1	—	c,d,h,i,j,k,r,u,w,aa	B,E,G
SIDE-BAGGING MODELS WITH ENGINE-KILL											
Lawn-Boy L21ZSM [D]	535	◕	◔	○	◕	◕	◕	○	◔	1	A,D,E,F,G,T	h,m,y,ff	A,I,M
Toro 16401	399	○	◕	◔	◕	○	—	○	○	1	F,L,V	e,i,k,bb,ff	B,E,F,I
Murray 22751 [S]	209	○	○	●	◕	◕	◕	◕	◔	1	E,H,M,O	g,h,i,aa,cc	D,E,I,J,L,N
Lawn Chief 35	279	○	○	●	◕	◕	◕	◕	◔	1	E,F,H,N,O,V	i,k,o,aa,cc	B,D,E,I,J,L
Dynamark C2204-500 [D]	330	◕	○	○	◕	◔	—	●	◔	1	—	g,h,i,k,u	B,E,I,L,N
Garden Pride 78-9222 [D]	308	◕	◕	○	◕	◕	◕	●	◔	1	A,H,M,O	d,i,k,r,aa	B,D,E,I,M
Wheeler WRSP-22 [D]	250	○	○	●	◕	◕	—	◕	◔	1	E,H,O	b,d,i,k,o,r,w,aa,cc	B,D,E,I,J,L,N
Sears Craftsman 37817 [D]	312	○	◕	◔	◕	○	◕	●	◔	1	E,G,O,T	d,h,i,k,o,q,r,w,y,z,bb	B,D,E,I,M,N,O

SELF-PROPELLED MOWERS 281

Successor Models (in Ratings order)
Lawn-Boy M21BMR is succeeded by 10591, $699; Snapper P21508B by PB21500V, $725; Yard-Man 122898 by 124-848L401, $399; Husqvarna R53S2 by R53S, $600; Snapper P21509B by P21500, $579; Murray 21711 by 21775, $269; Garden Pride 101-9221 by 101-9421, $300; Murray 22751 by 22755, $199.

Performance Notes
Except as noted: • Catcher convenience was good to excellent. • Changing modes was good to excellent. • Mulching evenness was very good. • Tall-grass performance was fair or poor.

Features in Common
Except as noted, all have: • Belt- or chain-driven transmission with differential or ratchet mechanism for easier turning. • 4-stroke, 3½- to 5½-hp. engine. • Rear-wheel drive. • Pull starter. • 21-in. cutting swath. • Steel deck. • Convenient way to fold handle and adjust its height. • Fuel- and oil-filler ports at or near top of engine. • Paper-element air filter that requires tools to change. • Fuel shutoff valve.
Except as noted, all side-bagging models: • Are at least 40 in. wide with bag.

Key to Advantages
A–Relatively few clippings collected under deck in mulching test.
B–Interlock prevents use without catcher, chute, or mulching plug or cover.
C–Electric start, with pull starter as backup.
D–Clutch easy to operate and could be engaged gradually.
E–U turns easier than most.
F–Easier to maneuver than most.
G–Narrower than most side-baggers; mower with bag only 24 to 30 in. wide.
H–Easier to push and pull than most.
I–Easier or more convenient than most to start.
J–Comfortable handle.
K–Relatively easy to shift.
L–Easy to change cutting height.
M–Not as noisy as most.
N–Catcher easy to remove and install.
O–Catcher easy to empty.
P–Single control adjusts height of all 4 wheels.
Q–Mixes oil and gasoline automatically; has oil/fuel sight-gauges at rear of engine housing; engine shuts off if oil too low.
R–Fuel sight-gauge on side of engine housing.
S–Very easy to drain engine oil.
T–No tools needed to service air filter.
U–Speed range relatively wide.
V–Tall-grass performance judged excellent or very good.

Key to Disadvantages
a–Clippings accumulated under deck in mulching test.
b–Clogged discharge chute in regular cutting.
c–Left clippings in clumps in regular cutting.
d–Drive engagement coupled with safety bail; inconvenient to operate; can't engage gradually except on **Toro 20107** and **20216.**
e–Drive engagement was abrupt.
f–U turns more difficult than with most.
g–Difficult to maneuver.
h–Hard to jockey from side to side.
i–Weak traction.
j–Catcher difficult to empty.
k–Did not track precisely in straight line.
l–Harder than most to push and pull.
m–Much harder to pull than most.
n–Front end felt light when catcher full.
o–Uncomfortable handle.
p–Handle vibrated more than most.
q–Slightly noisier than most.
r–Starter cord hard to pull or requires stooping.
s–Deadman control hard to actuate.
t–Inconvenient to change speeds.
u–Detent in throttle/choke control not precise.
v–Throttle lever judged flimsy.
w–Catcher difficult to remove and install.
y–Chute points at user when catcher off.
z–Exhaust blows up at user.
aa–Handle height not adjustable.
bb–Inconvenient to adjust or fold handle.
cc–Fueling and adding oil not convenient.
dd–Mower must be tipped to drain oil.
ee–Changing oil relatively messy.
ff–Catcher has inconvenient zipper closure.
gg–Speed range relatively narrow.
hh–Catcher convenience judged fair.
ii–Changing modes judged fair or poor.

Key to Comments
A–2-stroke engine.
B–Front-wheel drive.
C–Hydrostatic drive.
D–Fuel-primer bulb instead of choke.
E–No fuel shutoff valve.
F–Cast-aluminum deck. (Cast magnesium for **Lawn-Boy M21**; plastic, **Husqvarna.**)
G–Rear-discharge, rear-bagging deck.
H–Side-discharge, rear-bagging deck.
I–Side-discharge, side-bagging deck.
J–Oil-impregnated foam air filter.
K–Combination foam and paper air filter.
L–Starter cord mounts on left or right.
M–Mulching evenness was judged good.
N–22-in. swath (20 in. for **Homelite**).
O–Blade change required for mulching.

282 STRING TRIMMERS

RATINGS — STRING TRIMMERS

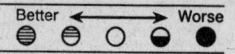

Better ⊕ ⊖ ○ ◐ ● Worse

▶ **See report, page 270.** From Consumer Reports, June 1992.

Recommendations: Choose any of the top six gasoline-powered models to tackle large property or heavy growth. If an extension cord is practical to reach your cutting tasks, consider the top two-handled electric models, the *IDC 120* and the *Homelite ST-70*. For very modest tasks, consider a one-handled electric like the *Toro 51230*.

Ratings order: Listed by types; within types, listed in order of estimated quality. Closely ranked models differed little in quality. The price is the manufacturer's suggested retail price for the trimmer and for a replacement spool of string; there may be an additional shipping charge. ⑤ indicates tested model has been replaced by successor model; according to the manufacturer, the performance of new model should be similar to the tested model but features may vary. See right for new model number and suggested retail price, if available. ⑩ indicates model discontinued.

Brand and model	Price (trimmer/string)	Cutting ability	Trimming next to wall	Edging	Balance	Handling	Vibration	Noise	Operating convenience	Advantages	Disadvantages	Comments
GASOLINE-POWERED MODELS												
Stihl FS-36	$140/$5	⊖	⊖	⊖	○	⊖	⊖	◐	◐	E,H,I	g,j,p,s	H
Echo GT-1100	150/8	◐	⊖	⊖	⊖	⊖	○	◐	◐	A,E,L,R	j,p	B,F,H,J
Sears Craftsman Weedwacker 79715	170/6	⊖	⊖	⊖	⊖	⊖	⊖	◐	⊖	G,H,I,J,N,S	—	D
Husqvarna 26LC	149/7	⊕	⊖	⊖	⊖	⊖	○	◐	○	G,H,I,N	r	D,H
Ryan 274 ⑤	89/4	⊕	⊖	⊖	⊖	⊖	○	◐	◐	A,F,I	p,t,w	—
Weed Eater XT 50	149/8	⊖	⊖	⊖	⊖	⊖	●	●	⊖	G,H,I,J,N	—	—
Sears Craftsman Weedwacker 79712 ⑩	130/6	⊖	⊖	⊖	⊖	⊖	●	◐	○	G,H,I,N,S	e	—
IDC 540 ⑤	109/4	⊖	⊖	—	⊖	○	⊖	◐	◐	B,H,K	h,j,p,t	G
Ryan 284	110/4	⊖	⊖	—	⊖	○	⊖	◐	◐	B,H,K	h,j,p,t,w	G
Homelite ST-185	160/7	⊖	●	⊖	●	⊖	⊖	◐	◐	B,C,H,M,O,P,Q,R	d,j,u	G,J
Poulan Pro 114	139/7	⊖	⊖	⊖	⊖	⊖	●	●	○	G,H,I,N	—	—
RedMax BT17	150/6	○	⊖	○	⊖	⊖	⊖	◐	○	I,O,P,Q	g,j,k,s,x	H,J
Weed Eater GTI 18 w/Blade	149/8	⊖	⊖	—	○	⊖	○	◐	○	B,H,J,N,O	c,f,h,j,q	C,G
IDC 500 ⑤	85/4	○	⊖	○	⊖	⊖	○	○	◐	—	a,p,t	—
Sears Craftsman Weedwacker 79710 ⑩	100/6	○	⊖	○	⊖	○	○	◐	○	E,I,N,S	a,i	—

STRING TRIMMERS 283

Brand and model	Price (trimmer/string)	Cutting ability	Trimming next to wall	Edging	Balance	Handling	Vibration	Noise	Operating convenience	Advantages	Disadvantages	Comments
Homelite ST-155	$110/$8	○	○	○	◓	◓	○	◐	○	M,P,Q,R	a,k,u	J
Poulan Pro 111	119/7	○	○	◓	◓	○	○	◐	○	E,I,N	a,i	—
Weed Eater GTI 15T	89/7	○	○	—	○	◓	○	◐	○	N,O	a,c,h,l,m,o,q	C
TWO-HANDLED ELECTRIC MODELS												
IDC 120 [S]	55/4	◓	◓	◓	◓	◓	◓	○	◓	D,E,F	—	—
Homelite ST-70 [D]	60/7	○	◓	◓	◓	◓	◓	●	○	D,E,J	k,u	A,I,J
Toro 51325	40/6	○	○	◓	◓	◓	◓	○	◓	G,H,	b,x	J
Weed Eater 1216	59/7	○	◓	◓	◓	◓	◓	◓	○	E,F	d,k,m	—
John Deere 72E	84/6	○	◓	◓	◓	◓	◓	◓	○	E,F	d,k	—
The Green Machine 1500/II [D]	80/7	◓	◓	—	◓	◓	○	○	○	—	d,e,h,k,v	—
Weed Eater 1212	39/5	◓	○	○	◓	◓	◓	○	○	—	b,k	—
ONE-HANDLED ELECTRIC MODELS												
Black & Decker 82300 [D]	30/7	◐	◐	—	○	○	◓	◓	○	—	b,h,	—
Toro 51230	25/5	●	◐	—	○	◓	◓	◓	◓	—	b,h,x	E,I,J
Weed Eater 1208	24/5	●	◐	—	○	◓	◓	◓	—	—	b,h	—
Sears Craftsman Weedwacker 79901	25/4	◐	◐	—	○	◓	◓	◓	—	—	b,h,x	—
Homelite ST-10 [D]	26/6	●	◐	—	◓	◓	◓	○	◓	J	b,h	I,J

Successor Models (in Ratings order)
Ryan 274 is succeeded by Ryobi 720R, $99; IDC 540 by Ryobi 740R, $149; IDC 500 by Ryobi 700R, $89; IDC 120 by Ryobi 130R, $59.

Performance Notes
Except as noted: • User comfort was good to excellent. • Spools were adequately easy to change.

Features in Common
Except as noted, all have: • Single string. • "Bump-feed" string advancement. • Curved shaft. • Assist handle that can be adjusted without tools. • Replaceable string. • 1-yr. warranty.
All gasoline models: • Have 2-stroke engine. • Weigh from 9 to 15 lb.
Except as noted, all gasoline-powered models have: • Engine mounted on upper end of shaft behind main handle. • Centrifugal clutch that lets the string coast to stop when throttle is released. • Air filter that requires tools to be removed. • Opaque fuel tank mounted on top or side of engine. • Shoulder strap available.
All electric models: • Weigh from 3 to 9 lb.
Except as noted, all electric models have: • Motor mounted low on shaft, just above cutting head. • Extension-cord retainer.

Key to Advantages
A—Compared with others, cut through heavy growth better than regular growth.
B—Comes with brush-cutter blades, judged effective (but least so with **Weed Eater GTI 18**).
C—Available with optional brush-cutting saw blade, $13, judged exceptionally effective.
D—Motor at top of shaft behind main handle; position enhances maneuverability.
E—Head shifted less than most in edging.
F—Trimmer head can be rotated to facilitate edging with handles in normal position.
G—Assist handle easier to adjust than most.
H—Assist handle more comfortable than most.

Ratings continued ▶

STRING TRIMMERS

I–Main handle more comfortable than most.
J–Fully automatic string-feeding.
K–Shoulder strap more comfortable and easier to adjust than on most others requiring one.
L–Air filter can be removed without tools.
M–Starter-cord handle larger and more comfortable than most.
N–Choke lever especially easy to operate.
O–Ignition-kill switch especially easy to reach.
P–Screws that adjust fuel mixture well exposed for easy access.
Q–Translucent fuel tank; easy to fill and check.
R–Fuel-tank filler opening located below engine, so fuel less likely to spill on engine than with others having top or side filler openings.
S–Retainer on fuel-tank cap.

Key to Disadvantages

a–No clutch. String spins continuously; judged an inconvenience and a possible safety shortcoming.
b–Judged too weak or otherwise unsuitable for trimming heavy growth.
c–Maneuverability and balance worsened when unit was raised or tilted.
d–Balance worsened considerably when unit was raised or tilted.
e–String broke fairly often in heavy growth.
f–User comfort judged fair.
g–Judged awkward for short people to use.
h–Not suitable for edging. No edging instructions provided. Mfr. of **The Green Machine 1500** specifically recommends against edging.
i–Edging required more stooping than with most.
j–Adjusting assist handle more difficult than with most.
k–Adjusting assist handle more irritating than with most; sharp-edged sheet-metal wing nuts tended to dig into fingers.
l–Assist handle can't be fully tightened.
m–Assist handle less comfortable than most.
n–Main handle less comfortable than most.
o–Weaker than other gasoline-powered models when cutting heavy growth.
p–Starter-cord handle uncomfortable.
q–Starter cord awkward to pull with right hand.
r–Ignition switch confusing to use.
s–Choke control less convenient than most.
t–Cover must be removed in order to reach screws that adjust fuel mixture.
u–Throttle trigger (or On/off switch on **Homelite ST-70**) tended to pinch user's finger.
v–On/off switch inconvenient.
w–Ignition-kill switch less convenient than most.
x–Tools required to change spool. On **Red-Max BT17**, additional line must be purchased in bulk ($13 for 400 ft.) and wound on spool by hand.

Key to Comments

A–Straight shaft; may help when trimming under shrubs and the like.
B–Optional cutting head with plastic blades ($14) judged ineffective in brush.
C–Vibration-isolation mounting for engine.
D–Vibration-isolation mounting for assist handle.
E–Assist handle molded with main handle, but unit is most comfortably used with one hand.
F–No carburetor-mixture adjustment.
G–Comes with shoulder strap.
H–No shoulder strap available.
I–No extension-cord retainer.
J–2-yr. warranty.

WHAT THE RATINGS MEAN

■ The Ratings typically rank products in order of estimated quality, without regard to price.

■ A product's rating applies only to the model tested and should not be considered a rating of other models sold under the same brand name unless so noted.

■ Models are check-rated (✓) when the product proved to be significantly superior to other models tested.

■ Products high in quality and relatively low in price are deemed Best Buys.

RATINGS — LAWN SPRINKLERS

Better ⬤ ⊖ ○ ⊖ ● Worse

▶ See report, page 273. From Consumer Reports, May 1993.

Recommendations: For an impulse sprinkler, choose from any of the models in the top half of the Ratings. Among rotary sprinklers, we recommend the *Nelson N-65*, $26, the *Melnor 876*, $16, the *Thompson 700*, $25. For an oscillating sprinkler, look to the eight models with the higher scores for Evenness of coverage.

Ratings order: Listed by types; within types, listed in order of estimated quality based mainly on evenness, speed of watering, and area covered. Closely ranked models differed little in quality. Models judged equal in quality are bracketed and listed alphabetically. Price is the manufacturer's suggested retail price. **Notes to table:** Coverage expressed as a single figure is the diameter of the circle irrigated; for traveling models, the width of the swath the sprinkler covers; two figures show the length and width of covered area.

Brand and model	Price	Coverage	Evenness	Speed	Versatility	Advantages	Disadvantages	Comments
IMPULSE SPRINKLERS								
Rain Bird WB-5 Pulsing Waters Rolling	$27	70 ft.	⊖	●	⊖	B	—	G
Rain Bird Timing Waters DD5	34	63	⊖	⊖	⊖	A,B	—	C,D
Melnor 9536C	28	70	⊖	⊖	⊖	G	—	C,E,F
Nelson 1172	16	70	⊖	●	⊖	—	a,c	C,I
Sun Mate 58017	4	70	⊖	⊖	⊖	—	a,c	C,F
Gilmour 967	28	75	⊖	●	⊖	—	a,c	C,E
Nelson 1162	10	70	⊖	●	⊖	—	a,c,k	C,F,I
Gilmour Pulsating 993NS-C	10	63	⊖	⊖	⊖	—	a,k	C,F
Sears Craftsman 79216	7	63	⊖	⊖	⊖	—	a,k	C,F
Sears Craftsman 79179 Pulsator	25	66	⊖	⊖	○	—	c,d,m	E,H
Thompson S505E	30	66	⊖	⊖	○	—	c,d,m	E,F,H
Gilmour 996S Pattern Master	31	70	○	●	⊖	A,C	a,c,k	C,F
Sears Programmable 79022	23	70	○	●	⊖	A,C	a,c	C
Gardena 6751	20	66	⊖	●	⊖	B,F	m	C,F
Gardena 6752	23	66	⊖	●	⊖	B,F	m	C
Green Thumb 157 677	10	64	⊖	⊖	○	—	a,c,d,m	C
Melnor Time-A-Matic 114	30	70	○	●	⊖	A	b,c	C,D
Gardena 6740	26	66	○	●	⊖	B,F	—	C,E,F
Nelson Rainpulse 90 1230	33	70	○	●	⊖	—	a,c	E

Ratings continued ▶

LAWN SPRINKLERS

▶ *Ratings continued*

Brand and model	Price	Coverage	Evenness	Speed	Versatility	Advantages	Disadvantages	Comments
Rain Bird Pulsing Waters PS-125	$38	70 ft.	○	●	⊖	—	a,c	C,E
ROTARY SPRINKLERS								
Nelson Metal Rainswirl N-65	26	50	⊖	○	⊖	D	a	E,G
Melnor 876	16	39	⊖	⊖	⊖	D	b,c	G
Thompson Aqua Dial 700	25	40	⊖	⊖	○	B	f	E
Gilmour 883	5	40	⊖	⊖	●	—	a,i	—
Rain Bird RO-345	8	36	⊖	⊖	●	—	a,i	—
Gardena 1955	9	45	⊖	⊖	●	F	i	—
Gilmour 884	19	32x32	⊖	⊖	◐	—	a,f	G
Melnor 368	7	30	⊖	⊖	●	—	a,i	—
Nelson Rainswirl 1945	8	21	⊖	⊖	●	—	a,i	—
Nelson Metal Rainswirl N-54	17	22x22	⊖	⊖	●	—	a,i	E,G
Sears Craftsman Revolving 79027	7	30	○	⊖	○	D	—	—
Thompson 433	12	24x24	○	⊖	●	—	a,f,i	C,E
Rain Bird RO-35-S Whirling Waters	14	18x18	◐	⊖	●	—	a,f,i	E
TRAVELING SPRINKLERS								
Melnor Travel-matic 2503	122	45	⊖	—	⊖	—	b,c	—
Sears Craftsman Traveling 79054	65	48	⊖	—	○	—	c	E
Thompson 605S	100	48	⊖	—	○	—	c	E
Nelson Metal Rain Train 200S 1865	107	57	○	—	○	—	—	E
OSCILLATING SPRINKLERS								
Nelson Rainshower N-055A	57	39x33	⊖	⊖	⊖	B	—	E
Nelson 1038	20	39x33	⊖	⊖	⊖	D	c	—
Green Thumb 531715	12	39x33	⊖	⊖	⊖	—	c	—
Gardena 1974	40	39x30	⊖	⊖	⊖	B,D,F	g	—
Gardena Polo 6991	14	39x27	⊖	⊖	⊖	B,F	e,g	—
Nelson Rainshower 1015	9	39x24	⊖	⊖	⊖	—	c,d	—
Sears Craftsman 79033	11	36x27	⊖	⊖	○	B	h	—
Sun Mate 58133	5	39x27	○	⊖	⊖	—	—	—
Sears Craftsman 79037	20	36x33	⊖	⊖	⊖	B	j	—
Rain Bird Dancing Waters RB-95	20	39x30	○	⊖	⊖	—	—	A

LAWN SPRINKLERS

Brand and model	Price	Coverage	Evenness	Speed	Versatility	Advantages	Disadvantages	Comments
Gilmour 8826	$9	33x27	○	◐	◐	—	—	—
Gilmour Pattern Master 8800	31	33x33	◐	◐	●	E	—	—
Sears Craftsman 79038	23	33x33	◐	◐	◐	E	—	—
Melnor 032	20	39x27	◐	◐	◐	—	b,c	B
Melnor Time-A-Matic 128	27	45x27	◐	◐	◐	—	b,c	D
Melnor 026	10	45x24	●	◐	◐	—	b,c	B
Rain Bird Impulsilator IO-28	20	45x33	●	◐	◐	B	j,l	A

Features in Common

Except as noted, all: • Have mostly plastic parts. • Have sledlike base. • Have free-spinning hose connector. • Impulse models have deflector that adjusts stream height and distance. • Rotary and traveling models have adjustable spray pattern; don't leave puddles around sprinkler. • Oscillating models have 4 basic patterns (left, right, narrow center, full), with extra detents between. • Have jet-cleaning pin on cleanout plug; plug is easily removed.

All impulse models: • Can cover full or partial circle. • Have diffuser screw to break up the water stream. • Tended to leave puddle near sprinkler.

All oscillating models: • Put more water at ends of spray pattern than in middle.

Key to Advantages

A–Evenness improved when set for back-and-forth motion.
B–Pattern adjustment easier than most.
C–Pattern shape somewhat adjustable.
D–Some nozzle holes can be plugged to change width of watering pattern.
E–Changing tube curvature alters pattern width.
F–Comes with quick-connect hose couplings.
G–Foot tab on spike base makes it easier to stick sprinkler in ground.

Key to Disadvantages

a–Hose connector not free-spinning.
b–Hose connector has sharp edges and can slip when wet.
c–Adjustable parts difficult to operate.
d–Lacks stream deflector.
e–Off-center pattern.
f–Tended to puddle, unlike most rotaries.
g–Removing cleanout plug requires tool.
h–Can't be set for narrow-center pattern.
i–Pattern not adjustable.
j–Broke in drop test.
k–Plastic spike may break in hard ground.
l–Stopped working after moderate drop in water pressure.
m–Evenness deteriorated when set for back-and-forth motion.

Key to Comments

A–Spray emerges in waves of different heights.
B–Rain gauge on housing; judged inaccurate.
C–Pass-through connector for adding another sprinkler in series.
D–Built-in mechanical timer.
E–Mostly metal operating parts.
F–Spike base.
G–Base has wheels; no practical use.
H–Can be adjusted for especially high or low water pressure; requires tools.
I–Separate rain gauge; judged accurate.

GARDEN HOSES

RATINGS GARDEN HOSES

Better ← → Worse
● ◐ ○ ◑ ●

▶ **See report, page 272.** From Consumer Reports, May 1993.

Recommendations: For 5/8-inch hoses, consider any of the models in the top half of the Ratings. For 1/2-inch hoses, look first to the *Gilmour Flexogen 10-12050*, $20; the *Teknor Apex Basic 7500*, $7; and the *Colorite WaterWorks WW1012*, $10. For 3/4-inch hoses, all the tested models are worth considering.

Ratings order: Listed by sizes; within sizes, listed in order of estimated quality. Closely ranked models differed little in quality. Models judged equal in quality are bracketed and listed alphabetically. Price is the mfr.'s suggested retail price. A * indicates the price CU paid. **Notes to table:** Weight is to the nearest pound. Material: **V** = vinyl; **R/V** = rubber/vinyl; **R** = rubber; and **N** = nylon. Reinforcement: **k** = knitted cords; **ds** = dual spiral; **sk** = combination of spiral and knit. ⓓ indicates model discontinued.

Brand and model	Price	Weight, lb.	Material	Reinforcement	Strength	Pulling damage [1]	Strength after pulling [2]	Coiling	Kinking	Comments
5/8-INCH HOSES										
Teknor Apex Ultra Flexible 8509	$17	8	V	k	●	●	●	●	●	K,T
Gilmour 23-58050	22	7	R/V	sk	●	●	●	●	●	F,I,L,T,V
Gilmour Flexogen 10-58050	29	8	V	sk	●	●	●	●	●	F,K,O,T
Teknor Apex Sure Flow 8585 ⓓ	20	11	R/V	k	●	●	●	●	●	J,K,M,S,T
Swan Soft & Supple SS5850	22	9	R/V	sk	●	○	●	●	●	K,O,T
Sears Best Craftsman 69210	22	9	R/V	sk	●	●	●	●	●	K,N,P,T
Radiator Speciality LTD Gold Cup	35	9	R/V	sk	●	○	●	●	●	B,K,N,O,W
Green Thumb Super Flex 224311	24	9	V	k	●	○	●	●	●	F,K,Q,T
Coast to Coast 485-1317	22	8	R/V	sk	●	◐	●	●	●	A,K,O,T
Colorite WaterWorks WW4558	18	6	V	k	●	○	●	●	●	B,K,O,S,T,V
Sears Best Craftsman 69202	18	11	R	ds	●	●	●	●	◑	A,K,P
Sears Craftsman 69282 ⓓ	27*	12	R	ds	●	●	●	●	●	A,K,U
Sears Craftsman 69022	8	6	V	k	●	●	●	●	●	B,P
Swan Permaflow PF5850	22	9	R/V	sk	●	○	●	●	●	J,K,M,N,T
Radiator Speciality Zero King 2657-50	23	6	V	k	●	◐	○	●	●	N,W
Servistar SSRO2064	20	9	R/V	ds	●	○	○	○	●	B,I,K,M,O,S,T,V
Radiator Speciality Trim-Lawn 1657-50	17	6	N	k	○	○	●	●	●	N,W
Sears Craftsman 69052	10	6	V	sk	●	●	●	○	●	C,L,P,X

GARDEN HOSES

Ratings are based primarily on performance tests. Symbols (left to right): ○ better, ◐, ⊖, ◑, ● worse.

Brand and model	Price	Weight, lb.	Material	Reinforcement	Strength	Pulling damage [1]	Strength after pulling [2]	Coiling	Kinking	Comments
Teknor Apex Basic 8500	$10	6	V	k	○	○	⊖	⊖	⊖	E
Colorite WaterWorks WW6958	25	8	R/V	ds	⊖	●	—	⊖	⊖	B,F,I,K, M,O,S,T
Swan Fairlawn FA 5850	9	6	V	k	○	⊖	⊖	⊖	⊖	B
Swan Weather Master WM5850	15	6	V	sk	⊖	◐	⊖	○	⊖	L,T,V
Ace 75400	22	9	R/V	ds	⊖	○	⊖	⊖	⊖	I,K,M, O,S,T,V
Teknor Apex 8650	25	10	R	ds	⊖	○	⊖	⊖	●	K,U
Swan Premium PM5850	25	9	R	ds	⊖	●	⊖	⊖	⊖	A,K,N,O,V
Gilmour Reinforced 19-58050 D	43*	10	R	ds	⊖	●	⊖	⊖	⊖	A,N,U,V
Colorite WaterWorks WW9058	25	11	R	ds	⊖	●	—	⊖	⊖	B,D,O,V
Colorite WaterWorks WW1058	10	6	V	k	○	⊖	⊖	○	○	B,D,O,V
Gilmour Greenlawn 15-58050	14	5	V	k	○	●	—	○	⊖	C,V
Moisture Master Multi-Purpose 21050	19*	8	R	ds	⊖	●	—	⊖	⊖	A,I,K,P, R,U
½-INCH HOSES										
Gilmour Flexogen 10-12050	20	5	V	sk	⊖	◐	⊖	⊖	⊖	—
Teknor Apex Basic 7500	7	4	V	k	⊖	◐	●	⊖	⊖	O,X
Radiator Speciality Zero King 2557-50	17	4	V	k	⊖	●	—	⊖	⊖	L,W,X
Colorite WaterWorks WW1012	10	4	V	k	○	⊖	⊖	⊖	⊖	O
Moisture Master Multi-Purpose 22050	16*	7	R	ds	⊖	●	—	⊖	⊖	A,K,P,R,U
Sears 69002	6	5	V	k	⊖	◐	⊖	⊖	⊖	G,P,V
Swan Medallion ME1250	7	4	V	ds	⊖	○	○	⊖	●	V
Servess 140392	5	4	V	—	○	◐	⊖	◑	○	B,H,V
Teknor Apex 7565	5	4	V	—	⊖	●	—	◑	⊖	B,H,V
¾-INCH HOSES										
Swan Soft & Supple SS3450	30	11	R/V	sk	⊖	⊖	⊖	⊖	⊖	A,K,O,T
Gilmour Flexogen 10-34050	42	9	V	sk	⊖	⊖	⊖	⊖	⊖	K,O
Swan Weather Master WM3450	19	9	V	sk	⊖	⊖	⊖	⊖	⊖	L,T,V
Colorite WaterWorks WW4534	26	9	V	k	⊖	⊖	⊖	⊖	⊖	I,K,O,S,T,V
Radiator Speciality Zero King 2757-50	39	8	V	k	○	⊖	⊖	⊖	⊖	A,L,W
Sears Craftsman 69284 D	33*	17	R	ds	⊖	⊖	⊖	⊖	●	K,U
Colorite WaterWorks WW6934	34	12	R/V	ds	⊖	●	—	⊖	○	A,F,I,K, M,O,S,T

[1] We applied a 150-lb. force at a right angle to the hose fitting to simulate a hard yank.
[2] After pulling test, we increased water pressure until hoses failed.

Ratings continued ▶

GARDEN HOSES

Features in Common
All: • Deliver enough water at the end of 50-ft. length to operate spray nozzle or sprinkler, assuming dynamic flow pressure of at least 25 psi at faucet.
Except as noted, all: • Have knurled brass fittings that discolored but did not corrode in our weathering tests. • Use flat washer to seal faucet fitting. • With dynamic flow pressure of 15 psi at faucet: 1/2-in. models had flow rate between 5 and 6 gal. per min. (gpm); 5/8-in. models, between 8 and 9 gpm; 3/4-in. models, between 15 and 17 1/2 gpm. • Fittings were damaged when run over by car. • Have clearly stated warranty ranging from 2 yr. to lifetime.

Key to Comments
A–Easier than most to coil at 40°F.
B–Harder than most to coil at 40°.
C–Virtually impossible to coil at 40°.
D–Less likely to kink at 40° than shown by score.
E–More likely to kink at 40° than shown by score.
F–More likely to kink at 95° than shown by score.
G–Deformed in kinking test at 95°.
H–Made of unreinforced vinyl; hose may be more likely to burst in time.
I–Flow rate somewhat lower than most of same diameter.
J–Fittings virtually undamaged when run over by car.
K–Octagonal faucet fitting; easier to thread and unthread on faucet.
L–Has collar over faucet fitting; much easier to thread and unthread on faucet.
M–Ribs or grooves inside hose permit water to flow even when hose is kinked.
N–Flow rate about 10 gpm.
O–O-ring instead of flat washer; washer suitable for replacement.
P–Nickel-plated fittings; did not discolor in weathering test.
Q–60-ft. length.
R–Mfr. claims hose made of 100-percent recycled rubber.
S–Mfr. claims hose material makes it safe to drink water (not tested).
T–Plastic sleeve at faucet fitting.
U–Mfr. claims hose can be used for hot water (not tested).
V–Warranty period not clearly specified.
W–No warranty.
X–Significant loss of burst strength after weathering test.

HOW TO USE THE RATINGS

■ Read the **article** for general guidance about types and buying advice.

■ Read **Recommendations** for brand-name advice based on our tests.

■ Read the **Ratings order** to see whether products are listed in order of quality, by price, or alphabetically. Most Ratings are based on estimated quality, without regard to price.

■ Look to the **Ratings table** for specifics on the performance and features of individual models.

■ A model marked Ⓓ has been discontinued, according to the manufacturer. A model marked Ⓢ indicates that, according to the manufacturer, it has been replaced by a successor model whose performance should be similar to the tested model but whose features may vary.

▶Home workplace

Telephones	292
Telephone answering machines	297
Home fax machines	299
Computer software systems	301
Computer printers	302
Ratings	304

Working at home has become so common that it's engendered a new term: telecommuting, meaning working at home but maintaining electronic contact with a central office by telephone, fax, and modem. Telecommuters, together with the millions of Americans who have home-based small businesses, are the primary customers of home-office equipment: computers plus all their adjuncts and software, fax machines, copiers, telephones from traditional to cellular, and telephone answering machines.

Fully outfitting a home workplace can run into many thousands of dollars, depending on your needs and tastes. But thanks to the sharp drop in the prices of the major pieces of equipment, you can equip a home workplace for less than ever. Computers that once cost thousands now cost less than a thousand. Faxes, once used only by large businesses, are now cheap enough for the mass market. Computer printers that print in color are at what black-and-white ink-jet printers were priced at a few years ago. Most dramatic of all has been the plunge of the price of the cellular telephone—from over a thousand to, in some cases, under a hundred dollars, particularly if you agree to a "bundled" deal, a phone with a contract for cellular service that typically binds you to a carrier for a year.

As demand for home equipment has increased, a new type of store has emerged—the discount office-supply store. Chains like Staples sell under one roof everything from rubber bands to executive desks, plus all the products discussed in this chapter.

Telephones—corded, cordless, and cellular—and answering machines continue to be redesigned and made more useful.

Telephones

▶ **Ratings start on page 304.**

If Alexander Graham Bell were alive today, he'd be amazed at how his invention has evolved in a little more than a century. Push buttons—some outsize, some that light up—have largely supplanted the rotary dial. Today's telephones let you put callers on hold while serenading them with Muzak. They dial themselves, answer themselves, fit in your pocket, leave the house or travel in the car with you. Advanced models display the name and number of the person calling or show the caller's picture. Decorator models look like Mickey Mouse or E.T. or the "French" phone back when the Eiffel Tower went up.

Telephones can be broken down into three broad categories: corded phones, cordless phones, and cellular phones.

Corded telephones

You can pay as little as $10 or more than $100 for a conventional phone—one consisting of a handset and a base that plugs into a wall outlet. Three manufacturers—AT&T, G.E., and Conair—sell more than half the phones on the U.S. market.

The choices

Console models. These are the modern version of the traditional Bell desk phone. They have a separate handset, an array of push buttons, and a handset cradle or base about eight inches deep and four to seven inches wide. They range in price from about $30 to more than $100.

Trim-style models. These are space-savers; the push buttons are on the handset itself, and the base is a bit more than two by eight inches. Trim-style phones now account for about half of the corded-phone market. Their price ranges from $10 to $50.

Features and conveniences

Ring sound. Few models actually ring. The most common sound is a chirp, although some emit a low warble.

Memory. This, more than anything is responsible for the major technological changes in "conventional" telephones. Memory-related capabilities that vary from model to model include: The quantity of numbers stored, automatic redial, one-touch speed dialing, one-touch save, scratch pad, and chain dialing.

Most phones with memory can store at least a dozen numbers of up to 15 digits—enough for all but some international calls. Larger memory capacity costs more.

Redial recalls the last number dialed. A few models can redial a busy number several times automatically.

One-touch speed dialing stores at least three numbers that you can then call by touching a single key. Many models expand speed dialing by using just two or three keys.

Scratch pads let you record a phone number during a conversation and, after you've hung up, dial the number. That's especially handy when you get a number from directory assistance.

Electronic banking and voice-mail systems require you to enter lots of numbers via the telephone dial. Phones with "chain dialing" memory can dial a long sequence of stored numbers.

Speakerphone. This lets you talk without the handset.

Easy-to-see keys. Lit keys let you dial in the dark. Big keys make dialing easy for kids or for those with poor eyesight.

Volume controls. One control raises or lowers the volume at the handset, as needed; the other does the same for the phone's ring. Speakerphones also have a volume control for the speaker in the base. A mute feature disconnects the mike so a caller won't hear sounds from your end of the line.

Pulse/tone dialing. Most phones have a switch that lets you switch pulse or tone dialing. That enables you to talk to computer or voice-mail systems even if you don't have tone service.

Flash. This button briefly disconnects a call, useful for call-waiting, a service that lets you take two calls on a single phone.

Capacitors. These battery alternatives keep a phone's memory intact for up to 24 hours if you unplug the phone or if the phone line fails. Batteries can do that job for longer, but need periodic replacement.

LCD display. This pricey feature shows the number dialed, time of day, and sometimes, length of call.

The tests

We test the phones in a variety of ways that simulate actual use. We note each model's ability to render speech, based on such factors as clarity, harshness, loudness, and the recognizability of the speaker's voice. We observe how clearly you can hear and be heard. We subject the phones to a variety of abuses that include 8000-volt electrical jolts, 800-volt current surges, and falls from a height of several feet onto a hard floor. And we make judgments of how convenient each phone is to use.

Buying advice

The telephone has been around for more than a century, and most quirks in performance were ironed out long ago. You should be okay if you buy features and price. A decent console or Trim-style model should cost no more than $40.

Once you've chosen a style, make a list of features you need. Expect to pay more for two-line models and speakerphones.

Cordless phones

A cordless phone is basically a walkie-talkie with a radio transmitter and receiver in both base and handset beaming the conversation between the two. The base stays plugged into your phone line; the handset is detachable, so you can make and take calls from hundreds of feet.

The technology, though much improved, is still not perfect. Cordless phones are often vulnerable to static. They may distort voices, pick up signals from other cordless phones, or simply quit when approaching the limit of their range. Your voice probably won't come through as clearly to people you call as theirs will to you, if they're using a regular phone. And if you're remiss about replacing the handset in its charger, the batteries are likely to give out at the worst possible time.

Models we've tested lately have had better sound quality and suffered less from background noise than models tested in the past. All now use a digital "combination code" linking handset and base to reduce interference from nearby cordless phones and to discourage eavesdropping.

The choices

Basic models. These usually cost $75 or less. Their main shortcoming: greater vulnerability to interference from nearby cordless phones operating on the same radio channel. More expensive models have up to 10 radio channels available while these have only one or two.

Full-featured models. These offer 10 radio channels; should interference occur, most let you change channels while continuing to talk. Some models automatically select a clear channel when you first pick up the phone.

Some models have a speakerphone in the base unit, which permits hands-free operation. On some, the base and handset can work as an intercom system. Some models have a dialing keyboard on the base, making the base, in effect, a complete phone.

Features and conveniences

Features adding to convenience include:
Two-way paging. Pushing a button on the base or handset sounds a paging signal on the other component. The signal can also lead you to a misplaced handset.
Ringer in base. When you're near the base, this alerts you to an incoming call no matter where the handset may be.
Out-of-range tone. It warns you the handset is too far from the base.
Speed-call memory. This stores frequently called numbers and lets you dial them using one or two buttons. Many phones can store more than 10 phone numbers of up to 16 digits each.
Volume control. This boosts the loudness of the handset's speaker.
Mute/hold. This lets you talk to someone in the room without letting the person on the phone hear you.

The tests

Like corded phones, we test cordless phones in ways that simulate actual use. We use them for making calls to and from regular phones, and check both sides of the conversation for loudness and voice quality. We measure the phones' maximum operating range in an open parking lot. We also subject each model to physical abuse—drops onto a hard floor and electrical jolts.

Buying advice

If you live in an uncrowded area, consider a basic model. Given the heavy discounting of phones, you may be able to find one for considerably less than $75

If you live in a densely populated area, a 10-channel phone will give you reasonable freedom from interference. By shopping around, you may even find a 10-channel cordless model at about the same price as a basic cordless phone.

Don't rely on a cordless phone to replace the regular phone in your house. Cordless phones won't work in the event of a power failure .

Cellular phones

Over the past five years, cellular phones have graduated from techno-toys for executives and owners of fancy cars to a practical consumer appliance. In a recent survey of CONSUMER REPORTS readers—10 percent of whom own a cellular phone—business use was the second-most-popular reason for buying a cellular phone. More readers bought their phone to use in emergencies and many to keep in touch with family members.

The increasing acceptance of cellular phones is partly due to the billions of dollars invested by cellular carriers—the companies that operate local cellular systems—to expand service areas.

The phones themselves also are changing. Permanently installed mobile phones and bulky, heavy "bag" phones have been joined by handheld portable models petite enough to fit in pocket or briefcase. Mobile and transportable models have more power and can make somewhat better connections than portables.

The way phones and phone service are sold has also attracted more users. In most areas, the price of the phone is contingent on signing up for service, a marketing technique called "bundling."

Motorola is by far the leading seller, accounting for one-fifth of cellular phones sold. Other brands include *AT&T*, *Audiovox*, *Mitsubishi*, *NEC*, *Nokia*, *NovAtel*, *Panasonic*, and *Uniden*.

The choices

Mobile phones. This, the grandfather of cellular phones, is permanently installed in a vehicle, usually by a professional. A mobile, or car, phone draws three watts of power from the vehicle's battery and requires an external antenna. Price (bundled—the phone plus the service contract): about $200.

Transportable phones. This is basically a mobile phone you can remove from a vehicle. It draws power from a rechargeable battery pack or a car's cigarette-lighter plug and comes with a carrying case. Though technically portable, such a phone can weigh more than you might care to tote—five pounds or so. Price (bundled): about $200.

Portable phones. Lightweight, handheld models are the best-selling type, though the most expensive. Battery-operated, a portable model looks like the handset of a cordless phone. Coverage in areas where cellular service is poor may be less than with mobile or portable units because of the transmitter's limited power—usually a mere 0.6 watts. A kit that boosts that power to 3 watts is available for some models. Price (bundled): about $250 to $400.

Features and conveniences

Cellular phones offer a host of features; here are the standard ones:

Memory and speed dialing. Most models store at least 30 numbers. You can usually speed-dial a number by pressing two or three buttons.

Call timer. Because cellular calls are so expensive, keeping track of air-time is important. Besides displaying elapsed time, some models have another timer to keep track of all your calls over a given period. You can also set most phones to beep at fixed intervals for time-keeping.

Battery-low indicator. Cellular-phone batteries, typically nickel-cadmium, sustain conversation for a minimum of an hour and standby status for a minimum of 8 hours. (Battery life may improve as nickel-metal batteries become more widespread.) An indicator warns visually or audibly that the battery is running low. If you're home, it's time to recharge the battery; on the road, it's time to insert a fresh battery.

Own-number display. Every cellular phone has its own phone number. Should you forget it, the phone's display can summon the number up.

Roaming features. In cellular parlance, "roaming" is is the term for leaving the area covered by your cellular carrier. Calls made outside your area are charged at a higher rate. Most models can be assigned more than one phone number so you can register with more than one carrier to reduce roaming charges All models can be programmed to temporarily halt roaming so you don't inadvertently run up extra charges.

Built-in help. With most phones, hitting a key or two will display instructions for features you don't use often.

Some cellular phones offer extra features and conveniences. Here are the ones you're likely to come across:

Automatic number selection. If you have numbers for more than one carrier, most models make you switch manually between them when you travel. This feature switches numbers automatically.

Battery-strength indicator. This shows whether the battery is low and, roughly, how much life it has left.

Fast recharge. A few models come with a rapid recharger that cuts recharging time from more than eight hours to one or two.

Any key/automatic answer. The any-key feature lets you answer incoming calls by pressing any key—not a particular key, as with many models. Handier still is the automatic-answer, which picks up for you after a couple of rings.

One-touch dial/speakerphone. To shorten dialing time when you're driving, a few phones have two dedicated keys that dial preset numbers. Most manufacturers offer an optional speakerphone kit; with a speakerphone in place, you can talk with both hands on the wheel.

Voice activation. Primarily on mobile phones, this expensive feature allows you to verbally send and receive calls and access the memory.

The tests

In our lab, we simulate such situations as a car moving far from a carrier's transmitter or traveling within the cacophony of reflected and competing signals found in a large city. We also test phones in the field, signing on with local carriers.

An experienced panel judges how well each model held its own against background noise and how natural the speaker's voice sounds.

We measure how weak a signal each phone could receive before background noise became overwhelming and how much noise there was on the line. We note how strong a signal was needed for a cellular station to establish a connection with each phone. Battery life is clocked, during use and when the phone is on standby and then checked against that claimed by the manufacturers.

And we assess convenience: the ease of placing and receiving calls, using the display and keypad, and storing and retrieving numbers in the phone's memory.

Buying advice

In cities or in areas with flat terrain, most barebones cellular models should be adequate. Suburban and rural areas, where cellular coverage may be spotty, make more demands of a cellular phone and carrier.

If you make most calls from a vehicle, a permanently installed mobile phone makes sense; it has more power for better connections and is usually less expensive than a portable model. Or consider a portable model with a kit that lets you power the phone from the car battery, boost transmitting power, and add an external antenna.

Because of the way cellular phones are bundled with the service commitment, identical models may differ in price by hundreds of dollars. Shop for a carrier and a contract as if they were part of the cost of the phone. Typically, you'll spend more for a year's service than you did for the phone itself. Monthly phone bills run $70 to $85, on average.

Telephone answering machines

Today's answering machine is smaller, smarter, and sleeker than the machines that first appeared in the late '70s. Improved technology has automated such functions as playing back your recorded messages and has shrunk the machine's size. The keypad of the touch-tone phone has replaced the remote beeper. Voice-actuated circuits and automatic "timeout" that hang up automatically if no one speaks have made the machines adroit at handling both long and short messages.

The choices

A phone answerer can be its own product or come integrated with a phone. An answerer with a built-in phone saves space and may be less expensive than buying a separate phone and answerer. But if either one fails, both go to the repair shop. Integrated phone/answering machines are typically priced at $70 or more. Answerers, with or without phones, use one of three recording technologies: single microcassette, dual cassette, or memory chips.

Single microcassette. This type records both the outgoing and incoming messages on a single microcassette. Individual messages are often limited to a minute or two and callers must wait for the tape to shuttle forward before they can leave a message because there's only one tape in the machine. Prices range from $40 to $60.

Dual cassette. The most versatile machines use two tapes—either full-sized cassettes or microcassettes. Callers can leave a message without delay and the greeting can be longer than on a single-cassette machine. A machine that uses an endless-loop tape for outgoing messages delays answering new calls for about 15 seconds after a call while the tape cycles back to the beginning. Prices range from $70 to $260.

Memory chips. Memory chips like those found in computers are used to store the greeting; a cassette records the message. Others, called all-digital machines, do away completely with the cassette, storing messages and greeting on memory chips. Both types are less likely to break down, since they use circuits instead of moving parts. Memory chips are expensive compared with tape, and limit recording time; a one-minute limit per call is typical. In our tests, voice quality on machines with chips was clear, but sounded less natural than messages on tape. These models tend to be small but pricey—ranging from about $100 to $400.

Features and conveniences

Certain basic features have become standard on many machines. These include:

Call screening. This lets you listen to a message as it comes in, so you can avoid nuisance calls and not miss important ones. If you decide to take a call, many machines automatically stop recording as soon as you pick up any phone in the house.

Number of rings. You can set the number of rings the machine will wait before it answers—no need to to race to the phone to beat the machine's pick-up.

Pause and Skip. These help control playback of recorded messages. Pause temporarily stops a message so you can jot down a name or number. Skip speeds things up by moving the tape back or forward exactly one message.

Call counters. Some machines use a blinking light to signal that at least one message is waiting. Better are ones that blink the light to tell you how many messages there are. The best displays provide a digital read-out of the number of calls. Most counters ignore hang-ups occurring before the beep.

Power backup. Most machines keep their memory at least for a short time in the event of power failure, but some reset the call counter to zero. The best designs use a battery-strength indicator and a battery backup that holds the settings for hours.

Remote control. All machines let you use a touch-tone phone to retrieve messages when away from home. Some let you set your own code; others are programmed. Those with two- or three-digit codes offer the most security.

Toll-saver. This lets you avoid a charge for calling your machine long-distance to check for possible messages. You set the machine to answer the first call after four or five rings and later calls after only one or two. You save money by hanging up after three rings—if the machine hasn't picked up by then, there are no messages.

Higher-priced machines offer features that may someday trickle down to basic models. These include:

Greeting bypass. Callers who don't want to listen to your outgoing message bypass it by pressing the right touch-tone key, usually the asterisk.

Time and date. With this, the machine notes the time and date of each message and announces them when you play the message back.

Announce-only. This lets you post a greeting—for example, a wedding announcement—without recording incoming calls.

Alternate greeting. This lets you program two greetings and switch between them at will, a feature useful for a home-based business.

Selective save and delete. Some digital answering machines do not store messages in a linear fashion as on tape. Messages can be stored or deleted in a random fashion while preserving ample storage for additional incoming messages.

Voice mailboxes. Some digital answerers provide voice mailboxes for people who share an answering machine. Callers are instructed as to how to leave messages for the specific party that they trying to reach.

Buying advice

If your needs are simple and you don't want a new telephone, look for a plain answerer with dual cassettes or with a memory chip for the greeting and a cassette for messages. A number are available for about $60 to $90. If you can live with just short messages, a machine that uses memory chips for greeting and messages is less likely to need repairs.

Among the answering machines with a built-in telephone, choices range from plain-vanilla telephones to cordless models with lots of features.

An alternative to a phone-answering machine is a service offered by many local phone companies. When you're out or if your line is busy, the phone company receives and stores messages; you can use a touch-tone phone to receive messages. The advantages are obvious—no machine to break down and an increased capability for receiving messages. The drawbacks are serious: there's no provision to screen incoming calls; no visible indicator to tell you if you have messages; network failures can destroy messages; and charges can run $5 to $10 per month or more.

Home fax machines
▶ **Ratings on page 309.**

With little fanfare, the facsimile machine has claimed considerable turf in the nation's offices and on the telephone network. It is hard to imagine a company of any size without a fax machine or to remember what life was like before faxes made it possible to send a page instantly across the country or around the world.

Trend seers say that the fax's next conquest will be the American home. More and more, people are using home faxes to order printed matter—newsletters, travel maps, reprints—or take-out food and mail-order purchases. A handful of pioneers use faxes in businesses operated from home or to "telecommute" to a traditional office—they work at home and use the fax to receive and return assignments.

Major brands of home fax machines include *Canon*, *Muratec* (formerly *Murata*), *Sharp*, and *Panasonic*, which calls its office-grade line *Panafax*.

The choices

Manufacturers aim their smaller models at the home-office market. Light-duty fax machines can be had for $300 to $600—and prices are falling. But there are compromises. Absent are features big businesses demand, like fast printing speeds and the ability to print on plain rather than "fax" paper. Such machines generally list for $1000 or more.

Home machines typically print incoming documents on long rolls of chemically treated stock, using a thermal system (tiny heating elements form the actual letters). That system helps keep both size and cost down.

The cheapest home fax machines—sometimes priced at less than $300—lack a document feeder and an automatic paper cutter. Not having a feeder means each page sent must be inserted manually by someone standing over the machine; no cutter means someone will have to cut scrolls of output into page-sized sheets.

But home fax machines also include amenities sometimes omitted on bigger models, features people running home offices will appreciate. The faxes can photocopy anything you can feed into the machine (the copies come out on fax paper); sometimes the fax can even enlarge or reduce modestly. Home models usually have a fax/voice switch, to make it easier for the machine to share the line with a regular phone. The circuitry listens for the data tone of a fax transmission to route incoming calls appropriately, to you or the machine. Home machines also usually offer an answering-machine interface, which allows an answerer to take voice calls and messages as it would normally when you're not there.

Features and conveniences

Sending modes. This determines the resolution of a faxed document and the speed at which it can be sent. In Standard mode, faxes break an inch of the page into 100 scan lines, each some 1700 dots across. Sending in Standard mode takes about a minute a page. Faxes can also be sent in Fine mode (twice the scan lines, double the time), for small print that might otherwise come out unreadable. Some models offer Superfine with yet higher resolution. And many offer a Halftone mode, for photos and artwork, rendering grays in 16 or more steps from black to white. (Sending such a document can take five minutes or more per page.)

One-touch dialing. A fax machine's

built-in memory typically sports at least a few buttons to program for frequently dialed numbers. More numbers can usually be programmed for speed-dialing (you press a special key, then a one- or two-digit code).

Auto retry. Typically, fax machines will persistently redial busy numbers for a few minutes until the receiving machine connects.

Delayed sending. Allows you to set up a document for transmission at a later time, to take advantage of cheaper phone rates.

Remote start. If you answer an extension phone that shares the fax's line and find the call is an incoming fax, this feature lets you start your fax receiving by pressing a short code. Without it, you'd have to press the Start button.

Memory, broadcasting. If a fax runs out of paper when receiving, some models can capture a few pages of text in memory for later printing. Typically, those models are also able to use their memory to "broadcast" a document you want distributed to a routing list of phone numbers.

Anti-curl system. This feature flattens thermal fax paper, which is notorious for curling and being hard to handle. Some models take a grade thermal paper that feels more like standard paper.

Activity reports. Most faxes print a listing of documents recently sent or received, along with phone numbers, times and dates, and whether or not the transmission went through.

The tests

Tests to evaluate sending capabilities measure a fax's optical scanner. To gauge transmission speed we fax three single-spaced typed pages in Fine mode, then look at the quality of the print received at the other end. We also transmit test photos in Halftone mode.

Receiving tests focus on immunity to telephone-line noise, as it is gradually added to a clear line. Noise slows down transmission and can stop a fax if it gets too bad.

To test printing, we send especially clean fax images sent by computer to each machine and transmit standard optical test charts by a high-quality fax machine.

Buying advice

Judging from our tests, sending and printing clear text are not a problem for modern light-duty fax machines. Features, however, can make or break a machine.

Don't cut corners on paper-handling features. Two musts: a document feeder, to send long faxes, and an automatic cutter, to receive multipage documents. Some models can take originals of various widths, a capacity you may need. Some can take a paper roll longer than the usual 98 feet, so they'll run out of paper less often. The anti-curl system available on a few models makes incoming pages easier to handle.

Look for a machine that makes it easy to share the phone line with a regular phone. Many home offices probably cannot afford to install a telephone line just for the fax. A built-in fax/voice switch that can be set to pick up after a few rings can route voice calls to you, fax calls to the machine. You'll also want the capability to start the fax from an extension, and an answering-machine interface (or built-in answering machine) that works smoothly and capably with the fax.

Special needs require special features. For faxing photographs or artwork, look for a machine with a Halftone mode; for lots of very small print, Superfine mode. If you'll be doing a lot of overseas faxing, choose a machine that lets you select a slower transmission speed to cope with electronic noise. For routinely sending the same documents to a roster of people, look for a built-in memory and the ability to "broadcast" to a routing list.

Computer software systems

For many years, shopping for a home computer meant choosing between a relatively low-priced, hard-to-master, IBM-compatible machine running DOS (for disk operating system) and the simpler, but more expensive, Apple *Macintosh*. Recently, though, there's a third choice: an IBM-compatible equipped with *Microsoft Windows* software.

The choices

Those three software systems vary as to how they govern the overall operation of your computer. They also determine which application software your computer can run. Here's how they work:

DOS. The standard for most computers for the past decade, this runs on IBM-compatible computers. Written in the days when computers were slow and monitors were black and white, it's now far from state-of-the-art. Still, it has three strong advantages: Many software packages are compatible with it; it requires a less powerful—and less expensive—computer than other systems; and it can often run software more quickly than *Windows*. The downside of DOS is the burden of learning its myriad commands and conventions, no small feat. Another disadvantage is that each software program that runs under DOS has its own unique set of commands, which must be separately mastered.

Macintosh. The hardware and software for this system were designed together, with the goal of making the computer's operating system less obtrusive. *Mac* software runs only on *Macs*, using a graphical user interface—known in the trade as a GUI (pronounced "gooey"). The interface lets you perform most actions by pointing to symbols on the screen with a "mouse," a handheld device. That eliminates the need to memorize commands or document names. *Macintosh* file operations are completely graphical: To copy a file, you use the mouse to move the cursor from one symbolic folder to another; to delete a file, you move it to an on-screen trash can. (You can do most tasks through keyboard commands, too.) Programs designed for the *Mac* all use similar approaches and commands, simplifying the learning process. The *Macintosh*'s only disadvantage is its price, typically hundreds of dollars more than an IBM-compatible of equivalent power. But that may be changing—prices of Macs are dropping.

Windows. *Windows* is Microsoft's answer to the *Mac*, designed to run on IBM-compatible computers. Because it is an operating environment—not a true operating system—it requires DOS. It has a graphical interface modeled after the *Mac's*. Programs written for *Windows*, like those for the *Mac*, use similar, if not identical commands. *Windows'* biggest drawback is that, underneath, the computer is still a DOS machine. That shows up mostly in its file management. You still have to use the DOS filing system to name and retrieve documents on the disk, a system that doesn't dovetail well with *Windows'* graphical interface. The result: *Windows* has something of a split personality.

Buying advice

Our tests, using a panel of users performing various tasks on each system with the corresponding version of Microsoft *Works*, showed *Windows* and *Macintosh* to be about equally easy to use overall; in both cases, far easier than DOS. In word processing, *Macintosh* and *Windows* were significantly easier than DOS.

Either system—*Windows* or *Macintosh*—is a better choice than DOS. If you prefer to learn as little as possible about technology, the extra money you'll pay for a *Macintosh* may be well spent. If you are willing to learn a bit about the computer as you go, a *Windows*-based machine will save money.

If you already have an old IBM-compatible using DOS, it will probably be cheaper to buy a new computer than upgrade to all the hardware needed for *Windows*. If you're happy with it, don't be stampeded into a costly purchase. DOS-based applications are likely to remain in widespread use for many years.

Computer printers

Technical innovation and competition are making computer printers better and cheaper than ever. The venerable daisy-wheel printer, an early standard bearer of print quality, has become virtually a relic. Even dot-matrix printers, the dominant breed for the past decade, may be on the brink of obsolescence, crowded out by the newest, most technologically advanced printers—ink-jet and laser models. Street prices for laser printers have dropped to less than $600. Nowadays, even color printers can be had for well under $300.

The printer market is enormous. There are more than 300 printer models available under more than 60 brand names, including such familiar names as *Panasonic, Epson, Star,* and *Tandy*.

The choices

Dot-matrix. These printers' tiny metal pins form characters by hitting the paper hundreds of times a second in a shrill whine. The more dots in a printhead's matrix, the smoother and crisper its print. Early dot-matrix models had only nine pins, which formed coarse, sometimes stunted, characters. Later models used more pins, or passed the printhead two or three times over a line, to create a smoother effect.

Today, most printer-makers offer a line of low-cost nine-pin models—typically priced below $200—and a line of 24-pin models priced in the $200- to $400-range. In our tests, 24-pin models turned out decent copy in near-letter-quality (NLQ) mode, their slowest. Nine-pin models are fine if text quality isn't important.

Ink-jet. This type, also called bubble-jet printers, uses an ink cartridge that feeds an array of nearly microscopic tubes, each with a heating element; when the element is energized, a small ink droplet in the corresponding tube squirts quietly onto the paper. Since the technology doesn't demand much electrical energy, it's often used in small, portable, battery-operated models. In our tests, most ink-jets' output quality was nearly as good as a laser printer's, with very little noise. Ink-jet cartridges are expensive, making operating costs about double that of laser or dot-matrix printers. Ink-jet printers typically are priced $350 to $600.

Laser. Using xerographic technology like that in photocopiers, these can reproduce an almost limitless variety of type forms and sizes, as well as complex graphics. Images are electronically created on a light-sensitive drum, usually with a scanning laser. Powdered toner adheres to areas where light touches the drum and then transfers to a sheet of paper, which is briefly heated to fuse the toner permanently. The output is clean and crisp. In our tests, laser printers produced—quietly—nearly perfect renditions of test pages. And they printed each page in half the time of an ink-jet or a dot-matrix printer in NLQ mode. Until recently, laser printers typically cost several thousand dollars. Now prices have dropped to less than $600 for basic models. Expect to pay more for those capable of printing postscript documents, such as those created by page-layout programs.

Features and conveniences

Typefaces. Most models can print in at least a couple of distinct typefaces—such as Times Roman, Helvetica, and Courier.

Paper feed. All printers can handle single sheets of letter-sized paper. Laser printers use an automatic feeder tray stacked with blank paper. That's an extra-cost option with most dot-matrix and some ink-jet models. Paper-tray capacity ranges from 30 sheets up to a ream of 20-pound paper.

Dot-matrix models typically use a tractor feed, a sprocketed, treadlike device that pushes or pulls perforated fanfold paper. Some designs put the sprockets on the roller itself. Those pin-feed printers work fine with standard-width continuous paper, but they can't adjust to narrow-width paper or standard one-across mailing labels. Least convenient with continuous paper are printers that have no tractor at all but rely instead on the friction of the roller to advance the paper. That may be OK for the first few sheets, but not long after that, the paper is likely to become misaligned.

Buying advice

If your needs are limited to routine tasks like correspondence and résumés or you need to print special tractor-feed documents such as checks, a 24-pin dot-matrix printer should do the job for relatively little expense. For a few dollars more, an ink-jet printer can provide near-laser quality without taking a toll on your ears. Ink jet refills cost about $20 to $35. Color cartridges, naturally, are more expensive.

Consider a laser model only if print quality and speed are extremely important. Prices and models change rapidly. Before buying, check prices in computer magazines and the business section of your newspaper.

HOW TO USE THE RATINGS

■ Read the **article** for general guidance about types and buying advice.

■ Read **Recommendations** for brand-name advice based on our tests.

■ Read the **Ratings order** to see whether products are listed in order of quality, by price, or alphabetically. Most Ratings are based on estimated quality, without regard to price.

■ Look to the **Ratings table** for specifics on the performance and features of individual models.

■ A model marked Ⓓ has been discontinued, according to the manufacturer. A model marked Ⓢ indicates that, according to the manufacturer, it has been replaced by a successor model whose performance should be similar to the tested model but whose features may vary.

CORDED TELEPHONES

RATINGS — CORDED TELEPHONES

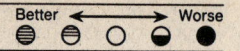

Better ◐ ◑ ○ ◉ ● Worse

▶ **See report, page 292.** From Consumer Reports, December 1992.

Recommendations: The top performers include the *AT&T 710*, $70, a console model with memory and the *GE 2-9210*, $25, a trim model with memory. Among speakerphones, the one-line *AT&T 720*, $60, and the two-line *732*, $130, stood out.

Ratings order: Listed in order of estimated quality, based on performance and convenience. Unless separated by a heavy rule, closely ranked models differed little in quality. Price is the manufacturer's suggested retail. **Notes to table:** Key to style: **C**=console model; **T**=trim model. Ⓢ indicates tested model has been replaced by successor model; according to the manufacturer, the performance of new model should be similar to the tested model but features may vary. See right for new model number and suggested retail price, if available. Ⓓ indicates model discontinued.

Brand and model	Price	Style	Speech quality: Listening	Speech quality: Speaking	Loudness: Listening	Loudness: Speaking	Ring	Memory, numbers/max. digits	Features	Advantages	Disadvantages	Comments
AT&T 710	$70	C	○	◐	◐	◐	◐	16/16	c,d,h,l,m	A,B,D,E	—	A,B
AT&T 230	40	T	○	◐	◐	○	◐	9/16	c,d,g,h,i,l,m	B,D,E	—	C,D,E,H,
AT&T 720	60	C	○	◐	◐	○	◐	16/16	a,c,d,g,h,l,m	A,B,D,E	b	A,B
AT&T Big Button Plus	60	C	○	◐	◐	●	○	3/16	c,d,j,l,m	B,D	—	A,C,E
AT&T 730	100	C	○	◐	○	○	◐	30/16	a,c,g,h,k,l,m	A,D,E	b,f	A,B,G
AT&T 732	130	C	○	◐	○	○	◐	30/16	a,b,c,g,h,k,l,m	A,D,E	b,f	A,B,G
Panasonic KX-T2335	50	C	○	◐	○	●	○	28/16	c,d,h,m	A,B,C,D,E	b	A,H
Panasonic KX-T2365	75	C	○	◐	○	●	○	28/16	a,c,d,f,g,k,m	A,B,C,D,E	b	A,H
Radio Shack ET-203 Ⓓ	45	C	○	◐	◐	◉	○	—	j,l,m	E	—	H
GE 2-9210	25	T	○	◐	○	●	○	12/16	c,d,m	D	—	C,D
GE 2-9266	40	C	○	◐	◐	◐	◐	6/18	c,d,j,l,m	—	—	A,C,E
ITT/Cortelco 3490	50	C	○	◐	○	●	○	22/20	c,d,g,h,m	A,D	—	A
Radio Shack ET-143	50	C	◐	◐	◐	○	○	20/15	c,h,m	C	—	A,B
Radio Shack ET-276 Ⓓ	50	T	○	◐	◐	◐	○	—	i,l	D	—	C,D,H,I

CORDED TELEPHONES

Brand and model	Price	Style	Listening	Speaking	Listening	Speaking	Ring	Memory; numbers/max. digits	Features	Advantages	Disadvantages	Comments
BellSouth 236V	$80	C	○	◒	◒	◒	○	20/15	a,c,e,f,h,l,m	A,C,D	b,d,f	A,F
BellSouth 840V	50	C	○	◒	○	◒	◒	9/15	c,e,h,l,m	A,C	d	A,H
GE 2-9175	30	C	○	◒	○	◒	◒	12/16	c,d,h,m	D	f	A
ITT/Cortelco 3494	65	C	○	◒	○	◒	○	22/20	a,c,g,h,m	A,D	b	A,C
ITT/Cortelco 8125	35	T	○	◒	○	◒	○	—	g,h,i,m	D	e	C,D,H
Radio Shack ET-272 [D]	25	T	○	◒	◒	◒	○	—1	m	D	a	C,D,H
Unisonic 9125 [D]	25	C	○	◒	○	◒	◒	13/16	c,d,m	D	—	A,H
BellSouth 473	35	T	○	◒	○	●	○	10/15	c,d,g,h,i	C,D	d,f	C,H,I
GE 2-9320	60	C	○	◒	○	◒	◒	12/16	a,c,d,g,h,m	—	b,f	A
GE 2-9435	80	C	○	◒	○	◒	○	32/16	a,b,c,d,f,g,h,m	A,B,C	b,f	A,G
ITT/Cortelco 8810	75	C	○	◒	◒	○	○	3/15	c,d,e,g,h,j,l,m	D,E	b,d,g	A,C,E,H,I
Radio Shack DuoFone 148	70	C	○	◒	○	◒	○	20/15	a,c,g,h,m	A,C	b,f	A,B,C,G
Conairphone PR304A [D]	22	T	○	◒	○	◒	○	9/16	c,i,l	D	—	C,D,E,H,I
GPX GP11C	25	T	○	◒	◒	○	◒	—	g,i	D	b,d	C,D,H
Unisonic Studio 6472	35	C	○	◒	○	◒	○	13/16	c,d,g,h,i	D	d	C,D,H,I
Conairphone PR6221G	70	C	○	◒	○	◒	○	14/16	a,c,d,e,m	—	b,f	A,E,H
Conairphone SW104A	20	T	○	◒	○	◒	—	—		D	a,e	C,D,H
Tozai TK-007AP [S]	10	T	○	◒	○	○	◐	—	g	E	a,c,d	C,D,H

Successor Models (in Ratings order)
Tozai TK-007AP is succeeded by ATC008.

Features in Common
All: • Have last-number redial. • Have ringer On/off switch. • Can sit on desk or be mounted on wall. • Memory phones can chain dial sequences of numbers from two or three memory locations.
Except as noted, all have: • Replaceable batteries that power memory when phone is unplugged. • Electronic ring sound. • Wall cord replaceable by user.

Key to Features
a–Speaker phone.
b–Two-line phone.
c–Speed-dialing.
d–Emergency call keys.
e–One-touch save.
f–Busy redial.
g–Mute.
h–Flash.
i–Lighted keys.
j–Big-button keys.
k–Time.
l–Earpiece volume.
m–Ringer volume.

Ratings continued ▶

PORTABLE CELLULAR TELEPHONES

Key to Advantages
A–Has more than 3 one-touch memory keys.
B–Has icons on emergency keys.
C–Can store and chain dial a mix of tone and pulse.
D–Has easy-to-reach pulse-to-tone switch.
E–Hearing-aid compatibility judged better than most.

Key to Disadvantages
a–Wall cord not replaceable by user.
b–May not work on special 6- or 20-volt line.
c–Can only dial pulse.
d–Operated poorly in worst-case line test.
e–Didn't work after drop test.
f–Didn't work after surge test.
g–Didn't ring on low-ring-voltage line.

Key to Comments
A–Has traditional, barbell-style handset.
B–Has battery test light.
C–No Hold button.
D–Handset has hook switch.
E–Can't put a pause into stored numbers.
F–Can redial last number or busy number only if phone is on hook.
G–Once pressed, Mute is on until repressed.
H–Lacks batteries; uses capacitor to save memory or last-number redial temporarily when phone is unplugged.
I–Has bell sound.

RATINGS PORTABLE CELLULAR TELEPHONES

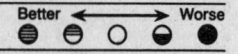

Better ← → Worse

▶ See report, page 294. From Consumer Reports, January 1993.

Recommendations: Any of the tested phones work well in an area with strong coverage such as a city or place with flat terrain. For use in suburban and rural areas, the *Audiovox MVX-500* (or its successor), the *Fujitsu Pocket Commander*, and the *Motorola Micro TAC Lite* are your best bets.

Ratings order: Listed in order of estimated quality, based primarily on performance and convenience. Bracketed models, which have only cosmetic differences, are listed in alphabetical order. Price is the suggested retail price of each phone when "bundled"—sold as part of a package that requires a contract for local cellular service, the terms of which vary with the carrier. ⓢ indicates tested model has been replaced by successor model; according to the manufacturer, the performance of new model should be similar to the tested model but features may vary. See right for new model number and suggested retail price, if available. ⓓ indicates model discontinued.

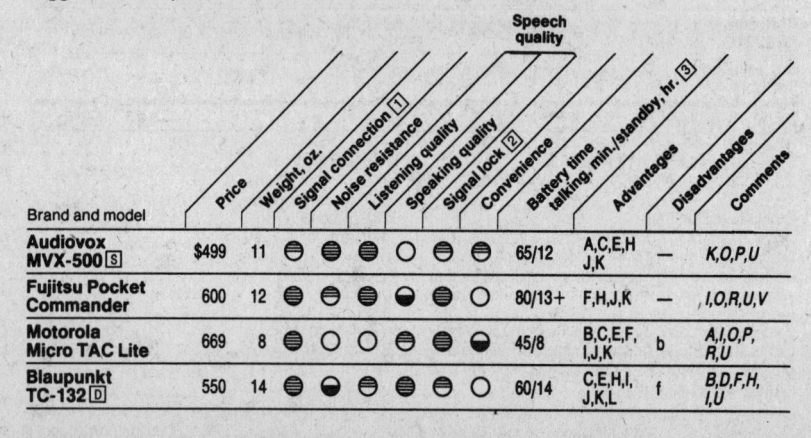

Brand and model	Price	Weight, oz.	Signal connection [1]	Noise resistance	Listening quality	Speaking quality	Signal lock [2]	Convenience	Battery time talking, min./standby, hr. [3]	Advantages	Disadvantages	Comments
Audiovox MVX-500 ⓢ	$499	11	◓	◓	◓	○	◓	◓	65/12	A,C,E,H,J,K	—	K,O,P,U
Fujitsu Pocket Commander	600	12	◓	◓	◓	●	◓	○	80/13+	F,H,J,K	—	I,O,R,U,V
Motorola Micro TAC Lite	669	8	◓	○	○	◓	◓	●	45/8	B,C,E,F,I,J,K	b	A,I,O,P,R,U
Blaupunkt TC-132 ⓓ	550	14	◓	●	◓	◓	◓	○	60/14	C,E,H,I,J,K,L	f	B,D,F,H,I,U

PORTABLE CELLULAR TELEPHONES

Brand and model	Price	Weight, oz.	Signal connection [1]	Noise resistance	Listening quality	Speaking quality (Speech quality)	Signal lock [2]	Convenience	Battery time talking, min./standby, hr. [3]	Advantages	Disadvantages	Comments
Antel STR1300 [D]	$207	14	⊖	⊖	⊖	⊖	○	⊖	80/12	C,F,I,J,K	—	K,P,R,U
AT&T 3730	460	13	○	⊖	⊖	⊖	⊖	⊖	65/12	C,D,E,G,I,J,K,L	d	D,I,N,P,R,U
Oki 900 [D]	399	12	○	⊖	⊖	⊖	⊖	⊖	60/10	C,D,E,G,I,J,K,L	d	D,E,I,O,P,R,U
Novatel PTR825	100	17	○	⊖	⊖	⊖	⊖	⊖	60/11	K	c,h,j	C,P,U
Technophone PC205A [D]	235	14	⊖	⊖	⊖	○	○	⊖	45/11*	B,C,F,H,I,J,K	—	D,M,P,Q,R,S,U
Panasonic EB-H60	467	9	⊖	⊖	⊖	⊖	○	⊖	55/11	C,H,I,J,K	d	F,G,I,Q
Nokia 101	299	10	○	⊖	⊖	⊖	⊖	⊖	45/11	C,I,J,K	i,j	C,J,L,Q,S
Motorola Metro One Ultra II [D]	200	17	⊖	⊖	⊖	⊖	◐	●	66/15	C,E,F,I,K	b,j	D,E,I,O,P,R,U
Uniden CP5500 [D]	235	10	○	⊖	⊖	⊖	●	●	72/10	H,J	a,e,f,g,h	F,H,I
NEC P600B	489	9	⊖	●	○	⊖	⊖	⊖	120/24+	C,E,F,I,J,K	g	G,I,R
DiamondTel 99X [D]	300	10	⊖	○	○	○	●	⊖	48/9	A,F,I,J,K	—	I,O,R
Mitsubishi 3000 [D]	299	10	⊖	⊖	⊖	⊖	⊖	⊖	48/9	A,F,I,J,K	—	I,O,R
Radio Shack (Tandy) CT-302 [D]	200	18	◐	⊖	⊖	○	○	⊖	60/14	—	g	C,F,H,J,L,P,Q
Murata MCT200 [D]	200	15	◐	⊖	⊖	⊖	⊖	⊖	60/12	E,F,H,I,K,L	g	D,G,I,L
GE TJA04	NA	15	○	◐	⊖	⊖	●	⊖	80/13*	C,I,J,K	—	H,I,P,T,U

[1] A measure of how strong a signal was needed for a cellular station to establish a connection.
[2] A measure of how weak a signal a phone could receive before background noise became overwhelming and how much noise was on the line when no one was speaking.
[3] + indicates an extended-life battery, when supplied with phone; * indicates our estimate where mfr. made no claim.

Successor Models (in Ratings order)
Audiovox MVX-500 is succeeded by MVX-525, $399.

Features in Common
All have: • Low-battery warning. • Received-signal-strength and roaming indicators. • Lighted keypad, with audible feedback. • Ability to send Touch-Tone signals, access all 832 channels authorized for cellular service, display their own phone number, be assigned multiple phone numbers, disable roaming, and select either cellular carrier. • Current and cumulative call timers. • Last-number redial. • Memory for at least 30 phone numbers. • Scratch-pad memory. • Ringer and earpiece volume controls. • Volume control or On/off switch for tone signals.
Except as noted, all have: • Speakerphone kit available. • Car battery adapter available. • Backlit LCD, dot-matrix display. • 0.6 watts of power. • 1-yr. parts and labor warranty.

Ratings continued ▶

- Incoming-call light. • 8- to 11-hr. charging for standard-life battery. • Retractable antenna. • Alphabetic memory search. • Ability to locate a free memory location automatically. • Ability to beep to indicate elapsed talk time. • Silent-ring feature for incoming calls. • Microphone mute. • Missed-call indicator; useful to voice-mail subscribers. • Automatic last-number redial.

Key to Advantages
A–Has one-touch dialing.
B–Rapid recharger; cuts recharge time by about 85 percent.
C–Can prevent accidental memory erasure.
D–Relatively easy to check for duplicate memory entries.
E–Can answer calls automatically.
F–Voice-activated circuitry conserves power in service areas that support the capability.
G–Can save a caller's phone number in memory even if you don't answer phone.
H–Has any-key answer.
I–Has built-in help.
J–Has battery-strength indicator.
K–Has alphanumeric directory.
L–Has automatic number selection.

Key to Disadvantages
a–Can't scroll through numbers in memory.
b–LED display turns off after several seconds; conserves power, but you don't see display.
c–No 911 lock override; drawback in an emergency.
d–Case-sensitive memory search.
e–Lacks incoming-call light.
f–Display is less readable than most.
g–No alphabetic memory search.
h–Cannot find free memory location automatically.
i–Listening loudness less than average.
j–Ringer loudness less than average.

Key to Comments
A–Compatible with NAMPS, possible future cellular standard.
B–Has 1.2-watt transmit mode.
C–Can't beep to indicate elapsed talk time.
D–Has removable, rather than retractable, antenna.
E–Comes with 2 batteries.
F–This manufacturer doesn't offer extended-life battery; other brands of battery may work.
G–Built-in clock and calendar.
H–No silent-ring feature for incoming calls.
I–Can put a pause into stored numbers.
J–No microphone mute.
K–No missed-call indicator.
L–No automatic last-number redial.
M–Can also display words in Spanish, French, Italian, or German.
N–2-yr. parts and labor warranty.
O–3-yr. parts and labor warranty.
P–External antenna adapter available.
Q–No speakerphone kit available.
R–3-watt power-booster kit available.
S–Can operate on household current.
T–No car battery adapter available.
U–Computer modem adapter available.
V–Now called **Pocket Commander Stylus**; mfr. says cosmetic changes only.

How Objective is CU?

Consumers Union is not beholden to any commercial interest. It accepts no advertising and buys all the products tested on the open market. CU's income is derived from the sale of CONSUMER REPORTS and other publications, and from nonrestrictive, noncommercial contributions, grants, and fees. Neither the Ratings nor the reports may be used in advertising or for any other commercial purpose. Consumers Union will take all steps open to it to prevent commercial use of its materials, its name, or the name of CONSUMER REPORTS.

HOME FAX MACHINES

RATINGS — HOME FAX MACHINES

Better ⬅ ⊜ ⊖ ○ ⊕ ● ➡ Worse

▶ **See report, page 299.** From Consumer Reports, November 1993.

Recommendations: The three paper-cutter faxes rated highest are all worthy of consideration. We rated two of them—the *Panasonic KX-F230*, $470, and the *Brother 600*, $390—Best Buys for their high quality and low price. Among models without a paper cutter, consider the *Sharp NX-1*, which often sells for less than $300. The most compact machines were the *Murata M750*, $330, and the *Canon Faxphone 16*, $350.

Ratings order: Listed by types; within types, listed in order of estimated quality. Price is the estimated average, based on prices paid in late 1993. **Notes to table:** Overall score is based largely on a model's features and its immunity to interruptions caused by a poor phone line. Convenience reflects factors including ease of changing the paper roll and capabilities to delay sending, adjust pickup delay, and store pages in memory should the machine run out of paper.

Brand and model	Price	Overall score	Convenience	Speed	Photos	Feeder	Receiving: One touch memory nos.	Receiving: Speed dial memory nos.	Poor lines	Sending: Remote start	Anticurl	Memory	Comments
PAPER-CUTTER MODELS													
Brother 800M	$600	92	⊜	⊜	⊜	20	40	100	⊜	✔	✔	✔	A,B,C,D,F,J,L
Panasonic KX-F230, A Best Buy	470	91	⊜	⊜	○	10	12	80	⊜	✔	✔	—	A,D,M
Brother 600, A Best Buy	390	88	⊜	○	⊜	10	5	10	⊜	✔	✔	—	A,C,D,F,L
Canon Faxphone 50II	400	81	⊕	○	⊜	10	16	—	⊜	—	✔	—	A,C,G,H,I,J,S
Panafax PX-150	500	79	○	⊜	○	10	16	70	○	—	—	✔	B,D,J,N
Sharp UX-172	395	78	○	⊜	⊕	10	20	30	⊜	✔	—	—	H
WITHOUT PAPER CUTTER													
Panasonic KX-F130	400	86	⊜	⊜	○	10	12	20	⊜	✔	✔	—	A,D,M
Sharp NX-1	300	83	⊜	⊜	⊕	—	5	15	⊜	✔	—	—	L,Q
Canon Faxphone 16	350	79	⊜	○	○	10	10	25	○	—	—	—	A,F,G,H,P,R
Muratec M750	330	78	○	○	○	—	5	20	○	—	—	—	E,G,K,P,R,T
Toshiba 5400	500	78	⊜	○	⊕	5	11	50	○	—	—	—	A,D,F,G
Sanyo SFX-11	320	77	⊜	○	○	5	8	20	○	—	—	—	A,D,G
Samsung FX-505	300	76	⊜	⊜	●	5	10	20	○	—	—	—	A,D,G,H,O

Ratings continued ▶

Performance Notes

All models: • Did a good job of sending, receiving, and printing ordinary typed text.

Features in Common

All have: • Built-in telephone with memory for frequently called numbers. • Built-in photocopier. • Ability to operate at high speed (9600 BPS, bits per second), to send text in Standard or Fine mode, and to transmit halftone images. • Small LCD window to display phone numbers, error messages.

Except as noted, all: • Use rolls of thermal fax paper, usually 98 ft. in length, at a cost of about 6¢ or 7¢ per page. • Have a fax/voice switch for sharing a phone line conveniently with incoming voice calls, and an answering-machine interface so an external answering-machine can be used. • Have a document feeder that holds 5 to 10 pages (page width varies from about 5¾ to 8½ in. • Have the ability to print stored phone numbers and reports of faxing activity. • Have a "footprint" of about 15 in. wide by 12 in. deep. • Automatic redial.

Key to Comments

A–Has delayed sending—can be programmed to send a fax at a later time, when phone rates are lower.
B–Can "broadcast" same document to list of phone numbers.
C–Slower transmisison speed can be set; makes long-distance faxing more reliable.
D–Has Superfine mode (resolution higher than Fine).
E–No automatic redial of busy numbers.
F–Setting to lighten dark originals when sending (all models listed can darken light originals).
G–Can activate fax remotely, but only from extension plugged directly into fax machine.
H–Cost per printed page cheaper than most (about 3¢ for **Canon Faxphone 50II**; 6½¢ for others).
I–Changing paper roll more difficult than most.
J–Takes paper roll longer than most (**Canon** 328 ft.; others, 164 ft.).
K–Takes paper roll that's shorter than most (49 ft.).
L–Can use mfr's. upgraded thermal paper (optional). More expensive (about 9¢ to 10¢ a page) but feels more like plain paper.
M–Has built-in answering machine, but no interface to work with external answering machine sharing same line.
N–Machine intercepts phone call after only one or two rings but doesn't require remote activation of fax from extension.
O–No fax/voice switch. When machine intercepts a voice call before owner picks up, it immediately sends the caller a fax tone.
P–Cannot print lists or activity report of faxing activity.
Q–Incudes bracket for mounting fax machine on wall.
R–Footprint is smaller than most.
S–Can fax sheets up to about 10 in. wide.
T–Can fax sheets as narrow as about 4 in.

HOW OBJECTIVE IS CU?

Consumers Union is not beholden to any commercial interest. It accepts no advertising and buys all the products tested on the open market. CU's income is derived from the sale of CONSUMER REPORTS and other publications, and from non-restrictive, noncommercial contributions, grants, and fees. Neither the Ratings nor the reports may be used in advertising or for any other commercial purpose. Consumers Union will take all steps open to it to prevent commercial use of its materials, its name, or the name of CONSUMER REPORTS.

▶ Home

Vacuum cleaners	312
Fans	315
Air-conditioners	317
Air cleaners	322
Water treatment	324
Lead in household water	329
Paint, stains, & finishes	330
Energy savers:	
Weather stripping	335
Exterior caulking compounds	336
Energy-saving thermostats	336
Furnaces	337
Heat pumps	338
Replacement windows	339
Ratings	341

Modern technology offers a variety of ways to keep the home healthy and comfortable. Vacuums play their part by cleaning dirt from various surfaces. Fans and air-conditioners make life bearable in summertime. Room air-cleaners make the air more tolerable to breathe, reducing dust and smoke from cigarettes and fireplaces (although they won't help much with allergies, odors, or dangerous gases). Water-quality tests can alert you to a hazard like lead or keep you from wasting money on water-treatment equipment you may not need. New types of thermostats and heating plants can keep a house comfortable in cold weather at much less energy cost than in the past. Other energy-saving measures include replacing rattly, single-paned windows and caulking up cracks.

Regular home maintenance involves protecting and beautifying the exterior and interior. Choosing the right color, though, is the easy part. You also need to choose the right finish for the job, whether it be paint, stain, or some other product.

Much of the work of painting comes before you pick up a brush. Surface preparation is critical. To ensure that the new finish will adhere properly, the surface should be clean and smooth. Sometimes that requires scraping, power-washing away chalking old paint, or scrubbing off mildew. The worst cases require stripping caked-on layers of old paint or varnish, which can make the job hazardous, too. Paint-stripping techniques commonly involve extreme heat, toxic chemicals, or abrasive tools, and old paint itself often contains lead.

The extra effort in preparation—scraping, sanding, and washing—improves your chances of ending up with a professional-looking job and long-lasting results.

Vacuum cleaners
▶ **Ratings on page 341.**

No vacuum works perfectly in all situations, unfortunately. The first question to ask in choosing a vacuum cleaner is thus pretty basic: What kind of surface will you be cleaning most? If your floors are largely carpeted, you'll need an upright vacuum or a canister model equipped with a power nozzle, which replicates the motorized brush of the upright. If you only have bare floors or if you expect to vacuum upholstered furniture, you need the kind of attachments and the suction available in a canister model or an upright model with a power nozzle.

For small jobs, handheld models fill the gap. Cordless models are best suited for quick pickups. For more power or better performance on carpet, look for a plug-in handheld model with a revolving brush.

The choices

Uprights. Uprights come in two basic designs: those with an old-fashioned, vertically mounted soft bag and those whose bag is enclosed in rigid plastic housing. Apart from looks, the two types differ mainly in how the dirt travels from floor to bag.

One reason uprights generally do better at carpet cleaning is their rotating brushes, which loosen and sweep up dirt lodged in the carpet's pile. But they generally have limited suction, so they're less capable on hard surfaces. Their business end tends to be large, often making them awkward in close quarters—too bulky to slip under a wing chair, too gangly for stairs. Uprights also tend to be more noisy than canisters. Price: $80 to $1600.

Canisters. Imbued with plenty of suction, canisters excel where uprights don't, on bare surfaces and upholstery.

With a canister, you push only the nozzle assembly. The squat tank follows along on wheels—a setup that usually makes the unit more agile than an upright, especially on stairs. But the canister's hose and numerous detachable wands are cumbersome to store, the bag is usually smaller than an upright's, and you have to give the hose a determined yank from time to time to keep the stubby body trailing behind you. As a group, canisters weigh more: 20 to 27 pounds versus 10 to 24 for uprights. Price: about $190 to $1100.

Compact canisters. Compact canisters have smaller tanks than their full-sized cousins. Their compact size and light weight—only 12 to 16 pounds—makes them easier to carry and store than full-sized canisters. But don't expect compacts to handle heavy chores. In our tests, compacts tended to be disappointing performers on all surfaces. They're inexpensive: $80 to $170.

Hand vacuums. Mini vacuums for mini messes now account for one of every three vacuum cleaners sold. Cordless, rechargeable models let users roam wherever grime might lead—from an overturned ashtray in the living room to an overturned flowerpot in the back of the car. Because cordless models rely mostly on suction for pickup, they work best on hard, smooth surfaces. Some models can even handle wet debris and liquids. At about two pounds, cordless models are a pound or so lighter than plug-in models. They run for about 10 minutes on a charge.

Plug-in hand vacuums tether the appliance's free-roaming spirit, although models with a long power cord—some extend 25 feet—are almost as convenient as their untethered siblings. They have no battery to deplete. Most come with revolving brushes like those in upright vacuum cleaners. Prices of cordless and plug-in vacuums overlap: about $30 to $90.

Car vacs. A variation on the portable vacuum, these resemble cordless models, except they include a 15- or 20-foot cord that plugs into the cigarette lighter. They can be used for extended periods of time without draining the car battery very much. Price: about $30 to $90.

Features and conveniences

Power nozzle. Most canisters, both full-sized and compact, come equipped with a power nozzle. This motorized brush helps canisters remove embedded dirt in carpeting. Look for an automatic shutoff mechanism that prevents the power-nozzle motor from overheating and burning out if an object gets stuck.

Assembly. An upright model requires little, if any, assembly to clean floors. A hose that's permanently attached to the cleaner on one end is the most convenient design for attaching tools. Some models make you snap an adapter over the carpet brush or, worse, unhook the drive belt to connect the hose.

Putting together a canister is slightly more cumbersome. You typically insert the hose, then attach a metal or plastic wand, which may consist of several pieces. Latches or clicking buttons hold metal wands together; plastic wands are held in place by friction. Apply too little force and the fittings can fall apart; apply too much and they're difficult to separate. The power nozzle and its wiring must be detached and set aside if you want to attach other tools.

Controls. An On/off switch high on an upright's handle is easy to reach. On most canisters and a few uprights, the switch is on the base, where it's easily worked by foot. Most canisters have a separate foot switch to turn off the power nozzle, helpful when you're cleaning flat-weave rugs, which can be damaged by heavy brushing.

Suction adjustment. When vacuuming loose or billowy objects, too much suction can cause the cleaner to inhale the fabric. Most canisters and some uprights let you reduce suction by uncovering a hole or valve near the handle. Models with more than one speed allow for varying degrees of suction as well.

Among hand vacs, a revolving brush improves carpet cleaning, but it also competes with suction, flinging coarser soils about instead of ingesting them. A few battery-powered models come with a power-brush attachment, which improves pickup but can quickly drain batteries.

Adjustable brush height. Look for a model that allows the brush to be raised or lowered. Most uprights and a few canisters have a dial, sliding lever, or foot pedal to adjust height. Some models make height adjustments automatically.

Hoses. The most convenient are ones that swivel. Non-swiveling hoses can form curlicues as you vacuum.

Pushing and carrying. Uprights equipped with power-assisted wheels glide over the plushest carpeting with hardly a push. Large wheels or rollers on models that require pushing, make the job easier.

Because they're one-piece units, uprights can usually be carried with one hand. Hoisting the tank and hose assembly of canisters requires two hands. Compact canisters sometimes come with a shoulder strap that makes them easy to carry and wield, especially on stairs.

Vacuum bags. Most full-sized cleaners collect dirt in a disposable paper bag; some have an indicator that helpfully tells you when the bag is full or when airflow is blocked. Soft-body uprights have the largest bags (about a four-quart capacity). Hand vacuums have the smallest, of course.

Replacing the bag is easiest when you can drop the bag's cardboard collar into a slot. It's less convenient on models that make you slide the bag's sleeve over a tube and secure it with a spring band.

Most cordless hand vacuums come with an internal dust cup, which holds only a cup or two of debris. Plug-ins with an external dust bag have the greatest capacity—6 to 11 cups.

Noise. No machine can be called quiet. The most offensive are uprights, especially the soft-bag models, according to our tests.

Dust emission and blow-by. We found that paper dust bags in uprights or canisters were better at trapping fine dust than water filtration or bagless dust collectors. The best solution for people who are severely allergic to dust may be to minimize carpeting.

Hand vacs are sometimes guilty of shooting dirt and dust out of vent holes. It's more of a problem with cordless vacs than plug-ins because of the rear-mounted fan.

Cord storage. It's simplest on machines that have a spring-driven button or pedal that slurps up the long power cord automatically. Others have two hooks around which you wind the cord. If one hook swivels or retracts, you can loosen the cord quickly. Some canisters make you wrap the cord around the tank.

The tests

To gauge deep-cleaning prowess, we grind silica and talcum into sections of medium-pile carpeting, then pass each cleaner back and forth over the carpeting eight times and weigh the carpet and the vacuum to see how much dirt is picked up. To judge suction, we measure airflow with a new bag, and then gradually feed each machine fine sawdust to measure how precipitously suction falls off.

The regimen is similar for hand-held models. We spread soils—sugar, sand, gravel, dog hair, potting soil—on wood flooring and on low-pile carpeting, then count the number of passes each machine takes to remove the debris.

We also check edge cleaning—how close to a wall each machine can vacuum—measure noise levels, and for full-sized cleaners, gauge how well the various models keep dust from kicking up.

Buying advice

Canisters have gained a reputation for versatility. They typically provide plenty of suction and do a decent job on carpeting, if equipped with a power nozzle. And their tools usually travel on board. But uprights, known primarily for their carpet-cleaning prowess, are becoming more versatile as well. In recent years, manufacturers have outfitted many models with a hose and attachments to bolster their effectiveness on bare surfaces. Some upright models also allow the hose and gadgets to ride on the cleaner, a far more convenient arrangement than having to rummage through the closet for them.

For small spaces, you might be satisfied with a compact canister model. But full-sized models outperformed compacts.

You needn't pay top dollar. Although you can spend more than $1000 for a *Kirby* or *Rexair Rainbow*, plenty of models that sell for $200 or so work quite well.

Most hand vacs should work well on spills and small messes. A plug-in model with a revolving brush can gobble up dirt on carpet better than battery-powered models, but a plug-in can also scatter heavier bits of debris such as gravel on hard flooring. And with a plug-in model, you lose much of the mobility that originally made handheld vacs popular.

The car vacs we've tested were mediocre workers. If there's an electric outlet close enough to your auto, you're better off using a regular hand-vac or full-sized vacuum.

Fans

▶ **Ratings start on page 344.**

Today's fans aren't very different from the ones CONSUMER REPORTS first reported on more than a half century ago. They're essentially just a motor, blades, switch, and housing. Manufacturers arrange those pieces into a few basic shapes for use in a window, the attic, or on the ceiling or floor.

Portable-fan brands include *Galaxy, Patton, Windmere,* and *Lakewood.* Major brands of ceiling fans include *Hunter, Emerson* and *Casablanca.* Some major chains carry their own brands—Home Depot's *Hampton Bay,* for instance, along with K Mart, Sears, and others.

The choices

Portable fans. They're meant for localized ventilation or cooling. Window models typically rest on the window sill, with sliding partitions to form the opening. Many box fans are suitable for window use, too. (Check manufacturer's recommendations for use.) Floor fans come with a pedestal or stand. Some window models can be converted to floor fans by rotating their legs or stands. The better air-movers tend to be noisier and create more turbulence. Portables have 9- to 20-inch blades and range in price from less than $20 to $100.

Ceiling fans. Fashionable as well as functional, these nostalgic appliances excel at circulating air within a room, particularly one with high ceilings. Their forte: The quiet, nearly imperceptible movement of air. Yet a large ceiling fan can, on higher speeds, recirculate cool air the way a portable fan does. Ceiling fans deliver a downdraft that's a foot or two wider than the diameter of the blades. Typically, the edge of this column of air moves briskly; the "eye" of the column moves more gently. If the fan is centered in the ceiling, the air column reaches the floor, spreads out toward the walls, and turns upward to be recirculated.

Ceiling fans require a ceiling at least eight feet high, so the blades hang at least seven feet from the floor. Models that can be flush-mounted against the ceiling provide more headroom than those that must be suspended.

Fans come with four, five, or six blades and may have blades anywhere from 29 inches to 62 inches across. A 52-inch blade sweep is the most common. Prices vary widely: from $25 to more than $1000, although most are priced at $80 to $180. The more expensive models—those priced at $200 and up—generally offer better workmanship and more durable parts than cheaper models. Their heavy-duty castings, sealed bearings, weighted and better-balanced blades contribute to smoother and quieter operation.

Whole-house fans. These large attic-mounted fans can quickly draw copious amounts of fresh air through the entire house. If the outside temperature drops from, say, 85° to 75°F in two hours, air temperature in a house will take another four hours to drop that much. A whole-house fan can do the job in a bit more than two hours.

A whole house fan requires the right kind of space and considerable effort to install. You need two openings, one from the living space to the attic and another from the attic to the outdoors. The most effective way to do the job is to cut and frame the needed openings and fit them with shutters. "Automatic" shutters are simple and cheap. They are moved by the fan's sucking or blowing action. Shutters that open mechanically are more effective because they restrict airflow less.

The fans, whose blades range from 24 to 36 inches, sell for about $200 to $400. Professional installation, adding louvers, shutters, remote-controlled switches, and other accessories, can double the cost.

Features and conveniences

Controls. Portable models sometimes come with a variable-speed control, which lets you set the speed precisely; some also have a thermostat that cycles the unit on and off at various temperature levels.

Typically, a ceiling fan will use a pullchain to cycle through two or three speeds and turn the fan on and off, with a switch on the fan housing to reverse the direction of the air flow.

A wall-mounted control is more convenient, especially for a fan mounted on a cathedral ceiling. Some fancier ceiling fans offer a handheld remote. On some models, the remote is the only means you have to control the fan. If you lose the gadget or it breaks, you're out of luck.

Whole-house fans typically have two or three speeds, controlled by a wall switch.

Lights. Ceiling fans typically come with a light fixture under the fan or allow one to be added.

Child safeguards. Child-safety features are especially important with portable fans because of their proximity to youngsters. Look for grilles and housings whose openings are small enough and rigid enough to keep out fingers. Some models have a child-resistant On/off switch that, like a pill bottle top, must be depressed and turned at the same time.

Sizing the fans

In general, the larger the blade diameter the greater a fan's air-moving capacity, but not always. Design differences help some smaller fans move more air than some of the larger models.

With a whole-house fan, there's a precise way to figure out what size machine to buy. First, figure out the cubic feet of the space to be ventilated. Include halls and stairways but exclude closets, pantries, store rooms, and the attic. If your summers are generally hot, you need a whole house fan that can change house air completely every two minutes when running at maximum speed. Thus, for a house with 12,000 cubic feet of living space, you need a fan that can move 6000 cubic feet of air per minute. In areas where the heat is less intense, a model with a lower capacity should suffice.

Manufacturers rate their fans working against resistance (usually as 0.1 inch of water) or for "free-air delivery," which indicates the breeze churned when nothing restricts air flow. A free-air delivery rate isn't very realistic, since windows, furnishings, and a house's layout can cut the flow. If the fan's air delivery when working against resistance isn't available, use 80 to 85 percent of the free-air delivery rating.

The tests

We assess both air-moving ability and air distribution. We also measure each model's noise output and efficiency—how much air is moved for each watt of power consumed. Depending on the type of fan, tests also include a "rain" test for electric-shock hazard and a stability test.

Buying advice

If you're considering a portable fan, first decide whether you want a fan that will sit in or near the window. Decide if you want the fan to ventilate the room or to just circulate the air within the room. For cooling a single room, consider a box fan or larger table and pedestal model. For ventilating more than one room, look to large fans or even an attic fan, whose 24- to 36-inch blades can vent an entire house in a matter of minutes.

Most portable fans do a fine job of circulating air in a room. If you don't mind the turbulence, a high-velocity unit will stir up quite a breeze. If you want a quiet fan, buy a large fan. On low speed, it may move as much air as a small fan moves on high, and do the job more quietly.

A ceiling fan's slow-turning blades create a quiet, gentle breeze. Money spent here buys better workmanship and more durable parts.

A whole-house fan can make the entire house feel cool in a hurry. In many parts of the country, drawing in the cool night air may be all you need to survive the summer.

Air-conditioners

▶ Ratings start on page 350.   ▶ Repair records on page 374.

Air-conditioning is often considered a necessity, particularly where summers are long and humid. But an air-conditioner's appetite for electricity exacts a high environmental cost—more fossil fuel burned at the power plant—as well as an economic one, in the form of high utility bills.

Choosing an efficient air-conditioner helps reduce costs. A model's efficiency rating—the EER (Energy Efficiency Rating) for a room unit, or SEER (Seasonal Energy Efficiency Rating) for other types—is on its yellow Energy Guide label. The higher the rating, the lower the unit's energy cost to produce a given amount of cooling. Among room models, we consider a rating of 9.0 or more to be high-efficiency.

Sears Kenmore is the leading brand of room air-conditioner. *Sears, GE, Whirlpool,* and *Fedders* account for about half of all room air-conditioners sold. Split-ductless models are a small, relatively new part of the market, but there are more than a dozen brands including *Mitsubishi* and *Sanyo*. Big names in central air-conditioning are *Carrier, Rheem, InterCity,* and *Goodman*.

The choices

All air-conditioners contain pretty much the same components: the outdoor compressor and condenser and the indoor fan and evaporator. The different types of units available in the market are simply different arrangements of these components, each with its own advantages and disadvantages:

Central units. The most popular type of central units are units that cool only. Another approach to central cooling is the heat pump, a central system that can switch from heating to cooling. Heat pumps make the most sense for homeowners who want to replace electric heating and those who cool more than heat. Both types put the noisier components outdoors and distribute air throughout the house through ducts in the walls. But they're also the most expensive way to cool. Systems are sold and installed by contractors. Price: at least $3000 to $4000 for a standard air-conditioner package that includes installation; $4000 to $5000 for a dual-purpose heat pump.

For maximum efficiency and cooling, proper sizing and installation of an air-conditioner are essential. A unit that's too large may not dehumidify adequately. A good contractor should calculate the needed capacity room by room, allowing for climate, house construction, and other factors. Avoid simplistic rules of thumb, such as one ton—12,000 Btu (British thermal units) per hour for every 1000 square feet.

Installation is easier and less expensive if your house has existing ducts that can be adapted for cooling or heating (with a heat pump). If not, you'll need new ducts. When installing ducts, the contractor should devote careful attention to balancing airflow into and out of each room to be cooled. Ducts should be firmly connected (not with duct tape), adequately supported so they don't bend sharply, and insulated where they pass through uncooled spaces.

Room models. Most of these are designed to fit in a double-hung window; others are designed for casement windows. Beyond that, they vary in size and capacity. The smallest, suitable for a small bedroom, are generally rated at 5000 Btu per hour. The largest made to run on normal household voltage are rated at 11,000 to 14,000 Btu per hour, enough to cool several rooms. Smaller units rated at 5000 to 5,800 Btu are priced at $300 to $450; units rated 6000 to 6,700 Btu, $300 to $425; units rated 7000 to 8,200 Btu, $400 to $750. To be sure, determine the size you need by using the worksheet on pages 320 and 321.

Two drawbacks of room air-conditioners are that they block most of a window and tend to be noisy. Manufacturers are making progress on both fronts. Some "low profile" designs put the bulk of the working parts outside and below the window, cutting noise and reducing the vertical window blockage by about half.

Performance continues to improve, too. In our tests, most units could adequately control temperature and humidity and most started up without incident under brownout conditions. When it comes to air distribution, most units tend to favor left or right.

Split-ductless models. Something of a cross between a room unit and central air-conditioning, this type is widely used in Europe and Japan, but fairly new to the U.S. Like a central system, its compressor and condenser are outdoors, but they connect by tubing directly to a wall-mounted fan and evaporator in the room or rooms to be cooled. No ductwork is needed. This arrangement insures quiet operation and the ability to place the room component where it will cool most effectively, without tying up a window. A ductless model makes the most sense if you need to cool more than one room, or for cooling an addition to a house with central air-conditioning.

Split-ductless models range in capacity from 8000 Btu per hour to 50,000. Some can double as a heat pump in winter. Ductless models are installed by contractors; prices range from $1100 to nearly $2000, plus installation. Most models we tested performed as well as and were quieter than room units.

Portable. A few portable models on the market are portable and don't need windows at all. Not only are such units expensive, but when we tested them, all proved disappointing. We rated two—the *Bionaire* and *Koldwave*—Not Acceptable as room air-conditioners in our May 1991 report.

Features and conveniences

Energy-saving options. A few room models have a 24-hour timer that lets you turn an air-conditioner on before you get home rather than leave it running all day. Common, but far less useful, is a timer that turns the unit on or off just once. You can also buy a separate timer specially designed to work with most room models. An Energy Saver setting, included on many room models, cycles the fan on and off with the compressor instead of letting it run continuously. These models can also provide better humidity control, but temperature control typically suffers and the lack of moving air can make the room feel stuffy.

Ductless models with a moisture-removal cycle dehumidify by turning the fan off when the compressor is off. They control the compressor's operating time and temperature setting.

Controls. Good design here can make it easier to keep the room comfortable. On room air-conditioners, look for a thermostat with clear markings. Even better—an electronic thermostat with LED readout of room temperature and a signal light showing that the power is on.

Because ductless units are typically mounted near the ceiling, all come with some type of remote control, either wired or wireless; we found a wireless infrared remote the most convenient. Look for models with LCD displays, which are easy to read in bright light.

Louvers. Many room models lack a good way to direct the cooled air. Directional control is especially important if the air-conditioner will be mounted in a corner or if you want spot-cooling. Models that let you close some of the louvers can throw cool air with more force through the open ones. A vent setting blows some air outdoors and should only be used when the unit isn't cooling. Some models can also draw fresh air in.

Slide-out chassis. This is found on a room air-conditioner, the only type of air-conditioner you can install yourself. It lets you secure the empty cabinet in the window, then slide the innards into position. That simplifies repairs and makes installation safer but time consuming. All room units should be installed by at least two people; low-profile models can easily become unwieldy.

The tests

CU tests air-conditioners by mounting them in an environmental chamber—a heavily insulated room partitioned down the middle, to create an "outside" and an "inside." Each unit's task is to maintain a temperature of 75°F or 80° when the "outdoor" temperature is kept at 95°. For room models, we also keep outdoor humidity at 70 percent and measure the ability to keep variations from exceeding five percent. Sensors mounted in front of the fan determine how uniformly each model distributes cool air. To simulate a heat-wave brownout, we boost the outside temperature to at least 115° and drop line voltage to as low as 100 volts. At the lower voltage, we run a unit for an hour, turn it off for three minutes, then try to start it again.

Reliability

Room air-conditioners are very reliable appliances. On average, only about one in 22 models purchased by our readers since 1987 has needed repairs. *Emerson Quiet Kool*, *Panasonic*, and *Sears* were among the most reliable brands. For central air-conditioners purchased from 1984 to 1992, *Trane* and *Lennox* have been among the brands requiring the fewest repairs to the outdoor components. See the brand Repair Histories on page 374.

Buying advice

If you live where the weather is hot for more than two or three months per year, consider central air-conditioning. Where summers are dry and nights cool, a window or whole-house fan may be a sufficient—and much cheaper—alternative. Otherwise, consider an air-conditioner that cools just part of the house—a room model for a room or two, a split-ductless model for two or more rooms.

Among room units, don't assume that the biggest unit that can fit is the best. Use the worksheet on pages 320 and 321 to determine the exact size you need. The higher the EER (or SEER, for central and ductless models), the lower the operating cost.

For a central or ductless air-conditioner, choose your installer with care, because you'll probably want to go back to that company for service or repairs.

How powerful an air-conditioner do you need?

This worksheet, adapted from one published by the Association of Home Appliance Manufacturers, can help you estimate how much cooling capacity you need. You'll need a tape measure, scratch paper, and a pocket calculator. The worksheet guides you through the measurements and the calculations to determine the size of the air-conditioner. Make the measurements listed. For each dimension or area, round it to the nearest whole number before entering it in the appropriate box, and multiply by the factor in bold. **(When two numbers are shown, use the factors in parentheses if the air-conditioner will be used only at night.)** If the room is connected to another by a permanently open door or by an archway more than 5 feet wide, consider the two rooms as one area and make all the necessary measurements in both rooms.

1. HEAT THROUGH WINDOWS. Calculate the area (height x width) of each window. Take the measurements in inches, then divide by 144 to determine the square footage. (Jot down the area of each window for use in step 6.) Add the areas, then enter that figure on the appropriate line below and multiply by the factor given.

For single glass .... _____ x 14 = _____
                                                            total window area, sq. ft.

For double glass or glass block .... _____ x 7 = _____
                                                            total window area; sq. ft.

2. WALLS. Measure the length of all walls, in feet. (Height assumed to be 8 feet.) Consider walls shaded by adjacent buildings as facing north. Write the lengths on the appropriate lines below and multiply by the factors given.

Uninsulated frame construction; masonry up to 8 inches thick

Outside, facing north +shaded +interior walls .... _____ x 30 = _____
                                                            total wall length, ft.

Outside, facing other directions .... _____ x 60(30) = _____
                                                            total wall length, ft.

Insulated frame construction; masonry more than 8 inches thick

Outside, facing north +shaded +interior walls .... _____ x 20 = _____
                                                            total wall length, ft.

Outside, facing other directions .... _____ x 30(20) = _____
                                                            total wall length, ft.

3. CEILING. Determine the ceiling area (length X width), in square feet. Enter that figure on the line that's appropriate for your house. Multiply by the factor given.

Uninsulated, no space above .... _____ x 19(5) = _____
                                                            ceiling area, sq. ft.

Uninsulated, attic above .... _____ x 12(7) = _____
                                                            ceiling area, sq. ft.

Insulated, no space above .... _____ x 8(3) = _____
                                                            ceiling area, sq. ft.

Insulated, attic above... _____ x 5(4) = _____
                                                            ceiling area, sq. ft.

Occupied space above.. _____ x 3 = _____
                                                            ceiling area, sq. ft.

4. DOORS AND ARCHES. Note: If the room has an archway more than 5 feet wide or a permanently open door, skip this step and go to step 5. Otherwise, enter the width of the door or archway and multiply by the factor shown.

                                                            _____ x 300(200) = _____
                                                            total width, ft.

5. FLOOR. Note: If the floor is on ground or over a basement, skip this step and move on to step 6. Otherwise, determine the floor area (length X width) in feet and multiply by the factor shown. The floor area is usually the same as the ceiling area.

                                                            _____ x 3 = _____
                                                            floor area, sq. ft.

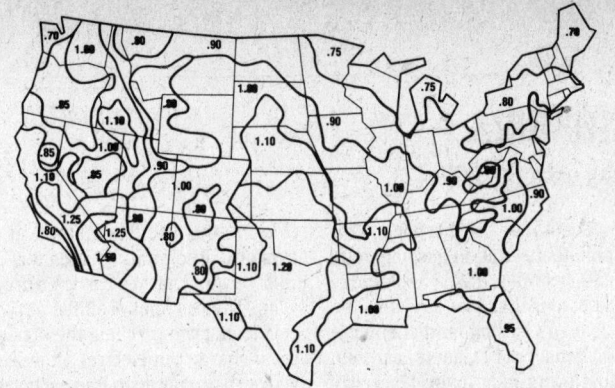

6. SUN THROUGH WINDOWS. Note: If the air-conditioner will be used only at night, or if all windows in the room face north, skip this step and go on to step 7. Using the measurements you made for step 1, enter the total window area for each wall on the appropriate line and multiply by the factor that best describes how the windows are shaded.

Wall orientation		No shades	Inside shades	Awnings	For glass block, multiply again by 0.5; for storm windows or double glass, by 0.8; for single glass. by 1	
Northeast	_____ area, sq. ft.	x 60	or x 25	or x 20=	x _____	= _____
East	_____ area, sq. ft.	x 80	or x 40	or x 25 =	x _____	= _____
Southeast	_____ area, sq. ft.	x 75	or x 30	or x 20 =	x _____	= _____
South	_____ area, sq. ft.	x 75	or x 35	or x 20 =	x _____	= _____
Southwest	_____ area, sq. ft.	x 110	or x 45	or x 30 =	x _____	= _____
West	_____ area, sq. ft.	x 150	or x 65	or x 45 =	x _____	= _____
Northwest	_____ area, sq. ft.	x 120	or x 50	or x 35 =	x _____	= _____

Use only the largest number.

7. SUBTOTAL. Add the figures from steps 1 through 5 and the largest figure calculated in step 6. Enter the sum here and in the box for step 8, below......................... _____

SUBTOTAL

8. CLIMATE CORRECTION. Enter the subtotal from step 7 on the line. Check the map above to find the climate-correction factor for your area. Enter the factor on the line below. Multiply the two numbers.

_____ x _____ = _____
subtotal from step 7   factor from map

9. HEAT FROM PEOPLE. Calculate the heat contributed by people in the room. In the box below, enter the number of people who normally use the room (use a minimum of 2). Multiply the figure by the factor given.

_____ x 600 = _____
people in room (min. 2)

10. HEAT FROM APPLIANCES. Add up the wattage of all lights and appliances in the room, not including the air-conditioner itself. Multiply the figure by the factor given.

_____ x 3 = _____
total wattage

11. TOTAL COOLING LOAD. Add the figures on lines 8, 9, and 10.
Enter the sum on the line at the right. _____

TOTAL

The number you derive tells how much heat builds up in the room each hour. The air-conditioner's cooling capacity (Btu per hour) should nearly match the number you calculated. A difference of about 5 percent between the number you calculated and the air-conditioner's capacity shouldn't be significant.

Air cleaners

▶ Ratings on page 357.

The air in your house can harbor a wide variety of pollutants—radon gas, cigarette smoke, cooking fumes, gases and smoke from furnaces and gas ranges, solvents from dry-cleaned clothing, and chemicals from paints, household cleaners, and bug sprays. Most eventually make their way outdoors through spaces around windows and doors, but in a tight house, the air-exchange rate can be so low that pollution levels may actually exceed government limits for outdoor air.

Opening windows and eliminating pollution sources are the most effective ways to control indoor pollution. Using an appliance to clear the air, our tests show, at best brings relief from only dust and smoke.

The choices

Many air contaminants are too small to see with the naked eye. To remove such small objects, air cleaners use filtration, electrical attraction, or ozone.

High-efficiency-particulate-arresting filters (HEPA, for short) are the most efficient and expensive filters. These filters snare at least 99.97 percent of particles as small as 0.3 microns. A variant, the pleated filter, traps up to 95 percent of the same particles. By comparison, a room air-conditioner's foam filter traps particles only 10 microns or larger, and no more than 30 percent of the particles at that. But even the best HEPA filter can't catch something as small as a gas molecule. Activated carbon or charcoal filters in HEPA or pleated-filter air cleaners are meant to handle that task but are usually inadequate.

With electrical attraction, airborne particles are given an electrical charge, then collected. There are three main types of cleaners that use this method. In an electrostatic-precipitating cleaner, a high-voltage wire charges particles drawn in by a fan. The particles are then attracted to a collection plate carrying the opposite electrical charge. An electret filter uses fibers with a static charge to trap particles. A negative-ionizer uses fine, electrically charged needles or wire to charge particles, which collect in a filter or, more typically, on walls and furnishings. None of the electrical-attraction cleaners removes gas molecules because the molecules tend to diffuse back into the air rather than stick to a collection plate.

A third approach to air-cleaning uses a high-voltage electrical charge to convert oxygen to ozone, a powerful but toxic gas commonly used to disinfect mildewy boats and deodorize fire-ravaged buildings. At sufficiently high concentrations, ozone attacks and destroys some gaseous odor molecules and microorganisms. Ozone has no effect on dust and other particulates, however. Further, the ozone generators sold for home use can actually foul the air. The two ozone generators we tested in 1992 generated unhealthy levels of ozone. Neither cleaned very well. We rated both Not Acceptable.

Air cleaners that use such technologies come in various configurations. The type to buy depends on the area you need to clean:

Tabletop. These are usually ionizers or devices that use electret filters. Their fans are quiet but move little air. They're suited to small rooms or the area around a smoker's chair. Price: less than $200.

Room cleaner. If you're cleaning any but the smallest room, you'll need this type with its stronger fan. Most room cleaners are either an electrostatic precipitator or use a HEPA filter. In our tests, most removed dust and smoke far better than even the best tabletop model. Price: about $200 to more than $600.

In-duct cleaners. These go in the ductwork of a central heating or air-conditioning system, where they clean the air for an entire house. There are several types, ranging from sophisticated to simple. The more effective in our tests included a simple filter (about $15) that replaces the existing one in your heating/cooling system. Better yet are complex electrostatic precipitators, which are priced at about $500 and must be installed by a contractor (about $300). Two potential drawbacks to in-duct cleaners: They work only when the system's fan is blowing, and they can slow air flow through the ducts, raising energy costs.

The tests

The closest thing to a performance standard for comparing air cleaners is the clean-air delivery rate (CADR), a measure that expresses the number of cubic feet of clean air a unit delivers each minute. The CADR, developed by the Association of Home Appliance Manufacturers, is used by some air-cleaner manufacturers on their products.

The CADR is based on both the percentage of particles removed and how quickly they are removed. Tests performed to the appliance association's specifications provide separate CADR numbers for dust, smoke, and pollen.

We believe the CADR numbers alone don't provide a complete picture of an air-cleaner's effectiveness. It's also necessary to know the unit's total air-flow rate to properly assess efficiency. For instance, two cleaners may have the same CADR, but the one with the lower total air flow will be the more efficient.

We measure air flow and determine the CADR inside a sealed chamber, using very fine laboratory dust and tobacco smoke. Contaminant concentrations are monitored by a laser spectrometer that counts the microscopic particles. To measure odor removal, we use human noses and an extremely sensitive monitor.

Buying advice

First, try to eliminate the source of the pollution or ventilate the room. If the trouble is pollen, an air-conditioner set to recirculate indoor air should work. An air cleaner should be tried if those measures fail. If the problem is cigarette smoke, odors, or gases, most air cleaners won't help.

The most effective room models in our tests were electrostatic precipitators and those using a HEPA filter. In general, tabletop units weren't nearly as good; the best were ionizers with electret filters.

We found the contractor-installed electrostatic precipitators nearly as effective as the best room models. Two do-it-yourself in-duct filters were about equally effective, on a par with a small tabletop unit, at best.

Stay away from ozone generators; the two models we tested can generate unhealthy levels of ozone.

Keep in mind that operating costs and maintenance are major considerations when choosing a cleaner. Energy and maintenance costs vary widely among models and, in some cases, can exceed the purchase price within just a year or two. Energy costs will range from about $20 to $60. The cost of replacement filters can be high, particularly for units using a HEPA filter. Expect to spend $30 to $120 for HEPA filters a year; for other types, $20 to $80.

Most air cleaners require little maintenance beyond filter changes and cleanings. If you choose an electrostatic precipitator you'll need to wash its electronic cell every few months. When the air cleaner makes a crackling sound, you'll know it's time for the cleaning.

Water treatment

▶ **Listings of water filters on page 355.**

Most people's drinking water in the U.S. is not seriously polluted. Public supplies are either comparatively clean to start with or are purified to bring them up to par. Some people who sell water filters and other treatment devices, though, hope you don't know that. The less you know, the more easily they can sell you equipment you may not need.

What gives high-pressure or deceitful tactics an air of credibility is that there are some very real drinking water problems. More than 70,000 water contaminants—industrial and agricultural wastes, heavy metals, radon, and microbes—have been identified. While such contaminants may affect only a fraction of the population, those people have justified concerns.

If you're wondering about your water quality, the first step is to find out what's in the water. If you use a community water system, ask for your utility's latest laboratory test results. If you use a well, try to get information on local water problems from your public works department or the local agricultural extension service.

Testing your water

The surest way to know what's in your water is to test it. The *Nordic Ware Water Test Kit,* about $8 at a hardware store, lets you run a few basic water-quality tests at home. It's easy to use and accurate enough for home use. For an extra $6, the *Nordic Ware* kit offers a mail-in test for lead, a useful option. Unfortunately the kit cannot detect most toxic pollutants. If you suspect you have a problem with, say, organic solvents or pesticides, you need to have your water tested by a professional.

If you have your water tested by someone else, use a reputable, state-certified, independent laboratory, not a company that sells water-treatment equipment. Here are three reliable labs we've identified and their prices for a lead test: Clean Water Fund, 704 251-0518, $12; Suburban Water Testing Labs, 800 433-6595, $35; National Testing Laboratories, 800 458-3330, $58. If a test report says your water has a high level of a contaminant, seek confirmation by having the water retested or sent to a second lab before taking costly action.

Pollutants to worry about

Of the thousands of water pollutants, three of the most widespread are lead, radon, and nitrate. Most organic pollutants present only localized problems. Treatment methods are listed in the chart on page 327.

Lead. Significant levels of this toxic metal are more widespread in drinking water than was once assumed (see "Lead in household water" on page 329), and levels once considered safe are now considered health concerns, particularly for infants and children. Even low-level lead exposure may affect learning ability in children and is associated with elevated blood pressure in adults.

Lead gets in water primarily from corrosion of household plumbing or water company service lines or both. Very soft water and slightly acidic water are especially likely to leach lead from soldered pipes and brass fixtures. To help minimize your exposure, use only cold water for cooking and drinking (hot water dissolves more lead). Running water for a minute or so to flush the pipes may help, but it's not a sure cure.

If you have more than 5 ppb (parts per

WATER TREATMENT

billion) of lead in your water even after letting it run, you should seriously consider doing something about it. This is especially true if your household includes someone at high risk for lead exposure or particularly vulnerable to lead—for example, an infant on a water-based formula (see page 329).

Radon. A naturally occurring radioactive gas, radon probably poses a greater health risk than all other environmental pollutants combined. According to the U.S. Environmental Protection Agency, radon may cause between 10,000 and 40,000 lung-cancer deaths each year. Most of the risk comes from radon that seeps into homes from the ground. But some well water contains dissolved radon, which escapes into the air in the home from sources like showers and washing machines. Exposure to radon from water may cause between 100 and 1800 deaths a year.

Water-borne radon is usually confined to wells in private or small community water systems. Larger systems generally remove any radon before it reaches the tap. Before you test your water for radon, test the air inside your house. If the level is high and you use ground (well) water, have the water tested. If the air level is low, don't worry about the water.

The level that should prompt remedial action is a matter of dispute. According to an EPA official, you should take action if you water's radon level is 10,000 picocuries per liter or higher (that corresponds to about 1 picocurie per cubic meter of airborne radon). Radon is easily dispersed in outdoor air, so aerating the water before it enters the house is usually the simplest solution. Ventilating the bathroom, laundry room, or kitchen may also help dissipate the radon. Other solutions include carbon filters.

Nitrate. High nitrate levels in water pose a risk mainly to infants. Bacteria in immature digestive tracts convert it into nitrite, which in turn combines with hemoglobin in the blood to form methemoglobin, which cannot transport oxygen. The resulting ailment, called methemoglobinemia, is rare but can result in brain damage or death. Some adults, including pregnant women, may also be susceptible to developing methemoglobinemia.

Nitrate in water comes mainly from agricultural activities. Rural families with private wells—especially those with infants or pregnant women—should have their water tested regularly. Some state health departments test wells for free. High nitrate levels may signal that other contaminants are also present.

Treatment choices

If tests show your water supply is contaminated, consider buying bottled water; CU's tests have shown that it's generally clean. If you have a well, you might also try digging deeper to an uncontaminated aquifer. Or you can treat your existing water supply with a water treatment device. Some products on the market use just one of the techniques explained here; others combine two or more. However, none of the types discussed below should be used to treat bacteriologically contaminated water. That may require sterilization methods such as UV, ozone, or chlorine.

Carbon filters. These treat a variety of problems, so they're the most popular water-treatment device. They remove residual chlorine, which improves the water's taste, and can also remove organic compounds—chemicals such as pesticides, solvents, or chloroform. But they won't remove hardness minerals or microbes (under certain conditions, they actually breed them).

Carbon filters come in many forms. In-line filters, which serve a single cold-water faucet, are suitable for a household that uses lots of water. Price: about $100 to $500.

Tiny, faucet-mounted filters with a couple of ounces of carbon cost $20 to $30. Pour-through or pitcher devices are priced from $10 to $25. Whole-house carbon filters, which have five-foot-high tanks and can be backwashed, are especially useful for removing radon from the whole house's water. They are priced $1500 and up.

The most practical method of carbon filtration is an in-line filter that treats water at a single location, such as at the kitchen sink. The two main designs are under-sink models and countertop models, which attach with flexible tubes.

Filters and cartridges have to be periodically replaced, at costs ranging from $5 to $100 each time. Manufacturers typically recommend replacing a filter after a certain time or after a given quantity of water has passed through. Some filters have a water meter built in. For a high-volume in-line filter, expect to change cartridges every six months or 1000 gallons.

Reverse-osmosis devices. Reverse-osmosis devices are best at removing inorganic contaminants, such as dissolved salts, ferrous iron, chloride, fluoride, nitrate, and heavy metals such as lead. A carbon filter is incorporated in most reverse-osmosis systems to remove organic chemicals.

Reverse-osmosis devices can be clogged by high levels of hardness minerals. They work slowly, producing only a few gallons of fresh water per day, and they waste several gallons of water for every purified gallon they produce.

At the heart of these devices lies a fine sieve of cellophanelike material—a semipermeable membrane that screens out all but the smallest molecules. Under pressure, only water and other small molecules are able to pass through.

Some versions attach to the cold-water line under the sink; others sit on the counter. Under-sink models run $500 to $850, countertop models about $350 to $500.

Reverse-osmosis membranes need replacement every few years; filters, more often. Replacement membranes cost $45 to $234; filters, another $25 or so.

Distillers. Distillers boil water, then cool the steam until it condenses. Some models include a tiny carbon filter. Countertop units hold from one-half to 2½ gallons. Prices range from $150 to $429.

Distillers are best for brackish water or water polluted with heavy metals; they demineralize it. Anything that won't boil or evaporate stays behind in the boiling pot. Boiling water can also kill microorganisms, but distillers shouldn't be relied on for that purpose. Distillers aren't effective against volatile organics like chloroform and benzene, which vaporize in the distiller and can wind up in the condensed water. A carbon filter might help remove such chemicals, but the filters incorporated into distillers are too small to do it reliably. Distillers are slow, taking a couple of hours to produce the first quart of water.

Since distillers collect and concentrate minerals, scale can build up quickly and must be cleaned out. And since they heat up, they use a lot of electricity—about three kilowatt-hours per gallon of water purified.

Water softeners. Water softeners remove minerals that cause soap deposits, and also remove iron and lead. They don't remove hazardous contaminants like radon, nitrate, or pesticides. They also take a lot of space. A water softener consists of a tank of tiny resin beads loosely coated with sodium ions. When hard water flows in, minerals—principally calcium and magnesium—take sodium's place on the resin. Periodically the softener reverses its flow, taking salt out of a reservoir tank to regenerate the resin beads. The minerals are flushed down the drain.

Some models regenerate at preset intervals, using a timer. More sophisticated models ("demand-control" models) regenerate according to water use. Softeners also differ in size. "Cabinet" units are the most compact size.

The average price for a softener is about $1000, but the price varies depending on installation, local water conditions, and competition among local dealers.

A water softener doesn't require very much care, except for the salt you add now

Water problems and solutions

Recommended if drinking water contains more than "action level" amounts.

	Action level	Carbon filter	Reverse osmosis	Distiller	Water softener	Iron remover	Activated alumina cartridge	Sediment filter	Aerator
AESTHETIC PROBLEMS									
Dissolved iron	—				✔	✔			
Rust stains	—			✔		✔		✔	
Calcium	—				✔				
Magnesium	—				✔				
Chlorine	—	✔							✔
Salty taste	—		✔	✔					
'Skunky' taste	—	✔							
Total dissolved solids (TDS)	500 ppm		✔	✔					
HEALTH HAZARDS - Organic									
Benzene	5 ppb	✔							✔
Carbon tetrachloride	5 ppb	✔							✔
Lindane	4 ppb	✔		✔					
Methoxychlor	100 ppb	✔		✔					
Trichloroethylene	5 ppb	✔							✔
Trihalomethanes (THM)	100 ppb	✔							
HEALTH HAZARDS - Inorganic									
Arsenic	50 ppb		✔	✔					
Barium	1 ppm		✔	✔	✔				
Cadmium	10 ppb		✔	✔	✔				
Chromium	5 ppb		✔	✔	✔				
Fluoride	4 ppm		✔	✔			✔		
Lead	15 ppb		✔	✔			✔		
Mercury	2 ppb	✔	✔	✔					
Nitrate	10 ppm		✔	✔					
Selenium	10 ppb		✔	✔			✔		
HEALTH HAZARDS - Radiological									
Dissolved radon	10,000 pc/l	✔							✔

and then. You can adjust the level of salt consumption. A high setting ensures softer water but means more frequent refills. A lower setting saves salt and money, but the resin may regenerate less completely.

Iron removers. Dissolved iron in water can leave rusty brown stains in the bathtub and sink. You can use a water softener to remove the iron, but special-purpose treatments are available for water where hardness is not a problem. An iron remover uses an oxidizing agent to precipitate the iron out. One common design is a canister similar to a water softener. Iron removers are priced anywhere from $400 to $650, and are best for removing clear ferrous iron.

Lead-removing filters. Reverse-osmosis or carbon filters designed specifically to remove lead come in different configurations: in-line filters (undersink or countertop), faucet filter, and carafe. Price: $65 to $350. If lead is your only problem, activated alumina cartridges are an effective treatment; cartridges cost $100, the housing $50. For more information, see the discussion of carbon filters on page 325.

The tests

Tests are geared to the type of device. We test the carbon filters using water spiked with chloroform, one of the most common organic compounds found in drinking water.

We test the reverse-osmosis devices using water laden with sodium chloride and 2 to 10 times the Federal limits for lead, cadmium, copper, and barium.

To test for lead removal, we feed tap water spiked with lead nitrate through the units until about 1000 gallons has been processed. For all the devices, we evaluated ease of installation and use.

Buying advice

The chart on page 327 sums up treatment methods recommended for the most common water problems. Before doing business with an unfamiliar water-treatment company, call the Better Business Bureau or a local consumer-protection agency to find out if there are unresolved complaints against it.

In a **carbon filter**, the more carbon the better. Based on our tests, small pour-through filters and fist-sized units that thread onto the faucet can improve the taste of water, but are simply too small to remove hazardous chemicals. High-volume under-the-sink or countertop filters do a much better job. Look for those with a replaceable filter cartridge. Cartridges made either with a "carbon block" or granulated carbon are better than those with powdered carbon.

If your carbon filter has a built-in sediment filter and your water contains a lot of undissolved solids, the sediment part may clog before the carbon is used up. To extend the filter's life, install a separate sediment prefilter upstream of the carbon. A 5- to 10-micron mesh is fine enough. A clear plastic sump on the filter housing indicates when the cartridge needs changing.

If you're considering a **distiller**, look at how easy it is to fill or clean. We found little variation in how well distillers removed inorganic compounds.

Any **water softener** will do an acceptable job of removing minerals, according to our tests. For greatest efficiency and minimum salt consumption where water use varies from week to week, a demand-control model is best.

For **iron removal**, costlier models have the advantage of removing more iron and regenerating automatically rather than manually. They're designed for high iron levels. Aeration devices can precipitate and remove iron and also radon.

Use the diagram on page 329 to determine whether you need a water-treatment device and, if so, what kind.

Lead in household water

To find out how common significant levels of lead are in drinking water, CU tested water from the homes of more than 2600 CONSUMER REPORTS subscribers in 1992. About 60 percent of those surveyed live in eight major cities and the rest are throughout the country. Samples included first-draw water, water that had stood in pipes for hours, and purged-line water, taken after running the tap for one minute. Both types were needed to distinguish lead due to household plumbing from that due to outside sources.

While results showed no sign that high lead levels in water are a widespread national problem among our readers, one region—the Northeast—had significantly more first-draw samples above the U.S. Environmental Protection Administration's "action level" of 15 parts per billion (ppb) than the rest of the country. Results from individual cities provided further reason for concern. Large numbers of households in Chicago and Boston had high levels of lead in both types of samples.

Lead levels were lower in New York, San Francisco, and Washington, but still above the national average. Households in Atlanta, Des Moines, and Seattle had relatively few high-lead samples.

Standard advice for houses with a potential lead problem has been to let the water run for a minute or two to clear the line of water into which lead has leached. Our tests showed that isn't always effective; in some cases, it seemed to worsen the problem. Our tests also point out that individual households can have high lead levels even if they're in communities that don't seem to carry a high risk.

Communities that fail the tests required of all public utilities by the EPA are legally required to institute some type of corrosion control by 1997.

WHAT ACTION SHOULD YOU TAKE?

If your water contains lead, you can use this diagram to decide whether you need a water-treatment device and, if so, what kind. First-draw water has stood in the pipe for a few hours; purged-line water is taken after you've let the tap run a minute or two.

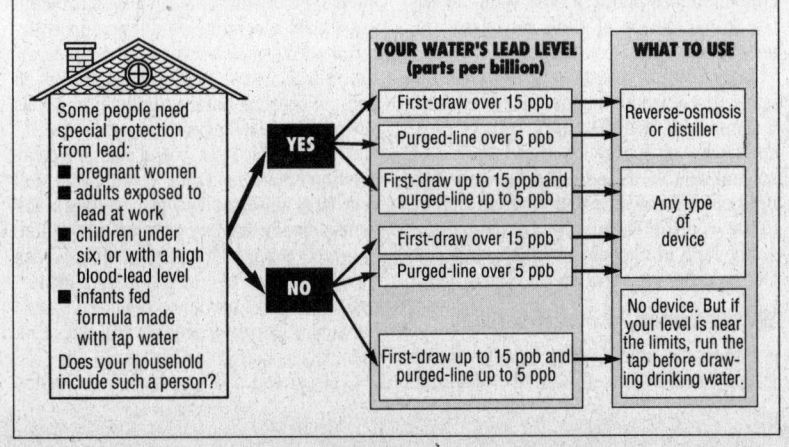

Some people need special protection from lead:
- pregnant women
- adults exposed to lead at work
- children under six, or with a high blood-lead level
- infants fed formula made with tap water

Does your household include such a person?

YES

YOUR WATER'S LEAD LEVEL (parts per billion)	WHAT TO USE
First-draw over 15 ppb / Purged-line over 5 ppb	Reverse-osmosis or distiller
First-draw up to 15 ppb and purged-line up to 5 ppb	Any type of device

NO

YOUR WATER'S LEAD LEVEL (parts per billion)	WHAT TO USE
First-draw over 15 ppb / Purged-line over 5 ppb	Any type of device
First-draw up to 15 ppb and purged-line up to 5 ppb	No device. But if your level is near the limits, run the tap before drawing drinking water.

Paints, stains, & finishes

▶ **Ratings of exterior paints & stains on page 359.**

Paint is the most common way to spiff up a surface. It provides a fairly tough film of resins and pigments that covers small blemishes and shields the surface from wear and weathering. It can be applied over primer or old paint and comes in almost every conceivable color.

Stain leaves less of a surface film, allowing the texture of the surface to show through to varying degrees. Some stains should be applied only to unfinished weathered wood; others, over "sealed wood" (wood treated with other finishes or primers). Colors are more limited, the most popular being browns, reds, and grays for exterior, and wood colors for interior.

The chemistry of paints and exterior stains is similar. Both contain pigment, binder, and solvent. The binder forms the film, holds the pigment, and helps adhesion. The solvent—water and alcohol in latexes and petroleum spirits in oil-based paints—determines how easily the paint goes on and helps with adhesion and coverage. Pigment provides the color. Paint contains more pigment than stain, and as the transparency of stain increases, the amount of pigment decreases.

Interior transparent stains and clear finishes reveal wood in all its glory. Surface finishes (like varnish) form a hard, durable coat; they also may be water-soluble or solvent-soluble. Penetrating finishes (like tung oil) use solvents to help them sink into the wood and harden the wood fibers.

For help in choosing a finish for a surface, see the charts on pages 332 and 333.

Water-based, solvent-based

Paints and stains come in water-based (latex) and oil-based (alkyd) versions. Generally, it's best to use the type of paint or stain that was used last time—oil over oil, latex over latex. That way, you'll minimize stresses in the coating that can lead to blistering and peeling.

Latexes. As the water evaporates in latex paint and exterior stain, it leaves behind a mesh of tiny plastic particles somewhat permeable to air and water.

Water-based paints and stains are very convenient. They're easier to apply than oil-based formulas. They can be applied to a damp surface, so you can use them even if it rained the day before. They dry quickly and without much odor. And, if you clean up right away, you can clean everything with soap and water. In addition, latex paints contain less of the air pollutants found in alkyd paints.

The properties that make latex easy to use also cause some problems. Latex paint is somewhat more vulnerable to damage from water and marring than alkyds. Latex, especially glossy latex, may remain tacky long after drying, causing books to stick to shelving and windows to sills—a problem known as "blocking." And if you apply exterior latex on a day with sudden showers, the rain can wash off the freshly applied paint. Freezing before application spoils latex paints, causing it to separate.

Alkyds. Alkyd paints and stains, typically compounds of alcohol, organic acid, and vegetable oil dissolved in petroleum solvents, usually dry by oxidation rather than by evaporation. As the paint combines with oxygen from the air, it forms a water-resistant skin of hardened resin. The initial hardening happens over several days, but the process may go on for years.

Consequently, oil-based paints and stains

PAINTS, STAINS, & FINISHES

are very tough, the right choice when you want smoothness, toughness, and extra resistance to water. Alkyds make sense for kitchens and bathrooms and for working surfaces such as bookshelves. They're especially adept at adhering to old painted surfaces, although latexes are catching up in that regard.

The petroleum-based chemistry of oil-based stains and paints, however, makes them messy to use. The brush may drag and leave drips and sags. Cleanup is a major nuisance as mineral spirits are required. For proper adhesion, oil-based finishes must be applied to a totally dry surface. They need about a day to dry between coats and, in the meantime, smell like solvent while drying.

The choices in paints

Interior paints. Latex paints are the typical choice for interior painting, a task often undertaken by do-it-yourselfers. Leading brands: *Glidden, Sears, Sherwin-Williams, Dutch Boy,* and *Benjamin Moore.* Colors, usually described in copywriters' fanciful language, cover the rainbow.

Both latex and alkyds come in various gloss levels. The general rule is to use a flat paint for ceilings and walls and a semigloss paint for most woodwork—moldings, baseboards, doors, windows. For the kitchen and bathroom, where you need a paint to resist dirt and endure scrubbing, choose a more glossy paint, particularly an alkyd. Gloss levels are not standardized—one brand's "satin" may gleam like another brand's "eggshell."

Exterior paints. Leading brands include *Sears, Glidden, Benjamin Moore, Sherwin Williams,* and *Dutch Boy.* Like interior paints, exterior paints come in a variety of sheens. House paint tends to be conservative white or subdued pastels, while trim hues are rich and bold.

Exterior latex and alkyd paints are formulated to withstand strong sunlight and the weather; most also combat mildew, though latexes usually do better than alkyds. A white paint that "chalks" continually sloughs off dirt along with the chalky powder, so it appears fresh and white longer. Formulations may vary by region. "Southern" formulations of white paint, for instance, usually contain more anti-mildew ingredients than standard white paints and are more apt to purposely chalk.

Specialty paints. Most *rust-protecting paints* contain rust-inhibiting compounds, but if the surface is prepped correctly, you don't need special products. Grind or sand off all existing rust to bright metal, prime it using a metal primer, and you can use almost any paint for the top coat. Brush-on coats are thicker, sturdier, and cover better than an aerosol enamel.

Basement-waterproofing paint might help if your basement suffers dampness or mild seepage. Don't count on any paint to halt outright leakage. Even the best basement-waterproofing paints we've tested allow a small amount of water to seep through. The most resistant to water are oil-based epoxies—expensive, strong-smelling coatings that harden through a chemical reaction between a resin and a catalyst. The epoxy must be mixed in precise amounts and applied promptly to a dry surface. Next best: oil-based paint specially formulated for use on masonry. Cement-based powder and water-based paint are not as effective, we've found.

The choices in stains

Interior stains. Unlike exterior stain, which resembles thinned paint, interior stain is more a dye. Colors are typically names of trees—walnut, cherry, mahogany. Many cabinet-quality stains are water-based. You brush them on, wipe the excess off, then seal the wood with varnish or polyurethane. Wiping off the stain takes a bit of finesse. Wipe too soon, and you may remove most of the color; wait too long, and the wood may be too dark. The water in stains may also raise the wood grain.

Oil stains are better suited for inexperienced hands. They're relatively simple to use, and their colors are easier to control.

Exterior stains. Stains are in latex (water-based) or alkyd (solvent-based). Solvent-based stains sell twice as much as water-based stains. Leading brands include *Olympic, Sherwin-Williams, Thompson's, Glidden,* and *Behr.*

Stains come in transparent, semitransparent, and opaque (solid color) varieties. Transparent and semitransparent stains provide less surface film and less pigment than paint, so they peel less but also tend to erode, hence fade more quickly.

The choices in clear finishes

Whether you're using a surface sealer or a penetrating finish, it's best to apply clear finish in several thin coats and sand between coats. Trying to do the job with only one or two heavy coats may result in sagging, wrinkling, or missed spots.

Varnish is essentially paint without the pigment, a combinations of oils and resins that coats the surface of the wood. The **polyurethane** widely used on floors is an oil-based varnish. **Water-based var-**

MATCHING EXTERIOR SURFACE TO FINISH

	Latex house	Alkyd house	Wood stain	Trim paint	Porch/deck paint	Cement powder paint	Polyurethane	Aluminum paint	Water-repellant preservative
WOOD									
Clapboard	✔	✔						✔	
Natural siding/trim			✔	✔			✔		
Shutters/trim	✔	✔		✔					
Window frames	✔	✔						✔	
Porch floor/deck					✔				✔
Shingle roof			✔						✔
MASONRY									
Brick	✔	✔				✔		✔	✔
Cement/cinder block	✔	✔				✔		✔	
Porches and floors	✔				✔				
Stucco	✔	✔				✔		✔	
METAL									
Aluminum windows	✔	✔		✔				✔	
Steel windows	✔	✔		✔				✔	
Metal siding	✔	✔		✔				✔	
Copper surfaces							✔		
Galvanized surfaces	✔	✔		✔				✔	
Iron surfaces	✔	✔		✔				✔	

Source: U.S. General Services Administration

PAINTS, STAINS, & FINISHES

nishes, which clean up with soap and water, are also available. Either type comes in several gloss levels.

Lacquer is a acrylic-derived resin that's dissolved in strong solvents. As the solvents evaporate, the lacquer dries to form a thin, tough film. **Penetrating oils** like tung oil or Danish oil soak into the wood's pores. They provide a natural-looking, low-luster finish.

Environmental considerations

The solvents used in paints and other finishes include hydrocarbons and other volatile organic compounds (VOCs). As the finish dries, those solvents evaporate. Some react with other gas pollutants in the presence of sunlight to produce ozone, a component of smog.

Until recently, both oil- and water-based finishes contained VOCs. Oil-based products contained 40 to 50 percent VOCs; latex, 2 to 7 percent. Although solvent-free paints have been used in Europe for several years, only one is available in the U.S.

Because of VOC regulations, the sale of oil-based paint has been restricted in some states, notably Arizona, California, New York, and Texas. In response to those restrictions, manufacturers are reformulating or, in some instances, eliminating oil-based paint from their product lines.

MATCHING INTERIOR SURFACE TO FINISH

	Latex, flat	Latex, gloss	Alkyd	Varnish	Shellac	Polyurethane	Stain	Floor varnish	Floor paint	Aluminum paint
WOOD										
Floors					✔	✔	✔	✔	✔	
Paneling	✔	✔	✔	✔	✔	✔	✔			
Stair risers		✔	✔	✔	✔	✔	✔			
Stair treads					✔	✔	✔	✔	✔	
Trim/furniture	✔	✔	✔	✔	✔	✔	✔			
MASONRY										
Concrete floors	✔								✔	
Kitchen/bath walls		✔	✔							
New masonry	✔	✔	✔							
Old masonry	✔	✔	✔							✔
Plaster	✔	✔	✔							
Wall board	✔	✔	✔							
METAL										
Aluminum windows	✔	✔								✔
Steel windows	✔	✔	✔							✔
Radiators/pipes	✔		✔							✔

Note: Unless surface has been previously finished, primer or sealer may be required. Consult manufacturer's instructions.

Until recently, most latex paints contained mercury compounds as bacteria- and fungus-fighting agents. In poorly ventilated rooms, mercury vapor escaping from drying paint could build up to high levels, posing a health hazard. The Government banned mercury from use in interior latex paint in 1990; outdoor paint containing mercury must be labeled that it is exclusively for exterior use.

Lead, once widely used as a pigment in paint and to help oil-based paint dry, was severely restricted in paint made after 1971. But old paint on walls and woodwork may contain lead, so care must be taken when using abrasive strippers to remove it.

The tests

We judge paint and stain after exposing them to typical conditions. For instance, samples of outdoor paint are applied to test panels and left outside for months, at our Yonkers headquarters and in Florida—where conditions favor mildew growth.

We evaluate each product for its workability—factors such as brushing ease, leveling (smoothness of the dried coating), and resistance to sagging (dripping) and blocking (residual tackiness).

We check how well interior products resist staining, scrubbing, blocking, spattering, and water. We measure gloss levels with an instrument called a glossmeter. We also test stain and paint for properties such as hiding ability.

Buying advice

Choose a finish that's compatible with the surface and make sure that surface is clean and smooth. In general, you're better off selecting products from the high end of the brand lines. Over the years, we've learned that bargain paints almost always fall down in important qualities such as hiding power and washability.

Prices for indoor and outdoor paints range from under $10 to $30 a gallon. Latexes tend to be cheaper than alkyd paints and flat-finish paints cheaper than glossy ones. Stains are priced similarly.

The color you choose affects how much paint you'll need. Muted blacks, browns, blues, dark reds, and greens generally hide best. Most pale colors, especially golds and yellows, may take more than one coat.

Claims of one-coat hiding assume that you'll spread the paint or stain thickly, typically around 450 square feet per gallon. On interior surfaces, that's easier to do with a brush than a roller. We've found that with normal rolling, a gallon can cover up to 650 square feet, which may offer a film too thin for one-coat hiding.

Any finish exposed to bright sunlight is apt to fade. Among exterior paints, alkyds tend to whiten, and white alkyds to yellow when shaded from the sun. Reds and yellows typically fade the most.

LEAD-TESTING KITS

Two kits address the need for quick reliable home lead testing of paint. While the readings they give aren't very precise, they reveal whether the paint you're testing contains some lead. (The kits aren't suitable for testing dishware as neither one can tell you how much lead is present. Nor are they sensitive to low levels of lead, so an item that tests negative may not be completely safe.)

■ *Leadcheck Swabs* (800-262-LEAD), $19.95 for 8 tests. It's the easier of the two to use, and it gives results within a minute.

■ *Frandon Lead Alert Kit* (800-359-9000), $19.95 for 40 tests. It's somewhat more difficult to use and requires as long as 30 minutes to give results.

Both kits have been revamped since our tests but should produce results comparable to the tested ones.

Energy savers

▶ Ratings start on page 361.

Twenty years ago, people conserved energy because of skyrocketing fuel prices and shortages. Today there's less economic incentive to conserve, but reducing energy use can still pay.

The reports in this section cover a number of ways to save energy and money: caulking, weather stripping, automatic setback thermostats. We also explain how to make an older furnace more efficient and discuss the new high-efficiency furnaces and heat pumps. Lastly, we report on the many choices now available in energy-saving windows.

Weather stripping

Weather stripping blocks drafts around doors and windows but won't save much energy. Studies show such drafts contribute little to heat loss. Still, plugging the gaps around windows and doors can make a house feel more comfortable. If, as a consequence, you don't turn up the heat as much, it may save energy indirectly.

The choices

Stripping comes in literally scores of designs and materials, costing from less than 20 cents per foot to over $1. The products are variations on these basic types:

Tape. Materials vary, as do widths and thicknesses, but all have the advantage of simple peel-and-stick installation. EPDM (ethylene-propylene-diene monomer), rubber, and nonporous closed-cell foam seal the best. Open cell foam, which looks like a foam air-conditioner filter, seals poorly. Tape works best along a door jamb or at the top or bottom of a window sash; it's not well suited for a window track.

Reinforced foam. Closed-cell foam tape attached to a strip of wood molding is best nailed in place around a window or door jamb. Installing it involves sawing, nailing, and painting the wood strip.

Tension seal. A strip of plastic that's folded to form a V or a springy bronze strip, whose sides seal the opening, can be installed in the track of a double-hung window or between a door and its jamb. Plastic strips are easier to install than bronze.

Felt. This type comes plain or reinforced with a flexible metal strip. Plain felt works in a door jamb; reinforced felt can seal around a door or window.

Pile. A narrow strip of fuzzy, carpetlike material that's best suited for recessed slots around the perimeter of a window sash, storm door, or sliding patio door.

Tubular rubber and vinyl. Tubes of sponge rubber or vinyl with a tacking flange, these are suited for sealing around a door.

Reinforced silicone. This tubular gasket attached to a metal strip seals well, but you need a hacksaw to install it. It' can be mounted on a door jamb or window stop.

Buying advice

No single type of weather stripping will work everywhere. Nor was any brand noticeably better than the rest in our tests. You'll probably need one type for doors, others for windows. Self-stick foam tape proabably has the widest range of uses. It's also the easiest type to install and provides the best seal.

Exterior caulking compounds

Every house needs caulk. Properly applied around windows, doors, and siding, it blocks drafts and prevents water damage to walls. A good caulk should be easy to apply, without running, sagging, drying out, or cracking, and it should stay flexible through heat and cold. A 10-ounce cartridge can typically run from $1 to $6.

The choices

Caulks come in several formulations, each with slightly different characteristics:

Silicone. This type won't mix with water, so you'll need mineral spirits to clean up hands and tools. And some brands can't be painted. Silicone dries to a rubbery consistency and, in our tests, shrank less over time than other types of caulk.

Latex. This is the easiest type to smooth, and it cleans up with water. Latex caulk can be painted. It's opaque when dry and shrinks more than silicone does.

Combinations. These include silicone/latex and acrylic latex. Characteristics vary widely from brand to brand. Some manufacturers claim that mixing silicone with latex improves caulk's performance, but that's not always the case.

The tests

To measure durability, we use caulk to fill half-inch wide channels between strips of wood or aluminum, then paint a portion of each caulk, leaving part bare. Some caulks spend a year in Florida's humidity and blistering sun, the rest suffer the seasonal extremes of the roof on our Yonkers, N.Y. laboratories. When the year is up, we inspect for shrinkage, cracking, mildew, and dirt. To test flexibility, we repeatedly stretch and compress each caulk at extreme temperatures.

Buying advice

Any caulk will be something of a compromise between convenience and durability, but silicone caulks performed the best overall in our tests. Some latex and silicone/latex caulks also perform well; they can be painted.

Energy-saving thermostats

An automatic-setback thermostat can save energy and money in the winter by automatically lowering temperature at night or when you're out. The savings generated by setting back the temperature can be substantial. For example, in the upper Midwest, reducing the nighttime temperature setting from 68°F to 55° in the winter can reduce a fuel bill by at least $10 to $20 a month.

The choices

There are two choices—electromechanical and electronic. Both are designed for do-it-yourself installation.

Electromechanical. This type, with the traditional round clock-timer, is the simplest. You program setback starting and ending times by placing movable tabs around the dial, and the temperatures by moving a couple of levers. The limitations of this type: You can only set one minimum and a single maximum temperature, and setback times can't vary from day to day.

Digital electronic. This type is more flexible but also more complicated. You can program multiple temperatures for different days of the week. A digital's display looks like a digital clock; the programming technique of some models is reminiscent of older VCRs—tedious and frustrating. You'll probably need to consult the instruction book or dial the manufacturer's help line.

Features and conveniences

You're likely to find the greatest number of features among the digital models.

Display. Look for one that has reasonably legible letters and numbers and displays the current set temperature.

Usage tracking. A light that shows when the unit is calling for heating or cooling is helpful. A display of cumulative on-time helps you track fuel use.

Ease of programming. Models that are easiest to program use few buttons and have a fairly straightforward sequence of steps. It's also helpful if the model gives sufficient time between programming steps. A few models we tried allowed only 15 seconds to decipher the instruction for the next step. Some models offer "armchair" programming, which simplifies the chore. They detach easily from the wall so you can program them while seated and in good light.

Programming capability. The most versatile units let you program up to four different temperatures per day, with a different set schedule for each day of the week. With any, you can temporarily override the settings at any time.

The tests

To test each thermostat's ability to maintain a temperature setting, its primary function, we put it in a 20-by-10 foot chamber designed to mimic a living room. Electric heaters substitute for a furnace and air-conditioning cools the room. We also program each thermostat and judge the quality of its display and controls.

Buying advice

If you conscientiously turn down the thermostat by hand, you probably don't need a setback thermostat. If you want a thermostat to do that for you but don't want to deal with programming, consider an electromechanical model. But keep in mind its limitation—the same two temperature levels every day unless you reset it. To have a variety of settings on weekdays and Saturday and Sunday, you'll need a digital electronic model. Models with "armchair" programming greatly simplify the chore of programming.

Furnaces: Upgrades & replacements

Today's furnaces are far more efficient and therefore much cheaper to run. But that doesn't necessarily mean the most efficient furnace makes economic sense.

Upgrading old furnaces

If your house has a furnace more than 20 years old, it probably wastes more than a third of the fuel it burns. Even at that, it probably doesn't pay to replace an older furnace unless your fuel bills are extremely high. Instead, have the furnace tuned up. As part of the tuneup consider the following ways to improve efficiency:

■ Replace the pilot light on a gas furnace with electronic ignition. Price: about $250.

■ Replace the fuel nozzle on an oil-fired furnace with a smaller one, a process called derating. Price: about $40.

■ Install a damper so warm air doesn't escape up the chimney when the furnace isn't running. Price: about $500.

Other ways to cut fuel use include installing an automatic-setback thermostat (see the report on page 336), plugging leaks in the duct system, and insulating exposed ducts that are routed through unheated spaces.

High-efficiency furnaces

Today's furnaces are required by Federal law to carry an Annual Fuel Utilization Efficiency rating (AFUE), which indicates what percent of fuel is converted to heat during the heating season. The minimum allowed is 78 percent. A furnace with an AFUE of around 80 percent, considered mid-efficiency, is priced about $1400 to $1700, depending on installation. High-efficiency units, with an AFUE of at least 90 percent, are priced from $2000 to $3000 or more.

High-effency furnaces rely on special technology to do their job, such as unusual burners and multistage heat exchangers. Unlike conventional furnaces, they do not require a chimney to carry away smoke and the other byproducts of combustion. These furnaces condense water vapor, which is usually routed to the sewer. Other combustion byproducts are typically vented to the outside through plastic pipe.

Being more complicated than other models, high-efficiency furnaces have had a reputation for needing more frequent repairs. Although manufacturers deny that this is still a problem, repair technicians confirm that it is still true to some degree. Warranties help, but they rarely cover labor costs, which can be considerable.

Buying advice

When you replace an old furnace, which is usually about 60 percent AFUE, greater efficiency doesn't necessarily translate into greater economy. It would take you 18 years to recoup the extra expense of a high-efficiency furnace (about $1300) over a mid-efficiency furnace if your current heating bill is $600. If you pay $1200 yearly for heat, you would recoup the difference in about 9 years.

Whatever type of furnace you choose, buy a maintenance contract from the installer to cover cleaning, checkups, and warranty work for at least five years.

Heat pumps

A heat pump is often described as an air-conditioner that can run in reverse. That's an oversimplification, but a heat pump's ability to both heat and cool makes it a possible substitute for both a furnace and central air-conditioner.

The choices

A heat pump works by transferring heat from the house to the outdoors in summer and in the opposite direction in winter. Heat-pump systems do that in either of two ways:

Air-to-air. In winter, outdoor coils draw what heat they can from the outside air to warm a refrigerant gas, which is then pumped indoors. In summer, heat drawn from indoors is pumped outside. The performance of an air-to-air system is very sensitive to outdoor temperature. For instance, cold spells can cause ice to form on the outdoor coils. Another winter-time complaint is that the indoor supply air often feels cool. Typical price for an installed air-to-air system: $3500 to $5000.

Ground-source. A closed-loop heat pump is less sensitive to winter weather than an air-to-air system because it draws heat through plastic pipes buried in the ground, where the temperature is relatively stable. But you need a great deal of space to lay piping—about as much room as your the square footage in your house—or a deep hole, if the pipes are laid vertically.

Typical price for a installed ground-source system: $7000 to $11,000.

The problems

A variety of problems have frustrated heat-pump users. One utility's study of 48 homes equipped with heat pumps found a host of problems. Not one of the heat pumps was functioning properly. Among the reasons: leaky or poorly assembled ductwork in the house; low airflow from the unit; leaky refrigeration systems, or systems kept at the wrong pressure; and thermostats used or installed improperly. That same study showed that efforts of the homeowners to repair the systems were met with further frustation: service technicians who were sometimes inadequately trained, often did slapdash work, lacked up-to-date equipment, and spent insufficient time diagnosing the problem.

Measuring efficiency

A heat pump's efficiency can be measured in several ways. For each way, the higher the number, the more effficient the heat pump is, the more it will cost to buy, and the less it will cost to operate.

Cooling efficiency is measured in air-to-air heat pumps by the Seasonal Energy-Efficiency Ratio and ground source heat pumps by the Energy-Efficiency Ratio. The minimum SEER for new air-to-air heat pumps is 10; the most efficient have a SEER of about 16.

Heating efficiency is measured in two ways: The Heating Seasonal Performance Factor, for air-to-air heat pumps, measures the total amount of heat a unit produces in a normal winter, given its wintertime energy consumption. HSPFs range from just under 7 to about 10. The Coefficient of Performance, which can refer to either type of heat pump, compares heating output with the amount of electricity used to provide that heat. A COP of 1 means you're receiving one unit of heat for an equivalent unit of electricity. The COP for heat pumps ranges from 1.5 to 3.5.

Buying advice

Consider a heat pump only if you experience mild winters or have a yard large enough to bury lots of pipes.

Replacement windows

There are two good reasons you might want to replace your home's windows: The old ones have deteriorated or you're remodeling. Saving energy is not a good reason. New windows for an entire house typically cost a couple of thousand dollars. We estimate most people would save only a small percentage of this in fuel costs each year.

Replacement windows are available as national brands, such as *Pella* and *Andersen*, or from local firms who custom build them.

Frame choices

The frame has a big effect on a window's thermal performance, price, and upkeep.

Wood. Wood-framed windows can be plain or clad in vinyl or aluminum. Of course, plain wood must be painted; clad wood requires minimal maintenance. Wood is a good insulator, but it's often the most expensive frame material.

Aluminum. This type of frame requires less maintenance than wood. But aluminum doesn't insulate as well. In cold weather, heat inside the house travels readily through the frame to the outdoors, making the indoor side of the window feel cold to the touch. When we tested a group of windows for accelerated durability, an aluminum-framed model fared the best. It's best suited for temperate climates.

Vinyl. A properly assembled vinyl frame—one whose corners have been welded rather than screwed together—is likely to be airtight, watertight, and relatively durable. It's as good or better an insulator as wood and generally less expensive. A well constructed vinyl frame can offer value for the money.

Glass choices

The glass you choose also affects a window's price and performance.

Single-pane. Inexpensive, but not a very effective insulator. In hot or cold climates, use of single-pane should be limited to garages and other unheated spaces.

Double-pane. Most new homes have this type. It consists of sealed glass panes typically separated by an aluminum spacer that includes a dessicant to keep moisture from condensing between the panes. Once that happens, you have to replace the glass.

Argon-filled. A step up in price and performance from double-pane, this type contains inert argon gas in the space between the panes, which slows heat loss.

Low-e. The name is short for low emissivity; it refers to a coating that alters the way the glass transmits visible and invisible light. A low-e coating helps reduce heat loss in winter and heat gain in summer.

Triple-pane. An extension of the double-pane concept, this isn't very popular because it's heavy and expensive.

Suspended-film. This is a lighter version of the triple-pane window. It sandwiches a polyester film between the panes. The film, which has a low-e coating, provides extra insulation without adding significantly to weight and thickness.

Measuring efficiency

Most manufacturers use the term U-value as a measure of insulating ability. More familiar is the R-value, the U-value divided into the number 1. The higher a window's R-value, the better it insulates. For a double-pane double-hung window, look for an R-value close to 2.

Some manufacturers quote numbers that are supposed to tell you how well a window retains heat. The makers have different ways to test windows or report the results, so the numbers are hard to compare. Only California now requires windows to be certified according to a standard test method developed by the National Fenestration Rating Council. Others states are considering a similar certification program.

Durability of the insulated glass is assessed by the Insulated Glass Certification Council. A window that displays the code "CBA," has passed a series of tests that exposes the glass and its seal to heat, cold, and water. Fewer than three letters means the window didn't pass extended tests.

The shading coefficient measures how well a window controls the sunlight coming through. Low numbers provide more shade; higher numbers, less.

Some manufacturers provide a "visible light" or "daylight transmission" number to help you compare different types of glazing. Untreated double-pane windows typically admit about 82 percent of visible light; low-e glass, no more than 79 percent. When in doubt abut the darkening effect of the glass, take a sample of the glass home.

Buying advice

New windows are usually not a major way to cut a home's energy bills. Even if you replaced single-pane wood-frame windows with the most energy-efficient, you'd see only a modest drop in heating and cooling costs.

But you may need windows because you've remodeled or because the old windows are past their prime. Then it makes sense to choose durable windows that keep out wind and water and that offer high thermal performance.

VACUUM CLEANERS

RATINGS — VACUUM CLEANERS

Legend: E VG G F P

▶ **See report, page 312.** From Consumer Reports, February 1993.

Recommendations: For vacuuming different surfaces, we recommend the *Panasonic MC-6250* upright (or its successor), $170 ($179), or the *Sears Kenmore* canister *22551*, $300. For just carpet cleaning, consider two *Eureka* upright models—the *Powerline Gold*, $120, and the *Boss Plus*, $90. Buy a compact canister only if your storage space is limited.

Ratings order: Listed by types; within types, listed in order of estimated quality. Closely ranked models differed little in quality. Price is the manufacturer's suggested retail. **Notes to table:** Key to type: For uprights, **S** = soft-body, **H** = hard-body; **P** = self-propelled. For canisters, which are all hard-bodies, **PN** = power nozzle, **SO** = suction-only. ⓢ indicates tested model has been replaced by successor model; according to the manufacturer, the performance of new model should be similar to the tested model but features may vary. See page 343 for new model number and suggested retail price, if available. Ⓓ indicates model discontinued.

UPRIGHTS

Brand and model	Price	Type	Weight	Overall score	Deep cleaning	Suction	Filtration	Noise	Overall convenience	Advantages	Disadvantages	Comments
Panasonic MC-6250 ⓢ	$170	H	15 lb.	92	E	E	E	G	E	A,D,I,K,S	h,o,u	P
Kirby Generation 3 G3D Ⓓ	1600	S,P	24	89	E	E	E	F	E	C,K,M,O,Q,U,Y	g,n,r,u	C,I,M
Eureka The Boss Plus 2134AT	90	S	13	88	E	F	E	E	G	—	b,c,g,r,u	C
Eureka Powerline Gold 9410	120	S	14	86	E	F	E	P	E	N	c,f	C,E,O
Eureka The Bravo Boss 9334AT	100	S	13	82	E	F	E	P	E	N	c,f,p	C,E,O
Royal 994	609	S	16	78	E	F	E	F	G	A,O,P,Q,S,V	g,u	K
Hoover Legacy 810 Ⓓ	180	S	15	78	G	F	E	E	E	H,N,V	a,d	O
Hoover Elite II 640 Ⓓ	140	S	14	78	E	E	E	P	E	—	a,d	O
Hoover Elite II 430 ⓢ	100	S	14	76	G	F	E	F	E	—	a,d	O
Sears Kenmore 39575 Ⓓ	270	S,P	18	74	E	F	E	F	E	B,C,K,M,N,O,P,Q,R,W	u	I,N
Singer SST1900 Ⓓ	299	S,P	17	73	E	P	E	F	G	B,C,N,X	d,g,r,t,u	N

Ratings continued ▶

VACUUM CLEANERS

▶ Ratings continued

Brand and model	Price	Type	Weight	Overall performance	Deep cleaning	Suction	Filtration	Noise	Overall convenience	Advantages	Disadvantages	Comments
Amway Clear Trak	$625	H	22 lb.	72	◓	○	◓	◓	◓	G,H,I,S	c,i,k,p,r,s	A,C,D,H,M
Hoover Power Max U3729-910 [S]	300	S,P	24	72	○	●	◓	●	◓	A,H,N,Q	n,t	O
Royal Dirt Devil 7200 [D]	140	H	16	71	○	◓	◓	◓	◓	C,H,K,T	d,f	O
Singer SST460 [D]	135	S	12	70	◓	◓	◓	◓	◓	B,C	c,g,n,r,u	C
Electrolux Genesis LX [D]	430	H	17	70	○	◓	◓	◓	◓	A,C,D,I,K,L,S,T,U,V	d,h,u	E,F,J,M,P
Royal Pro Series 7470 [D]	200	H	16	69	●	○	○	○	◓	C,H,I,K,T,V	d,f	H,O,P
Regina Housekeeper Plus H06307 [D]	140	H	15	65	◓	◓	◓	●	◓	B,C,H,I,K,T	a,c,f	O,P
Sears Kenmore Destiny 31999	400	H	22	64	◓	○	●	◓	◓	H,I,L,N	c,r,s	A,O
Oreck XL 9200	300	S	10	56	○	●	◓	◓	○	Q	e,h,i,n,t	C,H

CANISTERS

Brand and model	Price	Type	Weight	Overall performance	Deep cleaning	Suction	Filtration	Noise	Overall convenience	Advantages	Disadvantages	Comments
Sears Kenmore 22551	300	PN	26	84	◓	◓	○	◓	○	A,B,E,I,J,K,L,N,O,P,S,W	q	N,O,P
Sears Kenmore 2143090 [D]	250	PN	25	83	◓	◓	○	◓	○	E,J,K,L,N,O,P,W	q,v	C,N,O
Sanyo SCP-92	500	PN	24	77	○	◓	◓	◓	○	A,B,I,J,K,L,N,S,W	h,p,q	C,G,N,O,P
Miele S280i	599	SO	21	76	●	◓	◓	◓	○	B,I,J,N,W	h,l,p	C,N,O,P
Eureka Rally 3987 [D]	240	PN	21	75	◓	○	◓	◓	○	E,I,N,W	h,q	C,N,O,P
Nilfisk GS 90	654	SO	20	75	◓	◓	◓	◓	○	—	c,l,p,q	C,H
Panasonic MC-9530	300	PN	27	74	○	◓	○	◓	○	B,I,J,K,L,N,W	h	C,N,O,P
Singer System 90 SL1000	200	PN	27	74	○	◓	○	◓	○	I,K,N,W	h	C,N,O,P
Hoover Spectrum 900 S3595 [D]	280	PN	25	73	◓	○	○	●	○	A,B,I,J,K,N,Q,R,S,W	h,q	C,N,O,P
Hoover Futura 650 S3555 [D]	190	PN	22	68	○	◓	○	○	○	I,J,N,Q,R,W	h,q,v	C,N,O,P

VACUUM CLEANERS 343

Brand and model	Price	Type	Weight	Overall performance	Deep cleaning	Suction	Filtration	Noise	Overall convenience	Advantages	Disadvantages	Comments
Oreck XL Celoc 2	$400	PN	27 lb.	64	◐	⊖	⊖	●	⊖	F,I,K,W	h,p	C,E,L,N,P
Electrolux Diplomat LX [D]	650	PN	22	64	○	○	⊖	●	○	E,I,K,L,T,U,X	b,d,h	B,D,F,J,M,N,O,P
Princess III PN93	750	PN	26	61	◐	○	⊖	⊖	●	F	c,i,j,m,n,p,v	A,C,M,O,Q
Royal 4600	674	PN	27	59	◐	○	○	○	⊖	A,B,E,L	j	J,O
Rainbow SE	1100	PN	26	42	◐	⊖	⊖	⊖	●	L,M,U,Z	c,h,n,p,v	A,I,M,O
COMPACT CANISTERS												
Royal Dirt Devil Power Pak 3113	299	PN	16	52	◐	⊖	○	●	⊖	L,Q,S	c,h,i,p	C,H,O
Hoover Tempo 320 S1331 [D]	80	SO	12	51	●	◐	⊖	○	⊖	I,M,N,Q,S	c,h,p,q	O,P
Eureka Mighty Mite 3140 [D]	100	SO	12	48	●	◐	○	○	⊖	L,M,S,T	b,c,i,o,p	C,O

Succesor Models (in Ratings order)
Panasonic MC-6250 is succeeded by 6255, $179; Hoover Elite II 430 by U4617-930, $149; Hoover Power Max U3729-910 by U3729-930, $389.

Features in Common
Except as noted, all: • Have headlight. • Have rug-pile-height adjustment. • Have 20-to-30-ft. power cord. • Have powered carpet brush 11-12 in. wide. • Come with crevice tool and brushes for dusting and upholstery. • Use disposable dust bag. • Can be used on dry surfaces only. • Have 1-yr. warranty.
Except as noted, all canisters: • Can be used as blower. • Have suction control. • Can reach at least 3 ft. under furniture that has 3-to-4-in. clearance. • Have separate On/off switch for power nozzle.
Except as noted, all uprights: • Have on-board hose at least 5 ft. long. • Cannot be used as blower. • Can reach at least 3 ft. under furniture that has 9-in. clearance. • Lack separate On/off switch for carpet brush. • Lack suction control.

Key to Advantages
A—On/off switch located on handle.
B—Motor control with more than one speed.
C—Upright with suction control.
D—Upright with On/off switch for carpet brush.
E—Power-nozzle cord connects automatically at hand grip when reassembling.
F—Regular hose is extra-long: 10-11 ft.
G—Has second, extra-long hose.
H—Hose can remain attached.
I—Full-bag indicator.
J—Swivel joint on canister makes it easy to maneuver hose.
K—Carpet brush wider than 12 in.
L—Motor shuts off automatically when overheated or overloaded.
M—Cleaning gap at front of nozzle is 1/2 in. or less.
N—At least one cleaning gap at side edge of nozzle is 1/2 in. or less.
O—Rug-pile-height adjustment especially convenient.
P—Headlight easy to replace.
Q—Easy to push when cleaning high-pile carpet.
R—Judged easiest to use on carpet by persons with limited hand or arm function.
S—Easier to use on stairs than others of its type.
T—Bag replacement easier than most.
U—Comes with extra, useful attachments.
V—Power cord more than 30 ft. long.
W—Push-button cord rewind.
X—Pull-and-release cord rewind.
Y—Upright that can be used as blower.
Z—Has hose for use on wet surfaces.

Key to Disadvantages
a—On/off switch low on body.

Ratings continued ▶

PORTABLE FANS

b–Power cord less than 20 ft. long.
c–Cord storage or release is awkward.
d–Headlight difficult to replace.
e–Lacks crevice tool and brush attachments.
f–Hose less than 5 ft. long.
g–Hose difficult to set up or attach.
h–Lacks adjustment for rug-pile height.
i–Carpet brush narrower than 11 in.
j–Cleaning gap at side of nozzle is more than 1½ in.
k–Cleaning gap at front of nozzle is more than 1 in.
l–Optional carpet nozzle failed to improve deep cleaning.
m–Canister that lacks suction control.
n–Inconvenient for use on stairs.
o–Hard to push on high-pile carpet.
p–Lacks headlight.
q–Canister that cannot be used as blower.
r–Clearance under furniture worse than most.
s–Cannot reach more than 2 ft. under furniture, even when clearance is 14 in.
t–Because of low suction, may clean poorly when fine dust clogs bag.
u–Upright with hose not on board.
v–Canister that lacks independent On/off switch for power nozzle.

Key to Comments
A–Uses container or transparent bin instead of disposable dust bags.
B–Motor shuts off when bag is full or clogged.
C–On/off is by foot switch.
D–Grounded 3-prong plug.
E–Polarized plug.
F–Has small motorized brush for stairs.
G–Claims to kill dust mites by heating bag.
H–2-yr. warranty.
I–3-yr. warranty.
J–5-yr. warranty.
K–6-yr. warranty.
L–7-yr. warranty.
M–Sold only or mainly by home demos.
N–Has cord reel.
O–Has tool storage.
P–Has change-bag indicator.
Q–Also sold as **Filter Queen**.

RATINGS PORTABLE FANS

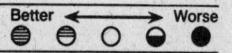

Better ← → Worse

▶ See report, page 315. From Consumer Reports, July 1992.

Recommendations: The top-rated *Patton* and *Lakewood* ventilating fans are high-speed models suited for large rooms or more than one room. Models adequate for single-room use include the *Duracraft DW-612* window model, or the *Lakewood P-223* box fan. For simple air circulation, we favor the *Duracraft DT-16* or the *Windmere KD-16WB*.

Ratings order: Listed by type of use; within use groups, listed in order of estimated quality. A model designed for or typically used in windows was considered a ventilating model, regardless of fan type. All others were considered circulating fans. Circulating fans listed below the bold rule on page 345 were significantly lower in quality than those above. Price is the manufacturer's suggested retail. **Notes to table:** Key to type: **W** = window; **B** = box; **F** = floor; **P** = pedestal; **T** = table; **H** = high-velocity. [D] indicates model discontinued.

Brand and model	Type	Price	Performance	Safeguards	Convenience	Noise (low/high)	Blade diameter, in.	Weight, lb. [1]	Advantages	Disadvantages	Comments
VENTILATING FANS											
Patton WF-1890	W/F/H	$75	◐	◐	●	◐/◐	18	16	C,E,G,O	f,h,i,l,t	A,C
Lakewood HV-18-WR	W/H	70	◐	○	◐	◐/○	18	20	D,F,L,O	m	A,C,D
Duracraft DW-612	W/F	45	○	◐	◐	◐/○	12	7	H	i,k,p	A,C,D

PORTABLE FANS 345

Model	Type	Price	Performance	Safeguards	Convenience	Noise (low/high)	Blade diameter, in.	Weight, lb.[1]	Advantages	Disadvantages	Comments
Vornado 280AE [D]	W/H	$149	○	○	⊖	⊖/●	11	13	D,G,N	p	A,E
Lakewood P-223	B	17	○	●	⊖	⊖/●	20	10	—	j,m	D
Holmes Air HAWF-1012ER	W/F	50	⊖	⊖	○	○/○	12	9	D,H,I	h,i,k,p	A,B,C,D
Toastmaster 4437	B	33	○	●	⊖	○/●	20	10	—	b,m,r	A,C,D,F
Galaxy 3746 [D]	B	30	○	○	⊖	⊖/●	20	12	L	b,d	C,D
Lakewood HV-12-WR	W	50	○	●	○	⊖/○	12	12	D,F	f,m,p	A,C,D
Robeson BF20-2393GW	B	20	●	⊖	⊖	⊖/●	20	9	—	j,m,o	A,D

NOT ACCEPTABLE

■ The following fan, whose instructions say it can be used in a window, had excessive current leakage in our rain tests.

Model	Type	Price	Performance	Safeguards	Convenience	Noise (low/high)	Blade diameter, in.	Weight, lb.[1]	Advantages	Disadvantages	Comments
Lakewood P-47/M [D]	B	40	⊖	●	⊖	○/●	20	15	L	m	C,D

CIRCULATING FANS

Model	Type	Price	Performance	Safeguards	Convenience	Noise (low/high)	Blade diameter, in.	Weight, lb.[1]	Advantages	Disadvantages	Comments
Duracraft DT-16	T	27	○	⊖	⊖	⊖/○	16	7	A,B,G	n	A
Windmere KD-16WB	T	30	○	○	⊖	⊖/○	16	8	B,G,N	—	A
Windmere KS-16WB	P	35	○	○	⊖	⊖/○	16	11	B,G,J,N	c	A
Galaxy 2151S	T	30	⊖	○	⊖	○/○	16	8	B,G	d,e,n	—
Patton U2-1887	F/H	60	⊖	⊖	○	○/●	18	14	E,G,K,O	f,t	A,C
Duracraft DS-1600	P	35	⊖	⊖	⊖	⊖/○	16	9	A,B,J	n	A
Holmes Air HAPF-1150 [D]	P/F	60	●	⊖	⊖	⊖/○	11	10	M	h,k	A,D,E
Lakewood HV-18-RA	P/H	70	⊖	⊖	○	●/●	18	21	E,G,J,K,O	c,d,g,l,t,v	A
Lakewood HV-18	F/H	50	⊖	⊖	○	●/●	18	15	E,G,K,O	d,l,s,t	A,C
Galaxy 2157RS	P/H	30	○	○	⊖	⊖/⊖	16	12	B,G,J	c,e,n	—
Galaxy 2150S	T	24	⊖	●	⊖	⊖/⊖	12	7	B,G	d,e,k,n	—
Holmes Air HAOF-1600	T	25	○	⊖	⊖	○/⊖	16	7	B,N	e,r,v	A
Vornado 280 SS	F/H	99	○	○	⊖	⊖/●	11	10	G,N	—	A,E
Lakewood 1645DX	P	35	⊖	○	⊖	⊖/○	16	8	B,G,J	c,e,k,r,u	D
Lakewood 1600DX	T	30	●	○	⊖	⊖/○	16	6	B,G	d,e,k,r,u	D
Galaxy 3723N	B	25	○	●	⊖	⊖/●	20	10	—	a,d,j,m	—
Galaxy 3521	F	25	●	○	●	○/●	20	9	G	f,k,o,q,v	—

[1] Rounded to the next higher pound.

Ratings continued ▶

PORTABLE FANS

Features in Common
All: • Operate on normal house current. • Use less than 300 watts on high speed.
Except as noted, all: • Have 3 speeds. • Provide 1-yr. warranty on parts and labor. • Require some assembly.

Key to Advantages
A–Child-resistant switch.
B–Horizontal oscillating range of 90 degrees.
C–Adapter for sliding windows is free.
D–Adjustable side panel.
E–3-prong grounded plug.
F–Installation template easy to use.
G–Airflow can angle at least 20 degrees up, at least 10 degrees down.
H–Grille rotates to disperse air.
I–Angles left/right in window, up/down on floor.
J–Adjustable stand height.
K–Can be used as ventilation fan (mfr. recommends using fan near, but not in, window).
L–Has thermostat control. On **Lakewood HV-18-WR,** On/off indicator light shows when thermostat has shut off fan.
M–Backlighted control switch.
N–Grille is easy to remove.
O–Thrust greater than most.

Key to Disadvantages
a–Box fan whose instructions recommend against use in window.
b–Box fan whose instructions don't say whether fan is suitable for use in window.
c–Extensive or difficult assembly.
d–Limited cautions and instructions (though some samples of **Galaxy 2151S** and **Lakewood 1600DX** had adequate instructions).
e–Grille ribs separate easily, can allow contact with blades.
f–Extensive or difficult disassembly needed to clean blades.
g–Stand design makes adjusting height difficult.
h–On some samples, small plastic parts broke in testing (but fan still operable).
i–Window can't close when fan is installed.
j–Rear support legs can break easily.
k–Thrust performance worse than most.
l–On High, fan may "walk" on smooth surfaces.
m–Large openings in motor housing can permit contact with electrical parts.
n–Plastic grille clips hard to use, broke in testing.
o–Less energy-efficient than most.
p–Ventilated worse than most.
q–Stability worse than others.
r–Controls poorly marked.
s–Vibrated more than most.
t–Has a lot of sharp edges or pointed corners.
u–Hard to adjust angle of fan up or down.
v–Wobbly stand.

Key to Comments
A–Warranty exceptions: **Vornado,** lifetime; **Patton,** 25 yr. on parts, 1 yr. on labor; **Lakewood,** 5 yr. on parts and labor; **Toastmaster,** 3 yr. on parts and labor; **Windmere,** 2 yr. on parts and labor; **Holmes Air,** 1 yr. extension for $1; **Duracraft, Holmes Air, Vornado, Windmere,** and **Robeson** charge fee for warranty service.
B–Grille bug screen available for $3.99.
C–Comes fully assembled.
D–Has polarized electrical plug.
E–Variable-speed motor.
F–May be sold as **4433** in some parts of country.

About Prices in the Buying Guide

Prices for most products have been updated for the Buying Guide. The prices we give, unless otherwise noted, are approximate or suggested retail as quoted by the manufacturer. Discounts may be substantial, especially for electronics and camera equipment.

CEILING FANS

RATINGS CEILING FANS

Better ◐ ◕ ○ ◔ ● Worse

▶ **See report, page 315.** From Consumer Reports, June 1993.

Recommendations: Among the large fans, the ultramodern and pricey *Beverly Hills Stratos* topped the Ratings, with high marks for air-moving ability and air distribution. We consider two models Best Buys: The *Harbor Breeze Wellington* and the *J.C. Penney 854-8968-03* (and its successor), both about $100. The *Casablanca Lady Delta*, $224, was the top small fan. It moved as much air as the best large fans but was a bit raucous and ran fast at high speed.

Ratings order: Listed in groups according to blade size; within groups, listed in order of estimated quality. Bracketed models were judged about equal in quality and are listed in order of increasing price. Similar models, those judged comparable in capacity and performance, are also listed at the end of the table. Price is the manufacturer's suggested retail. **Notes to table:** Mounting method: **D** = dropped with a ball and rod combination providing at least 7½ in. of clearance between blades and ceiling; **F** = flush to ceiling with only about 4½ in. to 6 in. of clearance. ⓢ indicates tested model has been replaced by successor model; according to the manufacturer, the performance of new model should be similar to the tested model but features may vary. See page 348 for new model number and suggested retail price, if available. Ⓓ indicates model discontinued.

Brand and model	Price	Mounting method	Blades	Speed, rpm, low/high	Air-moving ability	Air distribution	Airflow range	Noise at high speed	Comments
LARGE MODELS, 52-INCH									
Beverly Hills Stratos 4605	$287	D	4	55/205	◐	◐	◐	◐	A,C,I,L,P,R,S,T
Casablanca Panama Gallery Edition 12002R/12002T	549/489	D	4/5	30/205	◐	◐	◐	○	B,D,I,J,R,T,V,X,Y
Harbor Breeze Wellington 37771, A Best Buy ①	97	D/F	5	70/185	◐	◐	●	◐	A,J,R,V
J.C. Penney 854-8968-03, A Best Buy ⓢ	100	D/F	4/5	70/205	◐	◐	○	◐	J,Q,U,V,X
Emerson Northwind Designer CF755BK	129	D	5	55/155	◐	◐	○	◐	J,X
Hunter Studio Series Remote 25730	147	D/F	5	55/155	◐	◐	○	◐	H,O,T,U
Hunter Orion ORN-03 25827	300	D	5	60/175	◐	◐	○	◐	H,L,O,T,U,V,X
Homestead Wind 1 WN11000R-6 White ⓢ	330	D	6	55/170	◐	◐	◐	◐	H,J,T,X,Z
Fasco American Spirit Collection RM995BR	460	D	4/5	45/200	◐	◐	◐	◐	B,E,J,R,X

① *Sold at Lowe's, a home-center chain in the South and Midwest.*

Ratings continued ▶

348 CEILING FANS

▶ *Ratings continued*

Brand and model	Price	Mounting method	Blades	Speed, rpm, low/high	Air-moving ability	Air distribution	Airflow range	Noise at high speed	Comments
Wal-Mart DC52VB [D]	$36	D/F	5	75/185	◐	◐	○	◐	M,U
Encon Spectrum 5S-52WPB [S]	60	D/F	4/5	65/220	◐	◐	○	◐	M,R,V,X
K Mart Atlantic Air 61-86-35	60	D	5	60/170	◐	◐	○	◐	J,M,V
Hampton Bay—The Beacon Hill 623-067	94	F	4	60/170	○	◐	◉	◐	F,O,R,T,V,W
Hunter Low Profile 22426	98	F	4	70/195	○	◐	◉	◐	O,T,U
Crest 4500 Series 04-599	46	D/F	5	65/195	◐	◐	○	◐	M,N,U,V
Crest 04-775	46	D/F	5	45/135	◐	◐	○	◐	J,M,N,V
Wal-Mart DCKAD52A5C [D]	36	D/F	5	75/145	◉	◐	◉	◐	N,O,U
Encon Contempra 5CP52PBP [S]	60	F	4/5	70/165	◉	◐	◉	◐	B,K,M,O,U,V,X
SMALL MODELS, 42- to 44-INCH
Casablanca Lady Delta 16222D	224	D	4/5	70/275	◐	◐	◐	○	F,J,R,X,Y
Homestead Universal UV 460-1	200	D	4/6	80/250	◐	◐	○	○	A,J,T,X,Z
Emerson Legend CF3342PB	179	D	5	55/225	◐	◐	◐	○	J,M,U,X
Hunter Coastal Breeze CTL-01 23500	63	D/F	4	80/240	○	◐	◉	◐	A,F,G,M,O,T
K Mart Atlantic Air 61-93-50	50	D/F	5	60/175	◉	◐	◉	◐	J,N,V
Crest 5000 Series 05-001	35	F	4	95/250	◉	◐	◉	◐	J,M,U
Hunter Low Profile 22422 [D]	89	F	4	105/210	◉	◐	◉	◐	O,T,U,X
Beverly Hills Designer Colors 2003	113	D	5	105/245	○	○	◉	◐	F,J,M,R,S,T,X
Fasco Gulf Stream 975-42BR	114	D	4	105/220	◉	○	◉	◐	J,U,X
Wal-Mart 305D-42W [D]	25	D	4	115/255	◉	◉	◉	◐	J
Encon Premier Deluxe PF-42ABA [S]	45	D/F	4	105/230	◉	◐	◉	◐	K,R,U,V,Z

Successor Models (in Ratings order)
J.C. Penney 854-8968-03 is succeeded by 832-1424, $100; Homestead Wind 1 WN1 1000R-6 White by SC500R-SW, $299; Econ 5S-52WPB by 5S-P52EBA, $129; Econ 5CP52PBP by 5CP52PBT, $79; Econ PF-42ABA by PF-42ABT, $49.

Similar Models (in Ratings order)
Large models: Beverly Hills Stratos 4605 is similar to 4602, 4603, 4604, 4640, LA Fan Co. Cirrus; Casablanca Panama 12002R/12002T to 1225, 1226, 1227, 1228, 12C02, 12004, 12112, 12222, 12444, 12555, 12662, 12666, 121111, 121212, 121313, 121414, 121717,

CEILING FANS

121818; J.C. Penney 854-8968-03 to 854-8968-01, 854-8968-02; Emerson Northwind Designer CF755BK to CF755V, CF755R, CF755CH, CF755WPB, CF755W, CF755WW; Hunter Studio Series Remote 25730 to 25734, 25736, 25739; Hunter Orion ORN-03 25827 to 25826, 25821; Fasco American Spirit Collection RM995BR to RM995AB, 995BRCP, 995CR, 995GM, RM995W, RM995WBR; K Mart Atlantic Air 61-86-35 to 61-86-34; Hunter Low Profile 22426 to 22427, 22428; Econ Contempra 5CP52PBP to 5CP-52WHP.

Small models: Casablanca Lady Delta 16222D to 16112D, 16444D, 16555D, 16666D, 161111D, 161212D, 161313D, 161414D, 161717D, 161818D; Homestead Universal UV 460-1 to UV 460-2, UV 460-6, UV 460-61, UV 460-SW, UV 460-SW1; Emersen Legend CF3342PB to CF3342AB, CF3042W, CF3042WW, CF3042WPB; Hunter Coastal Breeze CTL-01 23500 to 23504, 23506; K Mart Atlantic Air 61-93-50 to 61-93-48, 61-93-49; Hunter Low Profile 22422 to 22423, 22429; Beverly Hills Designer Colors 2003 to 2000, 2014, 2023 to 2025, 2050, LA Fan Co. Basics; Fasco Gulf Stream 975-42BR to 975-42AN, 975-42CB, 975-42W, 975-42WBR; Econ Premier Deluxe PF-42ABA to PF-42PBC.

Features in Common

All: • Require assembly (usually fairly easy to do). • Are electronically reversible. • Must be mounted with blades at least 7 ft. above floor. • Have metal housing and wood blades. • Consumed less than 120 watts of electricity. • Do not require lubrication. • Have 1-yr. parts warranty.

Except as noted, all: • Mount using J-hook support plate. • Have 3 speeds. • Are operated by pull chain. • Moved 50-250 cubic feet of air per minute for each watt of power (running forward, at various speeds). • Have 5-yr. motor warranty.

Except as noted, all lack: • Light kit and light bulbs. • Blade-balance kit. • Reversible blades with different color or pattern on flip side.

Key to Comments

A—Judged more efficient than others; moved more air per watt of power consumed.
B—Judged less efficient than others.
C—Wall-mounted speed control instead of pull chain.
D—Model **12002T** has wall-mounted control (hand-held remote control is optional accessory); model **12002R** has hand-held remote (wall-mounted speed control available as option).
E—Operates with wall-mounted speed control, pull chain, or hand-held remote. Remote is free, but must be ordered from mfr.
F—Wall-mounted control can be purchased separately.
G—Hand-held remote can be purchased separately.
H—Operates by hand-held remote only; if remote is lost or broken, fan speed/blade direction can't be changed.
I—**Beverly Hills** has 4 blade speeds; **Casablanca** has 6 speeds.
J—Mounts to ceiling with hanger bracket; fan need only be lifted once during installation.
K—Warped blades on 2 samples. Also, motor vibrated or wobbled excessively in use.
L—Column mount provides same clearance from ceiling as downrod, but is less prone to wobble.
M—Motor made clicking or humming noise.
N—Metal tab that keeps downrod from rotating bends easily and could allow wires to become tangled, possibly causing short circuit.
O—Judged more difficult to assemble than most.
P—Must unscrew cap on housing to reach switch that reverses fan direction.
Q—Comes with extended downrod for ceilings higher than 8 ft.
R—Longer downrods sold separately.
S—Conversion kit for flush mounting sold separately.
T—Comes with blade-balance kit.
U—Blade sides differ in color and/or pattern.
V—Comes with light fixture kit. **Casablanca Panama Gallery Edition**, **Hunter Orion**, and **Hampton Bay** also come with light bulbs.
W—Lights positioned above blades; created a flickering and, in our view, annoying effect.
X—Motor warranty: Lifetime (**Beverly Hills Designer Colors, Casablanca Lady Delta, Emerson Legend, Fasco American Spirit, J.C. Penney**); 20 yr. (**Hunter Low Profile** and **Orion**); 15 yr. (**Emerson Northwind**); 10 yr. (**Casablanca Panama Gallery Edition, Encon Contempra** and **Spectrum, Fasco Gulf Stream, Homestead Wind 1** and **Universal**).
Y—Free in-home servicing during first 90 days of warranty, if installed as per instructions.
Z—No labor charge for repairs 90 days from purchase date.

ROOM AIR-CONDITIONERS

RATINGS ROOM AIR-CONDITIONERS

E ⊜ VG ⊖ G ○ F ⊕ P ●

▶ **See report, page 317.** From Consumer Reports, June 1993.

Recommendations: None of the models was superior to the others in every respect. Avoid the temptation to look only for the top-rated one; even models in the middle of the Ratings may do well in one or more aspects that matter to you. Among large models, for example, the top-rated *Panasonic* didn't score as well as the *White-Westinghouse* and the *Montgomery Ward Signature* in directional control. And the *Friedrich* is the most energy-efficient in the group. The first five medium-sized models were about equal overall. Among small models, the *Frigidaire* scored higher for its directional control and is much quieter indoors than the top-rated *Friedrich*.

Ratings order: Listed in groups according to cooling capacity. Within groups, listed in order of estimated quality. Except where separated by a bold rule, closely ranked models differed little in quality. Bracketed models, judged approximately equal in quality, are listed in order of increasing price. Similar models, those judged comparable in capacity and performance, are also listed at right. Price is the manufacturer's suggested retail.
Notes to table: EER = energy-efficiency rating as stated by the mfr. ⓢ indicates tested model has been replaced by successor model; according to the manufacturer, the performance of new model should be similar to the tested model but features may vary. See right for new model number and suggested retail price, if available. ⒹⒹ indicates model discontinued.

Brand and model	Price	Capacity, Btu/hr.	EER	Regular	Energy-saver	Moisture removal	Directional control left/right	Noise indoors, low	Advantages	Disadvantages	Comments
LARGE CAPACITY MODELS—7000 TO 8200 BTU
Panasonic CW-804JU	$530	8000	9.5	⊖	⊖	⊖	●/○	⊖	A,D,F	a,g,h,i,k,l,o	B,H
White-Westinghouse WAC089P7B ⓢ	399	8000	9.2	⊖	⊕	⊖	⊖/⊖	○	C,D,E,H,I	—	C,D,F
Quasar HQ5081DW ⓢ	415	8000	9.1	⊖	—	⊖	⊖/○	⊖	C,E,F,K	d,g,i,j,l,o	G,K,M
Montgomery Ward Signature 2000 5154	465	8000	9.2	⊖	⊖	⊖	⊖/⊖	○	C,D,E,H,I	j	C,D,F
General Electric AMD08FA ⓢ	489	8000	9.1	⊕	⊖	⊖	●/○	⊖	A,F	g,i	H
Panasonic CW-802HU	599	8000	9.1	⊖	⊖	⊖	⊖/○	○	C,E,F,K	a,d,g,i,l,o	G,K,M
Friedrich SS08H10A	739	8200	10.5	○	⊖	○	⊖/○	⊖	A,E,F,G,J,K,L,M,N	g,i,l	A,D,E
Sears Kenmore 77088	500	8000	9.7	⊖	⊕	⊖	○/●	⊖	I,M,N	a,b,c,e,j,l	D,F,N
Airtemp C1R08F2B	430	7500	8.5	○	—	⊖	⊖/○	⊖	E,J,L	f,o	B,D
Whirlpool ACM072XX ⓢ	379	7000	8.7	⊖	—	⊖	⊖/●	⊕	J	b,c,e,f	G
Whirlpool ACQ082XZ1 ⓢ	410	8000	9.0	○	—	○	○/⊖	⊖	A,C,F,K,M	g,m,n	F,H

ROOM AIR-CONDITIONERS 351

Comfort performance ratings legend columns: Price / Capacity, Btu/hr. / EER / Regular / Energy-saver / Moisture removal / Directional control left/right / Noise indoors, low / Advantages / Disadvantages / Comments

Brand and model	Price	Capacity	EER	Regular	Energy-saver	Moisture removal	Dir. control L/R	Noise	Advantages	Disadvantages	Comments
MEDIUM CAPACITY MODELS — 6000 TO 6700 BTU											
Carrier ZMB7061 [D]	$359	6200	9.4	◖	◖	◖	○/○	◖	A,D,F,J,K,L,M	g,o	E,I
Frigidaire FAC067P7B [S]	359	6100	10.0	◖	—	◖	◖/○	◖	C,E,I,J	I	D,F
Sharp AF-602M6 [S]	379	6500	9.5	○	◖	◖	○/◖	◖	J	a,o	—
General Electric AME06LA [S]	419	6000	9.5	◖	◖	○	●/◖	◖	A,D,F	g,i	H
Friedrich SQ06H10A [S]	429	6700	10.3	◖	◖	◖	◐/○	◖	A,B,F,H,K,L	a,g,i,l,m,o	I
Montgomery Ward Signature KMJ-5816	315	6000	8.5	○	○	○	●/○	◖	A,F	g,i,l,m,o	H,M
White-Westinghouse WAB067P7B [S]	359	6000	9.2	○	—	◖	◖/◖	◖	C,E,F,K,L	j	F,I,K
Whirlpool ACQ062XW [S]	339	6000	9.0	◖	—	◖	◖/●	◐	J,M	b,c,e,f,j,l	D
SMALL CAPACITY MODELS — 5000 TO 5800 BTU											
Friedrich SQ05H10B	399	5600	10.0	◖	◖	◖	◖/○	◖	A,B,F,H,L	e,g,i,o	B,I
Sharp AF-502M6 [S]	319	5500	9.5	◖	—	○	◖/◖	◖	J	o	B
Frigidaire FAB057P7B [D]	339	5000	8.4	○	—	◖	◖/◖	◖	C,E,F,K,L	—	B,I,K
Amana 5P2MC [S]	359	5300	9.6	◖	—	◖	○/◖	◖	E,F	f	B,L,N
General Electric APX05LA [D]	339	5400	9.0	◖	◖	◖	●/●	○	C,K,L	f,o	J,M
Sears Kenmore 71055 [S]	370	5000	9.5	◖	◖	◖	○/◐	◖	M,N	b,c,e,f,l	N
Fedders A3R06F2B [S]	470	5800	10.0	○	—	○	◖/◐	◖	E,J,L	f,h,o	D
Whirlpool ACQ052XY [S]	329	5000	9.5	◖	◖	◖	◖/◐	◖	J,N	a,b,c,e,f,l	—
Panasonic CW-500RU	330	5000	8.0	◖	—	○	●/●	○	K,L	f,j,m	G,J,M,N
Whirlpool ACM052XX [S]	299	5000	8.0	◖	—	○	◖/●	●	J	b,c,e,f	G

Successor Models (in Ratings order)
White-Westinghouse WAC089P7B is succeeded by WAC086T7A, $399; Quasar HQ5081DW by HQ5081GH, $500; GE AMD08FA by ASV08AB, $390; Whirlpool ACM072XX by ACM072XA, $379; Whirlpool ACQ082XZI by ACQ082XA, $410; Frigidaire FAC067P7B by FAC067T7A, $359; Sharp AF-602M6 by AF-604M6, $370; GE AME06LA by ASM06LA, $340; Friedrich SQ06H10A by SQ06H10A, $429; White-Westinghouse WAB067P7B by WAB067T7B, $379; Whirlpool ACQ062XW by ACQ062XA, $339; Sharp AF-502M6 by AF-504M6, $310; Amana 5P2MC by 5P2MCQ, $359; Sears Kenmore 71055 by 74055, $370; Fedders A3R06F2B by A3Q06F2A, $470; Whirlpool ACQ052XY by ACQ052XA, $329; Whirlpool ACM052XX by ACM052XA, $299.

Similar Models (in Ratings order)
Large models: Panasonic CW804JU is similar to General Electric ASM08FA, $410; Quasar HQ5081DW to Panasonic CW-802HU; Panasonic CW-802HU to Quasar HQ5081DW; Airtemp C1R08F2B to Fedders AZQ08F2B, $430. Medium models: Frigidaire FAC067P7B is similar to White-Westinghouse WAC067-

Ratings continued ▶

ROOM AIR-CONDITIONERS

T7A, $349; White-Westinghouse WAB067P7B to Frigidaire FAB067T7B, $379, Montgomery Ward Signature 2000 5134, $400, and Sears Kenmore 72060, $420. Small models: Fedders A3R06F2B is similar to Emerson Quiet Kool 6FR63, $490; Panasonic CW-500RU to Quasar HQ2051EH, $290; Whirlpool ACM052XX to Sears Kenmore 79051, $200.

Features in Common

All: • Large models fit window widths of 21-40 in., project inside 3½-6¼ in.; medium models, 25-42 in., project inside 3½-6¼ in.; small models, 23-39 in., project inside 3½-5¾ in. • Are rated at 115 volts. • Should be plugged into grounded outlet on 15-amp circuit protected by time-delay fuse or circuit breaker. • Are certified by the Assn. of Home Appliance Mfrs. (AHAM) for cooling capacity and amperage. • Are designed for installation in double-hung window, a task we think best handled by two people. • Keep window from being opened when properly installed. • Have removable air filter. • Use R-22 HCFC refrigerant, which has low ozone-depleting potential. • Have "slinger ring" to improve cooling and reduce dripping outdoors on humid days.
Except as noted, all have: • 3 cooling speeds. • Adjustable vertical and horizontal louvers. • Vent for exhausting some room air. • Expandable side panels. • At least 1 separate fan-only speed. • Ability to start immediately in low-voltage, high-temperature test. • Power cord at least 70 in. long. • No leveling provision, exterior support brace, or guard over condenser fins.

Key to Advantages

A–Slide-out chassis eases installation, service.
B–Low-voltage protection circuit; 3-minute delay may occur when turned on.
C–Handle steadies unit during installation.
D–Built-in timer for delayed start or stop.
E–Has exterior support bracket, at least 1 integral leveling provision, or both.
F–Judged to provide adequate security.
G–5 fan speeds.
H–Signal light shows when power is on; especially useful in "energy saver" mode.
I–Louvers can be partially closed to increase thrust or ventilation.
J–Easy access to coil for cleaning.
K–No sharp or pointed corners and edges on outside cabinet.
L–Rear guard on cabinet provides adequate protection from sharp cooling fins.
M–Insect screen on vent door.
N–Anti-icing device (not very effective for **Sears Kenmore 77088**).

Key to Disadvantages

a–Had minor difficulty operating at low voltage, low-cool setting, and in extreme heat.
b–Bottom of side-panel rail can come out of frame; may be dangerous if unit is picked up by side panels.
c–Side of grille facing room has pointed corners, sharp edges, or both.
d–Assembly screws didn't fit into brackets.
e–Filter judged harder than others to service.
f–Little or no movement from up/down louvers.
g–Takes longer to install than most.
h–Control door hard to open and close.
i–Side-curtains harder to assemble than most.
j–Ice formed on coil in our tests.
k–Left/right louvers harder to position than most.
l–Hinged door judged easy to break off.
m–Side panels attach only to window sash.
n–Power cord shorter than most.
o–No separate hardware to lock upper window.

Key to Comments

A–Side panels don't expand; requires cutting board to fit window.
B–When power resumed in low-voltage, high-temperature test, fan operated for 3 to 5 min. before compressor turned on.
C–Highly visible LED has filter check light that also indicates power failure.
D–Fiberglass insulation in discharge or intake side of unit.
E–Has fresh-air intake and room-air exhaust.
F–Ventilated room better than most.
G–Lacks vent feature.
H–Has drain pan for routing away condensate.
I–No identification of colder settings or numbers on thermostat.
J–Condensate may seep indoors if unit is installed level.
K–Low profile; more window viewing area.
L–Unit designed to mount flush against sill, projects inside only 1¾ in.; little exposure to sharp corners or edges.
M–Only 2 cooling speeds.
N–No fan-only speed; must adjust thermostat to minimum setting.

SPLIT DUCTLESS AIR-CONDITIONERS

RATINGS — SPLIT DUCTLESS AIR-CONDITIONERS

E ◐ VG ◐ G ○ F ◕ P ●

▶ **See report, page 317.** From Consumer Reports, June 1993.

Recommendations: Any of the units below will keep a good-sized room cool and dehumidified. Note: These models are designed so the fan and evaporator coil mount on a wall indoors and the compressor and condenser on a firm surface outdoors. They are suitable for cooling a medium to large room.

Ratings order: Listed in order of estimated quality, based on thermostat performance, directional control, and noise. Price is the manufacturer's suggested retail. Prices don't include installation, which can be costly. **Notes to table:** SEER = seasonal energy-efficiency rating per manufacturer. Remote control: **I** = wireless infrared; **W** = direct wired; **IW** = choice of types. Ⓢ indicates tested model has been replaced by successor model; according to the manufacturer, the performance of new model should be similar to the tested model but features may vary. See below for new model number and suggested retail price, if available.

Brand and model	Price	Capacity, Btu/hr.	SEER	Moisture removal, pt./hr.	Constant fan	Cyclical fan	Directional control	Noise outdoors, on high	Remote control	Indoor unit	Outdoor unit	Comments
Carrier 42KB009101/ 38KB009101	$1650	9700	11.0	2.4	◐	◐	◐	○	IW	15x38x8	23x31x10	A,C,D,H, L,O,T,V, W,X,Y,Z
Hitachi RAS-3098U/ RAC-3098UV	1550	8700	11.3	2.0	◐	◐	○	◐	I	15x33x8	21x32x10	E,F,H,I, K,M,V,W, X,Y,AA
Mitsubishi MS09EW/ MU09EW	1536	8800	10.7	2.9	◐	◐	○	○	I	15x32x7	22x33x11	C,I,K,M, U,V,W,X, Y,Z,AA
Friedrich MW09C1B/ MR09C1B	1518	9000	11.5	2.4	◐	◐	○	◕	I	15x33x8	24x33x11	E,F,I,K,M, V,W,X,AA
Sanyo K0911W/ C0911 Ⓢ	1100	9000	10.0	2.2	◐	—	◐	○	W	14x32x8	22x32x12	B,W,Y,Z
Burnham B870WHEB/ B870C Ⓢ	1500	8700	11.3	2.2	○	—	◕	◐	W	15x32x7	21x32x10	G,J,N,P, W,Y,AA
Toshiba RAS-09LK2U(W)/ RAS-09LA2U	1550	9000	11.0	2.0	◐	—	◐	◐	W	15x32x7	22x32x10	M,Q,R,S,Z

Successor Models (in Ratings order)
Sanyo K0911W/C0911 is succeeded by 09SK11, $1593; Burnham B870WHEB/B870C by RAS-3098, $1500.

Performance Notes
All were judged excellent in noise level inside, on high and low.

Features in Common
All: • Indoor sections mount permanently on wall near ceiling. • Should be installed by licensed heating/cooling contractor. • Use R-22 HCFC refrigerant, which has low ozone-depletion potential and will be phased out by the year 2030. • Allow at least 25 ft. of refrigerant line. • Can have 15-ft. height difference

Ratings continued ▶

354 SPLIT DUCTLESS AIR-CONDITIONERS

between indoor and outdoor units. • Require drainage for condensate. • Started and operated without problems in low-voltage, high-temperature test. • Have 2 permanent filters that are easy to remove and clean. • Have thermostat labeled in degrees. • Have 1-yr. parts-only warranty.

Except as noted, all: • Operate on 115-volt, 60-Hz electric power. • Have 5-yr. warranty on compressor, excluding labor. • Can vary fan speed with temperature and thermostat setting. • Had actual room temperature match thermostat setting within 2 degrees in our tests.

Key to Comments

- *A*–Has auto-sweep air louvers.
- *B*–Remote control displays room temperature.
- *C*–Shows relationship of room temperature to thermostat setting.
- *D*–Remote has backlight for viewing in low light.
- *E*–Remote displays time.
- *F*–Has the most sophisticated timer; can perform variety of on/off sequences.
- *G*–Can perform combined off and on timer sequence.
- *H*–Has filter monitor.
- *I*–Allows refrigerant lines approx. 50 ft. long.
- *J*–Has light sensor to alter thermostat setting.
- *K*–Thermostat judged to control wider range of temperatures than other tested models.
- *L*–Can direct air up as well as down.
- *M*–Stays off after power outage; must be turned on manually.
- *N*–In automatic-fan mode, fan will cycle only between medium and high speeds.
- *O*–Display symbols for mode and fan speed harder to interpret than others.
- *P*–Kept temperature 4 to 9 degrees higher than minimum and maximum thermostat settings.
- *Q*–Temperature scale not marked in whole numbers, a minor inconvenience.
- *R*–Indoor fan vibrated in our tests.
- *S*–Operates on 208/230-volt power.
- *T*–Based on mfr. suggested price, wireless remote costs $141 more than wired version.
- *U*–Has 6-yr. compressor warranty, excluding labor.
- *V*–Has LCD display.
- *W*–Has coil-freeze protection.
- *X*–Has moisture-removal cycle.
- *Y*–Has night setback.
- *Z*–Has outdoor coil guard.
- *AA*–Has indicator lights.

ABOUT THE REPAIR HISTORIES

Thousands of readers tell us about their repair experiences with autos, appliances, and electronic items on the Annual Questionnaire. Using that unique information can improve your chances of getting a trouble-free car, washing machine, TV set, or other product. See the automobile Frequency-of-Repair charts starting on page 178 and the brand Repair Histories starting on page 365.

WATER-TREATMENT DEVICES 355

LISTINGS WATER-TREATMENT DEVICES

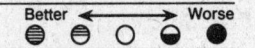

Better ← → Worse

▶ **See report, page 324.** From Consumer Reports, February 1993.

Recommendations: The reverse-osmosis systems and the distiller removed 98 to 99 percent of the lead in our tests. But nearly every other device tested, even the $25 *Brita* carafe, would serve well enough in a home where the lead problem isn't severe. All but one of the devices removed at least 80 percent of the water's lead. The one model we would recommend against, the *Glacier Pure* carafe, removed only half the lead.

Listings order: Listed by types; within types, except where separated by a bold rule, models differed little in performance and are listed alphabetically. Price is the manufacturer's suggested retail. Unless otherwise noted, price includes filters, filter housing, and any hardware that is necessary for installation. ⓢ indicates tested model has been replaced by successor model; according to the manufacturer, the performance of new model should be similar to the tested model but features may vary. See page 356 for new model number and suggested retail price, if available. ⓓ indicates model discontinued.

Brand and model	Price	Operating cost [1]	Lead removed	Life, mfr.	Minutes per gallon	Ease of installation	Comments
REVERSE-OSMOSIS DEVICES							
Culligan Aquacleer H-83 System	$800	$50	98%	3-5 yr.	180	●	A,F,J
Sears Kenmore 3490 ⓓ	399	45	99	3 yr.	120	●	A,E,O
DISTILLERS							
Sears Kenmore Distiller 3450 ⓢ	100	237	99	—	420	◐	G,P
UNDERSINK FILTERS							
Everpure QC4-VOC	300	226	92	500 gal./1 yr.	2.8	◐	J
Multipure MPC500B	330	76	92	500 gal./1 yr.	1.6	◐	J
Omni Total Plus OT-5	160	66	86	1 yr.	1.1	◐	—
Selecto Lead-Out 20	75	12	88 [2]	5000 gal.	0.3	◐	H,K
Teledyne WaterPik Instapure 100	189	44	92	1200 gal./1 yr.	1.6	○	B
COUNTERTOP FILTERS							
Ametek Water Filter CT CMR-10	102	36	88	750 gal./1 yr.	2.3	◐	—
Amway Water Treatment System E-9225	227	110	90	750 gal./1 yr.	0.6	◐	I,J
Sterling Spring CTS ⓢ	119	25	81 [2]	1 yr.	1.8	◐	—

[1] To treat 1000 gallons, about a year's supply of drinking water for four people.

[2] Although they performed well overall, these models removed much less lead in a few test runs than they did in all other test runs.

[3] Not calculated. Because the filters clogged quickly with our test water, replacement costs would be very high.

Listings continued ▶

356 WATER-TREATMENT DEVICES

▶ *Listings continued*

Brand and model	Price	Operating cost [1]	Lead removed	Life, mfr.	Minutes per gallon	Ease of installation	Comments
■ *The following two models became clogged very early in their expected life.*							
Bionaire H20 BT-820 [D]	$100	[3]	99%	700 gal./1 yr.	2.5	◒	D,L
Club Watermaster's K6795ASF [D]	499	[3]	99	700 gal./1 yr.	2.8	◒	J,M
FAUCET FILTERS							
Nordic Ware 78100	76	67	83	3 mo.	1.6	◒	N
CARAFE FILTERS							
Brita Water Filter System OB01/OB03	25	230	86	35 gal./1-2 mo.	20	◒	C,J
NOT ACCEPTABLE							
■ *During our tests, the following model removed only 50 percent of the lead.*							
Glacier Pure Water Filter 62290 [D]	10	100	50	50 gal.	60	◒	C

[1] To treat 1000 gallons, about a year's supply of drinking water for four people.

[2] Although they performed well overall, these models removed much less lead in a few test runs than they did in all other test runs.

[3] Not calculated. Because the filters clogged quickly with our test water, replacement costs would be very high.

Successor Models (in Ratings order)
Sears Kenmore Distiller 3450 succeeded by 3440, $120; Sterling Spring CTS by CTD, $100.

Key to Comments
A–Stores purified water in 2.7-gal. tank.
B–Easiest to install of undersink models.
C–Stores purified water in 1-gal. carafe.
D–Mfr. specifies minimum line pressure of 65 psi., above what we consider typical minimum household pressure.
E–Wastes 15 gal. of water per day.
F–Wastes 30 gal. of water per day; automatic shut-off valve is optional.
G–Consumes electrical energy; operating cost based on average U.S. cost of 8¼ cents per kilowatt-hour.
H–Needs tubing, connections, spigot; not included.
I–Needs tubing, connections; not included.
J–Certified by National Sanitation Foundation.
K–Couldn't confirm manufacturer's claim for filter life. Our test went to only 1000 gal.
L–Clogged at 100 gal.
M–Clogged at 150 gal.
N–Clogged at 200 gal.
O–Also sold as **Ecowater ERO-300**.
P–Also sold as **Ecowater Distiller 10001**.

ABOUT PRICES IN THE BUYING GUIDE

Prices for most products have been updated for the Buying Guide. The prices we give, unless otherwise noted, are approximate or suggested retail as quoted by the manufacturer. Discounts may be substantial, especially for electronics and camera equipment.

AIR CLEANERS

RATINGS — AIR CLEANERS

Ratings key: E ⊖ | VG ⊖ | G ○ | F ⊖ | P ●

▶ See report, page 322. From Consumer Reports, October 1992.

Recommendations: Give first consideration to the check-rated *Friedrich C90* room model. It was by far the most effective in our tests and its maintenance costs were among the lowest. The best tabletop air cleaner was the *Pollenex 1850;* however, its $80 annual operating cost is a drawback.

Ratings order: Listed by size; within sizes, listed in order of estimated quality, based primarily on effectiveness in removing dust and smoke. Bracketed models, judged approximately equal in quality, are listed alphabetically. Price is the manufacturer's suggested retail. ⑤ indicates tested model has been replaced by successor model; according to the manufacturer, the performance of new model should be similar to the tested model but features may vary. See page 358 for new model number and suggested retail price, if available. Ⓓ indicates model discontinued.

Brand and model	Price	Type[1]	Energy[2]	Filter[2]	Smoke removal	Dust removal	Noise High	Noise Low	Advantages	Disadvantages	Comments
ROOM MODELS											
✓ Friedrich C90	$439	EP	$25	$34	⊖	⊖	○	⊖	A,D	i	G
Honeywell F59A	600	EP	21	80	⊖	⊖	○	⊖	D,F	—	A,Q
Smokemaster P-600 Ⓓ	649	EP	27	40	⊖	⊖	○	⊖	D,E	i,d	O,Q
Enviracaire EV-35A ⑤	300	HEPA	57	73	⊖	⊖	●	⊖	A	e,j	G
Austin Air Sierra HEPA PFA-80-AC ⑤	395	HEPA	30	52	⊖	⊖	○	⊖	B	a,g,k	G,I
Trion Console 250 ③	279	EP	47	60	⊖	⊖	○	⊖	D	—	G,M
Vitaire H200	299	HEPA	24	69	○	○	○	○	A	a,d,g,k	A,F,H,I,J,Q
Hepanaire HP50 Ⓓ	495	HEPA	26	145	○	○	○	○	—	e,g,k	A,J
Cloud 9 Sterilaire 150	325	HEPA	32	139	○	○	○	○	A	e,g,k	A,J,L
Micronaire P-500	495	EP	34	98	●	●	○	⊖	D	f,l	A,J,M
NSA 7100A	489	HEPA	19	138	⊖	⊖	○	○	A,B,C,F,K	i	C,G
Space-Gard 2275	190	PF	12	26	●	⊖	⊖	⊖	—	a	F,G,H
TABLETOP MODELS											
Pollenex 1850 ⑤	60	I,EF	20	60	○	○	○	⊖	H,I	a,b,i	E,G
Bionaire F-150	180	I,EF	20	68	○	○	○	⊖	C,F,H	a,b,j	D,K,P
Trion Super Clean II ③	129	I,EP	12	40	⊖	⊖	○	⊖	D,J	i	G,M,O
Norelco CAM880	147	I,EF	16	120	⊖	○	○	⊖	F,H,I,J	—	E,G,I
Amcor Air Processor 2135 NI	99	I,EP	4	—	⊖	●	○	⊖	H	a,b	B,G,H,I,N,P

Ratings continued ▶

AIR CLEANERS

▶ *Ratings continued*

Brand and model	Price	Type[1]	Energy[2]	Filter[2]	Smoke removal	Dust removal	Noise High	Noise Low	Advantages	Disadvantages	Comments
Ecologizer Series 8000	$120	HEPA	19	108	●	●	●	—		a	C,P
NSA 1200A	179	EF	8	78	●	●	○	○	—	—	C,G,L

NOT ACCEPTABLE

■ *The following tabletop models can produce harmful levels of ozone and do not have an automatic control to limit ozone output. Listed alphabetically.*

Alpine 150	NA	OZ	5	—	●	●	●	◐	—	h,I	G,H,I
Quantum Panda Plus Q11	499	OZ	3	—	◐	●	○	◐	A,G	c,h	B,G,H

[1] *Key to type: EP = electrostatic precipitator; HEPA = high-efficiency particulate arresting filter; PF = pleated filter; I = ionizer; EF = electret filter; OZ = ozone generator.*

[2] *Our estimate of the cost to run each unit 8 hrs. each day on High, at the electricity rate of 8¼¢ per kwh. Filter cost is based on the suggested retail price and the shortest replacement interval recommended by the mfr.*

[3] *Product name changed: Trion 250 is now Kenmore 83143 and Sunbeam 2575, both $299; Trion II is Kenmore 83141 and Sunbeam 2571, both $129.*

Successor Models (in Ratings order)
Enviracaire EV-35A is succeeded by EV-35B, $300. Austin PFA-80-AC by Healthmate, $395; Pollenex 1850 by PA2000, $60.

Features in Common
Except as noted, all have: • 2 or more fan speeds. • Conveniently located controls. • Rubber or cork pads or legs. • Grounded or polarized plug. • Washable prefilter and/or postfilter. • Activated-carbon or charcoal filter to remove gaseous odors. • On/off light. • Easily accessible cell or filter.
Except as noted, all lack: • Handle, wheels, or casters. • Adjustable louvers. • Filter-replacement indicator.

Key to Advantages
A–Has handle.
B–Has wheels.
C–Adjustable louvers direct air flow.
D–Can't be operated if cover is removed.
E–Malfunction light and test button.
F–Filter-replacement indicator or schedule.
G–Self-clean switch cleans ozone power plate.
H–Separate On/off ionizer switch.
I–Separate indicator light for ionizer.
J–Can't run ionizer without fan on.
K–Has indicator light for both speeds.

Key to Disadvantages
a–No indicator light for normal operation.
b–Ionizer runs without fan on.
c–Has only 1 speed.
d–Inconveniently placed control knob.
e–No pads or legs.
f–Made annoying crackling sound.
g–Slight humming sound on Low.
h–High-pitched buzz at high ozone setting.
i–Humming, vibrating sound on High.
j–High-pitched whine on High.
k–Tools needed to replace filter.
l–Internal electrical and moving parts can be easily reached from outside by a small finger.

Key to Comments
A–Fan motor must be periodically lubricated.
B–Has spare prefilter.
C–Chemically treated filter system.
D–Has 4-stage filter cartridge.
E–Electret and charcoal filters in one cartridge.
F–No prefilter.
G–No postfilter.
H–No activated carbon or charcoal filter.
I–No grounded or polarized plug.
J–Front grille acts as a postfilter.
K–Fragrance cartridge.
L–Optional fragrance feature.
M–Has switch position that lets user dry precipitating cell after washing.
N–Comes with separate tester that indicates when ions are being produced.
O–Optional wall-mount kit.
P–Can be wall mounted.
Q–Optional casters.

RATINGS: EXTERIOR PAINTS & STAINS

E ◉ **VG** ◒ **G** ○ **F** ◐ **P** ●

▶ See report, page 330. From Consumer Reports, September 1993.

Recommendations: For the Ratings, we considered the ability to hide an old coat of paint or stain most important, but you may want to base your choice on other factors, like ease of application or ability to retain the color. Check the column that means the most to you, and buy a high-rated product that received an excellent score for that attribute.

Ratings order: Paints listed first, then stains. Within categories, listed by types, alkyd and latex; within types, in order of estimated quality. Bracketed products, judged approximately equal, are listed alphabetically. Price is the estimated average, based on prices paid nationally in June 1993. Prices may vary, up or down, by as much as $5. D indicates product discontinued.

Brand and product	Price	Gloss	Hiding	Application	Retaining color	Chalk resistance	Adhesion to chalk	Comments
ALKYD (OIL-BASED) PAINTS								
Devoe All-Weather Gloss House & Trim	$23	Satin	◒	◒	○	◐	◒	A,F
Glidden Spred House Dura-Gloss, A Best Buy	18	Gloss	◒	◒	○	◐	◒	C
Fuller O'Brien Weather King	23	Semi.	◒	○	○	○	◒	—
Pratt & Lambert Permalize Gloss	31	Semi.	◒	○	○	◐	◒	I
Pittsburgh Sun-Proof Gloss	26	Semi.	◒	◐	◒	◒	◒	—
Sherwin Williams SWP Gloss	28	Semi.	○	◒	◒	◒	◒	H
Valspar Our Best Quality Gloss	21	Semi.	○	○	○	◐	◒	B,G
Benjamin Moore High Gloss Enamelized	27	Semi.	○	◒	◐	◒	◒	C,E,G
LATEX (WATER-BASED) PAINTS								
Pratt & Lambert Accolade Eggshell	29	Flat	◒	◒	◒	◒	◒	—
Glidden Spred House Dura-Satin, A Best Buy	16	Egg.	◒	◒	◒	◒	[1]	—
Pratt & Lambert Vapex	22	Flat	◒	◒	◒	○	●	—
Sherwin Williams A-100	16	Flat	○	◒	◒	◐	●	—
Valspar Our Best Quality	20	Flat	○	◒	◒	◐	◐	—
Sears Weatherbeater Premium D	15	Flat	○	◒	◒	◐	[1]	B
Dutch Boy Dirt Fighter	14	Flat	○	◒	◒	○	[1]	—
Sherwin Williams A-100 Satin	18	Egg.	○	◒	◒	◒	◒	—
Benjamin Moore Moorgard	22	Egg.	○	◒	◒	○	◒	—
Sears Best Weatherbeater Satin	17	Egg.	○	◒	◒	◒	[1]	B
Glidden Spred	15	Flat	○	◒	◒	◒	○	—
Tru-Test Weatherall	16	Flat	○	◒	◒	◐	●	—
Olympic Overcoat	16	Flat	○	◒	◒	◐	[1]	—
Sherwin Williams SuperPaint	21	Flat	○	◒	◒	◐	[1]	—

[1] Product proved too variable in its different colors for us to make a single judgment.

Ratings continued ▶

EXTERIOR PAINTS & STAINS

▶ *Ratings continued*

Brand and product	Price	Gloss	Hiding	Application	Retaining color	Chalk resistance	Adhesion to chalk	Comments
Benjamin Moore Moorglo	$24	Semi.	○	◐	◐	◐	◐	—
Dutch Boy Dirt Fighter Gloss	18	Semi.	○	◐	◐	◐	[1]	—
Fuller O'Brien Weather King II	23	Egg.	○	◐	◐	●	[1]	—
Dutch Boy Dirt Fighter Satin	15	Egg.	○	◐	◐	●	◐	—
Glidden Spred House Dura-Flat	15	Flat	○	◐	◐	●	◐	—
Lucite	15	Flat	○	◐	◐	◐	●	—
Pittsburgh Sun-Proof	18	Flat	○	◐	◐	◐	○	—
Pittsburgh Sun-Proof	22	Semi.	○	◐	◐	◐	●	—
Sears Weatherbeater Premium Low Luster Satin	13	Flat	○	◐	◐	◐	[1]	B
Wal-Mart Our Best	8	Flat	○	◐	◐	◐	◐	—
Devoe Regency Soft Lustre	20	Flat	○	◐	◐	◐	●	F
Devoe Wonder-Shield	17	Flat	○	◐	◐	◐	●	F
Glidden Spred House Dura-Gloss	17	Semi.	○	◐	◐	◐	◐	—
Sears Weatherbeater Premium	18	Semi.	◐	◐	◐	◐	◐	B
OPAQUE ALKYD (OIL-BASED) STAINS								
Fuller O'Brien Ful-Stain	21	Flat	◐	◐	◐	—	◐	—
Pratt & Lambert Solid Hide	26	Flat	◐	◐	○	—	◐	D
Sears Weatherbeater Solid Color	13	Flat	◐	◐	◐	—	◐	—
Sherwin Williams Solid Color	18	Flat	◐	◐	○	—	◐	H
OPAQUE LATEX (WATER-BASED) STAINS								
Glidden Endurance Solid Color, A Best Buy	15	Flat	◐	◐	◐	—	[1]	—
Pratt & Lambert Solid Hide	21	Flat	◐	◐	◐	—	●	K
Benjamin Moore Moorwood Vinyl Acrylic	20	Flat	◐	◐	◐	—	◐	—
Fuller O'Brien Ful-Stain	18	Flat	◐	◐	◐	—	●	—
Cabot O.V.T. Solid Color Acrylic	21	Flat	◐	○	◐	—	◐	—
Dutch Boy Solid Color	14	Flat	○	◐	◐	—	○	—
Olympic Stain [D]	16	Flat	○	◐	◐	—	[1]	—
Olympic Weather Screen House & Trim	16	Flat	○	◐	◐	—	◐	—
Sherwin Williams Solid Color	15	Flat	○	◐	◐	—	◐	—
Behr Plus 10 Solid Color	14	Flat	◐	◐	◐	—	◐	—
Tru-Test Woodsman Solid Color (LS)	15	Flat	●	◐	◐	—	◐	—

[1] Product proved too variable in its different colors for us to make a single judgment.

Key to Comments
A–Lost more gloss than other paints.
B–We also tested "Southern" white paints.
C–Better than other paints at resisting dirt.
D–Label has no recommendation regarding use on painted surface.
E–We also tested **Benjamin Moore House &** **Trim High Gloss**, $28, another alkyd, in white. It performed extremely well and has a high resistance to chalking.
F–Sold east of the Rockies.
G–Not in Calif.
H–Not in Calif., N.Y., N.J. or parts of Ariz.
I–Not sold in Ariz.

EXTERIOR CAULKS

RATINGS: EXTERIOR CAULKS

Better ⬅ ➡ Worse

▶ **See report, page 336.** From Consumer Reports, October 1993.

Recommendations: Best overall were the *Ace*, *GE*, and *Red Devil* silicone caulks. Good as they were in our tests, they can't be painted and tools have to be cleaned up with solvent. The *M-D Paintable Silicone* is the highest-rated silicone that can be painted. The best of the latex and silicone/latex caulks are the *DAP '230,'* the *HWI Do-it Best*, and the *Macco Adhesive AC-138*.

Ratings order: Listed in order of overall quality. Price is approximate retail or what CU paid (marked with *) for a cartridge of about 10 ounces. **Notes to table:** Overall score reflects each caulk's performance, based on lab tests and a year's exposure to the elements. Weather scores tell how well the caulk adhered, and how well it resisted splitting and cracking. Flex scores show how flexible it stayed, in high and below-freezing temperatures. Mildew and dirt scores indicate how well it resisted mildew growth and dirt. Shrinkage shows how much it shrank. ⒹI indicates model discontinued.

Brand and model	Price	Type	Overall score	Weather	Flex	Mildew	Dirt	Shrinkage	Comments
Ace 50 Year Silicone	$4.29	Silicone	88	◒	◒	◒	◕	Very low	C,D,F
GE Silicone II Window & Door	4.50	Silicone	87	◒	◒	◒	◕	Very low	C,D,F
Red Devil 100% Silicone	5.00	Silicone	86	◒	◒	◒	◕	Very low	C,D,F
DAP '230' Advanced Latex	3.25	Latex	84	◒	◒	◒	○	High	K
HWI Do-it Best	2.10	Silicone/Latex	82	◒	○	◒	○	Medium	K
Macco Adhesive AC-138	3.00*	Silicone/Latex	80	◒	◒	○	○	Very high	D,J,L
M-D Paintable Silicone	5.99	Silicone	77	◒	○	◒	○	Very low	A,C
Elmer's Siliconized	3.29	Silicone/Latex	76	◒	◒	○	◕	Very high	H
DAP Alex Plus	2.10	Silicone/Latex	75	◒	◕	◒	○	Medium	K
Macco Super LC-130	3.00*	Silicone/Latex	73	◒	○	○	◕	High	—
M-D All Purpose	2.79	Acrylic latex	70	◒	◒	◕	○	Very high	—
DAP Dow Corning Silicone Plus	4.75	Silicone	69	○	◒	◒	○	Medium	D,E,G,K
M-D Painter's	1.59	Latex	69	◒	○	○	◒	Low	—
HWI Do-it	1.29	Acrylic latex	69	◒	◒	●	○	High	I,K
Red Devil Acrylic 15-Year	1.50	Acrylic latex	66	○	◒	◒	◕	Medium	—
UGL Duracalk	1.80	Latex	62	◒	◕	●	○	Low	J
Phenoseal Surpass	5.45	Acrylic latex	61	◒	○	◕	◕	Very high	—
Red Devil Siliconized 25-Year	1.90	Silicone/Latex	60	○	○	◒	◕	Medium	—

Ratings continued ▶

EXTERIOR CAULKS

▶ *Ratings continued*

Brand and model	Price	Type	Overall score	Weather	Flex	Mildew	Dirt	Shrinkage	Comments
Tru-Test WeatherAll	$2.68	Silicone/Latex	59	◓	○	○	●	Very high	H,K
Tru-Test Special [D]	1.50*	Latex	59	○	◓	◑	◑	Medium	J
Shur-Stik 1345 Siliconized	1.85	Silicone/Latex	59	◓	○	●	○	Medium	I
M-D 25 Year	2.19	Silicone/Latex	56	○	○	○	◑	High	K
Ace 25 Year Siliconized	1.79	Silicone/Latex	52	◑	○	◓	◑	Medium	—
Seamseal Plus	2.50*	Silicone/Latex	52	◑	○	○	○	Low	K
M-D Butyl Rubber	2.69	Butyl	50	◑	◓	◓	●	Medium	A,B,C
Elmer's Weather-Tite	1.89	Latex	36	◑	◑	◑	◑	Very high	H,J
DAP Butyl-Flex	2.60	Butyl	31	◑	○	●	●	High	A,B,C,G,I,K

Key to Comments
A–Harder to gun than most.
B–Sticky and messy to apply and level.
C–Solvent needed to clean caulking gun or putty knife after application.
D–Gave off strong odor while curing.
E–Painted sections stayed sticky and yellowish when left indoors for a year.
F–Manufacturer recommends against painting caulk.
G–Manufacturer recommends waiting at least 3 days before painting with oil-based paint.
H–At room temperatures, sagged considerably when applied in vertical aluminum channel, but not in vertical wood channel.
I–Mildewed more than most when painted with latex paint.
J–Unlike others, has no warranty information on label.
K–You must return caulk cartridge and proof of purchase to make claim under warranty.
L–Replaced with new formula carrying same model number.

INFORMATION FROM CONSUMER REPORTS

Consumers Union provides information in a variety of ways. Its publications include CONSUMER REPORTS; Zillions, a CONSUMER REPORTS for Kids; two newsletters, On Health and The Travel Letter; and a book list of more than 100 titles. CU also offers used car prices by telephone, computer printouts of new car prices, fax copies of recent articles in CONSUMER REPORTS, and an electronic version of CONSUMER REPORTS on America Online, CompuServe, Dialog, Nexis, and Prodigy.

THERMOSTATS

RATINGS THERMOSTATS

E ⊖ VG ⊖ G ○ F ◐ P ●

▶ See report, page 336. From Consumer Reports, October 1993.

Recommendations: If your family will be content with two temperature levels a day, then the three electromechanical models should do nicely. The *Emerson 7901* and the *Honeywell CT1501* are the easiest to use. For more versatility, any of the top four electronic thermostats would be a good choice. The *Sears Weekender* and the *Honeywell MagicStat* offer the convenience of completely independent programs for heating and cooling so you don't have to reprogram them when the seasons change.

Ratings order: Within types, listed in order of overall quality. Price is the manufacturer's suggested retail. **Notes to table:** Temperature choices: **M** = most flexible; **4** or **2** indicates the number of temperature choices you can program each week. ⒟ indicates model discontinued.

DIGITAL ELECTRONIC MODELS

Brand and model	Price	Overall score	Temp. swing	Programming ease	Programs	Temp. choices per week	Comments
Honeywell MagicStat 33	$90	90	⊖	⊖	Wkday/wknd.	M	C,E,F,G,S,AA,CC,DD
Honeywell PerfecTemp CT3400	130	84	⊖	⊖	Wkday/Sat./Sun.	M	B,C,F,S,Y,AA,CC
Sears Weekender 91112	70	78	⊖	⊖	Wkday/wknd.	M	C,F,G,AA,BB
Emerson 7907	100	72	⊖	○	Daily	4	A,C,F,W,AA,BB
Jameson Deluxe 0940	89	58	○	⊖	Daily	M	O,S,AA,BB
Robertshaw T60-1044 ⒟	50	58	⊖	◐	Daily	M	F,O,X,BB
Emerson 7903	60	46	⊖	●	Wkday/wknd.	2	G,J,L,M,T,W,BB,CC
Hunter Auto Temp 44402	55	46	●	○	Wkday/Sat./Sun.	M	C,D,N,P,R,U,V,DD
Robertshaw TX1000	39	45	◐	○	Wkday/Sat./Sun.	M	H,K,S,CC,DD
Hunter Set'n Save I 42204	28	43	◐	○	Wkday/wknd.	M	E,J,N,Q,R,S,Z,AA,CC
Jameson Economy 0925	49	42	◐	◐	Wkday/wknd.	4	D,I,O,S,T,BB

Ratings continued ▶

▶ *Ratings continued*

Performance

Brand and model	Price	Overall score	Temp. swing	Programming ease	Programs	Temp. choices per week	Comments
ELECTROMECHANICAL MODELS							
Emerson 7901	$50	65	Varies	◐	1	2	D,BB,CC
Honeywell CT1501	75	65	Varies	◐	1	2	D,X,BB,CC
Robertshaw T33-1044	49	60	Varies	○	1	2	D,BB,CC

Features in Common

All: • Control heating and cooling systems with a 24-volt control circuit. • Have battery backup, typically AA. • Displays time and room temperature. • Lets you adjust cycle time/temperature swing. • Can't automatically switch between heating and cooling.
All digital electronic models: • Let you override a temperature setting within a time period. • Use the same time periods for heating and cooling programs. • Let you program time to nearest 15 min. or less.

Key to Comments

A–7-day model simultaneously programs all days of week unless you override the setting.
B–Start of recovery from setback to comfort temperature varies according to room and outdoor temperature; feature can be overridden.
C–Digital display easy to read.
D–Lets you calibrate temperature display.
E–You can reach the batteries without opening main case.
F–"Armchair programming" lets you remove thermostat from wall to program.
G–Independent programs for heating, cooling.
H–Hard to display setpoint temperature.
I–Restricts weekend program to a single-setback version of weekday setting.
J–Battery change wipes out program.
K–Inconvenient to override temperature setting.
L–Requires daytime setback even if not wanted.
M–Keypad buttons somewhat hard to push.
N–Automatically switches out of programming mode after only 15 seconds.
O–Digital display hard to read.
P–Batteries hard to change.
Q–Must be reprogrammed when switching from heating to cooling season.
R–Temperature swing, cycle time not adjustable.
S–Heating system won't operate if thermostat batteries go dead.
T–Lets you program time settings in only 30-minute intervals.
U–Lets you program time settings in 1-minute intervals.
V–Has option for automatic heating/cooling changeover.
W–Temperature override effective for 2 hours.
X–**Honeywell CT1501** uses 2 AAA batteries. **Robertshaw T60-1044** uses one 9-volt battery.
Y–Largest of those tested.
Z–Smallest of those tested.
AA–Displays call for heat.
BB–Displays set point.
CC–Displays program period.
DD–Displays total on-time.

▶Repair histories

VCRs	366
TV sets	366
Compact-disc players	368
Camcorders	368
Dishwashers	369
Microwave ovens	370
Gas ranges	370
Refrigerators	371
Washing machines	372
Clothes dryers	372
Lawn mowers	373
Air-conditioners	374

Every year, CONSUMER REPORTS asks its subscribers to share their experiences with various products by answering questions on the Annual Questionnaire. One result is the automobile Frequency-of-Repair charts, beginning on page 178. Another result is what you'll find in this chapter—repair histories for various brands of major appliances, electronic items, and other products.

The graphs that follow represent the percent of products in each brand that have ever been repaired, as reported to us by subscribers in the survey. It's important to keep two things in mind: Repair histories apply only to brands, not to specific models of these products. And the histories, being histories, can only suggest future trends, not predict them exactly. A company can at any time change its products' design or quality control so substantially as to affect their reliability. But our findings over the years have been consistent enough that we are confident these repair histories presented can greatly improve your chances of getting a more trouble-free product.

Note, too, that the repair histories of different products are not directly comparable. Data for each graph have been adjusted differently—to compensate for differing age distributions, for instance—and the experiences summed up by different graphs may cover different years of purchase. The text associated with each graph explains exactly what type of product is covered and whether any special assumptions were made in the graph's preparation.

Use these graphs in conjunction with the product reports elsewhere in the Buying Guide. You'll find the most recent Repair Histories in the pages of the monthly CONSUMER REPORTS.

VCRs

Based on nearly 230,000 responses to our 1992 Annual Questionnaire. Readers were asked about any repairs to VCRs bought new between 1987 and 1992. Data have been standardized to eliminate differences among brands due solely to age and how much the VCRs were used. Differences of less than 3 points aren't meaningful.

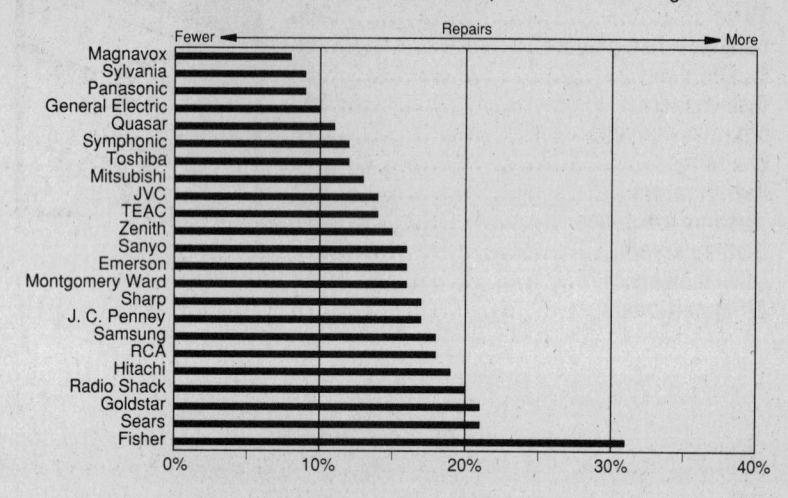

Brand	Repairs
Magnavox	~8%
Sylvania	~9%
Panasonic	~9%
General Electric	~10%
Quasar	~11%
Symphonic	~12%
Toshiba	~12%
Mitsubishi	~13%
JVC	~14%
TEAC	~14%
Zenith	~15%
Sanyo	~15%
Emerson	~16%
Montgomery Ward	~16%
Sharp	~17%
J. C. Penney	~17%
Samsung	~18%
RCA	~18%
Hitachi	~19%
Radio Shack	~20%
Goldstar	~21%
Sears	~21%
Fisher	~31%

Television sets: 13-inch

Based on more than 35,000 responses to our 1992 Annual Questionnaire. Readers were asked about any repairs to a 13-inch color TV with remote control bought new between 1987 and 1992. Data have been standardized to eliminate differences among brands due solely to age. Differences of less than 3 points aren't meaningful.

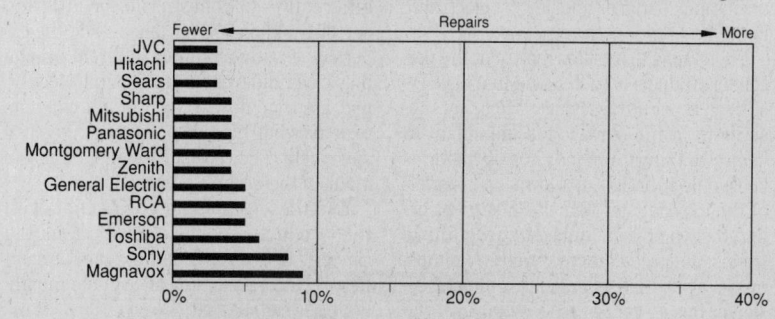

Brand	Repairs
JVC	~3%
Hitachi	~3%
Sears	~3%
Sharp	~4%
Mitsubishi	~4%
Panasonic	~4%
Montgomery Ward	~4%
Zenith	~4%
General Electric	~5%
RCA	~5%
Emerson	~5%
Toshiba	~6%
Sony	~7%
Magnavox	~9%

Television sets: 19-inch and 20-inch

Based on more than 100,000 responses to our 1992 Annual Questionnaire. Readers were asked about any repairs to a 19-inch or 20-inch color TV with remote control bought new between 1987 and 1992. Data have been standardized to eliminate differences among brands due solely to age. Differences of less than 4 points aren't meaningful.

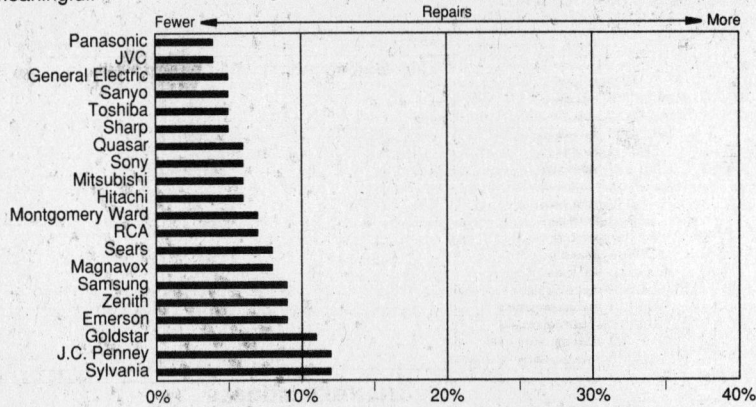

Fewer ← Repairs → More

- Panasonic
- JVC
- General Electric
- Sanyo
- Toshiba
- Sharp
- Quasar
- Sony
- Mitsubishi
- Hitachi
- Montgomery Ward
- RCA
- Sears
- Magnavox
- Samsung
- Zenith
- Emerson
- Goldstar
- J.C. Penney
- Sylvania

0% 10% 20% 30% 40%

Television sets: 25-inch to 27-inch

Based on more than 121,000 responses to our 1992 Annual Questionnaire. Readers were asked about any repairs to a 25-inch to 27-inch color TV with remote control bought new between 1987 and 1992. Data have been standardized to eliminate differences among brands due solely to age. Differences of less than 3 points aren't meaningful.

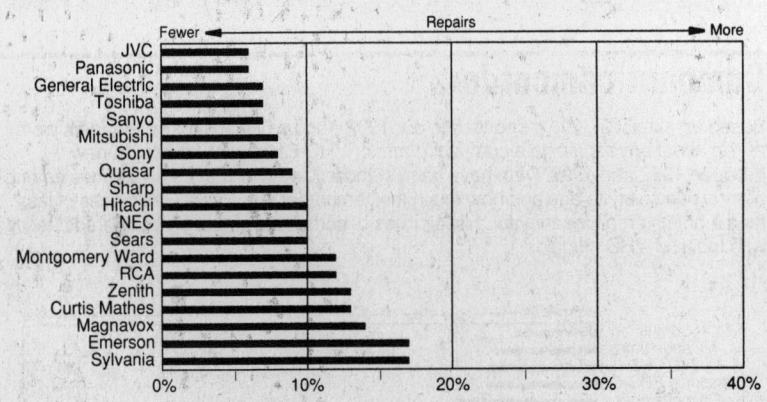

Fewer ← Repairs → More

- JVC
- Panasonic
- General Electric
- Toshiba
- Sanyo
- Mitsubishi
- Sony
- Quasar
- Sharp
- Hitachi
- NEC
- Sears
- Montgomery Ward
- RCA
- Zenith
- Curtis Mathes
- Magnavox
- Emerson
- Sylvania

0% 10% 20% 30% 40%

Compact-disc players

Based on more than 100,000 responses to our 1992 Annual Questionnaire. Readers were asked about any repairs to a single-play or changer tabletop model bought new between 1989 and 1992. Data have been standardized to eliminate differences among brands due solely to age and how much the CD players were used. Differences of less than 3 points aren't meaningful.

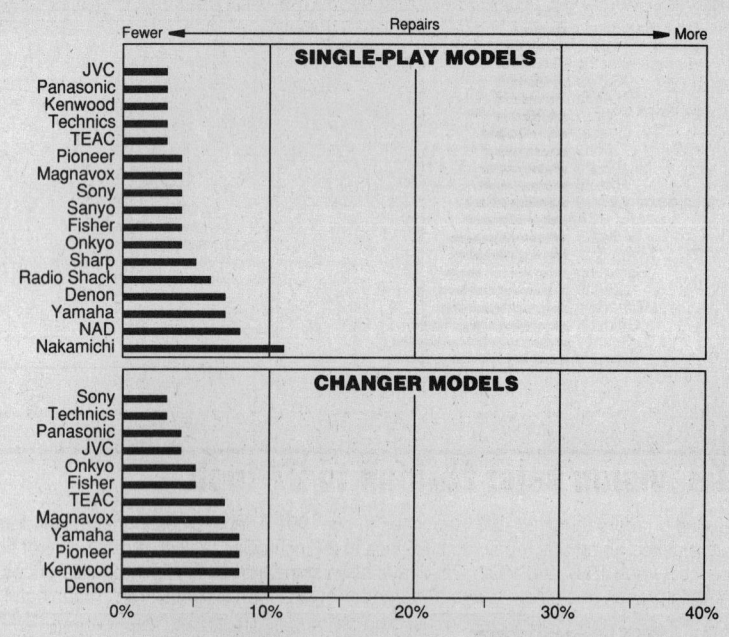

SINGLE-PLAY MODELS (Fewer ← Repairs → More)

- JVC
- Panasonic
- Kenwood
- Technics
- TEAC
- Pioneer
- Magnavox
- Sony
- Sanyo
- Fisher
- Onkyo
- Sharp
- Radio Shack
- Denon
- Yamaha
- NAD
- Nakamichi

CHANGER MODELS

- Sony
- Technics
- Panasonic
- JVC
- Onkyo
- Fisher
- TEAC
- Magnavox
- Yamaha
- Pioneer
- Kenwood
- Denon

(Scale: 0% – 40%)

Compact camcorders

Based on almost 37,000 responses to our 1992 Annual Questionnaire. Readers were asked about any repairs to a compact (8mm or VHS-C) camcorder bought new between 1987 and 1992. Data have been standardized to eliminate differences among brands due solely to age and how much the camcorder was used. Differences of less than 4 points aren't meaningful. Repair rates of compacts cannot be compared directly with those of VHS models.

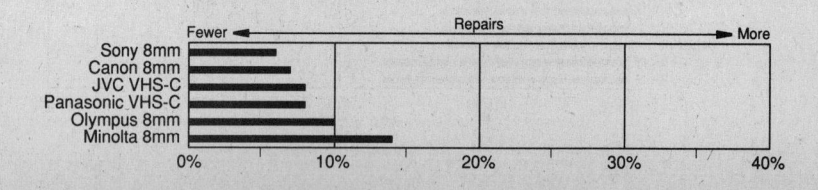

(Fewer ← Repairs → More)

- Sony 8mm
- Canon 8mm
- JVC VHS-C
- Panasonic VHS-C
- Olympus 8mm
- Minolta 8mm

(Scale: 0% – 40%)

REPAIR HISTORIES 369

VHS camcorders

Based on nearly 35,000 responses to our 1992 Annual Questionnaire. Readers were asked about any repairs to a VHS camcorder bought new between 1987 and 1992. Data have been standardized to eliminate differences among brands due solely to age and how much the camcorder was used. Differences of less than 4 points aren't meaningful. VHS repair rates cannot be compared directly with those of compact camcorders because the VHS models tended to be older than the compacts.

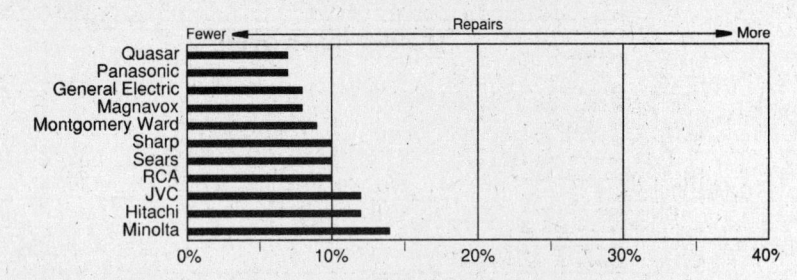

Fewer ← Repairs → More

- Quasar
- Panasonic
- General Electric
- Magnavox
- Montgomery Ward
- Sharp
- Sears
- RCA
- JVC
- Hitachi
- Minolta

0%   10%   20%   30%   40%

Dishwashers

Based on more than 137,000 responses to our 1992 Annual Questionnaire. Readers were asked about any repairs to installed dishwashers bought new between 1987 and 1992. Data have been standardized to eliminate differences among brands due solely to age. Differences of less than 3 points aren't meaningful.

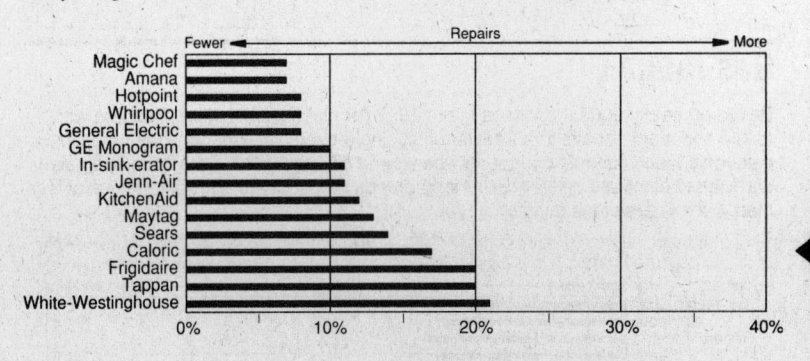

Fewer ← Repairs → More

- Magic Chef
- Amana
- Hotpoint
- Whirlpool
- General Electric
- GE Monogram
- In-sink-erator
- Jenn-Air
- KitchenAid
- Maytag
- Sears
- Caloric
- Frigidaire
- Tappan
- White-Westinghouse

0%   10%   20%   30%   40%

Microwave ovens

Based on more than 112,000 responses to our 1992 Annual Questionnaire. Readers were asked about any repairs to medium- and large-sized microwave ovens with electronic touch controls bought new between 1987 and 1992. Data have been standardized to eliminate differences among brands due solely to age. Differences of less than 3 points aren't meaningful.

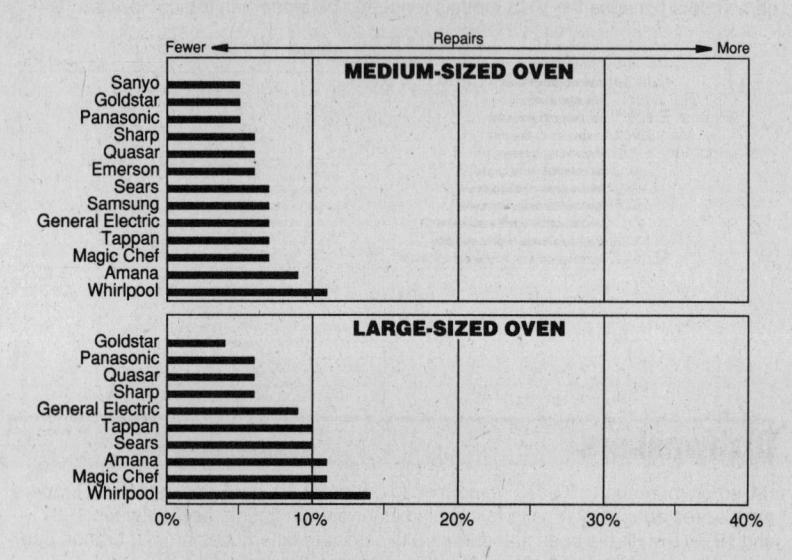

MEDIUM-SIZED OVEN
- Sanyo
- Goldstar
- Panasonic
- Sharp
- Quasar
- Emerson
- Sears
- Samsung
- General Electric
- Tappan
- Magic Chef
- Amana
- Whirlpool

LARGE-SIZED OVEN
- Goldstar
- Panasonic
- Quasar
- Sharp
- General Electric
- Tappan
- Sears
- Amana
- Magic Chef
- Whirlpool

Gas ranges

Based on nearly 9000 responses to our 1992 Annual Questionnaire. Readers were asked about any repairs to a freestanding, single-oven, self-cleaning gas range without electronic touch controls bought new between 1987 and 1992. Data have been standardized to eliminate differences among brands due solely to age. Differences of less than 4 points aren't meaningful.

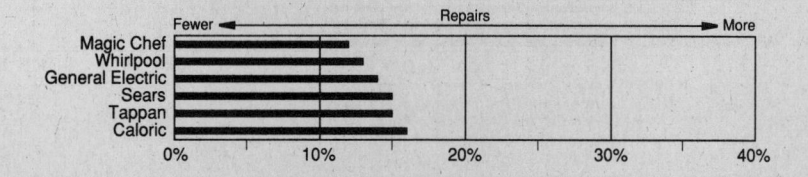

- Magic Chef
- Whirlpool
- General Electric
- Sears
- Tappan
- Caloric

Side-by-side refrigerators

Based on almost 33,000 responses to our 1992 Annual Questionnaire. Readers were asked about any repairs to side-by-side, two-door, no-frost refrigerators bought new between 1985 and 1992. Data have been standardized to eliminate differences among brands due solely to age. Differences of less than about 4 points aren't meaningful.

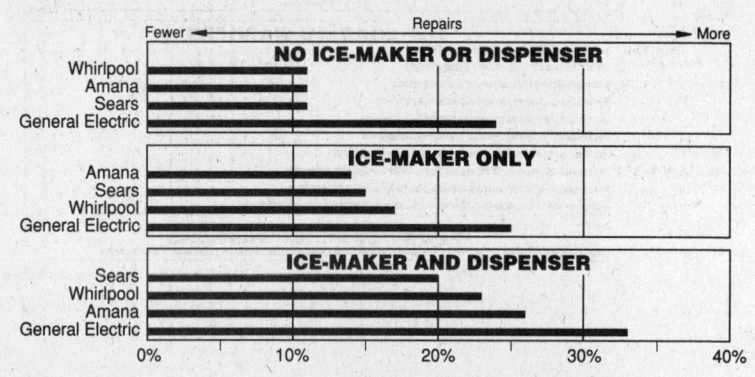

Fewer ◄──── Repairs ────► More

NO ICE-MAKER OR DISPENSER
- Whirlpool
- Amana
- Sears
- General Electric

ICE-MAKER ONLY
- Amana
- Sears
- Whirlpool
- General Electric

ICE-MAKER AND DISPENSER
- Sears
- Whirlpool
- Amana
- General Electric

0%   10%   20%   30%   40%

Top-freezer refrigerators

Based on more 97,000 responses to our 1992 Annual Questionnaire. Readers were asked about any repairs to top-freezer, two-door, no-frost refrigerators bought new between 1984 and 1992. Data have been standardized to eliminate differences among brands due solely to age. Differences of less than 4 points aren't meaningful.

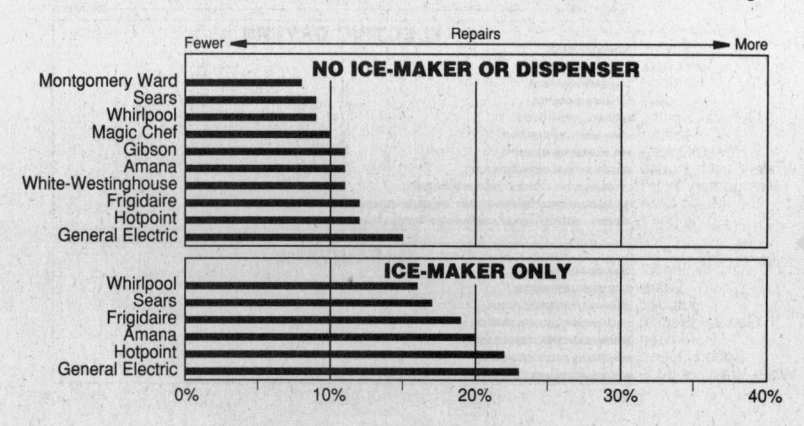

Fewer ◄──── Repairs ────► More

NO ICE-MAKER OR DISPENSER
- Montgomery Ward
- Sears
- Whirlpool
- Magic Chef
- Gibson
- Amana
- White-Westinghouse
- Frigidaire
- Hotpoint
- General Electric

ICE-MAKER ONLY
- Whirlpool
- Sears
- Frigidaire
- Amana
- Hotpoint
- General Electric

0%   10%   20%   30%   40%

Washing machines

Based on more than 200,000 responses to our 1992 Annual Questionnaire. Readers were asked about any repairs to a full-sized washer bought new between 1984 and 1992. Data have been standardized to eliminate differences among brands due solely to age. Differences of less than 4 points aren't meaningful.

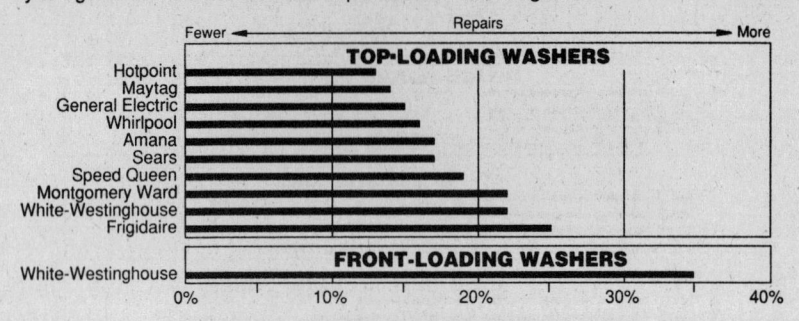

TOP-LOADING WASHERS (Fewer ← Repairs → More)

Brand	Repairs
Hotpoint	~12%
Maytag	~13%
General Electric	~14%
Whirlpool	~16%
Amana	~17%
Sears	~17%
Speed Queen	~19%
Montgomery Ward	~22%
White-Westinghouse	~22%
Frigidaire	~25%

FRONT-LOADING WASHERS

Brand	Repairs
White-Westinghouse	~35%

Clothes dryers

Based on more than 150,000 responses to our 1992 Annual Questionnaire. Readers were asked about any repairs to a full-sized electric or gas clothes dryer bought new between 1986 and 1992. Data have been standardized to eliminate differences among brands due solely to age. Differences of less than 4 points aren't meaningful.

ELECTRIC DRYERS (Fewer ← Repairs → More)

Brand	Repairs
Maytag	~6%
Whirlpool	~7%
Hotpoint	~7%
Sears	~7%
General Electric	~8%
Amana	~9%
Speed Queen	~9%
White-Westinghouse	~11%
Montgomery Ward	~15%
Magic Chef	~21%
Frigidaire	~25%

GAS DRYERS

Brand	Repairs
Whirlpool	~8%
Sears	~8%
Hotpoint	~10%
General Electric	~11%
Maytag	~11%
Speed Queen	~11%
White-Westinghouse	~17%

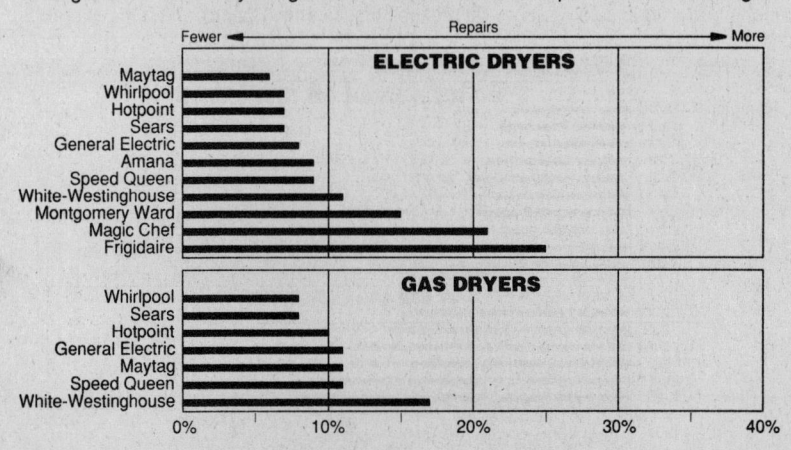

REPAIR HISTORIES 373

Lawn mowers & lawn tractors

Based on nearly 65,000 responses to our 1992 Annual Questionnaire. Readers were asked about any repairs to an electric or gasoline walk-behind mower, a riding mower, or a lawn tractor bought new between 1988 and 1992. Data have been standardized to eliminate differences among brands due solely to age and how much the lawn mowers/tractors were used. Differences of less than 2 points aren't meaningful.

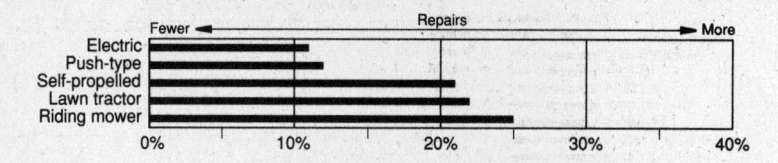

Fewer ← Repairs → More

- Electric
- Push-type
- Self-propelled
- Lawn tractor
- Riding mower

0% 10% 20% 30% 40%

Walk-behind lawn mowers

Based on more than 49,000 responses to our 1992 Annual Questionnaire. Readers were asked about any repairs to any push or self-propelled gasoline mower with an engine between 3.5 and 5.0 horsepower and a cutting swath of 20 to 22 inches that was bought new between 1988 and 1992. Data have been standardized to eliminate differences among brands due solely to age and how much the lawn mowers were used. Differences of less than about 5 points aren't meaningful.

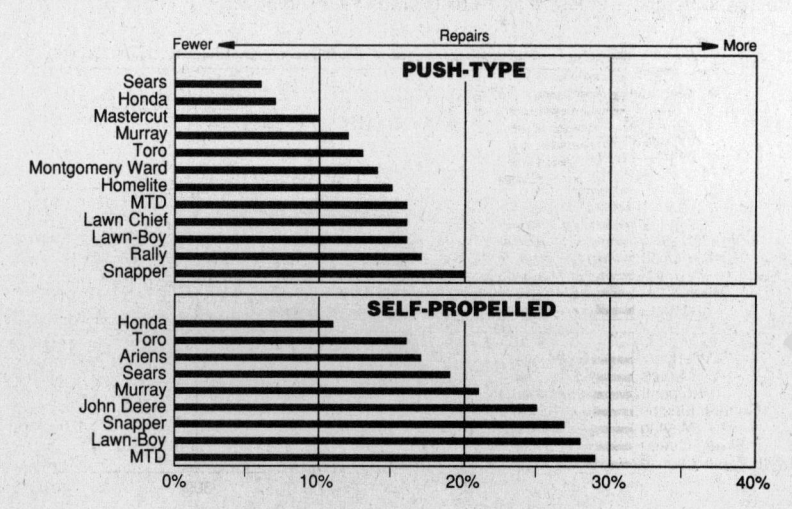

Fewer ← Repairs → More

PUSH-TYPE
- Sears
- Honda
- Mastercut
- Murray
- Toro
- Montgomery Ward
- Homelite
- MTD
- Lawn Chief
- Lawn-Boy
- Rally
- Snapper

SELF-PROPELLED
- Honda
- Toro
- Ariens
- Sears
- Murray
- John Deere
- Snapper
- Lawn-Boy
- MTD

0% 10% 20% 30% 40%

Room air-conditioners

Based on more than 17,000 responses to our 1992 Annual Questionnaire. Readers were asked about any repairs to a 115-volt room air-conditioner with cooling capacity under 10,000 BTUs/hour that was bought new between 1987 and 1992. Data have been standardized to eliminate differences among brands due solely to age. Differences of less than 3 points aren't meaningful.

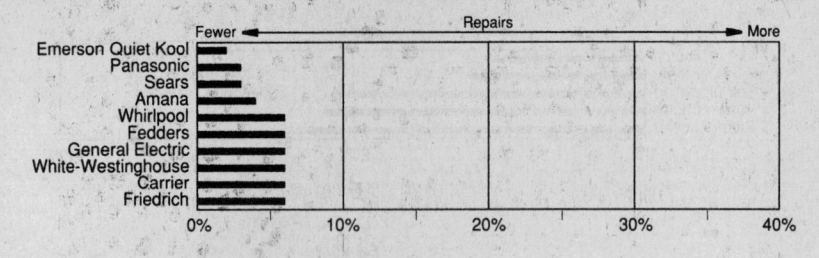

Central air-conditioners

Based on nearly 32,000 responses to our 1992 Annual Questionnaire. Readers were asked about any repairs to the outdoor compressor unit of a central air-conditioner installed between 1984 and 1992 in homes with between 1500 and 3000 square feet. Data have been standardized to eliminate differences among brands due solely to age. Differences of less than 2 points aren't meaningful.

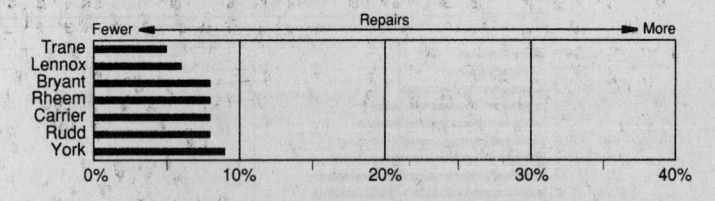

▶Product recalls

Children's products	375
Household products	381
Marine products	383
Cars	384
Trucks & vans	387
Child car seats	388
Motorcycles & bicycles	389
Motor homes	389
Vehicle accessories	390

Products ranging from cars to toys are recalled when there are safety defects. Various Federal agencies—the Consumer Product Safety Commission, the National Highway Traffic Safety Administration, the U. S. Coast Guard—monitor consumer complaints and injuries and, when there's a problem, issue a recall. A selection of those recalls are published monthly in CONSUMER REPORTS. This section covers recalls from October 1992 through October 1993. For the latest information, see the current issue of CONSUMER REPORTS.

Children's products

Le Roy pacifiers
Could come apart and choke child.

Products: Pink, blue, or ivory pacifiers sold in San Francisco Bay area 2/93-4/93 for $1.50. Pacifiers are 3-in. long, with 1½-in. round handle with cutout of stork in center of ring. Item came with 1½ in. plastic cap that covers fluid-filled nipple. "Le Roy" is on shield.
What to do: Return pacifier to store for refund. If you bought pacifier outside San Francisco Bay area, call Consumer Product Safety Commission at 800 638-2772.

Ultra Kip pacifiers, Infant Size
Could come apart and choke child.

Products: 165,400 pacifiers, model 1201, sold 1/90-9/92 for $3. Pacifiers have white plastic shield with green or blue plug on back and latex nipple in front. Lettering on shield reads: "(C) '90 the first years." Yellow duck or white and purple dog is on plug.
What to do: Return pacifier to store for refund.

376 PRODUCT RECALLS

Aviva Sports Inc. Sound Swing toy baseball bat
Plastic noisemaker end cap could fly loose and strike bystander.

Products: 125,000 lightweight 27-inch bats with foam exterior, model 31500, sold in 1992 for $13.

What to do: Return toy to store for refund, or mail bat to company for refund, postage reimbursement, and $2 coupon toward purchase of another Aviva product. Mail to: Nancy Nelson, Aviva Sports Inc., 15930 E. Valley Blvd., City of Industry, Ca. 91744.

Bamm-Bamm's Drum and Flute toy
Small parts could come off and choke child.

Products: 24,576 toys, sold 5/88-10/91 for $4 at following amusement parks: Kings Dominion, Doswell, Va.; Carowinds, Charlotte, N.C.; Kings Island, Cincinnati, Ohio; and Great America, Santa Clara, Calif. Toy, $7\frac{1}{2}$ in. long consists of whistle at one end and see-through hand-held drum at other. Handle has three circular holes. Two small plastic balls and 2 small metal bells are attached to drum. Whistle portion resembles flute. Each side of drum has transparent sticker that shows "Bamm-Bamm" (Flintstones cartoon character) wearing leopard loincloth and cap and carrying club.

What to do: Mail one side of drum to Laura Miranda, San Pacific International, Inc., 542 Brannan St., San Francisco, Calif. 94107 for refund, including postage.

Jaclyn Inc. "Barney" and "Baby Bop" carryall bags, plus vinyl bags featuring beach scenes with children or cats
Surface coating and colored inks may contain excess lead, which could be toxic to children who put bag in their mouth. Also, sunglasses, sold with some products, have lenses that could shatter.

Products: 650,000 bags sold 10/92-3/93 for $5-$32. Recalled Barney and Baby Bop bags include tote bags, shoulder bags, small handbags, "fanny" packs, and backpacks. Vinyl beach bags bear model nos. 3312, 3315, and 3371.

What to do: To exchange bag for similar item, mail to Jaclyn, c/o SPF, 415 Hamburg Tpk., Wayne, N.J. 07470. Consumers with questions can call 800 447-9279.

Benjamin-Sheridan CO2 and pneumatic air guns
Could accidentally discharge while safety is being disengaged.

Products: 65,000 air guns sold through hunting and sporting-goods catalogs and by specialty stores 2/7/91- 8/10/92. Recalled guns bear the following numbers on packaging: S397, S397W, 397, 397W, 397G, S397G, GS397W, 392, S392W, S392, 392W, 392G, S392G, GS392W, G392W, C9, CB9, CW9, CBW9, F9, FB9, FW9, FBW9, KP2, KP3. Guns are also subject to recall if they bear following designation on left side of action: 397P, 397G, 392P 392G, C9 Series, F9 Series, K Series.

What to do: For free repairs and shipping, note model and serial numbers and call 800 836-3101.

Brik Toy Co. 3-in-1 Construction Table for children
Small parts could come off and choke child.

Products: 50,000 tables sold 8/1/92-11/2/92 for $40-$60. Model 3630 came without chairs; model 3632 came with 2 matching chairs. Yellow and red plastic table is 17 x 20 inches wide and $19\frac{1}{2}$ inches high, with 4 removable plastic legs. "BRIK" is embossed on edge of table. Red or black vinyl caps under table frame, which hold legs in place during storage, pose choking hazard.

What to do: Table can be used safely if caps are removed. To receive free replacement table frame that allows legs to be stored under table, call 800 438-2745.

Plastic building blocks in 50- and 100-piece sets
Smallest blocks pose choking hazard.

Products: 9700 sets, in various colors, sold at Toys R Us stores in '92 for $8-$13. Each set, packaged in yellow or white plastic basket with white plastic handle, contains blocks of five different sizes. Small red "roof top" blocks pose choking risk. Label on side of basket reads, in part: "50 (or 100) Plastic Building Blocks, #50, 5 colors, Ages 18 Mos. & Up; Made in Israel by Palkar for Primex, New York, N.Y. 10001."

What to do: Return small red roof blocks to importer in exchange for 10 larger blocks. Mail to Palkar Plastics, c/o Primex International, 230 Fifth Ave., 7th Floor, N.Y.C. 10001.

Coynes Inc. Cordless Phone Organ musical telephone
Small parts could come off and choke child.

Products: 7000 toys sold 6/91-1/93 for $2-$3. Plastic telephone is blue or pink and measures 5 x $1\frac{5}{8}$ x $1\frac{1}{2}$ inches, with 2-inch black antenna. Telephone resembles cordless handset; keys play musical notes when pushed. Label on package reads, in part: ". . . Cordless Phone Organ...DO RE ME...Made in Taiwan...Model number D-6138..."

What to do: Return toy to store for refund.

PRODUCT RECALLS

Fisher-Price Kiddiecraft Racing Rover car
Small part could come off and choke child.

Products: 100,000 toys sold '91-92. Car is bright yellow, with white and black dog in driver's seat. Pushing down dog's head makes car move forward. Top of dog's head poses choking hazard.
What to do: For $10 refund, cut off dog's plastic ears and mail to Fisher-Price, Consumer Affairs, 636 Girard Ave., E. Aurora, N.Y. 14052. For information, call 800 355-8882.

Keds Flexibles sneakers for young children
Blue label on heel could come off and choke child.

Products: 20,000 pairs of sneakers sold since 2/92. Recalled sneakers, in sizes 2-10, come in high-lace, mid-lace, and mid-Velcro styles and bear the following model nos.: TH 2120; TH 2121; TH 2122; TH 2130; TH 2131; TH 2140; and TH 2141. Designation TW-206 or CH-206 follows model no. Sequence is at upper right corner on underside of sneaker tongue. Sole design features triangles, squares, circles.
What to do: Return sneakers to store for replacement or refund.

Taco Bell restaurant giveaways
Lowly Worm and Huckle Cat finger puppets could get stuck on child's tongue, and Rocky & Bullwinkle inflatable balls could cause dizziness during inflation.

Products: 500,000 finger puppets distributed 1/25-3/28/93 and 80,000 balls distributed 3/29-3/31/93 with Kid's Meal.
What to do: Return toy to restaurant in exchange for free Original Taco.

Fuzzy Puzzles "Farm Animals," "Pets," "Jungle Animals," and "Circus Animals" wooden jigsaw puzzles
Small parts could choke child.

Products: 14,400 puzzles sold 11/91-1/92 for $10. Animal-shaped puzzle pieces have textured surface that resembles fur or feathers. In center of each piece is peg. "Crafted by hand" is painted on bottom right of puzzle board. Label on back of board reads, in part: "FUZZY PUZZLES, Ages 1½ to 4 Made in Taiwan."
What to do: Return toy to store for replacement.

Gerber Gem Collection Decorator Pacifier with Travel Case
Could separate into small pieces and choke child.

Products: 460,300 pacifiers, sold individually and in double pack for $2 to $3 each. Pacifiers have tan nipple, tinted plastic shield, and plastic end cap decorated with marching bear, teddy bear with hearts, or rabbit. "Gerber" is embossed on shield. Travel case is transparent, plastic cover that fits over nipple. Recalled pacifiers were made 6/1/92-1/18/93. Date code, which ranges from 060192 (month, day and year) to 011893, appears on back of blister package, along with item no. 76407 or 76408.
What to do: Call 800 443-7237 for replacement pacifier. If blister package has been discarded, call for help in identifying recalled pacifiers.

Graduate booster seat sold by Pansy Ellen Prods.
Seat component could slide out of chair base and allow child to fall.

Products: 680,000 seats, models 415 and 4156, sold '87-91 for $11-$13. Product has white seat with blue base or red seat with white base. Back of both models is labeled, in part: "THE GRADUATE* Pansy Ellen."
What to do: If seat component doesn't fit securely into slots in base, send it to Pansy Ellen, 1245 Old Alpharetta Rd., Alpharetta, Ga. 30202 for $5 refund.

Dragons Are Too Seldom, Inc. infant heating pads
Pose burn hazard. Also, could leak hot liquid and scald child.

Products: 40,000 Snoopy Safe, Safe Heating, and Snooze Zoo Instant heating pads for babies, sold 11/88—03/92 for $15-$20. Product is sealed plastic pouch containing sodium acetate solution. It's heated by flexing metal disk inside pad.
What to do: Mail heating pad to Dragons Are Too Seldom, Inc., Box 8046, Rapid City, S.D. 57709, for replacement with Tub Buddie Puppet Washcloth. For more information, call 800-888-1495.

House of Lloyd Infant's Playmat and Special Skunk toys
Small parts could come off and choke child.

Products: 21,000 Special Skunk stuffed toys and 7200 Infant's Playmat toys sold at home-demonstration parties 5/89—12/89. Skunk sold for $12, Playmat for $35. Playmat, sold as catalog no. 3182, stock no. 130189, measures 36 x 32 in. It has furry tan bear face with black button eyes, plastic nose, 1 striped cloth ear and 1 dotted cloth ear, striped bow at neck, quilted stomach, and 4 stuffed tan paws. Toy also comes with rattle, teething toy, and mirror that can be attached to one of three paws with velcro. Fourth paw contains squeeze toy and applique of house. Front of paw says "TOUCH me." Black and white skunk, sold as catalog no. 4155, stock no. 510052, is 7½ in. high and

3½ in. wide, has plastic eyes and nose, curled tail, and suction cups attached to legs and arms. Message on stomach says "GOD MADE ME SPECIAL."
What to do: For refund, return toy to House of Lloyd Inc., Merchandise Recall, 601 S. 291 Hwy., 5555 W. GeoSpace Dr., Independence, Mo. 64056.

Jesty the Clown stuffed doll
Nose could come off and choke child.

Products: 6200 dolls, model 24501, sold at Target Stores 8/92-11/92 for $5. Fabric doll is 8 in. tall and 7½-in. wide, with tan face, black button eyes, red vinyl nose, brown stiched smile, multicolored yarn hair, and clown costume with two pom-poms attached to chest and one pom-pom on tip of hat. Label on clown suit reads in part: "1990 COMMONWEALTH TOY & NOVELTY CO. INC. NYC * * * MADE IN CHINA."
What to do: Return toy to store for refund.

My First Buddys Pop Pop Car
Small plastic balls under hood could choke child.

Products: 23,500 cars, model 4562, sold 1/91-6/92 for $8. Push-along car is 8 in. long, 4 in. wide, and 4¼ in. high, with white handle across top. As toy rolls, headlights, which are eyes, move up and down. Also, small colored balls under clear plastic hood pop up, and rear wheels make clicking noise. Car is red, white, and blue, with "My First Buddys Pop Pop Car" written on sides and "Turbo" on top of windshield.
What to do: Return toy to store for refund. For information, call importer, Target Stores of Minneapolis, at 612 370-6000.

Patty and Her Puppy and Triplet dolls
Arms or legs could come off and choke child.

Products: 10,000 Patty and Her Puppy dolls and 2000 Triplet dolls, sold 3/90-12/91 for $2 per set. Patty set consists of 6-in. vinyl doll and 3-in. vinyl puppy. Doll has short dress with velcro closure and white underpants. Triplet dolls include three vinyl dolls, 5 in. tall, with painted faces and curly hair. Each has multicolored halter dress and underpants.
What to do: Return doll set to store for refund.

Peg Perego high chair/youth chair
Leg restraint may not keep child from falling out of seat.

Products: 20,846 chairs, model 21-01-027, made 3/11/92-3/26/93. Chair has white molded-plastic seat and bears code no. 430311 through 440327 on underside of chair. Recall does not involve chairs with gray seat.
What to do: To get proper leg strap, call 800 238-7169.

Plastic Rattle and Flute toy sold at Dollywood amusement park
Small parts could come off and choke child.

Products: 4770 toys, model 42979, sold 4/91-6/92 for $2.50. Toy, 7½in. long, consists of flute-like whistle at one end and hand drum at other. Small black balls are attached to strings on side of drum. Whistle portion resembles flute. Pushing or pulling gray wand in clear plastic chamber of flute produces different sounds. "Dollywood" appears on white sticker in middle of drum.
What to do: Return toy to Dollywood Co., 1040 Dollywood Lane, Pigeon Forge, Tenn. 37863, for refund of purchase price and postage.

Playskool Travel-Lite portable cribs
Side rails could fold in use and suffocate child.

Products: 11,638 portable cribs, models 77101 and 77103, sold '90-'92. Crib has two nylon-mesh sides and two blue solid-plastic ends; "Playskool" appears in white letters on red background on each end. Crib folds in center.
What to do: Call 800 453-7673 for refund.

Jak Pak Inc. Rain or Shine doll
Small parts could come off and choke child.

Products: 6939 dolls, model JP #0137, sold 1/90-12/91 for $2-$3. Brown plastic doll stands 6¼ in., has brown-rooted hair and painted facial features. It comes with removable raincoat that fastens with velcro, removable shoes and socks, and nonremovable underwear. Doll's head, arms, and legs move at main body joints. Package label reads in part: "Rain or Shine Doll ... 1988 JAK PAK Inc. Milwaukee, WI 53201, Made in China."
What to do: Return toy to store for refund.

Aprica Rockin Rollin Rider toy car
Could tip and injure child.

Products: 400 toys, model 92090, sold in '91 for $110-$120. Ride-on car can be converted to rocking toy or push-walker. "Aprica" appears in white lettering on both sides and is molded into bottom of yellow plastic rocker base.
What to do: Return toy to store for refund.

Hedstrom and Sears swings with sling-type seats
V-shaped brackets connecting soft plastic belt seat to swing chain pose laceration hazard if their attachment hooks aren't fully closed.

Products: 2 million swing seats sold '87-'92 separately or in swing sets. Recall involves all Hedstrom swings

PRODUCT RECALLS

with sling-type seats. Also, Sears full sets, models 72026, 72096, 72098, 72262, 72558, 72725, 72730, and Sears accessory kits, models 70300, 70305, and 70320.
What to do: If hooks are open, close them with pliers until metal touches. Also call 800-233-3271 or 800-453-7077 for bracket guards to cover closed hooks.

Sesame Street nursery set
Small parts could come off and choke child.

Products: 12,000 toys, style 71700, sold 2/91-9/91 for $4. Set consists of Ernie finger puppet with orange and yellow rubber duck, orange and yellow swing set, and blue bath tub on feet with white faucet and white handles. Packaging reads in part: "Nursery Set Finger Puppets with Accessories, Made in China, F.W. Woolworth Co., New York, N.Y."
What to do: Return toy to store for refund.

Fisher-Price Snuggle Light dolls
Child could choke on pom-pom attached to doll's cap.

Products: 420,000 dolls, models 1372 and 1373, sold since 2/92. Pink or blue doll, whose face lights up when body is squeezed, has free-swinging cap to which pom-pom is attached. Recall does not involve modified version of doll, whose cap is sewn to head so it can't swing.
What to do: To get redesigned but unlighted doll, cut off pom-pom and product label and mail to Fisher-Price, Consumer Affairs, 636 Girard Ave., E. Aurora, N.Y. 14052.

Carlson Swing 'N Cradle and Swivel 'N Snooze cradle swings
Infant could suffocate if fully reclined.

Products: 7500 cradle swings sold 12/91-3/92.
What to do: Call 800-933-3309 to obtain cradle hanger frame to elevate infant's head.

Symphony Loco toy train
Could break into small parts and choke child.

Products: 3850 battery-operated toys, style no. 3037, sold at Toy Liquidators stores 1/89-12/91 for $8. See-through, red-plastic locomotive comes with built-in castanets, cymbals, xylophone, and drum. Stickers on both sides of engine show young boy conducting orchestra. Package reads in part: "Battery Operated Symphony Loco Mysterious Action, Made in Hong Kong, Distributed by Blue Box, New York, N.Y."
What to do: Return toy to store for refund.

Playskool teddy bear plush toy
Eyes could come off and choke child.

Products: 170,390 teddy bears, item no. 5149, sold 10/90-12/31/92 for $15. Soft plush toy is 13 inches high, with light-brown body, dark brown eyes, and black nose. Red sewn-in label says Playskool; white label lists item no. and washing instructions.
What to do: Return toy to store or mail to Playskool, Box 1990, Pawtucket, R.I. 02862, for refund of purchase price and postage.

Rainbow Mountain toddler bed with rails
Excessive space between mattress and side rails poses entrapment hazard.

Products: 1300 beds, model 3210, sold in East and Midwest 1/92-11/92. Red, white, or blue metal-framed bed was sold disassembled and includes headboard, footboard, 2 side guard rails, 2 mattress-support rails, and 6 mattress cross-support rails. Bed is designed for standard 27 x 52-inch crib mattress.
What to do: Return bed to store for refund, or ask at store or call 800 253-5410 for repair kit.

Toy Wooden Block Truck
Small parts could choke child.

Products: 10,944 toys sold 9/91-1/92 at Everything's A Dollar stores on East Coast and in Midwest. Unadorned wooden truck, 4¾ in. long, 2¾ in. wide, and 2½ in. high, consists of peg figure glued into driver's seat and open-lift bed with three removable colored building blocks.
What to do: Return toy to store for refund.

Toys R Us Magic Feeding Bottles
Could break into small pieces and choke child.

Products: 120,000 bottle sets sold 1/91-12/91 for $2. Set contains two plastic bottles, containing "milk" and "orange juice." When bottles are turned upside down, contents disappear. Packaging reads in part: "Magic Feeding Bottles with Safe Disappearing Fluid, Not to be Consumed, 5436B/2, SKN 330221, Made in Hong Kong."
What to do: Return toy to store for refund.

Rooster, Vegetable, Garden Tools, and Animals puzzles
Red paint contains excessive amounts of lead, which could be toxic to children who put pieces of puzzle in their mouth.

Products: 10,000 puzzles sold 1/1/80-12/31/91 (Animals puzzles sold until 5/31/92) for $15-$17. Puzzles have four to six pieces that form animals, (rooster, kitten, duck, fish, dog), vegetables (corn, carrot, lettuce, cucumber, tomato) or tools (saw, hammer, tool box, wrench, file). Rooster (model MTC-2033), Garden Tools (MTC-2028), and Vegetable (MTC-2026) puzzles measure 9½ x 12 in. with ¾ in. round wooden knobs on pieces. Animal puzzle (DL-

4002) is 21 x 6 in. with 1-in. knobs on pieces.

What to do: Return toy to store for replacement. If puzzle was bought through U.S. Toy Co. catalog, mail to: 1227 E. 119th St., Grandview, Mo. 64030. For information, call 816-761-5900.

Toy telephones by Handi-Craft Co
Small parts could choke child.

Products: 51,000 "Thin Line Play Phones," model 985, sold 8/91-4/92 for $5-$10; 36,865 "Talking Touch Tinkle Phones," model 3235, sold 1/92-4/92 for $5-$10; and 3600 911 Emergency Phone Centers, model 3675, sold 6/91-4/92 for $10-$15. Thin Line Phone is red, yellow, or green and measures 8 in. long, 2½ in. wide, and 2-in. high. Pushing any of 12 buttons on receiver rings bell. Talking Touch Tinkle Phone is battery operated and measures 8 in. long, 3½-in. wide, and 3-in. high. Pushing any of 10 buttons on face of phone rings bell. Toy also includes breakaway cord that comes apart when pulled. Pushing button on receiver plays one of 10 recorded messages. Battery-operated 911 Emergency Phone Center measures 8¾-in. long, 5-in. wide, and 6¼-in. high, has red roof, 12 push buttons, and yellow phone receiver with breakaway cord that comes apart when pulled. Pushing any button plays recorded message. Set also contains ambulance, fire truck, and police car. Models 985A, 3235A, and 3675A, sold after April 1992, have not been recalled.

What to do: Return toy to store for replacement with Handi-Craft toy of equal value.

Popper toy in boxes of Quaker's Cap 'n Crunch, Crunchberries, and Peanut Butter Crunch cereals
If child presses toy against face or eye, creating suction, toy could snap back, causing injury.

Products: 8.3 million toys included in 15- and 16-ounce cereal boxes sold since 4/1/93. Popper is 2-inch half-sphere that pops back to its original shape after being inverted and placed on flat surface.

What to do: Discard toy.

Sportcraft and Wilson Batting Tees
If child pulls on elastic cord or ball, metal washer that secures cord to base could fly loose and cause serious injury.

Products: 153,000 batting tees, Sportcraft model 06650 and Wilson model 96010, sold since 1/91. Batting tee includes ball tethered by elastic cord to plastic batting stand, which fits into rubber base. Cord is secured to base by 1¼-inch washer in recess under base.

What to do: For $5 refund, return tee to store or mail to Batting Tee Recall, General Sportcraft/Foremost, 140 Woodbine St., Bergenfield, NJ 07621.

Ranger International Corp. Wooden Pre-school Puzzles (no. 401) and Mini Wooden Puzzles (no. 404)
Pegs and clock hands could come off and choke child.

Products: 1400 toys sold 1/90-6/91 for $4. Puzzles depict various pictorial scenes. Package labeling reads in part: "SUMMCO, Wooden Puzzle with Easy-Lift Knobs for Little Fingers, Ranger...."

What to do: Return toy to store for refund.

Walk 'N' Roll baby walker
Could collapse and injure child.

Products: 14,000 baby walkers, model 882003-1, sold by Family Dollar stores in 1989 for $13 and by Venture stores in 1988 for $10-$20. Label sewn to seat says "Baby World Industries, Inc."

What to do: Return walker to store for refund.

Wind-up Row n Row Boat plastic water toy
Could break into small, sharp parts and injure child.

Products: 2000 toys sold since 1/91 for $3. Toy is 5½ in. long and 3½-in. wide and contains either an alligator or hippopotamus. Hippopotamus, which is green and has soft rubber head with painted facial features, comes in boat with yellow oars, red deck, white bottom, and blue wind-up key. Alligator, which has yellow body and green soft rubber head with painted facial features, comes in boat with beige oars, blue deck, white bottom, and red wind-up key. Both boats are decorated with decals that resemble blue water.

What to do: Return toy to store for refund.

Infant/toddler sweatshirts, jackets, and windbreakers sold at Macy's and Bullock's department stores
Zipper slide could come off and choke child.

Products: 1800 zipper-front hooded cotton sweatshirts labeled "MACY BABY" or "BULLOCK'S BABY" inside neck, in navy, red, or white, sold since 12/92 for $26. "CREW" appears on front of sweatshirt, "NAVIGATOR" and "DEPARTMENT CREW" appear on back. Garment came in infant/toddler sizes XS-XL. Also, 490 "MINE ALONE" zipper-front nautical-style hooded jackets, in white with navy trim, sold since 2/93 for $24. Nautical patch and "Sail Away" are on front. Jacket, with nylon shell and cotton lining, was sold in sizes 3-24 months. Also, 180 "MINE ALONE" zipper-front hooded windbreakers, in royal blue, lime green, and turquoise blocks, sold in '93 for $17. Windbreaker is nylon and was sold in sizes 3-24 months.

What to do: Return garment to store for refund.

Household products

DeLonghi 16-in. oscillating fans
Blade may break in use and injure bystanders. Also, retaining clips may not secure grills.

Products: 3360 brass- and platinum-plated fans, models BR-16 and BPED-16, made '90-1/91 and sold for $40 and $60. Model number and date of manufacture appear on label on bottom of fan base. First two digits of date code represent month; next two, the year.
What to do: Call 800-552-4240 for modification kit.

BRK, First Alert, and Family Gard AC-powered smoke detectors
Corrosion on electrical contacts could prevent alarm from sounding in fire.

Products: 3.5 million smoke detectors made 10/87-3/90 including the following models—BRK: 1839I, 1839WI-M, 1839WI-12, 1839I12R, 2839I, 2839WI, 2839TH; First Alert: SA1839WI; and Family Gard: FG1839I and FG1839IHD. Detectors were wired into the electrical circuits of new homes, apartments, and hotels.
What to do: Call 800 228-2250 for replacement detector and information on removing recalled units.

Megaflex Home Exerciser
Freely turning middle bar on bench-press mechanism could let user's feet slip, causing leg injury as mechanism returns forcefully.

Products: 66,000 exercisers, models 15-7500 and 15-7600, sold 2/91—1/92 for $400.
What to do: For repair kit to keep bar from turning, write to Diversified Prods., Box 100, Opelika, Ala. 36803. Also, manufacturer recommends that leg-press exercise not be attempted. For more information, call 800-633-5730.

Clairol Salon Power and Pazazz hairdryers
Prongs in plug can break off and remain in outlet. Touching prongs could cause electrocution.

Products: 130,000 hair dryers sold 1/92-9/92. Recalled units have large circuit-breaker plug with rectangular black test button on front and serial no. HGW0351 on back.
What to do: If plug breaks, call 800 843-3876 for follow-up instructions. Otherwise, return dryer (noting date of purchase) for replacement and postage reimbursement. Mail to: Dryer Plug Exchange, 80 Southfield Ave., Stamford, Conn. 06902

Manual French Fry Cutter sold at All For One, Odd Lot, and Big Lot stores
Sharp cutting blades are insecurely attached and pose laceration hazard.

Products: 37,656 french-fry cutters sold east of Mississippi River and in Missouri for $1. Cutter is 4 in. long and 2 3/4 in. wide, with eight blades mounted crisscross in plastic frame. Blister pack reads in part: "Dist. by: Midwestern Home Products, Inc., Wilmington, Delaware 19803 item No. 11010403 Made in Taiwan."
What to do: Return cutter to store for refund.

Sears Kenmore dishwashers
Timer could short-circuit, overheat, and cause fire.

Products: 400,000 dishwashers bought since 2/90. Recall involves 21 models including the following: 587.1400090; 587.1400190; 587.1400890; 587.1400990; 587.1440090; 587.1440590; 587.1469089; 587.1469589; 587.1510590; 587.1511590 (serial nos. 14912690492-15753461092 only); 587.1530590; 587.1540590; 587.1541590 (nos. 14056531191-15764571092 only);, 587.1550590; 587.1551590 (nos. 14056581191-15752861092 only); 587.1574590 (nos. 13637650991-15692691092 only); 587.1630590; 587.1640590; 587.1641590 (nos. 14203401291-15843721092 only); 587.1650590; and 587.1651590 (nos. 14186181191-15556951092 only). With door open, you can read model and serial nos. on plate along right front edge of tub.
What to do: Call 800 998-8470 for repair.

Sears Plug-in Light Control for automatic garage door openers
Tip of antenna poses shock hazard.

Products: 6000 controls with gray antenna wire, sold 9/92-1/93 for $20. (Those with white wire are not affected.) Recalled controls have model no. 139.53774 on back. Device, designed for Sears garage-door openers, also lets user turn on light inside house.
What to do: Return light control to store for replacement or refund.

Super Young Industrial Co. two-step aluminum ladder
Lower step could collapse and cause injury.

Products: 1 million ladders sold '85-11/89. Ladders have "SYC" marked on hinge and vertical grid lines across steps. Steel ladders aren't recalled.
What to do: Call 800-288-9315 for information on how to ship ladder to company for partial refund plus shipping costs.

PRODUCT RECALLS

Rival hand-held electric mixer
Cooling fan inside mixer could break apart, contaminating food.

Products: 600,000 mixers, model 433, sold 11/90-9/91 for $8-$14. Affected units bear date codes 3690 (36 being the week of manufacture, 90 denoting the year) to 5290 and 0191 to 2791. Model number and date code appear on bottom of mixer housing.
What to do: Call 800-793-0052 for replacement.

'88-'89 Lawn-Boy lawn mowers
Fuel tank could split along seams and leak, creating fire hazard.

Products: 160,000 lawn mowers sold since 9/1/89, including models 4262, 7073, 7073A, 8073, 8073AE, L20PRA, L20ZPR, L21ZPN, L21ZPNA, L21ZSN, and L21ZSNA. Recalled models have serial nos. beginning with F followed by nos. 273 and above, G followed by 111 through 295, and H followed by 001 through 241.
What to do: Have dealer replace fuel tank. Consumers who bought affected model before 9/1/89 should inspect fuel tank for leaks before each use and store mower with tank less than half full. If leak develops, have dealer replace tank free. Call 800 526-6937 for location of nearest dealer.

Toro and Lunalite 12-volt power packs for ground-mounted outdoor lights
Cable connectors could corrode, melt insulation, short-circuit, and cause fire.

Products: 25,000 Toro and Lunalite replacement power packs sold 1/88-3/92 for $35-$45 including the following models: 118-48, 118-DT, 118-IR, 160-IR, 52925, 52927, 52945, 52998, and 52999. (Original equipment is not being recalled.) Also recalled are a few Lunalite 12-volt power packs, rated at 108 or 118 watts, sold '86-'87 as part of light sets. Power packs are designed for installation near electrical outlet on exterior siding of house or garage. Model number of Toro units appears on back of power pack. Lunalite name appears on front of power pack with 108- or 118-watt rating on back; wiring connector is between power pack and first light.
What to do: Call 800-321-8676 for repair kit.

Battery-operated smoke alarms of various brands
May not sound in fire.

Products: 120,000 smoke detectors sold since 7/10/92, including: Black & Decker Slim Line, models SMK100, SMK200, and SMK300; Jameson Code 1 2000, models A, C, and D; Kidde Smoke and Fire Alarm, model KSA700; Safety First Baby's Room Smoke & Fire Alarm, model 244; Funtech Safety's Sake, model A; and Maple Chase Firex, models A and B. Except for Black & Decker models, recalled detectors bear date codes 92192-92231 (92 is year of manufacture; 192 is day of year). Recalled Black & Decker models bear codes 9228-9246 (first two digits are year of manufacture; second two, the week). Label with model information and date code appears on back of detector. Defective units may appear to be working properly and may sound alarm in test.
What to do: To get replacement for Black & Decker, phone 800-952-1331 for other brands, phone 800-492-4949.

Continental bar stools
Could collapse.

Products: 9650 unfinished 30 in. wooden stools, carrying UPC no. 87078-70122, sold throughout eastern U.S. at Bradlee's stores 7/1/91-2/13/92 for $10. "Continental Seat Corp." and date of manufacture appear on tag under seat.
What to do: Return seat to store for replacement or refund. For information, call 800 786-6421.

Aqua Swim 'N' Spa exercise pool with spa
Swimmer's hair could be drawn into suction covers when swim jets are on. That could cause drowning or serious scalp injury.

Products: 1300 swim spas, made by Rio Plastics Inc., sold '86-90, including models ASNS-16, ASNS-18, ASNS-19, ASJ-SP-14, and ASJ-SS-14. Products, made of thermoplastic/fiberglass, are 14-19 feet long and combine exercise pool with spa. (A few 14-foot models were sold as exercise pools without separate spa.) Wall separating exercise pool and spa houses control panel, 2 swim jets, and 2 suction openings. Each opening has cover that's supposed to prevent hair entrapment. Recalled models have 2 round 10-inch white-plastic suction covers, which should be replaced.
What to do: For replacement suction covers, call 210-831-2715 or write to Rio Plastics, Box 3709, Brownsville, Tex. 78523.

Berthoud and Tecnoma pump-type polypropylene sprayers
Could burst and cause serious injury.

Products: 17,000 one-, two-, and three-gallon sprayers sold 1/92-10/92, including: Berthoud F100, F200, F300, and F300 Plus (with yellow tank) and Tecnoma model T100 (with blue tank) and T200 (with orange tank only). Sprayers are used for gardening or applying stains or sealants.
What to do: Return empty sprayer to Exel NJ, Inc., 205 Commerce Pl., Randleman, NC 27317. Company will repair and return product and pay shipping costs.

PRODUCT RECALLS

Weider E-130 exercise benches
Leg-extension bar could trap and amputate fingers.

Products: 71,000 benches, models E130, E131, E131B, E133, E134, and E137, sold 4/91-12/91 for $80.
What to do: Call 800-685-5480 for protective cap to eliminate hazard.

Gampak outdoor floodlight
Extension cord poses shock and fire hazard.

Products: 2200 floodlights, model 15836, sold 10/92-12/92. Gray die-cast floodlight comes with 6-ft. cord; "Gampak" appears on side of light.
What to do: Return light to store for replacement.

"Worm Getter" worm probes
Pose electrocution hazard.

Products: 83,000 electric worm probes, models WG6-S and WG8-L, sold 1980-92 for $11-$28. Fishermen use probes to shock worms to soil's surface. Devices operate on AC current and consist of 21- or 26- inch metal rod enclosed in white plastic, with $7/8$-inch-diameter spring-loaded guard or sheath on one end, black-plastic bicycle grip on other. Short power cord is attached to grip. Both models have red end cap over probe tip.
What to do: If you bought probe from K Mart or other store, return it to store for refund. If you bought probe by catalog, call for instructions: Cabela's, at 800 237-8888; Bass Pro Shops, 800 554-5488; Gander Mountain, 800 426-3371; The Sportsman's Guide, 800 888-5222; and Fishing Hot Spots, 800 338-5957. If you bought probe elsewhere, call Consumer Product Safety Commission, 800 638-2772, to help identify other sources.

Marine products

'89-90 Kawasaki Jet Ski watercraft
Fuel leak could cause fire or explosion.

Models: 23,579 jet skis, model JF650-B1/B2, with hull identification nos. KAW90010B989 through KAW97712G989 and KAW40001G990 through KAW56341G090.
What to do: Have dealer replace fuel-filler neck and fuel-tank outlet gasket.

'91 Yamaha WR5000 Waverunner and WR6500 Waverunner LX engines
Fuel-filler neck could break off and allow fuel to spill into engine compartment, creating explosion or fire hazard.

Models: 5677 engines, including WR5000 model with serial numbers EUO-813603-EUO-817602 and WR6500 model with serial numbers FK7-811809-FK7-813105 and FK7-813306-FK7-813705.
What to do: Have dealer replace fuel tank.

'92 Bombardier Sea-Doo Watercraft 5851 XP jet ski
Could lose steering.

Models: 793 jet skis with serial nos. ZZN 20002K192-ZZN 21687L192. (First five numerals, 20002-21687, identify recalled models.)
What to do: Have dealer replace vessel-trim/ steering arm and jet venturi.

'92 Mercury Marine MCM 4.3L and 4.3LX Mercruiser V6 stern-drive engines
Distributor cap may not seal snugly, creating fire or explosion hazard.

Models: 18,199 engines with serial numbers 0D710079-0D817032.
What to do: Have dealer install gasket under cap.

'93 Yamaha Waverunner III boat
Steering could fail.

Models: 11,000 boats with following serial nos.: FJO-800101 to 801100, FJO-801201 to 802900, FJO-803001 to 808200, and FJO-808301 to 809500.
What to do: Have dealer inspect steering system.

Cars

'92 Audi 100
Brakes might not stop car adequately.

Models: 7000 cars with V6 engine and automatic transmission made 10/91-6/92.
What to do: Have dealer install redesigned brake-vacuum booster-valve assembly.

'85-91 Audi (various models)
Transaxle oil can evaporate over time, allowing gears and bearings to wear prematurely. In extreme cases, front wheels could lock abruptly, causing loss of control.

Models: 152,000 cars with 3-speed automatic transmission, made 10/84-1/91, including following models: 80, 90, 100, 200, 4000, and 5000.
What to do: Have dealer drain and refill differential with oil having higher performance characteristics.

PRODUCT RECALLS

'90-'91 Buick, Chevrolet, Oldsmobile, and Pontiac
Wiring for power seats or power recliner could short-circuit, igniting seat cushion.

Models: 319,181 cars, including '90-'91 Buick Century, Oldsmobile Ciera, and Pontiac 6000, and '90 Chevrolet Celebrity, made through 7/91.

What to do: Have dealer replace damaged wiring and reroute wiring harness.

'88-'89 Buick Skylark, Oldsmobile Calais, and Pontiac Grand Am
Fuel leak could cause fire.

Models: 108,836 cars with Quad 4 engine, made 1/88-7/89.

What to do: Have dealer replace front fuel-feed hose assembly.

BMW 318, 325, and M3
Excessive pressure in cooling system could allow coolant to escape and burn driver's leg or fog windows, reducing driver's vision.

Products: 375,000 cars made 1/83-1/93 including the following: '84-'85 and '91-'92 318; '84-'93 325; and '88-'91 M3.

What to do: Have dealer replace radiator cap and install thermostatically controlled bypass valve.

'89 BMW 525i and 525iA
Electrical-system failure could suddenly stop car and extinguish all lights.

Models: 15,900 cars made 8/88-6/89.

What to do: Have dealer reroute wiring in engine compartment and install new fusible link.

'91 BMW 318, 325, and M3
Windshield wipers may operate erratically or fail.

Models: 7650 cars made 1/91-6/91.

What for do: Have dealer relocate ground-wire attachment for wiper switch on steering column.

'91 BMW 535 and 735
Engine may not slow fully when accelerator is released.

Models: 637 cars made 3/91-4/91.

What to do: Have dealer inspect and, if necessary, replace nut that retains throttle valve shaft.

'91-'92 Buick Roadmaster,'91 Chevrolet Caprice,'91 Oldsmobile Custom Cruiser
Plastic cover on shoulder-belt guide loop could crack and allow steel underneath to cut belt webbing during crash.

Models: 219,571 cars made 3/90-7/91.

What to do: Have dealer install new guide loops.

'92 Chevrolet Caprice
Fuel line could crack, leak, and cause fire.

Models: 1771 cars with 4.3-liter engine made 7/91-7/92.

What to do: Have dealer replace fuel-feed line and fuel-return line.

'92-'93 Chevrolet Corvette
Power-steering fluid could leak into engine compartment and cause fire.

Models: 5152 cars, with LT1 engine, made 6/92-9/92

What to do: Have dealer replace power-steering gear-inlet hose.

'92 Chevrolet Beretta and Corsica
Stoplights may not come on during braking.

Models: 140,661 cars made 3/91-6/92.

What to do: Have dealer replace stoplight switch and change wiring.

'92 Chevrolet Camaro and Pontiac Firebird
Shifter cable for automatic transmission could break, preventing transmission from shifting. Gear indicator could show wrong gear position, resulting in unexpected vehicle movement.

Models: 43,413 cars made 2/92-8/92.

What to do: Have dealer replace shift cable.

'93 Dodge Intrepid and Eagle Vision
Front-suspension failure could cause loss of steering.

Models: 3000 cars made 6/92-8/92.

What to do: Have dealer replace front and rear strut-bar washers and nuts.

'91 Dodge Stealth RT Turbo and Mitsubishi 3000 GT VR-4
Oil could leak from transfer case, making all four wheels lock up suddenly while car is moving.

Models: 5854 cars made 4/90-4/91.

What to do: Have dealer repair or replace transfer case.

'89-'90 Ford Taurus and Mercury Sable,'91 Ford Explorer
Safety belts may not latch fully or may not release.

Models: 565,000 vehicles made 3/89-8/90.
What to do: Have dealer replace rigidly mounted safety-belt buckles. (Web-mounted buckles excluded.)

'91 Ford Escort and '92 Mercury Tracer
Steering could lock up suddenly.

Models: 91,000 cars made 7/90-5/91.
What to do: Have dealer modify ignition lock or, if necessary, replace it (along with other locks, so one key fits all).

'91-'92 Ford Escort and '91 Mercury Tracer
Fuel leak could cause fire.

Models: 22,000 cars made 4/91-8/91.
What to do: Check car's vehicle identification number and call Ford at 800-392-3673. If recall applies to your car, have dealer replace fuel-pump sending assembly.

'92 Ford Escort and Mercury Tracer
Stoplights may fail.

Models: 43,000 cars made 9/91-10/91.
What to do: Have dealer replace stoplight switch.

'93 Ford Probe
Open liftgate could drop suddenly.

Models: 3700 cars made 4/92-6/92.
What to do: Have dealer replace liftgate strut assemblies.

'93 Ford Taurus and Mercury Sable with antilock brakes
Incorrect brake-system parts may have been installed, impairing stopping ability.

Models: 212 cars made 1/93.
What to do: Have dealer make necessary repairs.

'90-'92 Geo Storm with driver's air bag
Center hub of steering wheel could crack during crash, possibly reducing driver control and air-bag protection.

Models: 211,306 cars made 11/89-4/92.
What to do: Have dealer attach reinforcement plate to steering-wheel hub.

'83-'87 Honda Accord and Prelude
Road salt could corrode fuel filler or breather pipe, creating fire hazard.

Models: 920,583 cars including '86-87 Accord, made 6/13/85-9/15/87, and '83-87 Prelude, made 9/9/82-5/7/87.
What to do: Have dealer inspect and, if necessary, replace fuel-system parts.

'90-'93 Honda Accord station wagon
Outside rear safety belts may not provide adequate protection.

Models: 45,958 cars made 6/89-11/92.
What to do: Have dealer replace sensor in belt retractors.

'90-'92 Isuzu Impulse and Stylus
Center of steering wheel could crack in a crash and impair driver control and air-bag protection.

Models: 25,059 cars made 10/89-2/92.
What to do: Have dealer reinforce steering-wheel hub.

'93 Jeep Cherokee and Wagoneer
Brakes could fail.

Models: 600 vehicles made 10/92.
What to do: Have dealer install new retainer clip to secure brake pedal.

'87-'92 Jeep Wrangler
Front brake hoses could rub against fender splash shield and leak, reducing stopping ability.

Models: 280,000 vehicles made 2/86-7/92.
What to do: Have dealer replace or reinforce one or both splash shields, as necessary, and inspect brake hoses for damage.

'91-'92 Mercury Capri
In hot weather, air bag could tear as it deploys.

Models: 648 cars made 8/91-2/92.
What to do: Have dealer replace air-bag module.

'87-'91 Mercedes-Benz 300
Throttle assembly could break, making engine lose power suddenly.

Models: 128,000 cars made 3/87-10/91.
What to do: Have dealer modify throttle assembly.

'90-'92 Mercedes-Benz 500SL
Brakes could lose power assist, lengthening stopping distances.

Models: 14,300 cars made 9/89-8/92.
What to do: Have dealer install new vacuum hose.

'92 Mercedes-Benz 400E
Brake hose could melt, leak, and cause fire.

Models: 845 cars with traction control made 8/91-5/92.
What to do: Have dealer inspect and, if necessary, route hose away from hot electrical component.

PRODUCT RECALLS

'93 Mazda MX6
Front suspension could fail, causing loss of control.

Models: 2450 cars made 2/92-4/92 at Flat Rock, Mich., plant. (Ask dealer to check vehicle identification no. to determine where car was made.)

What to do: Have dealer inspect and, if necessary, tighten retaining bolts for lower ball joints.

'93 Mercury Villager and Nissan Quest
Fuel leak could cause fire.

Models: 15,700 minivans made 4/92-10/92.

What to do: Have dealer replace fuel-filler hose.

'91 Pontiac Grand Prix
Operating low- and high-beam headlights and fog lights simultanously could overload circuit breaker and cause all lights to fail.

Models: 6013 cars made 1/91-8/91.

What to do: Have dealer replace electrical parts and modify lighting circuit to prevent fog lights and high beams from operating at same time.

'91 Porsche 928
Automatic transmission may not kick down into lower gear. Reduced acceleration could cause accident during passing or merging.

Models: 145 cars made 1/91-7/91.

What to do: Have dealer repair transmission.

'89-'92 Porsche 911
Cruise control could jam, preventing engine from slowing to idle speed.

Models: 11,091 Porsche Carrera 2 and Carrera 4 cars made 4/88-1/92.

What to do: Have dealer modify cruise-control linkage

'88-'89 Pontiac Grand Prix
Faulty stoplight switch could disable stoplights or engage cruise control.

Models: 112,765 cars made 7/87-11/88.

What to do: Have dealer install new stoplight switch.

'93 Saturn
Battery-cable terminal could touch starter-solenoid housing and short-circuit, creating fire hazard.

Models: 14,459 SC2, SL2, and SW2 coupes, sedans, and station wagons made 3/93-4/93.

What to do: Have dealer inspect and, if necessary, reposition terminal.

'91-'93 Saturn (all models)
If alternator shorts out, excessive heat could build up in wiring, creating fire hazard even if engine is off.

Models: 352,833 cars made 7/90 to 4/14/93.

What to do: Have dealer modify wiring.

'92 Saturn with auto transmission
Transmission may not be in Park or Neutral even though it appears so; engine could then be started while transmission is in Reverse or Drive, or car could move unexpectedly.

Models: 633 cars made 6/92.

What to do: Have dealer replace transaxle valve body.

'87-'90 Toyota Tercel
Replacing headlight bulb with brand other than Koito could cause inteference between bulb and headlight housing, reducing lighting.

Models: 315,000 cars made 7/86-8/90.

What to do: Have dealer inspect and, if necessary, install proper bulb.

'90-'92 Volkswagen GLI, GTI, & Passat
Engine may not slow fully when accelerator is released.

Models: 12,650 cars with 16-valve engine and California emission-control system, made 10/89-6/92.

What to do: Have dealer replace press-fit venturi tube in throttle-valve housing with thread-type tube.

'92 Volvo 244 and 245
Could lose steering control.

Models: 7526 cars made 2/92-6/92.

What to do: Have dealer inspect and, if necessary, replace ball-joint assemblies.

'93 Volvo 940 series
Plastic hood-insulation clips could get jammed in throttle housing and make throttle stick open.

Models: 1864 model 944 and 945 cars with turbo engine, made 8/92-2/93.

What to do: Have dealer remove any plastic clips that might have fallen into hose between charge-air cooler and throttle housing.

Trucks & vans

'91-'93 Jeep Wrangler
Engine could start by itself. If transmission is in gear, vehicle could move.

Products: 100,000 sport-utility vehicles with manu-

PRODUCT RECALLS

al transmission, made 7/90-2/93.
What to do: Have dealer route starter-solenoid wiring away from battery-feed wire.

'93 Jeep Cherokee and Wagoneer
Vehicle could swerve during braking and go out of control.
Products: 25,000 sport-utility vehicles made 1/93-3/93.
What to do: Have dealer replace front-suspension.

'89-'92 Chevrolet S10 and S15 trucks with 2.5-liter engine
Radiator-fan blades could break. If hood is open, pieces could injure anyone nearby.
Models: 215,052 light trucks, without air-conditioning, made 3/88-10/91.
What to do: Have dealer install new fan assembly.

'90-'91 Ford Econoline E250
Crossmember that holds rear shock absorbers could break loose and cause loss of control.
Models: 25,000 vans made 7/89-8/91.
What to do: Have dealer install new crossmember.

'91-'92 Mazda B2200 and B2600 pickups
Steel-spoked wheels could break or leak air.
Models: 15,822 pickups made 11/90-2/92.
What to do: Have dealer replace all four wheels.

'92 Chrysler Town & Country, Dodge Caravan, and Plymouth Voyager
Fuel leak could cause fire.
Models: 3000 minivans made 4/92.
What to do: Have dealer bend fuel-tank flanges and check fuel lines and mounting straps for damage.

'92 Ford Econoline and E150 vans
Label on vehicle incorrectly lists vehicle's tire requirements as P235/75R15 SL (standard load) rather than P235/75R15 XL (extra load). Incorrect replacement tires could fail suddenly.
Models: 29,052 vans made 9/91-2/92.
What to do: Check van's vehicle identification number and phone dealer. If label is incorrect, Ford will mail you replacement label.

'93 Mercury Villager and Nissan Quest
Brakes could fail partially. Also, front safety belts may not provide adequate protection.
Models: 5000 minivans made 4/92-8/92.
What to do: Have dealer replace brake master cylinder and tighten mounting bolts that secure track for automatic safety belts.

'93 Toyota 4X2 and 4X4 pickup trucks
Safety belts could fail in crash.
Models: 3655 pickups made 9/92.
What to do: Have dealer replace safety belts.

'88-93 Chevrolet and GMC light trucks
Heat buildup could force transmission fluid out of vent tube, possibly causing fire.
Models: 1,702,880 C and K series trucks, with 5.0-, 5.7-, and 7.4-liter engines and automatic transmission, made 12/86-8/92.
What to do: Have dealer install longer vent hose routed to left side of engine compartment.

'93 Dodge Dakota pickup truck
Antilock brake system may not work.
Models: 2000 pickups with antilock brakes, made 8/92-4/93.
What to do: Have dealer replace brake return check valve.

Child car seats

Fisher-Price model 9101 child safety seat
May not provide adequate protection in crash.
Products: 472,000 seats made 2/8/91-1/24/92. Model no. and manufacture date appear on label on back of seat.
What to do: Call 800 432-5437 for parts to prevent shoulder belts from coming loose.

Century child safety seats
Push-button latch could jam in crash, making it difficult to remove child.
Products: 969,182 child safety seats, including 3000 STE series (models 4353, 4365, 4366, 4367, 4368, 4369) made 10/89-4/92; 3500 STE series (model 4380) made 12/90-4/92; 5000 STE series (models 4450, 4460, 4470, 4475, 4476) made 9/89-4/92; and 5500 STE series (models 4480 and 4490) made 1/91-4/92. Label with model number and date code is on seat shell.
What to do: Call 800-231-2755 for repair kit.

Fisher-Price 9104 child safety seat
Red button on buckle assembly could become dislodged, making buckle impossible to latch securely.

Products: 14,000 seats made 6/15/92-9/4/92.
What to do: Call 800 432-5437 for choice of replacement seat, new buckle assembly, or refund.

Fisher-Price 9100 and 9101 child safety seats
Plastic layer on buckle shield could break with repeated use, making buckle hard to latch.

Products: 423,900 seats made 2/89-10/89.
What to do: Call 800 527-1034 to get replacement.

Gerry Guardian child safety seat
Child could release buckle and ride unprotected.

Products: 26,000 seats made 1/31/90-5/3/90. Label on side of seat shows date of manufacture.
What to do: Call 800-845-8813 for kit including buckle that requires more effort to open.

Century 2000STE child safety seats
Latch that secures child could fail in crash.

Products: 146,895 seats made 12/91-4/92, including models 4253, 4261, 4263, 4265, and 4266. Label on side of seat gives date of manufacture. First 2 digits indicate year; second 2, month.
What to do: Call 800 255-2220 for repair kit.

Renolux child safety seats
May not provide adequate protection in sudden stop or accident.

Products: 133,640 seats, models GT2000 and GT5500 ("Turn-A-Tot"), made 1/92-1/93. Model designation and date of manufacture appear on label on seat.
What to do: Phone company at 800 206-4400 for additional padding and installation instructions.

Century child safety seats
Wrong buckle-release button may have been shipped by manufacturer in earlier recall. Seat still may not adequately protect child in crash.

Products: 78,000 seats, series 3000STE, 3500STE, 5000STE, and 5500STE, made 9/89-4/92, including models 4353, 4365, 4366, 4367, 4368, 4369, 4380, 4450, 4460, 4470, 4475, 4476, 4480, 4490.
What to do: Call 800-554-5888 to find out whether red buckle-release button designed to replace original button is faulty. If so, manufacturer will send redesigned button.

Motorcycles & bicycles

'86-'92 Harley-Davidson motorcycles
After crash, fuel could leak from tank and cause fire.

Models: 29,986 FXD and FXR motorcycles made 4/86-3/92.
What to do: Have dealer make necessary repairs.

'89-'90 Harley-Davidson Softail FL & FX motorcycles recalled previously
Ignition, lights, and electrical accessories could fail.

Models: 6838 Softail FL and FX motorcycles made 6/88-7/90. Recall includes models whose faulty positive battery cable has already been replaced by dealer.
What to do: Have dealer replace cable again.

'89-'92 Harley-Davidson motorcycles
When vehicle is parked, starter relay could short-circuit and cause fire.

Models: 77,407 motorcycles, incl. FLSTC, FLSTF, FLSTS, FXST, FXSTC, and FXSTS models, made 1/88-7/92.
What to do: Have dealer replace starter relay.

'90-'91 Harley-Davidson motorcycles
Fuel could leak onto ground and cause fire.

Models: 66,046 motorcycles, including FL, FX, FXD, and FXR models, made 6/89-7/91.
What to do: Have dealer replace fuel-inlet needle.

'90-'92 BMW motorcycles
Front brake pads could come loose and reduce stopping ability.

Models: 2486 motorcycles made 7/89-5/92, including '90-92 K1 and K100, and '92 K1199 and R100.
What to do: Have dealer replace front brake pads.

'91-'92 Boss Hoss heavy motorcycles and motorcycle kits
Rear axle could crack, causing loss of control.

Models: 80 motorcycles made 3/91-10/92.
What to do: Have dealer install redesigned axle.

'93 Harley-Davidson motorcycles
Screws that secure front brake disc, jiffystand spring, and front-wheel cap could break, reducing stopping ability, cause loss of control, or allow front hub cap to fly off wheel.

Models: 4272 motorcycles of all models made 10/92-11/92.
What to do: Have dealer replace screws.

PRODUCT RECALLS

Huffy and Sears Free Spirit bicycles
Hand-brake levers could break, resulting in inability to stop.

Products: 14,000 20-, 24-, and 26-in. men's and women's bicycles made 2/17/93-3/15/93. Twenty-in. bicycle is Sledge Hammer (model 23583). Twenty-four-in. bicycles include: Beverly Hills (model 24233); Bull Run (44543); Dirt Thrower (34603); Double Take (24532); Essence (34213); Force One (44523); Highland (K4572); Jack Hammer (34563); Key Largo (84612); Laurel Bay (24253); Megaforce (24623); Mojave Gulch (24603, 24613); Mont Claire (K4532); Mt. Storm (54602, 54613); Mudslinger (24522); Night Heat (K4562); Paradise (44533); Pasadena (24533); Regatta (24612, 34613, 44613); Shock Treatment (34583); Sledge Hammer (K4583, 24583); Snake River (24523); Stomper 2 (84623); Street Heat (34533); Swamp Water (24563); Tide Water (44663); Tropic Bay (34253); Ultra Force (74623); Wild River (74533); Wild Slide (14642, 14652); Z18 (24643, 24653, 44653); and Z24 (K4522). Twenty-six-in. bicycles include: America (56563, 56573); Black Bear (86673); Cherokee (46523, 46533); Cross II (86203, 86213); Destroyer (36612); Expedition (K6613); Fastback (16653, 16643); Fire Mountain (26643); Key West (46672); Mojave Gulch (26622, 26623, 26632); Mojave Ridge (36632); Mt. Storm (56603, 56613); Rock Trail (26603, 26613); Sandy Creek (86623, 86633); Silhouette (26223, 26233); Sledge Hammer (36683); Snake Rock (46643); Stalker LX (26671); Thunder Ridge (26683, 26693, 76683EF, 76683J, 76693EF); and Titanium (K6662, K6672). Recalled bicycles also bear date-of-manufacture code: 90483 (first and last digits are year—'93; middle three numbers represent day of year— 048, in this case, is 48th day of '93, or 2/17); 90493; 90503; 90533; 90543; 90553; 90563; 90573; 90603; 90613; 90623; 90633; 90643; 90673; 90683; 90693; 90703; 90713; 90743. Date code and model no. are on pedal-crank housing. Recall doesn't include bicycles that have American flag label with "Huffy" on seat post.

What to do: Call Huffy at 800 462-7843 to get replacement brake levers. Company will provide name of nearest authorized service center to customers who don't want to replace levers themselves.

Motor homes

'80-'84 Holiday Rambler and Monitor motor homes
Gasoline or propane could leak from dual-fuel system, creating fire hazard.

Models: 3200 motor homes made 6/79-6/84 including Admiral, Aluma-Lite, Ambassador, Imperial, Monitor-Lite, Presidential, Ramblette, and Ramblette-Lite.

What to do: Have dealer repair fuel system.

'86-'92 Holiday Rambler motor homes
Front safety belts might not provide adequate protection in crash.

Models: 10,350 motor homes made 6/86-7/92, including: Aluma-Lite, Crown Imperial, HR100, Imperial, Limited, and Presidential.

What to do: Have dealer relocate safety-belt anchorages.

'89-'90 Coachmen Crosscountry and Pathfinder motor homes
Safety belts may not provide adequate protection. Also, windshield-wiper switch on dash may not be illuminated, a violation of Federal safety standards.

Models: 571 motor homes made 8/88-4/90.

What to do: Have dealer replace washers on belts and install light over wiper switch.

'91-'92 Spartan EC2000, Gulf Stream Sun Clipper, Sun Voyager, and Sunstream motor homes
Shock-absorber brackets could break, resulting in loss of vehicle control. Also, bracket on rear axle could separate and damage brake hose, reducing stopping ability.

Models: 1800 motor homes made 9/90-7/92.

What to do: Call Spartan Motors at 800-543-4334 for location of nearest service center, which will make repairs.

'92 Holiday Rambler Endeavor motor home
Electrical arcing could ignite liquid-propane gas, causing fire.

Models: 135 motor homes made 10/92-3/93.

What to do: Have dealer install grounding strap between LPG manifold and chassis frame.

'92 Itasca IKG 34RQ and Winnebago WKG 34RQ motor homes
Drinking-water tank could fall onto roadway.

Models: 200 motor homes made through 5/92.

What to do: Have dealer add extra water-tank bracket.

'92 Itasca and Winnebago motor homes
On rough roads, rear outside tire could rub against sidewall and fail.

PRODUCT RECALLS

Models: 403 motor homes made through 4/92, including following models: Itasca and Winnebago 422RG, 424RC, 427RC, 427RQ, 427RT, 524RC, 527RC, 527RQ. Also recalled are Itasca 522RS and Winnebago 522RG.
What to do: Have dealer modify sidewall assembly.

'93 Fleetwood Bounder and Southwind motor homes
In reverse, throttle could stick open.
Models: 359 motor homes made 5/92-5/93.
What to do: Have dealer make necessary repairs.

Vehicle accessories

Baby Beanie motorcycle safety helmet
May not provide adequate protection in crash.
Products: 10,251 helmets, manufactured by E&R Fiberglass Inc., made 8/91-4/92.
What to do: Return helmet to store for refund.

Kelly Springfield Summit Radial Trac 60 and Revenger Radial H/P all-season tires
Could fail.
Models: 1000 tires, size P235/60R15, made 6/92. Summit bears D.O.T. no. PJVE7CKR242; Revenger carries no. PJVEJDBR242.
What to do: Return tires to store for replacement.

'90-93 Mazda Miata
Hoist for lifting hardtop roof from car could break and allow suspended roof to fall.
Models: 3000 hoists made 6/89-7/92. Hoist, sold in kit form, is hanger-like apparatus used to suspend top from garage ceiling when top is not in use.
What to do: Have dealer replace hoist.

Multi-Mile Wild Country Radial RVT light-truck tires
Could fail if loaded as per incorrect labeling.
Products: 3634 tires, size LT265/75R16, with D.O.T. nos. PJW8TBBV402-452, made 10/92-11/92.
What to do: Return tires to store for replacement.

Interstate auto batteries
Hydrogen could leak into engine compartment and cause explosion.
Products: 19,441 batteries, models MB66-42A and MB88-42A, made 7/92. Recalled batteries have white case and cover and are designed for use in Audi, BMW, Mercedes-Benz, Peugeot, and Porsche cars.
What to do: Return battery to store for replacement.

Reliant and Star Sky Trak all-season radial-ply whitewall tires
Could fail.
Products: 2127 tires, size P165/80R13, made 6/92-8/92. Reliant tires bear identification no. PLJY-ACKR252; Star tires, no. PLJADR302.
What to do: Return tires to dealer for replacement.

Valeo replacement heater cores for Renault and Volkswagen models
Could rupture, spewing hot liquid into passenger compartment and burning driver's feet. Also, steam could cloud windows and impair driver's vision.
Products: 30,000 heater cores made 8/84-1/90 and installed as replacements in '83-87 Renault Alliance and Encore and '85-90 Volkswagen Golf, GTI, Jetta.
What to do: If heater core has been replaced, have Eagle or Volkswagen dealer install another one.

Trailer hitch for '92-93 Mitsubishi Montero
Hitch could break and allow trailer to separate from towing vehicle.
Models: 717 trailer hitches, made by Reese Prods. Inc., 4/92-10/92.
What to do: Have dealer replace hitch.

Norcold refrigerators in recreational vehicles and travel trailers
Electrical problem could cause fire when vehicle is connected to 115-volt AC source.
Products: 190,496 refrigerators, model nos. 838EG and 8310EG, made 3/83-9/86.
What to do: Have dealer replace panel, lights, and wiring.

Buying Guide index

This index is for information in the 1994 Buying Guide. For a one-year index of CONSUMER REPORTS, see page 393.

Air cleaners 322
   Ratings 357
Air-conditioners 317
   central, repair histories 374
   cooling-capacity worksheet 320
   room, Ratings 350
   room, repair histories 374
   split-ductless, Ratings 353
Audio cassette tapes 34
   Ratings 55
Automobiles
   buying a new car 166
   buying a used car 170
   Frequency-of-Repair records 178
   leasing 169
   1993 model year, Ratings 152
   owner satisfaction 224
   recommended 1993 cars 140

Bathroom scales 236
   Ratings 248
Bicycles 259
   exercise 256
   helmets 260
Blenders 113
   Ratings 126
Blood-pressure monitors 228
   Ratings 241

Camcorders 18
   compact, repair histories 368
   Ratings 45
   VHS, repair histories 369
Cameras, 35mm 60
   automation, 62
   compact 35mm, Ratings 70
   lenses 60
Cassette decks 29
Caulks, exterior 336
   Ratings 361
Clothes dryers 93
   Ratings 109
   repair histories 372
Coffee grinders 118
Compact-disc players 27
   Ratings 50
   repair histories 368
Computer printers 302

Computer software systems 301
Crib mattresses 235
Cribs 234
   Ratings 251
   safety 235

Detergents, laundry 95
Dishwashers 89
   Ratings 104
   repair histories 369
Drip coffee makers 117

Electric toothbrushes 239
   Ratings 246
Exercise bicycles 256
Eyeglasses 232
   chain stores, Ratings 243

Fabric softeners 96
Fans 315
   ceiling, Ratings 347
   portable, Ratings 344
Fax machines, home 299
   Ratings 309
Film, color print 66
   Ratings 78
Film-processing labs 67
Food processors 111
   Ratings 128
Furnaces, upgrades and replacements 337

Garden hoses 272
   Ratings 288
Grills, indoor 124
   Ratings 137

Headphones, stereo 32
Hearing aids 230
Heat pumps 338
Home gyms 254
   Ratings 265
Home theater 7
   and cable system 9
Hoses, garden 272
   Ratings 288

Indoor grills 124
   Ratings 137
Insect repellents 274

Juice extractors 120
   Ratings 131
Juicers 120
   Ratings 131

BUYING GUIDE INDEX

Laser-disc players 18
Laundry products 95
Lawn mowers 268
   repair histories 373
   riding, Ratings 276
   safety 268
   self-propelled, Ratings 279
Lawn sprinklers 273
   Ratings 285
Lawn tractors 269
   Ratings 276
   repair histories 373
   safety 268
Lead, in water 329
Loudspeakers 25
   3-piece, Ratings 52

Microwave ovens 80
   Ratings 101
   repair histories 370
Mixers, food 115
Mouthwash 238

Oral irrigators 239
   Ratings 244

Paints 330
   exterior, Ratings 359
   lead-testing kits 334
Pressure cookers 123
   Ratings 135
Printers, computer 302

Ranges 83
   electric, element types 84
   electric, Ratings 98
   gas, repair histories 370
Receivers 22
   amplifying power 24
   Ratings 41
Refrigerators 86
   side-by-side, repair histories 371
   top-freezer, repair histories 371
Remote controls 21
   universal, Ratings 57
Replacement windows 339
Running shoes 258

Scales, bathroom 236
   Ratings 248
Slow-cookers 122
   Ratings 133
Software systems 301
Sprinklers, lawn 273
   Ratings 285
Stains, wood 330
   exterior, Ratings 359

Stair climbers 256
   Ratings 262
String trimmers 270
   Ratings 282

Tapes
   audio cassette 34
   audio cassette, Ratings 55
   video 17
Telephones
   answering machines 297
   cellular 294
   cellular (portable), Ratings 306
   corded 292
   corded, Ratings 304
   cordless 293
Television sets 11
   large-screen, placement 13
   large-screen, Ratings 36
   19- and 20-inch, repair histories ... 367
   13-inch, repair histories 366
   25- to 27-inch, repair histories 367
Thermostats, energy-saving 336
   Ratings 363
Toaster ovens 119
Toasters 119
Toothbrushes, electric 239
   Ratings 246
Toothpastes 237
   types 237
Treadmills 255
Tripods 68
   Ratings 76

Used cars 170
   reliable 173
   to avoid 176

Vacuum cleaners 312
   Ratings 341
Video cassette recorders 15
   mid-priced, Ratings 39
   repair histories 366
Video tapes 17

Walkabout stereos 33
Walking shoes 258
Washing machines 91
   Ratings 107
   repair histories 372
Water
   lead content 329
   pollutants 324
   treatment 324
   treatment devices, Ratings 355
Weather stripping 335
Windows, replacement 339
Wood finishes 330

Consumer Reports one-year index

This index covers issues of CONSUMER REPORTS from October 1992 to September 1993. **Bold type** indicates Ratings reports or brand-name discussions; *italic type* indicates corrections or follow-ups. Numbers at the left of each entry are codes for ordering reports by fax or mail. (No code or * means a report is not available by fax.) To order, call 800 896-7788. You can use MasterCard or Visa. Each report is $7.75. When you call, have ready the report's code and your charge-card. Before ordering a report, check to see if it's in the Buying Guide.

Code	Entry	Page
9794	**A**dvertising	752 Dec 92
9773	Air cleaners	657 Oct 92
	Air-conditioners:	
	central,	374 Jun 93
9733	room	**364 Jun 93**
9733	split-ductless	**370 Jun 93**
	Automobile ratings:	
7914	Audi 90 CS Quattro Sport	**315 May 93**
9325	Cadillac Eldorado	**468 Jul 93**
7766	Chevrolet Astro	**628 Oct 92**
7948	Chrysler Concorde	**127 Mar 93**
7943	Dodge Caravan	**83 Feb 93**
7766	Dodge Grand Caravan	**628 Oct 92**
7948	Dodge Intrepid	**127 Mar 93**
7302	Eagle Summit ES	**517 Aug 93**
7936	Eagle Talon TSi AWD	**49 Jan 93**
7948	Eagle Vision TSi	**127 Mar 93**
7766	Ford Aerostar	**628 Oct 92**
7331	Ford Escort LX	**581 Sep 93**
7789	Ford Explorer	**729 Nov 92**
7936	Ford Probe GT	**49 Jan 93**
7914	Ford Taurus SHO	**315 May 93**
7302	Geo Prizm LSi	**517 Aug 93**
7936	Honda Prelude Si	**49 Jan 93**
7914	Infiniti J30	**315 May 93**
7789	Isuzu Trooper	**729 Nov 92**
7789	Jeep Grand Cherokee	**729 Nov 92**
9325	Lexus SC400	**468 Jul 93**
9325	Lincoln Mark VIII	**468 Jul 93**
9317	Mazda 626 ES	**381 Jun 93**
7766	Mazda MPV	**628 Oct 92**
7936	Mazda MX-6 LS	**49 Jan 93**
7948	Mercury Sable LS	**127 Mar 93**
7943	Mercury Villager	**83 Feb 93**
7331	Mitsubishi Expo LRV Sport	**581 Sep 93**
7789	Mitsubishi Montero	**729 Nov 92**
9317	Nissan Altima GLE	**381 Jun 93**
7943	Nissan Quest	**83 Feb 93**
9317	Pontiac Grand Am GT	**381 Jun 93**
7331	Saturn SW2	**581 Sep 93**
7789	sport/utility vehicles	**729 Nov 92**
7302	Subaru Impreza L	**517 Aug 93**
9317	Subaru Legacy LS	**381 Jun 93**
7948	Toyota Camry LE	**127 Mar 93**
7331	Toyota Corolla DX	**581 Sep 93**
7302	Toyota Corolla LE	**517 Aug 93**
7766	Toyota Previa	**628 Oct 92**
7943	Volkswagen Eurovan	**83 Feb 93**
7914	Volvo 850 GLT	**315 May 93**
	Automobiles & automotive equipment:	
	air cleaners, interior	192 Apr 93
9406	body dimensions	**258 Apr 93**
9984	buying a new car	207 Apr 93
9407	buying a used car	**265 Apr 93**
	cooler chests, electric-powered	193 Apr 93
9979	crash tests, NHTSA	199 Apr 93
1993	Frequency-of-Repair records	234 Apr 93
7315	jacks and jack stands	**305 May 93**
9983	leasing	204 Apr 93
9934	lemon law claims	40 Jan 93
9406	mechanical specifications	**258 Apr 93**
	motor oil, "recycling"	193 Apr 93
9985	optional equipment	211 Apr 93
9405	owner satisfaction	**256 Apr 93**
7315	ramps, drive-on	**305 May 93**
	summarized ratings, '93 models	213 Apr 93
9988	compact cars	**217 Apr 93**
9403	large cars	**220 Apr 93**
9989	mid-sized cars	**218 Apr 93**
9986	small cars	**214 Apr 93**
9404	small vans; sport/utility	**220 Apr 93**
9987	sporty cars	**215 Apr 93**
9945	tire-pressure gauges	**96 Feb 93**
	tire-pressure monitors	278 May 93
9946	tires, all-season	**100 Feb 93**
	Toyota Camry	*686 Nov 92; 8 Jan 93*
	Batteries, rechargeable	489 Aug 93
7903	Best-Buy gifts	789 Dec 92
	Bonds, municipal	106 Feb 93
9955	**C**amcorders	**151 Mar 93**
7795	Cameras, 35mm, compact	**758 Dec 92**
9959	Cassette decks	176 Mar 93
	digital compact	345 Jun 93
7783	Cereal	**688 Nov 92**
9785	Circular saws	**708 Nov 92**
	Cleaners, all-purpose	**589 Sep 93**
9786	Clock radios	**712 Nov 92**
9326	Clothes dryers	**476 Jul 93**
9958	Compact-disc players	**168 Mar 93**
9329	Computer software systems	570 Sep 93
9316	Consumer-protection agencies	312 May 93

CONSUMER REPORTS INDEX

Consumers Union:
awards .... 746 Dec 92; 414 Jul 93; 558 Sep 93
bylaws .... 116 Feb 93
9312—Cribs .... **284 May 93;** 558 Sep 93
mattresses .... **287 May 93**
portable .... **288 May 93**

D
Data Discman .... 686 Nov 92
3768—Diet & health .... 644 Oct 92; *745 Dec 92
9712—Dieting & weight loss .... 347 Jun 93
9724——weight-loss programs .... **353 Jun 93**

E
Electronic gear .... 139 Mar 93
testing, explanation of CU's .... 142; 162 Mar 93
9784—Environmental-awareness quiz .... 704 Nov 92
Extension cord, FlatPlug .... 7 Jan 93
9301—Eyeglass chain stores .... **495 Aug 93**

F
9713—Fans, ceiling .... **376 Jun 93**
9713—Fans, whole-house .... 380 Jun 93
Fast food, low-fat .... **574 Sep 93**
Flexible spending accounts .... 25 Jan 93
9769—Food labels .... *623, 654 Oct 92; 65 Feb 93
9311—Foods, no-fat .... **279 May 93**
Frankfurters .... **415 Jul 93**
9908—Frozen light entrées .... **27 Jan 93**
Furniture cleaners and polishes .... **358 Jun 93**

G
9949—Garment bags .... **134 Mar 93**
9944—Grills, indoor .... **90 Feb 93**

H
9778—Health care (pres. campaign) .... 696 Nov 92
9787—Hearing aids, how to buy .... 716 Nov 92
9314—Heart disease (women) .... 300 May 93
7313—Hoses, garden .... **290 May 93**
couplers .... **298 May 93**
9323—Household pests, controlling .... 455 Jul 93

I
Insect repellents .... **451 Jul 93**
Insurance:
automobile (fraud) .... 7 Jan 93
1327——life (interest-sensitive whole life) .... **525 Aug 93**
9322——life (term) .... **431 Jul 93**
1327——life (universal) .... **525 Aug 93**
1332——life (whole) .... **595 Sep 93**
Investing for retirement .... 289 May 93
Investing windfalls .... 361 Jun 93

J
9905—Jewelry, gold, purchasing .... 800 Dec 92
9793—Juice extractors .... **747 Dec 92**
9793—Juicers .... **747 Dec 92**

K
9796—Keyboards, electronic .... **767 Dec 92**
Knives, kitchen .... **511 Aug 93**
Kodak Photo CD player .... 413 Jul 93

L
9318—Lawn mowers, riding .... **388 Jun 93**
9318—Lawn tractors .... **388 Jun 93**

Lead, in water
Chicago .... 126 Mar 93
9938——national test .... 73 Feb 93; *126 Mar 93*
9775—Light-bulb dimmers .... **669 Oct 92**
9774—Light bulbs, compact fluorescent .... **664 Oct 92**
9774—Light bulbs, halogen .... **664 Oct 92**
Locks, door, "keyless" .... 687 Nov 92
9957—Loudspeakers, 3-piece .... **166 Mar 93**

M
9799—Microwave ovens .... **783 Dec 92**
7947—Mind/body medicine .... 107 Feb 93
Mortgages, reverse .... 637 Oct 92
7518—Mutual funds (bonds) .... **395 Jun 93**
3913—Mutual funds (stocks) .... **323 May 93**

N
3768—Nutrition .... 644 Oct 92

O
Oral irrigators, battery-powered .... 626 Oct 92
Oven convection fan, wind-up .... 490 Aug 93

P
Paint rollers .... 626 Oct 92
pump-powered .... 277 May 93
Paintbrushes, disposable .... 65 Feb 93
Paints, exterior .... **610 Sep 93**
Pantyhose .... 414 Jul 93
Peelers, electronic .... 346 Jun 93
Pressure cookers .... **427 Jul 93**
9324—Prostate disease .... 459 Jul 93

R
9335—Ranges, electric .... **604 Sep 93**
Razors, gender-specific .... 125 Mar 93
9956—Receivers .... **164 Mar 93**
Recycling plastic packaging .... 745 Dec 92
Refrigerator compressor, GE .... *558 Sep 93*
Remote controls .... 178 Mar 93
9904——universal .... **796 Dec 92**
voice-activated .... 278 May 93
Retirement funds, transferring .... 8 Jan 93

S
Salt blends (reduced sodium) .... 7 Jan 93
9909—Scales, bathroom .... **32 Jan 93**
9776—Scissors and shears .... **672 Oct 92**
Shirts, men's dress .... **504 Aug 93**
9788—Sleep sofas .... 724 Nov 92
9935—Slow cookers .... **45 Jan 93**
Solicitors, telephone, regulation .... 126 Mar 93
Sony minidisc player .... 345 Jun 93
Sports drinks .... **491 Aug 93**
7313—Sprinklers, lawn .... **292 May 93**
couplers .... **298 May 93**
timers .... **298 May 93**
Stain removers .... 125 Mar 93; **545 Aug 93**
Stains, wood, exterior .... **610 Sep 93**
9797—Stereo components .... **772 Dec 92**
Strollers, convertible .... 558 Sep 93
3328—Supermarkets .... **568 Sep 93**
shopping .... 559 Sep 93
Switches, wireless .... 8 Jan 93

CONSUMER REPORTS INDEX

9933—	Tapes, audio cassette	36 Jan 93	9937— Vacuum cleaners	67 Feb 93
	Taxes, property, assessment	723 Nov 92	9954—Video cassette recorders	148 Mar 93
	Telephone services, long-distance	277 May 93	9767—Vinyl floor coverings	639 Oct 92
9798—	Telephones	777 Dec 92		
7906—	——cellular	9 Jan 93	9321— Walking shoes	420 Jul 93
9953—	Television sets, large-screen	144 Mar 93	9939—Water treatment devices	79 Feb 93
9779—	Television sets, 13- and 20-inch	699 Nov 92	Weather radios	557 Sep 93
9907—	Tranquilizers	19 Jan 93	Wrenches, adjustable	540 Aug 93
	Tree pruners, electric	414 Jul 93	Wrenches, socket	541 Aug 93

STATEMENT OF OWNERSHIP, MANAGEMENT, AND CIRCULATION
(Required by 39 U.S.C. 3685)

1.Title of Publication: CONSUMER REPORTS. 1A .Publication No: 0010-7174. 2. Date of Filing: September 15, 1993. 3. Frequency of issue: Monthly, except semi-monthly in December. 3A. No. of Issues Published Annually: 13. 3B. Annual Subscription Price: $22.00. 4. Complete Mailing Address of Known Office of Publication: 101 Truman Avenue, Yonkers, New York 10703-1057. 5. Complete Mailing Address of the Headquarters of General Business offices of the Publisher: 101 Truman Avenue, Yonkers, New York 10703-1057. Full Names and Complete Mailing Address of Publisher, President, Editor, & Executive Editor. Publisher: Consumers Union of United States, Inc. 101 Truman Avenue, Yonkers, New York 10703-1057. President, Rhoda H. Karpatkin; Editor: Irwin Landau; Executive Editor: Eileen Denver. 7. Owner: (If owned by a corporation, the names and addresses of the individual owners must be given. If owned by a partnership or other unincorporated firm, its name and address, as well as that of each individual, must be given. If the publication is published by a nonprofit organization, its name and address must be stated.) Name: Consumers Union of United States, Inc., a nonprofit organization. Address: 101 Truman Avenue, Yonkers, New York 10703-1057. 8. Known Bondholders, Mortgagees, and Other Securities (if there are none, so state): None. 9. For Completion by Nonprofit Organizations Authorized to Mail at Special Rates (Section 424.12 DMM only). The purpose, function, and nonprofit status of this organization and the exempt status for Federal Income tax purposes has not changed during preceding 12 months. 10. Extent and Nature of Circulation.

	Average no. copies each issue during past 12 mo.	Actual no. copies of single issue published nearest to filing date
A. Total no. of copies (net press run)	5,505,000	5,386,000
B. Paid and/or requested circulation		
1. Sales through dealers and carriers, street vendors and counter sales	137,000	98,000
2. Mail subscription (Paid and/or requested)	5,102,000	5,031,000
C. Total paid and/or requested circulation (Sum of 10B1 and 10B2)	5,239,000	5,129,000
D. Free distribution by mail, carrier or other means Samples, complimentary, and other free copies	40,000	41,000
E. Total distribution (sum of C and D)	5,279,000	5,170,000
F. Copies not distributed		
1. Office use, left over, unaccounted, spoiled after printing.	45,000	44,000
2. Return from news agents	181,000	172,000
G. TOTAL (sum of E, F1 and 2—should equal net press run shown in A)	5,505,000	5,386,000

11. I certify that the statements made by me above are correct and complete.
Louis J. Milani, Director, Business Affairs

Give $1000. Get a whole lot more.

Giving away $1000 may not seem like a way to increase your assets. But consider all you get back when you give $1000 to Consumers Union:

1. You become a Lifetime Member of Consumers Union.

2. You receive Consumer Reports every month for the rest of your life.

3. Your name is inscribed on the permanent Honor Roll in the Consumer Reports National Testing and Research Center.

4. You get a tax deduction.

5. Your Lifetime Membership is acknowledged in a special listing published periodically in Consumer Reports—unless you'd prefer to remain anonymous.

6. Your contribution helps build a stronger Consumers Union. This means better values in the products and services you buy. Safer products for you and those you care about. More protection against fraud and deceit. A fairer world for the consumer—in so many ways.

As you may know, CU accepts no contributions from business. No outside advertising. No contributions larger than $5000 from anyone.

More than 5500 of our readers have increased their assets by contributing $1000 to Consumers Union. Join them by becoming a Lifetime Member today. Please use the coupon when you send your check.

Yes, I'd like to enjoy the benefits of Lifetime Membership in Consumers Union with a tax deductible contribution of:
- ☐ $1000   ☐ $1500   ☐ $2000
- ☐ Other $_____ (Maximum: $5000)
- ☐ My check is enclosed.
- ☐ I wish to contribute in quarterly installments.
- ☐ My first installment is enclosed.
- ☐ I cannot be a Lifetime Member now, but here is my gift for $_____

Name _____

Address _____

City_____ State_____ Zip_____

Name to be entered as Lifetime Member (if different):

_____

☐ Yes, you may list my name in Consumer Reports.
☐ Don't list my name.

Mail this coupon to:
CONSUMERS UNION
101 Truman Ave., Yonkers, N.Y. 10703   HLGGG

CONSUMERS UNION OF U.S., INC., 101 Truman Ave., Yonkers, N.Y. 10703, is a not-for-profit, tax-exempt organization, contributions to which are tax-deductible in accordance with law. Contributions are not accepted from any commercial interest. A copy of our latest financial report filed with the New York Department of State may be obtained by writing: Office of Charities Registration, Department of State, Albany, NY 12231, or from CU at the address above.

More Bestsellers

from Consumer Reports Books

- Mortgage Book. (#P511) $15.95
- How to Settle an Estate. (#H501) Hardcover $18.95
- Personal Computer Buying Guide. Rev. Ed. (#P560) $14.95
- Homeowner's Legal Guide. (#H529) Hardcover $22.95
- Take Control of Your Weight. (#H541) Hardcover $22.95
- How to Sell Your House, Condo, Co-op. (#P452) $15.95
- Hernia Book. (#H533) Hardcover $19.95
- 40+ Guide to Good Health. (#H535) Hardcover $27.95

Mail to:
Consumer Reports Books
9180 LeSaint Drive, Fairfield, OH 45014-5452

MONEY-BACK GUARANTEE

CODE	BOOK TITLE (*PLEASE PRINT CLEARLY*)	QTY.	PRICE EA.	TOTAL
			$	$
#P596	1994 DESK CALENDAR	1	~~$9.95~~	FREE

SHIPPING AND HANDLING: Order value (excluding premium)
Orders up to $25 (shipped via postal service.) — $2.50
$25.01-$35 (shipped via postal service.) — $3.50
Orders $35.01 or more (shipped via postal service) — FREE
UPS orders (any value) in continental U.S. — $5.00
Canadian and International orders (any value) (U.S. funds only) — $5.00

SUBTOTAL $
SHIPPING & HANDLING $
TOTAL $

Method of payment: ❑ Check enclosed for full amount
Charge to my: ❑ MasterCard   ❑ Visa   Exp. Date: Mo. ___ Yr. ___

Card Number ☐☐☐☐☐☐☐☐☐☐☐☐☐☐☐☐☐☐☐☐

Signature _____

Name _____

Address _____ Apt. ____

City _____ State ____ Zip ____

We will ship your order within 72 hours of receipt. Please allow four weeks for delivery via U.S. Postal Service. All books are paperback unless otherwise noted. CU publications may not be used for commercial purposes.

FREE with your order:
$9.95 value
Consumer Reports 1994 Desk Calendar

4P3CT

FOR FASTER ORDERING CALL 1-513-860-1178 OR FAX 1-513-874-1699

SEE BACK COVER FOR MORE BOOKS FROM CONSUMER REPORTS BOOKS

REPORTS FAXED TO YOU IN MINUTES FROM...

Consumer Reports FACTS By FAX

- Now you can get any recent CONSUMER REPORTS article faxed to you in minutes
- Don't have a fax? We'll send it First Class Mail by the next day
- Call the 24-hour faxline and put the information you need at your fingertips in minutes

Here's how Facts by Fax works:

Call anytime toll-free—800 896-7788. Each Report is $7.75. All you need is a touch-tone phone, the 4-digit Facts by Fax code (see the index at the back of The Buying Guide or the latest issue of CONSUMER REPORTS or call the Faxline and order the most recent index for $1.00), your Visa or MasterCard, and your fax number. Faxlines are open 24-hours a day, 7 days a week.

Call the 24-hour TOLL-FREE Faxline

(800) 896-7788

Not available outside the U.S.

How to Know A Used Car's Real Price

BUY · SELL · TRADE IN

Negotiate with confidence, deal from strength by calling for the facts.
- Hear CURRENT PRICES on 1984-1992 models for your region of the country. Cars, sport/utility vehicles, minivans, pickups. Prices based on vehicle age, mileage, options, and condition.
- Get 1993 MODEL PRICES beginning January 1994.

Call 1-900-446-0500 $1.75 per minute. Typical calls last 5 minutes or more.

You must call from a touch-tone phone. Service is available 7 days a week, 7 a.m. to 2 a.m. Eastern Time. You'll be charged on your phone bill. (Sorry, no service in Alaska, Canada, Hawaii, and certain areas in the continental United States.)

You'll be asked for:

- Zip Code
- Model name or number
  (example: "Cherokee" not Jeep)
- Model year
- Mileage
- Major options
- Number of cylinders
- Condition of vehicle

Consumer Reports

How to Buy a New Car for Less

YOU'RE IN CONTROL WHEN YOU KNOW THE FACTS

Save money on a new car with an up-to-date, factory invoice computer printout from *Consumer Reports*. What does that model cost the dealer? What does the dealer pay for that factory-installed option? **You** negotiate from strength and make **your** best deal when **you** have our information on the exact make and model **you** want. **You** get:

- Comparison of sticker price vs. dealer invoice.
- Factory options, both sticker and dealer prices.
- Rebate Information.
- *Consumer Reports'* Recommended Safety & Comfort Options.
- Low-cost Financing Information.

Example Please Print	*Ford*	*Taurus*	*GL 4dr Sedan*
	Make	Model	Exact Style

1st car _____
2nd car _____
3rd car _____
4th car _____
Name _____
Address _____
City _____ State _____ Zip _____

Prices: $11 for 1 car. $20 for 2 cars. $27 for 3 cars. Each additional, $5.
Mail with payment to: Consumer Reports, Box 8005, Novi, Michigan 48376

WF